D0146665

Luther College Library
University of Regina

MIDDLE ENGLISH LITERATURE

MIDDLE ENGLISH LITERATURE

edited by

Charles W. Dunn, HARVARD UNIVERSITY

and

Edward T. Byrnes, SETON HALL UNIVERSITY

HARCOURT BRACE JOVANOVICH, INC.

New York   Chicago   San Francisco   Atlanta

HBJ

LUTHER COLLEGE LIBRARY
University of Regina

© 1973 BY HARCOURT BRACE JOVANOVICH, INC.

All rights reserved. No part of this publication may be reproduced or transmitted in any form or by any means, electronic or mechanical, including photocopy, recording, or any information storage and retrieval system, without permission in writing from the publisher.

ISBN: 0-15-558762-5

Library of Congress Catalog Card Number: 73-2178

Printed in the United States of America

PREFACE

As the result of our individual experiences in teaching Middle English literature we decided to prepare an anthology that would provide our readers with complete works of genuine literary merit and appeal composed during the Middle English period (1100–1500) in England, Scotland, and Ireland, or at least large, self-contained extracts from such works. Our publisher sent out a request for comments on the details of our proposal to Professors Robert W. Ackerman of Stanford University, Jess B. Bessinger of New York University, Mortimer J. Donovan of University of Notre Dame, Richard H. Green of University of Florida, the late Merritt Y. Hughes of University of Wisconsin, Robert M. Lumiansky of University of Pennsylvania, Alan M. Markman of University of Pittsburgh, William Matthews of University of California at Los Angeles, Robert A. Pratt of University of Pennsylvania, Alain Renoir of University of California at Berkeley, and W. Edson Richmond of Indiana University. All of them graciously replied with numerous constructive suggestions. We personally consulted other medievalists for their opinions; and while the work was in progress, the late Professor James R. Kreuzer of Herbert H. Lehman College wrote a valuable critique of those sections that were available in first draft. There was a clear consensus about which of our suggested items should be included; predictably, there was no clear agreement about which items we should omit in the interest of space. And there was a division of opinion on the crucial question of how much linguistic assistance should be supplied. We hope we have satisfied the majority by our necessary compromises.

We decided to omit the works of Chaucer, the medieval dramatists, and Malory, since excellent editions are readily available. Most of the works finally chosen were included for their literary merit, while a few were included for their literary interest or as illustrations of some of the unfamiliar aspects of medieval culture.

We have provided glosses for all unfamiliar words and obscure phrases, and for every selection reference is made to at least one definitive edition where the details of recent scholarly opinions can be found. We have introduced modern punctuation and capitalization; we have consistently distinguished in spelling the words *of* and *off* and the words *the* and *thee* even when medieval scribes did not do so; and when scribes used various spellings for the same word, we have chosen their more intelligible alternate (such as *quene* rather than *whene* for *queen*).

We have based our texts on earlier scholarly editions no longer covered by international copyright, and we are thus especially indebted to the pioneering editors of the Early English Text Society, the Scottish Text Society, and similar enterprises. Whenever possible we have consulted facsimiles (listed in our headnotes) of original manuscripts, and we have occasionally introduced our own emendations or interpretations or have incorporated the suggestions of recent editors.

The Introduction is a brief guide to literary and linguistic questions; the head-notes and Bibliography supply extensive guidance to secondary sources; and the Appendices provide further details concerning linguistic matters.

We are indebted to a number of medievalists, including the late Professor Oscar Cargill of New York University and Professors B. J. Whiting of Harvard University, Morton Bloomfield of Harvard University, and Francis L. Utley of Ohio State University, as well as those already mentioned, for their advice and encouragement. We acknowledge the kind permission of the trustees of the British Museum and of the National Library of Scotland who allowed us to reprint their photographs of the manuscripts shown in Plates 1 to 6. Finally, as a personal matter, we thank our wives for their cheerful patience during our long periods of abstraction from the modern world, and we therefore dedicate the results of our labors to Elaine and to the memory of Pat.

CHARLES W. DUNN
EDWARD T. BYRNES

CONTENTS

vii

Contents

Contents

LIST OF SELECTIONS
BY AUDIENCE, CENTURY, AND GENRE

| Audience | Century | Genre | |
		Lyric	Verse Narrative
Religious	Twelfth	Poema Morale	
	Thirteenth	A Love Rune	Judas
	Fourteenth	The Five Joys of Mary	
	Fifteenth	Christ and His Mother On the Resurrection of Christ	St. Stephen and Herod The Dance of the Seven Deadly Sins
Learned	Twelfth		The Owl and the Nightingale
	Fourteenth		The Bruce
	Fifteenth	The Golden Targe	The Tale of Beryn The Siege of Thebes
Courtly	Twelfth		The Brut
	Fourteenth	Now Springs the Spray Alysoun Spring April Love in Paris	Sir Orfeo Morte Arthure Sir Gawain and the Green Knight The Lover's Confession
	Fifteenth		The Testament of Cresseid
Popular	Thirteenth		King Horn The Fox and the Wolf Dame Sirith
	Fourteenth		Halidon Hill Thomas of Erceldoun
	Fifteenth	The Blacksmiths	Robyn and Gandeleyn

	Genre	
Prose Narrative	*Verse Instruction*	*Prose Instruction*
William the Conqueror The Anarchy of King Stephen	The Proverbs of Alfred	Holy Maidenhood
	The Bestiary The Sayings of St. Bernard The Land of Cokayne	The Anchoresses' Rule
	Handling Sin The Parliament of the Three Ages Piers Plowman The Pearl	The Form of Living The Wyclyfite Bible A Defense of Translation
		The Properties of Things
	The Regiment of Princes	

MIDDLE ENGLISH
LITERATURE

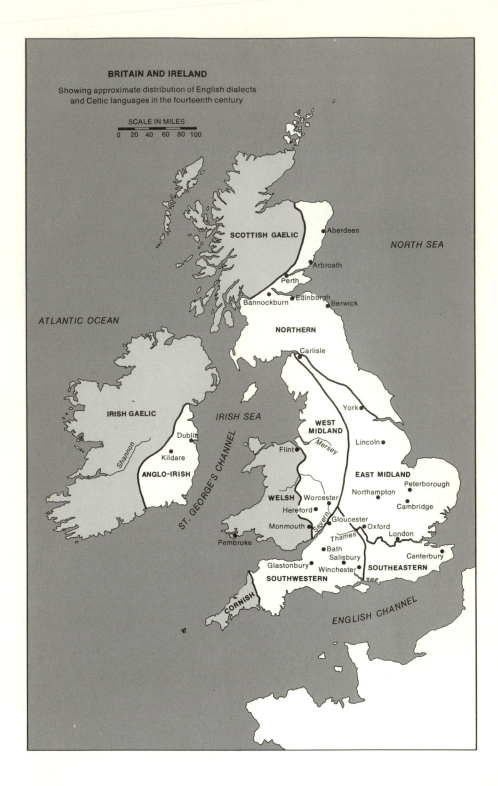

BRITAIN AND IRELAND

Showing approximate distribution of English dialects
and Celtic languages in the fourteenth century

SCALE IN MILES

0 20 40 60 80 100

SCOTTISH GAELIC

NORTH SEA

- Aberdeen
- Arbroath
- Perth
- Edinburgh
- Berwick
- Bannockburn

ATLANTIC OCEAN

NORTHERN

- Carlisle

IRISH GAELIC

IRISH SEA

- York

WEST MIDLAND

- Lincoln

- Dublin

ST. GEORGE'S CHANNEL

Mersey

- Flint

- Kildare

ANGLO-IRISH

EAST MIDLAND

- Peterborough

- Northampton

- Cambridge

WELSH

- Worcester

- Hereford

Severn

- Gloucester

- Oxford

- London

- Monmouth

Thames

- Pembroke

- Bath

- Salisbury

- Canterbury

SOUTHEASTERN

- Glastonbury

- Winchester

SOUTHWESTERN

CORNISH

ENGLISH CHANNEL

Shannon

Introduction

Middle English Literature

> Yf that olde bokes were aweye,
> Y-loren were of remembraunce the keye.
>
> Chaucer, *Legend of Good Women*

This anthology contains an abundant representation of the finest literature produced during the Middle English period. The term *Middle English* is awkward but convenient, for it identifies one distinct phase in the development of the English language (discussed below in the linguistic introduction) and also applies to a distinct epoch in the history of English culture that began with the Norman invasion of 1066 and ended at about the time that Caxton introduced printing in England, in 1476.

Old English literature, the predecessor of Middle English literature, differs greatly from what followed, emanating as it did from the pagan Germanic tribes who began to sweep into Britain in A.D. 449 and to subjugate the native Celtic-speaking British peoples. These Anglo-Saxon invaders maintained an interest in the traditions and legends of their continental fatherland and, even after they were Christianized, they composed works, such as the great epic *Beowulf*, that were cast in the conventional Germanic alliterative verse form and that reflected their ancient myths and legends. The arrival of the Normans in 1066 opened up new channels of cultural communications, and Britain subsequently shared with all the other countries of western Europe in the profound awakening of the renaissance of the twelfth century and became a productive and cosmopolitan center of letters.

During the long and eventful period from the Norman conquest to the end of the fifteenth century, Middle English was only one of several languages spoken and written within Great Britain and Ireland. The marvel is, indeed, that English succeeded in surviving as the primary language of the polyglot peoples who coexisted in the two small islands. The Normans brought with them their own dialect of French; the Cornish, the Welsh, the Irish, the Manx, and the Scottish Gaels continued to use their individual Celtic languages; Viking settlers used various Scandinavian dialects; Jewish scholars wrote in Hebrew; and other immigrants, such as the Bretons and the Flemings, retained their own languages, though their literary activities are unrecorded. Many men of letters were multilingual, and some of those who spoke and wrote Latin have left behind them outstanding works in that language.

RELIGIOUS LITERATURE

By far the largest proportion of surviving Middle English literature—and, for that matter, of medieval European literature in general—is devoted to some aspect of religion. Literacy was not widespread, but those men and women who were

3

literate tended to be in some way connected with the church, whose influence pervaded town and country—manors, villages, guilds, municipalities, schools, universities, and the royal court. Every parish had a priest subordinate to the bishop of the diocese, who was in turn subordinate to the hierarchy of archbishops and pope, so that even the remotest parish was linked potentially with the culture of the outside world. Furthermore, monks and nuns who were dedicated to the contemplative life settled in rural retreats, where they accumulated their own libraries. The Benedictines (Black Monks) had been established in England since 597; the Cistercians (White Monks) arrived in 1128; and other orders of monks and of regular canons (Augustinians, Premonstratensians, and Gilbertines) also founded their own houses. Members of the mendicant orders, who in their pursuit of the active life went out on preaching missions and were often interested in literary matters, arrived somewhat later—the Dominicans (Black Friars) in 1221, the Franciscans (Grey Friars) in 1224, the Carmelites (White Friars) in 1240, and the Austin Friars in 1248. Understandably, the literary works produced by the better-educated members of these various branches of the church tended to reflect their authors' personal piety and religious zeal.

Much of the most distinguished literature composed in Middle English, as in the other languages of Britain and Ireland, was thus basically religious in focus; and though the modern reader may find a purely literary pleasure in the survivals of a now submerged culture, he cannot appreciate such literature historically unless he recognizes its fundamental purpose. As the following brief analysis of the contents of this anthology will suggest, almost half of the items selected for inclusion on literary merit are the products of church or cloister.

The annals kept by the two Peterborough chroniclers were recorded for the sake of preserving a summary of events affecting their Benedictine monastery, and their selection and interpretation of these events reflect a thoroughly monastic, theocentric view of history. *The Proverbs of Alfred* contains popular, everyday sayings as well as religious advice, but the overall intention of the poem is religious. As the title suggests, the *Poema Morale* is likewise religious in intent. In *The Owl and the Nightingale*, the nightingale is notably sympathetic toward worldly lovers and the singers of amatory lays, but the churchly owl constantly draws the argument into the realms of religion. And, of all the early works selected here, the most centrally religious are the two tracts *Holy Maidenhood* and *The Anchoresses' Rule*, which both deal with the justification and observance of the recluse's way of life.

In the latter part of the thirteenth century the range of Middle English literature began to grow more diverse, but the emphasis on religion remained paramount. *The Bestiary* presents a vernacular popularization of the medieval theologian's interpretation of the works of God. *Judas*, which has been called one of the earliest of English ballads and is derived from popular international oral tradition, is essentially more didactic than dramatic in intention and more religious than secular in function. *A Love Rune*, which is directed by a Franciscan friar toward those girls who might wish to become brides of Christ, deals with spiritual rather than fleshly love. *The Sayings of St. Bernard*, which emanated from the Cistercian tradition, serves to warn mankind against the world, the flesh, and the devil; and *The Land of*

4

Cokayne is a satire composed by a Franciscan friar and aimed at the worldliness of monks such as the Cistercians.

In the early fourteenth century Mannyng dedicated his gift as a storyteller to the edifying task of composing *Handling Sin;* and Richard Rolle wrote *The Form of Living* for a female reader who had adopted a hermit's mode of life. This century also produced many fine religious lyrics, such as *The Five Joys of Mary*.

The latter part of the fourteenth century—the worldly age of Chaucer—produced even more important religious works. *The Parliament of the Three Ages*, which presents an allegory of the life of man, is amply illustrated with descriptions of the contemporary world and with allusions to secular history, but its intention is just as otherworldly as that of the early *Poema Morale* and its artistry much more distinguished. Langland's monumental *Piers Plowman* deals with the vast problems of the salvation of man and society. The brilliant *Pearl* raises a complex range of questions concerning the human soul. This period also produced the pioneering work of the Wyclifite translators of the Bible and Trevisa's enterprising translation of Bartholomew's Latin encyclopedia, the central purpose of which, like that of all the other works already mentioned, is specifically religious.

In the fourteenth century the members of the Lollard movement had already begun to attack corruption within the church and to flout ecclesiastical authority, just as the Wyclifite translators had done when they provided laymen with a vernacular translation of the very work on which that authority rested its claim, namely the Bible. Early in the fifteenth century a complete cleavage between the Catholic church and the new Protestant sects that emerged from the Reformation took place. Yet even the comparatively barren culture of the fifteenth century produced such religious gems as the artistic lyric *Christ and His Mother*, the popular ballad *St. Stephen and Herod*, and two impassioned poems of the Scottish priest William Dunbar, *The Dance of the Seven Deadly Sins* and *On the Resurrection*.

LEARNED, COURTLY, AND POPULAR LITERATURE

Despite the ubiquity of religion in medieval culture, some of the outstanding works surviving from the Middle English period were not primarily designed for purposes of religious instruction. The source of these works was not Biblical, and their purpose was not doctrinal; their authors were not necessarily churchmen, and their audiences were not immediately intent on salvation. Some were learned works, written by authors who had gained an education in school or college; these were characteristically artistic in form, carefully wrought, adorned with figures of speech and scholarly allusions, and frequently allegoric in significance. Some were courtly works, aimed at an aristocratic audience familiar with the concepts of courtly love and with the ideals of knighthood; these were frequently as artistic in their own way as learned works but were primarily imaginative and fantastic. Some were popular works, emanating from the simple residents of farms and towns, drawn from the endless resources of international folklore, fashioned orally and transmitted orally with no fixed text; these were as imaginative and fantastic as courtly works though they were artistically limited by the fact that they were molded by the unpretentious taste of an insatiable popular audience. Learned literature might be said to depend on the scribe, courtly literature on the harpist, and popular literature on the ballad-singer; and as a consequence, learned literature is the most fully preserved, while much of the graceful but ephemeral courtly literature and the robust popular literature have vanished without a trace.

The classification of particular literary works, however, is complicated by the fact that medieval culture was less stratified than medieval society. To be sure, the aristocrat enjoyed almost unbounded feudal privileges, while the villager enjoyed hardly any, yet upward social mobility was possible for those culture-carriers who had gained sufficient education to become teachers or clerks. In the following summary of the nonreligious works contained in this anthology, the fluidity of feudal society and the corresponding diffusion of culture are constantly evident.

To turn first to verse narrative, Lawman's *Brut* illustrates the impossibility of following any rigid system in classifying Middle English literature. Lawman was a secular priest; his work was a translation of an Anglo-Norman courtly poem, and his audience was presumably made up of his rural neighbors in the West Country. Furthermore, his Anglo-Norman source was itself an adaptation of Geoffrey of Monmouth's pseudohistorical *History of the Kings of Britain*, written in ornate Latin prose and aimed at a learned audience of clerics and courtiers. *The Brut* is thus not so much a folk epic as a popularization.

King Horn belongs to the genre of romance, and again the classification is not entirely unambiguous. A romance can be described as a narrative poem dealing with the trials of a hero in the service of his ladylove, his overlord, and God. Some romances are highly sophisticated, while others are popular and have often been reworked as simple ballads. *King Horn* belongs to the latter category, and the narrative, in fact, survived in oral ballad tradition until a very recent date, long after the romance had dropped from circulation.

Romances, however, were not necessarily restricted to the popular level. *Sir Orfeo* is derived from the classical myth of Orpheus, and its romantic emphasis on the power of love seems to address the work particularly to a courtly audience, although its basic narrative also circulated as a simple ballad. *Sir Gawain and the Green Knight* is even more clearly a sophisticated courtly romance. It assumes an understanding of Geoffrey of Monmouth's pseudohistorical concept of Arthur's destiny; it emphasizes the ethical challenges involved in knighthood; it subtly assesses the artificial code of courtly love, according to which a knight sought self-improvement through service to his ladylove; psychological realism overrides the fantastic elements within the plot; and allegoric implications enrich the entire romance. So far as is known, it was never reduced to ballad form; and if it was, the loss of force would have been lamentable.

At a simpler level, *Thomas of Erceldoun*, which also circulated as a ballad, is essentially a popular romance, describing a miraculous encounter between a knight and a supernatural ladylove, but in its extant form it has been specially adapted to support a political prophecy. *Robyn and Gandelyn* is a pure and simple ballad of outlawry, antiaristocratic in theme and attitude, which could hardly have been expanded into a courtly romance.

Romances, which are the counterpart of modern novels, and ballads, which are the counterpart of short stories, are thus difficult to characterize by any one criterion other than preoccupation with the obligations of heroism. There are, however, other medieval verse narratives that differ from the romance and the ballad and are generally called, for lack of a better term, tales. One of these, *The Fox and the Wolf*, contains a single anecdote of universal appeal, derived from the popular French cycle of tales dealing with the exploits of Reynard, the wily fox. Another is *Dame Sirith*, which is a popular *fabliau*, or comic story pertaining to bourgeois life, the plot of which also turns up in Middle English in a short bourgeois drama entitled *The Interlude of a Cleric and a Girl*. Similarly, *The Tale of Beryn* may be classified as a bourgeois tale, since it centers more on the hero's success as a merchant and lawyer than as a lover.

Some medieval verse narratives, it may be added, altogether elude even the relatively imprecise classifications presented here. *Morte Arthure* is frequently referred to as a romance because it deals with knightly deeds, but it is more learned than courtly in its treatment of the subject of King Arthur's conquest of Rome and his final downfall. It is colored by the historiographic vision of Geoffrey of Monmouth's *History of the Kings of Britain* and presents Arthur as a victim of the wheel of fortune—a philosophical concept dominant in the Middle Ages because of Boethius's highly influential work *The Consolation of Philosophy*. For lack of any better term, it might indeed be called a tragedy, in keeping with the groping definition of that medieval genre offered by Chaucer's Monk:

> Tragedie is . . . a certeyn storie . . .
> Of hym that stood in greet prosperitee
> And is y-fallen out of heigh degree
> Into myserie, and endeth wrecchedly.

A similar analysis can also be made of Henryson's *Testament of Cressid*, which deals with the tragic downfall of the heroine.

The same range of popular, courtly, and learned backgrounds appears in the medieval tradition of the lyric. *Now Springs the Spray* and the Harley lyrics *Alysoun*, *Spring*, *April*, and *Love in Paris* reflect the life of the wandering scholars of western Europe and carry with them the flavor of courtly love. Minot's violent political lyric *Halidon Hill* seems to be clerical in origin, but its tone is more bourgeois than courtly. *The Blacksmiths*, dealing as it does with noise pollution, is certainly the composition of a villager or townsman. Dunbar's *Golden Targe* is the work of a scholarly ecclesiastic who could express himself with equal facility in the realms of courtly love, as here, and religious devotion and morality, as in his other poems already cited.

The remaining four major works have in common one characteristic, the dependence on the learned tradition. Barbour's *Bruce*, which recounts the national history of Scotland, is the work of an erudite churchman. His learning is every-where apparent, but the primary materials of his verse chronicle were drawn largely from oral tradition, and the style of the work is more like that of a simple romance than of the classical epics whose orderly pattern he attempted vainly to imitate. Gower's *Lover's Confession* draws upon that encyclopedia of love, the Old French *Romance of the Rose*, both for its presentation of courtly love and for its analysis of the role of love in human life and in God's plan.

Hoccleve's *Regiment of Princes* is an ecclesiastical adaptation of earlier writings on statesmanship. Lydgate's *Siege of Thebes* is an epic adapted from a French prose romance whose author had reworked the familiar materials of classical legend to suit a medieval audience.

THE SCOPE OF MIDDLE ENGLISH LITERATURE

The works included in this anthology, then, represent both the religious and the secular aspects of medieval life and reflect the various educational and social levels of medieval audiences. From the surviving literature of the Middle English period the religious culture could be much more fully exemplified by the inclusion of saints' lives, miracle plays, sermons, and the like, since such materials were reverently recorded and preserved. The courtly tradition could be further illustrated, for instance, by romances of Charlemagne and of Alexander the Great; the learned tradition by treatises on such matters as medicine, dreams, and hunting; and the popular tradition by bawdy songs and tales, which, though seldom recorded, undoubtedly circulated vigorously. Yet, a wider survey would not reveal a portrait of medieval man any different from that already discernible in those works that have been selected here on the basis of their literary appeal.

What then, one may ask, are the characteristics that differentiate medieval man, as revealed in his literature, from modern man? Though the answers to this question lie far beyond the scope of this brief introduction, the question is one that every reader of medieval literature would do well to ask himself. Here it may be appropriate to stress the obvious by pointing to the dominance of the universal concepts of Christianity in the Middle Ages. God was thought in a very literal sense to be the controller of the universe; past, present, and future for him were one, and all events were affected by his providence; earthly rulers of church and state were responsible to him, and they exercised authority over lesser mortals only to the extent that they were God's regents.

In this sense, all literature was potentially religious. Thus, even the most fantastic medieval romances tended to deal with the hero's duties rather than, as is the case in modern fiction, with the hero's personal development and self-discovery. Similarly, in medieval works of social criticism, such as Langland's *Piers Plowman*, the author is concerned with man's obedience to the divine plan, whereas a contemporary author, such as Sartre, maintains that man is responsible to himself alone and must choose his own values.

As a result of their religious point of view, medieval writers constantly tended to enrich the significance of their works by means of allegory. The church fathers had shown that everything in the Bible could be interpreted allegorically. Each narrative item could be shown to have a concealed spiritual meaning, and the events recorded in the Old Testament could be shown to prefigure events in the New Testament and even events in secular history. So, for example, St. Augustine of Hippo, in his *City of God*, declared not only that Noah's Ark prefigured Christ's Church but also that Cain and Abel prefigured Romulus and Remus. Biblical commentators developed a system for the interpretation of texts at four different levels—the literal (based on the written word), the mystical (based on faith), the moral (based on charity), and the anagogical (based on hope):

> *Littera gesta docet, quid credas allegoria,*
> *Moralis quid agas, quo tendas anagogia.*

> The literal teaches the facts, the allegorical teaches what you should believe,
> The moral what you should do, the anagogical what you should aim for.

> (Augustine of Dacia)

This system was used not only by Biblical exegetes, as in the preface to the Wyclifite Bible, but also by men of letters, such as Langland in *Piers Plowman* and Gower in *The Lover's Confession*, and must have been familiar to every medieval layman who had listened to a sermon or had been taught the significance of the art that exemplified God's word in every Gothic cathedral. Authors also introduced morality into their writings by means of personification—a by-product of allegory —as in the lively characterizations of the Seven Deadly Sins in *Piers Plowman*, and by exemplification, as in the account of the Nine Worthies in *The Parliament of the Three Ages*. Even when the purpose was not explicitly religious, instruction was potentially present in much medieval literature.

Allegory is, of course, a difficult device. Sometimes it was employed very naively, as in *The Bestiary*, sometimes very subtly and even enigmatically, as in *The Owl and the Nightingale*, sometimes brilliantly, as in *The Pearl*. Sometimes, it should be added, allegory was certainly not intended, as in a simple romance such as *King Horn*, though any able exegete could no doubt have produced an edifying sermon even on this subject. Generally speaking, however, for medieval man the whole world was a symbol, and in this respect the medieval audience differs considerably from the modern. The modern reader does, to be sure, look for symbolic significance in a figure such as Moby Dick; but the medieval reader was prepared to discover in a whale four levels of allegory, for in a broad sense he had been trained, like Shakespeare's hero, to find "books in the running brooks, sermons in stone, and good in everything."

The other somewhat unfamiliar aspect of medieval culture that the modern reader should recognize is the general tendency of authors to approach the art of literature as apprentices who must serve a long course before they can become masters. At the popular level, for instance, minstrels were evidently expected to memorize traditional romances and lays before they could hope to compose anything new, and even as masters they consistently strove to rework traditional narratives rather than create completely original, imaginative topics. For them, as for other medieval artists and artisans, originality was irrelevant; what really counted was craftsmanship. The particular skill of the romancer lay in his ability

9

to cater to popular taste, and much of the charm of a romance such as *King Horn* arises from the attempts of a long succession of minstrels to perfect their performance of it in the presence of responsive, living audiences. The ultimate source of *King Horn* was an Anglo-Norman romance aimed at a courtly audience; the final native English product was a popular poem that was unoriginal and yet new.

At the level of courtly literature the scope is more complex, but the principle remains the same. Here also, craftsmanship outweighs originality. Thus, *Sir Gawain and the Green Knight*, for instance, is a supremely great work, but not because its plot is original. In fact, the plot was at least six hundred years old when the Middle English romancer was inspired to reinterpret it for his own courtly audience. Rather, *Sir Gawain* is great because of the author's combination of human perceptivity and artistic skill. His perceptivity may have been born within him, but his skill was surely not just instinctive. It must have been nurtured by wide reading, by the laborious study of rhetoric, by long practice in the arts of composition, and by the patient study of such kindred arts as music and architecture. He was the kind of poet who, like Chaucer, would feelingly exclaim: "The lyf so short, the craft so long to lerne!"

The craftsmanship of medieval culture has appropriately received much attention from recent literary critics, including some who reject the study of sources and backgrounds as irrelevant. Here, fortunately, the modern reader can join with them in an appreciation of the structure, texture, and architectonics of the Middle English masterpiece even if he has not himself absorbed any of the established literary-historical lore; for works such as *The Owl and the Nightingale*, *Sir Gawain and the Green Knight*, *The Pearl*, and *Piers Plowman* share in the general triumph attained by apprentices and masters during the flowering of Romanesque and Gothic art.

Their language, style, and concepts are medieval, but they deal with the universal experience of human life.

The Middle English Language

> Ye knowe ek that in forme of speche is chaunge
> Withinne a thousand yeer; and wordes tho
> That hadden pris now wonder nyce and straunge
> Us thinketh hem; and yet thei spake hem so.
>
> Chaucer, *Troilus and Criseyde*

Every language is liable to continual historical change and to local dialectal variation. The Old English language brought by the Anglo-Saxons from the Continent differentiated itself from the other Germanic languages spoken by the peoples who remained behind, even though all the Germanic languages belong to the same Indo-European family; and the Anglo-Saxons themselves spoke different dialects of Old English. Middle English similarly followed the inevitable processes of change and variation, so that it is not possible to present a single succinct description of the language that can apply equally to the Peterborough monk writing in Northamptonshire in 1121 and to William Dunbar writing in Southeastern Scotland in 1500.

The difficulty of describing Middle English is increased by the fact that language is a human oral behavior that is inadequately represented by even the most precise phonetic transcription and is only sketchily recorded by the usual haphazard processes of writing. Language is a signaling device dependent on an interconnected system of six different kinds of contrasts: phonemic contrasts between discrete sounds, both vowels (*bat/but*) and consonants (*bat/cat*); morphemic contrasts between forms (*cat/cats*); syntactic contrasts between constructions (*This is a cat/Is this a cat?*); semantic contrasts between words (*cat/dog*); stress contrasts between syllables (I'll *per-mít* you/I'll give you a *pér-mit*); and intonational contrasts between sentences (*This is a cat./This is a cat?*). English uses no contrasts other than these six (pitch provides intonational contrast but does not, as in Chinese, provide semantic tone contrast).

Despite the apparent simplicity of this signaling system, subtle historical changes and dialectal variations have differentiated our own Modern English from Middle English, so that we cannot be absolutely certain what a Middle English speaker sounded like or what he meant by what he said. Lacking native informants, we must therefore turn to the educated guesses of the philologists, which are briefly summarized below.

SOUNDS

For those readers who wish only the simplest possible advice, the following three rules provide the approximate sound contrasts intended by Middle English writers. The qualities of certain long stressed vowels, in particular, have changed considerably between the Middle English period and the present, even though the spelling of many of the words in which they occur has not changed at all.

(1) *Pronounce all written consonants as we do those in Modern English.* Also, pronounce the sound (now foreign to English) represented by *gh* in *night* as we pronounce the *h* sound in *how* but with a stronger breathing. (It is like the *ch* in the Scottish pronunciation of *loch*—not *lock*—or in the German pronunciation of *Bach*.)

(2) *Pronounce all final syllables*, even those represented by a final *-e*, no longer pronounced in Modern English. Middle English final *-e* has been marked *-è* in the following discussion. Thus, pronounce *damè* with two syllables as *dah-meh*, and *damès* as *dah-mess*. (The sound of the final *-è* is the same as that in the unstressed final syllable of the Modern English word *crooked*.)

(3) *Give all written vowels, both short and long, their so-called Continental sounds*, such as they would receive, for instance, in Modern French or Italian or in our modern pronunciation of Latin.

Therefore, pronounce the long vowel spelled `a` in Middle English *damè* as the *ah* sound of Modern French *dame* or Modern English *father*. Similarly, all of the following were pronounced with a stressed *ah* sound (and a final unstressed syllable, Rule 2): *barè, carè, famè, gamè, hatè, lamè, makè, namè, pagè, ragè, savè, takè, wakè.*

11

Pronounce the long vowel spelled *e* or *ee* in Middle English *regioun* as the *ay* sound of Modern French *région* or Modern English *rage*. Other instances are Middle English *be, he, me, she, thee*. For simplicity's sake, readers may ignore the set of words in which the *e* or *ee* as in Middle English *heeth* (modern *heath*) represents a distinctive vowel sound like that in Modern English *ebb*, but lengthened in duration.

Pronounce the long vowel spelled *i* or *y* in Middle English *fine* as the *ee* sound in Modern French *fine* or Modern English *machine*. Similarly: *bitè, glidè, kyndè, minè, primè, ridè, strivè, thinè, wyn* (modern *wine*).

Pronounce the long vowel *u* spelled *ou* or *ow* in Middle English *doutè* as the *ou* sound in Modern French *doute* or Modern English *rouge*. Similarly: *bour* (modern *bower*), *flour* (modern *flower*), *foul, hous, licour, mous, out, tour* (modern *tower*).

The other long vowels and diphthongs and all the short vowels have passed down into Modern English with less notable change, and the nonspecialist may therefore rely on his instinct for their pronunciation.

For a more detailed analysis of the Middle English sound system, see *Appendix I: Pronunciation of Middle English* (pp. 548–51).

FORMS

All obscure forms in the selections in this anthology have been interpreted in the marginal glosses, but a recognition of frequently recurring forms and constructions will facilitate the reading of Middle English.

Pronouns are the same as in Modern English, with the chief exception of two ambiguities that have now disappeared. The word variously spelled *her, here, hir, hire* is the Middle English equivalent not only of the modern *her* but also of the modern *their*, and the Middle English *his* is the equivalent not only of modern *his* but also of *its*.

In Old English the definite article, the adjective, and the noun were fully declined according to number, case, and gender. Early Middle English retained many of the inherited contrasting forms, which are interpreted in the glosses when necessary, but by the time of Chaucer, Middle English had reduced the number of contrasting forms so completely that it differed in usage only slightly from Modern English. Thus, in Old English the contrasting forms for the nominative singular, genitive singular, and nominative plural of the masculine article, adjective, and noun were respectively *sē gōda stān, thaes gōdan stānes, thā gōdan stānas;* in Chaucerian Middle English these became *the goodè ston, the goodè stonès, the goodè stonès;* and in Modern English, *the good stone, the good stone's* (or *of the good stone*), *the good stones*. The typical Old English feminine declension showed the following contrasting forms: *sēo gōdè caru, thaerè gōdan carè, thā gōdan cara;* the Chaucerian forms were *the goodè carè, the goodè carès, the goodè carès;* and the Modern English, *the good care, the good care's. the good cares.*

Verb forms generally resemble their modern counterparts, but the following peculiarities should be noted. The Middle English third person singular of the present usually appears as *he loveth*, rather than *he loves*. Verbs with roots ending

12

in *-d* or *-t*, however, regularly contracted the ending *-eth*, thus appearing as *he bit* (for *biddeth*), *fint* (*findeth*), *holt* (*holdeth*), *rit* (*rideth*), *stant* (*standeth*). Also, the commonly occurring *him lest* (or *list* or *lüst*) 'it pleases him,' is contracted from *lesteth* and has a past tense *him leste*, 'it pleased him.'

Many verb endings had a final *-n*, which by the fourteenth century was often dropped. Thus, the older form (*we, ye, they*) *lovèn* could optionally be replaced by *lovè* (the forerunner of the modern form *love*); (*we*) *lovedèn* by *lovedè* (modern *loved*); and *to lovèn* by *to lovè* (modern *to love*). Also the old prefix *y-* could optionally be dropped, so that *I have y-lovèd* could be replaced by *I have lovèd* (modern *I have loved*) and *I havè y-dronkè(n)* by *I have dronkè(n)* (modern *I have drunk*).

There were two alternative signs of the negative. One was the still familiar *not* (or its older variants *nought* and *naught*). The other was the now archaic *ne* (or *n'* before vowels). *Ne* combined with the following verb in certain frequently occurring collocations: *nadde* (*ne hadde*, modern *hadn't*), *nere* (modern *weren't*), *nolde* (modern *wouldn't*), *noot* (*ne woot*, modern *know not*), *nyl* (modern *will not*), *nyste* (*ne wiste*, modern *knew not*). *Ne* was often accompanied by other negative words, so that Chaucer's sentence *He nevere yet no vileynye ne sayde in al his lyf unto no maner wight* (literally, 'He never yet no villainy didn't say to no kind of person') was a perfectly grammatical expression of the statement *He never yet spoke any villainy to any kind of person.*

A frequent variant of the conjugated form of the past tense was provided by the verb *gan* (meaning literally 'began' followed by the infinitive, so that *he gan ridè(n)* could be used to mean either 'he began to ride' or 'he did ride' or simply 'he rode.'

For a more detailed account of the Middle English conjugational system, see *Appendix II: The Middle English Verb* (pp. 552–53).

SYNTAX

There are many subtle differences in syntax between Middle English and Modern English, but few will present any real difficulty to the reader. We occasionally may be surprised by the casual disregard for sentence structure and logic shown by such writers as Robert Mannyng and, ironically, the author of the preface to the Wyclifite translation of the Bible (notice his confusing attempt to coordinate ideas in the long sentence beginning "And these thre goostly understondingis," p. 486).

Many writers of Middle English, however, were masters of rhetorical control. In this respect, the highly literate author of *The Pearl* and *Sir Gawain and the Green Knight* particularly repays study. The poet knows instinctively how, for instance, to modulate *if*-clauses in Shakespearean style by means of inversion: *But wolde ye, lady lovely, then leve me grante* ("But, if you would, lovely lady, then grant me leave," p. 415). He develops long and intricate sentences with complete clarity, as in *Sir Gawain and the Green Knight*, page 425, lines 1508–1524, where he confidently inserts an eight-line, parenthetical sentence within a main sentence that, despite its extraordinary length, is not only completely comprehensible but also artistically effective. And these random examples of his virtuosity represent a norm and not an exception.

SEMANTICS

Readers should be constantly alert to the fact that words change their meanings through the ages. In a sense, a word conveys its meaning not so much by itself as by the contrast it implies between itself and other related words within the same semantic field; but words tend to shift unpredictably out of one field into another. The word *nice*, aptly used by Chaucer in the passage quoted above (p. 10), provides a good example. Borrowed through French from Latin *nescius* 'ignorant,' it used to mean 'ignorant,' in contrast to 'knowing.' But in the sense 'not knowing more than is immediately relevant,' it came to mean 'precise.' And in the sense 'not wishing to know too much,' it came variously to mean 'silly' or 'saintly' or 'pleasant,' according to the viewpoint of those who judged the "nice" person. We can, therefore, know what Chaucer intended by his use of the word only by examining his context and the available range of meanings recorded in the Middle English written during this period. Here dictionaries are more reliable than intuition, but the glosses in this anthology at least provide due warning of semantic traps.

STRESS AND INTONATION

In Middle English, syllabic stress tended to fall on the first syllable of words inherited from Old English, such as *lá-dy* (modern *lady*, unchanged in stress), and on the last syllable (not counting an unstressed final *-e*) of words borrowed from French, such as *li-cóur* and *cor-áge* (modern *líqu-or* and *cóur-age*, with stress now shifted to the first syllable). Thus, a rhyme between *rágė* and *corágė* was not artificial. Here again a dictionary is requisite.

Little can now be discovered about Middle English sentence intonation, but it probably did not differ considerably from that of Modern English.

WRITING

Writing is a device by which one records what one has said (or wishes one had said). As a device for communication between contemporaries who speak the same dialect, writing works well. But as a device for notifying readers who speak a later form of the language, it fails, for various technical reasons, to represent the living interplay of sounds, forms, arrangements, meanings, stresses, and intonations that constitutes an author's spoken utterance.

Furthermore, Middle English works seldom survive in manuscripts written by the author himself but have generally been copied or recopied from lost originals by scribes living in a later age and speaking some dialect other than the author's. Indeed, even under the author's supervision, scribes—like modern secretaries— could be fallible, as Chaucer attests in his *Words unto Adam His Own Scriven*:

14

Under thy long lokkes thou most° have the scalle°	may scale
But° after my makyng thou wryte more trewe,	Unless
So ofte a-daye I mot° thy werk renewe,	must
It to correcte and eek to rubbe and scrape,	
And al is thorough thy negligence and rape.°	haste

So that readers may have some idea of the nature of the manuscript tradition on which our knowledge of Middle English literature depends, we have reproduced, on pages 16–27, six pages (or columns of pages), all of which contain portions of the texts published in this anthology. (The manuscript sources of several other selections, as the headnotes indicate, are available in modern reproductions.) As will be clear from the literal transcriptions of the first few lines of these manuscript pages, Middle English scribes did not represent each contrasting sound by a contrasting letter, any more than Modern English writers do, nor did they indicate syllabic stress or sentence intonation. They sometimes used punctuation to indicate midpoints and end of poetic lines, but they seldom used it to indicate syntactic units; and their use of capitalization was individualistic rather than systematic.

of feole kineriche. And ardur
forþ wunede. mid wal þere bui
de. fiftene ʒeh after. feorðliche
wunden. von mihte þere lar
ce. tƕa glouen iþrafte. þa ƕat
þer þa mære. þan selfte to lare
ne. of tƕa hundred þusend
monnen. þa þer lereu to haiðie
Buten ardur þe king ane. 7 of
hit cnihtes tƕeien. Ak ardur ƕe
for wunded. Wunder ane sƕide.
þer to him com a cnihne. he ƕes
of hit cunne. he ƕes Cadores
sune. þe eorles of Corwnile.
Constantin hehte þe cnine. he
ƕes þan kinge deore. Ardur
hun lokede on þet he lai on
folden. And þas word seide.
mid sorhfulle heorte. Costen
tin þu art wilcume. þu weore
Cadores sone. Ich þe bitache
here. mine kineriche. And ƕi
re mine brittes. a to þines li
fes. And held heom alle þa la
ʒen. þa habbeoð istonden a
mine daʒen. And alle þe la
ʒen gode. þa bi uðeres daʒen
stode. And ich wulle uaren
to aualun. to ueirest alre mai
dene. To Argante þere quie
ne. Aluen sƕiðe scone. 7
heo sƕal mine wunden. ma
kien alle isunde. Al hal me

makien. Mid hale-berze dren
chen. And seoððich cume ƕil
le. to mine kineriche. And ƕu
men mid brutten. mid muþe
lere wunne. æfne þan worden
þer com of se wenden. þet ƕe
an sƕort þet liðen. seorien
mid uðen. And tƕa ƕimme
þer inne. Wunderliche idih
te. And heo nomen arður ana.
And ea ƕeouſte hine uereden.
And softe hine adun leiden.
7 forð gunnen hine liðen. þa
ƕes hit iwurðen. þet chlu
seide Wlwlen. þet ƕære um
mete care. of arðures forð si
re. Bruttes ileueð ʒete. þet he
bon on liue. And wunnen
in auelun. and fayrest alre
aluen. And lokieð euere þet
tes ʒete. When arður cume
lide. Þis nauer þe mon iboren
of nauer nane burde icoren
þe cunne of þan soðe. of ar
dure suggen mare. Bute Wh
ile ƕes an ulk þet et weorldin
hette. he ƕede mid worde
þischulder ƕearen soð. þet
du arður sculde ʒete. cum
anglen to fulſte. Costen
tin þul leouede on londe. 7
bruttes hine luueðe. And ƕi
de deore teomið. ƕes ſ ſ

PLATE 1   British Museum Manuscript (ca. 1225), Cotton Caligula A ix, folio 171 verso. The corresponding passage of Lawman's *Brut* (ca. 1200), printed on page 52, begins in the first column at the middle of line 10 (opposite the cropped marginal note [*Ar*]*ður*) and ends in the second column, four lines from the bottom. Lines 10–14 can be transliterated as follows:

> his cnihtes tweien. Arður wes
> forwunded, wunder ane swiðe.
> þer to him com a cnaue, þe wes
> of his cunne. he wes Cadores
> sune, the eorles of Corwaile.

The graphemes (contrasting letter forms) used by the scribe are for the most part still familiar, though *i* is also used without contrast for *j*, *r* in its familiar form alternates with a now extinct variant shaped like the number *2*, *s* alternates with a long *s* variant still used by eighteenth-century printers (∫, not *f*), and *u* is also used without contrast for *v*. Additionally, the scribe uses three graphemes that were inherited from Old English writing but have gradually dropped out of use: ȝ (Old English yogh, here equivalent to two different sounds, *y* and *gh*), ð (Old English eth, equivalent to the modern grapheme *th*), and þ (Old English thorn, also equivalent to *th*).

The scribe often uses contractions for letters, such as an abbreviated *s* above the vowel it follows, and a long mark over a vowel to indicate a following *n* (which, however, he forgets to insert over the *o* in *Cor*[*n*]*waile* 'Cornwall'). He also uses contrasting capital letters, but not in the same consistent way that they are used in Modern English writing. His punctuation is intended to mark metrical lines and half-lines, but not, as in Modern English, syntactic divisions. A period marks the end of each full line; a kind of inverted semicolon marks the end of a half-line.

þer is a wel fair abbei·
of white monkes & of grei·
þer beþ bowris & halles·
al of pasteus beþ þe walles·
of fleis of fisse & a rich met,
þe likfullist þat man mai et.
fluren cakes beþ þe scingles alle·
of cherch· cloister· bour & halle
þe pinnes beþ fat podinges·
rich met to princes & kinges·
man mai þerof et inoʒ·
al wiþ riʒt & noʒt wiþ woʒ·
al is commune to ʒung & old·
to stoute & sterne mek & bold·
þer is a cloister fair & liʒt·
brod & lang of sembli siʒt·
þe pilers of þe cloister alle·
beþ iturned of cristale·
wiþ har las & capitale·
of grene iaspe & rede corale·
In þe praer is a tre·
swiþe likful forto se·
þe rote is gingeuir & galingale·
þe siouns beþ al sedwale·
tender maces beþ þe flure·
þe rind canel of swet odur·

PLATE 2   British Museum Manuscript (ca.1308–18), Harley 913, folio 4 recto. The corresponding passage of *The Land of Cokayne* (ca. 1275–1300) is printed on pages 189–90, lines 51–76. The first six lines can be transliterated as follows:

> þer is a wel fair abbei.
> of white monkes & of grei.
> þer beþ bowris & halles.
> al of pasteiis beþ þe walles.
> of fleis of fisse & [*second & deleted*] rich met.
> þe likfullist that man mai et.

The shapes of letters and the forms of contractions in both this plate and in Plates 3 and 4 differ somewhat from those in Plate 1, but the graphemic system is the same. Poetic lines are written separately, and the end of each line is marked with a nonsyntactic period.

f ...ton wip outen hade
sum non armes nade ·
sum purth pe bodi hadde wounde ·
sum lay wode y bounde ·
sum armed on hors sete ·
sum astrangled as pai ete ·
sum were in water adreint ·
sum wip fire al for shreint ·
mes per lay onchis lede ·
...nd & sum awede ·
wonder fele p lay bisides ·
...t as pai slepe her vnder tides ·
...de was pus in pis warld y nome
...p fairi pider y come
...r he seie his owhen wiif ·
...me bewdit his his liif ·
...lepe vnder an ympe tre ·
...har cloper he knewe p it was he ·
Wen he hadde bihold pis ...alle
e went in to pe kinges halle ·
an seie he per a semly sizt ·
taber nade blisseful & brizt ·
...r in her manie kinges sete ·
...r quen fair & swete ·
...r crounes per cloper shine so brizt ·
...t vnnepe biolde he hem mizt ·
...en he hadde biholden alpat ping ·
e kneled adoun bifor pe king ·
lord he seyd zif it pi wille were ·
vnexstrat pou shust y here ·
e king answerd what man art...
...at art pider y to men noll ·
...ch no non pat is wip me ·
...o sent neuer after pe ·
...eppen pat ich here regni can ·
no fond neuer so fole hardi man ·
...at pider to ous durst wende ·
...ot pat ich him wald of sende ·
...rd quap pe tu welle ful wel ·
nam bot a pouer menstrel ·
sir it is pe maner of ous ·
...o seche mani a lordes hous ·
...ei we nouzt welcom nowe ·
...ete we mot profert forp our gle

B ...t for pe king he sat adoun ·
& tok his harp souns of soun
...en pley his harp as he wele can ·
blisseful notes he per gan ·
...at al pat in pe palays were ·
...om to hi forto here ·
...layden adoun to his fete ·
...em penkep his melody so swete ·
e king herknep & sitt ful stille ·
o here his gle he hap god wille ·
ok wunde he hadde of his gle ·
e riche quen al so hadde he ·
...en he hadde strut his harping ·
...an seyd to him pe king ·
...enstrel me likep wele pi gle ·
olk aske of me what it be ·
argelich ichil pe pay ·
olk speke & wolt mizt asay ·
...r he seyd ich biseche pe ·
...atow woldest ziue me ·
...at ich leuedi brizt on ble ·
...at slepep vnder pe ympe tre ·
...ay quap pe king pat nouzt nere ·
...son couple of zou it were ·
...or pou art lene rowe & blac ·
...he is louesum wip oute lac ·
...loplich ping it were forpi ·
...o sen hir in pi companyn ·
...sir he seyd gentil king ·
...ete were it a wele fouler ping
...o here a lesing of pi moupe ·
...o sir as ze seyd noupe ·
...hatt ich wold aske haue y shold ·
...nedes pou most pi word shold ·
...e king seyd seppen it is so ·
...ake hir bi pe hond & go ·
...f hir ichil patow be blipe ·
...e kneled adoun & ponked hi swipe ·
...is wiif he tok bi pe hond ·
...dede hi swipe out of pat lond ·
...went hi out of pat pede ·
...ut as he come pe way he zede ·
...o long he hap pe way y nome ·
...o winchester he is y come ·

PLATE 3   National Library of Scotland Manuscript (London?, ca. 1330–40), Auchinleck, Advocates 19.2.1, folio 302 recto. The corresponding passage from *Sir Orfeo* (ca. 1330) is printed on pages 225–27, lines 391–478. The first six lines of the second column can be transliterated as follows:

> Bifor þe king he sat adoun.
> & tok his harp so miri of soun.
> & tempreþ his harp as he wele can.
> & blisseful notes he þer gan.
> þat al þat in þe palays were.
> com to him forto here.

Skottes out of berwik and of abirdene
at þe banok burn war ȝe to kene
þare sloȝh ȝe many sakles als it was sene
and now has king Edward wroken it I wene
It es wroken I wene wele wurth þe while
war ȝit wrth þe skottes for þai er full of gile
Whare er ȝe skottes of saint Johnes toune
þe boste of ȝoure baner es beten all doune
When ȝe bosting will bede sir Edward es boune
forto kindel ȝow care and crak ȝoure croune
he has crakked ȝoure croune wele werth þe while
schame bryde þe skottes for þai er full of gile
Skottes of striflin war steren and stout
of god ne of gude men had þai no dout
now haue þai þe pelers prikes obout
bot at þe last sir Edward rifild þare rout
he has rifild þare rout wele wurth þe while
bot euer er þai vnder bot gaudes and gile
E nglisshe men rueling now kindels þi care
berebag with þi boste þi bigging es bare
fals wrecche and for sworn whider wilton fare
busk þe vnto brig and abide þare
þare wrecche saltou won and werp þe while
þi dwelling in donde es done for þi gile
Ye skottes gase in burghes and betes þe stretes
all þise inglis men harmes he betes
fast makes he his mone to men yf he metes
bot fone frendes he findes þat his bale betes
fune betes his bale wele wurth þe while
he vses all threting with gaudes and gile
Bot many man threetes and spekes full ill
þat sum tyme war better to be stane still
þe skot in his wordes has wind forto spill
for at þe last Edward sall haue al his will
he had his will at berwik wele wurth þe while
skottas broght him þe kayes bot get for þaire gile

Duke king
into braban
þe kayser Lo
þat in þat
he and als in
and oþer pr
visschopes a
þat had ful
princes and
al þat spac
all þai come
sir Edward
and pferd
forto hald
Ye duke of
swore for th
þat he sul
help sir Ed
in toun in
þe sWore
and al þe
and þarto
þan king
at andwe
and þare
þat no in
his mone
left in þ
and all þe
fars þe v
When pl
þarat þe
he gert a
princes a
At parisl
Whilk þe

PLATE 4   British Museum Manuscript (ca. 1400–25), Cotton Galba E ix, folio 52 verso, left-hand column. The corresponding version of Laurence Minot's *Halidon Hill* (ca. 1333) is printed in its entirety on pages 231–32. The first six lines can be transliterated as follows:

> Skottes out of berwik and of abirdene
> at þe bannok burn war ʒe to kene
> þare slogh ʒe many sakles als it was sene
> and now has king Edward wroken it I wene
> It es wrokin I wene wele wurth þe while
> war ʒit with þe skottes for þai er ful of gile

The grapheme *th* is now used alternately with the older form þ (thorn), and no punctuation is used at all. In line 2 ān represents *ann*.

How he þ[at] quauut was mayden marie
And say his loue floure and fructifie

Al þogh his lyfe be queynt þe resemblaunce
Of him hath in me so fressh lyflynesse
Þat to putte othir men in remembraunce
Of his p[er]sone I haue heere his lyknesse
Do make to þis ende in sothfastnesse
Þat þei þt haue of him left þought & mynde
By þis peynture may ageyn him fynde

The ymages þt in þe chirche been
Maken folk þenke on god & on his seyntes
Whan þe ymages þei be holden & seen
Were oft vnsyte of hem causith restreyntes
Of þoughtes gode whan a þing depeynt is
Or entailed if men take of it heede
Thoght of þe lyknesse it wil in hym brede

Yit somme holden oppynyon and sey
þt none ymages schuld maked be
þei erren foule & goon out of þe wey
Of trouth haue þei scant sensibilite
Passe ou[er] þt now blessid trinite
Vppon my maistres soule m[er]cy haue
ffor him lady eke þi m[er]cy I craue

More othir þing wolde I fayne speke & touche
Heere in þis booke but such is my dulnesse
ffor þt al voyde and empty is my pouche
þat al my lust is queynt w[i]t[h] heuynesse
And heuy spirit commaundith stilnesse

PLATE 5   British Museum Manuscript (ca. 1412), Harley 4866, folio 88 recto. The corresponding passage from Thomas Hoccleve's *Regiment of Princes* (ca. 1412) is printed on page 508, lines 13–40. The second stanza on the page begins as follows:

> Al þogh his lyfe be queynt þe resemblaunce
> Of him haþ in me so fressh lyflynesse
> þat to putte othir men in remembraunce
> Of his persone I haue heere his lyknesse

Thorn is still used optionally as a grapheme for *th*, along with the more modern *th*, but yogh has been replaced by *gh*. No punctuation is used.

The British Museum MS. Arundel 38 may once have contained what would have been a slightly earlier version of this portrait, but the page is missing now. The earliest portrait of Chaucer appears in the Ellesmere MS. of *The Canterbury Tales* (ca. 1400). See Margaret Rickert, *Painting in Britain: The Middle Ages* (Harmondsworth, 1954), p. 185; Jerome Mitchell, *Thomas Hoccleve* (Urbana, 1968), pp. 110–15.

And ned not fo with thy heuy hede
Tel vs fome thinge that draweth of to fpeke
Onely of iore and make no lenger fette
And when I fanghe it wolde be no bette
I obered vnto his byddynge
And as the lawe me bounde in alle thynge
As I koude with a ful pale chere
My tale I ganne anone as ye shal here

❧ Expliett prologus ❧

❧ Prima pars ❧

Here begynneth the Segge of Thebes ful
lamentably tolde by Iohn lidgate Monke of
Bury annexynge it to ye talys of Canturi

Irs quod I ficth of youre Curtefye
I entrede am in to youre Companye
And admytted a tale for to tele
By hym that hath power to compele
I mene oure hofte gouernere and gyde
Of youre erheone rydenge here by fyde
Thogh my wit barryne be and dulle
I wolle reherce a ftorry wonderfulle
Touchenge the fegge and deftruchyon
Of worthy Thebes the myghty royale Ton
Bilt and bygonne of olde antiquite
Vpon the tyme of worthy Iofue
By diligence of kynge Amphion
Cheeff caufe firft of this foundachon

PLATE 6   British Museum Manuscript (prepared either in 1455–56 or 1461–62), Royal 18 D ii, folio 148 recto, lower right-hand column. The corresponding passage from John Lydgate's *Siege of Thebes* (ca. 1421) is found on pages 510–12, lines 38–125.

The rubric beneath the miniature and the following three lines of poetry can be transliterated as follows:

PRIMA PARS

Here begynneth the Segge of Thebes ful
lamentably tolde by John Lidgate Monke of
Bury anneyynge it to þe tallys of Canterbury

Sirs quod I. sith of youre Curtesye
I enterde am. in to youre Companye
And admytted. a tale for to tele

As in Plate 5, thorn is still used optionally for *th*, and yogh has been displaced by *gh*. A period is used to mark each half-line, and no other punctuation appears.

This handsome manuscript was commissioned by Sir William Herbert (later Earl of Pembroke) as a gift for either Henry VI or Edward IV. The miniature of the Canterbury pilgrims, painted around 1509–19 by an artist of the Flemish school, was added in a space that had been reserved for it by the scribe.

The pictorial and symbolic details in the miniature deserve attention. The third figure from the left is certainly John Lydgate, dressed in the ascetic clothing mentioned in his prologue. The other characters are drawn from Chaucer's Prologue to *The Canterbury Tales*. The fourth figure from the left is probably Chaucer's worldly monk, with sleeves trimmed in fur, who is thought to have been, like Lydgate, a Benedictine, though certainly not a strict member of the order. (The artist has perhaps deliberately provided the Monk's horse with donkey's ears.) The second figure from the left is probably Chaucer; both rider and horse, in fact, closely resemble their early counterparts in the Ellesmere Manuscript (ca. 1400–10) of *The Canterbury Tales*.

The other pilgrims are ambiguous. The first figure on the left might be Chaucer's Yeoman, but according to *The Canterbury Tales*, he should bear a mighty bow rather than a spear. The young rider, fifth from the left, could be the Squire, for his sleeves are appropriately long and wide, even though he is not "embroidered like a meadow." The bearded rider on the extreme right might be the Merchant, with his Flemish beaver hat.

The miniature, as is to be expected in this period, does not render the setting in true perspective or in precise detail, but it is at least schematically accurate, and its pattern may have a symbolic intention. The pilgrims on their return journey to Southwark have appropriately left the walled town of Canterbury by the West Gate (still standing). The massive cathedral within the walls can be readily identified, although it is not accurately oriented.

The nearer of the two buildings outside the walls, at the upper left of the miniature, may correspond to the actual inn where pilgrims used to stay when the city gates were shut at night. The building behind the inn may be St. Dunstan's Church, though the proportions are exaggerated and its position is incorrect. Its inclusion in the miniature could well be intended as a tribute to St. Dunstan, who was renowned not only as an archbishop of Canterbury but also as a monastic reformer who introduced a new standard of piety and asceticism to the English branch of the Benedictine order, of which Lydgate himself was such an outstanding representative.

For the standard description of this manuscript, see Sir George F. Warner and Julius P. Gilson, *Catalogue of Western Manuscripts in the Old Royal and King's Collections* (London, 1921), II, 308–10.

VERSIFICATION

Middle English versification reflects a wide range of traditions and innovations. Alliterative verse, inherited from the native tradition, is represented, for instance, by the uncomplicated lines of Lawman's *Brut*, which do not fully meet the strict Old English requirements, and also by the alliterative stanzas of *Sir Gawain and the Green Knight*, which, because of their patterning, exceed these requirements. Similarly, rhyming verse, originally adopted from French usage, is represented not only by the erratic couplets of *King Horn* but also by the intricate concatenations of *The Pearl*.

The various types represented in this anthology are enumerated below. Terminology has been standardized and simplified as far as possible, but some of the alternate terms often used in descriptions of metrics have been included. The term *beat* has been used in preference to the term *stress*, which is best reserved for grammatical descriptions. The beat (marked with an acute accent in the examples quoted below) can be thought of as the segment of a poetic measure where the listener may expect to find a recurrence of the emphasis that is implicit within the poet's metrical pattern. Usually, the beat coincides with a syllable carrying emphatic syllabic stress and also the pitch stress of intonation; but poets in the Middle English period, just as in other eras, felt free to invert stresses, to elide unstressed finals, and to syncopate or expand their syllabic count in order to avoid metrical imprisonment.

In describing forms of versification, *A* signifies a stressed initial sound alliterating with another identical initial sound *A*, *X* signifies a nonalliterating stressed sound in the same line. In rhyming verse, *a* signifies an ending rhyming with an identical ending *a* in another line, and *x* signifies an ending that does not rhyme with an ending in any other line. A superscript with the rhyming letter indicates the number of beats per line (thus, a^3 indicates a three-beat line).

ALLITERATIVE VERSE

1. Conventional alliterative verse

Middle English alliterative verse, sometimes referred to as long-line alliteration, was inherited from Old English. Each long line is divided by a break, or caesura, into two half-lines. Each half-line carries two beats and an unrestricted number of unstressed syllables. The half-lines are linked by alliteration, designated as *A*, between at least one of the stressed syllables in the first half and at least one stressed syllable in the second half. Alliterating consonants must be phonetically identical, no matter how they are represented in spelling; a vowel may alliterate either with itself repeated or with any other vowel.

As in Old English, the nonalliterating stressed syllables, designated as *X*, provide a melodic contrast. Schematically, *AA* or *AX* or *XA* in the first half-line must alliterate with either *AA* or *AX* or *XA*; there were thus nine different possible combinations. In Old English the historically dominant pattern was *AA AX*, while full alliteration *AA AA* was apparently not felt to be essentially desirable. But in Middle English verse, every possible pattern occurs, including an optional tenth combination *AA BB*, in which each half-line alliterates only within itself.

The most artistic alliterative verse appears in the West Country in the latter half of the fourteenth century, during the period known as the Alliterative Revival (which should perhaps be called the Alliterative Survival, since the tradition was unbroken). Alliterative verse apparently seemed provincial and even rustic to London audiences, accustomed as they were to rhyming verse. Chaucer's Parson patronizingly remarks that, being a southern man, he cannot "rum, ram, ruf by letter." Many poets of the western counties, however, used the device with great ability and subtlety. The author of *Sir Gawain and the Green Knight* appraises more sympathetically than the Parson its characteristic distinction. He intends, he says in a memorable phrase, to recite his romance "as it is stad [recorded] and stoken [set down] in story stif [brave] and strong with lel [loyal] lettres loken [linked], as in lond so [as] has ben longe." A typical example of alliterative verse can be found in *The Parliament of the Three Ages*:

In the monethe of Maye · when mirthes bene fele

(l. 1, AA AX)

With auntlers one aythere syde · egheliche longe
(l. 28, vowel alliteration, AA AX)

And I slitte hym at the assaye · to see how me semyde
(l. 70, full alliteration, AA AA)

Other selections using this type are *Morte Arthure*, *Piers Plowman*, and *Blacksmiths*.

29

2. Alliterative stanzas

Sir Gawain and the Green Knight is an unusual poem that contains stanzas of twelve to thirty-eight alliterative lines, each terminated by five rhyming lines—a one-beat "bob" of two syllables and a heavily alliterated four-line "wheel" of either three-beat lines or alternating four-beat and three-beat lines (a^1 $b^{3/4}$ a^3 $b^{3/4}$ a^3).

> Sithen the sége and the assaut · was sésed at Tróyè,
>
> (l. 1, alliterating AA AX)

wyth wynnè,	a^1
Where werre and wrake and wonder	b^3
Bi sythès has wont ther-innè,	a^3
And óft bothe blysse and blunder	b^3
Ful skete has skyfted synnè.	a^3

(ll. 15–19, rhyming)

3. Semi-alliterative, semi-rhyming verse

An early and generally crude transitional form of Middle English verse, still depending basically on the inherited patterns of Old English alliteration, introduced lines of rhyming couplets as an optional variation in place of alliterating lines. The model for this variation was probably the Old French and Anglo-Norman eight-syllable (octosyllabic) rhyming couplet, such as that used by Wace (the source of Lawman's *Brut*). This example is drawn from *The Proverbs of Alfred*:

> And ek Eálvred, · Englenè hürdè
>
> (I, 5, alliterating AA AX)
>
> Byhüd hit on thirè heortè · that thee éft ne smeortè
>
> (XIII, 10, rhyming a a)

Other examples of this type of meter are *The Brut* and *The Bestiary*.

RHYMING VERSE

4. Three-beat couplets, a^3a^3

In *King Horn* alliteration within half-lines is frequent, and linking alliteration sometimes connects one line with the next, but the consistent rhyme scheme is the central device of versification. (Syllabic stress is often irregular.)

> Rymenild ros of benchè
>
> The beèr for tè shenchè.
>
> (ll. 1107–08, alliterating and rhyming)

5. Four-beat couplets, a⁴a⁴

The French and Anglo-Norman eight-syllable couplet was only incompletely adapted by the first Middle English alliterative poets (see type 3), but the four-beat couplet (short couplet) became the favorite form among Middle English rhyming poets and dominated verse until Chaucer turned from it to the five-beat couplet. The selections that use the short couplet are *The Owl and the Nightingale*, *The Fox and the Wolf*, *The Land of Cokayne*, *Handling Sin*, *Sir Orfeo*, *The Bruce*, and *The Lover's Confession*.

6. Five-beat couplets, a⁵a⁵

This iambic-pentameter couplet (heroic couplet) was introduced into English narrative poetry by Chaucer at some time shortly before 1386. The only example here is *The Siege of Thebes*.

7. Seven-beat couplets, x⁴a³x⁴a³

This measure is known variously as common meter, septenary, heptameter, fourteener, and ballad meter. It is often printed as a four-line tail-rhyme stanza, and there is always a break (caesura) between the x⁴ and the a³. (Compare type 11.) Examples are *Poema Morale*, *Judas*, where in some stanzas, the first half-line has only three beats, not four, *The Tale of Beryn*, which was intended as a supplement to *The Canterbury Tales*, though Chaucer never used this meter, *St. Stephen and Herod*, and *Robyn and Gandelyn*.

8. Four-line stanzas, a²b²a²b²

The first and the last stanzas of *Christ and His Mother* are a²b²x²b². The three symmetrical stanzas between these are linked by an a-rhyme: abab, acac, adad. Perhaps the poem is intended as an adaptation of the French *virelai*.

9. Four-line stanzas, a⁴b⁴a⁴b⁴

Thomas of Erceldoun is fundamentally built on four-line units but frequently has longer runs, such as abababab (ll. 41–48) or ababacac (ll. 11–16).

10. Four-line stanzas, a⁶a⁶a⁶a⁶

In *Love in Paris* the lines of the macaronic stanzas, though irregular, can be scanned as six-beat, except for the last stanza, which apparently has a⁵a⁶a⁵a⁶.

11. Eight-line, tail-rhyme stanzas, a⁴b³a⁴b³a⁴b³a⁴b³

April is written in the manuscript in long-line, seven-beat couplets, but it has been printed here in eight-line stanzas, since every stanza except the third contains rhymes linking the first and following four-beat lines. The concluding stanza varies the rhyme scheme but reinforces the eight-line structure ($a^4b^3a^4b^3a^4b^3c^4c^3$).

12. Six-line stanzas, $a^4a^4a^4a^4b^4b^4$

In *Halidon Hill* the meter is irregular but, as in conventional alliterative poetry, primarily four-beat. Alliteration sometimes does not appear (l. 1), sometimes links two stressed words (l. 4), sometimes three (l. 3), and sometimes all four (l. 10).

13. Six-line, tail-rhyme stanzas, $a^4a^4a^4b^3a^4b^3$

This stanza is used in *The Five Joys of Mary*.

14. Six-line, tail-rhyme stanzas, $a^4a^4b^3c^4c^4b^3$

The pattern in *The Sayings of St. Bernard* resembles that of the so-called romance six ($a^4a^4b^3a^4a^4b^3$) parodied by Chaucer in "The Tale of Sir Thopas" (in *The Canterbury Tales*) but is not dominated by the insistent a-rhyme. *Dame Sirith* is also of this type, though some a-lines have only three beats, some b-lines have only two beats, and some passages are four-beat couplets (type 5).

15. Seven-line, tail-rhyme stanzas, $a^4b^2a^4b^2b^2b^4a^2$

The only example here is *Now Springs the Spray*, which is introduced by a three-line refrain, rhyming $a^2c^4a^2$ with the first stanza.

16. Seven-line, tail-rhyme stanzas, $a^4b^{3/4}a^4b^{3/4}b^{3/4}b^{3/4}c^3$

Alysoun is of this type, with a four-line refrain, $d^4d^4d^4c^3$, whose final c-line rhymes with each of the final lines in all four stanzas.

17. Seven-line stanzas, $a^5b^5a^5b^5b^5c^5c^5$

This stanza was introduced into English by Chaucer at some time shortly before 1372 and was made famous by his use of it in *Troilus and Criseyde*. It was subsequently called rhyme royal because of its later use in *The King's Quair*, attributed to James I of Scotland. The two examples here are *The Regiment of Princes* and *The Testament of Cressid*.

18. Eight-line stanzas, $a^4b^4a^4b^4a^4b^4a^4b^4$

A Love Rune exhibits this type of versification, an extension of the four-line, $a^4b^4a^4b^4$ stanza (type 9).

19. Eight-line stanzas, $a^5b^5a^5b^5b^5c^5b^5c^5$

On the Resurrection of Christ is the only example here of this type.

20. Nine-line stanzas, $a^5a^5b^5a^5a^5b^5b^5c^5c^5$

The Golden Targe is the only example here of this type.

21. Twelve-line, tail-rhyme stanzas, $a^4a^4b^3c^4c^4b^3d^4d^4b^3e^4e^4b^3$

This stanza is an extension of the six-line, tail-rhyme stanza (type 13). It appears in *Spring*, in which every line also contains alliteration, either within itself or with the following line. *The Dance of the Seven Deadly Sins* uses the same stanza.

22. Twelve-line stanzas, $a^4b^4a^4b^4a^4b^4a^4b^4b^4c^4b^4c^4$

This stanza appears here only in *The Pearl*, in which approximately two-thirds of the lines also have internal alliteration. For a discussion of concatenation of the stanzas, see below, page 399.

THE
TWELFTH
CENTURY

A PETERBOROUGH CHRONICLER

William the Conqueror

(ca. 1121, East Midland)

❧

In the Benedictine monastery at Peterborough an anonymous scribe acquired a version of the *Old English Annals* and brought the compilation up to date as far as the year 1121. In summarizing the reign of King William I (1066–87) he presents a memorable prose account of the Conqueror, presumably drawn from his own observations. His extensive entry for the year 1087 (erroneously recorded as 1086) well illustrates the presence of a conscious literary style even at a time when Late Old English was about to become Early Middle English. The author writes critically, shows a real sense of history, understands the relation between cause and effect, and appreciates the significance of individual personality. He delights in rhetorical balance and, particularly in the passage quoted here, heightens his effects by the use of rhyme and alliteration. For the symbols ċ and ġ, see Appendix 1, page 548.

The best complete edition of all the *Old English Annals* is still Charles Plummer, *Two of the Saxon Chronicles Parallel* (Oxford, 1892), 2 vols. The best edition of *The Peterborough Chronicle* is edited by Cecily Clark (2nd ed., Oxford, 1970) and contains an important discussion of the development of prose style. The most convenient modernization is G. N. Garmonsway, *The Anglo-Saxon Chronicle* (London and New York, 1953). For the manuscript see *The Peterborough Chronicle*, in *Early English Manuscripts in Facsimile*, IV (Copenhagen and Baltimore, 1954). For bibliography see Wells, ch. 3.1; *CBEL*, 1.88–89, 5.84–86.

Witodliċe on his timan haefdon men myċel ġeswinc and swithe maniġe teonan. Castelas he let wyrċean and earme men swithe swenċean. Se cyng waes swa swithe stearc and benam of his undertheoddan man maniġ marc goldes and ma hundred punda seolfres, thet he nam be wihte and mid myċelan unrihte of his land-leode for
5 littelre neode. He waes on ġitsunge befeallan, and graedinaesse he lufode mid ealle.

He saette myċel deor-frith, and he laeġde laga thaerwith thet swa hwa-swa sloġe heort oththe hinde, thet hine man sċeolde blendian. He forbead tha heortas swylċe eac tha baras. Swa swithe he lufode tha hea-deor swilċe he waere heora faeder. Eac he saette be tham haran thet hi mosten freo faran. His rice men hit maendon,
10 and tha earme men hit beċeorodan. Ac he waes swa stith thet he ne rohte heora eallra nith. Ac hi moston mid ealle thes cynges wille folġian gif hi woldon libban oththe land habban—land, oththe eahta, oththe wel his sehta.

Wala-wa thet aeniġ man sċeolde modiġan swa, hine sylf upp ahebban, and ofer ealle men tellan! Se aelmihtiġa God cythae his saule mildheortnisse and do him
15 his synna forgifenesse!

36

[MODERNIZATION]

Truly in his time men had much toil and many, many troubles. He ordered castles to be built and poor men to toil exceedingly. The king was indeed most severe and seized from his subjects many a mark of gold and many more hundreds of pounds of silver. This he took by weight and with great injustice from the people of his land, with little need. He had fallen into avarice, and he was completely devoted to greed.

He established a great game preserve, and he laid down laws at the same time that, if anyone at all should slay a hart or a hind, he should be blinded. He closed the hunting of harts and also of boars. He loved the stags as much as if he were their father. As for the hares, also, he decreed that they were to travel free. His magnates complained about it, and the poor men grumbled about it. But he was so stubborn that he thought nothing of their unanimous hostility. They, however, had to follow the king's will completely if they wanted to survive or to have land—land, or possessions, or, indeed, his favors.

Alas that any man should be so proud, should exalt himself so high, and count himself above all men! May the Almighty God show mercy to his soul and grant him forgiveness for his sins!

The Anarchy of King Stephen

(ca. 1154, East Midland)

The final section of the Peterborough version of the *Old English Annals* was written by another anonymous scribe at the end of Stephen's reign (1135–54), a generation later than the entry concerning William the Conqueror.

A brief but dramatic portion of the entry for the year 1137 is presented here. In comparison with the earlier chronicler, the last chronicler relies less on rhyme and alliteration and more on parallelism and sentence structure to express his agitated emotions.

I ne can, ne I ne mai, tellen alle the wunder ne alle the pines that hi diden wrecċe men on this land, and that lastede tha nientiene wintre wile Stephne was king, and aevre it was werse and werse.

Hi laeiden ġaeildes on the tunes aevre umwile and clepeden it "tenserie." Tha
5 the wrecċe men ne hadden nan more to ġyven, tha raeveden hi and brendon alle the tunes, that wel thu myhtes faren al a daeis fare, sċuldest thu nevre finden man in tune sittende ne land tiled. Tha was corn daere, and flesċ and ċaese and butere, for nan ne waes o the land. Wrecċe men sturven of hungaer. Sume ieden on aelmes the waren sumwile riċemen; sume fluġen ut of lande.
10 Wes naevre ġaet mare wrecċehed on land, ne naevre hethen men werse ne diden than hi diden, for ofer sithon ne forbaren hi nouther ċirċe ne ċyrċe-iaerd oc namen al the god that tharinne was, and brenden sythen the ċyrċe and al tegaedere. Ne hi ne forbaren bisċopes land ne abbotes ne preostes ac raeveden munekes and clerekes, and aevriċ man other the overmyhte.
15 Ġif two men other thrie coman ridend to an tun, al the tunsċipe fluġaen for heom, wenden that hi waeron raeveres. The bisċopes and leredmen heom cursede aevre, oc was heom naht tharof, for hi weron al forcursaed and forsworen and forloren.

War-sae me tilede, the erthe ne bar nan corn, for the land was al fordon mid
20 swilċe daedes, and hi saeden openliċe that Christ slep and his halechen.

Swilċ, and mare thanne we cunnen saein, we tholeden nientiene wintre for ure sinnes.

38

[MODERNIZATION]

I neither know how, nor am able, to tell of all the horrors and all the tortures that they imposed upon the wretched men in this land, and this lasted for the nineteen winters while Stephen was king, and it was ever worse and worse.

They laid taxes upon the villages time after time and called it "protection." When the wretched men had no more to give, then they raided and burned all the villages, so that you could travel for a whole day's journey, yet would never find a man settled in a village, or land tilled. Then grain was dear, and meat and cheese and butter, for there was none in the land. Wretched men died of hunger. Some turned to alms who had once been rich men; some fled out of the country.

Never yet has there been a greater misery in any land, and heathen men never did worse than they did, for contrary to custom they spared neither church nor churchyard but took all the valuables that were within and then burned the church and all the rest together. They spared the land of neither bishop nor abbot nor priest but raided monks and clerics, and each one who could raided the other.

If two or three men came riding to a village, the entire community fled because of them, assumed that they were raiders. The bishops and clergymen anathematized them repeatedly, but that was nothing to them, for they were all utterly damned, forsworn, and abandoned.

Wheresoever one tilled, the earth bore no corn, for the land was all destroyed by such deeds, and they said openly that Christ and His saints were sleeping.

Such, and more than we are able to tell, we suffered for nineteen winters for our sins.

The Proverbs of Alfred

(ca. 1150–75, Southwestern)

ॐ

The work known as *The Proverbs of Alfred* survives in four manuscripts, all of which were copied at dates considerably later than that of the lost original. They differ from each other in language, arrangement, and meter; but all agree in attributing the collection to Alfred. Alfred the Great, who became king of Wessex in 871 and died in 899, was a patron of letters and himself an author. Yet it seems unlikely that he prepared the original version of this poem in Old English. The contents are timeless, being derived partly from written sources, such as the Old Testament, and partly from universal oral tradition, but the linguistic and metrical evidence suggests that *The Proverbs* was composed in Sussex around 1150 or a little later. The poem, though conventional in content, is lively in style and was apparently popular enough to impress both Lawman and the author of *The Owl and the Nightingale*.

The selection is based on the Jesus College (Oxford) Manuscript (ca. 1280), which contains an early revision (ca. 1200?, Southwestern) divided into twenty-two sections, totaling 458 short lines. Approximately one-third of this version is printed here. The lines, usually printed as half-lines, have been expanded as long lines, as have the comparable lines of Lawman's *Brut* (pp. 49–53). The meter is semi-alliterative, semi-rhyming; see Introduction, type 3, page 30.

The best edition and commentary is O. S. Arngart, *The Proverbs of Alfred* (Lund, 1942, 1955), 2 vols. (The stanza numbers given here are not those of the conflated texts but of the separately edited Jesus College MS.) For bibliography see Wells, ch. 7.5; *CBEL*, 1.180, 5.121.

I

At Sevorde sete theynes monye,
Fele biscopes, and feole boc-ilered,
Eorles prute, knyhtes egleche.
Thar wes the eorl Alvrich, of thare lawe swithe wis,
5   And ek Ealvred, Englene hürde,
Englene dürlyng; on Englelonde he wes kyng.
   Heom he bigon lere, so ye mawe i-hüre,
Hu hi heore lif lede scholden.
Alvred, he wes in Englelond an king wel swithe strong.
10   He wes king, and he wes clerk; wel he luvede Godes werk.
He wes wis on his word and war on his werke;
He wes the wysüste mon that wes Englelonde on.

[MODERNIZATION]

At Seaford[1] many thanes met, many bishops, and many scholars, proud earls, and warlike knights. There was Earl Aelfric,[2] most wise in the law, and Alfred also, the shepherd of the English, the darling of the English; in England he was king.

He began to teach them, as you may hear, how they should conduct their lives. Alfred was in England a king most strong indeed. He was king, and he was cleric; well he loved the work of God. He was wise of word and wary in action; he was the wisest man that there was in England.

[1] In Sussex.
[2] Unidentified.

XIII

Thus queth Alvred:
"If thu havest seorewe, ne seye thu hit than arewe.
Seye hit thine sadelbowe, and ryd thee singinde forth.
Thenne wile wene thet thine wise ne con
5   That thee thine wise wel thee lyke.
Serewe if thu havest, and the erewe hit wot,
Byfore, he thee meneth; byhynde, he thee teleth.
Thu hit myht segge swych mon that hit thee ful wel on;
Wythute echere ore he on thee muchele more.
10   Byhüd hit on thire heorte, that thee eft ne smeorte;
Ne let thu hyne wite al that thin heorte bywite."

XIV

Thus queth Alvred:
"Ne schaltu nevere thi wif by hire wlyte cheose,
For never none thinge that heo to thee bryngeth.
Ac leorne hire cüste—heo cutheth hi wel sone!
5   For mony mon for ayhte üvele i-auhteth,
And ofte mon of fayre, frakele i-cheoseth.
Wo is him that üvel wif bryngeth to his cotlif;
So him is alyve that üvele y-wyveth,
For he schal uppon eorthe dreori i-würthe.
10   Mony mon singeth that wif hom bryngeth;
Wiste he hwat he brouhte, wepen he myhte."

XV

Thus queth Alvred:
"Ne würth thu never so wod ne so wyn-drunke
That evere segge thine wife alle thine wille.
For if heo i-seye thee bivore thine i-vo alle,
5   And thu hi myd worde i-wreththed hevedest,
Ne schulde heo hit lete, for thing lyvyinde,
That heo ne scholde thee forth upbreyde of thine baleu-sythes.
"Wymmon is word-wod and haveth tunge too swift.
Theyh heo wel wolde, ne may heo hi nowiht welde."

42

[MODERNIZATION]

Thus said Alfred: "If you have a sorrow, do not tell it to one who is a betrayer. Tell it to your saddlebow, and ride forth singing. Then anyone who does not know your state of affairs will suppose that your state pleases you well. If you have a sorrow and the betrayer knows about it, in your presence he will commiserate with you; behind your back he will mock you. You might tell your sorrow to the very person who would heartily wish it on you; without any pity he will wish so much more on you. Conceal it in your heart, so that it may not bring you pain again; and do not let him know all that your heart may care about."

[MODERNIZATION]

Thus said Alfred: "You must never choose your wife by her looks, and never for anything that she brings to you. But learn to know her behavior—she will show that very quickly! For many a man because of wealth calculates amiss, and often a man chooses as one who is beautiful one who is vile. Woeful is he who brings an evil wife to his dwelling; so too is it for him in his life who marries badly, for he shall be miserable on the earth. Many a man sings who brings home a wife; if he knew what he brought, he might well weep."

[MODERNIZATION]

Thus said Alfred: "Never be so foolish or so drunk with wine that you ever tell all your counsel to your wife. For if she were to see all your enemies in front of you, and you had angered her with some word, she wouldn't be able to stop herself, for any living thing, from scolding you right then for your misfortunes.

"Woman is word-crazy and has too swift a tongue. Even though she might well wish to, she can't control it at all."

43

XVI

Thus queth Alvred:
"Idelschipe and overprute, that lereth yong wif üvele thewes,
And ofte that heo wolde do that heo ne scholde.
Thene unthew lihte leten heo myhte
5   If heo ofte a swote forswunke were.
Theyh hit is üvel to buwe that beo nüle treowe,
For ofte museth the kat after hire moder.
    "The mon that let wymmon his mayster i-würthe
Ne schal he never beon i-hürd his wordes loverd,
10   Ac heo hine schal steorne totrayen and toteone,
And selde würth he blythe and gled, the mon that is his wives qued.
    "Mony appel is bryht withute and bitter withinne;
So is mony wymmon on hyre fader bure
Schene under schete, and theyh heo is schendful.
15   So is mony gedelyng godlyche on horse
And is, theyh, lütel wurth—
Wlonk bi the glede and üvel at thare neode."

XVII

Thus queth Alvred:
"Nevre thu, bi thine lyve, the word of thine wyve
Too swithe thu ne arede.
If heo beo i-wreththed myd worde other myd dede,
5   Wymmon wepeth for mod oftere than for eny god,
And ofte, lude and stille, for to vordrye hire wille.
Heo wepeth otherhwile for to do thee gyle.
    "Salomon hit haveth i-sed that wymmon can wel üvelne red.
The hire red foleweth, heo bryngeth hine to seorewe,
10   For hit seyth in the Leoth as cuenes forteoth.
Hit is ifürn i-seyd that cold red is quene red;
Hu he is unlede that foleweth hire rede.
    "Ich hit ne segge nouht forthan that god thing nys god wymmon
The mon the hi may i-cheose and i-covere over othre."

[MODERNIZATION]

Thus said Alfred: "Idleness and conceit teach a young wife evil habits and often make her want to do what she should not. Vice she might easily avoid if often she were exhausted in sweat. Yet it is hard to bend that which does not wish to be straight, for often the kitten will chase mice in the same way as her mother.

"The man that lets a woman become his master will never be listened to as the lord of his own word, but she will severely torment and harass him, and seldom will he be contented and happy, the man who is his wife's victim.

"Many an apple is outwardly shiny and bitter within; so too many a woman in her father's bower is fair under the sheet and yet is disgraceful. So too, many a companion is handsome on horse and is yet worth little—brave at the fireside and useless at need."

[MODERNIZATION]

Thus said Alfred: "Never in your life accept the word of your wife too soon. If she is enraged by word or by deed, a woman will weep for anger more often than for any good reason, and often, loud or soft, to get her own way. At other times she will weep to cheat you.

"Solomon has said that woman well knows evil counsel. He who follows her counsel, she will bring him to sorrow, for it says in the Song[3] that women deceive. It is said of old that woman's counsel is cold counsel, that he is wretched who follows her counsel.

"I do not therefore say that a good woman is not a good thing for the man who can choose her and select her from among the others."

---

[3] Presumably in reference to Proverbs (attributed to Solomon) 7:5: ". . . keep thee from the strange woman, / from the stranger which flattereth with her words."

Poema Morale

(ca. 1175, Southwestern–West Midland)

Poema Morale provides a fine example of the homiletic tradition of the twelfth century. Like the last Peterborough chronicler (pp. 38–39), the preacher is concerned with the collective sins of the people, but he is also aware of personal sin. He begins his poem dramatically by confessing his own frailty and then goes on to lecture his listeners on how to behave toward God and their fellow man. The Last Judgment, he warns them, will condemn the unrighteous to hell and will admit to heaven only those who have loved both God and man.

The poem evidently retained its popularity for a long time after it was composed and was imitated in other lyrics as late as the fourteenth century. It is preserved in seven different manuscript versions, varying in length and in wording, that represent revisions made by adapters who admired the spirit of the now vanished original. The selection is based on the earliest extant version (contained in the Lambeth Manuscript), which contains only 270 long lines as compared to others that run to some 400 lines. The section printed here is the beginning of the poem.

The meter is as remarkable as the spirit and contents. It is the first known English adaptation of the Latin septenary; see Introduction, type 7, page 31. The long seven-beat lines have here been printed, as is customary, in alternate four-beat and three-beat lines.

A useful sketch of the background of the poem and a reconstruction of its text will be found in the edition by Hans Marcus, *Das frühmittelenglische Poema Morale*, Palaestra 194 (Leipzig, 1934). For bibliography see Wells ch. 7.25; *CBEL*, 1.180, 5.121.

[Lines 1–48]

Ich em nu alder° thene Ich wes	older
A wintre and a lare.°	A . . . In winters and in learning
Ich welde mare thene Ich dede;°	
Mi wit ahte bön° mare.	wit . . . sense ought to be
5 Wel longe Ich habbe child i-bön°	been
A worde and a dede;	

3. I possess more (experience now) than I had

46

Poema Morale

Thah° Ich bö° a wintre ald
  Too yung Ich em on rede.°
Unnet° lif Ich habbe i-led°
10 And yet,° me thingth, i-lede.°
Thenne° Ich me bithenche° wel,
  Ful sare° Ich me adrede;°
Mest al thet Ich habbe i-don
  Bifealt° to childhade.
15 Wel° late Ich habbe me bithocht,°
  Bute° God me nu rede.°
Föle° idel word Ich habbe i-quethen°
  Söththen° Ich speke kuthe;°
Föle yunge dede i-don
20 The me ofthincheth nuthe.°
Mest al thet me likede er°
  Nu hit me misliketh.
Tha müchel fülieth° his wil,
  Hine-sölf he biswiketh.°
25 Ich mihte habbe bet° i-don,
  Hefde Ich the i-selthe.°
Nu Ich walde,° ah° Ich ne mei°
  For elde° and for unhelthe.
Elde is me bistolen on°
30 Er° Ich hit wiste;°
Ne michte° Ich seon bifore me
  For smike° ne for miste.
Erghe° we beoth to done god,
  And to üfele° al too thriste.°
35 Mare eie stondeth men of monne
  Thanne höm do of Criste.°
The wel ne doth the hwile hö müghen,°
  Wel° oft hit schal rowen°
Thenne hö mawen sculen and repen°
40 Thet° hö er sowen.°
Do he to Gode thet he müghe°
  The hwile he bö° alive.
Ne lipnie na mon° too müchel
  To childe ne to wive;

Though   am
judgment
Useless led
still am leading
When consider
sorely dread

Pertains

Too considered
Unless advise
Many spoken
Since could

The ... Which I regret now
me ... pleased me before

Tha ... He who (too) much follows
Hine-sölf ... Himself deceives
better
Hefde ... If I'd had the fortune
would but can't
For elde Because of age
is ... has stolen on me
Before knew
Ne michte ... Nor could
smoke
Unwilling
evil bold

Very rue

That which **er sowen** sowed before
can
is
Ne ... Let no man trust

35–36. Men stand more in awe of man than they do of Christ.
37. Those who do not do well while they can
39. When they shall mow and reap

47

45 The him-sölve forget°
    For wive ne for childe,
He scal° cumen in üvel stüde°
    Bute° him God bö° milde.

The . . . He who forgets himself

shall   **üvel stüde** evil stead
Unless is

LAWMAN

The Brut

(ca. 1200, Southwestern–West Midland)

❧

Lawman was a priest at Areley Church near Redstone (north of Worcester) on the River Severn. His name, which is often modernized as Layamon (in the manuscript of *The Brut* it is spelled Laȝamon, Laweman, Loweman), means "man of law." His father's name was Leovenath. Otherwise, we know nothing of him. His *Brut* is, however, a distinguished achievement reflecting the strength of the native English tradition in the West Country, which was later to produce other great poets, such as Langland. Lawman's *Brut* is derived from Wace's Anglo-Norman poem the *Roman de Brut*, which Wace had dedicated to Queen Eleanor in 1155. The *Roman de Brut* was itself a translation of Geoffrey of Monmouth's prose *History of the Kings of Britain*, composed in Latin (ca. 1138–39). Geoffrey's pseudohistory was written primarily for learned clerics; Wace addressed his poem to the members of the court of King Henry II; Lawman aimed at his rural English audience, whose culture evidently still remained relatively unaffected by the Norman Conquest.

Lawman's materials were ultimately determined by Geoffrey's original inventions, which Wace had followed closely. The first 9,000 lines of *The Brut* tell how Brutus (hence the title), a legendary descendant of Aeneas of Troy, founded a royal line in Britain; the next 5,000 recount the rise and fall of Arthur; and the last 2,000 lines complete the enumeration of the British kings to A.D. 689, when the descendants of the Anglo-Saxon invaders took over.

The two passages printed below represent Lawman at his most original, but even these are expansions of his source rather than completely new inventions. The legend of the Round Table is not mentioned at all by Geoffrey but is briefly alluded to by Wace (*Roman de Brut*, ll. 9747–60). Arthur's departure to Avalon is described perfunctorily by Geoffrey in his *History* (XI, iii) and by Wace (ll. 13,275–81). The details of Arthur's reception by Morgen la Fée in the Island of Apples are recounted by Geoffrey in his Latin poem *The Life of Merlin* (ll. 908–40), and Lawman had evidently learned something of this tradition second-hand, though he or his scribe mistakenly refers to the otherworld queen Morgen as Argante.

Stylistically, Lawman's verse is more primitive than Wace's, and its effect more rousing, for it echoes the tone of Old English heroic poetry, particularly in battle scenes. Lawman resolutely avoids the adoption of foreign words, even when he is translating directly from Anglo-Norman. Indeed, his resulting lines, both in imagery and meter, frequently sound as if they had been composed in Old English.

> For heore múchele móde · morth-ȝomenn wrohten.
> (Because of their great spirit they wrought games of slaughter.)

The meter is semi-alliterative, semi-rhyming verse; see Introduction, type 3, page 30.

The only edition is *Laȝamons Brut*, edited and translated by Sir Frederick Madden (London, 1847), 3 vols. G. L. Brook has published *Selections from Laȝamon's Brut* (Oxford, 1963) and is publishing a definitive edition, *Laȝamon: Brut*, EETS 250– (London, 1963–). For manuscript see Plate 1, p. 16. For bibliography see Wells, ch. 3.3; *CBEL*, 1.163–65, 5.117. Also see: J. S. P. Tatlock, *The Legendary History of Britain* (Berkeley, 1950), pp. 483–531, and R. S. Loomis, "Layamon's *Brut*," in *Arthurian Literature in the Middle Ages*, ed. R. S. Loomis (Oxford, 1959), pp. 104–11.

The Round Table

Seoththen hit seith in there tale, the king ferde to Cornwale.
Ther him com to anan that waes a crafti weorcman,
And thene king i-mette, and feiere hine graette.
"Hail seo thu, Arthur, athelest kinge.
5 Ich aem thin aghe mon. Moni lond Ich habbe thurh-gan.
Ich con of treo-werkes wunder feole craftes.
Ich i-herde süggen biyeonde sae neowe tidende
That thine cnihtes at thine borde gunnen fihte
A midewinteres daei; moni ther feollen;
10 For heore müchele mode morth-gomenn wrohten;
And for heore hehghe cünne aelc wolde beon withinne.
"Ah Ich thee wülle wurche a bord swithe hende
That ther maghen setten to sixtene hundred and ma,
Al turn abuten, that nan ne beon withuten,
15 Withuten and withinne, mon to-yaeines monne.
Whenne thu wült riden, with thee thu miht hit leden,
And setten hit whar thu wülle after thine i-wille;
And ne dert thu navere adrede, to there worlde longen,
That aevere aeine modi cniht at thine borde makie fiht,
20 For ther scal the hehghe beon aefne than loghe.
Timber me lete biwinnen and that beord biginne."
To feouwer wikene virste that werc wes i-vorthed.
To ane heghe daeie that hired wes i-somned,
And Arthur himseolf beh sone to than borde,
25 And hehte alle his cnihtes to than borde forthrihtes.
Tho alle weoren i-seten cnihtes to heore mete,
Tha spaec aelc with other alse hit weore his brother.
Alle heo seten abuten; nes ther nan withuten.
Aevere aelches cünnes cniht there wes swithe wel i-diht.
30 Alle heo weoren bi ane, the hehghe and tha laghe;
Ne mihten ther nan yelpen for othere künnes scenchen,
Other his i-veren the at than beorde weoren.
This wes that ilke bord that Brüttes of yelpeth
And sügeth feole cünne lesinge bi Arthure than kinge.
35 Swa deth aver alc mon the other luvien con;
Yif he is him too leof, thenne wüle he lighen,
And süggen on him wurthscipe mare thenne he beon wurthe;
Ne beo he no swa lüther mon that his freond him wel ne on.
Aeft, yif on volke feondscipe arereth
40 An aever aei time betweone twon monnen,
Me con by than laethe lasinge süggen.

[MODERNIZATION]

Afterward, it says in the tale, the king went to Cornwall. There came to him then one who was a skillful carpenter and met the king and greeted him graciously.

"Hail to you, Arthur, noblest king. I am your own man. Many a land have I traveled through. In woodwork I am master of wondrous many skills. I have heard tell over the seas new tidings, that your knights at your table began to fight on a midwinter's day. Many fell there; out of their high pride they wrought deadly sport, and because of their high lineage each wished to be innermost.

"But I will construct for you a most convenient table, at which sixteen hundred men and more may sit down, all in turn around, so that none will be outermost— outer and inner, man opposite man. When you wish to ride forth, you can take it with you and set it up where you will according to your wish; and you need never fear, to the length of the world, that any proud knight will ever make strife at your table, for there the high shall be equal with the low. Allow me to gather the lumber and begin the table."

By the end of four weeks the work was completed. On a festival day the people were summoned, and Arthur himself came at once to the table and ordered all his knights to the table forthwith. When the knights were all seated for their meal, then each spoke to the next as if it were to his brother. They were all seated around; there was no one outermost. Every rank of knight was very well treated. They were all as one, the high and the low; nor could any there boast of a special serving of drinks different from that given his companions who were at the table.

This was the same table that the Bretons boast of and tell many kinds of lies about Arthur the king. Thus everyone does who loves someone else; if he is too dear to him, then he will lie and attribute more honor to him than he is worth; nor is there any man so base that his own friend will not wish him well. Again, if, among people, at any time enmity arises between two men, they will tell lies about the one who is loathed.

Theh he weore the bezste mon the aevere aet at borde,
The mon the him weore lath, him cuthe last finden.
Ne al soh ne al les that leod-scopes singeth;
45   Ah this is that soththe bi Arthure than kinge;
Nes naever ar swülc king, swa duhti thurh alle thing.
For that sothe stond a than writen hu hit is i-wurthen,
Ord from than aenden, of Arthure than kinge,
No mare no lasse buten alse his laghen weoren.

[Lines 28,589–651]

The Passing of Arthur

Arthur wes forwunded, wunder ane swithe.
Ther to him com a cnave the wes of his cünne.
He wes Cadores sune, the eorles of Cornwaile.
Constantin hehte the cnave; he wes than kinge deore.
5   Arthur him lokede on, ther he lai on folden,
And thas word seide mid sorhfulle heorte:
    "Constantin, thu art wilcume. Thu weore Cadores sone.
Ich thee bitache here mine kineriche.
And wite mine Brüttes a to thines lifes;
10   And hald heom alle tha laghen tha habbeoth i-stonden a mine daghen,
And alle tha laghen gode tha bi Utheres daghen stode.
    "And Ich wülle varen to Avalun to vairest alre maidene,
To Argante, there quene, alven swithe sceone;
And heo scal mine wunden makien alle i-sunde,
15   Al hal me makien mid haleweighe drenchen.
And seothe Ich cumen wülle to mine kineriche
And wunien mid Brütten mid müchelere wünne."
    Aefne than worden ther com of se wenden
That wes an sceort bat lithen, sceoven mid üthen;
20   And two wimmen therinne, wunderliche i-dihte;
And heo nomen Arthur anan and a-neouste hine vereden
And softe hine a-dun leiden, and forth gunnen hine lithen.
    Tha wes hit i-wurthen that Merlin seide whilen,
That weore unimete care of Arthures forthfare.
25   Brüttes i-leveth yete that he bön on live
And wunnien in Avalun mid fairest alre alven,
And lokieth evere Brüttes yete whan Arthur cumen lithe.
Nis naver the mon i-boren of naver nane bürde i-coren
The cunne of than sothe of Arthure sügen mare.
30   But while wes an witeghe, Merlin i-hate;
He bodede mid worde—his quithes weoren sothe—
That an Arthur sculde yete cum Anglen to fülste.

The Brut

[MODERNIZATION]

Though he were the best man that ever ate at table, they could find objection to the man who is loath to them. What the people's poets sing is neither all truth nor all lies. But this is the truth about Arthur the king: never before was there such a king, in all things so doughty. For the truth has been set down in writing how the deeds of Arthur the king came to pass, from beginning to end, neither more nor less, but just as his way of life was.

[MODERNIZATION]

Arthur was mortally wounded, grievously and severely. To him there came a youth who was of his kin. He was the son of Cador, the earl of Cornwall. Constantine the youth was called; he was dear to the king. From where he lay on the ground, Arthur looked upon him and spoke these words with sorrowful heart:

"You are welcome, Constantine. You were Cador's son. I here entrust my kingdom to you. And guard my Britons ever in your lifetime; and on their behalf keep all the laws that existed in my days and all the good laws that in Uther's days existed.

"And I will go to Avalon to the fairest of all maidens, to Argant the queen, an elf most beautiful; and she will make my wounds all sound, make me all whole with healing potions. And then I shall come back to my kingdom and dwell with the Britons in great bliss."

Even at these words, there came traveling from the sea a short boat, moving, driven by the waves, and two women in it, wondrously clad; and they took Arthur into it and went in beside him and laid him down gently, and they journeyed away.

Then was fulfilled what Merlin had previously said, that there would be unbounded sorrow at the departure of Arthur. The Britons still believe that he is alive and dwells in Avalon with the fairest of all elves, and the Britons ever look for the time, even yet, when Arthur will come back. Never has the man been born of any chosen woman that can tell more of the truth concerning Arthur. But once there was a wizard called Merlin; he announced by word—his sayings were true—that an Arthur was still to come as an aid to the Angles.

The Owl and the Nightingale

(ca. 1198–1216, Southwestern)

☞☜

The Owl and the Nightingale is a typical product of the intellectual renaissance of the twelfth century. The two argumentative birds in the poem sound remarkably like the London schoolboys of that era, who, according to William FitzStephen (d. 1190), delighted in debating:

> Some engage in disputation for display . . . , others for truth. . . . In epigrams, rimes, and verses . . . they pull their comrades to pieces without mentioning names; they fling at them scoffs and sarcasms; they touch the failings of their schoolmates or even of greater people with Socratic salt.

The genre of the poetic debate was understandably popular in the scholarly world of the twelfth century, and extant Latin examples, such as *The Debate Between Wine and Water*, parallel *The Owl and the Nightingale* in several respects. Even the title *Altercacio inter Filomenam et Bubonem*, given to the Middle English poem by the scribe, reflects its academic tone; and the author's language and his use of all the techniques of disputation similarly reflect the rhetorical tradition of the period.

In one respect, however, *The Owl and the Nightingale* is unique, for it is the only extant debate composed in English during the twelfth century. If for no other reason than this, the identity of the author has excited scholarly inquiry. Possibly he was the "Maister Nichole of Guldeforde" (ll. 191 and 1,746) whom the birds chose as their umpire. If so, we may surmise that he had been reared in Guildford, Surrey, that he knew the intellectual excitement of the nearby London area, was a scholar (hence called Master) equally at home in English, French, and Latin, served as a cleric in the remote village of Portisham (l. 1,752), in Dorset, and elected to compose his poem in English rather than in the more fashionable French or Latin because he hoped to gain the attention of a simple, rural audience. Like the poor but brilliant curate in many an English novel, he may have hoped to make the best of his unpromising situation.

The meaning of the poem has also aroused extensive discussion. The medieval encyclopedists had accumulated much strange lore concerning such birds as the owl (see *The Properties of Things*, p. 490), but the author relies on his own observations of nature. He treats the nightingale as what it is, namely, a sweet songster who comes to England only as a fair-weather visitor and seldom ventures farther north; he also appropriately portrays the owl as the faithful, if unappreciated, companion of man. The nightingale favors the foreign fashion of amorous lyrics and courtly love; the owl instinctively clings to the traditional music of the church and upholds the contemplative life of the monasteries. But why does the author not tell us which bird deserves to win the argument? Probably the answer lies in the twelfth-century attitude toward the definition of truth. Scholars allowed that two arguments, even if mutually incompatable, could both be true provided that each was self-consistent. The author may have felt that the logical position of the nightingale was philosophically true while the religious position of the owl was theologically true.

The Owl and the Nightingale

The meter is rhyming, four-beat couplets; see Introduction, type 5, page 31.

The best edition of the poem is *The Owl and the Nightingale*, ed. E. G. Stanley (London, 1960). For a modernization see the edition by J. W. H. Atkins (Cambridge, 1922). For the two extant manuscripts see *The Owl and the Nightingale Reproduced in Facsimile*, ed. N. R. Ker, EETS 251 (London, 1963). For bibliography see Severs, ch. 7.45.

Ich was in one sumere° dale;   **one sumere** a summer
In one swithe dighele hale°   **swithe** . . . very hidden corner
I-herde Ich° holde grete tale   **I-herde Ich** I heard
An ule and one nightingale.

5 That plait° was stif and starc° and strong,   debate   firm
Sum hwile softe, and lud among;°   between
And either aghen° other swal°   against   swelled
And let that üvele mod° ut al;   **üvele mod** bad temper
And either seide of otheres cüste°   manners
10 That alre-wörste° that hö wüste;°   **That alre-wörste** Worst of all   **hö wüste** she knew
And, hure and hure, °of otheres songe   **hure** . . . certainly
Hi holde plaiding swithe° stronge.   **Hi** . . . They held a debate very
      The nightingale bigon the speche
In one hurne° of one breche,°   **one hurne** a corner   field
15 And sat upone vaire boghe,°   **vaire boghe** fair bough
Thar° were abute blosme inoghe,°   Where   enough
In ore vaste,° thicke hegge°   **ore vaste** a tight   hedge
I-meind mid spire° and grene segge.°   **I-meind** . . . Mixed with grass   sedge
Hö° was the gladur for the rise°   She   branch
20 And song a vele cünne wise.°
Bet thughte° the dreim° that he° were   **Bet thughte** Rather seemed   sound   it
Of harpe and pipe, than he nere;°   **than** . . . than that it were not
Bet thughte that he were i-shote°   cast
Of harpe and pipe than of throte.
25   Tho° stod an old stoc° thar biside   Then   stump
Thar° the ule song hire tide,°   Where   **song** . . . sang her hours
And was mid° ivi al bigrowe;°   with   overgrown
Hit was thare ule earding-stowe.°   **thare** . . . the owl's dwelling-place
The nightingale hi i-segh°   **hi i-segh** . . . looked at her
30 And hi bihold and oversegh,°   looked her over
And thughte wel vul of thare ule,°   **thughte** . . . considered the owl most foul
For me hi halt lodlich and fule.°

20. And sang in many a kind of manner.
32. For people think her loathly and foul.

NIGHTINGALE

"Unwight," hö° sede, "awei thu flö!°
Me is° the würs that Ich thee sö.°
35 I-wis,° for thine vule lete°
Wel° oft Ich mine song forlete.°
Min hörte atflith, and falt° mi tonge,
Hwönne thu art to me i-thrunge,°
Me lüste bet speten° thane singe
40 Of° thine fule yoghelinge."°
    Thös ule abod forth° hit was eve.
Hö ne mighte no leng bileve,°
Vor hire hörte was so gret
That wel negh° hire fnast atschet,°
45 And warp° a word tharafter longe:

> Unwight, hö Monster, she   flee
> Me is I am   see
> Indeed   vule lete foul behavior
> Very   abandon
> atflith . . . flies off and fails
> art . . . have pressed upon me
> Me . . . I'd sooner spit
> Because of   fule yoghelinge foul hooti[ng]
> abod forth waited till
> Hö . . . She could no longer refrain
> wel negh very nearly   fnast atschet breath exploded
> uttered

OWL

"Hu thincthe° nu bi mine songe?
Wenst° thu that Ich ne cunne singe
Thegh° Ich ne cünne of writelinge?°
Ilome° thu dest° me grame°
50 And seist me° bothe töne° and schame.
Yif Ich thee hölde° on mine vote°—
So hit bitide° that Ich mote!°—
And thu were ut of thine rise,°
Thu sholdest singe an other wise."°
55 The nightingale yaf° answare:

> Hu thincthe How do you think
> Suppose
> Though   ne . . . don't know about chirp[ing]
> Often   cause   grief
> seist me utter against me   injury
> held   foot
> hit bitide might it happen   might
> branch
> tune
> gave

NIGHTINGALE

"Yif Ich me loki with the bare°
And me schilde with the blete,°
Ne reche° Ich noght of thine threte.
Yif Ich me holde in mine hegge,°
60 Ne reche Ich never what thu segge.°
Ich wot° that thu art unmilde
With höm that ne mughe° from thee schilde,
And thu tukest wrothe and üvele,°
Whar thu might, over° smale fughele.°
65 Vorthi° thu art loth° al fuel-künne,°
And alle hö° thee driveth hönne°
And thee bischricheth and bigredeth°
And wel narewe° thee biledeth;°
And ek, forthe,° the sülve möse,°
70 Hire-thonkes,° wolde thee totöse.°
    "Thu art lodlich° to biholde,
And thu art loth in monie volde.°

> loki . . . guard against the open
> schilde . . . hide against exposure
> care
> hedge
> say
> know
> ne mughe cannot
> tukest . . . pick angrily and maliciously
> on   birds
> Therefore   loathsome to   bird-kind
> alle hö they all   hence
> bischricheth . . . shriek at and scold
> wel narewe very closely   chase
> therefore   sülve möse very titmouse
> Gladly   tear to pieces
> loathly
> loth . . . loathsome in many ways

Thi bodi is short; thi swöre° is smal;   **neck**
Grettere is thin heved° than thu al;   **head**
75 Thin eyene böth° col-blake and brode   **eyene böth** eyes are
Right swo hö° weren i-peint mid wode.°   **Right** . . . Just as if they   **mid wode** with woad
Thu starest so° thu wille abiten°   as if   bite up
Al that thu mighst mid clivres° smiten.   talons
Thi bile is stif and scharp and hoked
80 Right so° an owel° that is croked;   **Right so** Just like   awl
Tharmid° thu clackest° oft and longe,   With it   chatter
And that is on° of thine songe!°   one   songs
Ac thu thretest to° mine fleshe;   **Ac** . . . But you threaten
Mid thine clivres woldest me meshe.°   **clivres** . . . talons you'd like to mash me
85 Thee were i-cündur to° one frogge   **Thee** . . . You'd be better suited for
That sit at mülne° under cogge!°   **sit** . . . sits at a mill   cog-wheel
Snailes, müs, and fule wighte°   **müs** . . . mice, and foul creatures
Böth° thine cünde° and thine righte.   Are   kind
   "Thu sittest a-dai and flighst a-night;
90 Thu cüthest° that thu art on unwight.°   show   **on unwight** a monster
Thu art lodlich° and unclene—   loathly
Bi° thine neste Ich hit mene   Regarding
And ek bi thine fule° brode;   foul
Thu fedest on höm a wel ful fode.°   **wel** . . . very foul progeny
95 Wel wostu that° hi döth tharinne: **wostu that** do you know what
Hi fuleth° hit up to the chinne.   dirty
Hö sitteth thar so hi bö bisne.°   **so** . . . as if they were blind
Tharbi men seggeth° a vorbisne:°   say   proverb
'Dahet habbe that ilke best°   **Dahet** . . . A curse on every beast
100 That fuleth his owe° nest.'   own
   "That° other yer a faukun bredde;°   The   **faukun bredde** falcon was breeding
His nest noght wel he ne bihedde.°   guarded
Tharto thu stele° in o day   stole
And leidest tharon thi fule ey.°   **fule ey** foul egg
105 Tho° hit bicom° that he haghte,°   When   happened   **he haghte** it hatched
And of his eyre briddes wraghte,°
He broghte his briddes mete,
Bihold his nest, i-segh hi° ete.   **i-segh hi** saw them
He i-segh bi one halve
110 His nest i-fuled uthalve.°   **i-fuled uthalve** befouled outside
The faucun° was wroth with his bridde°   falcon   chicks
And lude yal and sterne chidde:
'Seggeth° me, hwo haveth this i-do?   Tell
Öw nas never i-cünde° tharto.   **Öw** . . . You were never accustomed
115 Hit was i-don öw a lothe cüste.°   **öw** . . . to you in a loathsome way
Segge me yif ye hit wiste.'°   knew of

106. And from his eggs chicks were born

Tho quath that on° and quad that other,   **that on** the one
'I-wis,'° it was ure ower° brother,   Indeed   own
The yond° that haveth that grete heved.°   **The yond** That one there   head
120 Wai° that he nis° tharof bireved!   Alas   is not
Worp° hit ut mid° the alre-würste,°   Throw   with   worst of all
That his necke him toberste!"°   may burst
The faucun i-lefde° his bridde°   **faucun i-lefde** falcon believed   chicks
And nom° that fule brid amidde°   took   by the middle
125 And warp° hit of than° wilde bowe,   threw   **of than** off the
Thar pie° and crowe hit todrowe.°   **Thar pie** Where magpie   tore apart
   "Herbi men seggeth° a bispel,°   tell   parable
Thegh° hit ne bö fulliche spel.°   Though   **ne . . .** isn't completely a fable
Al so° hit is bi than ungode°   **Al so** Just as   **than ungode** the worthless person
130 That is i-cumen of fule brode
And is meind° with frö° mönne;   **is meind** has mingled   well-born
Ever he cüth° that he com thönne,°   shows   **com thönne** came thence
That he com of than adel eye,°   **than . . .** the addled egg
Thegh° he a° frö nest leie.°   Though   in a   might lie
135 Thegh appel trendli° from thon tröwe°   may roll   **thon tröwe** the tree
Thar° he and other mid° gröwe,   Where   together
Thegh he bö tharfrom bicume,°   **he . . .** it may have moved away
He cüth° wel whönene° he is i-cume."   **He cüth** It shows   whence
   Thös word ayaf° the nightingale,   uttered
140 And after thare° longe tale   that
Hö song so° lude and so scharpe   as
Right so me grülde schille° harpe.   **Right . . .** As if one plucked a shrill
Thös ule lüste thiderward°   **lüste thiderward** listened to it
And hold hire eye nötherward°   downward
145 And sat toswolle and i-bolwe°   **toswolle . . .** swollen and bursting
Al so° hö hadde one frogge i-swolwe,   **Al so** As if
For hö wel wiste° and was i-war   knew
That hö song hire a bisemar:°   **hire . . .** to her in mockery
And, notheles, hö yaf° andsware: gave

OWL

150 "Whi neltu flön° into the bare°   **neltu flön** won't you fly   open
And schewi hwether unker bö°   **hwether . . .** which of us is
Of brighter höwe,° of vairur blö?"°   hue   **vairur blö** fairer color

NIGHTINGALE

"No. Thu havest wel scharpe clawe,°   claws
Ne kepich noght° that thu me clawe.   **Ne . . .** And I don't wish
155 Thu havest clivres swithe° stronge;   **clivres swithe** talons very
Thu twengst tharmid so° döth a tonge.°   **twengst . . .** pinch with them as   pair of tongs
Thu thoghtest, so doth thine i-like,°   **thoghtest . . .** thought, as those like you d

Mid° faire worde me biswike.° — With   **me biswike** to betray me

Ich nolde don that° thu me raddest;° — **nolde** ... wouldn't do what   advised

160 Ich wiste° wel that thu me misraddest.° — knew   misadvised

Schamie thee° for thin unrede!° — **Schamie thee** Shame on you   bad advice

Unwroghen° is thi swikelhede.° — Exposed   treachery

Schild° thine swikeldom° vram the lighte, — Hide   villainy

And hüd that woghe° among the righte. — **hüd** ... hide the crooked

165 Hwane thu wilt thin unright spene,° — expend

Loke that hit ne bö° i-sene; — is

Vor swikeldom haveth schome and hete° — hate

Yif hit is ope and underyete.° — **ope** ... open and perceived

"Ne speddestu noght mid° thine unwrenche,° — **Ne** ... Nor did you succeed with   guile

170 For Ich am war° and can wel blenche.° — wary   dodge

Ne helpth noght that thu bö too thriste.° — bold

Ich wolde vighte bet° mid liste° — better   cunning

Than thu mid al thine strengthe.

Ich habbe on brede° and ek° on lengthe — in breadth   also

175 Castel god on mine rise.° — branch

'Wel fight that wel flighth,'° seith the wise. — **Wel fight** ... He fights well who flees well

"Ac° lete we awei thös cheste,° — But   strife

Vor swiche wordes böth unwreste;° — **böth unwreste** are useless

And fo we on° mid righte dome,° — **fo** ... let's begin   judgment

180 Mid faire worde,° and mid y-some.° — words   agreeable words

Thegh° we ne bö at one acorde, — Though

We mughe bet° mid fayre worde, — **mughe bet** can better

Withute cheste,° and bute° fighte, — strife   without

Plaidi mid foghe° and mid righte; — **Plaidi** ... Plead with relevance

185 And mai ure either hwat hö wile

Mid righte segge and mid skile."°

Tho quath the ule:

OWL

"Hwo schal us seme° — reconcile

That kunne° and wille right us deme?"° — may know how   **right** ... allot us justice

NIGHTINGALE

"Ich wot° wel," quath the nightingale. — know

190 "Ne tharf° tharof bö no tale. — **Ne tharf** There need not

Maister Nichole of Guldeforde°— — Guildford

He is wis and war° of worde, — wary

He is of dome swithe glew,° — **dome** ... judgment very wise

And him is loth evrich unthew.° — **him** ... he hates every vice

195 He wot insight in° eche songe— — **wot** ... has knowledge of

Hwo singeth wel, hwo singeth wronge;

185–86. And may each of us say whatever she will with right and with competence.

59

And he can schede° vrom the righte — distinguish
That woghe, that thüster° from the lighte." — That woghe . . . The wrong, the darkness
The ule one hwile hi° bithoghte — herself
200 And after than° this word upbroghte: — that

OWL

"Ich granti wel that he us deme,° — should judge
Vor, thegh° he were hwile breme,° — though **hwile breme** for a while wild
And löf him° were nightingale — **löf him** dear to him
And other wighte gente and smale,° — **wighte** . . . creatures gentle and slim
205 Ich wot° he is nu swithe acoled.° — know **swithe acoled** very much cooled down
Nis he vor thee noght afoled,° — **vor** . . . not deluded on your account
That° he for thine olde luve° — So that **thine** . . . former love of you
Me adun legge° and thee buve;° — **adun legge** may set down   up
Ne schaltu nevre° so him queme° — **Ne** . . . Nor shall you ever   please
210 That he, for thee, fals dom deme.° — **dom deme** judgment may utter
"He is him ripe and fast-rede,° — **him** . . . within himself mature and firm of counsel
Ne lüst him nu to none unrede.°
Nu him ne lüst na more pleie.° — to play
He wile gon a° righte weie." — in the
215 The nightingale was al yare;° — ready
Hö hadde i-lörned wel aihware.° — everywhere

NIGHTINGALE

"Ule," hö sede, "seie me soth,° — truly
Hwi dostu that unwightis° doth? — **that unwightis** what monsters
Thu singist a-night and noght a-dai,
220 And al thi song is 'Waila-wai!'° — Alas
Thu might mid thine songe afere° — frighten
Alle that i-hereth° thine i-bere.° — hear   carrying-on
Thu scrichest and yollest to thine fere° — companion
That hit is grislich° to i-here; — horrible
225 Hit thincheth bothe° wise and snepe° — **thincheth bothe** seems to both   foolish
Noght° that thu singe ac° that thu wepe. — Not   but
Thu flighst a-night and noght a-dai!
Tharof Ich wundri, and wel mai,
Vor evrich thing that schunieth° right, — shuns
230 Hit luveth thüster° and hatieth light; — darkness
And evrich thing that° is löf° misdede, — to whom   dear
Hit luveth thüster to his° dede. — **to his** for its
A wis word, thegh° hit bö unclene, — though
Is fele manne a muthe imene,° — **fele** . . . current in many men's mouths
235 For Alfred King[1] hit seide and wrot:

212. Nor does he now delight in any folly.
[1] King Alfred (referred to on twelve occasions in *The Owl and the Nightingale* as an authority on proverbial lore); see the headnote to *The Proverbs of Alfred* (p. 40).

'He schuneth° that hine vul wot.'°   shrinks back   **hine . . .** knows himself to be foul
Ich wene° that thu dost also,   Suppose
Vor thu flightst nightes ever mo.°   **nightes . . .** at night constantly
   "Another thing me is a-wene:°   **me . . .** I suppose
240 Thu havest a-night wel brighte sene;°   **wel . . .** very clear vision
Bi daie thu art stare° blind,   completely
That thu ne sichst ne bow ne rind.°   **ne sichst . . .** see neither bough nor bark
A-day thu art blind other bisne.°   **other bisne** or purblind
Thar-bi men seggeth a vorbisne:°   **seggeth . . .** utter a proverb
245 'Right° so hit farth° bi than ungode°   Just   fares   **than ungode** the evil one
That noght ne süth° to none gode   sees
And is so ful of üvele wrenche°   tricks
That him ne mai° no man atprenche°   **ne mai** cannot   outwit
And can° wel than thüstre° wai   knows   **than thüstre** the dark
250 And thane brighte lat awai.'°   **brighte . . .** bright way leaves aside
So doth that böth° of thine cünde;°   **that böth** those that are   kind
Of lighte nabbeth hi none imünde."°   **none imünde** no concern
   Thös hule lüste swithe° longe   **lüste swithe** listened very
And was oftöned° swithe stronge.   offended
255 Hö quath:

     OWL
   "Thu hattest° nightingale.   are called
Thu mightest bet hoten galegale,°   **bet . . .** better be called tattletale
Vor thu havest too monie° tale.   many a
Lat thine tunge habbe spale!°   time-out
Thu wenest that thes dai bö thin oghe.°   own
260 Lat me nu habbe mine throghe.°   turn
Bö nu stille and lat me speke.
Ich wille bön of° thee awreke;°   on   avenged
And lüst° hu Ich con me bitelle°   listen   defend
Mid righte sothe° withute spelle.°   **righte sothe** real truth   story
265 "Thu seist that Ich me hüde° a-dai.   hide
Tharto ne segge Ich 'nich' ne 'nai,'°
And lüst° Ich telle thee warevore,   listen
Al wi hit is and warevore.
"Ich habbe bile stif and stronge
270 And gode clivres° scharp and longe   talons
So° hit bicumeth to havekes cünne.°   As   **havekes cünne** hawk's kin
Hit is min highte,° hit is mi wünne,°   joy   delight
That Ich me draghe° to mine cünde,°   draw   kind
Ne mai me no man tharevore schende.°   scold
275 On me hit is wel i-sene,°   **wel i-sene** very clear
Vor righte cünde° Ich am so kene.°   **Vor . . .** By very nature   aggressive

266. To that I say neither 'not I' nor 'nay'

Vorthi° Ich am loth° smale foghle°   Therefore   loathsome to   birds
That flöth° bi grunde and bi thüvele.°   fly   thicket
Hi me bichermeth and bigredeth°   **bichermeth** . . . scream at and cry at
280   And höre flockes to me ledeth.
Me is löf° to habbe reste   **Me** . . . I like
And sitte stille in mine neste;
Vor nere Ich never no° the betere   **nere** . . . I'd never be any
Yif Ich mid chavling° and mid chatere   squabbling
285   Höm schende° and mid fule worde,   should scold
So herdes° doth, other mid schit-worde.°   shepherds   **other** . . . or with dirty words
Ne lüst me with the screwen chide;°
Forthi° Ich wende from höm wide.   Therefore
Hit is a wise monne dome°—   **wise** . . . judgment of wise men
290   And hi° hit seggeth wel ilome°—   they   frequently
That me° ne chide with the gidie°   one   foolish
Ne with than ofne me ne yonie.°

     "At sume sithe,° herde I telle   time
Hu Alvred sede on his spelle,°   utterance
295   'Loke that thu ne bö thare
Thar chavling böth and cheste yare.°
Lat sottes chide,° and vorth thu go.'   **sottes chide** fools debate
And Ich am wis and do also.°   so
And yet Alvred seide, an other side,°   **an** . . . on the other hand
300   A word that is i-sprunge wide:
'That° with the fule° haveth imene°   (He) that   foul   contact
Ne cumeth he never from him° cleine.'   it
Wenestu° that haveck° bö the worse   Do you suppose   hawk
Thogh crowe bigrede° him bi the mershe   **crowe bigrede** crows cry at
305   And göth to him mid höre chirme°   **höre chirme** their screaming
Right so° hi wille with him schirme?°   **Right so** As if   fight
The havek folgheth° gode rede°   follows   advice
And flighth his wei and lat him grede.°   **lat** . . . lets them cry
     "Yet thu me seist° of other thinge°   **me seist** speak against me   things
310   And telst° that Ich ne can noght singe,   complain
Ac° al mi rörde° is woning°   But that   voice   lamentation
And to i-hire grislich° thing.   **i-hire grislich** hear a horrible
That nis noght soth.° Ich singe efne°   true   evenly
Mid fulle dreme° and lude stefne.°   sound   voice
315   Thu wenist that ech song bö grislich
That thine pipinge nis ilich.°   **nis ilich** is not like
Mi stefne is bold and noght unorne;°   humble
Hö° is ilich one grete horne,   It

287. I don't like to debate with the shrews
292. Nor gape open in competition with the oven.
296. Where squabbling and strife are ready.

And thin is ilich one pipe
320 Of one smale wöde° unripe.   **one** . . . a narrow reed
Ich singe bet° than thu dest.   better
Thu chaterest so döth on Irish pröst.
Ich singe an eve a° righte time,   **an** . . . in evening (vespers) at the
And söththe wön° hit is bed-time,   **söththe wön** then when (compline)
325 The thridde sithe° ad middel-nighte,   **thridde sithe** third time (matins)
And so Ich mine song adighte°   prepare
Wöne Ich i-sö° arise vörre°   see   far off
Other dai-rim other° dai-sterre.   **Other** . . . Either daybreak (lauds) or
    "Ich do god mid mine throte
330 And warni men to höre note;°   **höre note** their profit
Ac° thu singest alle longe night   But
From eve forth° hit is dai-light,   until
And evre seist° thin o° song   utter   one
So longe so° the night is long,   **So** . . . As long as
335 And evre croweth thi wrecche crei°   craw
That he ne swiketh° night ne dai.   **he** . . . doesn't stop
Mid thine pipinge thu adünest°   deafen
Thas monnes earen thar° thu wunest°   **Thas** . . . The ears of man where   dwell
And makest thine song so unwürth°   worthless
340 That me ne telth of thar noght würth.°   **me** . . . one counts no value in it
Evrich mürghthe° mai so longe i-leste   pleasure
That hö shal liki wel unwreste,°   **hö** . . . it will satisfy very poorly
Vor harpe, and pipe, and fugheles° song   birds'
Misliketh° yif hit is too long.   Displeases
345 Ne bö the song never so mürie
That he ne shal thinche wel unmürie
Yef he i-lesteth over unwille;°
So thu might thine song aspille.°   waste
Vor hit is soth°—Alvred hit seidde—   true
350 And me° hit mai ine boke rede: one
'Evrich thing mai losen his godhede°   goodness
Mid unmethe° and mid overdede.'°   excess   superfluity
Mid este° thu thee might overquatie,°   pleasure   **thee** . . . can glut yourself
And overfulle maketh wlatie,°   **overfulle** . . . surfeit causes disgust
355 And evrich müreghthe mai a-gon°   **mureghthe** . . . pleasure can pass
Yif me hit halt evre-forth in on°
Bute° one, that° is Godes riche°   Except   which   kingdom
That evre is swete and evre iliche.°   the same
Thegh° thu nime° evere of than lepe,°   Though   take   **of** . . . from that basket
360 Hit is evre ful bi hepe.°   **ful** . . . heaping full

345–47. The song is (literally, 'Be the song') never so pleasant that it will not seem very unpleasant if it
lasts beyond the point of displeasure
356. If one persists in it evermore continually

63

	Wunder° hit is of Godes riche	A marvel
	That evre spenth° and ever is iliche.	expends
	"Yüt thu me seist° another shome	**me seist** utter against me
	That Ich am on mine eghen lome°	**eghen lome** eyes feeble
365	And seist, for that Ich flö° bi nighte,	fly
	That Ich ne mai i-sö° bi lighte.	**ne . . .** can't see
	Thu liest! On me hit is i-sene	
	That Ich habbe gode sene,°	sight
	Vor nis non so dim thüsternesse°	darkness
370	That Ich ever i-sö° the lasse.	see
	Thu wenest that Ich ne mighte i-sö,	
	Vor Ich bi daie noght ne flö.°	**noght . . .** don't fly at all
	The hare luteth° al dai,	hides
	Ac notheles i-sö he mai.	
375	Yif hundes ürneth° to him-ward,	run
	He gength wel swithe° awai-ward	**gength . . .** goes very fast
	And hoketh° pathes swithe narewe	winds along
	And haveth mid him his blenches yarewe°	**blenches yarewe** tricks prepared
	And hupth and stard° swithe cove°	**hupth . . .** hops and starts fast
380	And secheth pathes to the grove;	
	Ne sholde he, vor bothe his eghe,°	eyes
	So don yif he the bet ni-seghe.°	**yif . . .** unless he saw better
	Ich mai i-sön so wel so on° hare,	**i-sön . . .** see as well as a
	Thegh Ich bi daie sitte and dare.°	hide
385	Thar aghte° men böth in worre	**Thar aghte** Where bold
	And fareth bothe ner and förre°	far
	And overfareth fele thöde°	**overfareth . . .** overrun many nations
	And doth bi nighte gode nöde,°	service
	Ich folghi than° aghte manne°	**folghi than** follow those men
390	And flö° bi nighte in höre banne."°	fly **höre banne** their troop
	The nightingale in hire thoghte	
	Athold° al this and longe thoghte	Retained
	Wat hö tharafter mighte segge,	
	Vor hö ne mighte noght alegge°	refute
395	That° the hule hadde hire i-sed,	What
	Vor hö spac bothe right and red;°	reason
	And hire ofthughte° that hö hadde	**hire ofthughte** it annoyed her
	The speche so för vorth i-ladde°	**för . . .** far forward led
	And was oferd° that hire answare	afraid
400	Ne wurthe noght° aright i-fare.	**Ne . . .** Would not
	Ac notheles hö spac boldeliche—	
	Vor he is wis that hardeliche°	boldly
	With his vo° berth grete ilete,°	foe **grete ilete** a bold front
	That he vor areghthe hit ne forlete;°	**areghthe . . .** cowardice should not give
405	Vor swich worth° bold yif thu flighst°	**swich worth** such a foe becomes flee

That wile flö° yif thu vicst;° — flee fight
Yif he i-sith that thu nart aregh,° — **nart aregh** aren't afraid
He wile of bore würchen baregh.° — **of . . .** from boar became a piglet
And forthi,° thegh the nightingale — therefore
410 Were a-ferd, hö spac bolde tale.

NIGHTINGALE
"Ule," hö seide, "wi dostu so?
Thu singest a-winter 'wo-la-wo.'° — alas
Thu singest so° döth hen a-snowe; — as
Al that hö singeth hit is for wowe.
415 A-wintere thu singest wrothe and yomere,° — **wrothe . . .** angrily and mournfully
And evre thu art dumb a-sumere.
Hit is for thine fule nithe° — malice
That thu ne might° mid us bö blithe, — **ne might** cannot
Vor thu forbernest wel negh for onde° — **forbernest . . .** very nearly burn up because of envy
420 Wane ure blisse cumeth to londe.
Thu farest so döth the ille:° — malicious man
Evrich blisse him° is unwille;° — for him displeasing
Grucching and luring him böth rade°
Yif he i-söth° that men böth° glade. — sees are
425 He wolde that he i-seghe° — saw
Teres in evrich monnes eghe;° — eye
Ne roghte he thegh flockes were
I-meind bi toppes and bi here.°
Al° so thu dost on thire° side, — Just your
430 Vor wanne snow lith° thicke and wide, — lies
And alle wightes° habbeth sorghe,° — creatures care
Thu singest from eve fort a-morghe.° — **fort a-morghe** till morning
"Ac Ich alle blisse mid me bringe.
Ech wight is glad for mine thinge° — **for . . .** because of me
435 And blisseth hit° wanne Ich cume — **blisseth hit** rejoices
And highteth aghen° mine kume.° — **highteth aghen** looks forward to coming
The blostme ginneth° springe and sprede — **blostme ginneth** blossoms begin to
Bothe ine trö and ek on mede.
The lilie mid hire faire wlite° — face
440 Wolcumeth me, that thu hit wite;° — **that . . .** I'll have you know
Bit° me mid hire faire blö° — Bids countenance
That Ich shulle to hire flö.
The rose also mid hire rude° — radiance
That cumeth ut of the thorne-wode
445 Bit me that Ich schulle singe

423. Grumbling and scowling come quickly to him
427–28. Nor would he care though wool refuse were mixed in with choice wool and hair, *or* though flocks (of sheep or people?) were entangled by top-knots and by hair. (Both interpretations are possible.)

Vor hire luve° one skentinge,°   **hire luve** love of her   ditty
And Ich so do thurgh night and dai—
The more Ich singe, the more I mai°—   can
And skente hi° mid mine songe,   **skente hi** delight her
450 Ac notheles noght overlonge.
Wane Ich i-sö that men böth glade,
Ich nelle that hi bön too sade.°   **nelle** . . . don't want them to be oversated
Wan is i-do vor wan Ich com,°
Ich fare aghen° and do wisdom.   **fare aghen** go away
455 Wane mon hogheth of° his sheve,°   **hogheth of** thinks about   sheaves
And falewi° cumeth on grene leve,   fall coloring
Ich fare hom and nime° leve,   take
Ne recche° Ich noght of winteres reve.°   **Ne recche** Nor care   spoil
Wan Ich i-sö that cumeth that harde,°   hard time
460 Ich fare° hom to min erde°   go   abode
And habbe° bothe luve and thonc°   receive   gratitude
That Ich her com and hider swonk.°   **hider swonk** labored here
Wan min erende is i-do,°   done
Sholde Ich bileve?° Nai, warto?°   linger   what for
465 Vor he nis nother yep° ne wis   **nis** . . . is neither smart
That longe abid thar him nöd nis."°   **thar** . . . where he's not needed
    Thös hule lüste° and leide an hord°   listened   **an hord** in store
Al this mot,° word after word,   argument
And after thoghte hu heo mighte
470 Answere vinde° best mid righte,   find
Vor he mot hine ful wel bithenche°
That is aferd° of plaites wrenche.°   afraid   **plaites wrenche** tricks of pleading

OWL
    "Thu aishest° me," the hule sede,   ask
"Wi Ich a-winter singe and grede.°   cry
475 Hit is gode monne i-wone°—   **gode** . . . for good men customary
And was from the worlde frome°—   **worlde frome** world's beginning
That ech god man his frönd i-cnowe°   recognize
And blisse° mid höm sume throwe°   rejoice   **sume throwe** at some time
In his huse at his borde°   table
480 Mid faire speche and faire worde;
And hure and hure to° Cristesmasse,   **hure** . . . especially at
Wane riche and poure, more and lasse,
Singeth cundut° night and dai,   carols
Ich höm helpe what Ich mai.°   can
485 And ek° Ich thenche° of other thinge   also   think
Thane to pleien other° to singe.   or

453. When what I came for is done
471. For one must full well bethink himself

"Ich habbe herto gode answare
Anon i-redi and al yare.°   prepared
Vor sumeres-tide is al too wlonc°   **al ...** far too wanton
490 And doth misreken monnes thonk,°
Vor he ne recth noght of clennesse;°   **ne ...** cares naught for purity
Al his thoght is of golnesse.°   lechery
Vor none dör no leng nabideth,°   **none ...** no animal waits any longer
Ac evrich° upon other rideth.   each
495 The sülve stottes° ine the stode°   **sülve stottes** very horses   stud
Böth bothe° wilde and mere-wode.°   both   mare-crazy
And thu sülf art thar-among,
For of golnesse° is al thi song;   lechery
And aghen° thet thu wilt teme,°   toward the time   breed
500 Thu art wel modi° and wel breme.°   bold   wild
Sone so° thu havest i-trede,°   **Sone so** As soon as   coupled
Ne mightu leng° a word i-quethe°   **Ne ...** You can no longer   say
Ac pipest al so° döth a mose°   as   titmouse
Mid chokeringe° mid stevne hose.°   choking   **stevne hose** hoarse voice
505 Yet thu singst worse thon the hei-sugge°   hedge-sparrow
That flighth bi grunde among the stübbe.°   stumps
Wane thi lust is a-go,°   gone
Thonne° is thi song a-go also.   Then
A-sumere, chorles awedeth°   **chorles awedeth** churls go mad
510 And vorcrempeth° and vorbredeth.°   cramp up   contort themselves
Hit nis° for luve, notheles,   is not
Ac is the chorles wode res;°   **wode res** crazy impulse
Vor wane he haveth i-do° his dede,   done
I-fallen is al his boldhede.°   boldness
515 Habbe he i-stunge° under gore,°   **Habbe ...** When once he has thrust
Ne last° his luve no leng° more.   clothing
Al° so hit is on thine mode;°   lasts   longer
So sone so° thu sittest a-brode,°   Just   mood
Thu forlöst° al thine wise.°   **So ...** As soon as   on a brood
520 Al so thu farest° on thine rise;°   lose   song
Wane thu havest i-do° thi gome,°   behave   branch
Thi stevne° goth anon to shome.°   finished   game
     "Ac wane nightes cumeth longe   voice   ruin
And bringeth forstes° stark and stronge,   frosts
525 Thanne erest° hit is i-sene   for the first time
War° is the snelle,° war is the kene.°   Where   swift one   bold one
At than harde me° mai avinde°   **At ...** In bad times one   find out
Wo geth forth,° wo lith° bihinde.   **Wo ...** Who advances   lies
Me mai i-sön at thare nöde°   **thare nöde** the time of need
530 Wan° me shal harde wike böde.°   From whom   **wike böde** service demand

490. And causes man's thought to go astray

Thanne Ich am snel° and pleie and singe   **swift**
And highte me° mid mi skentinge.°   **highte me** rejoice   **skentinge** singing
On none° wintere Ich ne recche,°   **On none** For any   **ne recche** care not
Vor Ich nam non aswunde° wrecche.   **nam** ... am no feeble
535 And ek° Ich frouri vele wighte°   **also**   **frouri** ... comfort many creatures
That mid höm nabbeth none mightte;°   **mid** ... in themselves have no power
Hi böth hoghfule° and wel arme°   anxious   miserable
And secheth yörne to the warme.°   **secheth** ... seek eagerly for warmth
Oft Ich singe vor höm the more
540 For lütli° sum of höre° sore.   **For lütli** To lessen   their
Hu thincht thee?° Artu yüt i-nume?°   **thincht thee** seems it to you   caught
Artu mid righte° overcume?"   **mid righte** properly

NIGHTINGALE
"Nay, nay," sede the nightingale.
Thu shalt i-here another tale.
545 Yet nis thös speche i-broght to dome.°   verdict
Ac bö wel stille, and lüst° nu to me.   listen
Ich shal mid one bare worde
Do that° thi speche wurth forworthe."°   **Do that** Cause   **wurth forworthe** to become worthless

OWL
"That nere noht° right," the hule sede.   **nere noht** would not be
550 "Thu havest bicloped al so° thu bede,°   **bicloped** ... laid charge just as   asked to do
And Ich thee habbe i-yive answare.
Ac, ar° we to unker dome° fare,   before   **unker dome** the verdict on us
Ich wille speke toward thee
Al so thu speke° toward me,   spoke
555 And thu me answare, yif thu might.
Seie me nu, thu wrecche wight,°   creature
Is in thee eni other note°   use
Bute° thu havest schille° throte?   Except that   a shrill
Thu nart noght to non° other thinge   **nart** ... are useless for any
560 Bute thu canst of° chateringe,   **canst of** know about
Vor thu art lütel and unstrong,
And nis thi reghel° nothing long.   garment
Wat dostu godes° among monne   **dostu godes** good do you do
Na mo the° deth a wrecche wrann!°   **Na** ... Any more than   wren
565 Of thee ne cumeth non other god°   benefit
Bute° thu gredest swich° thu bö wod,°   Except that   **gredest swich** cry out as if   **bö wod** were wild
And, bö thi piping overgo,
Ne böth on thee craftes namo.°
"Alvred sede, that was wis—
570 He mighte wel, for soth° hit is: true

567–68. And when your piping has passed, there aren't any other skills in you.

'Nis° no man for his bare songe
Löf ne wurth° noght swithe longe,
Vor that is a forworthe° man
That bute singe noght ne can.'°
575 Thu nart bute on° forworthe thing;
On thee nis bute chatering.
Thu art dim and of fule höwe°
And thinchest° a lütel soti clöwe.°
Thu nart fair, no° thu nart strong,
580 Ne thu nart thicke, ne thu nart long.
Thu havest i-mist al of fairhede,°
And lütel is al thi godede.°
    "Another thing of thee Ich mene:°
Thu nart vair ne thu nart clene.
585 Wane thu cumest to manne haghe°
Thar° thornes böth and ris i-draghe°
Bi hegge° and bi thicke wöde°
Thar men göth oft to höre nöde,°
Tharto thu draghst,° tharto thu wunest,°
590 And other clene stede° thu schunest.
Wan Ich flö nightes after müse,°
I mai thee vinde° ate rum-huse.°
Among the wöde,° among the netle,
Thu sittest and singst bihinde the setle.
595 Thar me° mai thee ilomest° finde
Thar° men worpeth° höre bihinde!
    "Yet thu atwitest me° mine mete
And seist that Ich fule wightes ete.
Ac wat etestu—that thu ne lighe°—
600 Bute atter-coppe° and fule vlighe°
And wormes, yif thu might hi° finde
Among the volde° of harde rinde?°
Yet Ich can do wel gode wike,°
Vor Ich can loki manne wike;°
605 And mine wike böth wel gode,
Vor Ich helpe to° manne vode.°
Ich can nimen müs° at berne°
And ek° at chirche in the derne,°
Vor me is löf, to° Cristes huse,
610 To clansi° hit with° fule müse,°
Ne schal thar nevre come to
Ful° wight, yif Ich hit mai i-vo.°
And, yif me lüst° on mi skentinge°
To wernen° other wunienge,°
615 Ich habbe at wude trön° wel grete

Glosses:

There is
Löf . . . Loved or honored
useless
bute . . . knows nothing except how to sing
nart . . . are but a

hue
seem like   **soti clöwe** sooty ball
nor

i-mist . . . fallen entirely short of beauty
virtue
complain

manne haghe men's dwellings
Where   **ris i-draghe** branches drawn together
hedge   weeds
to . . . for their need
draw   dwell
places
mice
find   privy
weeds

one   most often
Where   set down
atwitest me reproach me about

ne lighe may not lie
Bute atter-coppe But spiders   flies
them
folds   bark
services
loki . . . guard men's dwellings

with   food
nimen müs catch mice   barn
also   dark
me . . . I love, in
cleanse   of   mice

Any foul   catch
me lüst it pleases me   singing
refuse   dwellings
at . . . in the woods a tree

Mit thicke boghe nothing blete°   **nothing blete** in no way bare
Mid ivi grene al bigrowe°   grown over
That evre stont iliche i-blowe°   **evre** . . . stands unchangingly in leaf
And his höw° never ne vorlöst°   **his höw** its hue   loses
620   Wan hit sniuth° ne wan hit fröst.°   snows   freezes
Tharin Ich habbe god ihold,°   **god ihold** a good stronghold
A-winter warm, a-sumere cold.
Wane min hus stont° bright and grene,   stands
Of thine nis nothing i-sene.
625   "Yet thu me telst° of other thinge;   reproach
Of mine briddes seist gabbinge°   lies
That höre nest nis noght clene.
Hit is fale° other wighte imene,°   of many   common
Vor hors a-stable and oxe a-stalle
630   Doth° al that höm wüle° thar falle,   Let   **höm wüle** they wish
And lütle children in the cradele,
Bothe chörles and ek athele,°   **chörles** . . . low-born and also noble
Doth al° that in höre yoethe°   **Doth al** All do   youth
That° hi vorleteth° in höre dughethe.°   Which   abandon   maturity
635   Wat! Can that yongling hit bihede?°   **yongling** . . . youngster prevent it
Yif hit misdeth,° hit mod nede.°   misbehaves   **mod nede** must necessaril▌
A vorbisne° is of olde ivürne°   proverb   **olde ivürne** long ago
That nöde° maketh old wif ürne.°   need   run
     "And yet Ich habbe another andsware.
640   Wiltu to mine neste vare°   go
And loki° hu hit is i-dight?°   look   made
Yif thu art wis, lörni° thu mighst.   learn
Mi nest is holgh and rum° amidde,   **holgh** . . . hollow and roomy
So hit is softest mine° bridde.   for my
645   Hit is broiden° al abute   woven
Vrom the neste vör withute.°   **vör withute** far outward
Tharto hi goth to höre nöde;°   necessity
Ac that thu menest,° Ich höm forböde.°   complain of   forbid
We nimeth yeme of manne bure,°   **nimeth** . . . take example from men's bedrooms
650   And after than° we maketh ure;°   **after than** like them   ours
Men habbeth, among other iwende,°   devices
A rum-hus° at höre bures ende   privy
Vor that hi nelleth too vör go,°   **nelleth** . . . don't want to go too far
And mine briddes doth al so.°   **al so** the same
655   "Site nu stille, chaterestre!°   chatterbox
Nere thu never i-bunde vastre.°   **i-bunde vastre** bound more fast
Herto ne vindestu never andsware.
Hong up thin ax! Nu thu might fare!"°   **might fare** can go
     The nightingale at thisse worde
660   Was wel negh ut of rede i-worthe°   **negh** . . . nigh run out of ideas

70

And thoghte yörne° on hire mode°   eagerly   mind
Yif hö oght elles understode,°   **oght** . . . knew anything else
Yif hö kuthe° oght bute singe,°   understood   **bute singe** except how to sing
That mighte helpe to other thinge.°   **to** . . . for other purposes
665 Herto hö moste andswere vinde
Other mid alle bön° bihinde;   **Other** . . . Or completely be
And hit is swithe strong° to fighte   hard
Aghen soth° and aghen righte.   **Aghen soth** Against truth
He mot gon to° al mid ginne°   **mot** . . . must go at   ingenuity
670 Wan the hörte böth on winne;°   **böth** . . . is at strife
And the man mot on other segge°—   **on** . . . talk differently
He mot bihemmen and bilegge°—   **bihemmen** . . . decorate and gloze
Yif muth withute mai biwro,°
That me° the hörte noght ni-sö.°   **That me** So that one   **noght ni-sö** doesn't see
675 And sone° mai a word misreke°   quickly   miscarry
Thar° muth shal aghen° hörte speke;   Where   against
And sone mai a word misstörte°   misstart
Thar muth shal speken aghen hörte.
Ac notheles yüt, upe thon°   **upe thon** concerning that
680 Her is to red, wo hine kon;°
Vor never nis° wit so kene   is
So wane red him is a wene.°
Thanne erest° cumeth his yephede°   for the first time   **his yephede** its ingenuity
Wöne hit is alremest on drede;°   **alremest** . . . most of all in doubt
685 For Alvered seide of olde quide,°   a saying
And yüt hit nis of hörte i-slide:°   **of** . . . hasn't slipped from mind
'Wone the bale° is alre-hecst,°   trouble   highest of all
Thonne is the bote alre-necst.'°   **bote alre-necst** remedy nearest of all
Vor wit west among his sore,°   **west** . . . increases while on trial
690 And for his° sore hit is the more.   **for his** because of its
Vorthi nis nevere mon redles°   without a plan
Ar° his hörte bö witles.   Until
Ac, yif that he forlöst° his wit,   loses
Thonne is his red-purs° al to-slit;°   bag of schemes   split apart
695 Yif he ne kon° his wit atholde,°   **ne kon** can't   retain
Ne vint he red° in one volde.°   **Ne** . . . He won't find counsel   **one volde** a single fold
Vor Alvrid seide, that wel kuthe°—   knew how
Evre he spac mid sothe° muthe: truthful
'Wone the bale° is alre-hecst,°   trouble   highest of all
700 Thanne is the bote alre-nest.' "°   **bote alre-nest** remedy nearest of all
The nightingale al hire hoghe°   mind
Mid rede° hadde wel bitoghe;°   counsel   exercised

673. If the mouth is to conceal outwardly
680. There is a remedy available for him who knows it (probable interpretation)
682. As when a plan of action (*red*, literally, 'counsel') is still in doubt for it (the debater's *wit*, 'mind').

71

Among the harde, among the toghte°   strained arguments
Ful wel mid rede hire bithoghte;°   had bethought herself
705 And hadde andswere gode i-funde
Among al hire harde stunde.°   moments

NIGHTINGALE

"Hule, thu axest me," hö seide,
"Yif Ich kon° eni other dede   can do
Bute singen in sumere tide°   **sumere tide** summertime
710 And bringe blisse för° and wide.   far
Wi axestu of craftes mine?
Betere is min on° than alle thine.   one craft
Betere is o° song of mine muthe   one
Than al that evre thi kün kuthe.°   **kün kuthe** kind could do
715 And lüst—Ich telle thee warevore.
Wostu to wan° man was i-bore?°   **Wostu ...** Do you know for what   born
To thare° blisse of hövene-riche°   the   heaven's kingdom
Thar° ever is song and mürghthe iliche.°   Where   **mürghthe iliche** pleasure consistently
Thider fundeth° evrich man   strives
720 That eni thing of gode kan.°   **gode kan** good knows
Vorthi me° singth in holi chirche,   **Vorthi me** For this reason one
And clerkes ginneth° songes wirche,°   undertake   to compose
That man i-thenche° bi the songe   may ponder
Wider he shal° and thar bön longe,   is destined
725 That he the mürghthe ne voryete°   **mürghthe ...** pleasure may not forget
Ac tharof thenche and biyete°   attain
And nime yeme of chirche stevene°
Hu mürie is the blisse of hövene.
Clerkes, munekes, and kanunes,°
730 Thar° böth thos gode wicke-tunes,°   Where   communities
Ariseth up to midel-nighte
And singeth of the hövene lighte,°   **hövene lighte** heavenly light
And pröstes upe londe° singeth   **upe londe** in country parishes
Wane the light of daie springeth;
735 And Ich höm helpe wat I mai.
Ich singe mid höm night and dai,
And hö böth alle for° me the gladdere   because of
And to the songe böth the raddere.°   readier
"Ich warni° men to here° gode   warn   **to here** for their
740 That hi bön° blithe on höre mode°   **hi bön** they should be   spirit
And bidde° that hi moten i-seche°   urge   **moten i-seche** must seek
Than ilke° song that ever is eche.°   **Than ilke** The same   eternal
Nu thu might,° hule, sitte and clinge!   **thu might** may you

727. And take heed from the church's voice
729. Clerics, monks, and canons (living according to religious rule)

72

Her among nis° no chateringe.   **Her . . .** In this there is

745 Ich graunti° that we go to dome   agree

Tofore the sülfe° Pope of Rome!   very

    "Ac abid yete, notheles.

Thu shalt i-here another thes;°   thing about this

Ne shaltu, for° Engelonde,   for all of

750 At thisse worde me atstonde.°   withstand

Wi atwitestu me mine unstrengthe°   **atwitestu . . .** do you twit me about my weakness

And mine ungrete° and mine unlengthe°   smallness   shortness

And seist that Ich nam noght strong,

Vor° Ich nam nother° gret ne long?   Just because   neither

755 Ac thu nost never wat° thu menst;°   **nost . . .** don't know at all what   say

Bute lese° wordes thu me lenst.°   **Bute lese** Nothing but false   offer

For Ich kan° craft, and Ich kan liste,°   know   ingenuity

And tharevore Ich am thus thriste.°   bold

Ich kan wit and song mani eine,°   **mani eine** many a one

760 Ne triste° Ich to° non other maine;°   trust   in   power

Vor soth hit is that seide Alvred:

'Ne mai° no strengthe aghen red.'°   can prevail   counsel

Oft spet° wel a lüte liste°   speeds   **lüte liste** little ingenuity

Thar° muche strengthe sholde miste;°   Where   fail

765 Mid lütle strengthe thurgh ginne°   stratagem

Castel and burgh me° mai i-winne;   **burgh me** stronghold one

Mid liste me mai walles felle

And worpe of° horsse knightes snelle.°   **worpe of** throw off   bold

Üvel° strengthe is lütel wurth,   Brute

770 Ac wisdom ne wurth° never unwurth;°   becomes   worthless

Thu myht i-seo° thurh alle thing   **myht i-seo** can see

That wisdom naveth non evening.°   **naveth . . .** has no equal

An hors is strengur than a mon,

Ac, for° hit non i-wit ne kon,°   because   **non . . .** has no understanding

775 Hit berth° on rügge° grete semes°   carries   its back   loads

And draghth° bi sweore° grete temes°   draws   its neck   plough-chains

And tholeth° bothe yerd° and spure   suffers   stick

And stont° i-teid at mülne dure;°   stands   **mülne dure** the mill door

And hit deth that° mon hit hot.°   **deth that** does what   orders

780 And, for than that° hit no wit not,°   **for . . .** because   **no . . .** knows no understanding

Ne mai his strenthe hit i-shilde

That hit nabughth the lütle childe.°

Mon deth° mid strengthe and mid witte   **Mon deth** Man brings it about

That other thing nis non his fitte.°   **other . . .** no other thing is his equal

785 Thegh alle strengthe at one were,°   **alle** the strength of all things was united

Monnes wit yet more were;°   would be

Vorthe,° mon mid his crafte   Therefore

781–82. Its strength cannot shield it from having to yield to the small child.

73

Overkumeth al örthliche shafte.°   **örthliche shafte** earthly creatures

Al so Ich do mid mine one songe

790   Bet° than thu al the yer longe.   Better

Vor mine crafte men me luvieth;°   love

Vor thine strenghte men thee shunieth.

Telstu bi me° the wurs for than°   **Telstu** . . . Do you count me **for than** because

That Ich bute anne° craft ne kan?°   **bute anne** only one know

795   "Yif tweie° men goth to wraslinge,   two

And either other faste thringe,

And the on can swenges swithe fele°

And kan his wrenches° wel forhele,°   tricks conceal

And the other ne can sweng but anne,°   **ne** . . . knows just one hold

800   And the° is god with° eche manne,   that against

And mid thon one leith° to grunde   **thon** . . . that one he lays

Anne after other a lütle stunde,°   **a** . . . in little time

Wat tharf° he recche of a mo° swenge   need **of** . . . for one more

Wone the on him° is swo genge?°   **the** . . . one for him **swo genge** so effective

805   "Thu seist that thu canst fele wike,°   **canst** . . . know how to do many services

Ac ever Ich am thin unilike.°   **thin unilike** unlike you

Do° thine craftes alle togadere,   Put

Yet is min on hörte° betere.   **on hörte** essentially

Oft wan hundes foxes driveth,

810   The kat ful wel himselve liveth°   survives

Thegh he ne kunne wrench bute anne.°   **ne** . . . may know just one trick

The fox so godne ne can nanne°   **so** . . . knows none so good

Thegh he kunne so vele° wrenche   many

That he wenth° eche hunde atprenche,°   expects to outwit

815   Vor he can° pathes righte and woghe,°   knows **righte** . . . straight and crooked

And he kan hongi bi the boghe,°   bough

And so forlöst° the hund his fore°   loses trail

And turnth aghen eft° to than more.°   **aghen eft** once more **than more** the moor

The vox kan cröpe° bi the heie°   **kan cröpe** knows how to creep hedge

820   And turne ut from his forme° weie   former

And eft sone° kume tharto.   **eft sone** again quickly

Thonne° is the hundes smel fordo;°   Then destroyed

He not,° thurgh the i-meinde smak,°   doesn't know **i-meinde smak** confused scent

Wether he shal avorth the abak.°   **avorth** . . . go forward or back

825   Yif the vox mist of° al this dwöle,°   **mist of** escapes by deception

At than ende he cröpth° to hole;   creeps

Ac natheles mid alle his wrenche

Ne kan he hine so bithenche,°   **Ne** . . . He can't so contrive

Thegh he bö yep° and swithe snel,°   smart quick

830   That he ne löst° his rede vel.°   **ne löst** doesn't lose **rede vel** red pelt

The cat ne kan wrench bute anne°   **ne** . . . knows no trick but one

796–97. And each presses the other hard, and one knows very many holds

Nother bi dune ne bi venne,°   By that   continues to wear
Bute he kan climbe swithe wel;
Tharmid° he wereth° his greie vel.   concerning
835 Al so Ich segge bi° mi sölve,
Betere is min on° than thine twelve."   one

OWL

"Abid! Abid!" the ule seide.
"Thu gest al to° mid swikelede.°   **gest** ... go at things entirely   treachery
Alle thine wordes thu bileist°   disguise
840 That hit thincth° soth al that thu seist.   **That** ... So that it seems
Alle thine wordes böth i-sliked°   smoothed over
And so bisemed and biliked°   **bisemed** ... plausible and likely
That alle tho° that hi avoth°   those   **hi avoth** hear them
Hi weneth° that thu segge soth.   suppose
845 Abid! Abid! Me shal thee yene.°   **Me** ... You are to be countered
Nu hit shal wurthe° wel i-sene   become
That thu havest müchel i-loghe°   **müchel i-loghe** greatly lied
Wone thi lesing° böth unwroghe.°   deception   revealed
    "Thu seist that thu singist mankünne°   for mankind
850 And techest höm that hi fundieth hönne°   **fundieth hönne** strive to go hence
Up to the songe that evre i-lest;°   endures
Ac hit is alre wunder mest°   **alre** ... of all wonders most
That thu darst lighe so opeliche.°   openly
Wenest thu hi bringe° so lightliche°   **hi bringe** to bring them   easily
855 To Godes riche° al singinge?   kingdom
Nai, nai! Hi shulle wel avinde°   find
That hi mid longe wope mote°   **wope mote** weeping must
Of höre sünnen bidde bote°   **Of** ... For their sins ask relief
Ar° hi mote° ever kume thare.   Before   may
860 Ich rede thi° that men bö yare°   **rede thi** advise so   ready
And more wepe thane singe,
That fundeth° to than höven-kinge,   strive
Vor nis no man withute sünne.
Vorthi he mot,° ar he wende hönne,°   must   hence
865 Mid teres and mid wope bete,°   **wope bete** weeping amend
That him bö sur that er was swete.°
Tharto Ich helpe, God hit wot,
Ne singe Ich höm no foliot;[2]
For al my song is of longinge,

832. Either by hill or by fen
866. So that, for him, that may be sour which previously was sweet.
[2] 'Nor do I sing them any folly.' The rare word *foliot* would inevitably convey to the poet's contemporaries an additional punning connotation, for Bishop Foliot (d. 1187) was widely known as a supporter of Henry II against Becket. The churchly owl instinctively scorns the king's party; the courtly nightingale predictably ignores the jibe and later (l. 1091) praises the king.

870 And i-meind sumdel° mid woninge,°
That mon bi° me hine bithenche°
That he groni° for his unwrenche.°
Mid mine songe Ich hine pülte,
That he groni for his gülte.

875   "Yif thu gest herof to disputinge,
Ich wepe bet° thane thu singe.
Yif right goth forth, and abak wrong,
Betere is mi wop° thane thi song.
Thegh sume men bö thurghut° gode

880 And thurghut clene on höre mode,°
Höm longeth hönne,° notheles.
That° böth her,° wo is höm thes,°
For, thegh hi bön hömsölve i-borwe,°
Hi ne söth her nowight° bote sorwe;

885 Vor other men hi wepeth sore
And for höm biddeth° Cristes ore.°
Ich helpe monne on either halve;
Mi muth haveth tweire künne salve:
Than gode° Ich fülste° to longinge,

890 Vor wan him longeth, Ich him singe;
And than sünfulle° Ich helpe alswo,
Vor Ich him teche ware° is wo.
    "Yet Ich thee yene° in other wise,
For wane thu sittest on thine rise,

895 Thu draghst men to fleses lüste,°
That wülleth° thine songes lüste.°
Al° thu forlöst° the mürghthe° of hövene,
For tharto nevestu none stevene.°
Al that thu singst is of golnesse,°

900 For nis on thee non holinesse,
Ne weneth na man for° thi pipinge
That eni preost in chirche singe!
    "Yet I thee wülle another° segge,
Yif thu hit const ariht bilegge:°

905 Wi nültu° singe an° other theode°
Thar hit is müchele° more neode?°
Thu neaver ne singst in Irlonde,
Ne thu ne cumest noght in Scotlonde.
Hwi nültu fare to Noreweie

910 And singen men° of Galeweie°?
Thar° beoth men that lütel kunne°
Of songe that is bineothe the sunne.
Wi nultu thare preoste° singe
And teche of thire writelinge,°

i-meind sumdel mixed somewhat lament
through **hine bithenche** bethink
  himself
may groan   fault
hine pülte pelt him

better

weeping
throughout
spirit
Höm ... They long to go hence
Those who here   therefore
saved
ne ... see here nothing

beseech   mercy

tweire künne two kinds of
Than gode The good man   help

than sünfulle the sinful
where
refute

fleses lüste flesh's lust
That wülleth Who will   listen to
Completely lose   bliss
nevestu stevene you have no voice
lust

Ne ... Nor does any man suppose because
  of

another thing
construe
won't you among   people
much need

singen men sing to men   Galloway
  (Scotland)
There know

nultu ... won't you there to priests
of ... by your warbling

915 And wisi° höm mid thire° stevene   direct   your
    Hu engeles singeth ine heovene?
    Thu farest° so doth an ydel wel°   act   **ydel wel** useless spring
    That springeth bi burne° that is snel°   **bi burne** beside a brook   swift
    And let fordrüe the dune°
920 And flohth on idel° thar adune.°   **flohth** . . . flows uselessly   below
    Ac Ich fare bothe north and south;
    In everich londe Ich am cuth;°   known
    East and west, fer and ner,
    I do wel faire° mi mester°   **wel faire** very fairly   office
925 And warni men mid mine bere°   performance
    That thi dweole° song heo ne forlere.°   deceiving   **heo** . . . mislead them not
    Ich wisse° men mid mine songe   direct
    That hi ne sünegi nowiht° longe.   **ne** . . . they sin not
    I bidde° höm that hö i-swike°   beg   desist
930 That hömsölve ne biswike,°   **That** . . . From deceiving themselves
    For betere is that hö wepen here
    Than elleswhar to bön dövlene fere."°   **dövlene fere** devils' mates
       The nightingale was i-gremet,°   enraged
    And ek hö was sumdel ofschamed°   **sumdel ofschamed** somewhat ashamed
935 For the hule hire atwiten° hadde   twitted
    In hwücche stüde° hö sat and gradde°   **In** . . . About the place in which   wept
    Bihinde the bure° among the wede   bedroom
    Wher men goth to here nöde;°   **to** . . . for their need
    And sat sumdel,° and hö bithohte,°   a while   bethought herself
940 And wiste° wel on hire thohte   knew
    That wraththe binimeth° monnes red.°   takes away   judgment
    For hit seide the king Alfred,
    "Selde° endeth wel the lothe,°   Seldom   loathsome person
    And selde plaideth° wel the wrothe."°   pleads   angry
945 For wraththe meinth° the hörte° blod   disturbs   heart's
    That° hit floweth so° wilde flod   So that   like a
    And al the heorte overgeth,°   overwhelms
    That hö naveth nothing bute breth°
    And so forleost° al hire liht,   loses
950 That heo ne sith soth ne° riht.   **ne** . . . sees neither truth nor
       The nightingale hi understod°   **hi understod** bethought herself
    And overgan lette° hire mod.   **overgan lette** let pass by
    Hö mihte bet speken a sele°   **a sele** in good spirits
    Than mid wraththe° wordes deale.   **mid wraththe** in wrath

               NIGHTINGALE
955 "Ule," heo seide, "lüst nu hider.
    Thu schalt falle; the wei is slider.°   slippery

919. And lets the hill dry up
948. So that it has nothing but anger

Thu seist Ich fleo° bihinde bure.°   fly   the bedroom
Hit is riht; the bur is ure.°   ours
Thar laverd liggeth and lavedi,°   **Thar** ... Where lord lies and lady
960   Ich schal heom° singe and sitte bi.   **schal heom** must for them
Wenstu° that wise men forlete,°   Do you think   would abandon
For° fule venne,° the righte strete;   Because of   mud
Ne sunne the later shine°
Thegh hit bö ful in neste thine?
965   Sholde Ich, for one hole brede,°   **one** ... a plank with a hole
Forlete mine righte stede,°   place
That Ich ne singe° bi the bedde   **That** ... So that I wouldn't sing
Thar loverd° haveth his löve i bedde?   **Thar loverd** Where lord
Hit is mi right, hit is mi laghe,°   law
970   That to the hexst° Ich me draghe.°   highest   **me draghe** draw myself
    "Ac yet thu yelpst° of thine songe   boast
That thu canst yolle wrothe° and stronge   angrily
And seist thu wisest° mankünne   direct
That hi biwepen höre sünne.°   **biwepen** ... lament their sin
975   Solde euch° mon wonie° and grede°   **Solde euch** Should each   weep   wail
Right swich° hi weren unlede?°   **Right swich** Just as if   accursed
Solde hi yollen also thu dest?°   **also** ... as you do
Hi mighte oferen here pröst."°   **oferen** ... frighten their priests
Man shal bö stille and noght grede.
980   He mot° biwepe his misdede;   must
Ac war° is Cristes heriynge°   where   praise
Thar me° shal grede° and lude singe?   one   wail
Nis nother° too lud° ne too long,   neither   loud
At righte time, chirche-song.
985   Thu yolst and wonest,° and Ich singe;   weep
Thi stevene is wop,° and min, skentinge.°   weeping   amusement
Ever mote° thu yolle and wepen   may
That° thu thi lif mote forleten,°   As if   **mote forleten** must abandon
And yollen mote thu so heye
990   That ut berste bo° thin eye!   both
Wether° is betere of twere twom:°   Which   **twere twom** the two
That mon bö blithe, other grom?°   **other grom** or gloomy
So bö hit ever in unker sithe°   **unker sithe** our situation
That thu bö sori and Ich blithe.
995   "Yüt thu aisheist wi Ich ne fare
Into other londe and singe thare?
No! Wat sholde Ich among höm do
Thar never blisse ne com to?
That lond nis god, ne hit nis este,°   pleasant

963. Or that the sun will shine any the later

1000	Ac wildernisse hit is and weste.	
	Knarres and cludes höven-tinge,°	**Knarres** ... Crags and hills sky-high
	Snou and haghel höm° is genge.°	**haghel höm** hail for them usual
	That lond is grislich and unvele.°	**grislich** ... horrible and unprosperous
	The men böth wilde and unisele;°	unpeaceful
1005	Hi nabbeth nother grith ne sibbe;°	**nother** ... neither truce nor concord
	Hi ne reccheth hu hi libbe.°	live
	Hi eteth fish and flesh unsode°	uncooked
	Swich° wulves hit hadde tobrode;°	As if torn apart
	Hi drinketh milc and hwei tharto.	
1010	Hi nüte° elles wat hi do.°	don't know should do
	Hi nabbeth nother° win ne bör°	neither beer
	Ac libbeth also° wilde dör.°	like animals
	Hi goth bitight° mid rugh felle°	clad **rugh felle** rough skins
	Right swich° hi comen° ut of helle.	**Right swich** Just as if had come
1015	"Thegh eni god man to höm come,	
	So hwile düde sum from Rome,[3]	
	For höm to lere° gode thewes°	teach customs
	And for to leten° höre unthewes,°	halt vices
	He mighte bet sitte stille,	
1020	For al his wile° he sholde spille.°	time waste
	He mighte bet teche ane böre°	**ane böre** a bear
	To weghe° bothe sheld and spere	wield
	Thane that wilde folc i-bringe°	persuade
	That hi me wolde i-here° singe.	**wolde i-here** would wish to hear
1025	Wat soldich° thar mid mine songe,	should I do
	Ne sunge Ich höm never° so longe?	**Ne** ... Even if I sang to them ever
	Mi song were i-spild ech del,°	**i-spild** ... wasted every part
	For höm ne mai halter ne bridel	
	Bringe vrom höre wode wise°	**wode wise** crazy manner
1030	Ne mon° mid stele ne mid ire.°	**Ne mon** Nor a man iron
	"Ac war° lond is bothe este° and god,	where pleasant
	And war men habbeth milde mod,	
	Ich noti mid° höm mine throte,	**noti mid** use among
	Vor Ich mai do thar gode note°	service
1035	And bringe höm löve tithinge,°	**löve tithinge** welcome news
	Vor Ich of chirche-songe singe.	
	Hit was i-seid in olde laghe°—	tradition
	And yet i-last thilke soth-sagh°—	**yet** ... still lasts that saw
	That man shal erien° and sowe	plow
1040	Thar he wenth after° sum god mowe,°	**wenth after** expects afterward to reap
	For he is wod° that soweth his sed	crazy

[3] 'As on one occasion a certain one did come from Rome.' Probably a reference to Cardinal Vivian's embassy (1176) to Scotland, Ireland, and Norway.

Thar never gras ne sprinth ne bled."°   sprinth . . . springs nor blade
  The hule was wroth, to cheste rad;°   to . . . ready for conflict
Mid thisse worde hire eyen abrad:°   eyen abrad eyes she widened

OWL

1045 "Thu seist thu witest manne bures,°   witest . . . guard men's bedrooms
Thar leves böth and faire flores,
Thar two i-löve° in one bedde   lovers
Liggeth biclopt° and wel bihedde.°   Liggeth biclopt Lie clasped together guarded
Enes° thu sunge—Ic wod° wel ware°—   Once know where
1050 Bi° one bure and woldest lere°   At instruct
The lefdi° to an üvel luve   lady
And sunge bothe loghe and buve°   loghe . . . low and high
And lerdest hi° to don shome   lerdest hi taught her
And unright of hire licome.°   body
1055 The loverd° that sone underyat;°   lord perceived
Liim and grine and wel eiwat°
Sette° and leyde thee for to lacche.°   He set catch
Thu come sone to than hacche.°   casement
Thu were i-nume° in one grine;   caught
1060 Al hit aboghte thine shine.°   aboghte . . . your shins paid for
Thu naddest non° other dom ne laghe°   naddest non had no dom . . . verdict or law
Bute mid wilde horse were todraghe.°   drawn
Vonde° yif thu might eft misrede°   Try eft misrede again misadvise
Wather° thu wült, wif the° maide!   Whichever or
1065 Thi song mai bö so longe genge°   effective
That thu shalt wippen° on a sprenge."°   flutter snare
  The nightingale at thisse worde
Mid sworde and mid speres orde,°   point
Yif hö mon° were, wolde fighte;   a man
1070 Ac, tho° hö bet do ne mighte,   since
Hö vaght° mid hire wise tunge.   fought
"Wel fight° that wel specth," seith° in the songe.   Wel fight He fights well it says
Of hire tunge hö nom red.°   nom red took counsel
"Wel fight that wel specth," seide Alvred.

NIGHTINGALE

1075 "Wat! Seistu this for mine shome?
The loverd° hadde herof grame.°   lord herof grame harm from this
He was so gelus of his wive
That he ni mighte for his live
I-sö that man with hire speke
1080 That his hörte nolde° breke.   wouldn't
He hire bileck° in one bure°   locked up bedroom
That hire° was bothe stronge and sure.   for her

1056. Lime and snare and almost everything

Ich hadde of hire milse and ore° | milse . . . pity and compassion
And sori was for hire sore
1085 And skente hi° mid mine songe | **skente hi** entertained her
Al that Ich mighte rathe° and longe. | early
Vor than° the knight was with me wroth; | that
Vor righte nithe° Ich was him loth.° | **righte nithe** sheer malice   loathsome
He düde° me his oghene° shome, | put on   own
1090 Ac al him° turnde it to grome.° | on him   harm
That underyat° the king Henri⁴— | learned
Jesus his soule do merci!
He let forbonne thene knight° | **let** . . . had the knight outlawed
That hadde i-don so müchel° unright | much
1095 Ine so gode kinges° londe | a king's
Vor righte nithe° and fule onde° | **righte nithe** sheer malice   spite
Let thane lütle fughel nime
And him fordeme lif an lime.⁵
Hit was wurthsipe° al mine künne;° | an honor to   kin
1100 Forthon° the knight forles his wünne° | For this   happiness
And yaf° for me an hundred punde, | paid
And mine briddes seten i-sunde° | **seten i-sunde** sat safe
And hadde soththe blisse and highte° | joy
And were blithe, and wel mighte.
1105 Vorthon° Ich was so wel awreke,° | Thus   avenged
Ever eft° Ich dar° the bet° speke. | after   dare   more boldly
Vor° hit bitidde ene swo,° | Because   **bitidde** . . . happened once thus
Ich am the blithur ever mo.° | more
Nu Ich mai singe war Ich wülle,
1110 Ne dar me never eft mon agrülle.° | **eft** . . . again anyone annoy
    "Ac thu, ereming!° Thu wrecche gost, | wretch
Thu ne canst finde, ne thu nost,° | **ne** . . . nor do you know
An holgh stok thar° thu thee might hüde | **holgh** . . . hollow stump where
That me ne twengeth° thine hüde.° | **That** . . . So that no one will pluck   skin
1115 Vor children, gromes, heme, and hine,° | **gromes** . . . boys, servants, and yokels
Hi thencheth alle of thire pine.° | **thire pine** tormenting you
Yif hi mughe° i-sö thee sitte, | **hi mughe** they can
Stones hi doth° in höre slitte° | put   pockets
And thee totorveth and toheneth° | **thee** . . . pelt and stone you
1120 And thine fule bon toshenneth.° | **bon tosheneth** bones smash
Yif thu art i-worpe other i-shote,° | **i-worpe** . . . hit or shot
Thanne thu might erest to note,° | **might** . . . can finally be useful
Vor me thee hoth in one rodde,° | **me** . . . people hang you on a stick
And thu, mid thine fule codde° | paunch

⁴ Henry II (d. 1189), here referred to as already dead. See page 75, footnote 2.
⁵ 'As to have the little bird taken and have it condemned illegally life and limb.' Under the laws of Henry II only the king could condemn a culprit to loss of life and limb, and the crime had to be a serious one.

1125	And mid thine ateliche swöre,°
	Biwerest manne corn vrom döre.°
	Nis nother noght,° thi lif ne° thi blod,
	Ac thu art shewles° swithe god.
	Thar nöwe° sedes böth i-sowe,°
1130	Pinnuc,° golfinc, rok,° ne crowe
	Ne dar° thar never cumen ihende°
	Yif thi buc° hongeth at than ende.°
	Thar trön° shulle a yere blowe,°
	And yunge sedes springe and growe,
1135	Ne dar no fughel° tharto vonge°
	Yif thu art tharover i-honge.°
	Thi lif is evre lüther and qued;°
	Thu nard noght bute° ded.
	"Nu, thu might wite sikerliche,°
1140	That thine leches° böth grisliche°
	The wile° thu art on lif-daghe,°
	Vor wane thu hongest i-slaghe,°
	Yüt° hi böth of thee ofdradde,°
	The fugheles that thee er bigradde.°
1145	Mid righte° men böth with thee wrothe,
	For thu singist ever of höre lothe;°
	Al that thu singst rathe° other late,
	Hit is ever of manne unwate.°
	Wane thu havest a-night i-grad,°
1150	Men böth of thee wel sore ofdrad.
	Thu singst thar sum man shal be ded;
	Ever thu bodest sumne qued.°
	Thu singst aghen eighte lüre°
	Other° of summe fröndes rüre,°
1155	Other thu bodest huses brüne°
	Other ferde° of manne other thöves rüne,°
	Other thu bodest cwalm° of oreve°
	Other that lond-folc wurth i-dorve°
	Other that wif löst° hire make,°
1160	Other thu bodest cheste and sake.°
	Ever thu singist of manne° harme;
	Thurgh thee hi böth sori and arme.°
	Thu ne singst never one sithe°
	That hit nis for sum unsithe.°
1165	Hervore hit is that me° thee shuneth
	And thee totorveth and tobuneth°
	Mid stave and stoone and turf and clute°
	That thu ne might nowar atrute.°
	Dahet° ever swich büdel° in tune

ateliche swöre horrid neck
Biwerest . . . Protect men's grain from animals
Nis . . . It's otherwise useless   or
a scarecrow
new   sown
Sparrow   rook
dare   near
body   boundary
trees   **a** . . . in spring bloom

bird   molest
hung
lüther . . . useless and evil
nard . . . are useless unless
wite sikerliche know certainly
looks   horrible
The wile While   **on lif-daghe** alive
hongest i-slaghe hang slain
Still   afraid
thee . . . previously berated you
Mid righte Rightly
dislikes
early
manne unwate men's misfortunes
cried out

sumne qued some disaster
aghen . . . concerning loss of property
Or   **fröndes rüre** friend's ruin
burning
invasion   **thöves rüne** thief's pursuit
plague   cattle
lond-folc . . . people will be distressed
will lose   mate
cheste . . . quarrel and strife
man's
miserable
one sithe once
disaster
people
totorveth . . . pelt and thrash
clods
escape
A curse on   **swich büdel** such a herald

82

1170 That ever bodeth unwreste rune° — **bodeth** . . . prophesies bad news
And ever bringeth üvele tithinge° — tidings
And that ever specth of üvele thinge!
God Almighti wurthe him wroth° — **wurthe** . . . be angry with him
And al that werieth linnene cloth."[6]
1175 The hule ne abot noght° swithe longe — **ne** . . . didn't wait
Ah yef ondsware starke° and stronge: — **Ah** . . . But gave answer fierce

OWL

"Wat?" quath hö. "Hartu i-hoded,° — **Hartu i-hoded** Are you ordained
Other thu kursest al unihoded?[7]
For prestes wike,° Ich wat,° thu dest.° — **prestes wike** the office of priest know are performing
1180 Ich not° yef thu were yare° prest; — don't know formerly
Ich not yef thu canst masse singe.
Inoh° thu canst° of mansinge,° — Enough know cursing
Ah° hit is for thine alde nithe° — But **alde nithe** ancient malice
That thu me akursedest other sithe.° — **other sithe** a second time
1185 Ah tharto is lihtlich ondsware.° — **lihtlich ondsware** an easy answer
'Drah to thee!'° cwath the cartare.° — **Drah** . . . Slow up carter
"Wi attwitestu me° mine insihte° — **attwitestu me** do you twit me about wisdom
And min iwit° and mine mighte?° — insight ability
For Ich am witi, ful i-wis,° — **witi** . . . wise, most certainly
1190 And wod° al that to kumen is. — know
Ich wot of hunger, of her-gonge;° — invasion
Ich wot yef men schule libbe° longe; — live
Ich wat yef wif lüst° hire make;° — loses mate
Ich wat war° schal beo nith and wrake;° — where **nith** . . . malice and vengeance
1195 Ich wot hwo schal beon anhonge° — hung
Other elles fulne° deth afonge.° — a foul receive
Yef men habbeth bataile i-nume,° — **bataile i-nume** undertaken judicial combat
Ich wat hwather° schal beon overkume. — which one
Ich wat yif cwalm° scal comen on orfe° — pestilence cattle
1200 And yif dör° schul ligge astorve.° — animals **ligge astorve** lie prostrate
Ich wot yef treon° schule blowe;° — trees blossom
Ich wat yef cornes° schule growe; — grains
Ich wot yef huses schule berne;
Ich wot yef men schule eorne other erne;° — **eorne** . . . run or ride
1205 Ich wot yef sea schal schipes drenche;° — sink
Ich wot yef smithes schal üvele clenche;° — **üvele clenche** rivet badly
And yet Ich con müchel° more. — **con müchel** know much
Ich con inoh° in bokes lore, — enough

[6] 'All that wear linen underclothing,' the upper classes and the clergy, but not the lower classes and monks.
[7] 'Or do you curse (excommunicate) even though you are not hooded (ordained)' (and therefore not entitled to do so)? The owl refers to the nightingale's two curses (ll. 99 and 1169).

And eke° Ich can of the Goddspelle° — also Gospel

1210 More than Ich nüle° thee telle, — will

For Ich at chirche come ilome° — frequently

And muche leorni of wisdome.

Ich wat al of the tacninge° — allegorical interpretation

And of other feole° thinge. — other feole many another

1215 Yef eni mon schal rem abide,° — rem abide be pursued by hue and cry

Al Ich hit wot ear° hit i-tide.° — before happens

Ofte, for° mine müchele iwitte,° — because of müchele iwitte great insight

Wel sori-mod and wroth° Ich sitte. — sori-mod . . . sorry-hearted and angry

Wan Ich i-seo that sum wrechede° — misery

1220 Is manne neh, innoh° Ich grede.° — manne . . . near to man, enough wail

Ich bidde° that men beon iwarre° — pray aware

And habbe gode reades yarre,° — reades yarre counsels ready

For Alfred seide a wis word—

Euch mon hit schulde legge° on hord:° — lay store

1225 'Yef thu i-sihst er he° beo i-cume, — i-sihst . . . see ahead before it (misery)

His° strenchte is him wel neh binume.'° — Its him . . . well nigh taken from it

And grete duntes° beoth the lasse° — blows less

Yef me i-kepth° mid iwarnesse,° — me i-kepth one looks out awareness

And flo° schal thee toward misyenge° — arrow thee . . . miscarry toward you

1230 Yef thu i-sihst° hu fleo° of strenge,° — see it flew string

For thu might blenche° wel and fleo° — might blenche can dodge flee

Yif thu i-sihst heo° to thee teo.° — it coming

"Thauh eni man beo falle in odwite,° — shame

Wi schal he me his sor atwite?° — me . . . blame me for his suffering

1235 Thah Ich i-seo° his harm bivore, — see

Ne cometh hit noght of me tharvore.

Thah thu i-seo that sum blind mon

That nanne rihtne wei ne con° — nanne . . . knows no straight way

To thare diche his dweole fulieth° — his . . . follows his wrong way

1240 And falleth and tharone sulieth,° — tharone sulieth is dirtied in it

Wenest° thu, thah Ich al i-seo, — Suppose

That hit for° me the rathere beo?° — because of the . . . came to be any the sooner

"Al swo hit fareth bi mine witte.

Hwanne Ich on mine bowe sitte,

1245 Ich wot and i-seo swithe brihte° — clearly

An summe men° kumeth harm tharrihte.° — An . . . To some man directly

Schal he that tharof nothing not° — knows

Hit wite me for° Ich hit wot? — Hit . . . Blame it on me because

Schal he his mishap wite me

1250 For Ich am wisure thane he?

Hwanne Ich i-seo° that sum wrechede° — see misery

Is manne neh, inoh° Ich grede° — manne . . . near to man, enough wail

And bidde inoh that hi heom schilde,° — heom schilde shield themselves

For toward heom is harm unmilde.°   cruel

1255 Ah,° thah Ich grede° lude and stille,   But   cry out

Al hit i-tid° thurh Godes wille.   happens

Hwi wülleth men of me hi mene°   **hi mene** complain to themselves

Thah Ich mid sothe heo awene?°   **heo awene** grieve them

Thah Ich hi warni al that yer,°   **that yer** the year

1260 Nis heom tharfore harem no the ner.°

Ah° Ich heom singe for Ich wolde°   But   wish

That hi wel understonde schulde

That sum unselthe heom is ihende°   **unselthe** . . . disaster is near them

Hwan Ich min huing° to heom sende.   hooting

1265 Naveth no man none sikerhede°   **Naveth** . . . No one has any assurance

That he ne mai wene and adrede°   **wene** . . . expect and fear

That sum unhwate neh him beo°   **unhwate** . . . misfortune may be near him

Thah he ne conne hit i-seo.

Forthi seide Alfred swithe wel—

1270 And his worde was Goddspel°—   Gospel

That evereuch° man, the bet him beo,°   every   **bet** . . . better off he may be

Eaver the bet he hine beseo;°   **hine beseo** should look out for himself

Ne trüste° no mon to his weole°   **Ne trüst** Nor rely   wealth

Too swithe° thah he habbe veole.°   much   much

1275 Nis nout° so hot that hit na coleth,°   nothing   **na coleth** doesn't cool

Ne noght so hwit that hit ne soleth,°   doesn't soil

Ne noght so leof° that hit ne alotheth,°   dear   doesn't grow loathsome

Ne noght so glad that hit ne awrotheth;°   doesn't grow angry

Ac eavereuch° thing that eche° nis   every   eternal

1280 Agon° schal, and al this worldes blis.   Pass away

"Nu thu might wite readliche°   **might** . . . can know readily

That eavere thu spekest gideliche,°   giddily

For al that thu me seist for schame

Ever thee-seolve° hit turneth to grome.°   upon yourself   reproach

1285 Go so hit go, at eche fenge°   bout

Thu fallest mid thine ahene swenge.°   **ahene swenge** own attack

Al that thu seist for me to schende°   **me** . . . to shame me

Hit is mi wurschipe° at the ende.   **mi wurschipe** in my favor

Bute° thu wille bet aginne,°   Unless   start out

1290 Ne shaltu bute schame i-winne."

The nightingale sat and sighte°   sighed

And hohful° was—and ful wel mighte—   anxious

For the hule swo i-speke° hadde   **swo i-speke** so spoken

And hire speche swo i-ladde.°   conducted

1295 Heo was hohful and erede°   uncertain

Hwat heo tharafter hire sede,°   **hire sede** should say to her

Ah° neotheles heo hire understod.°   But   **hire understod** bethought herself

1260. Harm is not for that reason any the nearer to them.

NIGHTINGALE

"Wat!" heo seide. "Hule, artu wod?° crazy
Thu yeolpest° of seolliche° wisdome; boast wondrous
1300 Thu nüstest wanene he° thee come nüstest . . . didn't know whence it
Bute° hit of° wicchecrefte were. Unless from
Tharof thu, wrecche, moste thee skere° moste . . . must keep yourself clear
Yif thu wült among manne beo,
Other thu most of londe fleo,° most . . . must flee from the land
1305 For alle theo° that therof cuthe° those therof cuthe are expert at it
Heo were ifürn of° prestes muthe ifürn of previously by
Amanset.° Swüch° thu art yette!° Excommunicated So too now
Thu wiecchecrafte neaver ne lete.° neaver . . . have never abandoned
Ich thee seide nu lütel ere,° thee . . . told you so just a little while ago
1310 And thu askedest yef Ich were—
A bisemere°—to° prest i-hoded.° A bisemere Asked in scorn as ordained
Ah the mansing° is so i-broded,° the mansing excommunication
   widespread
Thah no preost a londe nere,° a . . . were in the land
A wrecche° neotheles thu were,° outcast would be
1315 For eavereuch° child thee cleopeth fule,° every thee . . . calls you foul
And evereuch man a wrecche hule.
Ich habbe i-herd—and soth hit is—
The mon mot beo wel större-wis
That wite inoh of wücch thing kume
1320 So thu seist thee is i-wune!° do you know stars
Hwat canstu,° wrecche thing, of större° Except bihaltest . . . behold them from
Bute° that thu bihaltest hi feorre?° afar
Alswo deth mani dör° and man Alswo . . . So does many an animal
Theo° of swücche nawiht ne con.° Who swücche . . . such knows nothing
1325 On° ape mai a boc° bihalde, An book
And leves wenden and eft folde,° wenden . . . turn and close again
Ac he ne con the bet° tharvore ne . . . doesn't know any the better
Of clerkes lore° top ne more.° learning ne more or bottom
Thah thu i-seo° the steorre alswa,° may see also
1330 Nartu the wisure° neaver the mo.° Nartu . . . You aren't any the wiser mor
   "Ah yet thu, fule thing, me chist° chide
And wel grimliche me atwist° reproach
That Ich singe bi manne huse° manne huse men's houses
And teache wive breke spuse.° wive . . . wives to break wedlock
1335 Thu liest, i-wis,° thu fule thing! indeed
Thurh me nas° neaver i-schend spusing.° was i-schend spusing marriage
   destroyed
Ah soth hit is, Ich singe and grede° cry
Thar lavedies beoth° and faire maide; lavedies beoth ladies are

1317–20. I have heard—and true it is—that the man must be very wise in stars (astrology) who could
know enough of what may come as you say is customary with you!

And soth hit is, of luve Ich singe.
1340 For god wif mai i° spusing — within
Bet luvien° hire oghene were° — love **oghene were** own man
Than awer° hire copenere;° — somewhere else lover
And maide mai luve cheose
That hire wurthschipe ne forleose° — **wurthschipe** ... honor she won't forfeit
1345 And luvie mid rihte luve
Thane the° schal beon hire buve.° — **Thane the** Him who above
Swiche luve Ich i-tache and lere;° — **i-tache** ... recommend and teach
Therof beoth al mine ibere.° — utterance
Thah sum wif beo of nesche mode°— — **nesche mode** yielding mood
1350 For wummon beoth of softe blode—
That heo,° thurh sume sottes lore° — **That heo** So that she **sottes lore** fool's instruction
The yeorne bit and siketh° sore, — **The** ... Who eagerly begs and sighs
Misrempe and misdo sumne stunde,°
Schal Ich tharvore beon i-bunde?° — blamed
1355 Yif wimmen luvieth unrede,° — indiscretion
Witestu me° höre misdede? — **Witestu me** Do you blame me for
Yef wimmon thencheth luvie derne,° — **thencheth** ... decide to love in secret
Ne mai Ich° mine songes werne.° — **Ne** ... I cannot abandon
Wummon mai pleie under clothe° — clothes
1360 Wether° heo wile, wel the wrothe,° — Whichever **wel** ... virtuously or wickedly
And heo mai do bi mine songe
Hwather heo wüle, wel the wronge,° — or wrongly
For nis a worlde° thing so god — **a worlde** in the world
That ne mai do sum ungod° — evil
1365 Yif me° hit wüle turne amis. — someone
For gold and seolver, god hit is;° — **hit is** they are
And notheles tharmid° thu might° — with it can
Spus-brüche büggen° and unright. — **Spus-brüche büggen** Procure adultery
Wepne° beoth gode, grith° to halde; — Weapons peace
1370 Ah neotheles tharmide beoth men acwalde° — killed
Agheines riht an fale° londe — **Agheines** ... Against the law in many
Thar theoves hi bereth° an honde. — **hi bereth** bear them
Alswa° hit is bi mine songe: — So
Thah he° beo god, me hine mai misfonge° — it **me** ... one can misuse it
1375 And drahe hine° to sot-hede° — **drahe hine** apply it folly
And to othre üvele dede.
   "Ah schaltu, wrecch, luve tele?° — blame
Bö wüch hö° bö, uich° luve is fele° — **Bö** ... Be whatever it each proper
Bitweone wepmon and wimmane;° — **wepmon** ... man and woman
1380 Ah yef heo° is atbroide,° thenne — it extorted
Heo is unfele and forbrode.° — **unfele** ... improper and corrupt

1353. May go astray and misbehave sometime

Wroth wurthe heom the Holi Rode

The rihte ikunde swo forbreideth!°   **1382-83**

Wunder hit is that heo na wedeth.°   heo . . . they don't go crazy

1385   And swo heo doth,° for heo beoth wode°   do go   mad

The bute° nest goth to brode.   **The bute** Who without

Wummon is of nesche° flesche,   yielding

And flesches lust is strong to cwesse;°   suppress

Nis wunder nan° thah heo abide.°   **Nis . . .** It's no wonder   **heo abide** she persist

1390   For° flesches lustes hi° maketh slide,   Even though   them

Ne beoth heo nowt° alle forlore   **Ne . . .** They aren't

That stumpeth at° the flesches more,°   **stumpeth at** trip on   stumbling block

For moni° wummon haveth misdo°   many a   misbehaved

That arist op of° the slo.°   **arist . . .** arises from   mire

1395   "Ne beoth nowt ones° alle sünne,°   **Ne . . .** Nor are alike   sins

Forthan° hi beoth tweire künne.°   Since   **tweire künne** of two kinds

Sum arist° of the flesches lüste,°   arise   lust

And sum of the gostes cüste.°   **gostes cüste** spirit's nature

Thar° flesch draheth° men to drunnesse°   Whereas   draws   drunkenness

1400   And to wrouehede° and to golnesse,°   irritability   lechery

The gost misdeth thurch nithe and onde°   **misdeth . . .** misbehaves through malice and spite

And seoththe° mid mürhthe of monne shonde°   also   **mürhthe . . .** pleasure in a man's shame

And yeoneth after° more and more   **yeoneth after** yawns open for

And lütel rehth of milce and ore°   **rehth . . .** cares for mercy and compassion

1405   And stighth° on heh° thurh modinesse°   climbs   high   pride

And overhoheth thanne lasse.°   **overhoheth . . .** scorns the lowlier

"Sei me soth, yef thu hit wost.°   know

Hwether° deth würse, flesch the° gost?   Which   or

Thu might segge,° yef thu wült,°   **might segge** can say   will

1410   That lasse° is the flesches gült.   less

Moni° man is of his flesche clene   Many a

That is mid mode deovel imene;°   **mid . . .** in pride a match for the devil

Ne schal non mon wumman bigrede°   berate

And flesches lustes hire upbreide;°   **hire upbreide . . .** reproach her for

1415   Swüch he may telen of golnesse

That sünegeth würse i modinesse.°

Hwet yif Ich schulde a luve° bringe   **a luve** to love

Wif other maide hwanne Ich singe?

Ich wolde with the maide holde.°   **wolde . . .** would like to encourage the maid

1420   Yif thu hit const ariht atholde,°   **const . . .** can properly understand

Lüst nu, Ich segge thee hwarvore

Up to the toppe from the more.°   bottom

1382-83. May the Holy Cross show anger upon (literally, 'become angry with') those who thus pervert natural instincts!

1415-16. Such a woman he may reprove for lechery while he himself sins in a worse way through pride (literally, 'he may . . . that sins . . .').

Yef maide luveth dernliche,° secretly
Heo stumpeth and falth icündeliche,° **stumpeth** ... trips and falls by natural
instinct
1425 For, thah° heo sum hwile° pleie, even though **sum hwile** for a while
Heo nis nout feor ut of the weie.° **nis** ... isn't far astray
Heo mai hire güld atwende° **güld atwende** guilt escape
A° rihte weie thurh chirche-bende° In the church rites
And mai eft° habbe to hire make° then **to** ... as her mate
1430 Hire leofmon° withute sake° sweetheart blame
And go to him bi daies lihte
That er stal to° bi theostre° nihte. **That** ... Whom she previously stole to
dark
An yungling not° hwat swüch thing is; **yungling not** young girl doesn't know
His° yunge blod hit drageth° amis, Her **hit drageth** draws her
1435 And sum sot° mon hit tihth° tharto foolish **hit tihth** leads her
Mid alle than that° he mai do. **than that** that
He cometh and fareth and beod and bid° **beod** ... demands and begs
And heo bistant and oversid°
And bisehth i-lome° and longe. **bisehth i-lome** beseeches often
1440 Hwat mai that child thah hit misfonge?° **Hit** ... She never knew
Hit nüste neaver° hwat hit was; **Forthi** ... She thought to try it
Forthi hit thohte fondi thas°
And wite i-wis hwüch beo the gome°
That of so wilde° maketh tome.° wild a creature a tame one
1445 Ne mai Ich for reothe lete,
Wanne Ich i-seo the tohte ilete
The luve bring on the yunglinge,
That Ich of mürghthe him ne singe.°
Ich teache heom bi mine songe
1450 That swücch luve ne lest noght° longe, **ne** ... lasts not
For mi song lütle° hwile i-lest,° only a little lasts
And luve ne deth noght bute rest° **ne** ... does but alight
On swüch childre° and sone ageth,° girls goes away
And falth adun° the hote breth.° **falth adun** subsides passion
1455 Ich singe mid heom one throghe,° **one throghe** a while
Biginne on heh, and endi laghe,° **heh** ... high, and finish low
And lete mine songes falle
An lütle wile adun mid alle.°
That maide wot, hwanne Ich swike,° cease
1460 That luve is mine songes iliche,° like
For hit nis bute a lütel breth
That sone kumeth and sone geth.° goes

1438. And urges her and sits over her
1440. How can that child (girl) help it though she (it) go wrong?
1443. And know for sure what is the sport
1445–48. Nor can I, when I see the drawn face that love brings on the young girl, resist out of pity singing (literally, 'that I sing') of pleasure to her.
1457–58. And let my songs subside in a little while completely.

That child bi° me hit understönd°
And his unred° to red i-wend,°
1465 And i-seghth° wel, bi mine songe
That düsi° luve ne last noght° longe.
    "Ah wel Ich wüle that thu hit wite,°
Loth° me beoth wives utschüte;°
Ah° wif mai of° me nime yeme:°
1470 Ich ne singe nawt hwan Ich teme.°
And wif ah lete sottes lore,°
Thah spusing-bendes thüncheth° sore.
Wundere me thüngth° wel starc and stor°
Hu eni mon so eavar for°
1475 That he his heorte mighte drive
To do hit to others° mannes wive.
For other° hit is of twam° thinge,
Ne mai that thridde° no man bringe:
Othar the laverd° is wel aht°
1480 Other aswunde and nis naht.°
Yef he is wurthful° and aht man,
Nele no man that wisdom can
Hure of his wive do him schame,°
For he mai him adrede grame°
1485 And that he forleose that° ther hongeth°
That him eft° tharto noght ne longeth.°
And thah he that noght ne adrede,°
Hit is unright and gret sothede°
To misdon° one gode manne
1490 And his ibedde° from him spanne.°
Yef hire laverd is forwurde°
And unorne° at bedde and at borde,
Hu mighte thar beo eni luve
Wanne a cheorles buc hire ley buve?°
1495 Hu mai thar eni luve beo
War swüch man gropeth° hire theo?°
Herbi thu might wel understonde,
That on° is harm, that other schonde,°
To stele to othres mannes bedde;
1500 For yif aht° man is hire ibedde,°
Thu might wene° that thee mistide°
Wanne thu list° bi hire side;
And yef the laverd is a wrecche,°
Hwüch este° mightistu thar vecche?°
1505 Yif thu bithenchest° hwo hire ofligge,°
Thu might° mid wlate° the este bügge.°

child bi girl through   understands
his unred her folly   red i-wend wisdom turns
she sees
giddy   ne . . . lasts not
know
Loathsome to   wives utschüte wives' excesses
And a   from   nime yeme take example couple
ah . . . ought to ignore a fool's instruction
spusing-bendes thüncheth marriage-bonds seem
Wundere . . . A wonder it seems to me great
behaved

another
either one   two
the third
lord   able
aswunde . . . feeble and is useless
an honorable

him . . . fear harm for himself
forleose that may lose what   pertains
That . . . So that he again   yearn
noght . . . doesn't fear
folly
betray
wife   entice
incapable
useless

cheorles . . . churl's belly lay upon her

feels   thighs

That on The one alternative   shame

an able   bedmate
might wene can expect   thee mistide you'll have trouble
lie
impotent
Hwüch este What satisfaction   get
think   hire ofligge may have lain on her
may   disgust   pay for

1482–83. No man who possesses wisdom will wish at all to do him (the lord) shame through his wife

Ich not° hu mai eni freo° man   don't know   well-bred
For hire sechen° after than.°   seek   that
Yef he bithencth bi hwan° he lai,   whom
1510 Al mai the luve gan awai."
     The hule was glad of swüche tale.
Heo thoghte that the nihtegale,
Thah heo wel speke° atte frume,°   spoke   first
Hadde at then ende misnume;°   miscarried
1515 And seide:

OWL

     "Nu Ich habbe i-funde°   found
That maidenes beoth of thine imunde.°   **thine imunde** concern to you
Mid heom thu holdest and heom biwerest,°   defend
And overswithe° thu hi herest.°   excessively   praise
The lavedies° beoth to me i-wended;°   ladies   inclined
1520 To me heo hire mode° sendeth,   feelings
For hit i-tit° ofte and ilome°   happens   frequently
That wif and were° beoth unisome;°   husband   disunited
And therfore the were gülte°   is guilty
That leof is other wummon to pülte°
1525 And speneth on thare° al that he haveth   **speneth** ... spends on her
And siweth thare° that no riht naveth°   **siweth thare** follows her   has
And haveth attom° his righte spuse,   at home
Wowes weste, and lere° huse,   **Wowes** ... Waste walls, and empty
Wel thünne i-schrud, and i-ved wrothe°   **thünne** ... thinly clad and badly fed
1530 And let heo bute° mete and clothe.   **let** ... leaves her without
Wan he cometh ham° eft to his wive,   home
Ne dar° heo noght a word i-schire.°   dare   speak
He chid and gred swüch° he beo wod°   **chid** ... chides and screams as if   crazy
And ne bringth hom non other god.°   good
1535 Al that heo° deth, him is unwile;°   she   **him** ... he dislikes
Al that heo speketh, hit is him ille;
And oft hwan heo noght ne misdeth,°   **noght** ... does nothing wrong
Heo haveth the füst° in hire teth.   fist
Ther is nan mon that ne mai i-bringe°   send
1540 His wif amis mid swücche thinge.
Me° hire mai so ofte misbeode°   One   maltreat
That heo do wüle° hire ahene neode.°   **heo** ... she will fulfill   **ahene neode** own needs
La, Godd hit wot, heo nah i-weld°   **nah i-weld** can't help it
Thah heo hine makie kukeweld!°   **hine** ... make him a cuckold
1545 For hit i-tit lome° and ofte   **i-tit lome** happens frequently
That his wif is wel nesche° and softe,   yielding
Of faire bleo° and wel i-diht;°   complexion   shaped

1524. Who likes to assail another woman

91

Thi° hit is the more unriht°   *Thi° Though*   *So unjust*
That he his luve spene° on thare°   *spend*   *someone else*
1550 That nis wurth one of hire heare,°   *hairs*
And swücche men beoth wel manifolde
That wif ne kunne noght aright holde.°   **wif** . . . *can't adequately retain a wife*
Ne mot non° mon with hire speke;   **Ne** . . . *Nor can any*
He weneth° heo wüle anon tobreke°   *thinks*   **anon tobreke** *at once break*
1555 Hire spusing° yef heo loketh°   *marriage vow*   *looks*
Other with manne faire° speketh.   *nicely*
He hire biluth° mid keie and loke.   *locks up*
Tharthurh° is spusing° ofte tobroke,°   *Thereby*   *marriage*   *broken up*
For yef heo is tharto i-broht,°   **tharto i-broht** *brought to that point*
1560 Heo deth that° heo nadde ear i-thoht.°   *what*   **nadde** . . . *hadn't thought of before*
Dahet° that too swüthe hit bispeke°   *A curse on him*   **too** . . . *condemns it too much*
Thah swücche wives heom awreke!°   **heom awreke** *avenge themselves*
Herof the lavedies° to me meneth°   *ladies*   *complain*
And wel sore me ahweneth;°   *grieve*
1565 Wel neh° min heorte wüle tochine°   *nearly*   *break*
Hwon Ich biholde hire pine.°   *pain*
Mid heom Ich wepe swithe sore
And for heom bidde° Cristis ore°   *beg*   *mercy*
That the lavedi° sone aredde°   *lady*   *he may rescue*
1570 And hire sende betere i-bedde.°   *bedfellow*
   "Another thing Ich mai thee telle
That thu ne schald,° for thine felle,°   **ne schald** *won't*   *skin*
Ondswere none° tharto finde.   **Ondswere none** *Any answer*
Al thi sputing° schal aswinde.°   *disputation*   *fail*
1575 Moni chapmon° and moni cniht   **Moni chapmon** *Many a merchant*
Luveth and hald° his wif ariht,   *holds*
And swa° deth moni bondeman.°   *so*   *serf*
That° gode wif deth after than°   *The*   **deth** . . . *acts accordingly*
And serveth him to bedde and to borde
1580 Mid faire dede and faire worde
And yeorne fondeth° hu heo muhe°   **yeorne fondeth** *eagerly seeks out*   *can*
Do thing that him beo i-dughe.°   **him** . . . *may be useful for him*
The laverd into thare theode°   *country*
Fareth ut on thare beire nede,°   **on** . . . *for the needs of both*
1585 And is that gode wif unblithe°   *unhappy*
For hire laverdes oudsithe,°   *departure*
And sit and sihth,° wel sore oflonged,°   *sighs*   **sore oflonged** *sorely longing*
And hire sore an hörte ongred,°
Al for hire loverdes sake
1590 Haveth daies° kare and nightes wake;°   *by day*   **nightes wake** *by night sleeplessness*
And swüthe longe hire° is the hwile,   *for her*

1588. And grieves herself sorely at heart

And ech steape hire thünth° a mile.   **hire thünth** seems to her
Hwanne othre slepeth hire abute,
Ich one° lüst thar withthute   alone
1595 And wot of hire sore mode°   **sore mode** sad spirits
And singe a-night for hire gode;
And mine gode song, for hire thinge,°   situation
Ich turne sumdel° to murninge.°   somewhat mourning
Of hüre seorhe° Ich bere sume;   sorrow
1600 Forthan° Ich am hire° wel welcume.   Thus to her
Ich hire helpe hwat I mai,
For hö geth thane° rehte wai.   **geth thane** goes the
    "Ah thu me havest sore i-gramed°   vexed
That° min heorte is wel neh alamed,°   So that paralyzed
1605 That Ich mai unneathe° speke.   hardly
Ah yet Ich wüle forthure reke.°   continue
Thu seist that Ich am manne ylath,°   **manne ylath** loathsome to man
And evereuch° man is with me wroth   every
And me mid stone and lugge threteth°   **lugge threteth** sticks threatens
1610 And me tobusteth and tobeteth,°   **tobusteth . . .** batters and beats to pieces
And hwanne heo habeth me ofslahe,°   slain
Heo hongeth me on heore hahe,°   hedge
Thar Ich aschewele pie° and crowe   **aschewele pie** scare away magpie
From than the° thar is i-sowe.°   **than the** that which sown
1615 Thah hit beo soth, Ich do heom god,
And for heom Ich schadde° mi blod.   shed
Ich do heom god mid mine deathe;
Warvore thee is wel unneathe,°
For, thah thu ligge dead and clinge,°   waste away
1620 Thi deth nis nawt° to none° thinge!   **nis nawt** is nothing any
Ich not neaver to hwan thu might,°
For thu nart bute° a wrecche wight.   **nart bute** are but
Ah thah mi life me beo atschote,°   **me . . .** be spent from me
The yet° Ich mai do gode note;°   **The yet** Still service
1625 Me° mai upone smale sticke   One
Me sette a° wude ine the thicke,°   in thicket
And swa mai mon tolli him to°   **tolli . . .** lure to himself
Lütle briddes and i-vo,°   catch them
And swa me° mai mid me biyete°   one obtain
630 Wel gode brede° to his mete.   roasts
Ah thu nevre, mon to gode,°   **mon . . .** for man's good
Lives ne deathes stal ne stode.°   **Lives . . .** Alive or dead gave help
Ich not to hwan° thu breist° thi brod;   **not . . .** don't know for what breed

1618. Whence it is very troublesome for you (to argue on this matter, since you are useless whether alive or dead)
1621. I don't know ever what good you are (literally, 'for what you are capable')

93

Lives ne deathes ne deth hit god."°   **ne deth** . . . it does no good

1635   The nihtegale i-herde this

And hupte° uppon on blowe ris°   hopped   **blowe ris** a flowering branch

And herre° sat than heo düde ear.°   higher   previously

NIGHTINGALE

"Hule," heo seide, "beo nu wear.°   warned

Nülle Ich with thee plaidi° na more,   debate

1640   For her thee mist° thi rihte lore.°   fails   wisdom

Thu yeilpest° that thu art manne° loth   boast   to man

And evereuch° wiht is with thee wroth;   every

And mid yülinge° and mid igrede°   yelling   crying

Thu wanst° wel that thu art unlede.°   lament   miserable

1645   Thu seist that gromes° thee i-foth°   boys   catch

And heie on rodde° thee anhoth°   a stick   hang up

And thee totwichet and toschaketh,°   **totwichet** . . . pluck and shake to pieces

And summe of thee schawles° maketh.   a scarecrow

Me thüncth° that thu forleost that° game.   **Me thüncth** It seems to me   the

1650   Thu yülpest of thire oghe° schame.   **thire oghe** your own

Me thüncth that thu me gest an honde.°   **me** . . . fall into my hands

Thu yülpest of thire oghene° schomme."   own

Tho° heo hadde theos word i-cwede,°   When   uttered

Heo sat in one faire stüde°   place

1655   And tharafter hire stevene dihte°   **stevene dihte** voice prepared

And song° so schille° and so brihte   sang   clearly

That feor° and ner me° hit i-herde.   far   one

Tharvore anan° to hire cherde°   at once   came

Thrusche and throstle and wudewale°   **throstle** . . . mavis and oriole

1660   And fuheles bothe grete and smale,

Forthan heom thühte° that heo° hadde   **Forthan** . . . For it seemed to them   she

The houle overcome vorthan heo gradde,°   **vorthan** . . . because she cried out

And sungen alswa vale wise,°

And blisse was among the rise.°   branches

1665   Right swa me gred° the manne a° schame   **me gred** one calls out at   in

That taveleth° and forleost that gome.   gambles

OWL

Theos hule, tho° heo this i-herde,   when

"Havestu," heo seide, "i-banned ferde?°   **i-banned ferde** called up an army

And wültu, wreche, with me fighte?

1670   Nai, nai! Navestu none mighte.

Hwat gredeth theo° that hider come?   **gredeth theo** do those cry out

Me thüncth thu ledest ferde to me.

1663. And they sang also many songs

Ye schule wite, ar ye fleo heonne,°   hence
Hwüch° is the strenthe of mine künne,   What   kin
1675   For theo the° haveth bile i-hoked   **theo the** those that
And clivres° scharpe and wel i-croked,   talons
Alle heo beoth° of mine künrede   **Alle** ... They all are
And walde° come yif Ich bede.°   would   should ask
The seolfe coc,° that wel can fighte,   **seolfe coc** cock himself
1680   He mot° mid me holde mid° righte,   must   by
For bothe we habbeth stevene brighte
And sitteth under weolcne° by nighte.   the clouds
Schille Ich an utest uppen öw grede,°
Ich shal swo° stronge ferde° lede   such a   army
1685   That öwer prude° schal avalle°—   **öwer prude** your pride   collapse
A tort° ne give Ich for öw° alle!—   turd   you
Ne schal, ar hit beo fulliche° eve,   fully
A wreche° fether on öw bileave.°   wretched   leave
    "Ah hit was unker voreward°   **unker voreward** our agreement
1690   Tho° we come° hiderward   When   came
That we tharto holde scholde
Thar riht dom us give wolde.°
Wültu nu breke foreward?
Ich wene,° dom thee thingth° too hard!   suppose   **thee thingth** seems to you
1695   For° thu ne darst domes abide,°   Because   **ne** ... dare not wait for judgment
Thu wült nu, wreche, fighte and chide.
Yöt Ich öw° alle wolde rede°   you   advise
Ar Ich utheste° uppon öw grede°   hue and cry   call
That öwer fihtlac leteth beo°   **öwer** ... your fight you let be
1700   And ginneth rathe° awei fleo.°   **ginneth rathe** begin quickly   to flee
For, by the clivres that Ich bere,
Yef ye abideth° mine here,°   wait for   army
Ye schule on other wise singe
And acursi° alle fightinge,   curse
1705   Vor nis of öw non so kene°   brave
That dürre° abide mine onsene."°   would dare   gaze
    Theos hule spac wel baldeliche,°   boldly
For, thah° heo nadde swo hwatliche°   though   **nadde** ... wouldn't have so quickly
I-fare° after hire here,°   Gone out   army
710   Heo walde neotheles yeve° answere   **walde** ... wanted nevertheless to give
The° nightegale mid swücche worde.   To the
For moni man mid speres orde°   point
Haveth lütle strencthe and mid his schelde,
Ah neotheles in one felde°   battlefield

1683. If I'm going to have to call out a hue and cry against you
1691–92. That we were to agree in accordance with whatever a legal judgment would award us.

1715 Thurh belde° worde and mid ilete°   bold   bearing
Deth° his ivo° for arehthe swete.°   Causes foe **arehthe swete** cowardice to
      sweat
    The wranne,° for heo cuthe° singe,   wren **heo cuthe** knew how to
Thar com° in thare moregheninge   came
To helpe thare° nightegale,   the
1720 For, thah° heo hadde stevene° smale,   though   voice
Heo hadde gode throte and schille°   clear
And fale manne song a wille.°
The wranne was wel wis i-holde,°   **wel** ... considered very wise
Vor, thegh heo nere i-bred a wolde,°   **nere** ... wasn't bred in the woods
1725 Hö was i-toghen° among mankenne°   raised   mankind
And hire wisdom brohte thenne.°   thence (from man)
Heo mighte speke hwar heo walde°—   would
Tovore the king thah° heo scholde.°   though   should wish to

WREN

    "Lüsteth,"° heo cwath. "Lateth me speke.   Listen
1730 Hwat, wülle ye this pes tobreke°   **pes tobreke** peace break
And do than kinge swüch schame?[8]
Ye,° nis he nouther ded ne lame.   Yea
Hünke° schal i-tide° harm and schonde°   On both of you come disgrace
Yef ye doth grith-brüche° on his londe.   **doth grith-brüche** commit breach of peac
1735 Lateth beo, and beoth i-some,°   reconciled
And fareth riht° to öwer° dome,   **fareth riht** go directly your
And lateth dom this plaid tobreke°   **this** ... settle this dispute
Alswo° hit was erur bispeke."°   As **erur bispeke** previously agreed

NIGHTINGALE

    "Ich an wel,"° cwath the nightegale.   **an wel** agree willingly
1740 "Ah, wranne, nawt for thire° tale   **for thire** because of your
Ah do° for mire lahfulnesse.°   do so **mire lahfulnesse** my respect for
      law
Ich nolde° that unrihtfulnesse°   wouldn't wish illegality
Me at then° ende overkome.   the
Ich nam ofdrad° of none° dome.   **nam ofdrad** I am not afraid any
1745 Bihote° Ich habbe—soth hit is—   Promised
That Maister Nichole, that is wis,
Bitwüxen us deme schülle.   judge
And yet° Ich wene° that he wüle,   still expect
Ah war mihte we hine° finde?"   him
1750 The wranne sat in ore linde.°   **ore linde** a linden tree

1722. And sang for the delight of many men.
[8] 'And cause such shame to the king.' The king referred to is apparently Richard I (reigned 1189–99). According to Anglo-Norman law, anyone creating a public disturbance could be charged before a royal court with breach of the king's peace.

WREN

"Hwat? Nüste ye,"° cwath heo, "his hom?   **Nüste ye** Didn't you know
He wuneth at Porteshom,°   Portesham
At one tune° ine Doresete°   village   Dorset
Bi thare° see in ore utlete.°   Near the   **ore utlete** an outlet

1755 Thar he demeth° manie righte dom   judges
And diht and writ° mani wisdom,   **diht . . .** composes and writes
And thurh his muthe and thurh his honde
Hit is the betere into° Scotlonde.   **the . . .** as far off as
To seche hine is lihtlich° thing;   an easy

1760 He naveth bute° one woning.°   **naveth bute** has only   dwelling
That is bischopen muchel° schame   **bischopen muchel** for the bishops a great
And alle than° that of his nome°   those   name
Habbeth i-hert° and of his dede!°   heard   deeds
Hwi nülleth° hi nimen heom to rede°   won't   **nimen . . .** adopt as their plan

1765 That he were mid heom ilome°   often
For° teche heom of his wisdome,   To
And give him rente a vale stüde°   **rente . . .** revenues in many places
That he mighte heom ilome be mide?"°   **heom . . .** often be with them

OWL

"Certes,"° cwath the hule, "that is soth.   Certainly

1770 Theos riche° men wel muche misdoth°   powerful   do wrong
That leteth thane° gode mon   **leteth thane** abandon the
That of so feole° thinge con°   many   knows
And giveth rente wel misliche°   **rente . . .** revenues very erratically
And of him leteth° wel lihtliche.°   **of . . .** esteem him   casually

1775 With heore cünne° heo beoth mildre°   kin   more kind
And yeveth rente° litle childre!   revenues to
Swo heore wit hi demth a dwole
That ever abid Maistre Nichole.°
"Ah ute we thah° to him fare,   **ute . . .** let us then

1780 For thar is unker° dom al yare."°   our   ready

NIGHTINGALE

"Do we," the nightegale seide.
"Ah wa° schal unker speche rede°   who   **unker . . .** present our pleas
And telle tovore unker deme?"°   **telle . . .** speak before our judge

OWL

"Tharof Ich schal thee wel i-cweme,"°   satisfy

1785 Cwath the houle, "for al, ende of orde,°   **ende . . .** from end to end
Telle Ich con word after worde.

1777–78. Thus their intelligence condemns them as being in error in that Master Nichole is still waiting (to receive additional ecclesiastical revenues).

And yef thee thincth° that Ich misrempe,°
Thu stond aghein and do me crempe."°
   Mid thisse worde forth hi ferden°
1790   Al bute here° and bute ferde°
To Portesham, ther° heo bicome.°
Ah hu heo spedde of heore dome°
Ne can Ich eu namore telle.
Her nis namore of this spelle.°

thee thincth it seems to you   go wrong
Thu . . . Protest and make me stop
went
Al . . . Without army   troops
where   arrived
judgment

story

Holy Maidenhood

(ca. 1200, Southwestern)

Hali Meidenhad (or *Hali Meiðhad*) was written by an unknown author to encourage girls to enter into religious life. His arguments are drawn from an ancient Christian tradition. In the early days of the hermitic movement in the fifth century, when Jovinian argued that the celibate's life was not necessarily better than that of a married person, Jerome directed against the heretic an angry tract that was still being quoted in the days of Chaucer's Wife of Bath. In a similarly violent tone the Middle English preacher attacks marriage in order to defend virginity.

Despite the vehemence of his argument, the preacher basically has much in common with the gentle author of *The Anchoresses' Rule* (pp. 106–13). He warns maidens against human marriage in order that he may recommend a more satisfying spiritual marriage with Christ, in which the recluse's soul may mystically conceive virtues rather than children as her offspring. He recognizes the danger of spiritual pride and warns his listeners that "a mild wife or a meek widow is better than a proud maiden." And he couples his rhetorical brilliance with the same perceptivity of everyday human affairs displayed by the author of the *Rule*.

The edition of *Hali Meidenhad*, ed. F. J. Furnivall, revised by Oswald Cockayne, EETS 18 (London, 1866, 1922), contains a modernization; the latest edition is *Hali Meiðhad*, ed. A. F. Colborn (Copenhagen, 1940). For the manuscript see *Facsimile of Ms. Bodley 34*, ed. N. R. Ker, EETS 247 (London, 1960). For bibliography see Wells, ch. 5.1; *CBEL*, 1.168, 5.118.

Ah schawi we yet witerlüker, as we ear biheten, hwet drehen the i-weddede thet thu i-cnawe therbi hu mürie thu maht libben meiden i thi meithhad over thet heo libbeth, to eche the mürhthe and the menske in Heovene thet muth ne mei nümnen. . . .

5 Thus, wümmon, yif thu havest were after thi wil and wünne ba of weorldes weole, thee schal nede i-tiden. And hwat yif ha beoth thee wone that thu nabbe thi wil with him ne weole nowther, and schalt greni godles inwith wasti wahes, and in breades wone bredes thi barn-team, and, t'eke this, liggen under lathest mon that, thah thu hafdest alle weole, went hit thee to weane?

10 For beo hit nu that thee beo richedom rive, and thine wide wahes wlonke and welefulle, and habbe monie under thee, hirdmen in halle, and thi were beo thee wrath and i-wurthe thee lath swa that inker either heasci with other, hwat worldlich weole mei beo thee wünne? Hwen he beoth ute, havest ayain his ham-cume sar, care, and eie. Hwil he bith at hame, alle thine wide wanes thüncheth

15 thee too narewe. His lokinge on thee agasteth thee; his ladliche mürhth and his untohe bere maketh thee to agrisen. Chit thee and cheoweth thee and schent thee schomeliche; tuketh thee to bismere as huler his hore; beateth thee and busteth thee as his i-bohte threl and his ethell theowe. Thine banes aketh thee, and thi flesch smerteth; thin heorte inwith thee swelleth of sar grome, and thi neb utewith

20 tendreth ut of tene.

Hwüch schal beo the somnunge bituhhen öw i bedde? Me theo that best luvieth ham tobeoreth ofte thrin, thah ha therof na semblaund ne makien inne marhen; and ofte of moni nohtunge, ne luvien ha ham neaver swa, bitterliche bi hamseolf teonith either. Ha schal his wil, müchel hire unwil, drehen, ne luve

25 ha him neaver swa wel, with muche weane ofte. Alle hise ful-itoheschipes and hise unhende gomenes—ne beon ha neaver swa with fülthe bifunden, nomeliche i bedde—ha schal, wülle ha nülle ha, tholien ham alle. Crist schilde euch meiden to freinen other to wilnen for to wite hwücche heo beon! For theo that fondeth ham meast i-findeth ham forcuthest and clepeth ham selie i-wis the nüten neaver

30 hwat hit is and hatieth that ha haunteth. Ah hwa-se lith i leiven deope bisunken, thah him thünche üvel thrin, he ne schal nawt up acoveren hwen he walde. . . .

Ga we nu forthre! Loke we hwüch wünne ariseth therafter i burtherne of bearne hwen that streon i thee awakeneth and waxeth. Hu moni earmthen anan awakeneth therwith that würcheth thee wa inoh, fehteth o thi selve flesch, and weorreth with

35 fele weanen o thin ahne cünde. Thi rudie neb schal leanen and as gres grenen. Thin ehnen schulen doskin and underthon wonnen, and of thi breines turnunge thin heaved ake sare; inwith thi wombe swelin the bitte, that beoreth forth as a water bulge. . . .

After al this, cumeth of that bearn i-boren thus wanunge and wepunge that

40 schal abute midniht makie thee to wakien, other theo that thi stede halt, that thu most fore carien. . . .

[MODERNIZATION]

But let us, as we promised earlier, show more clearly what those who are married suffer, so that you may thus perceive how happily you can live as a maiden in your virginity in comparison to the way they live, in addition to the bliss and honor in Heaven which mouth cannot describe. . . .

Thus, woman, if you do have a husband according to your desire and the pleasure also of worldly wealth, necessity will still befall you. And what if these are lacking to you, so that you have neither pleasure in him nor wealth either, and must groan penuriously within your waste walls, and in dearth of bread give birth to your brood, and, besides, must lie under a most hateful man who, even if you possessed every wealth, would turn it into misery for you?

For now, even if you abound in riches, and your wide walls are splendid and luxurious, and you have many people under you as servants in hall, and your husband should become enraged with you and loathsome to you so that each of you quarrels with the other, what worldly wealth can be a delight for you? When he is out, you have sorrow, care, and fear for his home-coming. While he is at home, all your wide dwellings seem too narrow for you. His looking at you terrifies you; his hateful merriment and his rude behavior make you shudder. He chides you and bickers with you and scolds you shamefully; he mocks you as a lecher does his whore; he beats you and mawls you as his purchased slave and his family servitor. Your bones ache, and your flesh smarts; your heart swells within you from sore mortification, and your face flushes outwardly from anger.

What sort of coupling will there be between you in bed? Even those that love one another best often disagree in that, even if they may show no semblance of it in the morning; and often over many a frustration, though they love each other ever so much, one or other suffers bitterly by himself. She must endure his will, much against her own, however well she love him, often with much misery. All his lasciviousness and his improper pranks—no matter with what impurity they be conceived, especially in bed—she must suffer them all, willy nilly. May Christ prevent every maiden from asking or from wishing to know what they may be! For those that try them out the most find them to be the most despicable and call those blessed indeed who have never known what this is and who hate what such ones practice. But whoever lies deep sunken in a bog, though it seems ill to him to be in it, is not going to recover when he would wish to. . . .

Let us continue further! Let us see what joy ensues afterward in the bearing of children when the seed awakens and grows within you. How many miseries from this at once ensue that cause you woe aplenty, contend with your own body, and with many tribulations war on your own nature. Your radiant face will grow lean and turn green as grass. Your eyes will cloud and fail at this time, and your head will sorely ache from the whirling of your brains; within your belly your womb will swell and bulge out like a water bag. . . .

After all this, from the child born thus will come lamentation and weeping that will force you to wake up at midnight, or the one who takes your place, so that you must tend to it. . . .

And hwat yif ich easki yet, thah hit thünche egede, hu that wif stonde that ihereth, hwen ha cumeth in, hire bearn screamen, seoth the cat at the flicke, and the hund at the huide? Hire cake bearneth o the stan, and hire calf suketh; the croh eorneth i the für, and the cheorl chideth. Thah hit be egede sahe, hit ah, meiden, to eggi thee swithre therframward, for nawt ne thünche hit hire egede that hit fondeth!

Ne tharf that seli meiden that haveth al i-don hire ut of thüllich theowdom ase Godes fre dohter and his Sunes spuse drehe nawt swücches. Forthi, seli meiden, forsac al thüllich sorhe for utnume mede, that thu ahes to don withuten euch hüire.

Holy Maidenhood

[MODERNIZATION]

And what if I ask still further, though it may seem silly, how the wife is placed who, when she comes in, hears her baby screaming, sees the cat at the bacon and the dog at the hide? Her cake is burning on the stone, and her calf is sucking up the milk; the pot is running over into the fire, and the servant is grumbling. Though it may be a silly story, it ought to urge you away from it all the more strongly, maiden, for it does not seem in the least silly to the one who tries it!

The blessed maiden who as God's free daughter and the spouse of his Son has excluded herself completely from such servitude need not endure anything like this. So, blessed maiden, forsake all such sorrow in exchange for an exceptional reward, as you ought to do without any payment.

THE
THIRTEENTH
CENTURY

ॐ

The Anchoresses' Rule

(ca. 1200, Southwestern)

The Anchoresses' Rule was prepared by an unknown cleric for a group of three aristocratic ladies who had decided to retire from the world into a life of spiritual contemplation. Usually such candidates would have joined a nunnery. The Benedictines had established convents for women in England even before the Norman Conquest and admitted new orders of nuns after the conquest; by 1200, the Gilbertines had admitted nuns to their order; and the Augustinians and Premonstratensians had founded orders for canonesses. The three anchoresses, however, had evidently decided to live by themselves, and their adviser therefore undertook to warn them of their duties and of what might be called the psychological hazards of their profession. Within the eight brief and clearly organized divisions of his manual the author (1) advocates observance of the divine services, (2) shows how the five senses may be directed toward the worship of God, (3) explains allegorically how the inner self should be controlled, (4) enumerates the temptations of the Seven Deadly Sins and prescribes remedies, (5) advocates confession, (6) advocates penance, (7) extolls the love of Christ as the highest form of love, and (8) appends some practical suggestions concerning the recluse's everyday life.

His treatment follows the method to be expected from someone trained in the scholastic tradition of the twelfth century. His convenient subdivisions within each topic are often more arbitrary than logical, and his allegorical interpretations of the scriptures are not intended so much to explain the passages quoted as to support his own arguments. Despite his scholastic method, however, his tone and style are highly personal and intimate. The concept of divine love that illuminates the works of the two great Cistercians he so frequently quotes—Bernard of Clairvaux and Ailred of Rievaulx—provides a similar warmth in his own writing.

His rule is thus not a series of restrictions. In the first excerpt included here, from his Introduction, he minimizes the importance of the outer or external regulations compared to the basic principles of the inner rule. In the second excerpt, from Book 2, when he turns to the dangers associated with the five senses, he recognizes that a small, defenseless group of ladies may be exposed to the unscrupulous advances of seducers skilled in the deceptive dalliance of courtly love. In a contemporary treatise on *The Art of Courtly Love*, the author, a French chaplain known as Andreas Capellanus, admits that he himself had once been drawn into a love affair with a nun. His reasons for discontinuing provide a striking contrast with the advice the unknown cleric gives the anchoresses. Andreas claims that he desisted for fear of God's wrath, of punishment by the civil authorities, and of the loss of his reputation, while the idealistic English confessor upholds the love of Christ rather than fear as a sufficient reason for overcoming untimely passions. In the third excerpt, from Book 8, when he deals with the problems of daily living, he praises the example of Mary Magdalen, who, on the occasion of Christ's visit, showed her love toward him, while her sister Martha was "cumbered about much serving" (Luke x.40); characteristically, he applies this commonly maintained distinction in an eminently practical and positive manner.

The *Ancrene Riwle*, as it was called in Middle English, was a widely disseminated and influential work. (The alternate title *Ancrene Wisse* 'Anchoresses' Guide' is sometimes applied by scholars to the Corpus Manuscript version and sometimes to the work as a whole.) Amplifications were introduced in the text for the sake of larger conventual communities, both male and female, and translations were prepared in both Latin and Anglo-Norman.

The Nero Manuscript version has been excerpted here; the latest edition of this is EETS 225, ed. Mabel Day (London, 1946); a modernization was prepared by James Morton (Camden Society, 1853; later eds. 1905, 1926). The Corpus Manuscript, containing the author's own revisions, has been published under the title *Ancrene Wisse*, eds. J. R. R. Tolkien and N. R. Ker, EETS 249 (London, 1960), and in modernization as *The Ancrene Riwle*, ed. M. B. Salu (London, 1955). The best introduction to the anchoritic tradition is *Ancrene Wisse: Parts Six and Seven*, ed. Geoffrey Shepherd (London, 1959). For bibliography see Severs, ch. 6.1.

The Inner and the Outer Rule

[INTRODUCTION]

Nu, aski ye hwat riwle ye ancren schullen holden? Ye schullen alles weis, mid alle mihte, and mid alle strencthe, wel witen the inre and the uttre vor hire sake. The inre is evere iliche; the uttre is misliche, vor everich schal holden the uttre efter thet the licome mei best mid hire servi the inre. . . .

5 The uttre riwle, thet Ich thuften cleopede and is monnes findles, nis for nothing elles i-stald bute forto servie the inre. Thet maketh festen, wakien, kold, and here werien, and swüche othre heardschipes thet moni flechs mai tholien and moni ne mai nout.

Vor-thi mot theos riwle chaungen hire misliche efter euch ones manere and
10 efter hire efne. Vor sum is strong; sum is unstrong and mei ful wel beo cwite and paie God mid lesse. Sum is clergesse, and sum nis nout and mot the more wurchen and an other wise siggen hire ures. Sum is old and atelich and is the leasse dred of; sum is yung and livelich and is neode the betere warde.

Vor-thi schal efrich ancre habben the uttre riwle after schriftes read and, hwat
15 se he bit and hat hire, don in obedience, the cnoweth hire manere and hire strencthe. He mai the uttre riwle chaungen efter wisdom alse he i-sihth thet the inre mai beon best i-holden.

Non ancre bi mine read ne schal makien professiun, thet is, bihoten ase hest, bute threo thinges, thet is, obedience, chastete, and stude-stathelvestnesse (thet heo ne
20 schal thene stude never more chaungen bute vor neod one, als strengthe, and deathes dred, obedience of hire bischope other of hire herre). Vor hwoa-se nimeth thing on hond and bihat hit God alse heste to donne, heo bint hire therto and sünegeth deadliche ithe brüche yif heo hit breketh willes and woldes. Yif heo hit ne bihat nout, heo hit mai don thauh and leten hwon heo wel wüle, alse of mete,
25 and of drünch, fleschs forgon other visch, and alle other swüche thinges of weriunge, liggunge, of vres, of beoden. Sigge so monie and o hwüche wise so heo ever wüle. Theo and swüche othre beoth alle ine freo wille to donne other to leten hwon me ever wüle bute heo beon bihoten.

Auh cherite (thet is, luve), and edmodnesse, and tholemodness, treoweschipe, and
30 holding of the Tene olde Hesten, schrift and penitence—theos and swüche othre thet beoth summe of the Olde Lawe, summe of the Neowe, ne beoth nout monnes fündles, ne riwle thet mon stolde, ah beoth Godes hesten. And for-thi, everiche mon ham mot nede holden, and ye over alle thing!

The Anchoresses' Rule

[MODERNIZATION]

Now, you ask what rule you anchoresses are to follow? You must in all ways, with all your power and all your strength, know the inner rule well and the outer for its sake. The inner rule is always the same; the outer is varied, for each person must follow the outer in such a way that the body can best serve the inner rule by means of it. . . .

The outer rule, which I have called a handmaiden and which is the invention of man, is established for no other reason but to serve the inner. It requires fasting, keeping vigil, enduring cold, and wearing haircloth, and such other hardships that the flesh of many can endure and of many others cannot.

Therefore this rule must change variously according to the manner and nature of each. For some are strong; some are not and can be perfectly well acquitted and satisfy God with less. Some are scholarly, and some are not and must strive the more and in another way recite their hours. Some are old and ugly and are to be less feared for; some are young and lively and in need of better protection.

Therefore each anchoress ought to follow the outer rule according to the advice of a confessor, and whatever he, who knows her manner and strength, orders and commands her, she should perform in obedience. He can change the outer rule at discretion as he sees that the inner rule can best be observed.

No anchoress, by my advice, ought to make profession, that is, promise as an obligation, except for three matters, namely, obedience, chastity, and permanence of residence (that she will never change her place of residence unless because of absolute necessity, such as force, fear of death, and obedience to her bishop or to her superior). For whoever undertakes something and promises it to God under obligation to do it, commits herself to it and sins mortally in breaking it if she breaks it willingly and intentionally. If she does not promise, she can still perform it and cease to perform it whenever she wishes, as for instance with eating and drinking, abstaining from meat or fish, and all other such matters concerning clothing, resting, reciting hours, and prayers. Let her recite them as many and in such manner as she may wish. These and such other matters are all within free choice to be performed or not whenever one wishes, unless they have been promised.

But charity (that is, love), and humility, and long-suffering, fidelity, and the observation of the Ten Commandments of old, of confession, and of penitence— these and such other matters that are partly of the Old Law and partly of the New, are not the invention of man or a rule that man instituted but are the commands of God. And therefore everyone must observe them, and you in particular!

The Love of Man and of Christ

[BOOK 2]

Vor-thi, mine leove süstren, yif eni mon bit fort i-seon ou, asketh of him hwat god therof muhte lihten, vor moni üvel Ich i-seo therinne and none biheve. And yif he is methleas, i-leveth him the wurse. And yif eni wurtheth so wod and so awed that he worpe his hond forth touward the thurl-cloth, swiftliche anonriht
5 schutteth al the thurl to and letteth hine i-wurden. And also sone ase eni mon valleth into lüther speche thet falle touward fule live, tüneth thet thurl anonriht, and ne answerie ye him nowiht, auh wendeth awei mit thisse vers thet he hit muwe i-heren: "Narraverunt mihi iniqui fabulaciones sed non ut lex tua." And goth forth bivoren ower weovede mit the *Miserere*.
10 Ne chastie ye never nenne swüchne mon bute o thisse wise, vor mit the chastiement he muhte onswerien so and blowen so litheliche thet sum sperke muhte acwikien. No wouhleche nis so culvert ase is o pleinte wis, ase hwo se thus seide: "Ich nolde, vor to tholien deathe, thenche fülthe touward thee. Auh Ich hevede i-sworen hit, luvien Ich mot thee. And nu me is wo thet thu hit wost. Auh foryif
15 hit me nu thet Ich hit habbe i-told thee, and, thauh Ich schulde i-wurthe wod, ne schalt thu never more eft witen hu me stont."
Ant heo hit foryiveth him, for he speketh thus feire, and speketh theonne of otherwhat. Auh "ever is the eie to the wude leie; therinne is thet Ich luvie!" Ever is the heorte in there vorme speche; and yet, hwon he is forthe, heo went in hire
20 thuhte ofte swüche wordes hwon heo schulde otherhwat yearneliche yemen. He eft secheth his point vorte breke voreward and swereth thet he mot nede, and so waxeth the wo se lengre se wurse. Vor no freondschipe nis so üvel ase is fals freondschipe; feond thet thüncheth freond is swike over alle swike.
Vor-thi, mine leove süstren, ne yive ye to none swüche monne non inyong to
25 spekene, for ase Holi Writ seith, "Höre speche spret ase cauncre." Auh for alle onsweres wendeth ou ant wrencheth frommard him. . . .
This beoth nu two thinges thet beoth i-luved swüthe: swete speche and schene hwite. Hwo-se ham haveth togederes, swüche cheoseth Jesu Crist to leofmon and to spuse. Yif thu wilt beon swüch, ne scheau thu none monne thi hwite, ne ne lete
30 blitheliche i-heren thine speche. Auh turn bothe to Crist, to thi deorewurthe spus, ase he bit theruppe, ase thu wilt thet thi speche thünche him swete, and thi hwite schene, and habben him to leofmon thet is a thusentfold schenre then the sunne.

[MODERNIZATION]

If, then, my dear sisters, a man asks to see you, ask him what good might come of it, for here I forsee many evils and no advantage. And if he is importunate, consider him the worse for it. And if any man becomes so wild and so disturbed that he thrusts his hand forth toward the curtain, at once shut the window swiftly and let him be. And as soon as any man falls into seductive speech pertaining to an impure way of life, close the window at once and answer him nothing, but turn away with this verse so that he may overhear it: "The wicked have told me fables, but not as thy law." And go in before your altar with the psalm "Have mercy upon me."

Never reprove any such man in any other way than this, for upon the reproof he might answer and blow so subtly that some spark might be kindled. No seduction is so subtle as that which is in a plaintive manner, as if he were to say:

"I would not, on pain of death, think of indecency directed toward you. But, even if I had sworn the contrary, I must love you. And now I regret that you know it. But forgive me now that I have told you, and even if I should turn mad, you will never again know how things stand with me."

And she forgives him, for he speaks so gracefully, and then she speaks of something else. But "ever is the eye toward the shelter of the woods; the one whom I love is there!" Ever is the heart on the previous speech; and when he is gone, still she often turns such words in her thoughts when she ought to attend diligently to other matters. Still he seeks his opportunity to break his promise and swears that he must needs do so, and thus the longer the worse the calamity grows. For no friendship is so evil as is false friendship; an enemy who seems a friend is a villain above all villains.

So, my dear sisters, give no admittance to any such man to speak, for as Holy Writ says, "Their speech spreadeth as a cancer." But in place of all answers, turn and draw away from him. . . .

Now these are two things that are much beloved: sweet speech and fair beauty. Whoever has both of these together, such a one Jesus Christ chooses as his beloved and his bride. If you wish to be such, do not show any man your beauty, and do not blithely let him hear your speech. But turn both to Christ, for your precious spouse, as he summons you thither, as you wish that your speech may seem sweet and your beauty seem fair to him, and choose as your beloved him who is a thousandfold more beauteous than the sun.

Domestic Life

[BOOK 8]

Ye, mine leove süstren, ne schulen habben no best bute kat one. Ancre thet haveth eihte thüncheth bet husewif ase Marthe was then ancre, ne none wise ne mei heo beon Marie mid grithfulnesse of heorte. Vor theonne mot heo thenchen of the kues foddre and of heorde-monne huire, oluhnen thene heiward, warien
5 hwon me punt hire, and yelden thauh the hermes. Wat Crist, this is lodlich thing hwon me maketh mone in tune of ancre eihte. Thauh, yif eni mot nede habben ku, loke thet heo none monne ne eilie ne ne hermie, ne thet hire thouht ne beo nout theron i-vestned.

Ancre ne ouh nout to habben no thing thet drawe utward hire heorte. None
10 cheffare ne drive ye. Ancre thet is cheapild, heo cheapeth hire soule the chepmon of helle. Ne wite ye nout in oure huse of other monnes thinges, ne eihte, ne clothes; ne nout ne undervo the chirche vestimenz ne thene caliz bute yif strencthe hit makie other muchel eie, vor of swüche witunge is i-kumen muchel üvel oftesithen. . . .

Vor-thi thet no mon ne i-sihth ou, ne ye i-seoth nenne mon, wel mei don of
15 ower clothes, beon heo hwite, beon heo blake, bute thet heo beon unorne and warme and wel i-wrouhte, velles wel i-tauwed; and habbeth ase monie ase ou to-neodeth to bedde and eke to rügge.

The Author's Prayer

[EPILOGUE]

O thisse boc redeth everiche deie hwon ye beoth eise, everiche dei lesse other more. Vor Ich hopie thet hit schal beon ou, yif ye redeth ofte, swüthe biheve thuruh Godes grace—and elles ich hevede üvele bitowen muchel of mine hwüle! God hit wot, me were leovere vorto don me touward Rome then vorto biginnen hit eft
5 forto donne.

And yif ye i-vindeth thet ye doth al so ase ye redeth, thonketh God yeorne; and yif ye ne doth nout, biddeth Godes ore, and beoth umbe ther abuten thet ye hit bet hol holden efter ower mihte.

Veder and Sune and Holi Gost, and on Almihti God, he wite ou in his warde.
10 He gledie ou, and froure ou, mine leove sustren. And for al thet ye vor him drieth and suffreth, he ne yive ou never lesse huire then altogedere himsülven. He beo ever i-heied from worlde to worlde, ever on ecchenesse. Amen.

[MODERNIZATION]

My dear sisters, you must not keep any animal except for a cat. An anchoress that has property seems more like a housewife such as Martha was than an anchoress, nor can she in any way be Mary in peacefulness of heart. For then she must think of the cow's fodder and the herdsman's hire, must flatter the heyward, guard against the impounding of her cattle, and furthermore pay damages. Christ knows, it is a sorry matter when complaint is made in town over the property of anchoresses. However, if any anchoress, absolutely must have a cow, see that it neither annoys nor harms anyone and that her concern is not attached to it.

An anchoress ought not to have anything that might draw her heart outward. Deal in no business. An anchoress who is a dealer sells her soul to the tradesman of hell. Do not store in your house other people's possessions or property or clothes; and do not accept the church vestments and chalice unless compulsion or some great alarm require it, for great harm has often come from such custody. . . .

Since no man sees you and since you see no man, you may well be satisfied with your clothes, whether they be white or black, provided that they be simple and warm and well made, and the leather-skins well prepared; and have as many as you need both for bed and for your back.

[MODERNIZATION]

Read in this book every day when you are free, either less or more each day. For I hope that, if you read it often, it will by the grace of God be very profitable for you—otherwise, I would have ill spent much of my time! God knows, I would sooner set out for Rome than begin to do it again.

And if you find that you are doing exactly what you read, thank God heartily; and if you are not doing so, pray for God's mercy, and attempt to follow it better according to your ability.

May the Father, Son, and Holy Ghost, the one Almighty God, keep you in his care. May he gladden you and comfort you, my dear sisters. And for all that you endure and suffer on his behalf, may he never grant you a recompense less than himself entirely. May he be ever exalted from generation to generation, ever in eternity. Amen.

King Horn

(ca. 1225, Southwestern)

❧

King Horn is an outstanding example of what may be called a primitive romance. The composer is resolutely concerned with the basic and universal ingredients of romance—religion, love, and warfare (Dante's *salus, venus,* and *virtus*)—but he is not concerned with the attendant subtleties of pictorialization, characterization, and motivation. Here, as with the ballad, the listeners provided their own interpretations. The highly developed art of *Sir Gawain and the Green Knight* (p. 376) with all its ethical, courtly, and chivalric nuances was not to emerge in England until a century and a half later. Yet the very simplicity of *King Horn* gives it a universal appeal.

It is not only the earliest surviving English romance but also one of the most enduringly popular. The oldest recorded form of the tale is an Anglo-Norman poem composed around 1170–80 by a certain Master Thomas. The Middle English romance printed here is preserved in three closely similar manuscript versions. An alternate and inferior version known as *Horn Child* was composed around 1320; and this or some other later form entered the popular oral tradition of balladry with such vigor that the ballad of *Hind Horn* was still being sung in the nineteenth century.

The version that follows is based on the Harley Miscellany (2253), compiled in Hereford around 1330–39. Two lines, unnumbered, have been borrowed from the Laud Manuscript, and a few variants have been introduced from the other manuscripts when the Harley version seems inconsistent. The composer of *King Horn* may have had a clear sense of geography, but the minstrels who transmitted his romance and the scribes who recorded it were evidently indifferent. For clarification, his movements between Sudene (his home), Westnesse (his sweetheart's home), Ireland (his place of exile), and Reynis or Reme (the unwanted suitor's home) have therefore been supplied in the text. The reader will also note that Horn's father, Allof, is alternately called Murry in some passages.

The meter is rhyming, three-beat couplets; see Introduction, type 4, page 30.

The standard edition of the three manuscript versions (and of *Horn Child*) is *King Horn, A Middle English Romance*, ed. Joseph Hall (Oxford, 1901); for *Hind Horn* see F. J. Child, ed., *English and Scottish Popular Ballads* (Cambridge, Mass., 1882), No. 17 (cf. No. 252). The manuscript followed here is reproduced in *Facsimile of British Museum MS. Harley 2253*, ed. N. R. Ker, EETS 255 (Oxford, 1965), item 70. For bibliography see Severs, ch. 1.1.

Alle heo ben° blythe	**Alle . . .** May they all be
That to my song y-lythe.°	listen
A song Ychülle ou° singe	**Ychülle ou** I will to you
Of Allof the gode kynge—	

King Horn

[HORN IN SUDENE]

5   Kyng he wes by° weste,   in the
    The whiles hit y-leste°—   lasted
    Ant Godylt his gode quene—
    No feyrore myhte bene—
    Ant hüere° sone hihte° Horn—   her   called
10 Feyrore child ne myhte° be born;   **ne myhte** couldn't
    For reyn ne myhte byryne°   touch on
    Ne sonne myhte shyne°   shine on
    Feyrore child then he was,
    Bryht so° ever eny glas,   as
15 So whit so eny lylye flour,
    So rose red wes his colour.
    He wes feyr ant eke° bold   also
    Ant of fyftene wynter old.
    Nis non° his yliche°   **Nis non** There is none   like
20 In none kinges ryche.°   realm
      Tweye feren° he hadde   **Tweye feren** Two companions
    That he with him ladde,
    Alle riche menne° sones,   **riche menne** powerful men's
    Ant alle swythe° feyre gomes,°   very   lads
25 Wyth him for te° pleye.   to
    Mest° he lovede tweye.   Most
    That on° wes hoten° Athulf Chyld,   **That on** The one   called
    Ant that other Fykenyld.
    Athulf wes the beste,
30 Ant Fykenyld the werste.
      Hyt was upon a someres day,
    Also° Ich ou° telle may,   As   you
    Allof the gode kyng
    Rod upon ys pleyghyng°   **ys pleyghyng** his sport
35 Bi the see side,
    Ther° he was woned° to ryde.   Where   accustomed
    With him ne ryde bote° two.   **ne ... rode** only
    Al too fewe hüe° were tho.°   they   then
    He fond by the stronde
40 Aryved on is° londe   his
    Shipes fyftene
    Of Sarazynes kene.°   bold
    He askede whet hüe sohten°   sought
    Other° on is lond brohten.   Or
45 A payen° hit y-herde   pagan
    Ant sone° him onswerede: at once
      "Thy lond-folk° we wölleth slon° people   **wölleth slon** will slay
    That° ever Crist leveth on,°   Who   **leveth on** believe in

Ant thee we wölleth° ryht anon.   will slay
50 Shalt thou never henne gon."°   **henne gon** go hence
     Thy kyng lyhte of° his stede,   **lyhte of** alighted from
   For tho° he hevede nede,   then
   Ant his gode feren° two.   companions
   Mid y-wis, hüem wes ful wo.°   **Mid . . .** Certainly, they were very woeful
55 Swerd° hy gonne° gripe   Swords   began to
   Ant togedere smyte.
   Hy smyten under shelde
   That hy somme y-felde.
   The kyng hade too fewe
60 Agheyn° so monie schrewe.°   Against   villains
   So fele° myhten ethe°   many   easily
   Bringe thre to dethe.
   The payns° come to londe   pagans
   Ant nomen° hit an° honde.   took   in
65 The folk hy gonne quelle°   **gonne quelle** began to kill
   Ant cherches for to felle.
   Ther ne myhte° libbe   **ne myhte** couldn't
   The fremede° ne the sibbe°   stranger   relation
   Bote° he is° lawe forsoke   Unless   his own
70 Ant to hüere° toke.   theirs
     Of alle wymmanne
   Werst wes Godyld thanne.
   For Allof hy° wepeth sore   she
   Ant for Horn yet more.
75 Godild hade so muche sore
   That habbe myhte hüe° na more.   she
   Hüe wente out of halle
   From hire maidnes alle
   Under a roche of stone,
80 Ther° hüe wonede° alone.   Where   dwelt
   Ther hüe servede Gode
   Agheyn° the payenes forbode;°   Despite   **payenes forbode** pagans' prohibition
   Ther hüe° servede Crist   she
   That° the payenes hit nüst;°   So that   didn't know
85 Ant ever hüe bad° for Horn Child   prayed
   That Crist him wurthe° myld.   **him wurthe** to him might be
     Horn wes in payenes hond
   Mid is feren° of the lond.   **Mid . . .** With his companions
   Muche wes the feyrhade°   attractiveness
90 That Jhesu Crist him° made.   in him
   Payenes° him wolde slo,°   Pagans   **wolde slo** wanted to slay
   Ant summe him wolde flo.°   flay

Yyf Hornes feyrnesse nere,°   it hadn't been for
Y-slawe° this children were.°   Slain   would have been
95 Tho spec on admyrold°—   **Tho . . .** Then spoke an emir
Of wordes he wes swythe° bold: very
"Horn, thou art swythe kene,°   bold
Bryht of hewe, ant shene;°   beautiful
Thou art fayr ant eke° strong   also
100 Ant eke eveneliche long.°   **eveneliche long** proportionately tall
Yef thou to-lyve mote° go   **to-lyve mote** alive may
Ant thyne feren° also,   companions
That Y may byfalle:°   suffer
That ye shule slen° us alle.   slay
105 Tharefore thou shalt to streme° go,   sea streams
Thou ant thy feren also;
To° shipe ye shule founde°   On a   go
Ant sinke to the grounde.°   bottom
The see thee shal adrenche,°   drown
110 Ne shal hit us ofthenche,°   distress
For, yef thou were alyve,
With swerd other° with knyve   **swerd other** sword or
We shulden alle deye,
Thy fader° deth to beye."°   father's   atone for
115   The children ede° to the stronde,   went
Wryngynde hüere° honde,   their
Ant into shipes borde
At the fürste worde.°   words
Ofte hade Horn be wo°   **be wo** been woeful
120 Ah° never wors then him° wes tho.°   But   **then him** than he   then
The see bygon to flowen,
Ant Horn faste to rowen,
Ant that ship wel swythe° drof,   **wel swythe** very quickly
Ant Horn wes adred° therof.   afraid
125 Hüe wenden mid y-wisse°   **Hüe . . .** They expected certainly
Of hüere lyve to misse.°   **Of . . .** To lose their lives
Al the day ant al the nyht
Othat° sprong the day-lyht   Until
Flotterede° Horn by the stronde   Hovered
130 Er° he seye° eny londe.   Before   saw
"Feren," quoth Horn the yynge,°   young
"Y telle ou° tydynge.   you
Ich here foules° singe   birds
Ant se the grases springe.
135 Blythe° be ye alyve;   Happy
Ur ship is come to ryve."°   shore

[HORN IN WESTNESSE]

Of° shipe hy gonne founde° — By **gonne founde** did go
Ant sette fot to grounde.
By the see syde
140 Hüre° ship bigon to ryde. — Their
Thenne spec him° Child Horn— — **spec him** spoke
In Sudenne he was y-born:
"Nou, ship, by the flode
Have dayes gode.
145 By the see brynke
No water thee adrynke.° — **No** ... May no water sink you
Softe mote° thou sterye° — **Softe mote** Gently must steer
That water thee ne derye.° — **ne derye** doesn't harm
"Yef thou comest to Sudenne,
150 Gret° hem that me kenne;° — Greet know
Gret wel the gode
Quene Godild, mi moder,
Ant sey thene hethene° kyng, — **thene hethene** to the heathen
Jhesu Cristes wytherlyng,° — adversary
155 That Ich hol ant fere° — **hol** ... whole and well
In londe aryvede here,
Ant say that he shal fonde° — undergo
Then deth of° myne honde." — **Then** ... Death from
The ship bigon to fleoten° — sail
160 Ant Horn Child to weopen.
By dales ant by doune° — upland
The chidren eoden° to toune.° — went town
Metten hüe° Eylmer the kyng— — they
Crist him yeve° god tymyng— — give
165 Kyng of Westnesse.
Crist him myhte blesse!
He spec° to Horn Child — spoke
Wordes swythe° myld: — very
"Whenne° be ye gomen° — From where lads
170 That büeth her a° londe y-comen, — **büeth** ... are here to
Alle threttene° — thirteen
Of bodye swythe kene?° — bold
By God that me made,
So feyr a felaw-rade° — company
175 Ne seh° Y never stonde — saw
In Westnesse londe.
Say me whet ye seche."° — seek
Horn spec hüere° speche. — **spec hüere** spoke their
Horn spac for hüem alle,
180 For so hit moste byfalle;

He wes the wyseste
Ant of wytte the beste.
    "We büeth° of Sudenne,   are
Y-come° of gode kenne°   Descended   kin
185 Of Cristene blode,
Of cünne swythe° gode.   **cünne swythe** kin very
Payenes° ther connen° aryve   Pagans   did
Ant Cristine brohten of lyve,°   **brohten** ... killed
Slowen ant todrowe°   **Slowen** ... Slaughtered and drew to pieces
190 Cristine men ynowe.°   enough
    "So Crist me mote rede,°   **mote rede** may counsel
Ous hy düden° lede   **Ous** ... Us they did
Into a galeye
With the see to pleye.
195 Day is gon ant other°   **Day** ... For a day and another
Withoute seyl ant rother°   rudder
Ure ship flet° forth y-lome,°   sailed   steadily
Ant her to londe hit ys y-come.
    "Now thou myht us slen° and bynde   strike
200 Oure honde us bihynde,
Ah,° yef hit is thi wille,   But
Help us that we ne spille."°   **ne spille** don't perish
    Tho spac° the gode kyng—   **Tho spac** Then spoke
He nes° never nythyng:°   was   a niggard
205   "Sey, Child, whet is thy name?
Shal thee tide bote game."°
    The child him onswerede
So sone° he hit y-herde: **So sone** As soon as
    "Horn Ych am y-hote,°   called
210 Y-come out of this bote
From the see side.
Kyng, wel thee bitide."°   **wel** ... may well befall you
    "Horn Child," quoth the kyng,
"Wel brouc° thou thy nome yyng.°   enjoy   **nome yyng** young name
215 Horn him° göth so stille°   **Horn him** A horn   quietly
Bi dales ant by hülles;
Horn hath loude soune°   sound
Thurhout üch-a toune.°   **üch-a toune** each town
So shal thi nome springe
220 From kynge to kynge
Ant thi feirnesse
Aboute Westnesse.
Horn, thou art so swete,
Ne shal Y thee forlete."°   desert

206. You shall receive nothing but kind treatment.

225   Hom rod Aylmer the kyng,
    Ant Horn with him, his fundlyng,°   foundling
    Ant alle his yfere°   companions
    That him were so düere.°   dear
       The kyng com into halle
230   Among his knyhtes alle.
    Forth he clepeth° Athelbrus,   calls
    His stiward, ant him seide thus:
      "Stiward, tac° thou here   take
    My fundlyng° for to lere°   foundling   instruct
235 Of thine mestere°   profession
    Of wode ant of ryvere°   river
    And toggen o° the harpe   **toggen o** to play on
    With is nayles sharpe,
    And tech him alle the listes°   skills
240 That thou ever wystest°   knew
    Byfore me to kerven°   carve
    Ant of my coupe to serven,
    Ant his feren° devyse   **his feren** for his companions
    With ous° other servise.   us
245 Horn Child—thou understond—
    Tech him of harpe ant of song."
      Athelbrus gon leren°   **gon leren** instructed
    Horn and hyse feren.
    Horn mid herte lahte°   **mid . . .** took to heart
250 Al that mon him tahte.
    Withinne court and withoute
    Ant overal aboute
    Lovede men Horn Child,
    Ant most him lovede Rymenyld,
255 The kynges oune dohter,
    For he wes in hire thohte.
    Hüe° lovede him in hire mod,°   She   heart
    For he wes feir and eke° god;   also
    Ant, thah° hüe ne dorste° at bord°   though   **ne dorste** dared not   table
260 Mid° him speke ner a word   With
    Ne in the halle
    Among the knyhtes alle,
    Hyre sorewe ant hire pyne°   pain
    Nolde° never fyne°   Would   cease
265 Bi daye ne by nyhte
    For hüe° speke ne myhte°   **For hüe** Because she   **ne myhte** couldn't
    With Horn that wes so feir ant fre°   noble
    Tho° hüe ne myhte with him be.   When
      In herte hüe hade care° ant wo,   sorrow

270 Ant thus hüe bithohte hire tho.° — **bithohte . . .** bethought herself then
 Hüe sende hyre sonde° — messenger
 Athelbrus to honde° — **Athelbrus . . .** To Athelbrus
 That he come hire to
 Ant also shulde Horn do° — bring
275 Into hire boure,
 For hüe° bigon to loure.° — she   look ill
 Ant the sonde° sayde — messenger
 That seek° wes the mayde — sick
 Ant bed° him come swythe,° — bade   quickly
280 For hüe nis nout° blythe. — **nis nout** isn't
 The stiward wes in hüerte wo,° — **hüerte wo** heart woeful
 For he nüste° whet he shulde do. — didn't know
 What Rymenild bysohte
 Gret wonder him thohte° — seemed to him
285 Aboute Horn the yinge° — young
 To boure for te° bringe. — to
 He thohte on is mode° — **is mode** his mind
 Hit nes° for none gode. — was
 He tok° with him another, — took
290 Athulf, Hornes brother.
 "Athulf," quoth he, "ryht anon
 Thou shalt with me to boure gon° — go
 To speke with Rymenild stille° — secretly
 To wyte° hyre wille. — know
295 Thou art Hornes yliche;° — image
 Thou shalt hire byswyke.° — deceive
 Sore me adrede° — **me adrede** I fear
 That hüe° wole Horn mysrede."° — she   lead astray
 Athelbrus ant Athulf bo° — both
300 To hire boure beth y-go.° — **beth y-go** have gone
 Upon Athulf Childe
 Rymenild con waxe° wilde. — **con waxe** grew
 Hüe wende° Horn it were — supposed
 That hüe hade there.
305 Hüe seten° adoun stille° — **Hüe seten** They sat   quietly
 Ant seyden hüre wille.° — **hüre wille** what they wanted to
 In hire armes tweye° — two
 Athulf he con leye.° — **con leye** lay down
 "Horn," quoth heo, "wel longe
310 Y have loved thee stronge.
 Thou shalt thy treuthe plyhte° — pledge
 In myn hond with ryhte
 Me to° spouse welde° — as   to take
 Ant Ich thee loverd° to helde."° — as lord   hold

315   So stille so° hit were,   **So** ... As quietly as
Athulf seyde in hire eere,
"Ne tel thou no more speche,
May,° Y thee byseche.   Maiden
Thi tale gyn thou lynne,°   **Thi** ... Cease from your talk
320 For Horn nis nout° herynne;   **nis nout** isn't
Ne be we nout yliche,°   **Ne** ... Nor are we alike
For Horn is fayr ant ryche,
Fayrore by one ribbe[1]
Then ani mon that libbe.°   lives
325 Thah° Horn were under molde,°   Though   earth
Other ellewher° he sholde°   **Other ellewher** Or elsewhere   should be
Hennes° a thousent milen,°   Hence   miles
Y nülle° him bigilen."   won't
Rymenild hire bywente,°   **hire bywente** turned around
330 Ant Athelbrus thus heo shende:° scolded
"Athelbrus, thou foule thef,
Ne worthest thou me never lef!°
Went° out of my boure.   Go
Shame thee mote byshoure,°   **Shame** ... May shame shower on you
335 Ant evel hap° to underfonge,°   fate   suffer
Ant evele rode° on to honge.°   cross   hang
Ne speke Y nout° with Horne;   **Ne** ... I'm not speaking
Nis he nout° so unorne."°   **Nis** ... He isn't ugly
Tho Athelbrus a stounde°   **a stounde** at once
340 Fel akneu° to grounde.   on his knees
"Ha, levedy° myn owe,°   lady own
Me lythe° a lütel throwe,°   hear while
Ant list° werefore Ych wonde°   listen hesitate
To bringen Horn to honde,
345 For Horn is fayr ant riche;
Nis° non his ylyche.°   There is **his ylyche** like him
Aylmer the gode kyng
Düde° him me in lokyng.°   Put **me** ... in my care
Yif Horn thee were aboute,
350 Sore Ich myhte doute°   fear
With him thou woldest pleye
Bitwene ou selven tweye.°   **ou** ... your two selves
Thenne shulde, withouten othe,° question
The kyng us make wrothe.°   **us** ... show anger on us
355 "Ah foryef° me thi teone,°   **Ah foryef** But forgive **thi teone** for grieving you
My levedy° ant my quene.   lady
Horn Y shal thee fecche,

[1] 'Fairer by a rib.' The rib is a measure of beauty, since fair Eve is made of Adam's rib.
332. You'll never be dear to me!

Wham so° hit y-recche."°   **Wham so** Whomever   may vex
    Rymenild, yef heo couthe,°   could have
360 Con lythe° with hyre mouthe.   **Con lythe** Listened
Heo loh ant made hire blythe,°   **loh** . . . laughed and rejoiced
For wel° wes hyre o lyve.°   happy   **hyre** . . . she alive
    "Go thou," quoth heo, "sone,°   at once
    Ant send him after none°   noon
365 A skuyeres wyse°   **A** . . . In squire's clothing
When the king aryse.°   arises
He shal myd° me bileve°   with   stay
That° hit be ner eve.   Till
Have Ich° of him mi wille,   **Have Ich** If I have
370 Ne recchi° whet men telle."   **Ne recchi** I don't care
    Athulbrus goth with alle;
Horn he fond in halle,
Bifore the kyng o° benche   on
Wyn for te shenche.°   **for** . . . to pour out
375   "Horn," quoth he, "thou hende,°   noble one
To boure gyn thou wende°   **boure** . . . the bower go
To speke with Rymenild the yynge,°   young
Dohter oure° kynge.   of our
Wordes swythe° bolde   very
380 In hörte gyn thou holde.°   **In** . . . Hold in your heart
Horn, be thou me° trewe,   **be** . . . if you're to me
Shal thee nout arewe."°   **Shal** . . . You will not regret it
    He eode° forth to ryhte°   went   **to ryhte** directly
To Rymenild the bryhte.
385 Aknewes° he him sette   On his knees
Ant swetliche hire grette.°   greeted
Of is fayre syhte°
Al that bour gan lyhte.°   **gan lyhte** began to lighten
He spak faire is° speche,   his
390 Ne durth non° him teche.   **Ne** . . . And no one needed to
    "Wel thou sitte° ant softe,   **thou sitte** may you sit
Rymenild, kinges dohter,
Ant thy maydnes here
That sitteth thyne yfere.°   **thyne yfere** as your companions
395 Kynges styward oure°   **Kynges** . . . Our king's steward
Sende° me to boure   Sent
For te y-here, levedy° myn,   **For** . . . To hear, lady
Whet be wille thyn."
    Rymenild up gon stonde°   **gon stonde** stood
400 Ant tok° him by the honde.   took
Heo made feyre chere

387. From the fair sight of him

Ant tok him bi the swere.°   neck
Ofte heo him cüste°   kissed
So wel hyre lüste.°   **So . . .** As well as she wished
405   "Welcome, Horn," thus sayde
Rymenild that mayde,
"An° even ant a° morewe   On   on
For thee Ich habbe sorewe
That Y have no reste
410 Ne slepe me ne lyste.°   **Ne slepe . . .** Nor want to sleep
   "Horn, thou shalt wel swythe°   **wel swythe** very quickly
Mi longe sorewe lythe.°   lessen
Thou shalt withoute strive°   opposition
Habbe me to wyve.
415 Horn, have of° me reuthe,°   on   pity
Ant plyht° me thi treuthe."   pledge
   Horn tho hym bythohte
Whet he speken ohte.
   "Crist," quoth Horn, "thee wisse,°   direct
420 Ant yeve° thee hevene° blisse   give   heaven's
Of thine hosebonde
Who° he be a° londe.   Whoever   on
   "Ich am y-bore thral,°   **y-bore thral** born a thrall
Thy fader fundlyng° withal.   **fader fundlyng** father's foundling
425 Of künde me ne felde°
Thee to spouse welde.°   **to . . .** as spouse to have
Hit nere° no fair weddyng   would be
Bitwene a thral ant the kyng!"
   Tho gon° Rymenild mislyken,°   began   to grieve
430 Ant sore bigon to syken,°   sigh
Armes bigon unbowe,°   to unclasp
Ant doun heo fel y swowe.°   **y swowe** in a swoon
Horn hire up hente°   took
Ant in is armes trente.°   folded
435 He gon° hire to cüsse°   began   kiss
Ant feyre for te wisse.°   **te wisse** to direct
   "Rymenild," quoth he, "düere,°   dear
Help me that Ych were°   may be
Y-dobbed° to be knyhte,   Dubbed
440 Swete, bi al thi myhte°   power
To° mi loverd° the kyng   Over   lord
That he me yeve° dobbyng.   give
Thenne is my thralhede°   thralldom
Al wend° into knyhthede.   turned
445 Y shal waxe more°   **waxe more** grow greater

425. By nature it wouldn't befit me

Ant do,° Rymenild, thi lore."°   perform   instruction
    Tho Rymenild the yynge°   young
Aros of hire swowenynge.°   swoon
"Nou, Horn, to sothe,°   **to sothe** in truth
450 Y leve° thee by thyn othe.°   believe   oath
Thou shalt be maked knyht
Er then° this fourteniht.   **Er then** Before
Ber thou her thes° coppe   this
Ant thes ringe theruppe°   also
455 To Athelbrus the styward,
Ant say him he holde foreward.°   **holde foreward** should hold agreement
Sey Ich him biseche
With loveliche° speche   loving
That he for thee falle°   **for . . .** on your behalf should fall
460 To the kynges fet in halle
That he with is° worde   his
Thee knyhty° with sworde.   may knight
With selver ant with golde
Hit worth him° wel y-yolde.°   **worth him** will be to him   paid
465 Nou, Crist him lene° spede.   give
Thin erndyng° do bede."°   errand   declare
    Horn tok° is leve,   took
For hit wes neh° eve.   nearly
Athelbrus he sohte
470 Ant tok him that° he brohte,   what
Ant tolde him thare
Hou he hede y-fare.
He seide° him is nede   told
Ant him bihet° is mede.°   promised   reward
475   Athelbrus so blythe°   happy
Eode° into halle swythe°   Went   quickly
Ant seide, "Kyng, nou leste°   hear
O° tale mid° the beste.   A   among
Thou shalt bere coroune
480 Tomarewe in this toune.°   town
Tomarewe is thi feste;°   festivity
Thee bihoveth geste.°   **Thee . . .** You need an occasion
Ich thee rede mid° al my myht   **rede mid** advise with
That thou make Horn knyht.
485 Thin armes do him welde.°   **do . . .** let him have
God° knyht he shal thee yelde."°   A good   **thee yelde** make for you
    The kyng seide wel sone,°   promptly
"Hit is wel to done.°   do
Horn me wel quemeth.°   pleases
490 Knyht him° wel bysemeth.°   he   seems

125

He shal have mi dobbyng
Ant be myn other derlyng,°   favorite
Ant hise feren twelve
He shal dobbe himselve.
495 Alle Y shal hem knyhte
Byfore me to fyhte."
     Al that° the lyhte day sprong   **Al that** Till
Aylmere thohte long.
The day bigon to springe;
500 Horn com byfore the kynge
With his twelf fere.
Alle ther y-were.°   **ther y-were** were there
Horn knyht made he
With ful gret solempnité,°   pomp
505 Sette him on a stede
Red so° eny glede,°   as   glowing coal
Smot° him a lüte wiht,°   Tapped   **lüte wiht** little bit
Ant bed° him büen° a god knyht.   bade   be
Athulf vel akne° ther   **vel akne** fell on his knees
510 Ant thonkede kyng Aylmer.
     "Nou is knyht Sire Horn,
That in Sudenne wes y-born.
Lord he is of londe
Ant of us that by him stonde.
515 Thin armes he haveth ant thy sheld
For te fyhte in the feld.
Let him us alle knyhte
So° hit is his ryhte."   As
     Aylmer seide ful y-wis:°   **ful y-wis** very certainly
520 "Nou do that° thi wille ys."   what
     Horn adoun con lyhte°   **con lyhte** alighted
Ant made hem alle to knyhte,°   **alle . . .** all knights
For müchel° wes the geste,°   great   occasion
Ant more wes the feste.°   festivity
525   That Rymenild nes nout° there   **nes nout** wasn't
Hire thohte seve° yere.   **Hire . . .** Seemed to her like seven
Efter Horn hüe sende;°   **hüe sende** she sent
Horn into boure wende.°   went
He nolde gon is one;°   **nolde . . .** wouldn't go alone
530 Athulf wes hys ymone.°   companion
Rymenild welcometh Sire Horn
Ant Athulf knyht him biforn.°   **him biforn** before him
     "Knyht, nou is tyme
For to sitte by me.
535 Do nou that° we spake;°   what   spoke of

To thi wyf thou me take.
Nou° thou hast wille thyne,   Now that
Unbynd me of this pyne."°   pain
    "Rymenild, nou be stille.
540 Ichülle don° al thy wille.   **Ichülle don** I will do
Ah her° hit so bitide,   **Ah her** But before
Mid spere Ichülle ryde
Ant my knyhthod prove
Er then° Ich thee wowe.°   **Er then** Before   woo
545 We büeth° now knyhtes yonge   are
Alle today y-spronge,°   sprung forth
Ant of the mestere°   profession
Hit is the manere
With sum other knyhte
550 For his lemmon° to fyhte   sweetheart
Er ne° he eny wyf take   **Er ne** Before
Other° wyth wymmon forewart° make.   Or   agreement
Today—so° Crist me blesse°—   as   may bless
Y shal do pruesse°   prowess
555 For thi love mid° shelde   with
Amiddewart° the felde.   Amid
Yef Ich come to-lyve,°   alive
Ychül° thee take to wyve."   I will
    "Knyht, Y may y-leve° thee.   **may y-leve** can trust
560 Why, ant° thou trewe be,   if
Have her this gold ring.
Hit is ful god° to thi dobbyng.   **ful god** very appropriate
Y-graved is on the rynge:
'Rymenild thy lüef° the yynge.'°   sweetheart   young one
565 Nis° non betere under sonne   There is
That eny mon of conne.°   **of conne** knows of
For mi love thou hit were,°   wear
Ant on thy fynger thou hit bere.
The ston haveth suche grace°   power
570 Ne shalt thou° in none place   **Ne ...** That you will
Deth underfonge°   suffer
Ne büen y-slaye° with wronge   **Ne ...** Nor be slain
Yef thou lokest theran
Ant thenchest o° thi lemman;°   **thenchest o** think of   sweetheart
575 Ant Sire Athulf thi brother
He shal han° enother.   have
Horn, Crist° Y thee byteche°   to Christ   commend
Mid mourninde° speche.   anxious
Crist thee yeve° god endyng   give
580 Ant sound ayeyn thee brynge."°   **sound ...** bring you back safe

The knyht hire gan° to cüsse,°   **began   kiss**
Ant Rymenild him to blesse.
Leve at° hyre he nom,°   **Leve at** Leave from   took
Ant into halle he com.
585 Knyhtes eode° to table,   went
Ant Horn eode to stable.
Ther he toc° his gode fole,°   took   foal
Blac so ever eny cole.
With armes he him sredde,°   **him sredde** clad himself
590 Ant is° fole he fedde.   his
The fole bigon to springe
Ant Horn mürie to synge.
    Horn rod one whyle
Wel more then a myle.
595 He seh° a shyp at grounde°   saw   **at grounde** at the shore
With hethene hounde.°   **hethene hounde** heathen hounds
He askede wet hüe° hadden   **wet hüe** what they
Other° to londe ladden.°   Or   brought
An hound him gan biholde°   **gan biholde** beheld
600 Ant spek wordes bolde:
    "This land we wölleth° wynne   will
Ant sle that° ther büeth° inne."   **sle that** slay those who   are
    Horn gan is swerd gripe°   **swerd gripe** sword to grip
Ant on is arm hit wype.
605 The Sarazyn he hitte so
That is hed fel to ys to.°   toes
Tho gonne° the houndes gone°   began   to go
Ayeynes° Horn ys one.°   Against   **ys one** alone
He lokede on is rynge
610 Ant thohte o° Rymenyld the yynge.   of
He sloh° therof the beste,°   slew   best
An houndred at the leste;
Ne mihte no mon telle°   **Ne . . .** No man could count
Alle that he gon quelle.°   **gon quelle** killed
615 Of that° ther were oryve°   those who   ashore
He lafte lüt olyve.°   **lüt olyve** few alive
    Horn tok the maister heved°   **maister heved** great head
That he him hade byreved°   bereft of
Ant sette on is swerde°   sword
620 Aboven o then orde.°   **o . . .** on the tip
He ferde° hom to halle   went
Among the knyhtes alle.
    "Kyng," quoth he, "well thou sitte°   **thou sitte** may you sit
Ant thine knyhtes mitte.°   with you
625 Today Ich rod o my pleyyng°   **rod . . .** rode out in sport

After my dobbyng.
I fond a ship rowen°   rowing
In the sound byflowen°   afloat
Mid unlondisshe° menne foreign
630 Of Sarazynes kenne°   kin
To dethe for te pyne°   **To . . .** To put to the death
Thee ant alle thyne.
Hy gonne° me asayly.°   began to assail
Swerd° me nolde fayly.°   Sword **nolde fayly** wouldn't fail
635 Y smot hem alle to grounde
In a lütel stounde.°   while
The heved° Ich thee bringe head
Of the maister kynge.
Nou have Ich thee yolde° repaid
640 That thou me knyhten woldest."° **knyhten woldest** were willing to knight
  The day bigon to springe;
 The kyng rod on° hontynge **rod on** rode out
To the wode wyde
Ant Fykenyld bi is syde
645 That fals wes ant untrewe,
Who se° him wel y-knewe. **Who se** Whoever
  Horn ne thohte nout him on° **him on** about him
Ant to boure wes y-gon.
He fond Rymenild sittynde
650 Ant wel° sore wepynde   very
So whyt so the sonne,
Mid terres° al byronne.°   **Mid terres** With tears drenched
Horn seide, "Lüef,° thyn ore.° Sweetheart favor
Why wepest thou so sore?"
655   Hüe° seide, "Ich nout ne wepe, She
Ah° Y shal er° Y slepe.   But before
Me thohte o° my metyng° **Me . . .** It seemed to me in dream
That Ich rod o° fysshyng **rod o** rode out
To see my net y-caste,
660 Ant wel fer° hit laste.°   **wel fer** very far extended
A gret fyssh at the ferste
My net made berste.
That fyssh me so bycahte° overcame
That Y nout ne lahte.°   **nout . . .** caught nothing
665 Y wene° Y shal forleose° suppose lose
The fyssh that Y wolde cheose."° prefer
  "Crist ant Seinte Stevene,"
Quoth Horn, "areche° thy swevene!° interpret dream
No shal Y thee byswyke° **No . . .** I won't deceive you
670 Ne do that° thee mislyke.° what may displease

Ich take thee myn owe°   **myn owe** as my own
To holde ant eke° to knowe   also
For° everüch other wyhte.°   Before   person
Therto my trouthe Y plyhte."°   pledge
675   Wel° muche was the reuthe°   Very   sorrow
That wes at thilke treuthe.°   **thilke treuthe** that betrothal
Rymenild wep° wel ylle,°   wept   sadly
Ant Horn let terres stille.°   **let . . .** stilled the tears
"Lemmon,"° quoth he, "dere,°   Sweetheart   dear
680 Thou shalt more y-here.
Thy sweven° shal wende.°   dream   come about
Summon° us wole shende.°   Someone   **wole shende** wants to harm
That fyssh that brac° thy net,   broke
Y-wis,° it is sumwet°   Indeed   something
685 That wol us do sum teone.°   injury
Y-wys,° hit worth y-sene."°   Indeed   **worth y-sene** will be seen
Aylmer rod° by Stoure,°   rode   the River Stour
Ant Horn wes yne boure.
Fykenhild hade envye
690 Ant seyde theose folye:°   **theose folye** this slander
"Aylmer, Ich thee werne,°   warn
Horn thee wole forberne.°   **wole forberne** wants to destroy
Ich herde wher he seyde—
Ant his swerd he leyde°—   wagered
695 To brynge thee of lyve°   **of lyve** from life
Ant take Rymenyld to wyve.
He lyht° nou in boure   lies
Under covertoure°   bedclothes
By Rymenyld thy dohter,
700 Ant so he döth wel ofte.
Do° him out of londe   Put
Er he do more shonde."°   harm
Aylmer gon hom turne°   **gon . . .** turned home
Wel mody° ant wel sturne.   angry
705 He fond Horn under arme°   her arm
In Rymenyldes barme.°   bosom
"Go out," quoth Aylmer the kyng,
"Horn, thou foule fundlyng,°   foundling
Forth out of boures flore°   **boures flore** the bedroom floor
710 For° Rymenild thin hore.°   Because of   whore
Wend° out of londe sone.°   Go   at once
Her nast° thou nout to done.°   have   **nout . . .** nothing to do
Wel sone, bote° thou flette,°   unless   flee
Myd swert° Y shal thee sette."°   sword   **thee sette** set on you
715   Horn eode° to stable   went

Wel modi° for that fable.°   angry   slander
He sette sadel on stede;
With armes he gon him shrede;°   **gon** ... dressed himself
His brünie° he con lace,°   coat of mail   **con lace** laced
720 So he shulde, into place;
His swerd he gon fonge,°   **gon fonge** took
Ne stod° he nout too longe.   tarried
To° is swerd he gon teon,°   For   **gon teon** reached
Ne durste non wel° him seon.°   **Ne** ... Nor would anyone dare willingly   see
725   He seide, "Lemmon,° derlyng,   Sweetheart
Nou thou havest thy swevenyng.°   dream
The fyssh that thyn net rende°   tore
From thee me he sende.°   has sent
The kyng with me gynneth° strive;   begins to
730 Awey he wole° me dryve.   wants to
Tharefore have nou godne-day.°   good day
Nou Y mot founde and fare° away   **mot** ... must set out and go
Into uncouthe° londe   unknown
Wel° more for te fonde.°   Much   **for** ... to attempt
735 Y shal wonie° there   live
Fulle seve° yere.   seven
At the seve yeres ende,
Yyf Y ne come ne sende,°   **ne come** ... don't come or send for you
Tac thou hosebonde;
740 For me that thou ne wonde.°   **that** ... don't hesitate about that
   "In armes thou me fonge,°   take
Ant cüs° me swythe longe."   kiss
   Hy cüsten hem° a stounde,°   **Hy** ... They kissed   while
And Rymenyld fel to grounde.
745 Horn toc his leve;
He myhte nout byleve.°   **myhte** ... couldn't stay
He toc° Athulf is fere   clasped
Aboute the swere°   neck
Ant seide, "Knyht so trewe,
750 Kep° wel my love newe.   Guard
Thou never ne forsoke°   **ne forsoke** failed
Rymenild to kepe ant loke."°   **kepe** ... guard and watch
   His stede he bigan stryde,
Ant forth he con hym ryde.°   **con** ... rode
755 Athulf wep with eyyen,
Ant alle that hit y-seyyen.°   saw
Horn forth him ferde.°   **him ferde** went
A god ship he him herde°   **him herde** hired
That him shulde passe
760 Out of Westnesse.

The wynd bigon to stonde°   rise
Ant drof hem up o londe.°   **londe** on land (Ireland)

      [HORN IN IRELAND]
    To° londe that hy fletten°   On the   reached
Fot out of ship hy setten.
765 He fond bi the weye
Kynges sones tweye.°   two
That on° wes hoten° Athyld,   **That on** The one   called
Ant that other Beryld.
Beryld hym con° preye   did
770 That he shulde seye
What he wolde° there   wanted
Ant what ys nome° were.   name
    "Godmod," he seid, "Ich hote,°   am called
Y-comen out of this bote
775 Wel fer° from by-weste°   far   the west
To seche° myne beste."°   seek   advantage
    Beryld con ner him ryde°   **con . . .** rode nearer to him
Ant toc him bi the bridel.
    "Wel be thou, knyht, y-founde.
780 With me thou lef° a stounde.°   stay   while
Also° Ich mote sterve,°   As sure as **mote sterve** must die
The kyng thou shalt serve;
Ne seh° Y never alyve   **Ne seh** Nor saw
So feir knyht her aryve."
785   Godmod he ladde to halle,
Ant he adoun gan° falle   did
Ant sette him a-knelyng
Ant grette thene° gode kyng.   **grette thene** greeted the
Tho saide Beryld wel sone,°   **wel sone** at once
790   "Kyng, with him thou ast done.
Thi lond tac° him to werie,°   choose   guard
Ne° shal thee no mon derye,°   Nor   **no . . .** anyone harm
For he is the feyreste man
That ever in this londe cam."
795   Tho seide the kyng wel dere,
"Welcome be thou here.
Go, Beryld, wel swythe,°   quickly
Ant make hym wel blythe,°   happy
Ant when thou farest° to wowen,°   set out   woo
800 Tac him° thine gloven!°   for him   gloves as pledge
Ther° thou hast münt° to wyve   Where   intended
Awey he shal thee dryve.
For° Godmodes feyrhede°   Because of   attractiveness

Shalt thou nower spede."°   **nower spede** nowhere succeed

805   Hit wes at Cristesmasse,
Nouther° more ne lasse,   Neither
The kyng made feste°   festivities
Of° his knyhtes beste.   For
Ther com in at none
810 A geaunt swythe sone°   **geaunt** . . . giant very fast
Y-armed of paynyme°   **of paynyme** from pagandom
Ant seide thise ryme:
    "Site kyng bi° kynge,   beside
Ant herkne my tidynge.
815 Her° büeth paynes aryve.   Here
Wel more then fyve
Her beth upon honde,°   **beth** . . . are at hand
Kyng, in thine londe.
On° therof wol fyhte   One
820 Toyeynes° thre knyhtes.   Against
Yef eure° thre sleh oure on,°   your   **sleh** . . . slay one of ours
We shulen of° eure londe gon.°   from   go
Yef ure on° sleh eure thre,   **ure on** one of ours
Al this lond shal ure° be.   ours
825 Tomorewe shal be the fyhtynge
At the sonne upspringe."
    Tho seyde the kyng Thurston,
"Godmod shal be that on;°   **that on** the one
Beryld shal be that other;°   second
830 The thridde,° Athyld is brother;   third
For hüe büeth strongeste
Ant in armes the beste.
Ah° wat shal us to rede?°   But   **shal** . . . is our best plan
Y wene° we büeth dede."°   suppose   dead
835   Godmod set° at borde°   was sitting   the table
Ant seide theose wordes:
"Sire kyng, nis no ryhte°   **nis** . . . it's not right
On° with thre fyhte°—   One   to fight
Ayeynes° one hounde   Against
840 Thre Cristene to founde.°   strive
Ah, kyng, Y shal alone
Withoute more ymone°   companion
With my swerd ful ethe°   **ful ethe** very easily
Bringen hem alle to dethe."
845   The kyng aros a-morewe;
He hade muche sorewe.
Godmod ros of bedde;
With armes he him shredde;°   **him shredde** clad himself

His brünye° he on caste   coat of mail
850 Ant knütte° hit wel faste°   tied firmly
    Ant com him to the kynge
    At his uprysynge.
        "Kyng," quoth he, "com to felde
    Me for te byhelde
855 Hou we shule flyten°   contend
    Ant togedere smiten."
        Riht at prime tide°   **prime tide** the first hour
    Hy gonnen out to ryde.
    Hy founden in a grene
860 A geaunt° swythe kene,°   giant bold
    His feren him biside,
    That day for to abyde.°   endure
    Godmod hem gon asaylen;°   **hem . . .** began to attack them
    Nolde he nout° faylen.   **Nolde . . .** He didn't want to
865 He yef duntes ynowe;°   **yef . . .** gave blows enough
    The payen fel y swowe.°   **y swowe** into a faint
    Ys feren gonnen° hem withdrawe,   began to
    For hüere maister wes neh slawe.°   **neh slawe** nearly slain
    He° seide, "Knyht, thou reste   He (the giant)
870 A whyle yef thee leste.°   **thee leste** you wish
    Y ne hevede ner° of monnes hond   **ne . . .** never had
    So harde duntes in non lond
    Bote° of the kyng Murry,°   Except Allof
    That wes swithe sturdy.
875 He wes of Hornes kenne.°   kin
    Y sloh° him in Sudenne."   slew
        Godmod him gon agryse,°   **gon agryse** began to shudder
    Ant his blod aryse.°   began to rise
    Byforen him he seh° stonde   saw
880 That drof° him out of londe   **That drof** The one who drove
    Ant fader his aquelde.°   **fader . . .** killed his father
    He smot him under shelde;
    He lokede on is rynge
    Ant thohte o Rymenild the yynge;
885 Mid god swerd at the fürste°   **at . . .** directly
    He smot him thourh the hüerte.
        The payns bigonne to fleon°   flee
    Ant to hüere shype teon.°   withdraw
    To ship hüe° wolden erne;°   they run
890 Godmod hem con werne.°   **con werne** prevented
    The kynges sones tweyne°   two (Beryld and Athyld)
    The paiens slowe beyne.°   **slowe beyne** slew both
    Tho wes Godmod swythe wo,°   woeful

Ant the payens he smot so
895 That in a lütel stounde°   while
The paiens hy felle to grounde.
Godmod ant is men
Slowe° the payenes everüchen.°   Slew   each one
His fader° deth ant ys lond   father's
900 Awrek° Godmod with his hond.   Avenged
The kyng with reuthful° chere   sorrowful
Lette leggen is sones° on bere°   **Lette ...** Had his sons laid   bier
Ant bringen hom° to halle.   **bringen hom** had them brought home
Muche sorewe hüe maden alle.
905 In a chirche of lym ant ston
Me buriede hem° with ryche won.°   **Me ...** They were buried   display
The kyng lette forth calle
Hise knyhtes alle
Ant seide, "Godmod, yef thou nere,°   **thou nere** it weren't for you
910 Alle ded we were.
Thou art bothe god ant feyr.
Her Y make thee myn heyr,
For my sones büeth y-flawe°   gone
Ant y-broht° of lyfdawe.°   bereft   life
915 Dohter Ich habbe one—
Nis° non so feyr of blod ant bone—   There is
Ermenild that feyre may,°   maiden
Bryht so eny someres day.
Hire wolle Ich yeve° thee,   give
920 Ant her kyng shalt thou be."
He seyde, "More Ichül° thee serve,   I will
Kyng, er then° thou sterve.°   **er then** before   die
When Y thy dohter yerne,°   yearn for
Heo ne shal me nothyng werne."°   refuse
925   Godmod wonede° there   lived
Fulle six yere,
Ant, the sevethe yer bygon,°   being past
To Rymynyld sonde° ne sende he non.   messenger
Rymenyld wes in Westnesse
930 With muchel sorewenesse.
A kyng ther wes aryve
Ant wolde hyre han° to wyve.   have
At one° were the kynges   **At one** Agreed
Of° that weddynge.   About
935 The dayes were so sherte,°   short
Ant Rymenild ne derste°   **ne derste** dared not
Latten° on none wyse.   Delay
A wryt hüe düde devyse;°   **düde devyse** composed

135

	Athulf hit düde wryte,	
940	That Horn ne lovede nout lyte.°	
	Hüe sende hire sonde°	messenger
	Into everüche° londe	each
	To sechen° Horn knyhte	seek
	Whe-so-er me myhte.°	**Whe-so-er . . .** Wherever one could seek
945	Horn therof nout herde	
	Til o° day that he ferde°	one went
	To wode for te shete,°	shoot
	A page he gan° mete.	did
	Horn seide, "Leve° fere,	Dear
950	Whet dest thou nou here?"	
	"Sire, in lütel spelle°	space
	Y may thee sone telle.	
	Ich seche° from Westnesse	seek
	Horn knyht of Estnesse,	
955	For Rymenild, that feyre may,°	maiden
	Soreweth for him nyht ant day.	
	A kyng hire shal wedde	
	A Sonneday° to bedde—	**A Sonneday** On Sunday
	Kyng Mody of Reynis,	
960	That is Hornes enimis.°	enemy
	"Ich habbe walked wyde	
	By the see side,	
	Ne mihte Ich him never cleche°	
	With nones künnes° speche,	**nones künnes** any kind of
965	Ne may Ich of him here°	hear
	In londe fer no nere.	
	Weylawey° the while!°	Alas delay
	Him may hente gyle."°	**hente gyle** treachery capture
	Horn hit herde with earen°	ears
970	Ant spec with wete tearen:	
	"So wel, grom,° thee bitide!°	page may betide
	Horn stond° by thi syde.	stands
	Ayeyn° to Rymenild turne,	Back
	Ant sey that hüe ne murne.°	**ne murne** shouldn't grieve
975	Y shal be ther bi° time	on
	A Sonneday° er prime."°	**A Sonneday** On Sunday the first hour
	The page wes wel blythe°	happy
	Ant shipede° wel swythe.	embarked
	The see him gon adrynke;°	**gon adrynke** drowned
980	That Rymenil may ofthinke!°	regret
	The see him con ded throwe°	**con . . .** threw dead

940. Who loved Horn not a little.
963. Nor could I ever catch him

Under hire chambre wowe.°   wall
Rymenild lokede wide
By the see syde
985 Yef heo seye° Horn come   might see
Other° tidynge of eny gome.°   Or   lad
Tho fond hüe° hire sonde°   **Tho** . . . Then she found   messenger
Adronque° by the stronde   Drowned
That shulde° Horn brynge.   **That shulde** Who was going to
990 Hire hondes gon hüe wrynge.
     Horn com to Thurston the kynge
Ant tolde him thes tidynge,
Ant tho° he was biknowe°   then   **was biknowe** revealed
That Rymenild wes ys owe°   own
995 Ant of his gode kenne°   **gode kenne** true kindred
The kyng of Sudenne
Ant hou he sloh a-felde°   **sloh a-felde** slew on the field
Him that is fader aquelde,°   killed
Ant seide, "Kyng so wyse,
1000 Yeld° me my service.   Repay
Rymenild help me to wynne
Swythe, that thou ne blynne,°   **ne blynne** may not fail
Ant Y shal do to house°   **do** . . . have at home
Thy dohter wel to spouse,°   **wel** . . . well married
1005 For hüe shal to spouse have
Athulf my gode felawe.°   companion
He is knyht mid the beste
Ant on of the treweste."
     The kyng seide so stille,°   quietly
1010 "Horn, do al thi wille."
He sende° tho by sonde°   sent   messenger
Yend° al is londe   Throughout
After knyhtes to fyhte
That were° men so lyhte.°   would be   agile
1015 To him come ynowe°   **come ynowe** came enough
That into shipe drowe.°   embarked
     Horn düde him in° the weye   **düde** . . . set out on
In a gret galeye.
The wynd bigon to blowe
1020 In a lütel throwe.°   while
The see bigan with ship to gon,°   go
To Westnesse hem brohte anon.°   soon

Hüe striken° seyl of maste | lowered
Ant ancre gonnen caste.° | **ancre . . .** cast anchor
1025 Matynes° were y-ronge | Matins
Ant the masse y-songe
Of Rymenild the yynge° | young
Ant of Mody the kynge;
Ant Horn wes in watere,
1030 Ne mihte he come no latere.
He let° is ship stonde° | had   stand to
Ant com him up to londe.
His folk he made abyde° | wait
Under a wode syde.
1035 Horn eode forh al one° | **eode . . .** went forth alone
So° he sprong of the stone. | As if
On° palmer he y-mette | A
Ant with wordes hyne grette:° | **hyne grette** greeted him
"Palmere, thou shalt me telle,"
1040 He seyde, "of thine spelle.° | news
So brouke thou° thi croune, | **So . . .** So may you save
Why comest thou from toune?"° | town
  Ant he seide on is tale,
"Y come from a brüdale,° | wedding
1045 From brüdale wylde
Of maide Remenylde,
Ne mihte hüe nout dreye
That hüe ne wep with eye.° |
Hüe seide that hüe nolde° | didn't want to
1050 Be spoused° with golde. | married
Hüe hade hosebonde,° | a husband
Thah° he were out of londe. | Though
  "Ich wes in the halle
Withinne the castel walle.
1055 Awey Y gon glide;° | **gon glide** stole
The dole° Y nolde abyde.° | sad event   **nolde abyde** didn't want to stand
Ther worth° a dole reuly.° | is happening   sorrowful
The brüde° wepeth bitterly." | bride
  Quoth Horn, "So Crist me rede,° | counsel
1060 We wölleth° chaunge wede.° | will   clothes
Tac thou robe myne,
Ant Y sclaveyn° thyne. | cloak
Today Y shal ther drynke
That° summe hit shal ofthynke."° | Where   regret
1065 Sclaveyn he gon doun legge° — | **gon . . .** laid down

1047–48. Nor could she manage not to weep with her eyes.

    Ant Horn hit düde on rügge°—   **düde** . . . put on his back

    Ant toc Hornes clothes,

    That nout him were lothe.°   **nout** . . . weren't unwelcome to him

    Horn toc bordoun ant scrippe°   **bordoun** . . . staff and wallet

1070 Ant gan° to wrynge° is lippe;   began twist

    He made foule chere°   **foule chere** a foul appearance

    Ant bicollede° is swere.°   blackened neck

    He com to the yateward,°   porter

    That him onswerede froward.°   defiantly

1075 Horn bed undo° wel softe°   **bed und**o asked to open gently

    Moni tyme ant ofte;

    Ne myhte he y-wynne°   **Ne** . . . But he couldn't manage

    For to come therynne.

    Horn the wyket puste°   **wyket puste** door pushed

1080 That° hit open fluste.°   So that sprang

    The porter shulde abügge;°   **shulde abügge** had to make atonement

    He threw him adoun the brügge°   **adoun** . . . over the drawbridge

    That thre ribbes crakede.

       Horn to halle rakede°   went

1085 Ant sette him doun° wel lowe   **sette** . . . sat down

    In the beggeres rowe.

    He lokede aboute

    Myd is collede snoute.°   **collede snoute** blackened nose

    Ther seh he Rymenild sitte

1090 Ase° hüe were out of wytte,°   As if her wits

    Wepinde sore;

    Ah he seh nower thore°   **seh** . . . saw nowhere there

    Athulf is gode felawe

    That trewe wes in üch plawe.°   **üch plawe** each engagement

1095   Athulf wes o tour° ful heh°   **o tour** in a tower high

    To loke fer ant eke neh°   **fer** . . . far and also near

    After° Hornes comynge   For

    Yef water him wolde brynge.

    The see he seh flowe

1100 Ah Horn nower rowe.°   **nower rowe** nowhere sailing

    He seyde on is songe,

    "Horn, thou art too longe.

    Rymenild thou me bitoke°   **me bitoke** entrusted to me

    That Ich hire shulde loke.°   guard

1105 Ich have y-loked evere,

    Ant thou ne comest nevere."

       Rymenild ros of benche

    The beer al for te shenche°   pour out

    After mete in sale,°   hall

1110 Bothe wyn ant ale.

An horn° hüe ber an° honde,   **drinking horn**   **ber an** carried in her
For that wes lawe° of londe.   the custom
Hüe dronc of the beere
To knyht ant skyere.°   squire
1115   Horn set at grounde;
Him thohte° he wes y-bounde.°   **Him thohte** It seemed as if   overwhelmed
He seide, "Quene so hende,°   gracious
To me hyderward thou wende.°   come hither
Thou shenh us° with the vürste;°   **Thou . . .** Pour for us   foremost
1120 The beggares büeth afurste."°   thirsty
Hyre horn hüe leyde adoune
Ant fülde him° of the broune°   **fülde him** filled for him   brown jug
A bolle of a galoun;°   **bolle . . .** gallon tankard
Hüe wende° he were° a glotoun.   expected   must be
1125 Hüe seide, "Tac the coppe,
Ant drync this ber al uppe.
Ne seh Y° never, Y wene,°   **Ne . . .** I saw   suppose
Beggare so kene."°   bold
    Horn toc hit hise y-fere°   **toc . . .** gave it to his companion
1130 Ant seide, "Quene so dere,
No beer nüllich i-bite°   **nüllich i-bite** will I take
Bote° of coppe white.   Except
Thou wenest° Ich be a beggere.   suppose
Y-wis,° Ich am a fysshere   Indeed
1135 Wel fer° come by weste°   far   **by weste** westward
To seche° mine beste.°   seek   advantage
Min net lyht° her wel hende°   lies   convenient
Withinne a wel feyr pende.°   enclosure
Ich have leye there°   **leye there** placed the net there
1140 Nou is this the sevethe yere.
Ich am i-come to loke
Yef eny fyssh hit toke.
Yef eny fyssh is therinne,
Therof thou shalt wynne.°   gain
1145 For° Ich am come to fyssh,   Since
Drynke nüll° Y of dyssh.   won't
Drynke to Horn of horn.
Wel fer° Ich have y-orne."°   far   traveled
    Rymenild him gan bihelde;°   **gan bihelde** beheld
1150 Hire herte fel to kelde.°   **fel . . .** ran cold
Ne kneu° hüe noht is° fysshyng   **Ne kneu** Neither recognized   **hüe . . .** his reference to
Ne° himselve nothyng,°   Nor   in any way
Ah wonder hyre gan thynke°   **hyre . . .** it seemed to her
Why for Horn he bed° drynke.   bade
1155 Hüe fülde the horn of wyne,

140

Ant dronk to that pelryne.°   pilgrim
Hüe seide, "Drync thi felle,
Ant seththen° thou me telle   then
Yef thou Horn ever seye°   saw
1160 Under° wode leye."°   In grove
     Horn dronk of horn a stounde°   while
Ant threu is ryng to grounde,°   the bottom
Ant seide, "Quene, thou thench°   **thou thench** think about
What Y threu° in the drench."°   have thrown drink
1165 The quene eode to boure
Mid hire maidnes foure;
Hüe fond that° hüe wolde,°   what wanted
The ryng y-graved° of golde   engraved
That Horn of her hedde.
1170 Ful sore hyre adredde°   **hyre adredde** she feared
That Horn ded were,
For his ryng was there.
Tho sende° hüe a damoisele   sent
After thilke° palmere.   that
1175   "Palmere," quoth hüe, "so trewe,
The ryng that thou yn threwe,
Thou sey° wer thou hit nome°   **Thou sey** Say   got
Ant hyder hou thou come."
     He seyde, "By Seint Gyle,
1180 Ich eode mony a myle
Wel fer yent° by weste   away
To seche° myne beste,°   seek advantage
Mi mete for te bydde,°   **for . . .** to beg
For so me tho bitidde.°   it happened to
1185 Ich fond Horn knyht stonde°   heading
To shipeward° at stronde.   **To shipeward** For a ship
He seide he wolde gesse°   **wolde gesse** was planning
To aryve at Westnesse.
The ship nom into flode°   **nom . . .** took to the sea
1190 With me ant Horn the gode.
Horn bygan be sek° ant deye   **be sek** to sicken
Ant for his love me preye°   begged
To gon with the rynge
To Rymenild the yynge.
1195 Wel ofte he hyne keste,°   **hyne keste** kissed it
Crist yeve is soule reste!"
     Rymenild seide at the firste,
"Herte, nou toberste.°   break
Horn worth thee° no more   **worth thee** exists for you
200 That haveth thee pyned° sore."   **That . . .** Who has tormented you

141

Hüe fel adoun a bedde
Ant after° knyves gredde° — for   cried out
To slein mide hire kyng lothe° — **slein** . . . slay her loathed king with
Ant hireselve bothe° — too
1205 Withinne thilke° nyhte, — that very
Come yef Horn ne myhte.° — **Come** . . . If Horn couldn't come
To herte knyf hüe sette.° — would set
Horn in is armes hire kepte.° — took
His shürte-lappe° he gan take — shirt's edge
1210 Ant wypede awey the foule blake
That wes opon his swere° — neck
Ant seide, "Lüef° so dere, — Sweetheart
Ne const° thou me y-knowe?° — **Ne const** Don't   recognize
Ne am Ich Horn thyn owe?° — own
1215 Ich, Horn of Westnesse,
In armes thou me kesse."
Y-clüpten° ant kyste — They embraced
So longe so hem lyste.° — **hem lyste** they wished
"Rymenild," quoth he, "Ich wende° — am going
1220 Doun to the wodes ende,
For ther büeth myne knyhte,
Worthi men ant lyhte,° — eager
Armed under clothe;° — their outer clothing
Hüe° shule make wrothe° — They   angry
1225 The kyng and hise gestes
That büeth at thise festes;° — festivities
Today Ychülle° hüem cacche. — will
Nou Ichülle hüem vacche."° — fetch
Horn sprong out of halle;
1230 Ys sclavin° he let falle. — cloak
Rymenild eode of boure;
Athulf hüe fond loure.° — **fond loure** found hiding
"Athulf, be wel blythe,° — happy
Ant to Horn go swythe.
1235 He is under wode bowe° — boughs
With felawes ynowe."° — enough
Athulf gon froth° springe — forth
For that ilke° tydynge. — same
Efter Horn he ernde;° — ran
1240 Him thohte° is herte bernde. — **Him thohte** It seemed as if
He oftok° him, y-wisse,° — overtook   indeed
Ant cüste° him with blysse. — kissed
Horn tok is preye° — band
Ant düde him° in the weye. — **düde him** set them
1245 Hüe comen° in wel sone— — came

142

	The yates° weren undone—	gates
	Y-armed swithe thicke°	heavily
	From fote to the nycke.	
	Alle° that ther evere weren,	All those
1250	Withoute° is trewe feren	Except for
	Ant the kyng Aylmare,	
	Y-wis° hüe hade muche care.	Indeed
	Monie that ther sete,	
	Hüre lyf hy gonne lete.°	**gonne lete** lost
1255	Horn understondyng ne hede°	**understondyng** ... had no idea
	Of Fykeles falssede.	
	Hüe sworen alle ant seyde	
	That hüre non° him wreyede°	**hüre non** none of them betrayed
	Ant swore othes holde°	**othes holde** to maintain their oaths
1260	That hüere non ne sholde°	would
	Horn never bytreye	
	Thah° he on dethe leye.	Though
	Ther hy ronge the belle	
	That wedlake° to fulfülle.	wedding
1265	Hüe wenden höm with eyse°	**Hüe** ... They went at leisure
	To the kynges paleyse.	
	Ther wes the brüdale° swete,	wedding feast
	For riche° men ther ete.°	noble ate
	Telle ne mihte no tonge	
1270	The gle° that ther was songe.	music
	Horn set in chayere	
	Ant bed° hem alle y-here.°	bade to listen
	He seyde, "Kyng of londe,	
	Mi tale thou understonde.	
1275	Ich wes y-bore in Sudenne;	
	Kyng wes mi fader of kenne.°	**of kenne** by descent
	Thou me to knyhte hove;°	raised
	Of knyhthod habbe Y prove.	
	Thou dryve° me out of thi lond	drove
1280	Ant seydest Ich wes traytour strong.	
	Thou wendest° that Ich wrohte°	assumed did
	That° Y ner ne thohte,°	What **ner** ... never thought of
	By Rymenild for te lygge.°	lie
	Y-wys,° Ich hit withsügge,°	Indeed deny
1285	Ne° shal Ich hit ner agynne°	Nor **hit** ... ever begin it
	Er Ich Sudenne wynne.	
	"Thou kep hyre me° a stounde,°	**Thou** ... Guard her for me while
	The while that Ich founde°	attempt to go
	Into myn heritage	
1290	With this Yrisshe page.	

That lond Ichülle thorhreche°　　　　recover
Ant do mi fader wreche.°　　　　**do . . .** avenge my father
Ychül be kyng of toune°　　　　the community
Ant lerne kynges roune.°　　　　**kynges roune** a king's lore
1295　Thenne shal Rymenild the yynge
Ligge° by Horn the kynge."　　　　Lie
　　　Horn gan to ship drawe°　　　　come
With hyse Yrisshe felawe,°　　　　companion
Athulf with him, his brother;
1300　He nolde habbe non other.
The ship bygan to croude;°　　　　push forward
The wynd bleu wel loude.
Wythinne dawes° fyve　　　　days
The ship began aryve.
1305　Under° Sudennes side°　　　　At　shore
Hüere ship bygon to ryde
Aboute the midnyhte.

　　　　[HORN IN SUDENE]
　　　Horn eode wel rihte.°　　　　**wel rihte** directly
He nom° Athulf by honde　　　　took
1310　Ant ede° up to londe.　　　　went
Hüe fonden° under shelde　　　　found
A knyht liggynde° on felde.　　　　lying
O° the shelde wes y-drawe°　　　　On　drawn
A croyz° of Jhesu Cristes lawe.°　　　　cross　religion
1315　The knyht him lay on slape,°　　　　**on slape** asleep
In armes wel y-shape.°　　　　provided
　　　Horn him gan y-take°　　　　**gan y-take** seized
Ant seide, "Knyht, awake.
Thou sei° me whet thou kepest°　　　　**Thou sei** Tell　are guarding
1320　Ant here whi thou slepest.
Me thüncheth,° by crois liste,°　　　　**Me thüncheth** It seems to me　**crois liste** the
　　　　　　　　devices of the cross
That thou levest on° Criste.　　　　**levest on** believe in
Bote° thou hit wolle shewe,°　　　　Unless　reveal
My swerd shal thee tohewe."°　　　　hew to pieces
1325　　The gode knyht up aros;
Of° Hornes wordes him agros.°　　　　At　**him agros** he shuddered
He seide, "Ich servy ille°　　　　**servy ille** serve miserably
Paynes toyeynes° mi wille.　　　　against
Ich was Cristene sumwhile.°　　　　once
1330　Y come° into this yle;°　　　　came　isle
Sarazyns lothe° ant blake　　　　loathsome
Me made Jhesu forsake.
[Bi God, on wam Y leve,°　　　　believe

Tho° hüe makeden me reve°]²   Then   warden
To loke° this passage   guard
For° Horn that is° of age,   Against   has come
1335 That woneth her by weste,°   **woneth . . .** lives west of here
God° knyht mid the beste.   A good
     "Hüe slowe° mid hüere honde   slew
The kyng of thisse londe
Ant with him mony honder.°   **mony honder** many hundred
1340 Therfore me thüncheth wonder°   **me . . .** it seems to me strange
That he° ne cometh to fyhte.   he (Horn)
God yeve him the myhte°   opportunity
That wynd him hider dryve°   may drive
To don° hem alle of° lyve!   put   out of
1345 Hüe slowen° kyng Mury,°   slew   Allof
Hornes cünesmon° hardy;   kinsman
Horn, of londe hüe senten;
Twelf children with him wenten.
With hem wes Athulf the gode,
1350 Mi child, myn oune fode.°   offspring
Yef Horn is hol° ant sounde,   whole
Athulf tit° no wounde.   suffers
He lovede Horn with mihte,
Ant he° him with ryhte.   he (Horn)
1355 Yef Y myhte se hem tweye,°   both
Thenne ne roht I for te deye."°   **ne . . .** I wouldn't care if I died
     "Knyht, be thenne blythe
Mest° of alle sythe.°   Most now   times
Athulf ant Horn is fere,
1360 Bothe we beth here."
     The knyht to Horn gan skippe
Ant in his armes clippe.°   embraced him
Muche joye hüe maden yfere°   together
Tho° hüe togedere y-come were.   When
1365 He saide with stevene° thare,   voice
"Yunge men, hou habbe ye yore y-fare?°   **yore y-fare** fared up to now
Wolle ye this lond wynne
Ant wonie° therynne?"   live
He seide, "Swete Horn child,
1370 Yet° lyveth thy moder Godyld.   Still
Of joie hüe ne miste°   **ne miste** wouldn't be lacking
Olyve° yef hüe thee wiste."°   Alive   knew to be
     Horn seide on is ryme,°   speech
"Y-blessed be the time!
1375 Ich am i-come into Sudenne

² These lines from another manuscript supply a necessary connection.

With fele° Yrisshemenne.   many
We shule the houndes kecche°   catch
Ant to the deghe vecche;°   **to . . .** bring to death
Ant so we shulen hem teche
1380 To speken oure speche."
     Horn gon is horn blowe.
Is folc hit con y-knowe;°   **con y-knowe** recognized
Hüe comen out of hürne°   hiding
To Horn swythe yürne.°   eagerly
1385 Hüe smiten° ant hüe fyhten°   struck   fought
The niht ant eke° the ohtoun.°   also   early dawn
The Sarazyns hüe slowe°   slew
Ant summe quike todrowe;°   **quike todrowe** alive tore to pieces
Mid speres ord° hüe stong°   point   pierced
1390 The olde and eke the yonge.
     Horn lette sone würche°   **lette . . .** had built
Bothe chapel and chyrche.
He made belle rynge°   **made . . .** ordered bells to be rung
Ant prestes masse synge.
1395 He sohte is moder° halle   mother's
In the roche° walle.   rock
He cüste° hire ant grette°   kissed   greeted
Ant into the castel fette.°   brought
Croune he gan werie°   **gan werie** began to wear
1400 Ant make feste° merye.   festivities
Mürie° he ther wrohte,°   Happiness   produced
Ah Rymenild hit abohte.°   **hit abohte** suffered for it
     The whiles Horn wes oute,
Fikenild ferde° aboute.   went
1405 The betere for te spede,°   succeed
The riche° he yef mede,°   **The riche** To the powerful **yef mede** gave bribes
Bothe yonge ant olde,
With him for te holde.°   retain
Ston he düde lade°   **düde lade** had delivered
1410 Ant lym therto° he made.   for it
Castel he made sette°   **made sette** caused to be placed
With water byflette,°   surrounded
That° theryn come ne myhte°   So that   **ne myhte** couldn't
Bote foul° with flyhte;   **Bote foul** Anything but a bird
1415 Bote when the see withdrowe,
Ther mihte come ynowe.°   enough
Thus Fykenild gon bywende°   **gon bywende** proceeded
Rymenild for te shende.°   **for . . .** to disgrace
To° wyve he gan hire yerne;°   As   **gan . . .** yearned for her
1420 The kyng ne durst° him werne°   dared   refuse

Ant habbeth set the day
Fykenild to wedde the may.°   maiden
Wo° was Rymenild of mode;°   Woeful   **of mode** in spirit
Terres° hüe wepte of blode.   Tears
1425   Thilke° nyht Horn swete   That
Con wel harde mete°   **Con . . .** Dreamed very vividly
Of Rymenild his make°   mate
That into shipe wes take.
The ship gon overblenche;°   **gon overblenche** began to overturn
1430 Is lemmon shulde adrenche;°   **lemmon . . .** sweetheart was to drown
Rymenild mid hire honde
Swymme wolde° to londe;   was trying to
Fykenild ayeyn hire pylte°   **ayeyn . . .** pushed her back
Mid his swerdes hylte.
1435 Horn awek in is bed;
Of° his lemmon he wes adred.°   For   afraid
    "Athulf," he seide, "felawe,°   my companion
To shipe nou we drawe.°   **we drawe** let us go
Fykenild me hath gon under°   **gon under** betrayed
1440 Ant do° Rymenild sum wonder.°   has done   **sum wonder** something strange
Crist, for his wondes° fyve,   wounds
Tonyht thider us dryve!"
    Horn gon to shipe ride,
His knyhtes bi his side.
1445 The ship bigon to stüre°   sail
With wynd god of cüre;°   choice
Ant Fykenild, her° the day-springe,   before
Seide° to the kynge   Spoke
After° Rymenild the bryhte°   For   radiant
1450 Ant spousede° hyre by nyhte.   married
He ladde hire by derke
Into is newe werke.°   castle
The feste° hüe bigonne   festivities
Er then aryse° the sonne.   **Er . . .** Before arose

     [HORN IN WESTNESSE]
1455   Hornes ship atstod° in Stoure   stood to
Under Fykenildes boure.
Nüste° Horn alyve°   Didn't know   at all
Wher he wes aryve.
Thene° castel hüe ne knewe,   The
1460 For he° was so newe.   it
The see bigon to withdrawe;
Tho seh Horn his felawe°   companion
The feyre knyht Arnoldyn,

147

That wes Athulfes cosyn,
1465 That ther set° in that tyde   sat
Kyng Horn to abide.°   wait for
    He seide, "Kyng Horn, kynges sone,
Hider thou art welcome.
Today hath Sire Fykenild
1470 Y-wedded thi wif Rymenild.
White thee° nou this while,   **White thee** Guard yourself
He haveth do thee gyle.°   **do** . . . deceived you
This tour he düde make
Al for Rymenildes sake;
1475 Ne may ther comen ynne
No mon with no gynne.°   **no gynne** any stratagem
    "Horn, nou Crist thee wisse°   direct
Rymenild that thou ne misse."
    Horn couthe° alle the listes°   knew   tricks
1480 That eni mon of wiste.°   **of wiste** knew of
Harpe he gon shewe
Ant toc him to felawe°   **him** . . . to him as companions
Knyhtes of the beste
That he ever hede of weste.°   **of weste** from the west
1485 Oven o° the sherte   **Oven o** Over
Hüe gürden hüem° with swerde.   **gürden hüem** equipped themselves
Hüe eoden on the gravele
Towart the castele.
Hüe gonne mürie singe
1490 Ant makeden hüere gleynge°   music
That Fykenild mihte y-here.
    He axede who hit were.
Men seide hit were harpeirs,
Jogelers, ant fythelers.
1495 Hem me düde in lete.°   **Hem** . . . They were allowed in
At halle dore hüe sete.°   sat down
Horn sette him a° benche;   **him a** himself on a
Is harpe he gan clenche.°   **gan clenche** began to pluck
He make Rymenild a lay,
1500 Ant hüe seide "Weylawey."°   Alas
Rymenild fel y swowe;°   **y swowe** in a swoon
Tho nes ther° non that lowe.°   **nes ther** there was   laughed
Hit smot Horn to herte;
Sore con him smerte.°   **con** . . . he smarted
1505 He lokede on is rynge
Ant o Rymenild the yynge.
He eode up to borde.°   the table
Mid his gode sworde

Fykenildes croune°   head
1510 He fel° ther adoune,   cut
Ant alle is men a rowe°   **a rowe** in turn
He düde adoun throwe,
Ant made Arnoldyn kyng there,
After kyng Aylmere
1515 To be kyng of Westnesse,
For° his mildenesse;   Because of
The kyng ant is baronage
Yeven° him truage.°   Gave   tribute
    Horn toc Rymenild by honde
1520 Ant ladde hire to stronde
Ant toc with him Athelbrus,
The gode stiward of hire fader° hous.   father's
The see bigan to flowen,
Ant hy° faste to rowen.   they

      [HORN IN REYNIS]
1525   Hüe aryveden under Reme°   **under Reme** at Reynis
In a wel feyr streme.
Kyng Mody wes kyng in that lond,
That Horn sloh° with is hond.   slew
Athelbrus he made ther kyng
1530 For his gode techyng;
For Sire Hornes lore°   instruction
He wes mad kyng thore.°   there

      [HORN IN IRELAND]
  Horn eode to ryve;°   the shore
The wynd him con wel dryve.
1535 He aryvede in Yrlonde,
Ther Horn wo couthe er fonde.°   **wo** . . . previously found woe
He made ther Athulf Chyld
Wedde mayden Ermenyld;
Ant Horn com to Sudenne,
1540 To is oune kenne.°   kin

      [HORN IN SUDENE]
  Rymenild he made ther is quene,   be
So hit myhte bene.°
In trewe love hüe lyveden ay,   law
Ant wel hüe loveden Godes lay.°
1545   Nou hüe beoth bothe dede.
Crist to heovene us lede.
        Amen.

The Bestiary

(ca. 1225–50, East Midland)

The lore of beasts, birds, and fishes provided a rich and enduring popular source of Christian allegory throughout the Middle Ages. As early as the fifth century, a scholar now known only as Physiologus prepared an allegorical bestiary in Greek, and his work was subsequently imitated throughout the western world. The Old English bestiary contained in the *Exeter Book* (ca. 970–80), though fragmentary, is typical of the tradition; it demonstrates that the panther betokens Christ, the whale betokens the devil, and the partridge betokens God. For the Norman aristocracy Philipe de Thaun produced a much more extensive Anglo-Norman *Bestiaire* (ca. 1125), which was soon followed by other Anglo-Norman versions. The bestiary excerpted here is the only extant example of the genre recorded in Middle English. It is based on a Latin adaptation composed in the eleventh century by Theobald the Italian and contains 802 lines.

The Middle English author includes Theobald's lion, eagle, worm (serpent), ant, hart, fox, spider, whale, mermaid, elephant, turtledove, and panther; he omits Theobald's centaur and adds from another source the culver (dove). He matches the artistic variations of Theobald's Latin meters by moving between the older English alliterative patterns and the newer rhyming lines; see Introduction, type 3, p. 30.

Naive and derivative though it may be, this remnant of the Middle English period serves well to indicate the continuity of medieval allegory in the native English tradition. Chaucer's Nun's Priest blandly cites Physiologus as the authority for his assertion that mermaids sing. Even in the Elizabethan period the fashionable euphuistic style of John Lyly depended heavily, as Drayton complained, on the ancient topics:

> Talking of stones, stars, plants, of fishes, flies,
> Playing with words and idle similes.

And in seeking an appropriate epic simile for Satan, Milton resorted to the familiar figure of the deceptive whale, already expounded in the Old English and the Middle English bestiaries.

The best edition of the Middle English bestiary is in Joseph Hall, *Selections from Early Middle English* (Oxford, 1920), I, 176–96; II, 579–626. For background see Beatrice White, "Medieval Animal Lore," *Anglia*, 72 (1954), 21–30, and Francis Carmody, "Bestiary," *New Catholic Encyclopedia*, II (Washington, 1967), 367–69. For bibliography see Wells, ch. 2.24; *CBEL*, 1. 182–83, 5.122.

The Bestiary

[Lines 384–455]

Natura Wulpis[1]

	A wilde der is°	**der is** creature there is
	That is ful of fele° wiles;	many
	Fox is hire to name.	
	For hire quethsipe°	wickedness
5	Husebondes° hire haten,	Householders
	For hire harm-dedes.	
	The coc and the capun	
	Ge° feccheth ofte in the tun,°	She enclosure
	And the gandre and the gos	
10	Bi the necke and bi the nos°	beak
	Haleth is° to hire hole.	**Haleth is** She brings them
	For-thi° man hire hatieth,	Therefore
	Hatien and hulen°	howl at her
	Bothe men and fules.°	birds
15	Listneth° nu a wunder	Hear
	That this der° doth for hunger:	**this der** this creature
	Goth o felde° to a furgh°	**Goth . . .** She goes afield furrow
	And falleth tharinne,	
	In eried° lond er° in erth-chine,°	ploughed or gully
20	For to bilirten fugeles.°	**bilirten fugeles** deceive birds
	Ne stereth ge noght of° the stede°	**Ne . . .** She doesn't stir from spot
	A god stund deies°	**stund deies** part of a day
	Oc dareth so° ge ded were;	**Oc . . .** But lies still as if
	Ne drageth° ge non onde.°	draws breath
25	The raven is swithe° redi,	very
	Weneth° that ge rotieth,°	Assumes **ge rotieth** she (the fox) is decaying
	And othre fules hire fallen bi°	**hire . . .** alight beside her
	For to winnen fode	
	Derflike° withuten dred.°	Boldly fear
30	He° wenen that ge° ded beth.°	They she is
	He wüllen on° this foxes fel,°	**wüllen on** want to get onto skin
	And ge° it wel feleth.°	she perceives
	Ligtlike° ge lepeth up	Quickly
	And letteth° hem sone;°	stops at once
35	Gelt° hem here billing°	She repays **here billing** for their jabbing
	Rathe° with illing;°	Swiftly malice
	Tetoggeth° and tetireth° hem	She rends rips
	Mid hire teth sharpe;	
	Fret° hire fille	Devours
40	And goth than ther ge° wille.	**ther ge** where she

[1] The nature of the fox.

151

Significacio prima[2]

Twifold forbisne° in this der°
To frame° we mugen° finden her,
Warsipe° and wisedom
With° devel and with ivel man
45   The devel dereth dernelike.°
He lat° he ne wile us nogt biswike.°
He lat he ne wile us don° non loth°
And bringeth us in a sinne
And ther° he us sloth.°
50   He bit° us don ure bukes° wille,
Eten and drinken with unskil,°
And in° ure skemting°
He doth rathe a foxing.°
    He billeth one° the foxes fel°
55   Wo-so° telleth idel spel,°
And he tireth on° his ket°
Wo-so him° with sinne fet,°
And devel geld swilk billing°
With shame and with sending°
60   And, for his sinfule werk,
Ledeth man to helle merk.°

Twifold forbisne A twofold example   creature
To frame Of use   may
Prudence
Against
dereth dernelike lies secretly
pretends   **ne . . .** will not deceive us
do   harm

there   slays
bids   **ure bukes** our belly's
imprudence
during   amusement
doth . . . swiftly acts the fox's role
billeth one jabs at   skin
Whosoever   **idel spel** a lying tale
tireth on rips at   carrion
himself   feeds
geld . . . repays such jabbing
disgrace

helle merk hell's darkness

Significacio secunda[3]

The devel is thus the fox ilik°
Mid ivele breides° and with swik;°
And man° also the foxes name
65   Arn° wurthi to haven shame.°
For wo-so seieth other god°
And thenketh ivel on his mod,°
Fox he is and fend i-wis.°
The Boc ne legeth nogt° of this.
70   So was Herodes fox and flerd°
Tho° Crist kam into this middel erd;°
He seide he wulde him leven on°
And thogte he wulde him fordon.°

like
ivele breides evil tricks   deception
men
Are   in shame
wo-so . . . whoever says good to another
mind
fend i-wis fiend indeed
ne . . . does not lie
deceiver
When   earth
leven on believe in
destroy

---

[2] First allegorical meaning.
[3] Second allegorical meaning.

Judas

(ca. 1250, Southwestern)

❧

Judas has been called the earliest recorded example of an English ballad, though strictly speaking, it belongs to the genre of religious carol. The narrative is drawn in part from the New Testament and in part from the medieval traditions associated with Judas. Here, in a unique development, it is the sister of Judas who is ultimately responsible for the betrayal of Christ—a thoroughly antifeminist invention in keeping with the medieval assumption that Eve was the origin of evil.

The meter is seven-beat couplets; see Introduction, type 7, page 31.

The ballad may be found in F. J. Child, ed., *English and Scottish Popular Ballads* (Cambridge, Mass., 1882), No. 23, and in Carleton Brown, ed., *English Lyrics of the Thirteenth Century* (Oxford, 1932), pp. 38–39. For bibliography see Wells, ch. 5.48; Chambers, OHEL, pp. 51–53.

Hit wes upon a Scere° Thorsday	Maundy	
That ure Loverd° aros.	Lord	
Ful milde were the wordes		
He spec° to Judas.	spoke	
5 "Judas, thou most° to Jurselem	must go	
Oure mete for to bügge.°	buy	
Thritti platen° of selver	pieces	
Thou bere upo° thi rügge.°	**Thou** . . . Carry upon back	
"Thou comest fer i° the brode stret,	**fer i** far in	
10 Fer i the brode strete.		
Summe of thine tunesmen°	townspeople	
Ther thou meight i-mete."°	**meight i-mete** may meet	
I-mette° wid is söster,°	He met **is söster** his sister	
The swikele wimon.°	**swikele wimon** treacherous woman	
15 "Judas, thou were würthe°	**were würthe** deserve that	
Me stende° thee wid ston.	**Me stende** People stone	
"Judas, thou were würthe		
Me stende thee wid ston		

153

For the false prophete
20   That thou bilevest upon."

"Be stille, leve söster.°   **leve söster** dear sister
    Thin herte thee tobreke!°   **Thin . . .** May your heart shatter
Wiste min loverd Crist,°   **Wiste . . .** If my lord Christ knew
    Ful wel he wolde be wreke."°   avenged

25   "Judas, go thou on the roc,
    Heie upon the ston.
Lei thin heved i° my barm.°   **heved i** head on   bosom
    Slep thou thee° anon."   **Slep . . .** Sleep

Sone so° Judas   **Sone so** As soon as
30   Of° slepe was awake,   From
Thritti platen° of selver   pieces
    From hym weren i-take.

He drou° hymselve bi the cop°   tore   crown
    That° al it lavede a° blode.   So that   **lavede a** was bathed in
35   The Jewes out of Jurselem
    Awenden° he were wode.°   Assumed   crazy

Foreth hym com° the riche Jeu **Foreth . . .** Forth came
    That heighte° Pilatus.   was called
"Wolte sülle° thi Loverd°   **Wolte sülle** Will you sell   Lord
40   That hette° Jesus?"   is called

"I nül° sülle my Loverd   won't
    For nones cünnes eighte°   **nones . . .** any kind of property
Bote° hit be for the thritti platen° Unless   pieces
    That he me bitaighte."°   entrusted

45   "Wolte sülle° thi Lord Crist **Wolte sülle** Will you sell
    For enes° cünnes golde?"   any
"Nay, bote hit be for the platen
    That he habben wolde."

In him com ur Lord gon°   **In . . .** In came our Lord
    As is postles seten° at mete.° **is . . .** his apostles sat   their meal
50   "Wou° sitte ye, postles,   Why
    Ant wi nüle° ye ete?   won't

"Wou sitte ye, postles,
    Ant wi nüle ye ete?
55   Ic am i-bought ant i-sold today
      For oure mete."

Up stod him Judas:
    "Lord, am I that?
    I nas° never o° the stüde°   was   in   place
60   Ther me thee° evel spec."°   **Ther** ... Where people against you   spoke

Up him stod Peter
    Ant spec wid al is° mighte: his
"Thau° Pilatus him come   Though
    Wid ten hundred cnightes,

65 "Thau Pilatus him com
    Wid ten hundred cnightes,
Yet Ic wolde, Loverd,
    For thi love fighte."

"Still thou be, Peter.
70   Wel I thee i-cnowe.
Thou wolt fursake me thrien°   thrice
    Ar° the coc him crowe."   Before

THOMAS OF HAILES

A Love Rune

(ca. 1224–72, Southwestern)

༄

Nothing is known about the author of this remarkable poem except that, according to the scribe of the only surviving manuscript, "Frater Thomas de Hales" belonged to the order of Fratres Minores (the Minorites, or Franciscans, who first came to England in 1224) and composed the work for a girl who had dedicated herself to God. Presumably Friar Thomas or his family originated in the village of Hailes (near Gloucester); the Southwestern dialect of the piece supports this likelihood.

The friar's transfer of the language of love to the language of religion is a standard medieval device; his argument that the girl should find contentment by becoming the bride of Christ is a familiar one, already fully developed in *The Anchoresses' Rule* (p. 106); and the various reminders of the vanity of the world are commonplace. Yet the poem has a striking individuality because of the rich allusiveness of its imagery. The *love rune* (l. 2), which the girl requests, according to medieval usage would normally be a love spell by which to bind an earthly lover to herself; but the friar redirects the incantation toward heavenly love. The heroes and lovers whom he mentions (ll. 65–70) are the favorite exemplars of medieval narrative: Hector and Caesar, two of the Nine Worthies; Paris and Helen, from the classical tradition; Amadas and Ydoine, from Anglo-Norman romance; and Tristram and Isolde, from Celtic legend. But the friar introduces these names only to epitomize all that is transitory. The precious stones (ll. 169–76) that he lists are such that, in a courtly lay, bedeck a heroine, but the friar subordinates all of these to the gemstone of virginity. His theme is *fyn amur* (l. 182), but the usual sense of 'refined courtly love' is here irrelevant, for the friar has exalted his poem to the higher level of spiritual love.

The meter is eight-line stanzas, with four beats to a line; see Introduction, type 18, page 32.

The best edition is found in Carleton Brown, ed., *English Lyrics of the Thirteenth Century* (Oxford, 1932), pp. 68–74. For bibliography see Wells, ch. 13.173; Legge, pp. 227–28.

A mayde Cristes me bit yörne°
    That Ich hire würche° a luve ron
For-whan heo° myhte best i-leorne
    To taken onother soth lefmon°
5 That treowest were° of alle berne°
    And best wyte cuthe° a freo° wymmon.
Ich hire nüle nowiht werne;°
    Ich hire wüle teche as Ic con:

bit yörne is asking eagerly
hire würche compose for her
For-whan heo So that she
soth lefmon true lover
treowest were most faithful would men
wyte cuthe would know how to prot⸱ noble
nüle . . . will in no way refuse

156

"Mayde, her thu myht biholde°   **myht biholde** can see that
10   This worldes luve nys bute o res°   **nys . . .** is only on the run
And is byset° so fele-volde,°   harassed   variously
    Vikel and frakel and wok and les.°
Theos theines° that her weren bolde   **Theos theines** The leaders
    Beoth aglyden so° wyndes bles;°   **Beoth . . .** Have glided away like   gust
15 Under molde° hi liggeth° colde   earth   lie
    And faleweth so° döth medewe gres.°   **faleweth so** fade as   grass

"Nis° no mon i-boren o lyve°   There is   **i-boren . . .** born alive
    That her may beon stüdevest,°   **may . . .** can be steadfast
For her he haveth seorewen ryve,°   **seorewen ryve** sorrows rife
20 Ne tyt° him never ro° ne rest.   **Ne tyt** Nor befall   **never ro** ever peace
Toward his ende he hyeth blyve,°   **hyeth blyve** hastens fast
    And lütle hwile he her i-lest.°   survives
Pyne° and deth him wile ofdryve°   Pain   kill
    Hwenne° he weneth° to libben° best.   Just when   expects   live

25 "Nis° non so riche ne non so freo°   There is   noble
    That he ne schal heonne° sone away;   **ne . . .** shall not go hence
Ne may hit never his waraunt beo
    Gold, ne seolver, vouh, ne gray.°
Ne beo he no the° swift, ne may he fleo°   **Ne . . .** Be he ever so   **ne . . .** he can't fly
30 Ne weren° his lif enne° day.   **Ne weren** Or save   for one
Thus is thes world, as thu mayht seo,°   see
    Also° the schadewe that glyt° away.   Just like   glides

"This world fareth hwilynde;°   **fareth hwilynde** passes in transition
    Hwenne on° cumeth, another göth;   one
35 That° wes bifore nu is bihynde;   What
    That er° was leof,° nu hit is loth.°   once   dear   hated
Forthi° he doth as the blynde°   Therefore   blind man does
    That in this world his luve döth.°   puts
Ye mowen i-seo° the world aswynde.°   **mowen i-seo** can see   decay
40 That wouh° göth forth,° abak that soth.°   **That wouh** Wrong   forward   **abak . . .** backward truth

"The luve that ne may her abyde,°   **ne . . .** can't last here
    Thu treowest hire° myd müchel wouh,°   **treowest hire** trust it   **müchel wouh** much wrong
Also° hwenne hit schal toglide,°   As   **schal toglide** is to vanish
    Hit is fals, and mereuh, and frouh,°   **mereuh . . .** weak, and brittle
45 And fromward° in üych-on tide.°   perverse   **üych-on tide** every occasion
    Hwile hit lesteth is° seorewe inouh;°   **lesteth is** lasts there is   enough
An° ende, ne werie mon so syde,°   In the   **ne . . .** even if a man guard ever so widely
    He schal todreosen so° lef on bouh.°   **todreosen so** decay like   bough

12. Fickle and foul and weak and deceiving.
27–28. Nor can gold or silver or striped fur or gray ever be his guarantee.

"Monnes luve nys buten o stunde;° nys . . . lasts but awhile
50 Nu he luveth, nu he is sad;° sated
Nu he cumeth, nu wile he funde;° go
Nu he is wroth,° nu he is gled. angry
His luve is her and ek a lunde.° her . . . here and also away (?)
Nu he luveth sum that he er bed.° er bed previously challenged
55 Nis he never treowe i-funde;°
That° him tristeth,° he is amed.° He who trusts mad

"Yf mon is riche of° worldes weole,° in wealth
Hit maketh his heorte smerte and ake.
If he dret° that me° him stele,° dreads people rob
60 Thenne döth° him pyne° nyhtes wake.° causes torment to lie awake
Him waxeth° thouhtes monye and fele° Him waxeth In him rise various
Hu he hit may witen° withuten sake.° guard strife
An° ende, hwat helpeth hit to hele?° In the conceal
Al deth° hit wile from him take. death

65 "Hwer is Paris and Heleyne,
That weren so bryht and feyre on bleo;° on bleo of feature
Amadas, Tristram, and Ideyne,
Yseude, and alle theo;° those
Ector with his scharpe meyne,° scharpe meyne fierce retinue
70 And Cesar riche of° worldes feo?° in possessions
Heo beoth° i-glyden ut of the reyne° Heo beoth They have realm
So the schef° is of the cleo.° sheaf hill (?)

"Hit is of heom al-so° hit nere.° heom al-so them as if had never been
Of heom me° haveth wunder i-told,° people wunder i-told related marvels
75 Nere hit reuthe° for to heren° Nere . . . Were it not pity hear
Hu hi° were with pyne aquold° they pyne aquold torment destroyed
And hwat hi tholeden° alyve here. suffered
Al is heore hot i-turnd to cold.
Thus is thes world of false fere.° appearance
80 Fol° he is the° on hire° is bold. A fool who it

"Theyh° he were so riche mon Though
As Henry° ure kyng Henry III (r. 1216–72)
And al-so veyr° as Absalon, al-so veyr as fair
That nevede° on eorthe non evenyng,° had not non evenyng any equal
85 Al were sone his prüte agon.° prüte agon pride gone
Hit nere, on° ende, wurth on heryng!° nere, on wouldn't be, in the wurth . .
  worth a herring
Mayde, if thu wilnest after leofmon,° wilnest . . . wish a lover
Ich teche° thee enne treowe° king. direct enne treowe to a true

55. He is never found to be faithful

"A, swete,° if thu i-knöwe°
90 The gode thewes° of thisse childe!°
He is feyr and bryht of heowe,°
    Of glede chere, of mode° mylde,
Of lufsum lost, of truste treowe,°
    Freo° of heorte, of wisdom vilde.°
95 Ne thurhte thee° never rewe,°
    Myhtestu do thee° in his ylde.°

"He is ricchest mon of londe
    So wide so° mon speketh with muth.
Alle heo beoth to° his honde,
100 Est and west, north and suth.
Henri king of Engelonde
    Of° him he halt° and to hym buhth.°
Mayde, to thee he send° his sonde°
    And wilneth° for to beo thee cuth.°

105 "Ne byt he° with thee lond ne leode,°
    Vouh° ne gray, ne rencyan.°
Naveth° he therto none neode;°
    He is riche and weli° man.
If thu him woldest luve beode°
110 And bycumen° his leovemon,°
He brouhte° thee to such wede°
    That naveth king ne kayser° non.

"Hwat spekestu° of eny bolde°
    That wrouhte the wise Salomon
115 Of jaspe,° of saphir, of merede° golde,
    And of mony onother ston?
Hit is feyrure of feole-volde°
    More than Ich eu telle con.
This bold,° mayde, thee° is bihote°
120 If that thu bist° his leovemon.°

"Hit stont° uppon a treowe mote°
    Thar° hit never truke° ne schal;
Ne may no mynur hire underwrote°
    Ne never false thene grund-wal.°
125 Tharinne is üich balewes bote,°
    Blisse and joye and gleo and gal.°
This bold,° mayde, is thee bihote°
    And üych-o° blisse thar wythal.

123. Nor can any sapper undermine it

---

Glosses (right column):

swete sweetheart   i-knöwe only knew
thewes virtues   childe squire
heowe hue
mode spirit
lufsum ... lovable spirit, true of trust
Freo Noble   vilde filled
Ne ... You would need   rewe regret
Myhtestu ... If you could put yourself
    protection

So ... As far as
Alle ... All these lands are in

Of ... From   halt holds as vassal   buhth yields
send sends   sonde messenger
wilneth wishes   beo ... be known to you

Ne ... He doesn't demand as dowry
    leode people
Vouh Striped fur   rencyan fine cloth
Naveth Has   therto ... no need for that
weli wealthy
beode offer
bycumen become   leovemon lover
brouhte would bring   wede clothing
kayser emperor

spekestu do you say   bolde building

jaspe jasper   merede refined

of feole-volde many times

bold building   thee to you   bihote promised
bist will be   leovemon lover

stont stands   treowe mote secure eminence
Thar Where   truke fail

false ... breach the foundation
üich ... each sorrow's cure
gleo ... mirth and song
bold building   bihote promised
üych-o every

159

"Ther ne may° no freond fleon other,°
130   Ne non furleosen° his i-ryhte.°
Ther nys° hate ne wretth nouther,°
    Of prüde° ne of onde° of none wihte.°
Alle heo schule° wyth engles pleye
    Some and sauhte° in heovene° lyhte.
135 Ne beoth heo,° mayde, in gode weye°
    That° wel luveth ure dryhte?°

"Ne may no° mon hine i-seo°
    Also° he is in his mihte
That may withuten blisse beo°
140   Hwanne he i-sihth° ure drihte.
His sihte° is al joye and gleo;°
    He is day wythute nyhte.
Nere he,° mayde, ful seoly°
    That myhte wunye° myd such a knyhte?

145 "He haveth bitauht° thee o° tresur
    That is betere than gold other pel°
And bit° thee luke° thine bur°
    And wilneth° that thu hit wyte° wel.
Wyth theoves,° with reveres,° with lechurs
150   Thu most beo waker and snel.°
Thu art swetture° thane eny flur
    Hwile thu witest thene° kastel.

"Hit is ymston of feor i-boren;°
    Nys° non betere under heovene grunde.°
155 He° is tofore° alle othre i-coren;°
    He heleth alle luve wunde.°
Wel were° alyve i-boren°
    That° myhte wyten° this ilke stunde,°
For, habbe thu hine enes forloren,°
160   Ne byth he° never eft° i-funde.

"This ilke ston that Ich thee nemne°
    Maydenhod i-cleoped° is.
Hit is o derewurthe° gemme.
    Of alle othre he berth that pris°
165 And bryngeth thee withute wemme°
    Into the blysse of Paradis.
The hwile° thu hyne witest° under thine hemme,°
    Thu ert swetture° than eny spis.°

ne may can   avoid another
non furleosen anyone lose   rights
is no   **ne . . .** or wrath either
pride   envy   person
Alle . . . They are all destined to
Some . . . United and reconciled   heaven's
Ne . . . Are they not   circumstances
Who   lord

Ne . . . Nor can any   **hine i-seo** see him
As

withuten . . . remain joyless
sees
His sihte The sight of him   happiness

Nere he Would not he be   blessed
dwell

granted   a
other pel or purple
orders   to close   bower
wishes   guard
Wyth theoves Against thieves   robbers
most . . . must be watchful and quick
sweeter
witest thene guard the

ymston . . . gemstone brought from afar
It is   **heovene grunde** the floor of heaven
It (virginity)   before   chosen
luve wunde the wounds of love
would be   born
Anyone who   guard   **ilke stunde** same state
habbe . . . once you have lost it
Ne . . . It will be   again

thee nemne name to you
Maydenhod i-cleoped Virginity called
o derewurthe a precious
he . . . it wins the prize
flaw

The hwile As long as   guard it   clothing
ert swetture are sweeter   spice

160

"Hwat spekstu° of eny stone   do you say
170   That beoth in vertu other in° grace—   **beoth** ... possesses power or
    Of amatiste, of calcydone,°   chalcedony
        Of lectorie° and tupace,°   cock-stone   topaz
    Of jaspe, of saphir, of sardone,°   sardonyx
        Smaragde,° beril, and crisopace?°   Emerald   chrysoprase
175 Among alle othre ymstone°   gemstones
        Thes beoth deorre[1] in uyche° place.   every

"Mayde, also° Ich thee tolde,   as
        The ymston of thi bur°   bower
    He° is betere an hundred-folde   It
180   Than alle theos in heore° culur.   their
    He is i-don° in heovene° golde   set   heavenly
        And is ful of fyn amur.°   **fyn amur** pure love
    Alle that myhte hine wite° scholde,   **myhte** ... might be able to guard it
        He schyneth so bryht in heovene bur.

185 "Hwen thu me dost in thine rede°   **me** ... consult me
        For thee to choose a leofman,°   lover
    Ich wile don as thu me bede°   ask
        The beste that Ich fynde con.
    Ne doth he,° mayde, on üvele° dede   **Ne** ... Doesn't he commit   **on üvele** an evil
190   That may cheose of two that on°   **that on** the one
    And° he wile withute neode   If
        Take thet wurse, the betere let gon?

"This rym, mayde, Ich thee sende
        Open and withute sel.°   seal
195 Bidde° Ic that thu hit untrende°   Ask   unroll
        And leorny bute bok üych del°
    Herof° that thu beo swithe hende,°   Of it   **beo** ... may be very apt
        And tech hit° other maydenes wel.   **tech hit** teach it to
    Hwo-so cuthe° hit to than° ende,   **Hwo-so cuthe** Whoever might know   the
200   Hit wolde him stonde müchel stel.°   **stonde** ... give much aid

"Hwenne thu sittest in longynge,
        Drauh thee forth° this ilke wryt.°   **Drauh** ... Draw you out   **ilke wryt** same composition
    Mid swete stephne° thu hit singe,   voice
        And do also° hit thee byt.°   as   commands

---

[1] 'These are precious.' Nine of the ten stones mentioned here belong to the group of twelve precious stones enumerated in Rev. xxi. 19–20 (referred to in *The Pearl*, ll. 999 ff.); the other stone, *lectorie* (properly, *alectorie*), according to Bartholomew de Glanville, "exciteth the service of Venus."
196. And learn without book (i.e., by heart) each part

205 To thee he haveth send one° gretynge.   **he** . . . it has sent a
     God almyhti thee beo myd°   **beo myd** be with
     And leve cumen° to his brüdthinge°   **leve cumen** grant you to come   bridal
     Heye° in heovene ther° he sit."°   High   where   sits

     And yeve° him god endynge   give
210   That haveth i-wryten this ilke wryt.°   **ilke wryt** same composition
          Amen.

The Sayings of St. Bernard

(ca. 1275, West Midland or East Midland)

ᏆᏆ

This powerful poem survives in five manuscripts, each of which contains a slightly different version. The Digby Manuscript contains thirty-one stanzas, and the last ten stanzas, which are printed here, were set apart by the scribe under a separate heading.

In the first part of the poem the author warns his listeners against their three foes, the world, the flesh, and the Devil, and he then turns to the familiar question, "Where are those who were before us?" The poem is attributed to St. Bernard of Clairvaux (1090–1153), the great Cistercian leader, but does not correspond to any of his writings except in its spiritual fervor.

The poem is cast in six-line, tail-rhyme stanzas; see Introduction, type 14, page 32.

The best edition of the various versions is still *The Minor Poems of the Vernon MS*, ed. F. J. Furnivall, EETS 117 (London, 1901), 511–22, 757–63. For the Harley manuscript see *Facsimile of British Museum MS. Harley 2253*, ed. N. R. Ker, EETS, 25 (London, 1965), item 74. For bibliography see Wells, ch. 7.30; Brown and Robbins, *Index*, items 2865, 3310.

Ubi sunt qui ante nos fuerunt ?

Were beth they° biforen us weren,   **Were . . .** Where are they who
Houndes ladden,° and hawekes beren,°   led   bore
    And hadden feld and wode?
The riche levedies° in hoere° bour,   ladies   their
5   That wereden gold in hoere tressour,°   coiffures
    With hoere brightte rode,°   complexions

Eten and drounken and maden hem° glad;   themselves
Hoere lif was al with gamen i-lad;°   **gamen i-lad** games spent
    Men keneleden° hem biforen.   knelt
10 They beren hem° wel swithe heye,°   **beren hem** bore themselves   **swithe heye**
                                                      very high
And in a twincling of on° eye   an
    Hoere° soules weren forloren.°   Their   lost

Were° is that lawing° and that song,   Where   laughter
That trayling° and that proude yong,°   **That trayling** The trailing clothes   walking
15   Tho° hawekes and tho houndes?   Those

Al that joye is went away;
That wele° is comen te weylaway,°   well-being **te weylaway** to woe
   To manie harde stoundes.°   trials

    Hoere° paradis hy nomen° here,   Their **hy nomen** they took
20 And now they lien° in helle ifere.°   lie together
   The füir° hit brennes hevere.°   fire **brennes hevere** burns ever
    Long is ay,° and long is ho;°   aye always
    Long is wy,° and long is wo.   alas
      Thennes ne cometh they nevere.

25 Dreghy° here, man, thenne, if thou wilt,   Endure
    A lüitel pine° that me° thee bit.°   torment people offer
     Withdrau° thine eyses° ofte.   Draw from pleasures
    They° thi pine be ounrede,°   Though extreme
    And° thou thenke on thi mede,°   If reward
30   Hit sal° thee thinken° softe.   shall seem

    If that fend,° that foule thing,   **that fend** the fiend
    Thorou wikke roun,° thorou fals egging,   **wikke roun** wicked spell
     Nethere° thee haveth i-cast,°   Down cast
    Oup and be god chaunpioun.
35   Stond, ne° fal namore adoun   and
     For a lüytel blast.

    Thou tak the rode to° thi staf,   **rode to** cross as
    And thenk on him that thereonne yaf°   gave
     His lif that wes so lef.°   precious
40   He hit yaf for thee. Thou yelde° hit him;   repay
    Ayein° his fo that staf thou nim,°   Against take
     And wrek° him of that thef.°   avenge thief

    Of rightte bileve° thou nim that sheld   **Of** . . . In true faith
    The wiles that° thou best° in that feld.   **The** . . . While are
45   Thin hond to strenkthen fonde,°   try
    And kep° thy fo with staves ord,°   oppose point
    And do that° traytre seien that word.°   **do that** make the **seien** . . . surrender
     Biget° that mürie londe.   Gain

    Thereinne is day withhouten night,
50 Withouten ende strenkthe and might,
     And wreche° of everich° fo,   vengeance every
    Mid God himselven eche° lif,   eternal
    And pes and rest withoute strif,
     Wele withouten wo.

55 Mayden Moder, Hevene° Quene,   Heaven's
    Thou might° and const and owest° to bene°   may ought be
      Oure sheld ayein° the fende.°   against fiend
    Help ous sünne for to flen,°   flee
    That we moten° thi sone i-seen°   may see
60   In joye withouten hende.

The Fox and the Wolf

(ca. 1275–1300, Southwestern)

∽∾

An ancient form of literature, numbering among its early examples the Indian *Panchatantra* and the Greek fables attributed to Aesop, the beast fable is represented in extant Middle English literature before Chaucer's "Nun's Priest's Tale" only by *The Fox and the Wolf*. Nevertheless, the beast fable represents a long and important tradition. Aesop's tales appeared early in Latin collections in the first and fourth centuries and again in a widely popular prose collection of the tenth century. An English translation of the latter is said to have been prepared for Henry I. Perhaps Marie de France was alluding to that lost translation when she declared that her Anglo–Norman *Fables* (ca. 1189) were translated from English.

A number of literary works in this genre appeared on the Continent. A late eighth-century poem by Paulus Diaconus was followed by the efforts of a Cistercian monk, the *Ecbasis Captivi* (ca. 1043–46). Several years later in Flanders a Master Nivardus produced a long Latin poem *Ysengrimus*. In addition to this literary tradition, there sprang up out of oral tradition and international folklore a number of fables concerning Reynard the Fox: the French beast epic *Roman de Renart* (ca. 1175–1250), a German *Reinhart Fuchs* (ca. 1180), by Heinrich Glichezaere, and two Middle Dutch versions (in the thirteenth and fourteenth centuries). The lasting popularity of the tales is demonstrated by the editions in Dutch and English in the later fifteenth century and thereafter, including two editions by Caxton.

The Fox and the Wolf is memorable not only as the earliest humorous beast fable in English but also as the only early example in English of a versified story dealing with Reynard the Fox. Though it corresponds in general to Branch II of the French *Roman de Renart*, no specific source has been positively identified.

Found in the same manuscript as *Dame Sirith*, *The Fox and the Wolf* is composed in four-beat couplets; see Introduction, type 5, page 31. The simplicity and clarity of style fit the subject matter, and even if the poem lacks some of the wit and descriptive powers of its French counterpart and ignores the allegorical potentialities of its theme, it compensates for these weaknesses by its downright humor, as when we are told of the hungry fox:

> Him were levere meten one hen / Then half an oundred wimmen.

Useful editions and commentaries are in G. H. McKnight, *Middle English Humorous Tales in Verse* (Boston, 1913) and J. A. Bennett and G. V. Smithers, *Early Middle English Verse and Prose* (New York, 1968), pp. 65–76, 297–303. For bibliography see Wells, ch. 2.25.

	A vox gon° out of the wode go,	**vox gon** fox did
	Afingret° so that him° wes wo.°	Hungry he woeful
	He nes° nevere in none wise°	was manner
	Afingret erour° half so swithe.°	before much
5	He ne hoeld° nouther wey ne strete,°	kept to **wey** . . . road nor street
	For him° wes loth° men to mete;	to him hateful
	Him were levere° meten one hen,	**Him** . . . He would sooner
	Then half an oundred° wimmen.	hundred
	He strok swithe° over al,	**strok swithe** went quickly
10	So that he ofsei ane° wal.	**ofsei ane** saw a
	Withinne the walle wes on° hous,	a
	The vox° wes thider swithe vuous;°	fox **swithe vuous** very ready
	For he thohute° his hounger aquenche,	intended
	Other mid mete, other mid drünche.°	
15	Abouten° he biheld wel yerne;°	About **biheld** . . . looked very eagerly
	Tho eroust° bigon the vox to erne,°	**Tho eroust** Then first run
	Al fort° he come to one° walle.	Until a
	And som therof wes afalle,°	fallen down
	And wes the wal over al to-broke,°	broken down
20	And on yat° ther wes i-loke.°	**on yat** a gate shut
	At the fürmeste brüche° that he fond,	**fürmeste brüche** first opening
	He lep in, and over he wond.°	went
	Tho° he wes inne, smere° he lou,°	When scornfully laughed
	And therof he hadde gome i-nou;°	**gome i-nou** sport enough
25	For he com in withouten leve	
	Bothen of haiward° and of reve.°	**of haiward** from hayward reeve
	On° hous ther wes, the dore wes ope,°	A open
	Hennen weren° therinne i-crope,°	**Hennen weren** Hens had crept
	Five—that maketh anne° flok—	a
30	And mid° hem sat on kok.°	with cock
	The kok him wes flowen on hey,°	high
	And two hennen him seten ney.°	near
	"Vox,"° quod the kok, "wat dest° thou thare?	Fox do
	Go hom. Crist thee yeve kare!°	**yeve kare** give sorrow
35	Houre° hennen thou dest ofte shome."°	Our insult
	"Be stille, Ich hote, a° Godes nome!"°	**hote, a** command, in name
	Quath the vox. "Sire Chauntecler,	
	Thou fle° adoun, and com me ner.	fly
	I nabbe° don her nout bote° god,	have not **her** . . . here anything but
40	I have leten thine hennen blod.	
	Hy° weren seke° ounder the ribe,	They sick
	That hy ne mightte non lengour libe,°	**ne** . . . couldn't live any longer
	Bote here heddre° were i-take.	**Bote** . . . Unless their blood (from veins)
	That I do for almes° sake.	charity's

14. Either with food or with drink.

45 Ich have hem leten eddre-blod,°   vein blood
And thee, Chauntecler, hit wolde don° god.   do
Thou havest that ilke° ounder the splen;°   same sickness spleen
Thou nestes nevere daies ten,°
For thine lif-dayes beth° al ago,°   are gone
50 Bote° thou bi mine rede° do.   Unless counsel
I do° thee lete blod ounder the brest,   advise
Other° sone axe° after the prest."   Or else ask
"Go wei," quod the kok; "wo thee bigo!°   befall
Thou havest don oure künne° wo.   kin
55 Go mid than° that thou havest nouthe;°   **mid than** with this   now
Acoursed be thou of Godes mouthe.
For were I adoun,° bi Godes nome,°   down below   name
Ich mighte ben siker° of othre shome.°   **ben siker** be sure   insult
Ac weste° hit houre° cellerer,   But if knew   our
60 That thou were i-comen her,°   **were** ... had come here
He wolde sone after thee ghonge°   go
Mid° pikes and stones and staves stronge.   With
Alle thine bones he wolde to-breke;
Then we weren wel awreke."°   avenged
65   He wes stille, ne spak namore,°   **spak namore** spoke no more
Ac° he werth° athürst wel sore.°   But was **wel sore** very sorely
The thürst him dede° more wo   caused
Then hevede rather° his hounger do.°   **hevede rather** had earlier done
Over al he ede and sohute.°   **ede** ... went and sought
70 On aventure° his wiit° him brohute°   **On aventure** By chance wits broug
To one pütte° wes water inne,   **one pütte** a pit where
That wes i-maked mid° grete ginne.°   with ingenuity
Tuo boketes° ther he founde: buckets
That other wende° to the grounde,   **That** ... The one goes
75 That wen me° shulde that on opwinde,°   one **that** ... the one wind up
That other wolde adoun winde.°   go
He ne hounderstod nout of the ginne;°   trap
He nom° that boket and lep ther-inne,   took
For he hopede i-nou° to drinke.   enough
80 This boket° beginneth to sinke.   bucket
Too late the vox° wes bithout,°   fox concerned
Tho° he wes in the ginne i-brout.°   When brought
I-nou he gon him bithenche,°   **gon** ... reflected
Ac° hit ne halp mid° none wrenche.°   But helped with trick
85 Adoun he moste,° he wes ther-inne;   must go
I-kaut he wes mid swikele ginne.°   **swikele ginne** treacherous trap
Hit mighte han i-ben wel° his wille   **han** ... well have been
To lete that boket hongi stille.

48. You have not lain with a woman for ten days (literally, 'You nest never for ten days')

Wat mid serewe° and mid drede, sorrow
90 Al his thürst him overhede.° disappeared
Al thus he com to the grounde,° bottom
And water i-nou° ther he founde. enough
Tho° he fond water, yerne° he dronk; When   eagerly
Him thoute° that water there stonk, **Him thoute** It seemed to him
95 For hit wes toyeines° his wille. against
    "Wo wörthe,"° quath the vox,° "lust and wille,° **Wo wörthe** Cursed be   fox   pleasure
That ne con meth too his mete.° **ne . . .** knows not moderation in   food
Yef Ich nevede° too muchel° i-ete, hadn't   much
This ilke shome neddi nouthe,° **ilke . . .** same insult I had not now
100 Nedde lust i-ben of mine mouthe.°
Him is wo° in eche londe, **Him . . .** Woe to him
That is thef mid his honde.
Ich am i-kaut mid swikele ginne,° **swikele ginne** treacherous trap
Other° soum devel me broute her-inne. Or
105 I was woned° to ben° wiis, accustomed   being
Ac° nou of° me i-don hit hiis."° But   for   is
    The vox° wep, and reuliche° bigan. fox   piteously
Ther com a wolf gon °after than° walking   this
Out of the depe wode blive,° quickly
110 For he wes afingret swithe.° **afingret swithe** very hungry
Nothing he ne founde in al the nighte,
Wer-mide° his honger aquenche mightte. Wherewith
He com to the pütte,° thene vox i-herde. pit
He him kneu wel by his rerde,° voice
115 For hit wes his neighebore
And his gossip, of children bore.°
Adoun bi the pütte he sat.
    Quod the wolf: "Wat may ben° that be
That Ich in the pütte i-here?
120 Hertou Cristine other° mi fere?° **Hertou . . .** Are you Christian or
                                        companion
Say° me soth,° ne gabbe° thou me nout, Tell   the truth   lie
Wo° haveth thee in the pütte i-brout?" Who
The vox hine° i-kneu wel for his kün,° him   kin
And tho eroust° kom wiit° to him; **tho eroust** then first   an idea
125 For he thoute, mid somme ginne,° trick
Himself houp° bringe, thene° wolf ther-inne. up   and the
Quod the vox, "Wo is nou there?
Iche wene° hit is Sigrim that Ich here." suppose
    "That is soth,"° the wolf sede, true
130 "Ac° wat art thou, so God thee rede?"° But   help
    "A!" quod the vox, "Ich wille thee telle,

100. Had it not been for the pleasure of my mouth.
116. And his close friend, since they were children.

169

On alpi° word Ich lie nelle.°   **On alpi** One single   will not
Ich am Reneuard thi frend,
And yif Ich thine come hevede i-wend,°   **thine** . . . your coming had expected
135 Ich hedde° so i-bede° for thee,   had   prayed
That thou sholdest comen to me."
     "Mid thee?" quod the wolf. "War-to?
Wat shulde Ich in the pütte do?"
     Quod the vox, "Thou art ounwiis;°   unwise
140 Her° is the blisse of paradiis.   Here
Her Ich mai evere wel fare
Withouten pine,° withouten kare.°   pain   sorrow
Her is mete,° her is drinke,   food
Her is blisse withouten swinke;°   work
145 Her nis° hounger never mo,°   is   more
Ne non other künnes° wo;   **Ne** . . . Nor other kinds of
Of alle gode her° is i-nou."°   **gode her** good things here   enough
Mid thilke° wordes the wolf lou.°   **Mid thilke** At those   laughed
     "Art thou ded, so God thee rede,°   help
150 Other° of the worlde?" the wolf sede.   Or
Quod the wolf, "Wenne storve° thou,   died
And wat dest° thou there nou?   do
Ne beth nout° thre daies ago   **Ne** . . . It was only
That thou and thi wif also,
155 And thine children, smale and grete,
Alle togedere mid me hete."°   ate
     "That is soth,"° quod the vox.   true
"Gode thonk,° nou hit is thus,   **Gode thonk** Thank God
That Ich am to Criste wend.°   gone
160 Not° hit non of mine frend.   Knows
I nolde,° for al the worldes god,°   wouldn't   goods
Ben° ine the worlde ther° Ich hem fond.   Be   where
Wat° shuld Ich ine the worlde go,   Why
Ther nis bote kare° and wo,   **Ther** . . . There is only sorrow
165 And livie° in fülthe° and in sünne?°   live   filth   sin
Ac her beth° joies fele cünne.°   **her beth** here are   **fele cünne** of ma
Her beth bothe shepe and get."°   kinds
     goats
     The wolf haveth hounger swithe° gret,   very
For he nedde yare° i-ete,   **nedde yare** had not for a long time
170 And tho° he herde speken of mete,°   when   food
He wolde bletheliche° ben thare.   gladly
     "A!" quod the wolf, "gode i-fere,°   companion
Moni god mel° thou havest me binome.°   meal   deprived of
Let me adoun to thee kome,
175 And al Ich wole thee foryeve.°   forgive
     "Ye," quod the vox, "were thou i-srive,°   absolved

And sünnen hevedest al forsake,°   **sünnen** ... had forsaken all sins
And to klene lif i-take,°   turned
Ich wolde so bidde° for thee   pray
180 That thou sholdest comen to me."
    "To wom° shuld Ich," the wolf seide,   whom
"Ben i-knowe° of mine misdede?   **Ben i-knowe** Be confessed
Her nis° nothing alive   is not
That me kouthe° her nou srive.°   could   absolve
185 Thou havest ben ofte min i-fere;°   companion
Woltou nou mi srift° i-here,   confession
And al mi liif I shal thee telle?"
    "Nay," quod the vox, "I nelle."°   won't
    "Neltou,"° quod the wolf, "thin ore?°   Won't you show   mercy
190 Ich am afingret swithe sore.°   **afingret** ... very sorely hungry
Ich wot° tonight Ich wörthe° ded,   know   will be
Bote° thou do me somne reed.°   Unless   **somne reed** some counsel
For Cristes love, be mi prest."
The wolf bey° adoun his brest,   bent
195 And gon° to siken° harde and stronge.   began   sigh
    "Woltou,"° quod the vox, "srift ounderfonge,°   Will you   **srift ounderfonge** undertake confession
Tel thine sünnen on and on,°   **sünnen** ... sins one by one
That ther bileve° never on?"   remain
    "Sone,"° quod the wolf, "wel i-faie.°   At once   **wel i-faie** very gladly
200 Ich habbe ben qued° al mi lif-daie.   evil
Ich habbe widewene kors,°   **widewene kors** widows' curse
Ther-fore Ich fare the wors.
A thousent shep Ich habbe abiten,°   bitten
And mo, yef hy° weren i-writen.   they
205 Ac hit me ofthinketh sore.°   **me** ... I repent sorely
Maister, shall I tellen more?"
    "Ye," quod the vox, "al thou most sügge,°   **most sügge** must say
Other° elles-wer thou most abügge."°   Or   atone
    "Gossip,"° quod the wolf, "foryef° hit me,   Close friend   forgive
210 Ich habbe ofte sehid qued bi° thee.   **sehid** ... said evil about
Men seide that thou on thine live
Misferdest° mid mine wive.   Misbehaved
Ich thee aperseivede° one stounde,°   perceived   moment
And in bedde togedere ou° founde.   you
215 Ich wes ofte ou ful ney,°   near
And in bedde togedere ou sey.°   saw
Ich wende,° al-so othre doth,°   thought   **al-so** ... as others do
That° Ich i-seie° were soth,°   What   saw   true
And ther-fore thou were me loth.°   **me loth** hateful to me
220 Gode gossip,° ne be thou nohut wroth."°   Close friend   **nohut wroth** not angry
    "Wolf," quod the vox him tho,°   then

"Al that thou havest her° bifore i-do,°   *here done*

In thohut,° in speche, and in dede,   *thought*

In eche otheres künnes quede,°   **eche** ... *every other kind of evil*

225 Ich thee foryeve° at thisse nede."°   *forgive* **thisse nede** *this hour of need*

  "Crist thee foryelde,"° the wolf seide.   *reward*

"Nou Ich am in clene live,°   **clene live** *pure life*

Ne recche° Ich of° childe ne of wive.   *care about*

Ac sei° me wat I shal do,   *tell*

230 And ou° Ich may comen thee to."   *how*

  "Do?" quod the vox. "Ich wille thee lere.°   *instruct*

I-siist° thou a boket hongi° there?   *See* **boket hongi** *bucket hanging*

Ther is a brüche of hevene° blisse   **brüche** ... *opening to heaven's*

Lep ther-inne mid i-wisse,°   *certainty*

235 And thou shalt comen to me sone."°   *at once*

  Quod the wolf, "That is light° to done."   *easy*

He lep in, and way sumdel;°   **way sumdel** *weighed much*

That weste° the vox ful wel.   *knew*

The wolf gon sinke,° the vox arise.   **gon sinke** *began to sink*

240 Tho° gon the wolf sore agrise.°   *Then become frightened*

Tho° he com amidde° the pütte,°   *When in the middle of pit*

The wolf thene° vox opward mette.   *the*

  "Gossip,"° quod the wolf, "wat nou?   *Close friend*

Wat havest thou i-münt?° Weder° wolt thou?"   *decided Whither*

245 "Weder Ich wille?"° the vox sede.   *wish to go*

"Ich wille oup, so God me rede!°   *help*

And nou go doun with thi meel.°   *meal*

Thi biyete wörth wel° smal;   **biyete** ... *gain will be very*

Ac Ich am therof glad and blithe

250 That thou art nomen° in clene live.°   *taken* **clene live** *pure life*

Thi soule-cnül° Ich wille do ringe,   *death knell*

And masse for thine soule singe."

  The wrecche binethe nothing ne vind°   *finds*

Bote cold water, and hounger him bind.

255 To colde gistninge° he wes i-bede;°   *feast invited*

Vroggen° haveth his dou° i-knede.   *Frogs dough*

  The wolf in the pütte° stod,   *pit*

Afingret° so that he wes wod.°   *Hungry mad*

I-nou° he cursede that° thider him broute.   *Enough him who*

260 The vox therof lüitle route.°   *cared*

The püt him wes the house ney°   *near*

Ther freren woneden swithe sley.°

Tho that° hit com to the time   *When*

That hoe° shulden arisen ine°   *they within*

265 For to süggen° here houssong,°   *say matins*

262. Where very shrewd friars dwelled.

172

O° frere ther wes among,
Of here° slep hem shulde awecche,°
Wen hoe shulden thidere recche.°
He seide, "Ariseth on and on,°
270 And kometh to houssong heverechon."°
    This ilke° frere heyte° Ailmer;
He wes hoere° maister curtiler.°
He wes hofthürst swithe stronge,°
Right amidward° here houssonge.°
275 Alhone° to the pütte° he hede,°
For he wende bete° his nede.
He com to the pütte, and drou,°
And the wolf was hevi i-nou.
The frere mid al his maine tey°
280 So longe that he thene° wolf i-sey.°
For° he sei thene wolf ther sitte,
He gradde,° "The devel is in the pütte."
    To the pütte hy gounnen gon°
Alle, mid pikes and staves and ston,
285 Ech mon mid that° he hedde.
Wo wes him that wepne nedde.°
Hy comen to the pütte, thene° wolf opdrowe.°
Tho hede° the wreche fomen° i-nowe
That weren egre° him to slete°
290 Mid grete houndes, and to bete.°
Wel and wrothe° he wes i-swonge,°
Mid staves and speres he wes i-stounge.°
The vox bicharde° him mid i-wisse,°
For he ne fond nones künnes° blisse
295 Ne hof düntes foryevenesse.°

**Glosses (right column):**

A
Of here Who from their awake
reach
on . . . one by one
everyone
same was named
their gardener
hofthürst . . . very greatly thirsty
in the middle of matins
Alone pit went
wende bete intended to remedy
drew up

maine tey might pulled
the saw
Since
cried out
hy . . . they did go

what

the drew up
Tho hede Then had enemies
eager tear
beat
cruelly beaten
stung
tricked certainty
nones künnes any kind of
hof . . . remission of blows

---

286. Woe to him who had not weapons.

Dame Sirith

(ca. 1275–1300, Southwestern)

❧

Nearly 150 *fabliaux* (comic bourgeois tales) appear in French literature between 1150 and 1320. Only one from that period survives in English. The reason is not that the stories of the *fabliaux* were unknown in England, for the existence of a number of ballads based on these ribald stories indicates the contrary. Such ballads as "The Friar in the Well" (Child 276), "The Wife Wrapped in Wether's Skin" (277), and "The Farmer's Curst Wife" (278) were probably of such an origin. The reason that only one such story has survived in written literature is probably best expressed by Chaucer when he apologizes for the greatest of all Middle English *fabliaux*, "The Miller's Tale," as a "cherles tale," and bids his readers:

> ... therfore, whoso list it nat y-heere,
> Turne over the leef and chose another tale;
> For he shal fynde ynowe, grete and smale,
> Of storial thyng that toucheth gentillesse
> And eek moralitee and hoolynesse.

Certainly Chaucer gave the *fabliau* a place in Middle English literature that it had not held before, but the frequency of complaints about such tales during this period suggests both the moralistic objections to them and their deeply embedded popularity, such as the references to "harlotrie" in *Piers Plowman* (IV, 115; V, 419, below, p. 306) and to "merye tales" in the same work (XIII, 352). After Chaucer a number of *fabliaux* appear, including "The Pardoner and the Tapster," prefixed to *The Tale of Beryn* (p. 504), and *The Freiris of Berwik*, sometimes attributed to Dunbar.

The only extant *fabliau* written in English before Chaucer's time, *Dame Sirith* is composed in lively but irregular tail-rhyme stanzas; see Introduction, type 14, page 32. Portions of the poem are set in couplets, suggesting that the anonymous poet was transforming an earlier source into stanzas. The existence of a fragmentary *Interludium de Clerico et Puella*, dating about fifty years later than *Dame Sirith* and paralleling even verbally the earlier work, further suggests, though by no means conclusively, that the nonexistent source of both pieces may have been an early secular dramatic piece.

On the relation of *Dame Sirith* to the interlude, see W. Heuser, "Das Interludium 'De Clerico et Puella,'" *Anglia*, XXX (1907), 306–19. Useful editions and commentaries are in G. H. McKnight, *Middle English Humorous Tales in Verse* (Boston, 1913), J. A. Bennett and G. V. Smithers, *Early Middle English Verse and Prose* (New York, 1968), pp. 77–95, 303–12, and Larry D. Benson and Theodore M. Andersson, *The Literary Context of Chaucer's Fabliaux: Texts and Translations* (Indianapolis, 1971), pp. 372–87. For bibliography see Wells, ch. 2.20.

Dame Sirith

As I com bi an waie,
Hof on° Ich herde saie,   **Hof on** Of one
    Ful modi° mon and proud.   high-spirited
Wis he wes of lore,
5 And gouthlich° under gore,°   goodly   garments
    And clothed in fair sroud.°   dress

To lovien he bigon
On° wedded wimmon;°   A   woman
    Therof he hevede° wrong.   did
10 His herte hire° wes alon;°   for her   only
That reste nevede° he non,   had not
    The love wes so strong.

Wel yerne° he him bithoute°   **Wel yerne** Very eagerly   **him bithoute**
Hou he hire gete moute°   considered
15   In ani cünnes° wise.   **gete moute** might get
That befel° on an day,   manner
The loverd wend° away   **That befel** It happened
    Hon° his marchaundise.°   **loverd wend** lord goes
        On   business

He wente him° to then inne,°   **wente him** went   **then inne** the dwelling
20 Ther hoe wonede° inne,   **Ther . . .** Where she dwelled
    That wes riche won;°   **riche won** a splendid dwelling
And com into then halle,
Ther hoe wes srud° with palle,°   clothed   rich cloth
    And thus he bigon:

WILEKIN

25 "God almightten be herinne!"

MARGERI

"Welcome, so Ich ever bide wenne,"°   **bide wenne** feel joy
    Quod this wif.
"His hit° thi wille, com and site,   **His hit** If it is
And wat is thi wille let me wite,°   know
30   Mi leve lif.°   **leve lif** dear love

"Bi houre Loverd, Hevene° King,   **houre . . .** our Lord, heaven's
If I mai don° ani thing   do
    That thee° is lef,°   to you   dear
Thou mightt finden me ful fre,°   **ful fre** very generous
35 For bletheli willi° don for thee,   **bletheli willi** happily will I
    Withouten gref."°   hesitation

WILEKIN

"Dame, God thee foryelde,°   reward
Bote on that° thou me nout bimelde,°   **Bote** . . . Provided that   **nout bimelde**
Ne make thee wroth;°   may not betray
40   Min hernde° willi to thee bede,°   **make** . . . become angry
Bote wraththen° thee for ani dede   business   announce
Were me loth."°   to anger
     Would be hateful to me

MARGERI

"Nai, i-wis,° Wilekin,   indeed
For nothing that ever is min,
45   Thau° thou hit yirne,°   If   yearn for
Houncurteis° ne willi° be,   Ungracious   **ne willi** I will not
Ne con° I nout on vilté,°   know   **on vilté** of meanness
Ne nout I nelle° lerne.   **Ne** . . . Naught will I

"Thou mait saien° al thine wille,   **mait saien** can say
50   And I shal herknen° and sitten stille,   listen to
     That° thou have told.   What
And if that thou me tellest skil,°   **me** . . . speak to me right
I shal don after° thi wil,   **don after** act according to
     That° be thou bold.°   Of that   sure

55   "And thau° thou saie me° ani same,°   if   **saie me** speak to me   shame
Ne shal I thee nowight° blame   not
     For thi sawe."°   saying

WILEKIN

"Nou Ich have wonne leve,°   **wonne leve** gained permission
Yif that I me shulde greve,°   grieve
60   Hit were hounlawe.°   wrong

"Certes,° dame, thou seist as hende,°   Surely   **seist** . . . speak courteously
And I shal setten spel on° ende,   **setten** . . . speak my speech to the
     And tellen thee al,
Wat Ich wolde° and wi Ich com.   want
65   Ne con° Ich saien non falsdom,   **Ne con** Cannot
     Ne non I ne shal.°   **Ne** . . . Nor shall I

"Ich habbe i-loved thee moni yer,
Thau° Ich nabbe° nout ben her   Though   have
     Mi love to schewe.
70   Wile thi loverd° is in toune   lord
Ne mai no mon with thee holden roune°   talk
     With no thewe.°   good manners

"Yürstendai° Ich herde saie,   Yesterday
As Ich wende° bi the waie,   went
75   Of oure sire.°   **oure sire** your husband
Me° tolde me that he was gon   One
To the feire of Botolfston°   Boston
    In Lincolnshire.

"And for° Ich weste° that he wes houte,°   because. knew out
80 Thar-fore Ich am i-gon aboute
    To speken with thee.
Him bürth° to liken wel his lif,   **Him bürth** It behooves him
That mightte welde selc° a wif   **welde selc** rule such
    In privité.°   privacy

85 "Dame, if hit is thi wille,
Both dernelike° and stille°   secretly quietly
    Ich wille thee love."

         MARGERI
"That woldi don° for non thing,   **woldi don** would I do
Bi houre Loverd, Hevene° King,   **houre . . .** our Lord, Heaven's
90   That ous° is bove!°   us above

"Ich habbe mi loverd that is mi spouse,
That maiden broute me to house,
    Mid menske i-nou.°   **menske i-nou** honor aplenty
He loveth me and Ich him wel;
95 Oure° love is also° trewe as stel,   Our as
    Withouten wou.°   wrong

"Thau° he be from hom on his hernde,°   Though business
Ich were ounseli,° if Ich lernede   **were ounseli** would be unhappy
    To ben on hore.°   **ben . . .** be a whore
00 That ne shal nevere be,
That I shal don selk falseté,   **selk falseté** such deceit
    On bedde ne on flore.°   floor

"Never more his lif-while,
Thau° he were on° hondred mile   Though a
05   Biyende° Rome,   Beyond
For no thing ne shuld I take
Mon on erthe to ben° mi make,°   be mate
    Ar° his hom-come."   Before

WILEKIN

"Dame, dame, torn thi mod.°   torn ... change your mind
110 Thi curteisi wes ever god,
        And yet shal be.
     For the Loverd° that ous° haveth wrout,°   Lord   us   made
     Amend thi mod, and torn thi thout,°   thought
        And rew on° me."   rew on pity

MARGERI

115 "We, we! Holdest° thou me a fol?   Consider
     So Ich ever mote biden Yol,°   mote ... must await Yule
        Thou art ounwis.°   unwise
     Mi thout ne shalt thou never wende.°   turn
     Mi loverd° is curteis° mon and hende,°   lord   courteous   gracious
120   And mon of pris.°   excellence

     "And Ich am wif bothe god and trewe.
     Trewer womon ne mai no° mon cnowe°   ne ... cannot any   know
        Then Ich am.
     Thilke° time ne shal never bitide°   That   come
125 That mon for wouing° ne thoru prüde°   wooing   thoru prüde through pride
        Shal do me scham."

WILEKIN

     "Swete levemon,° merci!   lover
     Same° ne vilani   Shame
        Ne bede° I thee non;   offer
130 Bote derne° love I thee bede,   secret
     As mon that wolde of° love spede°   from   prosper
        And finde won."°   great store

MARGERI

     "So bide° Ich evere mete other° drinke,   expect   mete other food or
     Her thou lesest° al thi swinke.°   waste   toil
135 Thou might gon hom, leve° brother,   dear
     For wille Ich thee love ne non other
     Bote mi wedde houssebonde.
     To tellen hit thee ne wille Ich wonde."°   hesitate

WILEKIN

     "Certes,° dame, that me forthinketh;°   Surely   that ... I repent of that
140 And wo is° the mon that muchel swinketh,°   wo is woe to   muchel swinketh toils
     And at the laste leseth° his sped!°   much
     To maken menis is him ned.°   loses   success
                                                 To ... He needs to make lamentations

Bi me, I saie ful i-wis,
That love the love that I shal mis.°
145 And, dame, have nou godne dai!°   **have** . . . good day
And thilke° Loverd, that al welde mai,°   that   **welde mai** can rule
Leve° that thi thout° so tourne,°   Allow   thought   change
That Ich for thee no leng° ne mourne.''   longer

Dreri-mod° he wente awai,   Sad-hearted
150 And thoute bothe night and dai
    Hire° al for to wende.°   Her   change
A frend him radde° for to fare,°   advised   go
And leven al his muchele kare,°   **muchele kare** great sorrow
    To Dame Sirith the hende.°   courteous

155 Thider he wente him° anon,   **wente him** went
So swithe so° he mightte gon,   **So** . . . As quickly as
    No mon he ne mette.
Ful he wes of tene° and treie.°   grief   sorrow
Mid° wordes mild and eke sleie°   With   **eke sleie** also shrewd
160   Faire he hire grette.°   greeted

          WILEKIN
''God thee i-blessi, Dame Sirith!
Ich am i-com to speken thee with,
    For ful muchele nede.°   **ful** . . . very great need
And° Ich mai have help of thee,   If
165 Thou shalt have—that thou shalt se—
    Ful riche mede.''°   reward

          SIRITH
''Welcomen art thou, leve sone.°   **leve sone** dear son
And if Ich mai other cone°   **other cone** or can
In eni wise° for thee do,   manner
170 I shal strengthen me° therto.   **strengthen me** try
For-thi,° leve sone, tel thou me   Therefore
Wat thou woldest I düde° for thee.''   did

          WILEKIN
  ''Bote,° leve nelde.° Ful evele I fare;   Help   **leve nelde** dear old woman
I lede mi lif with tene° and kare.°   grief   sorrow

143–44. Concerning myself, I say it very certainly, I who love the loved one that I shall lose.

179

175 "With muchel hounsele° Ich lede mi lif,   **muchel hounsele** much unhappiness
    And that is for on° swete wif°   a   woman
      That heighghte° Margeri.   is called
    Ich have i-loved hire moni° dai,   many a
    And of hire love hoe seith° me nai.   **hoe seith** she says
180   Hider Ich com for-thi.°   therefore

    "Bote if° hoe wende° hire mod,°   **Bote if** Unless   changes   mind
    For serewe mon° Ich wakese wod,°   **serewe mon** sorrow must   **wakese wo**
      Other miselve quelle.°   grow mad
             Other . . . Or kill myself
    Ich hevede° i-thout miself to slö.°   had   slay
185 For-then radde° a frend me go   **For-then radde** Wherefore advised
      To thee mi serewe telle.

    "He saide me, withouten faille,
    That thou me couthest helpe° and vaile,°   **couthest helpe** could assist   help
      And bringen me of° wo   from
190 Thoru° thine crafftes° and thine dedes.°   Through   skills   deeds
    And Ich wile yeve° thee riche mede,°   give   reward
      With that° hit be so."   **With that** Provided that

SIRITH

    "*Benedicite*° be her-inne!   Blessing
    Her havest thou, sone, mikel senne.°   **mikel senne** great sin
195 Loverd, for his swete nome,°   name
    Lete thee ther-fore haven no schome!
    Thou servest affter Godes grome,°   anger
    Wen thou seist on° me silk blame.°   **seist on** tell to   **silk blame** such a cha
    For Ich am old, and sek,° and lame;   sick
200 Seknesse haveth maked me ful° tame.   very
    Blesse thee, blesse thee, leve knave,°   **leve knave** dear boy
    Leste thou mesaventer° have   misadventure
    For this lesing° that is founden°   deceit   found
    Oppon me, that am harde i-bounden.°   pressed
205 Ich am on° holi wimon;°   a   woman
    On witchecrafft nout I ne con,°   **nout . . .** I know nothing
    Bote with gode men° almesdede   men's
    Ilke° dai mi lif I fede,   Each
    And bidde° mi pater-noster and mi crede,   pray
210 That God hem helpe at höre nede°   **höre nede** their need
    That helpen me mi lif to lede,
    And leve° that hem mote° wel spede.°   grant   may   prosper
    His lif and his soule wörthe i-shend°   **wörthe i-shend** be disgraced

That° thee to me this hernde° haveth send.   Who business

215 And leve me to ben i-wreken°   **ben i-wreken** be avenged

On him this shome me haveth speken."°

WILEKIN

"Leve nelde, bi-lef° al this.   **Leve** . . . Dear old woman, stop

Me thinketh° that thou art onwis.°   **Me thinketh** It seems to me unwise

The mon that me to thee taute°   directed

220 He weste° that thou hous couthest saute.°   knew **hous** . . . could reconcile us

Help, Dame Sirith, if thou maut,°   can

To make me with the sweting saut,°   **sweting saut** darling a reconciliation

And Ich wille geve thee gift ful stark,°   **ful stark** very great

Moni a pound and moni a mark,

225 Warme pilche° and warme shon,°   furs shoes

With that° mi hernde° be wel don.   **With that** When business

Of muchel godlec° might thou yelpe,°   **muchel godlec** much goodness boast

If hit be so that thou me helpe."

[SIRITH]

"Ligh me° nout, Wilekin! Bi thi leute,°   **Ligh me** Lie to me faithfulness

230 Is hit thin hernest° thou tekest° me?   sincere purpose show

Lovest thou wel Dame Margeri?"

WILEKIN

"Ye, nelde, witerli.°   **nelde, witerli** old woman, surely

Ich hire love; hit mot° me spille°   must ruin

Bote° Ich gete hire to mi wille."   Unless

SIRITH

235 "Wat!° God Wilekin, me reweth° thi scathe;°   Oh **me reweth** I pity harm

Houre° Loverd sende thee help rathe!°   Our at once

"Weste Hic° hit mightte ben forholen,°   **Weste Hic** If I knew that **ben forholen** be concealed

Me wolde thünche° wel folen°   **Me** . . . It would seem to me suited

Thi wille for to füllen.°   fulfill

240 Make me siker° with word ond honde   sure

That thou wolt helen,° and I wile fonde°   conceal try

If Ich mai hire tellen.

"For al the world ne woldi nout°   **ne** . . . I would not

That Ich were to chapitre° i-brout   ecclesiastical court

245 For none selke° werkes.   such

216. On him who has said this shameful thing about me.

181

Mi jugement were sone i-given
To ben with shome somer-driven°
   With° prestes and with clerkes."   By

WILEKIN

"I-wis, nelde, ne woldi°
250 That thou hevedest vilani°   baseness
   Ne shame for mi goed.°   benefit
Her° I thee mi trouthe plightte,°   Here **trouthe plightte** word pledge
Ich shal helen° bi mi mightte,°   conceal power
   Bi the holi roed!"°   cross

SIRITH

255 "Welcome, Wilekin, hiderward.
Her havest° i-maked a foreward°   you have agreement
   That thee mai ful° wel like.°   very please
Thou maight° blesse thilke sith,°   may **thilke sith** that time
For thou maight make thee ful blith;°   happy
260   Dar thou namore sike.°   **Dar** ... You need nevermore sigh

"To goder hele° ever come thou hider,   **To** ... For good fortune
For sone will I gange° thider   go
   And maken hire hounderstande.
I shal kenne° hire sülke° a lore°   teach such lesson
265 That hoe° shal lovien thee mikel° more   she much
   Then ani mon in londe."

WILEKIN

"Also havi° Godes grith,°   **Also havi** As I have peace
Wel havest thou said, Dame Sirith,
   And Godes hile° shal ben° thin.   prosperity be
270 Have her twenti shiling.
This Ich yeve° thee to meding°   give **to meding** as reward
   To büggen° thee sep and swin."°   buy **sep** ... mutton and pork

SIRITH

"So° Ich evere brouke° hous other flet,°   As may enjoy **other flet** or floor
Neren° never penes° beter biset°   Were not pence employed
   Then thes shulen ben.°   **Then** ... Than these shall be
For I shal don° a juperti,°   make venture
And a ferli maistri,°   **ferli maistri** wonderful trick
   That thou shalt ful wel sen.

247. To be made to ride shamefully upon an ass
249. Indeed, old woman, I would not wish

182

Dame Sirith

"Pepir° nou shalt thou eten;¹   Pepper
280 This mustart shal ben° thi mete,°   be   food
       And gar° thin eien° to renne.°   make eyes run
     I shal make a lesing°   deception
     Of thin heie-renning,°   eye-running
       Ich wot° wel wer and wenne."   know

WILEKIN

285 "Wat!° nou const° thou no god,   Oh   can do
     Me thinketh that thou art wod.°   crazy
     Yevest thou° the welpe° mustard?"   **Yevest thou** Do you give   dog

SIRITH

     "Be stille, boinard!°   fool
     I shal mit° this ilke gin°   with   same trick
290 Gar° hire love to ben° al thin.   Make   be
     Ne shal Ich never have reste ne ro,°   quiet
     Til Ich have told hou thou shalt do.
     Abid° me her° til min hom-come."   Wait for   here

WILEKIN

     "Yüs, bi° the somer blome,°   **Yüs, bi** Yes, until   **somer blome** summer
295 Hethen nulli ben binomen,°   bloom
     Til thou be ayein° comen."   back
       Dame Sirith bigon to go,
     As a wrecche that is wo,°   woeful
     That hoe com hire° to then inne°   **hoe . . .** she came   **then inne** the dwelling
300 Ther° this gode wif wes inne.   Where
     Tho hoe° to the dore com,   **Tho hoe** When she
     Swithe reuliche° hoe bigon: **Swithe reuliche** Very pitifully

SIRITH

     "Loverd," hoe seith, "wo is holde° wives   **wo . . .** woe to old
     That in poverté ledeth ay° lives;   ever
305 Not° no mon so muchel of pine°   Knows not   suffering
     As povre wif that falleth in ansine.°   **povre wif** poor woman   want
     That mai ilke° mon bi me wite,°   each   know
     For mai I nouther gange° ne site.   walk
     Ded woldi ben° ful fain.°   **woldi ben** would I be   **ful fain** very
310 Hounger and thürst me haveth nei° slain;   gladly
     Ich ne mai° mine limes on-wold°   nearly
     For mikel° hounger and thürst and cold.   can   control
     War-to° liveth selke° a wrecche!   great
     Wi nül° God mi soule fecche?"   Why   such
                                                  Wi nül Why will not

---

¹ As line 287 makes clear, this stanza (ll. 279–84) is spoken by Dame Sirith to her dog.
295. Hence I will not be taken away

183

MARGERI

315 "Seli wif,° God thee hounbinde!°   **Seli wif** Good woman unbind
    To-dai wille I thee mete° finde   food
       For love of God.
    Ich have reuthe° of thi wo,   pity
    For evele° i-clothed I se thee go,   poorly
320   And evele i-shoed.

    "Com her-in, Ich wile thee fede."

SIRITH

    "God Almightten do thee mede,°   reward
    And the Loverd that wes on rode i-don,°   **rode i-don** the cross slain
    And faste° fourti daws to non,°   fasted **daws . . .** days to the ninth hour
325 And hevene and erthe haveth to welde,°   rule
    As thilke Loverd thee foryelde."°

MARGERI

    "Have her fles° and eke° bred,   **her fles** here meat also
    And make thee glad, hit is mi red.°   counsel
    And have her the coppe° with the drinke."   cup

SIRITH

330 "God do° thee mede° for thi swinke,"°   give reward toil
    Thenne spac° that olde wif°—   spoke woman
    Crist awarie° hire lif—   curse
    "Alas, alas! that ever I live!
    Al the sünne° Ich wolde forgive   sin
335 The mon that smite off min heved!°   head
    Ich wolde mi lif me were bireved!"°   taken from

MARGERI

    "Seli wif,° wat eilleth° thee?"   Good woman ails

[SIRITH]

    "Bote ethe° mai I sori be.   **Bote ethe** Yet easily
    Ich hevede° a douter feir and fre,°   had noble
340 Feirer ne mightte no mon se.
    Hoe° hevede a curteis° hossebonde,   She courteous
    Freour° non mightte no mon fonde.   Nobler
    Mi douter lovede him al too wel;
    For-thi° mak I sori del.°   Therefore **sori del** sorrowful grief
345 Oppon a dai he was out wend,°   gone
    And thar-thoru° wes mi douter shend.°   thereby disgraced

    326. May that same Lord reward you.

Dame Sirith

He hede° on ernde° out of toune; — went errand
And com a modi clarc° with croune,° — **modi clare** proud clerk tonsure
To mi douter his love beed,° — offered
350 And hoe nolde nout° folewe his red.° — **nolde nout** would not counsel
He ne mightte his wille have
For nothing he mightte crave.
Thenne bigon the clerc to wiche,° — use witchcraft
And shop° mi douter til° a biche.° — changed to bitch
355 This is mi douter that Ich of speke;
For del° of hire min herte mot° breke. — grief must
Loke hou hire heien greten,° — **heien greten** eyes cry
On hire cheken the teres meten.
For-thi,° dame, were hit no wonder — Therefore
360 Thau° min herte burste assunder. — If
And wose-ever° is yong houssewif, — whosoever
Hoe loveth ful lüitel hire lif,
And° eni clerc of love hire bede,° — If offer
Bote° hoe grante and lete him spede."° — Unless succeed

MARGERI

365 "A! Loverd Crist! Wat mai I thenne do?
This enderdai° com a clarc° me to, — other day clerk
And bed me love on his manere,
And Ich him nolde nout i-here.° — **nolde ...** would not hear
Ich trowe° he wolle° me forsape.° — believe will transform
370 Hou troustu, nelde,° Ich mowe ascape?"° — **troustu, nelde** do you believe, old woman **mowe ascape** can escape

SIRITH

"God Almightten be thin help,
That thou be nouther bicche ne welp!
Leve dame, if eni clerc
Bedeth° thee that love werc,° — Offers work
375 Ich rede° that thou grante his bone° — advise request
And bicom his lefmon sone.° — **lefmon sone** lover at once
And if that thou so ne dost,
A worse red° thou ounderfost."° — counsel receive

MARGERI

"Loverd Crist, that me is wo,° — **that ...** I am sorry for that
380 That the clarc° me hede fro,° — clerk **hede fro** went from
Ar° he me hevede biwonne.° — Before **hevede biwonne** had won
Me were levere° then ani fe° — **Me ...** I would rather money
That he hevede enes leien° bi me — **enes leien** once lain
And efftsones° bigunne. — again

185

385 "Evermore, nelde, Ich wille be thin,
With that° thou feche me Willekin,   **With that** Provided that
    The clarc° of wam° I telle.   clerk   whom
Giftes will I geve thee
That thou maight ever the betere be,
390   Bi Godes houne° belle!"   own

SIRITH

"Sothliche,° mi swete dame,   Truly
And if I mai withoute blame,
    Fain° Ich wille fonde.°   Gladly   try
And if Ich mai with him mete
395 Bi eni wei other° bi strete,   or
    Nout ne will I wonde.°   hesitate

"Have god dai, dame. Forth willi° go."   will I

MARGERI

"Allegate° loke that thou do so   At any rate
    As Ich thee bad.°   asked
400 Bote that° thou me Wilekin bringe,   **Bote that** Unless
Ne mai I never lawe° ne singe   laugh
    Ne be glad."

SIRITH

"I-wis,° dame, if I mai,°   Indeed   can
Ich wille bringen him yet todai,
405   Bi mine mightte."°   power
Hoe wente hire° to hire inne,   **wente hire** went
Ther° hoe founde Wilekinne,   Where
    Bi houre Drightte!°   **houre Drightte** our Lord

SIRITH

"Swete Wilekin, be thou nout dred,°   afraid
410 For of thin hernde° Ich have wel sped.°   business   succeeded
Swithe° com forth thider with me,   Quickly
For hoe haveth send affter thee.
I-wis° nou maight thou ben above,   Indeed
For thou havest grantise° of hire love."   grant

WILEKIN

415   "God thee foryelde,° leve nelde,   reward
That hevene and erthe haveth to welde!"
This modi° mon bigon to gon   proud
With Sirith to his levemon°   lover

186

In thilke stounde.°   **thilke stounde** that time
420   Dame Sirith bigon to telle,
And swor bi Godes owene belle,
    Hoe hevede° him founde.   She (Sirith) had

SIRITH
"Dame, so have Ich Wilekin sout,°   sought
For nou have Ich him i-brout."

MARGERI
425   "Welcome, Wilekin, swete thing,
Thou art welcomore° then the king."   more welcome

"Wilekin the swete,
Mi love I thee bihete,°   promise
    To don al thine wille.
430   Turnd° Ich have mi thout,°   Changed   thought
For I ne wolde nout
    That thou thee shuldest spille."°   destroy

WILEKIN
"Dame, so° Ich evere bide noen,°   as   **bide noen** expect the ninth hour
And Ich am redi and i-boen°   prepared
435   To don al that thou saie.
Nelde, *par ma fai!*°   *par* ... by my faith
Thou most gange° awai,   go
    Wile° Ich and hoe shulen plaie."   While

SIRITH
"Goddot° so I wille.   God knows
440   And loke that thou mid° hire tille°   with   till
    And strek° out hire thes.°   stretch   thighs
God yeve° thee muchel kare°   give   sorrow
Yeif that° thou hire spare   **Yeif that** If
    The wile thou here bes.°   are

445   "And wose° is onwis,°   whoever   unwise
And for non pris°   price
    Ne con geten his levemon,°   lover
I shal, for mi mede,°   reward
Garen° him to spede,°   Make   succeed
450   For ful wel I con."

187

The Land of Cokayne

(ca. 1275–1300, Anglo-Irish)

❧

The Land of Cokayne is a forerunner of the Anglo-Irish literature of the nineteenth and twentieth centuries. The poem survives in a unique manuscript, which contains a variety of works in English, French, and Latin, some of which may have been composed by English-speaking settlers in Ireland. Since the manuscript is associated with the Franciscan abbey in Kildare, it has been argued that the poem is a satire aimed by a Franciscan friar specifically against the Cistercian monks in Kildare. More generally, perhaps, the poem is a universal parody of a monk's notion of the "earthly paradise," where he would be relieved of vigils, fasts, and celibacy. Despite this ambiguity of intention and the frivolity of its tone, the stern voice of the preacher is unmistakable.

The word *cokayne* is French, meaning probably "the land of cakes." There are various parallels to this poem: the Old French *Le Fabliau de Coquaigne*, the Anglo-Norman *L'Ordre de Bel Eyse*, and the Irish satire *MacConglinne's Vision*. The Anglo-Irish treatment of the topic, however, is unique in its delightfully racy anticlerical satire and its blend of the frivolous with the didactic.

The meter is rhyming couplets; see Introduction, type 5, page 31.

A useful recent edition of *The Land of Cokayne* is in J. S. Bennett and G. V. Smithers, *Early Middle English Verse and Prose* (New York, 1968), pages 136–44, 336–41. For the manuscript see the facsimile of British Museum MS. Harley 913 (Kildare MS), folio 4r., which contains lines 51–76, reproduced here on page 18. For bibliography see Wells, ch. 4.29; *CBEL*, 1.161.

	Fur in see° bi west Spaygne	**Fur . . .** Far over the sea
	Is a lond i-hote° Cokaygne;	called
	Ther nis° lond under heven riche°	is not **heven riche** heaven's realm
	Of wel,° of godnis hit i-liche.°	**Of wel** In well-being **hit i-liche** like it
5	Thogh paradis be miri° and bright,	merry
	Cokaygn is of fairir sight.°	appearance
	What is ther in paradis	
	Bot grasse and flure° and grene ris?°	flowers branches
	Thogh ther be joi and gret dute,°	rejoicing
10	Ther nis met bote° frute;	**nis . . .** is no food but
	Ther nis halle, bure, no° benche,	**bure, no** bower, nor
	Bot watir manis thursto quenche.°	

12. There is only water to quench man's thirst.

188

Beth° ther no men bot two,   Are
Hely° and Enok also.¹   Elijah
15 Elinglich° may hi° go,   Wretchedly   they
Whar ther wonith° men no mo.°   dwell   more
   In Cokaigne is met° and drink   food
Withute care, how, and swink.°   **care** ... sorrow, trouble, and toil
The met is trie,° the drink is clere°   choice   bright
20 To none, russin,° and sopper.   **To** ... At noon, afternoon snack
I sigge° for soth, boute were,°   say   **soth** ... truth, without doubt
Ther nis° lond on erthe is pere;°   is no   **is pere** its peer
Under heven nis lond i-wisse°   indeed
Of so mochil° joi and blisse.   much
25 Ther is mani° swete sighte;   many a
Al is dai, nis° ther no nighte.   there is
Ther nis baret nother° strif;   **nis** ... is no struggle nor
Nis ther no deth, ac° ever lif;   but
Ther nis lac of met no° cloth;   **met no** food nor
30 Ther nis man no womman wroth;°   angry
Ther nis serpent, wolf, no fox;
Hors no capil,° kowe no ox;   nag
Ther nis° schepe no swine no gote,   is no
No non horwgh, la,° God it wote.°   **horwgh, la** filth, indeed   knows
35 Nother harace, nother stode;°   **Nother** ... Neither horse breeding, nor stud
The lond is ful of other gode.°   goods
Nis ther flei,° fle, no lowse   fly
In cloth, in toune,° bed, no house.   farmstead
Ther nis dunnir,° slete, no hawle,°   thunder   hail
40 No non vile worme° no snawile;°   serpent   snail
No non storme, rein, no winde.
Ther nis man no womman blinde,
Ok° al is game,° joi and gle;   But   mirth
Wel is him that ther mai be.
45 Ther beth° rivers gret and fine   are
Of oile, melk, honi, and wine;
Watir servith ther to° no thing   for
Bot to sight° and to waiissing.°   looking at   washing
Ther is al maner frute;
50 Al is solas° and dedute.°   amusement   delight
   Ther is a wel° fair abbei   very
Of white monkes and of grei.
Ther beth bowris° and halles;   **beth bowris** are bowers
Al of pasteiis° beth the walles,   pies
55 Of fleis,° of fisse,° and rich met,°   meat   fish   food
The likfullist° that man mai et.   most delicious

¹ See 2 Kings 2.11; Gen. 5.24.

	Fluren° cakes beth the schingles alle	Flour
	Of cherche, cloister, boure, and halle.	
	The pinnes° beth fat podinges,°	pinnacles sausages
60	Rich met to° princes and kinges.	for
	Man mai ther-of et inogh,°	enough
	Al with right and noght with wogh.°	sin
	Al is commune° to yung and old,	common
	To stoute and sterne,° mek and bold.	**stoute** . . . proud and fierce
65	Ther is a cloister fair and light,	
	Brod and lang, of sembli sight.°	**sembli sight** fair appearance
	The pilers of that cloister alle	
	Beth° i-turned of cristale,	Are
	With har bas° and capitale	**har bas** their base
70	Of grene jaspe° and rede corale.	jasper
	In the praer° is a tre	meadow
	Swithe likful° for to se.	**Swithe likful** Very delightful
	The rote is gingevir and galingale,	
	The siouns beth° al sedwale.°	**siouns beth** shoots are setwall (zedoary)
75	Trie maces° beth the flure;°	Choice mace blossom
	The rind, canel° of swet odur;	**rind, canel** bark, cinnamon
	The frute, gilofre° of gode smakke;°	gillyflower (clove) flavor
	Of cucubes° ther nis no lakke.	cubebs
	Ther beth rosis of rede ble°	color
80	And lilie likful° for to se.	delightful
	Thai faloweth° never dai no night;	wither
	This aght° be a swet sight.	ought to
	Ther beth fower willis° in the abbei,	wells
	Of triacle and halwei,°	**triacle** . . . treacle (medicine) and healing w:
85	Of baum and ek peiment,°	**baum** . . . balm and also spiced wine
	Ever ernend° to right rent°—	running **right rent** good profit
	Of thai stremis al the molde°—	
	Stonis preciuse and golde.	
	Ther is saphir and uniune,°	pearl
90	Carbuncle and astriune,°	astrion (star sapphire?)
	Smaragde, lugre, and prassiune,°	**Smaragde** . . . Emerald, ligure, and chrysop:
	Beril, onix, topasiune,°	topaz
	Ametist and crisolite,°	chrysolite
	Calcedun and epetite.°	**Calcedun** . . . Chalcedony and hepatite
95	Ther beth briddes° mani and fale:°	birds brownish yellow
	Throstil, thruisse,° and nightingale.	**Throstil, thruisse** Throstle, thrush
	Chalandre and wodwale,°	**Chalandre** . . . Lark and green woodpecke:
	And other briddes without tale°	count
	That stinteth° never bi har° might	stop their
100	Miri° to sing dai and night.	Merrily

87. From these four wells all the earth thereabout overflows

Yite° I do° yow mo,° to witte: — Yet tell more
The gees i-rostid on the spitte
Flees to that abbai, God hit wot,° — knows
And gredith:° "Gees, al hote, al hot!" — cry out
105 Hi bringeth garlek gret plenté,° — quantity
The best i-dight° that man mai se. — dressed (stuffed)
The leverokes°—that beth cuth°— — larks well known
Lightith adun° to manis° muth, — **Lightith adun** Alight down   man's
I-dight° in stu° ful swithe° wel, — Prepared stew very
110 Pudrid° with gilofre and canel.° — Powdered **gilofre** ... cloves and cinnamon
Nis no spech of no drink,° — **of** ... needed to get a drink
Ak° take inogh° withute swink.° — But enough toil
Whan the monkes geeth° to masse, — go
Al the fenestres° that beth of glasse — windows
115 Turneth in to cristal bright
To yive° monkes more light. — give
Whan the masses beth i-seiid
And the bokes up i-leiid,° — laid
The cristal turnith into glasse,
120 In state that hit rather wasse.° — **rather wasse** earlier was
   The yung monkes ech dai
Aftir met° goth to plai. — food
Nis ther hauk no fule° so swifte — bird
Bettir fleing bi° the lifte° — **fleing bi** flying through sky
125 Than the monkes heigh° of mode° — high spirit
With har slevis° and har hode.° — **har slevis** their sleeves hood
Whan the abbot seeth ham flee,
That he holt° for moch glee; — considers
Ak° natheles al ther amang — But
130 He biddith ham light to evesang.° — **light** ... alight for evensong (vespers)
The monkes lightith noght adun,
Ac fürre° fleeth in o randun.° — farther **o randun** a rush
Whan the abbot him i-seeth,
That is° monkes fram him fleeth, — his
135 He taketh a maidin of the route° — company
And turnith up hir white toute° — buttocks
And betith the taburs° with is hond, — small drums
To make is monkes light° to lond. — alight
Whan is monkes that i-seeth,
140 To the maid dun° hi fleeth — down
And geth° the wench al abute — go
And thakketh° al hir white toute° — pat buttocks
And sith° aftir her swinke° — then **her swinke** their toil
Wendith meklich hom° to drinke — **Wendith** ... Go meekly home
45 And geth to har collacione,° — collation

191

A wel° fair processione.   very
  An other abbei is ther bi,
For soth,° a gret fair nunnerie,   truth
Up a river of swet milke,
150 Whar is plenté gret° of silk.   **plenté gret** great quantity
Whan the someris° dai is hote,   summer's
The yung nunnes takith a bote
And doth ham° forth in that river,   **doth ham** go
Bothe with oris° and with stere.°   oars   rudder
155 Whan hi° beth für° fram the abbei,   they   far
Hi makith ham° nakid for to plei   themselves
And lepith dune° in to the brimme°   down   stream
And doth ham sleilich° for to swimme.   slyly
The yung monkes, that hi° seeth,   them
160 Hi doth° ham up, and forth hi fleeth   get
And commith to the nunnes anon,
And ech monke him° taketh on°   for himself   one
And snellich berrith° forth har prei   **snellich berrith** quickly bears
To the mochil° grei abbei   great
165 And techith the nunnes an oreisun°   prayer
With jamblevé° up and dun.   raised leg
The monke that wol be stalun° gode   stallion
And kan set aright is hode,°   **is hode** his hood
He schal hab° withoute danger°   have   difficulty
170 Twelve wives eche yere,
Al throgh right and noght throgh grace,
For to do himsilf solace.
And thilk° monke that slepith best   that
And doth is likam° al to rest,   **doth . . .** gives his body
175 Of him is hoppe,° God hit wote,°   hope   knows
To be sone vadir° abbot.   father
  Whose wol° com that lond to,   **Whose wol** Whoever will
Ful grete penance he mot° do: must
Seve° yere in swineis dritte°   Seven   **swineis dritte** swine's dung
180 He mote wade, wol° ye i-witte,°   well   know
Al anon up to the chynne,
So he schal the lond winne.
  Lordinges gode and hend,°   courteous
Mot° ye never of° world wend,°   May   from   go
185 Fort° ye stond to° yure cheance   Unless   **stond to** encounter
And fulfille that penance,
That ye mote that lond i-se°   see
And never more turne awé.°   away
Prey we God, so mote hit be,
190 Amen, pur° Seint Charité.   by

THE EARLY
FOURTEENTH
CENTURY

ॐ

ROBERT MANNYNG

Handling Sin

(1303–ca. 1317, Northeast Midland)

‿❦‿

Robert Mannyng describes himself as belonging to Bourne (Brunne), in Lincolnshire. He was born not later than the year 1283 and studied at Cambridge (ca. 1298–1302). In 1302 he became a canon of the Gilbertine order at Sempringham priory (six miles from Bourne) and in 1303 began the writing of *Handling Sin*. In his prologue written in 1317 or later, which is reprinted below, he tells us that he lived in the priory for fifteen years. The only other definite information we have about him is that he completed his *Story of England* in 1338 at the Gilbertine priory of Sixhills, also in Lincolnshire. Mannyng may also be the author of an adaptation (ca. 1300–25) of the Latin *Meditations on the Life of Christ*, ascribed to St. Bonaventura. In any case, his fame rests secure on his two major poems.

Both are works of considerable size and scope. *Handling Sin* surveys in some twelve thousand lines the entire range of the Ten Commandments, the Seven Deadly Sins, the Sin of Sacrilege, the Seven Sacraments, the Twelve Points of Shrift, and the Eight Joys of Grace. *The Story of England* in some seventeen thousand lines summarizes history from Noah to King Edward I. Both of Mannyng's works are, inevitably, derivative, but Mannyng adapts his sources freely and adds a wealth of anecdotes, observations, and opinions of his own.

The framework of *Handling Sin* is determined by its source, *Le Manuel des Péchés*, an Anglo-Norman poem attributed dubiously to William of Waddington, probably composed around 1260 in Lincolnshire. The tale of the sacrilegious carolers well illustrates the freedom with which Mannyng reworked the cautionary tales contained in his original. He gains immediacy for the miraculous curse of the dancers of Kölbigk by transferring the incident from Saxony to England. From his reading of the *Life of St. Edith of Wilton* (who died in 984) he adds the fascinating sequel concerning the cure of one of the victims. He provides credibility by blandly citing the Bishop of "St. Toulouse" (actually "holy Toul") as his authority. And he softens the theological severity of his *exemplum* by personally sympathizing more with the sacrilegious dancers than with the impatient priest who cursed them.

Mannyng's syntax is often awkward, and his style shows little influence of the rhetorical manuals that he must have studied at Cambridge; but he writes as he probably spoke—colloquially, conversationally, unassumingly. If, as is likely, he was Master of Novices at Sempringham, he naturally thought of himself not as an author seeking literary fame but as a responsible canon teaching young laymen about life. Despite his limitations, Mannyng deserves to be recognized as a worthy predecessor of Gower and Chaucer, the great raconteurs.

The meter is rhyming four-beat couplets; see Introduction, type 5, page 31.

The only convenient edition is Robert of Brunne, *Handlyng Synne*, ed. F. J. Furnivall, EETS 119, 123 (London, 1901–03). For the legend of the dancers, see Kenneth Sisam, *Fourteenth Century Verse and Prose* (Oxford, 1921), pages xxxvi–xxxvii, 204–05. For bibliography, see Wells, ch. 6.2 (and ch. 3.7); *CBEL*, 1.183, 5.122; Legge, 213–14.

Prologue

[Lines 43–88]

For lewde° men Y undyrtoke   unlearned
On° Englyssh tunge to make thys boke,   In
For many ben° of swyche° manere   are   such
That talys and rymys wyl blethly° here.   gladly
5   Yn gamys and festys and at the ale
Love men to lestene trotevale°   **lestene trotevale** hear trifles
That may falle ofte to vylanye,°   bawdry
To dedly synne, or other folye.
For swyche° men have Y make this ryme   such
10   That they may weyl dyspende here tyme
And theryn sumwhat for to here
To leve° al swyche foul manere°   desist from   behavior
And for to kunne° knowe therynne   be able to
That they wene° no synne be ynne.   may suppose
15   To alle Crystyn men undir sunne,
And to gode men of Brunne,°   Bourne (Lincolnshire)
And speciali alle be° name   by
The felaushepe of Symprynghame,°   Sempringham
Roberd of Brunne greteth yow
20   In al godenesse that may to prow,°   **to prow** tend to profit
Of Brunnewake° yn Kestevene°   Bourne   Kesteven (Lincolnshire)
Syxe myle besyde Sympryngham evene.
   Y dwelled yn the pryorye
Fyftene yere yn cumpanye.
25   In the tyme of gode Dane Jone°   **Dane Jone** Don John
Of Camelton, that now is gone,
In hys tyme was Y there ten yeres
And knewe and herd of hys maneres;
Sythyn° with Dane Jone of Clyntone   Then
30   Fyve wyntyr wyth hym gan° Y wone.°   did   dwell
Dane Felyp° was mayster that tyme   **Dane Felyp** Don Philip (Master, 1298–1332)
That Y began thys Englyssh ryme.
The yeres of grace fyl than to be
A thousynd and thre hundred and thre.
35   In that tyme turnede Y thys
On° Englyssh tunge out of Frankys°   Into   French
Of a boke as Y fonde° ynne.   found it
Men clepyn° the boke *Handlyng Synne*.   name
In Frenshe, ther° a clerk° hyt sees,   where   scholar
40   He clepyth hyt *Manuel de Pécchés*.
Manuel ys "handlyng with honde."
Pécchés ys "synne," Y undyrstonde.

195

These twey° wurdys that beyn otwynne,°   two   **beyn otwynne** are separated
Do° hem togedyr, ys "handlyng synne"   Put
45 And weyl ys clepyd° for thys skyle,°   named   reason
And, as Y wote,° yow shew Y wyle.   know best

The Sin of Sacrilege

[Lines 8987–9252]

Karolles,° wrastlynges, or somour games,   Round-dance songs
Whosoever haunteth any swyche° shames   such
Yn cherche other° yn cherche-yerd,   or
Of sacrylage he may be aferd.°   afraid
5 Or° entyrludes or syngynge   Either
Or tabure-bete° or other pypynge.   drumming
Alle swyche thyng forbodyn es°   **forbodyn es** is forbidden
Whyle the prest stondeth at messe.
Alle swyche° to every gode preste ys lothe,°   such   hateful
10 And sunner wyl he make hym wroth°   **hym wroth** himself (the priest) angry
Than he wyl that hath no wyt°   learning
Ne° undyrstondeth nat Holy Wryt.   And
And specyaly at hyghe° tymes   solemn
Karolles° to synge and rede rymys   Round-dance songs
15 Noght yn none° holy stedes°   **Noght** . . . In any   places
That myght dysturble° the prestes bedes,°   disturb   prayers
Or° yyf he were yn orysun°   Either   supplication
Or any outher devocyun,
Sacrylage ys alle hyt tolde,°   counted
20 Thys and many other folde.
But for to leve° yn cherche to daunce,°   desist   **to daunce** from dancing
Y shal yow telle a ful° grete chaunce,°   very   event
And Y trow,° the most° that fel°   believe   greatest part   happened
Ys as soth° as the gospel.   true
25 And fyl° thys chaunce yn thys londe,   happened
Yn Ingland, as Y undyrstonde;
Yn a kynges tyme that hyght Edward°   **hyght Edward** is called Edward (r. 1042–66)
Fyl thys chaunce° that was so hard.   event
Hyt was uppon a Crystemesse nyght
30 That twelve folys a karolle dyght.°   **folys** . . . foolish people set up a round-dan[ce]
Yn wodehed, as° hyt were yn cuntek,°   **wodehed, as** madness, as if   strife
They come° to a tounne men calles Colbek.°   came   Kölbigk (Germany)
The cherche of the tounne that they to come
Ys of Seynt Magne,° that suffred martyrdome;   Magnus

196

35 Of Seynt Bukcestre hyt ys also,
     Seynt Magnes' süster, that they come to.
     Here° names of alle thus fonde° Y wryte,   *Their found*
     And as Y wote,° now shul ye wyte.°   *know know*
     Here lodesman° that made hem glew,°   *leader **hem glew** music for them*
40 Thus ys wryte,° he hyghte° Gerlew.   *written was called*
     Twey° maydens were yn here coveyne,°   *Two band*
     Mayden Merswynde and Wybessyne.
     Alle these come thedyr for that enchesone°   ***for** . . . because*
     Of the prestes doghtyr of the tounne.°   ***prestes** . . . town priest's daughter*
45   The prest hyght° Robert, as Y kan ame;°   *was called report*
     Azone hyght hys sone by name;
     Hys doghter that these men wulde have
     Thus ys wryte° that she hyght Ave.   *written*
     Ech oune consented to o° wyl   *one*
50 Who shuld go Ave oute to tyl;°   *entice*
     They graunted° ech one out to sende   *agreed*
     Bothe Wybessyne and Merswynde.
     These wommen yede° and tolled here° oute   *went **tolled here** enticed her*
     Wyth hem° to karolle the cherche aboute.   *them*
55 Bevne ordeyned here° karollyng;   ***ordeyned here** directed their*
     Gerlew endyted what they shuld syng.
       Thys ys the karolle that they sunge,
     As telleth the Latyn tunge:

        Equitabat Bevo per silvam frondosam;
60   *Ducebat secum Merswyndam formosam.*
        Quid stamus? Cur non imus?

        By the leved° wode rode Bevolyne;   *leafy*
        Wyth hym he ledde feyre Merswyne.
        Why stonde we? Why go we noght?

65 Thys ys the karolle that Grysly wroght.
     Thys songe sunge they yn the cherche-yerd—
     Of foly were they nothyng aferd°—   ***nothyng aferd** in no way afraid*
     Unto° the matynes were alle done,   *Until*
     And the messe shuld bygynne sone.°   *at once*
70   The preste hym revest° to begynne messe,   ***hym revest** robed himself*
     And they ne left° therfore, neverthelesse,   ***ne left** didn't desist*
     But daunsed furthe as they bygan;
     For alle the messe they ne blan.°   *desisted*
     The preste, that stode at the autere°   *altar*
75 And herde here° noyse and here bere,°   *their clamor*
     Fro the auter down he nam,°   *betook himself*
     And to the cherche porche he cam

And seyd, "On Goddes behalve, Y yow forbede
That ye no lenger do swych° dede,   such
80 But cometh° yn on° feyre manere   come in
Goddes servyse for to here,°   hear
And doth at° Crystyn mennys lawe.   **doth at** attend to
Karolleth no more, for Crystys awe!
Wurschyppeth hym with alle youre myght
85 That of the Vyrgyne was bore° thys nyght."   born
    For° alle hys byddyng lefte° they noght   Despite desisted
But daunsed furth as they thoght.°   wished
The prest tharefore was sore agreved.
He preyd God, that° he on belevyd,°   whom **on belevyd** believed in
90 And for Seynt Magne, that he wulde so werche°—   bring it about
Yn whos wurschyp sette was the cherche—
That swych a venjaunce were° on hem° sent,   would be them
Are° they out of that stede° were went,   Before place
That they myght ever ryght so wende°   **ryght** . . . continue just so
95 Unto° that tyme twelvemonth ende.   Until
    (Yn the Latyne that Y fonde thore,
He seyth nat "twelvemonth" but "evermore"!)
    He cursed hem there al saume°   together
As they karoled on here° gaume.   their
100 As sone as the preste hadde so spoke,
Every hande yn outher° so fast was loke°   other locked
That no man myght with no wundyr°   **no wundyr** any miracle
That° twelvemonthe parte hem° asundyr.   During that them
    The preste yede° yn, whan thys was done,   went
105 And commaunded hys sone Azone
That he shulde go swythe° aftyr Ave,   quickly
Oute of that karolle algate° to have.   **karolle algate** round-dance song under circumstances
But al too late that wurde was seyd,
For on hem alle was the venjaunce leyd.
110 Azone wende° weyl for to spede.°   expected succeed
Unto the karolle as swythe° he yede;°   quickly as possible went
Hys systyr by the arme he hente,°   seized
And the arme fro the body wente.
Men wundred alle, that there wore,°   were
115 And merveyle mowe° ye here more,   may
For, sethen° he had the arme yn hande,   after
The body yede furth karoland,°   **yede** . . . went on dancing
And nother° body ne the arme   neither
Bledde never blode, colde ne warme,
120 But was as drye with al the haunche
As of° a stok were ryve° a braunche.   **As of** As if from torn
    Azone to hys fadyr went

And broght hym a sory present.
"Loke, fadyr," he seyd, "and have hyt here,
125 The arme of thy doghtyr dere
That was myn owne syster Ave
That Y wende° Y myght a save.°   supposed   **myght...could have saved**
Thy cursyng now sene hyt ys
With venjaunce on thyn owne flessh.
130 Fellyche° thou cursedest and over-sone.°   Maliciously   too quickly
Thou askedest venjaunce. Thou hast thy bone!"°   request
    You thar° nat aske yyf there was wo   need
With the preste and with many mo.°   more
The prest that cursed for that daunce,
135 On some of hys fyl° harde chaunce.   **hys fyl** his kin fell
He toke hys doghtyr° arme forlorn   daughter's
And byryed° hyt on the morn;   buried
And nexte day the arme of Ave
He fonde hyt lyggyng° above the grave.   lying
140 He byryed hyt on anouther° day,   a second
And eft° above the grave hyt lay;   again
The thrydde tyme he byryed hyt,
And eft was hyt kast oute of the pyt.
The prest wulde byrye° hyt no more;   bury
145 He dredde° the venjaunce ferly sore.°   dreaded   **ferly sore** very sorely
Ynto the cherche he bare the arme
For drede and doute° of more harme.   fear
He ordeyned hyt for to be
That every man myght° with ye° hyt se.   could   eye
150   These men that yede° so karolland°   went   carol dancing
Alle that yere hand yn hand,
They never oute of that stede° yede,   place
Ne none myght hem thenne lede.°
There° the cursyng fyrst bygan,   Where
155 Yn that place aboute they ran,
That° never ne felte they no werynes,°   So that   weariness
As many bodyes for goyng dös,°   do
Ne mete° ete ne drank drynke,   **Ne mete** Nor food
Ne slepte onely alepy° wynke.   a single
160 Nyght ne° day they wyst° of none,   or   knew
Whan hyt was come, whan hyt was gone.
Frost ne snogh, hayle ne reyne,
Of colde ne hete felte they no peyne.
Heere ne nayles never grewe,
165 Ne solowed° clothes, ne turned hewe.°   soiled their   complexion
Thundyr ne lyghtnyng dyd hem° no dere;°   them   harm

153. Nor could anyone lead them thence.

Goddes mercy dyd hyt fro hem were;°   shield
But sungge° that songge that the wo wroght: they sang
"Why stonde we, why go we noght?"
170   What man shuld thyr be yn thys lyve
That ne wulde hyt see and thedyr dryve?
The Emperoure Henry° come fro Rome   Henry II (r. 1014–24)
For to see thys harde dome.°   judgment
Whan he hem say,° he wepte sore   saw
175 For the myschefe that he sagh° thore.   saw
He ded come wryghtes° for to make   **ded . . . had carpenters come**
Coveryng over hem for tempest sake;
But that° they wroght, hyt was yn veyn,   what
For hyt come to no certeyn,°   **come . . . had no effect**
180 For that they sette on oo° day,   one
On the touther° downe hyt lay.   next
Ones, twyys, thryys, thus they wroght,
And alle here° makyng was for noght.   their
Myght no coveryng hyle° hem fro colde   shield
185 Tyl tyme of mercy that Cryst hyt wolde.
     Tyme of grace fyl° thurgh hys myght   happened
At the twelvemonth ende on the Yole° nyght.   Yule
The same oure that the prest hem banned,°   cursed
The same oure atwynne° they woned;°   separated became
190 That houre that he cursed hem ynne,
That same oure they yede° atwynne;   went
And, as° yn twynkelyng of an ye,°   as if eye
Ynto the cherche gyn° they flye,°   did fly
And on the pavement they fyl alle downe
195 As they hade be dede or fal° yn a swone.   fallen
     Thre days styl they lay ech° one,   each
That° none steryd other° flesshe or bone,   So that **steryd other** stirred either
And at the thre days ende
To-lyfe° God grauntede hem to wende.°   Alive go
200 They sette hem upp and spak apert°   **spak apert** spoke openly
To the parysshe prest, Syre Robert:
     "Thou art ensample and enchesun°   **ensample . . . precedent and cause**
Of oure long confusyun.
Thou maker art of oure travayle,
205 That ys to many grete mervayle;
And thy traveyle shalt thou sone° ende,   at once
For to thy long home sone shalt thou wende."°   go
     Alle they ryse° that yche tyde°   rose **yche tyde** same time
But Ave; she lay dede besyde.
210 Grete sorowe had here° fadyr, here brother;   her
Merveyle and drede had alle outher—

Y trow° no drede of soule dede,°   suppose   **soule dede** her soul's death
But with pyne° was broght the body dede.°   torment   **broght . . . the body** killed
The fyrst man was the fadyr, the prest,
215 That deyd aftyr the doghtyr nest.°   next
Thys yche° arme that was of Ave   same
That none myght leye yn grave,
The Emperoure dyd a vessel werche°   have made
To do° hyt yn and hange yn the cherche,   put
220 That° alle men myght se hyt and knawe   So that
And thenk on the chaunce° when men hyt sawe.   incident
    These men that hadde go° thus karolland°   gone   carol dancing
Alle the yere fast hand yn hand,
Thogh that they were than° asunder,   then
225 Yyt alle the worlde spake of hem wunder.
That same hoppyng that they fyrst yede,°   went with
That daunce yede they thurgh land and lede,°   nation
And as° they ne myght fyrst° be unbounde,   just as   **ne . . .** couldn't at first
Ne myght they never° come agheyn   **Ne . . .** They could now never
230 Togedyr to oo stede certeyn.°   **oo . . .** one fixed place
    Foure yede to the courte of Rome,
And ever hoppyng aboute they nome.°   continued
With sundyr lepys° come they thedyr,   **sundyr lepys** separate leaps
But they come never efte° togedyr.   again
235 Here° clothes ne roted,° ne nayles grewe,   Their   **ne roted** didn't rot
Ne heere ne wax,° ne solowed hewe,°   grew   **solowed hewe** faded their complexion
Ne never hadde they amendement°   remedy
That we herde° at any corseynt°   heard of   saint's relic
But at° the vyrgyne Seynt Edyght.°   **But at** Except from   Edith (d. 984)
240 There was he botened,° Seynt Teodryght.°   cured   Theodoric
On Oure Lady-Day° yn Lenten tyde,   March 25
As he slepte here° toumbe besyde,   her (Edith's)
There he hade hys medycyne
At Seynt Edyght, the holy vyrgyne.
245   Brunyng° the bysshope of seynt Tolous°   Bruno   **seynt Tolous** holy Toul (France)
Wrote thys tale so merveylous;
Seththe° was hys name of more renoun—   Later
Men called hym the Pope Leoun.°   Leo IX (Pope, 1049–54)
Thys° at the court of Rome they wyte,°   This story   know
250 And yn the kronykeles hyt ys wryte°   written
Yn many stedys° beyounde the see   places
More than ys yn thys cuntré.
Tharfor men seye, and weyl° ys trowed:°   well   believed
"The nere° the cherche, the fyrther fro God."   nearer to
255   So fare° men here by thys tale: behave
Some holde hyt but a trotevale;°   trifle

Yn other stedys° hyt ys ful dere,°
And for grete merveyle they wyl hyt here.°
A tale hyt ys of feyre shewyng,°
260 Ensample° and drede° aghens cursyng.
Thys tale Y tolde yow to make yow aferde°
Yn cherche to karolle or yn cherche-yerde,
Namely aghens° the prestys wylle.
Leveth° whan he byddeth yow be stylle!

places **ful dere** very precious
hear

feyre shewyng fine significance
An example   warning
afraid

Namely aghens Particularly against
Cease

Now Springs the Spray

(ca. 1300, West Midland)

ᴥ

This song belongs to the common heritage of western European lyrics, in Latin, Old French, Provençal, Anglo-Norman, and Middle English. Most of them have survived in undatable manuscripts bereft of the musical settings associated with them. Specifically, it follows the pattern of the *chanson d'aventure*—'song of chance meeting.' The genre eventually sank to the level of nursery rhymes, such as "Where Are You Going, My Pretty Maid?" The brilliance of meter, alliteration, and refrain, however, clearly elevates *Now Springs the Spray* above most examples of the genre, whether early or late. The author of the religious lyric *The Five Joys of Mary* (p. 205, below) may have deliberately imitated the opening line of the first stanza.

The meter is seven-line, tail-rhyme stanzas; see Introduction, type 15, page 32.

The best edition of this lyric is in *English Lyrics of the Thirteenth Century*, ed. Carleton Brown (Oxford, 1932), pages 119–20. For bibliography see Wells, ch. 13.25.

Nou sprinkes the sprai.°	foliage
Al for love Icche am so seek°	sick
That slepen I ne mai.°	*ne mai* cannot
Als° I me rode this endre° dai	As **me** ... rode out the other
O° mi playinge,°	On sport
Seih° I hwar a litel mai°	Saw maiden
Bigan to singge:	
"The clot him clingge!	
Wai es him i louve-longinge	
Sal libben ai."°	
Nou sprinkes the sprai.	
Al for love Icche am so seek	
That slepen I ne mai.	

5 (line 5 marker)
10 (line 10 marker)

8–10. May the sod cling to him! Woeful it is for the one who must always live in (unrequited) longing for love.

Son° Icche herde that mirie note,   As soon as
15   Thider I drogh.°   drew
I fonde hire° in an herber swot°   her **herber swot** fragrant arbor
Under a bough
With joie inogh.°   enough
Son° I asked: "Thou mirie mai,°   At once maiden
20   Hwi sinkestou° ai?"   do you sing

   Nou sprinkes the sprai.
Al for love Icche am so seek
That slepen I ne mai.

   Than answerde that maiden swote
25   Midde wordes fewe:
"Mi lemman° me haves bihot°   sweetheart **haves bihot** has promised
Of louve trewe.
He chaunges anewe.
Yif I mai, it shal him rewe°   **it** . . . he shall rue it
30   Bi this dai."

   Nou sprinkes the sprai.
Al for love Icche am so seek
That slepen I ne mai.

The Five Joys of Mary

(ca. 1330, Southwestern)

ᖙᖕ

The religious lyric *The Five Joys of Mary* and the four love lyrics following (pp. 208–215) are all found in the Harley Miscellany (MS. 2253), which was compiled in Hereford around 1330–39 and includes works of various ages, such as *King Horn* (p. 114, above, ca. 1225) and *The Sayings of St. Bernard* (p. 163, above, ca. 1275), some composed in Middle English, some in Anglo-Norman or French, and some in Latin.

The celebration of the joys of the Virgin was a popular medieval theme. More than a dozen extant Middle English poems deal in one way or another with the topic, and passing references, as in *Sir Gawain and the Green Knight* (p. 376), occur frequently. The Harley *Five Joys* is neither the oldest nor the most extensive of these poems, but it is certainly the most striking because of the compelling way in which it moves from the secular tone of the *chanson d'aventure*, already familiar in *Now Springs the Spray* (p. 203, above), to its devout religious purpose. The joys here celebrated are the Annunciation, the Nativity, the Epiphany (not referred to in the other Middle English treatments), the Resurrection, and the Ascension of Mary; the Assumption, which is handled separately in the other Middle English treatments, is subsumed under the Ascension.

The meter is seven-line, tail-rhyme stanzas; see Introduction, type 19, page 33.

The best edition of the lyric is in George L. Brooks, ed., *The Harley Lyrics: The Middle English Lyrics of MS. Harley 2253*, 2nd ed. (Manchester, 1956), pages 65–66. The manuscript is reproduced in *Facsimile of British Museum MS. Harley 2253*, ed. N. R. Ker, EETS 255 (London, 1965), item 67. For bibliography see Wells, ch. 13.209.

Ase Y me rod this ender° day	**me** . . . rode out the other
By grene wode to seche° play,	seek
Mid herte Y thohte al on a may,°	maiden
Suetest of alle thinge.	
5 Lythe,° and Ich ou° telle may	Listen you
Al of that swete thinge.	
This maiden is suete ant fre° of blod,	noble
Briht, and feyr, of milde mod.°	spirit
Alle heo mai don us° god	**Alle** . . . She may do all of us
10 Thurh hire bysechynge.°	**Thurh** . . . Through beseeching her
Of hire he tok fleysh and blod,	
Jesu Crist, hevene Kynge.	

With al mi lif Y love that may.°   maiden
Heo° is mi solas nyht and day,   she
15 My joie, and eke° my beste play,°   also   pleasure
    Ant eke my love-longynge.°   longing for love
Al the betere me° is that day   for me
    That Ich of hire° synge.   her

Of alle thinge Y love hir mest,°   most
20 My dayes blis, my nyhtes rest.
Heo° counseileth and helpeth best   She
    Bothe elde and yynge.°   **elde . . .** old and young
Nou Y may, yef Y wole,°   wish
    The fif joyes mynge.°   enumerate

25 The fürst joie of that wymman:°   woman
When Gabriel from hevene cam
Ant seide God shulde bicome man
    Ant of hire be bore°   born
And bringe up of helle pyn°   **helle pyn** hell's torment
30   Monkyn° that wes forlore.°   Mankind   lost

That other° joie of that may°   second   maiden
Wes o° Cristesmasse day,   on
When God wes bore, on thoro lay,°   **on . . .** a perfect light
    Ant brohte us lyhtnesse.°   illumination
35 The ster° wes seie° byfore day;   star   seen
    This hirdes° bereth wytnesse.   **This hirdes** The shepherds

The thridde joie of that levedy:°   lady
That, men clepeth° the Epyphany,   call
When the kynges come wery
40   To presente hyre° sone   her
With myrre, gold, and encenz,
    That wes mon bicome.°

The furthe joie we telle mawen:°   may
On Ester-morewe,° when hit gon dawen,°   Easter morning   **gon dawen** dawned
45 Hyre sone that wes slawen°   slain
    Aros in fleysh and bon.
More joie ne mai me haven,°   **ne . . .** one cannot have
    Wyf ne mayden non.

42. The son who had become man.

The fifte joie of that wymman:°   woman
50 When hire° body to hevene cam,   her
The soule to the body nam°   united
    Ase hit wes woned to bene.°   **woned** ... accustomed to be
Crist, leve° us alle with that wymman   grant
    That joie al for te sene.°   **te sene** to see

55 Preye we alle to oure Levedy°   Lady
Ant to the sontes° that woneth hire by°   saints **woneth** ... dwell with her
That heo° of us haven merci   they
    Ant that we ne misse
In this world to ben° holy   be
60   Ant wynne hevene blysse.
                        Amen.

Alysoun

(ca. 1330, Southwestern)

Unlike Thomas of Hailes's *Love Rune* (p. 156, above), this courtly *roun* (l. 44) deals with the perennial sufferings of an earthly lover. The meter is seven-line, tail-rhyme stanzas; see Introduction, type 16, page 32.

The best edition is in George L. Brooks, ed., *The Harley Lyrics: The Middle English Lyrics of MS. Harley 2253*, 2nd ed. (Manchester, 1956), page 33. For the manuscript see *Facsimile of British Museum MS. Harley 2253*, ed. N. R. Ker, EETS 255 (London, 1965), item 29. For bibliography see Wells, ch. 13.12.

Bytuene Mersh and Averil°	**Mersh** . . . March and April
Whan spray° biginneth to springe,	foliage
The lütel foul° hath hire° wyl	birds their
On hyre lüd° to synge.	**On** . . . In their language
5 Ich libbe in love-longinge°	longing for love
For semlokest° of alle thynge.	the comeliest
Heo° may me blisse bringe.	She
Ich am in hire baundoun.°	**hire baundoun** her power
An hendy hap Ichabbe y-hent;°	*hendy* . . . gracious fortune I have won
10 *Ichot° from hevene it is me sent.*	I know
From alle wymmen mi love is lent°	turned
And lyht° on Alysoun.	lights
On heu hire her° is fayr ynoh,°	**On** . . . In hue her hair abundantly
Hire browe broune, hire eye blake.	
15 With lossum chere heo° on me loh,°	**lossum** . . . loving look she smiled
With middel smal and wel y-make.	
Bote° heo me wolle to hire take	Unless
For te büen° hire owen make,°	be **owen make** own mate
Longe to lyven Ichulle° forsake	I shall
20 And feye° fallen adoun.	death-fated

208

Alysoun

An hendy hap Ichabbe y-hent;
Ichot from hevene it is me sent.
From alle wymmen mi love is lent
    And lyht on Alysoun.

25   Nihtes when Y wende° and wake,   pace
      Forthi° myn wonges waxeth won,°   Whereby   **wonges** ... cheeks grow wan
    Levedi,° al for thine sake   Lady
      Longinge is y-lent me on.°   **y-lent** ... imposed on me
    In world nis non so wyter mon°   **nis** ... there is no man so wise
30   That al hire bounté telle con.°   **hire** ... her excellence can count
    Hire swyre° is whittore then the swon,   neck
      And feyrest may° in toune.   **feyrest may** she the fairest maiden

    An hendy hap Ichabbe y-hent;
    Ichot from hevene it is me sent.
35   *From alle wymmen mi love is lent*
        And lyht on Alysoun.

    Ich am for wowyng° al forwake°   loving   weary from sleeplessness
      Wery so° water in wore,°   as   a whirlpool (?)
    Lest eny reve me° my make°   **reve me** rob me of   mate
40   Ychabbe y-yyrned yore.°
    Betere is tholien whyle sore°   **tholien** ... to suffer sorely for a while
    Then mournen evermore.
    Geynest° under gore,°   Loveliest one   clothing
      Herkne to my roun!°   song

45   *An hendy hap Ichabbe y-hent;*
    Ichot from hevene it is me sent.
    From alle wymmen my love is lent
        And lyht on Alysoun.

40. Whom I have yearned for long.

Spring

(ca. 1330, Southwestern)

∽

Spring is a fine example of the *reverdie*, the song inspired by the return of spring. The combination of rhyme and alliteration is particularly striking, though sound sometimes overwhelms sense. Line 20 is especially difficult. Perhaps it should read, *Meles meres with hüere makes*, 'Mares murmur with their mates,' but it seems unlikely that the Harley scribe understood what he was writing at this point.

The meter is twelve-line, tail-rhyme stanzas; see Introduction, type 21, page 33.

The best edition of the lyric is in George L. Brooks, ed., *The Harley Lyrics: The Middle English Lyrics of MS. Harley 2253*, 2nd ed. (Manchester, 1956), pages 43–44. For the manuscript see *Facsimile of British Museum MS. Harley 2253*, ed. N. R. Ker, EETS 225 (London, 1965), item 43. For bibliography see Wells, ch. 13.14.

Lenten ys° come with love to toune,° — **Lenten ys** Spring has   men's dwellings
With blosmen,° and with briddes roune,° — blossoms   **briddes roune** birds' songs
   That° al this blisse bryngeth,° — Spring which   brings
Dayes-eyes° in this° dales, — Daisies   the
5 Notes swete of nyhtegales.
   Uch foul° song singeth. — **Uch foul** Each bird a
The threstel-coc him threteth oo.° — **threstel-coc** . . . thrush scolds ever
Away is hüere° wynter woo° — their   sorrow
   When woderove° springeth. — woodruff
10 This° foules singeth ferly fele° — The   **ferly fele** marvelously much
Ant wlyteth° on hüere wynter wele° — look back   state
   That° al the wode ryngeth. — So that

The rose rayleth hire rode;° — **rayleth** . . . puts on her red hue
The leves on the lyhte° wode — gay
15   Waxen° al with wille.° — Grow   a will
The mone mandeth° hire bleo;° — sends out   radiance
The lilie is lossom° to seo,° — lovely   see
   The fenyl,° and the fille.° — fennel   chervil
Wowes this° wilde drakes; — **Wowes this** Woo the
20 Miles mürgeth hüere makes° — **Miles** . . . Creatures (?) delight their mates
   Ase strem that striketh stille.° — **striketh stille** glides silently

Mody meneth;° so doth mo!°
Ichot° Ych am on° of tho°
  For° love that likes ille.°

Mody meneth The passionate lament **doth mo** do others
I know one those
Because of **likes ille** ill satisfies

25 The mone mandeth hire° lyht;
  So döth the semly° sonne bryht
    When briddes° singeth breme.°
  Deawes donketh° the dounes;°
  Deores° with hüere derne rounes°
30   Domes for te deme;°
  Wormes woweth° under cloude;°
  Wymmen waxeth wounder° proude,
    So° wel hit wol hem seme.°
  Yef me° shal wonte° wille of on,°
35   This wünne weole° Y wole forgon°
    Ant wyht° in wode° be fleme.°

mandeth hire sends out her
fair
birds loudly
Deawes donketh Dews soak hills
Animals **hüere...** their secret converse
Domes... To express their feelings
make love clod
waxeth wounder grow wondrous
As **wol...** will suit them
I fail to have my one
wünne weole wealth of joy abandon
at once the woods an exile

April

(ca. 1330, Southwestern)

ɷ

Like *Spring*, this Harley lyric is another fine example of the *reverdie*. The lover complains (l. 32) that his longing is making him turn, literally, "green," but there is presumably no intention of comic exaggeration here, for the adjective had a more neutral sense in Middle English than it does in Modern English.

The meter is eight-line (four long-line), tail-rhyme stanzas; see Introduction, type 11, pages 31–32.

The best edition of the lyric is in George L. Brooks, ed., *The Harley Lyrics: The Middle English Lyrics of MS. Harley 2253*, 2nd ed. (Manchester, 1956), page 63. The manuscript is reproduced in *Facsimile of British Museum MS. Harley 2253*, ed. N. R. Ker, EETS 255 (London, 1965), item 65. For bibliography see Wells, ch. 13.20.

When the nyhtegale singes,
    The wodes waxen° grene.   grow
Lef ant gras ant blosme springes
    In Averyl,° Y wene.°   April   suppose
5   Ant love is to myn herte gon
    With one° spere so kene,   a
Nyht ant day my blod hit drynkes;
    Myn herte deth° me tene.°   causes   suffering

Ich have loved al this yer
10   That° Y may love na more.   So that
Ich have siked moni syk,°   **siked . . .** sighed many a sigh
    Lemmon,° for thin ore.°   Sweetheart   favor
Me nis° love never the ner,°   **Me nis** To me is   nearer
    Ant that me reweth° sore.   grieves
15   Suete lemmon, thench° on me;   think
    Ich have loved thee yore.°   long

Suete lemmon, Y preye thee
    Of love one° speche.   a
Whil Y lyve in world so wyde,
20   Other nülle Y seche.°   **nülle . . .** I won't seek

With thy love, my suete leof,°   dear
   My blis thou mihtes eche.°   **mihtes eche** could increase
A suete cös° of thy mouth   kiss
   Mihte be my leche.°   physician

25   Suete lemmon,° Y preye thee   lover
   Of° a love-bene:°   For   love-boon
Yef thou me lovest ase men says,
   Lemmon, as I wene,°   suppose
Ant yef hit thi wille be,
30   Thou loke° that hit be sene.   **Thou loke** Look to it
So müchel° Y thenke upon thee   much
   That al Y waxe grene.°   **waxe grene** grow pale

Bituene Lyncolne ant Lyndeseye,°   Lindsey (Suffolk)
   Norhamptoun ant Lounde,°   London
35   Ne wot° I non so fayr a may°   know   maiden
   As° I go fore y-bounde.°   As the one   in bondage
Suete lemmon,° Y preye thee   sweetheart
   Thou lovie me a stounde.°   while
Y wole mone° my song   direct
40   On wham° that hit ys on ylong.°   **On wham** To whom   **on ylong** due

Love in Paris

(ca. 1330, Southwestern)

ↈ

The following spirited love lyric from the Harley Miscellany serves as a useful reminder of the multilingual and cosmopolitan culture of the fourteenth century. It is written in perfectly rhymed macaronic stanzas that move effortlessly between Latin and Anglo-Norman and conclude dramatically in English. The reference to the lover's lodging in Paris suggests that he is an English student abroad; and the dialect form *sügge* 'say' (l. 19) may indicate that he belongs to the Southwestern area of England, but all the Harley lyrics are recorded in the same dialect.

The meter is four-line stanzas; see Introduction, type 10, page 31.

The best edition of *Love in Paris* is in George L. Brooks, ed., *The Harley Lyrics: The Middle English Lyrics of MS. Harley 2253*, 2nd ed. (Manchester, 1956), page 55. For the manuscript see *Facsimile of British Museum MS. Harley 2253*, ed. N. R. Ker, EETS 255 (London, 1965), item 55. For bibliography see Wells, ch. 13.24a (s6).

> *Dum ludis floribus velud lacinia,*
> Le dieu d'amour moi tient en tiel *angustia,*
> Merour me tient de duel e de *miseria*
> Si je ne la ay *quam amo super omnia.*
>
> 5   *Eius amor tantum me facit fervere*
> Qe je ne soi *quid possum inde facere.*
> Pur ly covent *hoc seculum relinquere*
> Si je ne pus l'amour de li *perquirere.*
>
> Ele est si bele e gente dame *egregia*
> 10   Cum ele fust *imperatoris filia,*
> De beal semblant e *pulcra continencia;*
> Ele est la flur *in omni regis curia.*
>
> Quant je la vey, je su *in tali gloria*
> Come est la lune *celi inter sidera.*
> 15   Dieu la moi doint *sua misericordia*
> Beyser e fere que *secuntur alia.*
>
> *Scripsi hec carmina in tabulis.*
> Mon ostel est enmi la vile de Paris.
> May Y sügge namore, so wel me is.
> 20   Yef Hi deye for love of hire, duel hit ys!

Love in Paris

[TRANSLATION]

While you sport with the lace-like flowers,
The god of love holds me in such constraint
That he holds me as a mirror of sorrow and misery
If I don't get her whom I love beyond all others.

5 My love for her makes me rage so violently
That I don't know what I can do about it.
For her I shall have to abandon this world
If I can't win her love.

She is an illustrious lady, as beautiful and refined
10 As if she were the emperor's daughter,
Beautiful in appearance and charming in modesty.
She is the flower in the court of any king.

When I see her, I am in the same glory
As the moon in the sky among the stars.
15 God in his mercy bestow her on me
To kiss and to do whatever else follows.

I have written out these verses in my notebook.
My lodging is in Paris town.
I can say no more, so blissful am I.
20 If I die for love of her, a pity it is!

Sir Orfeo

(ca. 1330, East Midland)

❧

The relation of the Middle English lay of Sir Orfeo to the classical myth of the cult hero Orpheus is obscure. For Vergil and for Ovid the connotations of the myth were tragic: the great musician failed in his attempt to regain his beloved Eurydice from the underworld and died of grief (see *Georgics*, IV, and *Metamorphoses*, X–XI). For Boethius the tale served as a warning against the futility of looking backward into hell (see *Consolation of Philosophy*, III, m. 12). But the Middle English minstrel tells a very different version of the tale. Dame Heurodis is abducted by an otherworld lover into a Celtic fairyland, from which Orfeo happily regains her.

The prologue to *Sir Orfeo* claims that the source of the tale is a Breton lay. This origin would explain the Celtic coloration; unfortunately, however, not a single lay composed in the Breton language has survived. Many of the so-called Breton lays composed by Marie de France (ca. 1170–89) and her imitators either in Anglo-Norman or Old French may have been derived from Breton sources; and it is known that an Old French *Lai d'Orphey* (now lost) was in circulation in the twelfth century. Consequently, there is a strong likelihood that Breton minstrels played some part in the shaping of the original poem, which has survived only in this later English redaction.

As a graceful lay celebrating the triumph of marital devotion, *Sir Orfeo* has always been popular; and it is one of those rare works that, like *King Horn* (p. 114), survived in the oral tradition as a ballad (Child, No. 19) down to the nineteenth century.

The version of *Sir Orfeo* printed below is based on the Auchinleck Manuscript (ca. 1330–39), which was apparently compiled in a London bookshop by a group of professional redactors and translators. They were possibly responsible for the bold interpretation of the town of Traciens (l. 47; actually Old French, meaning 'Thracian') as Winchester and of Orfeo as an English king (ll. 25–26) who favors the election of a successor by parliament (l. 216). Lines 1–24 and 33–46 have been supplied from a later manuscript.

The meter is rhyming couplets; see Introduction, type 5, page 31.

The best edition of the lay is *Sir Orfeo*, ed. A. J. Bliss (London, 1954). For the manuscript see facsimile of Auchinleck MS (National Library of Scotland, Advocates 19.2.1), folio 302 r., containing lines 391–478, reproduced on page 20. For bibliography see Severs, ch. 1.86, and John B. Friedman, *Orpheus in the Middle Ages* (Cambridge, Mass., 1970).

We redyn° ofte and fynde y-wryte,°	read written
As clerkes don° us to wyte,°	make know
The layes that ben of harpyng°	**ben** . . . are sung with the harp
Ben y-founde° of frely thing.°	composed **frely thing** noble matter

216

5 Sum ben of wele° and sum of wo,	prosperity
And sum of joy and merthe also,	
Sum of trechery and sum of gyle,	
And sum of happes° that fallen by whyle,°	events **fallen ...** happen now and then
Sum of bourdys° and sum of rybaudry,°	jests ribaldry
10 And sum ther ben° of the feyré.°	are fairy
Of alle thing that men may se,	
Moost to lowe forsothe° they be.	**to ...** for praise indeed
In Brytayn this° layes arne y-wrytt,°	**Brytayn this** Brittany these written
Fürst y-founde° and forthe y-gete°	composed **forthe y-gete** brought forth
15 Of aventures that fellen by dayes,°	**fellen ...** happened long ago
Wherof Brytouns made her layes.	
When they myght o-wher heryn°	**o-wher heryn** anywhere hear
Of aventures that ther weryn,	
They toke her harpys° with game,°	**her harpys** their harps pleasure
20 Maden layes and yaf° it name.	gave
Of aventures that han befalle,	
Y can sum tell, but nought alle.	
Herken, lordyngys, that ben° trewe,	are
And Y wol you telle of Syr Orphewe.	
25 Orfeo was a ryche king,	
In Ingland an heighe° lording,	noble
A stalworth° man and hardi bo,°	stalwart **hardi bo** bold as well
Large and curteys° he was also.	**Large ...** Generous and courteous
His fader was comen of° King Pluto,	from
30 And his moder of King Juno,	
That sum time were as godes y-hold°	considered
For aventours that thai dede and told.	
Orpheo most of ony thing	
Lovede the gle° of harpyng.	minstrelsy
35 Syker° was every gode harpure	Sure
Of hym to have moche honour.	
Hymself loved for to harpe,	
And layde ther-on his wittes scharpe.	
He lerned so, ther nothing° was	not at all
40 A better harper in no plas.°	place
In the world was never man born	
That onus° Orpheo sat byforn,	ever
And° he myght of his harpyng her,°	If hear
He schulde° thinke that he wer	**He schulde** Who would not
45 In one of the joys of paradys,	
Suche joy and melody in his harpyng is.	
This king sojournd in Traciens,	
That was a cité of noble defens.°	fortification
(For Winchester was cleped tho°	**cleped tho** called then

217

50	Traciens withouten no.°)	denial
	The king hadde a quen of priis°	excellence
	That was y-cleped Dame Heurodis,	
	The fairest levedi° for the nones°	lady while
	That might gon° on bodi and bones,	walk
55	Ful of love and of godenisse;	
	Ac° no man may telle hir fairnise.	But
	Bifel° so in the comessing° of May—	It happened beginning
	When miri and hot is the day,	
	And oway° beth winterschours,°	away winter showers
60	And everi feld is ful of flours,	
	And blosme breme° on everi bough	**blosme breme** fresh blossom
	Overal wexeth° miri anough°—	grows enough
	This ich° quen, Dame Herodis,	same
	Tok to° maidens of priis°	two excellence
65	And went in an undrentide°	morning
	To play bi an orchard side,	
	To se the floures sprede and spring,	
	And to here the foules° sing.	birds
	Thai sett hem° doun al thre	themselves
70	Under a fair ympe-tre,°	orchard tree
	And wel° sone this fair quene	very
	Fel on slepe° opon the grene.	**on slepe** asleep
	The maidens durst hir nought awake,	
	Bot let hir ligge° and rest take.	lie
75	So sche slepe til afternone,	
	That undertide° was al y-done.°	morning gone
	Ac° as sone as sche gan awake,°	But **gan awake** awoke
	Sche crid and lothli bere° gan make.	**crid . . .** cried and a horrible scream
	Sche froted° hir honden and hir fet,	wrung
80	And crached° hir visage;° it bled wete.°	scratched face wet
	Hir riche robe hye° al torett°	she tore
	And was reveyd° out of hir witt.	driven
	The two maidens hir biside	
	No durst° with hir no leng° abide,	**No durst** Dared not longer
85	Bot ourn° to the palays ful right°	ran straight
	And told bothe squier and knight	
	That her quen awede wold,°	**awede wold** was going crazy
	And bad hem go and hir at-hold.°	seize
	Knightes urn and levedis° also,	**urn . . .** ran and ladies
90	Damisels sexti and mo.°	**Damisels . . .** Maidens sixty and more
	In the orchard to the quen hye° come	they
	And her up in her armes nome°	took
	And brought hir to bed atte last	
	And held hir there fine° fast.	very

95   Ac° ever she held° in o° cri   But   persisted   one
     And wold° up and owy.°   wished to go   away
          When Orfeo herd that tiding,
     Never him nas wers for nothing.°
     He come with knightes tene°   ten
100 To chaumber right bifor the quene
     And biheld° and seyd with grete pité: looked
          "O lef liif,° what is° thee,   **lef liif** dear life   is wrong with
     That ever yete hast ben so stille,°   quiet
     And now gredest wonder schille?°   **gredest** . . . cry wonderfully loud
105 Thi bodi, that was so white y-core,°   excellently
     With thine nailes is al totore!°   torn to pieces
     Alas, thi röde,° that was so red,   face
     Is al wan, as° thou were ded!   as if
     And also thine fingres smale
110 Beth al blodi and al pale!
     Allas! thi lovesum eyghen to°   **lovesum** . . . two lovely eyes
     Loketh so° man döth on his fo!   as
     A! Dame, Ich biseche merci!
     Lete ben° al this reweful° cri,   **Lete ben** Stop   pitiful
115 And tel me, what thee is° and hou,   is wrong with
     And what thing may thee help now!"
          Tho° lay sche stille atte last   Then
     And gan° to wepe swithe fast°   began   **swithe fast** very hard
     And seyd thus the king to:
120 "Allas, mi lord, Sir Orfeo!
     Seththen° we first togider were,   Since
     Ones wroth° never we nere;°   **Ones wroth** Once angry   were
     Bot ever Ich have y-loved thee
     As mi liif, and so thou me.
125 Ac° now we mot delen ato;°   But   **mot** . . . must part
     Do thi best, for Y mot go!"
          "Allas!" quath he, "forlorn Ich am!
     Whider wiltow° go and to wham?   will you
     Whider thou gost, Ichil° with thee,   I will go
130 And whider Y go, thou schalt with me."
          "Nay, nay, sir, that nought nis.°   **nought nis** can't be
     Ichil thee telle al hou it is.
     As Ich lay this undertide°   morning
     And slepe under our orchard side,
135 Ther come to me to° fair knightes   two
     Wele y-armed al to rightes°   **to rightes** properly
     And bad me comen an heighing°   **an heighing** in haste
     And speke with her° lord the king.   their

98. He was never so unhappy over anything.

219

And Ich answerd at° wordes bold, with
140 Y durst nought, no y nold.° no . . . nor would I
  "Thai priked oyain, as° thai might drive.° priked . . . spurred again, as fast as ride
 Tho° com her king al so blive° Then quickly
 With an hundred knightes and mo° more
 And damisels° an hundred also maidens
145 Al on snowewhite stedes;
 As white as milke were her wedes.° **her wedes** their clothes
 Y no seighe° never yete bifore saw
 So fair creatours y-core.° excellent
 The king hadde a croun on hed,
150 It nas° of silver no of gold red, was not
 Ac° it was of a precious ston; But
 As bright as the sonne it schon.
  "And as son as he to me cam,
 Wold Ich, nold Ich,° he me nam° **nold Ich** would I not took
155 And made me with him ride
 Opon a palfray bi his side,
 And brought me to his palays,
 Wele atird° in ich ways,° clothed **ich ways** every way
 And schewed me castels and tours,° towers
160 Rivers, forestes, frith° with flours, parks
 And his riche stedes ichon,° each one
 And seththen° me brought oyain° hom then again
 Into our owhen° orchard, own
 And said to me thus afterward:
165 'Loke, dame, to-morwe thatow° be that you
 Right here under this ympe-tre,° orchard tree
 And than thou schalt with ous° go us
 And live with ous ever mo.° more
 And yif thou makest ous y-let,° delayed
170 Whar° thou be, thou wörst y-fet° Wherever **wörst y-fet** will be fetched
 And totore° thine limes al torn to pieces
 That nothing help thee no schal.
 And thei° thou best so totorn, though
 Yete thou wörst with ous y-born.'"° carried off
175 When King Orfeo herd this cas,° matter
 "O, we!" quath he. "Allas, allas!
 Lever me were° to lete° mi liif **Lever . . .** I would prefer lose
 Than thus to lese the quen mi wiif!"
 He asked conseyl at ich° man, **at ich** of each
180 Ac no man him help no can.
 Amorwe° the undertide° is come, On the next day morning
 And Orfeo hath his armes y-nome,° taken
 And wele ten hundred knightes with him,

Ich y-armed stout and grim,
185 And with the quen wenten he
Right unto that ympe-tre.°   orchard tree
Thai made scheltrom° in ich a side°   phalanx   **ich** ... each side
And sayd thai wold there abide
And dye ther everichon°   everyone
190 Er° the quen schuld fram hem gon.°   Before   **hem gon** them go
   Ac yete amiddes hem ful right°   **ful right** straightway
The quen was oway y-twight,°   **oway y-twight** snatched away
With fairi° forth y-nome,°   magic   taken
Men wist° never wher sche was bicome.°   **Men wist** One knew   gone
195 Tho° was ther criing, wepe, and wo!   Then
The king into his chaumber is go°   gone
And oft swoned° opon the ston°   fainted   stone floor
And made swiche diol° and swiche mon°   **swiche diol** such sorrow   lament
That neighe° his liif was y-spent.   nearly
200 Ther was non amendement.°   remedy
   He cleped° togider his barouns,   called
Erls, lordes of renouns,
And when thai al y-comen were,
"Lordinges," he said, "bifor you here,
205 Ich ordainy min heighe steward
To wite° mi kingdom afterward.   direct
In mi stede ben° he schal   **stede ben** place be
To kepe mi londes over al.
For now Ichave° mi quen y-lore,°   I have   lost
210 The fairest levedi° that ever was bore.°   lady   born
Never eft° Y nil° no woman se.   again   will
Into wildernes Ichil te°   **Ichil te** I will go
And live ther ever more
With wilde bestes in holtes hore.°   **holtes hore** gray woods
215 And when ye understond that Y be spent,°   dead
Make thou than a parlement
And chese° you a newe king.   choose
Now doth your best with al mi thing."
   Tho° was ther wepeing in the halle   Then
220 And grete cri among hem° alle.   them
Unnethe might° old or yong   **Unnethe might** Hardly could
For wepeing speke a word with tong.
Thai kneled adoun al yfere°   together
And praid him, yif his wille were,
225 That he no schuld nought fram hem go.
"Do way,"° quath he, "it schal be so."   **Do way** Stop
   Al his kingdom he forsoke.
Bot° a sclavin° on him he toke,   Only   pilgrim's robe

He no hadde kirtel no hode,°   **kirtel** ... tunic nor hood

230   Schert, ne non other gode.°   goods

Bot his harp he tok algate°   at any rate

And dede him barfot° out atte yate.°   **dede** ... went barefoot   gate

No man most° with him go.   might

O way! What,° ther was wepe and wo,   Lo

235   When he that hadde ben king with croun

Went so pouerlich° out of town.   poorly

     Thurch wode° and over heth°   **Thurch wode** Through woods   heath

Into the wildernes he geth.°   goes

Nothing he fint° that him° is ays,°   finds   for him   comfort

240   Bot ever he liveth in gret malais.°   discomfort

He that hadde y-werd° the fowe and griis°   worn   **fowe** ... spotted fur and gray fur

And on bed the purper biis,°   **purper biis** purple linen

Now on hard hethe° he lith;°   heath   lies

With leves and gresse he him writh.°   wraps

245   He that hadde castels and tours,°   towers

River, forest, frith° with flours,   parks

Now, thei° it comenci to snewe and frese,   though

This king mote° make his bed in mese.°   must   moss

He that had y-had knightes of priis°   excellence

250   Bifor him kneland and levedis,°   **kneland** ... kneeling and ladies

Now seth° he nothing that him liketh,°   sees   pleases

Bot wilde wormes° bi him striketh.°   serpents   glide

He that had y-had plenté

Of mete and drink, of ich deynté,°   **ich deynté** every delicacy

255   Now may he al day digge and wrote,°   root in the soil

Er° he finde his fille of rote.   Before

     In somer he liveth bi wild frut

And berien° bot gode lite.°   berries   **gode lite** little good

In winter may he nothing finde

260   Bot rote, grases, and the rinde.°   bark

Al his bodi was oway dwine°   **oway dwine** dwindled away

For missays,° and al to-chine.°   suffering   scarred

Lord! Who may telle the sore°   trouble

The king sufferd ten yere and more!

265   His here° of his berd blac and rowe°   hair   rough

To his girdel-stede° was growe.   waist

     His harp, wheron was al his gle,°   merriment

He hidde in an holwe tre.

And when the weder was clere and bright,

270   He toke his harp to him wel right°   properly

And harped at his owhen° wille.   own

Into alle the wode the soun gan schille,°   **soun** ... sound resounded

That alle the wilde bestes that ther beth

For joie abouten him thai teth.° — go
275 And alle the foules° that ther were — birds
Come and sete on ich a brere° — **ich** ... each twig
To here his harping afine,° — to the end
So miche° melody was therin. — much
And when he his harping lete° wold, — stop
280 No best bi him abide nold.° — would
He might se him bisides° — **him bisides** beside him
Oft in hot undertides° — mornings
The King o Fairy° with his rout° — **o Fairy** of Fairyland   company
Com to hunt him al about,
285 With dim cri and bloweing,
And houndes also with him berking.
Ac no best thai no nome,° — took
No never he nist° whider thai bicome.° — knew   went
And other while he might him° se, — **might him** could
290 As a gret ost,° bi him te° — host   go
Wele atourned° ten hundred knightes, — equipped
Ich° y-armed to his rightes,° — Each   **to** ... fittingly
Of contenaunce stout and fers,° — **stout** ... strong and fierce
With mani desplaid° baners, — unfurled
295 And ich his swerd y-drawe hold,°
Ac never he nist° whider thai wold.° — knew   would go
And other while he seighe° other thing: — saw
Knightes and levedis° com daunceing — ladies
In queynt° atire gisely,° — elegant   skillfully
300 Queynt pas° and softly. — **Queynt pas** Graceful step
Tabours and trunpes yede° hem bi — **Tabours** ... Drums and trumpets went
And al maner menstraci.° — minstrelsy
And on a day he seighe him biside° — **seighe** ... saw beside him
Sexti levedis on hors ride,
305 Gentil and jolif° as brid° on ris,° — **Gentil** ... Well bred and gay   bird   a branch
Nought o° man amonges hem° ther nis.° — one   them   is
And ich a faucon on hond bere° — bore
And riden on haukin° bi o° rivere. — **riden** ... rode out hawking   a
Of game thai founde wel° gode haunt:° — very   plenty
310 Maulardes, hayroun,° and cormeraunt. — **Maulardes, hayroun** Mallards, heron
The foules of° the water ariseth; — **foules of** birds from
The faucons hem° wele deviseth;° — them   descry
Ich faucon his pray slough.° — slew
That seighe° Orfeo and lough.° — saw   laughed
315 "Parfay,"° quath he, "ther is fair game. — Indeed
Thider Ichil,° bi Godes name. — I will go
Ich was y-won swiche° werk to se." — **y-won swiche** accustomed such

295. And could see each knight holding his sword drawn

223

He aros and thider gan te.°   **gan te** went
To a levedi he was y-come,
320 Biheld, and hath wele undernome,°   recognized
And seth° bi al thing, that it is   sees
His owhen° quen Dam Heurodis.   own
Yern° he biheld hir, and sche him eke,°   Eagerly   also
Ac noither° to other a word no speke.   neither
325 For messais° that sche on him seighe°   discomfort   saw
That had ben so riche and so heighe,°   noble
The teres fel out of her eighe.°   eye
The other levedis this y-seighe
And maked hir oway° to ride;   away
330 Sche most° with him no lenger abide.   might
     "Allas," quath he, "now me is wo!
Whi nil° deth now me slo!°   will not   slay
Allas wreche, that Y no might°   **no might** could not
Dye now after this sight!
335 Allas, too long last° mi liif,   lasts
When Y no dar° nought with mi wiif   dare
No hye° to me o° word speke.   **No hye** Nor she   one
Allas, whi nil° min hert breke!   will not
Parfay,"° quath he, "tide wat bitide,°   Indeed   **tide . . .** happen what may
340 Whider so this° levedis ride,   these
The selve° way Ichil streche.°   same   **Ichil streche** I will go
Of liif no deth me no reche!"°   **me . . .** I care not
     His sclavain° he dede° on al so spac°   pilgrim's robe   put   quickly
And henge his harp opon his bac
345 And had wel gode wil° to gon;°   **wel . . .** very great desire   go
He no spard° noither stub° no ston.   avoided   tree trunk
In at a roche° the levedis rideth,   rock
And he after and nought abideth.°   delays
When he was in the roche y-go
350 Wele thre mile other mo,°   **other mo** or more
He com into a fair cuntray
As bright so° sonne on somers day,   as
Smothe and plain and al grene;
Hille no dale was ther non y-sene.
355 Amidde the lond a castel he sighe,°   saw
Riche and real° and wonder heighe;°   regal   **wonder heighe** wonderfully noble
Al the utmast° wal   outermost
Was clere and schine° as cristal.   bright
     An hundred tours° ther were about   towers
360 Degiselich and bataild° stout.   **Degiselich . . .** Wonderful and battlemented
The butras° com out of the diche,°   buttress   moat
Of rede gold y-arched riche.

The vousour° was avowed° al   vaulting   adorned
Of ich maner divers° aumal.°   **maner divers** different kind of   enamel
365 Within ther wer wide wones°   chambers
Al of precious stones.
The werst piler° on to biholde   **werst piler** worst pillar
Was al of burnist gold.
Al that lond was ever light,
370 For when it schuld be therk° and night,   dark
The riche stones light gonne°   **light gonne** shone
As bright as döth at none° the sonne.   noon
No man may telle no thenche° in thought   think
The riche werk that ther was wrought.
375 Bi al thing him think° that it is   **him think** it seems to him
The proude° court of paradis.   splendid
    In this castel the levedis alight.
He wold° in after yif he might.   would go
Orfeo knokketh atte gate;
380 The porter was redi ther-ate
And asked what he wold have y-do.
    "Parfay,"° quath he, "Icham° a minstrel, lo,   Indeed   I am
To solas thi lord with mi gle,°   minstrelsy
Yif his swete wille be."
385   The porter undede the yate° anon   gate
And lete him into the castel gon.°   go
Than he gan bihold° about al   **gan bihold** beheld
And seighe liggeand° within the wal   lying
Of folk that were thider y-brought
390 And thought dede and nare nought.°   head
Sum stode withouten hade,°   head
And sum non armes nade;°   had
And sum thurch° the bodi hadde wounde,   through
And sum lay wode,° y-bounde,   crazy
395 And sum armed on hors sete,
And sum astrangled as thai ete,
And sum were in water adreynt,°   drowned
And sum with fire al forschreynt.°   shrivelled
Wives ther lay on child-bedde,
400 Sum ded, and sum awedde.°   gone mad
And wonder fele° ther lay bisides,   **wonder fele** wonderfully many
Right as thai slepe her undertides.
Eche was thus in this warld y-nome,°   taken
With fairi° thider y-come.   **With fairi** By magic
405   Ther he seighe his owhen° wiif,   own
Dame Heurodis his lüf liif,°   **lüf liif** dear life

390. And considered dead but were not.

Slepe under an ympe-tre;°   orchard tree
Bi her clothes he knewe that it was he.°   she
And when he hadde bihold this mervails alle,
410 He went into the kinges halle.
Than seighe he ther a semly sight:
A tabernacle° blisseful and bright,   canopy
Ther-in her° maister king sete   **Ther-in her** In which their
And her quen fair and swete.
415 Her crounes, her clothes schine so bright,
That unnethe° bihold he hem might.   hardly
    When he hadde biholden al that thing,
He kneled adoun bifor the king:
"O lord," he seyd, "yif it thi wille were,
420 Mi menstraci° thou schust y-here."   minstrelsy
    The king answerd: "What man artow°   are you
That art hider y-comen now?
Ich no non° that is with me   **Ich** ... Neither I nor any
No sent never after thee.
425 Seththen that° Ich here regni gan,°   **Seththen that** Since   **regni gan** began to reign
Y no fond so folehardi man
That hider to ous° durst wende,°   us   come
Bot that Ichim wald ofsende."°   **Ichim** ... I would send for him
    "Lord," quath he, "trowe° ful wel,   believe
430 Y nam bot° a pouer menstrel,   **nam bot** am only
And, sir, it is the maner of ous
To seche° mani a lordes hous;   seek
Thei° we nought welcom no be,   Though
Yete we mot proferi° forth our gle."°   **mot proferi** must offer   minstrelsy
435   Bifor the king he sat adoun
And tok his harp so miri of soun°   sound
And tempreth° his harp, as he wele can,   tunes
And blisseful notes he ther gan,°   began
That al that in the palays were
440 Com to him for to here,°   hear
And liggeth° adoun to° his fete;   lie   by
Hem thenketh° his melody so swete.   **Hem thenketh** Seemed to them
The king herkneth° and sitt ful stille;   listens
To here his gle° he hath gode wille.   minstrelsy
445 Gode bourde° he hadde of his gle;   pleasure
The riche quen al-so hadde he.°   she
    When he hadde stint° his harping,   stopped
Than seyd to him the king:
"Menstrel, me liketh° wele thi gle.   pleases
450 Now aske of me what it be,
Largelich Ichil° thee pay.   **Largelich Ichil** Generously I will

Now speke and tow might asay."°   **and . . .** if you can try
"Sir," he seyd, "Ich biseche thee
Thatow woldest yive° me   give
455 That ich° levedi bright on ble°   same   complexion
That slepeth under the ympe-tre."°   orchard tree
"Nay," quath the king, "that nought nere!°   **nought nere** would not be fitting
A sori couple of you it were,
For thou art lene, rowe,° and blac,   rough
460 And sche is lovesum° withouten lac.°   lovely   fault
A lothlich° thing it were forthi°   repulsive   therefore
To sen° hir in thi compayni."   see
"O sir," he seyd, "gentil king,
Yete were it a wele° fouler thing   much
465 To here° a lesing of° thi mouthe.   hear   **lesing of** lie from
So, sir, as ye seyd nouthe,°   just now
What Ich wold aski, have Y schold,°   I should have
And nedes° thou most° thi word hold."°   necessarily   must   keep
The king seyd, "Seththen° it is so,   Since
470 Take hir bi the hond and go.
Of hir Ichil thatow° be blithe."   **Ichil thatow** I wish that you
He knelyd adoun and thonked him swithe.°   greatly
His wiif he tok bi the hond
And dede him swithe° out of that lond   **dede . . .** went quickly
475 And went him out of that thede.°   country
Right° as he come the way he yede.°   Just   went
So long he hath the way y-nome,°   taken
To Winchester he is y-come,
That was his owhen° cité;   own
480 Ac no man knewe that it was he.
No forther than the tounes ende
For knoweleche° he no durst wende.°   **For knoweleche** Because of recognition   go
Bot with a begger y-bilt° ful narwe,°   lodged   poorly
Ther he tok his herbarwe°   lodging
485 To° him and to his owhen wiif   For
As a minstrel of pouer liif,
And asked tidings of that lond,
And who the kingdom held in hond.
The pouer begger in his cot°   cottage
490 Told him everich a grot:°   **everich . . .** every bit
How her quen was stole owy
Ten yer gon with fairy,°   **gon . . .** ago by magic
And hou her king en° exile yede,°   in   went
Bot no man nist° in wiche thede;°   knew   country
495 And hou the steward the lond gan° hold,   did
And other mani thinges him told.

Amorwe, oyain none tide,°   **Amorwe . . .** The next day, toward noontime
He maked his wiif ther abide;
The beggers clothes he borwed° anon,   borrowed
500 And heng his harp his rigge° opon,   back
And went him into that cité,
That men might him bihold and se.
Erls and barouns bold,
Burjays° and levedis him gun° bihold.   Burgesses   did
505 "Lo," thai seyd, "swiche° a man!   such
How long the here° hongeth him opan!   hair
Lo, hou his berd hongeth to his kne!
He is y-clongen also° a tre!"   **y-clongen also** shrivelled like
And as he yede° in the strete,   went
510 With his steward he gan mete,
And loude he sett on him a crie:
"Sir steward," he seyd, "merci!
Ich am an harpour of hethenisse.°   foreign lands
Help me now in this distresse!"
515 The steward seyd, "Com with me, come!
Of that Ichave° thou schalt have some.   **that Ichave** what I have
Everich° gode harpour is welcom me to   Every
For mi lordes love, Sir Orfeo."
In the castel the steward sat atte mete,°   the meal
520 And many lording was bi him sete.
Ther were trompours and tabourers,°   **trompours** . . . trumpeters and drummers
Harpours fele and crouders.°   **fele** . . . many and fiddlers
Miche melody thai maked alle,
And Orfeo sat stille in the halle
525 And herkneth.° When thai ben° al stille,   listens   are
He toke his harp and tempred schille.°   tuned loudly
The blissefulest notes he harped there
That ever ani man y-herd with ere.°   ear
Ich man liked wele his gle.
530 The steward biheld and gan y-se°   see
And knewe the harp als blive.°   **als blive** at once
"Menstrel," he sayd, "so mot° thou thrive,°   may   prosper
Where hadestow this harp and hou?
Y pray that thou me telle now."
535 "Lord," quath he, "in uncouthe thede°   **uncouthe thede** strange country
Thurch° a wildernes as Y yede,°   Through   went
Ther Y founde in a dale
With lyouns a man totorn smale,°   **totorn smale** torn to pieces
And wolves him frete° with teth so scharp.   gnawed
540 Bi him Y fond this ich° harp,   same
Wele ten yere it is y-go."

"O," quath the steward, "now me is wo!
That was mi lord, Sir Orfeo.
Allas wreche, what schal Y do,
545 That have swiche° a lord y-lore!°   **such**   **lost**
Away° that Ich was y-bore!°   **Alas**   **born**
That him was so hard grace y-yarked°   **hard** ... cruel a fortune ordained
And so vile deth y-marked!"°   appointed
     Adoun he fel aswon° to grounde.   fainting
550 His barouns him toke up in that stounde°   moment
And telleth him hou it geth;°   goes
It nis no bot of° manes deth.   **It** ... There is no remedy for
King Orfeo knewe wele bi than°   **bi than** from that
His steward was a trewe man,
555 And loved him, as he aught to do,
And stont° up and seyt° thus: "Lo,   **stands**   **says**
Steward, herkne° now this thing: listen to
Yif Ich were Orfeo the king,
And hadde y-suffred ful yore°   **ful yore** long ago
560 In wildernisse miche sore,°   **miche sore** great sorrow
And hadde y-won mi quen owy
Out of the lond of fairy,°   magic
And hadde y-brought the levedi hende°   courteous
Right here to the tounes ende,
565 And with a begger her in y-nome,°   **her** ... provided lodging for her
And were miself hider y-come
Pouerlich to thee, thus stille,
For to asay° thi gode wille,   test
And Ich founde thee thus trewe,
570 Thou no schust° it ever rewe.°   **should**   **regret**
Sikerlich° for love or ay°   **Surely**   **fear**
Thou schust be king after mi day.
And yif thou of mi deth hadest ben blithe,
Thou schust ben voided also swithe."°   **voided** ... banished at once
575   Tho° al tho° that ther-in sete   **Then**   **those**
That it was King Orfeo underyete,°   understood
And the steward him wele knewe.
Over and over the bord° he threwe°   **table**   **knocked**
And fel adoun to his fet.
580 So dede everich° lord that ther sete,   **dede everich** did every
And al thai seyd at o° criing: one
"Ye beth our lord, sir, and our king!"
Glad thai were of his live.°   life
To chaumber thai ladde him als blive°   **als blive** at once
585 And bathed him and schaved his berd
And tired° him as a king apert.°   **dressed**   **openly**

229

And seththen° with gret processioun   then
Thai brought the quen into the toun
With al maner menstraci.°   **maner menstraci** kinds of minstrelsy

590   Lord, ther was grete melody!
For joie thai wepe with her eighe,°   eyes
That° hem so sounde° y-comen seighe.   Those that   safe
Now King Orfeo newe coround is
And his quen Dame Heurodis,

595   And lived long afterward,
And seththen° was king the steward.   then
    Harpours in Bretaine° after than°   Brittany   that
Herd hou this mervaile° bigan,   marvel
And made herof a lay of gode likeing°   charm

600   And nempned° it after the king.   named
That lay "Orfeo" is y-hote;°   called
Gode is the lay, swete is the note.
Thus com Sir Orfeo out of his care.°   sorrow
God graunt ous alle wele to fare.

LAURENCE MINOT

Halidon Hill

(ca. 1333, Northern)

All we know of Laurence Minot is that he composed eleven political poems celebrating the triumphs achieved by King Edward III against the Scots and the French during the period between 1333 and 1352. The poems are written in the Northern English dialect, but that clue merely places the author somewhere in the northeast of England between Yorkshire and the Scottish border.

Halidon Hill is the first of these poems. Edward II had been defeated by the Scots at Bannockburn in 1314 (see Barbour's *Bruce*, p. 271, below). Edward III temporarily regained control of the border in 1333 by a victory at Halidon Hill, near Berwick. In commemorating the victory, Minot was still concerned, however, by the possibility that the Scottish merchants might be able to wrest the advantage from England in Bruges and elsewhere in the Low Countries.

The meter of the poem is six-line stanzas; see Introduction, type 12, page 32.

The best edition is in Joseph Hall, ed., *The Poems of Laurence Minot*, rev. ed. (Oxford, 1914), pages 4–6. For a facsimile of the manuscript see Plate 4 and accompanying notes, pages 22–23. For bibliography see Wells, ch. 4.12.

Skottes out of Berwik and of Abirdene,	
At the Bannok Burn war ye too kene.°	bold
Thare slogh° ye many sakles, als° it was sene,	slew **sakles, als** innocent, as
And now has King Edward wroken° it, I wene.°	avenged trust
5 It es wrokin, I wene; wele wurth° the while!°	**wele wurth** good luck to event
War yit with° the Skottes, for thai er° ful of gile.	**War . . .** Still beware are
Whare er ye Skottes of Saint Johnes toune?°	**Saint . . .** Perth
The boste of yowre baner es betin all doune.	
When ye bosting will bede,° Sir Edward° es boune°	offer Edward III ready
10 For to kindel yow care and crak yowre crowne.	
He has crakked yowre croune; wele wurth° the while!°	**wele wurth** good luck to event
Schame bityde the Skottes, for thai er° full of gile.	are
Skottes of Striflin° war steren° and stout;	Stirling stern
Of God ne° of gude men had thai no dout.°	or fear
15 Now have thai, the pelers, priked° obout,	**pelers, priked** ravagers, raced
Bot at the last Sir Edward rifild° thaire rout.°	despoiled band

231

He has rifild thaire rout; wele wurth° the while!°
Bot ever er° thai, under, bot gaudes° and gile.

Rugh-fute riveling,° now kindels thi care.
20 Bere-bag° with thi boste, thi biging° es bare.
Fals wretche and forsworn, whider wiltou fare?°
Busk thee° unto Brig,° and abide thare.
    Thare, wretche, saltou won, and wery° the while.°
    Thi dwelling in Dondé° es done° for thi gile.

25 The Skottes gase° in Burghes° and betes° the stretes.
Al° thise Inglismen harmes he hetes.°
Fast° makes he his mone° to men that he metes,
Bot fone° frendes he findes that his bale betes.°
    Fune° betes his bale; wele wurth° the while!°
30 He uses al threting with gaudes° and gile.

Bot many man thretes and spekes ful ill
That sumtyme war° better to be stane-still.
The Skot in his wordes has wind for to spill,
For, at the last, Edward sall have al his will.
35 He had his will at Berwik; wele wurth° the while!
Skottes broght him the kayes;° bot get° for thaire gile!

wele wurth good luck to   ever
are   **under**...underneath,
    nothing but tricks

Rugh-fute riveling Rough-sho
    brogue-wearer
Bag-carrier   dwelling
wiltou fare will you go
Busk thee Hasten   Bruges
saltou...you shall dwell, and
    curse event
Dundee   destroyed

go   Bruges   walk
To all   promises
Continually   complaint
few   **bale betes** torment reliev
Few   **wele wurth** good luck to
    event
al...every kind of threat along
    with tricks

would be

wele wurth good luck to

keys of the town   look out

RICHARD ROLLE

The Form of Living

(1349, Northern)

∞

The most famous of the fourteenth-century English mystics was the hermit Richard Rolle (d. 1349), of Hampole in the West Riding of Yorkshire. He wrote *The Form of Living* for the anchoress Margaret Kirkby, of Anderby in the North Riding, near whom he had earlier resided. In this work Rolle achieved a clear and orderly if austere prose style, but the intimate and personal nuances of *The Anchoresses' Rule* (p. 106, above) were beyond or beneath him. Though *The Form of Living* is couched in the form of a letter to an individual anchoress, the brief set of general instructions it provides is suitable for anyone interested in pursuing a mystical experience. Nowhere does Rolle give the sort of personal allusion or specific advice that the unknown author of the earlier work gave his three spiritually minded young ladies. Characteristic of Rolle, however, is his incessant emphasis on the sweetness and joy of the mystical life and on the importance of the *calor* ('warmth'), *canor* ('splendor,' literally, 'song'), and *dulcor* ('sweetness') of divine love.

The selection below consists of the final two chapters. For the most dependable edition see Hope Emily Allen, *The English Writings of Richard Rolle, Hermit of Hampole* (Oxford, 1931). The best study of the man and his work is *Writings Ascribed to Richard Rolle, Hermit of Hampole, and Materials for his Biography*, by the same author (New York, 1927). For bibliography see Wells, ch. 11.5; *CBEL*, 1. 191–94.

Chapter XI

The sevene gyftes of the Haly Gaste that ere° gyfene to   are
men and wymmene that er ordaynede to the joye of
hevene and ledys° theire lyfe in this worlde reghtwysely,   lead
thire° are thay: Wysdome, Undyrstandynge, Counsayle,   these
5 Strenghe, Connynge, Peté, the Drede of God.
  Begynne we at Consaile, for thareof es myster° at the   need
begynnynge of oure werkes, that us myslyke° noghte   may displease
aftyrwarde. With thire sevene gyftes the Haly Gaste teches
sere° mene serely.°   various   individually
10 Consaile es doynge awaye of worldes reches and of all
delytes of all thynges that mane may be tagyld° with in   entangled
thoghte or dede, and tharwith° drawynge intill° contem-   thereby   into
placyone of Gode.
  Undyrstandynge es to knawe whate es to doo and whate

233

15 es to lefe,° and that sall° be gyffene, to gyffe it to thaym that
has nede, noghte till° other that has na myster.°

Wysedome es forgetynge of erthely thynges and
thynkynge of heven, with discrecyone of° all mens
dedys.° In this gyfte schynes° contemplacyone, that es,
20 Saynt Austyne° says, a gastely dede° of fleschely affec-
cyones,° thurghe the joye of a raysede° thoghte.

Strenghe es lastynge to fulfill gude purpose, that it be
noghte lefte for wele° ne for waa.°

Peté es that a man be mylde and gaynesay noghte Haly
25 Writte whene it smyttes his synnys, whethire he undyr-
stand it or noghte; bot in all his myghte purge he the
vilté° of syne in hyme° and other.

Connynge es that makes a man of gude hope, noghte
ruysand hyme of° his reghtewysnes, bot sorowand of his
30 synnys, and that man gedyrs erthely gude anely to the
honour of God and prow° to other mene thane hymselfe.

The Drede of God es that we turne noghte agayne till°
oure syne thurghe any ill eggyng.° And than es drede
perfite° in us and gastely,° when we drede to wrethe° God
35 in the leste syne that we kane knawe, and flese° it als°
venyme.

leave alone	**that sall** whatev[er]
	shall
to	need
discrecyone of separation	
	from
deeds	shines forth
Augustine	**gastely dede**
	spiritual act
desires	elevated
happiness	woe
vileness	himself
ruysand . . . glorying in	
benefit	
to	
egging on	
perfect	spiritual anger
flee	as

Chapter XII

Twa lyves thar er° that Cristen men lyfes.° Ane es
called actyve lyfe, for it es in mare° bodili warke. Another,
contemplatyve lyfe, for it es in mare swetnes gastely.°
Actife lyfe es mykel° owteward, and in mare travel° and
5 in mare peryle for the temptacions that er in the worlde.
Contemplatyfe lyfe es mykel inwarde, and for-thi° it es
lastandar and sykerar,° restfuller, delitabiler,° luflyer, and
mare medeful.° For it hase joy in Goddes lufe and savowre
in the lyf that lastes ay° in this present tyme, if it be right
10 ledde. And that felyng of joy in the lufe of Jesu passes al
other merites in erth. For it es swa° harde to com to for°
the freelté of oure flesch and the many temptacions that we
er umsett° with, that lettes° us nyght and day. Al other
thynges er lyght at° com to, in regarde tharof, for that may
15 na man deserve, bot anely° it es gifen of Goddes godenes til°
tham that verrayli gifes tham° to contemplacion and til
quiete for Cristes luf.

are	live
more	
spiritually	
much	labor
therefore	
lastandar . . . more lasting a[nd]	
more secure	more deligh[t]
rewarding	
forever	
so	because of
er umsett are surrounded	
	hinder
lyght at easy to	
bot anely only if	to
themselves	

Til men or wymen that takes tham° til actife lyfe, twa
thynges falles.° Ane, for to ordayne thair meyné° in drede
20 and in the lufe of God, and fynd tham thaire necessaries,
and thamself kepe enterely the commandementes of God,
doand til° thar neghbur als° thai wil that thai do til tham.
Another es that thai do at thar power the seven werkes of
mercy, the whilk° es: to fede the hungry; to gyf the
25 thristi a drynk; to cleth the naked; to herbar hym that
hase na howsyng; to viset the seke; to comforth tham that
er° in prysoun; and to grave° dede men. Al that mai,° and
hase cost,° thai may noght be qwyt° with ane or twa of
thir,° bot tham behoves° do tham al, if thai wil have the
30 benyson° on Domesday that Jesu sal til al gyf° that dose
tham. Or els may thai drede the malysoun° that al mon°
have that will noght do tham when thai had godes° to do
tham wyth.

Contemplatife lyf hase twa partyes,° a lower and a heer.
35 The lower party es meditacion of haly wrytyng, that es
Goddes wordes, and in other gude thoghtes and swete that
men hase of the grace of God abowt the lufe of Jesu Criste,
and also in lovyng° of God in psalmes and ympnes° or in
prayers. The hegher party of contemplacion es behaldyng
40 and yernyng of° the thynges of heven, and joy in the Haly
Gaste. That men hase oft, and° if it be swa° that thai be
noght prayand with the mowth, bot anely thynkand of
God and of the fairhede° of aungels and haly sawles.° Than
may I say that contemplacion es a wonderful joy of Goddes
45 luf, the whilk° joy es lovyng of God, that may noght
be talde. And that wonderful lovyng es in the saule, and
for abundance of joy and swettenes it ascendes in til° the
mouth, swa° that the hert and the tonge acordes° in ane,
and body and sawle joyes° in God lyvand.°

50 A man or woman that es ordaynd til contemplatife
lyfe, first God enspires tham to forsake this worlde and
al the vanité and the covayties and the vile luste tharof.
Sythen° he ledes tham by thar ane,° and spekes til thair
hert, and, als the prophete says, he gifes tham at sowke°
55 the swetnes of the begynnyng of lufe, and than he settes
tham in will° to gyf tham haly° to prayers and meditacions
and teres. Sithen, when thai have sufferd many temptacions and foule noyes° of thoghtes that er° ydel and of
vanitées the whilk° wil comber° tham that can noght
60 destroy tham, er° passand away, he gars tham geder° til
tham thair hert, and fest° anely in hym, and opens til the
egh° of thair sawls° the yates° of heven, swa° that the ilk°

---

takes tham devote themselves
are ordained   household

doand til doing to   as

the whilk which

are   bury   can
hase cost have enough money
 released
these   it behooves to
sal . . . shall give to all
curse   must
goods

parts

praising   hymns

for

even   so

fairness   souls

the whilk which

to
so   agree
sawle joyes soul rejoice
 living

Then   **by . . .** by themselves
at sowke to suck

settes . . . makes them wish
 wholly

annoyances   are
the whilk which   encumber
before   **gars . . .** makes them
 gather
fix

eye   souls   gates   so   same

egh lokes in til heven; and than the fire of lufe verrali
ligges° in thair hert and byrnes tharin and makes clene of   lies
65 al erthly filth; and sithen forward° thai er° contemplatife   **sithen forward** from then on
men and ravyst° in lufe. For contemplacion es a syght, and   are
thai se in til heven with thar gastly egh.° Bot thou sal witt°   ravished
that na man hase perfite syght of heven whils thai er   **gastly egh** spiritual eye **sal**
lifand bodili here; bot als° sone als thai dye thai er broght   **witt** shall know
70 before God and sese° hym face til face and egh til egh,   as
and wones° with hym withouten ende. For hym thai soght   see
and hym thai covayted and hym thai lufed in al thar   dwell
myght.

Loo, Margarete, I have schortly sayde° thee the forme of   told
75 lyvyng and how thou may com til perfection and to lufe
hym that thou hase taken thee til.° If it do thee gude and   **thee til** to you
profit til thee, thank God and pray for me. The grace of
Jesu Criste be with thee and kepe thee. Amen.

THE AGE
OF
CHAUCER

The Parliament of the Three Ages

(ca. 1350, East Midland)

❧

The Parliament (that is, 'Discussion') employs two medieval conventions, the dream framework and the debate format, the latter comparable to *The Owl and the Nightingale* (p. 54, above). The closest analogues are to be found in a series of medieval French poems on 'The Three Dead Men and the Three Living Men,' a theme often represented in medieval paintings and illumination.

In *The Parliament*, however, the central issue in Age's argument is the medieval tradition of the Nine Worthies, which seems to have sprung immediately from a French romance on Alexander, *The Vows of the Peacock* (*Voeux de Paon*, ca. 1312), by Jacques de Longuyon, and ultimately from Celtic sources, probably from the traditional Welsh triads. The Nine Worthies appear in Middle English literature most frequently in the north, the two most notable occurrences being in the alliterative *Morte Arthure* and the present poem. An anonymous translation of the *Voeux de Paon* was made at a later date into Middle Scots octosyllabic verse and was entitled *The Avowis of Alexander* (1438). No one version, even the *Voeux*, is clearly identifiable as a source for *The Parliament*, though the author refers to the theme of the peacock with familiarity (p. 252, l. 34). Presumably the author based his own account of the Worthies on a wide acquaintance with romance literature and learned tradition.

Age relates this account of the Worthies as clear evidence of the vanity of all worldly things, and he continues his moral lecture with a brief survey of wise men and famous lovers, all underscoring the theme of *Ubi sunt qui ante nos fuerunt?* ('Where are those who were before us?'), a common medieval motif found in Thomas of Hailes's *Love Rune* (p. 156, above) and *The Sayings of St. Bernard* (p. 163, above), and most memorably expressed at the end of the era by François Villon. The entire *Parliament of the Three Ages* is thus not so much a treatise on the Nine Worthies as it is a moral lesson on the evanescence of everything worldly, showing at least some originality in the author's blending of the separate themes of the Ages, the Worthies, and *Ubi sunt* into an effective didactic piece.

Originality is even more apparent in the description of the setting (p. 239, ll. 1–20), the hunt (pp. 239–41, ll. 21–65), and falconry (pp. 240–41, ll. 40–77)—passages based more on the author's actual experiences and observations than on his erudition. The description of the handling of the slain deer (ll. 66–96) bears comparison with a similar passage in the later *Sir Gawain and the Green Knight* (pp. 419–20, ll. 1323–61) for vivid realism. The passages stand out in what would otherwise be a good but undistinguished representative of the alliterative revival in Northern England. For the meter see Introduction, type 1, page 29.

A useful edition is *The Parlement of the Thre Ages*, ed. I. Gollancz (London, 1915), in which are printed a number of analogues on the Nine Worthies. The best edition and commentary are *The Parlement of the Thre Ages*, ed. M. Y. Offord, EETS 246 (London, 1959). For bibliography see Wells, ch. 4.49.

Prologue

In the monethe of Maye when mirthes bene fele°   **bene fele** are many
And the sesone of somere when softe bene the
    wedres,°   breezes
Als° I went to the wodde° my werdes° to dreghe,°   As   wood   chances   try
Into the schawes° myselfe a schotte me to gete   thickets
5 At ane hert or ane hynde, happen as it myghte,
And as Dryghten° the day drove frome the heven,   the Lord
Als I habade one° a banke be° a bryme° syde,   **habade one** waited on   by   brook's
There° the gryse° was grene, growen with floures—   Where   grass
The primrose, the perwynke, and piliole° the riche—   **perwynke** . . . periwinkle, and pennyroyal
10 The dewe appon daysés donkede° full faire,   spread moisture
Burgons,° and blossoms, and braunches full swete,   Buds
And the mery mystes full myldely gane falle,°   **gane falle** fell
The cukkowe, the cowschote, kene° were thay   **cowschote, kene** wood-pigeon, lively
    bothen,°   both
And the throstills° full throly threpen° in the bankes,   throstles   **throly threpen** eagerly contend at singing
15 And iche foule° in that frythe faynere° than other   **iche foule** each bird   **frythe faynere** wood gladder
That the derke was done and the daye lightenede.
Hertys and hyndes one° hillys thay gowen;°   on   gaze about
The foxe and the filmarte° thay flede to the erthe;   polecat
The hare hurkles° by hawes° and harde thedir   crouches   hedges
    dryves
20 And ferkes° faste to hir fourme° and fatills° hir to   goes   **hir fourme** her nest   readies
    sitt.
    Als I stode in that stede,° one° stalkynge I thoghte.   place   on
Bothe my body and my bowe I buskede° with leves   dressed
And turnede towardes a tree and tariede there a
    while.
And als° I lokede to a launde° a littill me besyde,°   as   glade   **me besyde** away from me
25 I seghe ane° hert with ane hede,° ane heghe for the   **seghe ane** saw a   antlered head
    nones.°   **heghe** . . . high one indeed
Alle unburneschede was the beme, full borely the
    mydle,
With iche feetur, as thi fote, forfrayed in the
    greves,°
With auntlers one° aythere syde egheliche° longe.   on   fearfully

26–27. All unburnished (with hair rubbed off but not yet the skin) was the main stem of the antlers, very strong was the middle, with each tine, looking like your foot, frayed (with hair rubbed off) against trees in the groves

The ryalls full richely raughten frome the myddes,

30 With surryals full semely appon sydes twayne;

And he assommet and sett of six and of fyve,°

And therto borely° and brode and of body grete, strong he was

And a coloppe° for a kynge, cache hym who tasty bit
myghte.

Bot there sewet° hym a sowre° that servet hym full followed   buck
yerne,° eagerly

35 That woke and warned hym when the wynde
faylede

That none so sleghe° in his slepe with sleghte° clever   cunning
scholde hym dere,° harm

And went the wayes hym byfore when any wothe
tyde.° **wothe tyde** danger happens

My lyame° than full° lightly lete I doun falle, leash   very

And to the bole° of a birche my berselett° I trunk   hound
cowchide.° made lie down

40 I waitted wiesly° the wynde by waggynge of leves, **waitted wiesly** watched carefully

Stalkede full stilly, no stikkes to breke,

And crepit° to a crab tre and coverede me ther- crept
under.

Then I bende up my bowe and bownede me° to **bownede me** prepared
schote,

Tighte° up my tylere and taysede° at the hert, Set   **tylere . . .** crossbow stock and ai[m]

45 Bot the sowre° that hym sewet° sett up the nese° buck   followed   nose

And wayttede wittyly° abowte and wyndide° full **wayttede wittyly** looked carefully   s[m]
yerne.° eagerly

Then I moste° stonde als° I stode and stirre no fote had to   as
ferrere,° farther

For, had I myntid° or movede or made any synys,° aimed   signs

Alle my layke° hade bene loste that I hade longe sport
wayttede.° awaited

50 Bot gnattes gretely me grevede and gnewen° myn bit
eghne.° eyes

And he stotayde and stelkett° and starede full brode,° **stotayde . . .** paused and moved carefu[lly]   **full brode** very widely

Bot at the laste he loutted° doun and laughte till° his bent   **laughte till** took up
mete,° food

And I hallede to° the hokes° and the hert smote, **hallede to** pulled back   crossbow cat[ch]

And happenyd that I hitt hym byhynde the lefte
scholdire

55 That the blode braste° owte appon bothe the sydes, burst

29-31. The royals (second branches of the antlers) extended very splendidly from the middle, with very fair surroyals (crown antlers) on both sides; and he displayed antlers fully formed and was furnished with six branches on one antler and with five on the other

And he balkede° and brayed and bruschede° thurgh the greves,° — stopped rushed groves

As° alle had hurlede one ane hepe° that in the holte longede,° — As if **hurlede** . . . dashed together in one bunch dwelled

And sone° the sowre° that hym sewet resorte° to his feris,° — at once buck **sewet resorte** followed returned companions

And thay, forfrayede° of his fare,° to the fellys° thay hyen.° — frightened behavior moors hurry

60 And I hyede to my hounde and hent hym up° sone — **hent** . . . took him

And louset° my lyame° and lete hym umbycaste.° — loosed leash cast about

The breris° and the brakans° were blody byronnen,° — briars bracken **blody byronnen** covered with blood

And he assentis to that sewte° and seches° hym aftire, — pursuit searches

There° he was crepyde° into a krage and crouschede° to the erthe. — Where **was crepyde** had crept **krage** . . . cave and crouched

65 Dede als° a dore-nayle doun was he fallen. — as

And I hym hent° by the hede and heryett° hym uttire,° — took dragged out

Turned his troches and tachede° thaym into the erthe, — **troches** . . . tines and fastened

Kest° up that keudvart° and kutt of° his tonge, — Turned rascal off

Brayde° owte his bewells° my berselett° to fede, — Drew entrails hound

70 And I slitte hym at the assaye° to see how me semyde,° — breast (where flesh was usually tested) **me semyde** it seemed to me

And he was floreschede° full faire of two-fyngere brede.° — lined with fat breadth

I chese to° the chawylls chefe° to begynn — **chese to** chose at **chawylls chefe** jowls especially

And ritte° doun at a rase° reght to the tayle, — ripped rush

And than the herbere anone° aftir I makede. — **herbere anone** arber (first stomach) next

75 I raughte° the righte legge byfore, ritt° it theraftir, — seized ripped

And so fro legge to legge I lepe° thaym aboute, — leaped

And the felle° fro the fete fayre I departede° — skin separated

And flewe° it doun with my fiste faste° to the rigge.° — flayed right spine

I tighte° owte my trenchore° and toke of° the scholdirs, — drew knife off

80 Cuttede corbyns° bone and keste it awaye. — raven's

I slitte hym full sleghely° and slyppede in my fyngere — **full sleghely** very cleverly

Lesse° the poynte scholde perche° the pawnche or the guttys. — Lest pierce

I soughte owte my sewet and semblete° it togedire — **sewet** . . . suet and gathered

And pullede oute the pawnche and putt it in an hole.° — hole in the ground

85 I grippede owte the guttes and graythede° thaym besyde, — put

241

And than the nombles anone name° I thereaftire,　　**nombles** ... entrails next took

Rent up fro the rygge° reghte to the myddis,°　　spine middle

And than the fourches° full fayre I fonge° fro the sydes　　haunches took

And chynede° hym chefely° and choppede of° the nekke,　　split along spine especially off

90　And the hede and the haulse homelyde° in sondree.　　**haulse homelyde** neck cut

The fete of the fourche I feste° thurgh the sydis　　fastened

And hevede° alle into ane hole and hidde it with ferne,　　heaved

With hethe and with hore° mosse hilde° it about　　gray hid

That no fostere of the fee° scholde fynde it theraftir;　　**fostere** ... forester by inheritance

95　Hid the hornes and the hede in ane hologhe° oke　　hollow

That no hunte° scholde it hent° ne have it in sighte.　　hunter take

　　I foundede° faste therefro for ferde° to be wryghede°　　hastened fear discovered

And sett me° oute one a syde to see how it chevede,°　　**sett me** seated myself fared

To wayte° it frome wylde swyne that wyse bene° of nesse.°　　guard are nose

100　And als° I satte in my sette, the sone was so warme,　　as

And I for slepeles was slome and slomerde° a while　　**slome** ... heavy with sleep and slumbered

And there me dremed, in that dowte,° a full dreghe swevynn,°　　uncertainty / **dreghe swevynn** long dream

And whate I seghe° in my saule the sothe° I schall telle.　　saw truth

The Three Ages

I seghe thre thro° men threpden° full yerne°　　earnest who argued eagerly

And moteden° of myche-whate° and maden thaym full tale.°　　spoke many things lively in speech

And° ye will, ledys,° me listen ane hande-while,°　　If men moment

I schall reken° thaire araye redely,° for sothe,°　　describe **araye redely** attire promp‑ / truth

5　And to yowe neven° thaire names naytly° there-aftire.　　name exactly

　　The firste was a ferse freke,° fayrere than thies° othire,　　**ferse freke** fierce man these

A bolde beryn one° a blonke, bownne° for to ryde,　　**beryn one** knight on / steed, ready **blonke, bown**

A hathelle° on ane heghe horse with hauke appon hande.　　noble

He was balghe° in the breste and brode in the scholdirs,　　deep

242

10 His axles° and his armes were i-liche° longe,   *shoulders   correspondingly*
    And in the medill als a mayden menskfully°   *gracefully*
       schapen.
    Longe legges and large and lele° for to schewe,   *fair*
    He streghte hym° in his sterapis and stode uprightes.   **streghte hym** *stretched*
    He ne hade no hode ne no hatte bot his here one,°   **here one** *hair only*
15 A chaplet one his chefe-lere, chosen for the nones,°   **chefe-lere . . .** *head of hair, choice indeed*
    Raylede° alle with rede rose, richeste of floures,   *Adorned in rows*
    With trafoyles and trewloves° of full triede° perles,   **trafoyles . . .** *trefoils and love knots fine*
    With a chefe charebocle chosen° in the myddes.   **chefe . . .** *fine choice carbuncle*
    He was gerede° alle in grene, alle with golde   *dressed*
       bywevede,°   *interwoven*
20 Embroddirde alle with besanttes and beralles° full   **besanttes . . .** *bezants and beryls*
       riche.
    His colere° with calsydoynnes° clustrede full thikke,   *collar   chalcedonies*
    With many dyamandes full dere dighte° one his   **dere dighte** *costly arranged*
       sleves.
    The semys with saphirs sett were full many,
    With emeraudes and amatists° appon iche° syde,   **emeraudes . . .** *emeralds and amethysts*
       each
25 With full riche rubyes raylede° by the hemmes.   *arrayed*
    The price of that perry° were worthe powndes full   *jewelry*
       many.
    His sadill was of sykamoure that he satt inn,
    His bridell alle of brente° golde with silke brayden°   *burnished   plaited*
       raynes.
    His cropoure° was of Tartaryne° that traylede to the   *crupper   Tartar silk*
       erthe,
30 And he throly° was threven° of thritty yere of elde   *eagerly   grown up*
    And therto yonge and yape,° and Youthe was his   *active*
       name,
    And the semelyeste segge° that I seghe° ever.   **semelyeste segge** *fairest man   saw*
      The seconde segge in his sete satte at his ese,
    A renke° alle in rosette° that rowmly° was schapyn,   *man   russet clothes   amply*
35 In a golyone° of graye girde° in the myddes,°   *tunic   belted   middle*
    And iche bagge° in his bosome bettir than othere.   **iche bagge** *each money bag*
    One his golde and his gude° gretly he mousede,°   *goods   mused*
    His renttes and his reches rekened° he full ofte—   **reches rekened** *riches counted*
    Of mukkyng,° of marlelyng° and mendynge of   *manuring   fertilizing with marl*
       howses,
40 Of benes° of his bondemen,° of benefetis many,   *extra services   serfs*
    Of presanttes of polayle,° of pufilis als,°   *poultry*   **pufilis als** *plots of land also*
    Of purches° of ploughe-londes, of parkes full faire,   *acquisition*
    Of profettis of his pasturs that his purse mendis,°   *fill*
    Of stiewardes, of storrours, stirkes° to bye,°   **storrours, stirkes** *storekeepers, heifers*
       buy
45 Of clerkes, of countours° his courtes to holde—   *legal pleaders*

And alle his witt° in this werlde was one° his wele   thought   on
   one.°   **wele one** wealth only
Him semyde,° for to see to,° of sexty yere elde,   **Him semyde** He seemed   **see to** look
And therfore men in his marche Medill-elde° hym   **marche Medill-elde** district Middle-/
   callede.
   The thirde was a laythe lede lenyde° one his syde,   **laythe . . .** ugly man bent
50 A beryne bownn° alle in blake with bedis in his   **beryne bownn** man dressed
   hande,
Croked and courbede,° encrampeschett for elde.°   bent   **encrampeschett . . .** contorted because of old age
Alle disfygured was his face and fadit° his hewe,   faded
His berde and browes were blanchede full whitte,
And the hare one his hede hewede° of the same.   colored
55 He was ballede° and blynde and alle babir-lippede,°   bald   thick-lipped
Totheles and tenefull,° I tell yowe for sothe.°   peevish   truth
And ever he momelide and ment,° and mercy he   **momelide . . .** mumbled and moaned
   askede
And cried kenely one Criste and his Crede sayde,°   **Crede sayde** Credo recited
With sawtries° full sere° tymes to sayntes in heven,   psalms   various
60 Envyous and angrye, and Elde° was his name.   Age
I helde° hym be° my hopynge° a hundrethe yeris of   considered   by   belief
   age,
And bot° his cruche and his couche he carede for no   except for
   more.
   Now hafe I rekkende° yow theire araye redely°   described to   **araye redely** attire promptly
   the sothe,°   truth
And also namede yow thaire names naytly° there-   exactly
   aftire,
65 And now thaire carpynge° I sall kythe,° knowe it if   talk   make known
   yowe liste.°   it pleases

The Parliament

   Now this gome° alle in grene so gayly attyrede,   man
This hathelle one° this heghe horse with hauke one   **hathelle one** noble on
   his fiste,
He was yonge and yape and yernynge° to armes,   **yape . . .** lively and eager
And pleynede hym one° paramours and peteuosely   **pleynede . . .** lamented about
   syghede.°   **peteuosely syghede** piteously sighed
5 He sett hym° up in his sadill and seyde theis wordes: **sett hym** seated himself
   "My lady, my leman° that I hafe luffede ever,   sweetheart
My wele° and my wirchip in werlde where thou   happiness
   dwellys,

My playstere° of paramours, my lady with pappis° full swete, — balm; breasts

Alle my hope and my hele,° myn herte es thyn ownn. — well-being

10 I byhete° thee a heste, and heghely° I avowe — pledge; **heste . . .** promise, and solemnly

There schall no hode ne no hatt one my hede sitt

Till that I joyntly° with a gesserante justede° hafe onere° — steadily; **gesserante justede** coat of mail jousted; with honor

And done dedis for thi love, doghety° in armes." — valiant

Bot then this gome° alle in graye greved with this wordes — man

15 And sayde: "Felowe, be my faythe thou fonnes° full yerne° — act like a fool; eagerly

For alle fantome and foly that thou with faris.° — deal

Where es the londe and the lythe° that thou arte lorde over? — people

For alle thy ryalle araye,° renttis hase thou none, — attire

Ne for thi pompe and thi pride penyes° bot fewe. — pennies

20 For alle thi golde and thi gude gloes° one thi clothes. — **gude gloes** goods glow

And° thou hafe caughte thi kaple,° thou cares for no fothire.° — If; horse; wagonload

Bye° the stirkes° with thi stede and stalles thaym° make; — Buy; heifers; for them

Thi brydell of brent° golde wolde bullokes thee gete; — burnished

The pryce of thi perrye° wolde purches thee londes; — jewelry

25 And wonne, wy, in thi witt,° for wele-neghe thou spilles."° — **wonne . . .** keep, man, your wits; ruin yourself

Than the gome° alle in grene greved full sore — man

And sayd, "Sir, be° my soule, thi consell es feble; — by

Bot° thi golde and thi gude° thou has no god ells,° — Except for; goods; **god ells** other god

For, be the Lorde and the laye° that I leve° inne, — faith; believe

30 And by the Gode that me gaffe goste° and soule, — spirit

Me were levere° one this launde lengen° a while, — **Me . . .** I would rather; stay

Stoken° in my stele-wede° on my stede bakke, — Enclosed; steel garment

Harde haspede° in my helme and in my here-wedys,° — **Harde haspede** Firmly buckled; war dress

With a grym grounden glayfe graythely° in myn honde, — **grym . . .** cruelly sharpened sword ready

35 And see a kene° knyghte come and cowpe° with myselven — bold; exchange blows

That I myghte halde that° I hafe highte and heghely° avowede — **halde that** keep what; **highte . . .** promised and solemnly

And parfourme my profers° and proven my strengthes, — promises

245

Than alle the golde and the gude° that thoue gatt ever, — goods

Than alle the londe and the lythe° that thoue arte lorde over; — people

40 And ryde to a revere redily° thereaftir, — **revere redily** river bank promptly

With haukes full hawtayne° that heghe willen flye, — proud

And when the fewlis bene° founden, fawkoneres hyenn° — **fewlis bene** birds are / hurry

To lache° oute thaire lessches and lowsen° thaym sone° — take **lessches** . . . leashes and loose / at once

And keppyn of° thaire caprons° and casten fro honde, — **keppyn of** pull off hoods

45 And than° the hawteste° in haste hyghes° to the towre, — then proudest hurry

With theire bellys so brighte blethely° thay ryngen, — happily

And there they hoven appon heghte° as it were heven° angelles. — **hoven** . . . hover on high / heaven's

"Then the fawkoners full fersely° to floodes° thay hyen,° — eagerly streams / hurry

To the revere° with thaire roddes° to rere° up the fewles, — river bank beating rods rouse

50 Sowssches° thaym full serely° to serven thaire hawkes. — Beat separately

Than tercelettes° full tayttely telys° doun stryken; — male falcons **tayttely telys** swiftly t[e]

Laners and lanerettis lightten° to thes endes, — **Laners** . . . Female falcons and hawks swoop down

Metyn° with the maulerdes° and many doun striken. — Meet mallards

Fawkons thay founden freely° to lighte,° — **founden freely** hasten quickly swo[op] down

55 With 'Hoo' and 'Howghe'° to the heron thay hitten hym full ofte, — Huff

Buffetyn hym, betyn hym, and brynges° hym to sege° — bring / seat (defensive position)

And saylen° hym full serely and sesyn° hym there-aftire. — assail **serely** . . . separately and seiz[e]

Then fawkoners full fersely founden° tham aftire, — **fersely founden** eagerly hasten

To helpen thaire hawkes thay hyen thaym° full yerne,° — **hyen thaym** hurry / eagerly

60 For° the bitt° of his bill bitterly° he strikes. — Because of sharp edge fiercely

They knelen doun one theire knees and krepyn full lowe,

Wynnen to his° wynges and wrythen° thaym togedire, — **Wynnen** Get at its twist

Brosten° the bones and brekyn thaym in sondire, — Crush

Puttis° owte with a penn° the maryo° one his° glove, — Put feather marrow his (the falc[on]

65 And quopes° thaym to the querrye° that quelled
    hym° to the dethe.

whoops   quarry

quelled hym tormented it (heron)

He quyrres° thaym and quotes° thaym, quyppeys°
    full lowde,

quarries   calls   whips his rod

Cheres° thaym full chefely ecchekkes° to leve,

Encourages   **chefely ecchekkes** especially lesser quarry

Than henntis° thaym one honde and hodes thaym
    theraftire,

takes

Cowples° up theire cowers° thaire caprons° to
    holde,

Draws   leather thongs   hoods

70 Lowppes° in thaire lesses° thorowe vertwells° of
    silvere.

Loops   leashes   rings

Than he laches to° his luyre° and lokes to his horse

laches to takes up   hawk lure

And lepis upe one the lefte syde als the laghe askes.°

laghe askes custom demands

"Portours° full pristly putten upe° the fowlis°

Bearers   **pristly . . .** swiftly make rise from cover   birds

And taryen° for theire tercelettis° that tenyn° thaym
    full ofte,

wait   male falcons   annoy

75 For some chosen to the echecheke,° thoghe some
    chefe° bettire.

lesser quarry

achieved

Spanyells full spedily thay spryngen abowte,

Bedagged° for dowkynge° when digges ben
    enewede;°

Muddied   plunging

digges . . . ducks are driven into water

And than kayre° to the courte that I come fro,

I return

With ladys full lovely to lappyn° in myn armes

clasp

80 And clyp° thaym and kysse thaym and comforthe
    myn hert,

embrace

And than with damesels dere to daunsen in thaire
    chambirs,

Riche romance to rede, and rekken° the sothe°

tell   truth

Of kempes° and of conquerours, of kynges full
    noblee,

knights

How thay wirchipe° and welthe wanne° in thaire
    lyves;

honor   won

85 With renkes° in ryotte° to revelle in haulle,

men   merriment

With coundythes° and carolles and compaynyes
    sere,°

part-songs

various

And chese° me to the chesse,° that chefe es of
    gamnes.°

betake   chess

games

"And this es life for to lede while I schalle lyfe
    here,

And thou with wandrynge and woo schalte wake
    for° thi gudes,

wake for watch over

90 And be thou dolven° and dede, thi dole° schall be
    schorte,

buried   lamentation

And he that thou leste luffes° schall layke hym°
    therewith

leste luffes least love   **layke hym** amuse himself

And spend that° thou haste longe sparede.° The devyll spede° hym ells!"°   what   saved   help   otherwise

Than this renke° alle in rosett rothelede° thies wordes.   man   **rosett rothelede** russett clothes rattled

He sayde, "Thryfte and thou have threpid° this thirtene wynter.   argued

95   I seghe° wele samples bene sothe° that sayde bene ful yore:°   see   **samples . . .** proverbs are true   **sayde . . .** have been said long ago

'Fole° es that with foles delys.'° Flyte° we no lengare."   Fool   deals   Argue

Than this beryn° alle in blake bownnes hym° to speke   man   **bownnes hym** prepared

And sayde: "Sirres, by my soule, sottes° bene ye bothe.   fools

Bot will ye hendely° me herken ane hande-while,°   courteously   moment

100   And I schalle stynte° your stryffe and stillen your threpe.°   stop   argument

I sett ensample bi myselfe and sekis° it no forthire.   seek

While I was yonge in my youthe and yape° of my dedys,   lively

I was als everrous° in armes as outher° of youreselven   greedy for glory   either

And as styffe° in a stourre° one my stede bake,   firm   battle

105   And as gaye in my gere als any gome ells,°   **gome ells** other man

And as lelly byluffede° with ladyse and maydens.   **lelly byluffede** faithfully beloved

My likame° was lovely as lothe° nowe to schewe,   body   loathsome

And as myche wirchip° I wane, i-wis,° as ye bothen.   **myche wirchip** much honor   **wane, i-wis** won, indeed

And aftir irkede me° with this, and ese was me levere°   **irkede me** I became tired   **me levere** dearer to me

110   Als man in his medill elde° his makande° wolde have.   age   comfort

Than I mukkede and marlede° and made up my howses   **mukkede . . .** manured and fertilized v marl

And purcheste me ploughe-londes and pastures full noble,

Gatte gude° and golde full gaynly° to honde.   **Gatte gude** Got goods   readily

Reches° and renttes were ryfe° to myselven.   Riches   plentiful

115   "Bot elde undiryode° me are° I laste wiste°   undermined   before   **laste wiste** lea knew

And alle disfegurede my face and fadide my hewe.

Bothe my browes and my berde blawnchede full whitte,

And when he sotted° my syghte, than sowed° myn hert,   dulled   grieved

Croked° me, cowrbed° me, encrampeschet° myn hondes   Made crooked   bent   twisted

120 That I ne may hefe° tham to my hede ne noghte ne . . . can't raise
    helpe myselven

Ne stale° stonden one my fete bot° I my staffe have.   firmly   unless

"Makes° youre mirrours bi me, men, bi youre   Make
    trouthe;

This schadowe in my schewere schunte° ye no   **schewere schunte** mirror avoid
    while.

And now es dethe at my dore that I drede moste.

125 I ne wot° wiche daye ne° when ne whate tyme he   **ne wot** know not   nor
    comes,

Ne whedirwardes° ne whare ne whatte to do aftire;   whither

Bot many modyere° than I, men one this molde,°   prouder   earth

Hafe passed the pase° that I schall passe sone,   path

And I schall neven° yow the names of nyne of the   name
    beste,

130 That ever wy° in this werlde wiste° appon erthe,   man   knew

That were conquerours full kene and kiddeste° of   **kene** . . . bold and most famous
    other.

The Nine Worthies : Hector

"The firste was Sir Ector,° and aldeste° of tyme,   Hector   oldest

When Troygens° of Troye were·tried to fighte°   Trojans   **tried** . . . tested by fighting

With Menylawse° the mody° kynge and men out   Menelaus   proud
    of Grece

That° thaire cité assegede and sayled° it full yerne°   Who   **assegede** . . . besieged and attacked
                                                       eagerly

5 For Elayne° his ownn quene that thereinn was   Helen
    halden

That Paresche,° the proude knyghte, paramours°   **That Paresche** Whom Paris   passionately
    lovede.

Sir Ectore was everous,° als the storye telles,   eager for glory

And, als clerkes in the cronycle cownten the sothe,°   truth

Nowmbron° thaym to nynety and nyne mo° by   Number   more
    tale°   count

10 Of kynges with crounes he killede with his handes

And full fele° other folke, als ferly were ellis.°   many   **als** . . . who were otherwise as wonder-
                                                              ful

    "Then Achilles his adversarye undide with his
        werkes,

With wyles and no wirchipe° woundede hym to   honor
    dethe

Als he tentid to° a tulke° that he tuke° of were,°   **tentid to** took care of   man   took prisoner
                                                         war
15 And he was slayne for that slaughte sleghely°   **slaughte sleghely** slaughter cunningly
        theraftir

With the wyles of a woman as he had wroghte° byfore. — done

Than Menylawse the mody° kynge hade myrthe at his hert — proud

That Ectore,° hys enymy, siche auntoure° hade fallen,° — Hector **siche auntoure** such mischa[nce] befallen

And with the Gregeis° of Grece he girde° over the walles; — Greeks rushed

20 The prowde paleys° dide he pulle doun to the erthe — palace

That was rialeste° of araye° and rycheste undir the heven. — most royal adornment

And then the Trogens of Troye teneden° full sore — grieved

And semblen thaym° full serely, and sadly° thay foughten; — **semblen thaym** assemble **serely** . . order, and stoutly

Bot the lüre° at the laste lighte° appon Troye, — defeat fell

25 For there Sir Priamus the prynce put was to dethe,

And Pantasilia the quene paste° hym byfore. — died

Sir Troylus, a trewe knyghte, that tristyly° hade foghten, — faithfully

Neptolemus, a noble knyghte, at nede that wolde noghte fayle,

Palamedes, a prise° knyghte and preved° in armes, — excellent proved

30 Ulixes° and Ercules,° that full everrous° were bothe, — Ulysses Hercules eager for glory

And other fele° of that ferde° fared of the same — many company

As Dittes and Dares[1] demeden° togedir. — declared

---

[1] Dictys Cretensis, reputed author of a pro-Greek diary of the Trojan War. What purported to be a Latin translation (fourth century A.D.) of this nonextant work was popular throughout the Middle Ages. Dares Phrygius, a priest in the *Iliad* (V, 9), was the supposed author of a pro-Trojan work translated into Latin in the fifth century A.D., *De Excidio Trojae*.

Alexander

"Aftir this, Sir Alysaunder alle the worlde wanne,° — won

Bothe the see and the sonde° and the sadde° erthe, — sand solid

The iles° of the Oryent to Ercules boundes,° — islands **Ercules boundes** Hercules' pillars

Ther° Ely and Ennoke[1] ever hafe bene sythen,° — Where since

5 And to° the come of Antecriste unclosede° be thay never; — until released

And conquered Calcas° knyghtly theraftire — Colchis

---

[1] According to widespread belief, Elias and Enoch were staying in an earthly paradise (*iles of the Oryent*) awaiting the coming of the Antichrist, whom they were to oppose.

Ther jentille Jazon° the Grewe wane° the flese of golde. — **Ther** ... Where noble Jason / **Grewe wane** Greek won

Then grathede° he hym to Gadres° the gates° full righte,° — prepared to go   Gaza   ways / straight

And there Sir Gadyfere the gude the Gaderayns° assemblet — people of Gaza

10 And rode oute full ryally to rescowe the praye;° — booty

And than Emenyduse° hym mete and made him full tame — Emenidus

And girdes° Gadyfere to the grounde, gronande° full sore, — strikes   groaning

And there that doughty was dede, and mekill dole makede.°

"Then Alixander the emperour, that athell° kyng hymselven, — noble

15 Arayed hym° for to ryde with the renkes° that he hade: — **Arayed hym** attired   men

Ther was the mody Meneduse,° a mane of Artage,° — **mody Meneduse** pro: Emenidus / Arcadia

He was duke of that douth° and a dussypere;° — noble company   one of twelve peers

Sir Filot and Sir Florydase, full ferse men of armes;

Sir Clyton and Sir Caulus, knyghtis full noble;

20 And Sir Garsyene the gaye, a gude man of armes;

And Sir Lyncamoure thaym ledys° with a lighte° will. — leads   cheerful

And than Sir Cassamus thaym kepide,° and the kyng prayede — detained

To fare into Fesome° his frendis to helpe, — Epheson

For one Carrus the kynge was comen owte of Inde

25 And hade Fozome affrayede and Fozayne asegede° — besieged

For Dame Fozonasc° the faire that he of lufe bysoughte. — Fesonas

The kynge agreed hym to goo and graythed° him sone — prepared

In mendys of Amenyduse° that he hade mysdone. — **mendys** ... amends for Emenidus

Then ferde° he towarde Facron° and by the flode abydes,° — went   Phasis River / **flode abydes** water stays

30 And there he tighte° up his tentis and taried there a while. — set

"There knyghtis full kenely caughten° theire leve — **kenely caughten** eagerly took

To fare into Fozayne° Dame Fozonase° to see — Epheson   Fesonas

And Idores and Edease² alle bydene.° — together

13. And there that valiant one (Gadifer) was dead, and Emenidus made great lamentation.
25. And had frightened Fesonas (Gadifer's daughter) and besieged Epheson
² Idores and Edias, daughters of Antigonus and nieces of Fesonas.

And there Sir Porus and his prynces to the poo
    avowede;³

35 Was never speche byfore spoken sped° bettir aftir,   that succeeded
For als thay demden° to doo thay deden full even.°   declared   **deden** ... did exactly
For there Sir Porus the prynce into the prese
    thrynges°   **prese thrynges** thick of the fight pushe
And bare the batelle one bake and abaschede thaym
    swythe.°
And than the bolde Bawderayne bowes° to the kyng   turns
40 And brayde° owte the brighte brande° owt of the   drew   sword
    kynges hande,
And Florydase full freschely foundes° hym aftir   **freschely foundes** keenly hastens
And hent° the helme of° his hede and the halse°   takes   off   neck
    crakede.
Then Sir Gadefere the gude⁴ gripis his axe
And into the Indyans ofte auntirs hym sone,°   **auntirs** ... ventures at once
45 And thaire stiffe standerte to stikkes he hewes.
And than Sir Cassamus the kene° Carrus releves;   bold
When he was fallen appon fote, he fet° hym his   brought
    stede,
And aftir that Sir Cassamus Sir Carus he drepitt,°   killed
And for that poynte° Sir Porus perset° hym to   deed   pierced
    dethe.
50 And than the Indyans ofte uttire tham droghen°   **uttire** ... betook themselves off
And fledden faste of the felde, and Alexander suede.°   pursued them
  "When thay were skaterede and skayled and
    skyftede in sondere,°   **skayled** ... dispersed and split asunde
Alyxandere, oure athell° kyng, ames hym° to   noble   **ames hym** decides
    lenge°   tarry
And fares into Fozayne, festes° to make,   **Fozayne, festes** Epheson, celebration
55 And weddis wy unto wy° that wilnede° togedire.   **wy** ... person to person   wished to be
Sir Porus, the pryce° knyghte moste praysed of   excellent
    othere,°   **of othere** by others
Fonge Fozonase to fere, and fayne° were thay bothe.   **Fonge** ... Took Fesonas as his wife an
The bolde Bawderayne of Baderose, Sir Cassayle   glad
    hymselven
Bele° Edyas, the faire birde, bade° he no nother.   Beautiful   **birde, bade** maiden, asked
60 And Sir Betys, the beryne° the beste of his tyme,   knight
Idores, his awnn lufe, aughte° he hymselven.   **awnn** ... own love, obtained
Then iche lede° hade the love that he hade longe   **iche lede** each man
    yernede.

³ 'Made vows to the peacock.' At a banquet where a roast peacock was the chief dish, Porrus vowed to
unhorse Emenidus, while his companion Baudrain (l. 39) vowed to disarm Alexander.
38. And forced the battle line back and confounded them quickly.
⁴ Sir Gadifer of Epheson, whose father Gadifer of Larris was slain by Emenidus (ll. 11–13, above).

Sir Alixander, oure emperour, ames hym° to ryde   **ames hym** decides
And bewes° towardes Babyloyne with the beryns   turns
    that were levede°   left
65 Bycause of dame Candace that comforthed hym
    moste.
And that cité he bysegede and assayllede it aftire
While° hym the yatis° were yete, and yolden° the   Until gates **yete** . . . surrendered, and
    keyes.   given up
And there that pereles prynce was puysonede° to   poisoned
    dede;°   death
Thare he was dede of a drynke—as dole es to here—
70 That the curssede Cassander in a cowpe° hym   cup
    broghte.
He conquered with conqueste kyngdomes twelve
And dalte° thaym to his dussypers° when he the   distributed   twelve peers
    dethe tholede,°   suffered
And thus the worthieste of this werlde wente to his
    ende.

Julius Caesar

"Thane Sir Sezere° hymselven that Julyus was   Caesar
    hatten,°   named
Alle Inglande he aughte° at his awnn° will   obtained   own
When the Bruyte in his booke Bretaygne it callede.°
The trewe toure° of Londone in his tyme he   tower
    makede,
5 And craftely the condithe° he compaste° there-   conduit   contrived
    aftire,
And then he droghe hym° to Dovire and dwellyde   **droghe hym** withdrew
    there a while
And closede° ther a castelle with cornells° full heghe,   fortified   battlements
Warnestorede° it full wiesely,° als witnesses the   Provisioned   wisely
    sothe,
For there es hony° in that holde holden sythen° his   honey   **holde** . . . stronghold retained since
    tyme.
10 Than rode he into Romayne and rawnsede° it sone,   **Romayne** . . . the Roman realm and
And Cassabalount the kynge conquerede there-   ransomed
    aftire.
Then graythed he hym° into Grece and gete° it   **graythed** . . . he prepared to go   conquered
    belyve.°   quickly

3. At a time when the Brut (Lawman's *Brut*?) called it Britain (not England).

The semely cité Alexaunder seside° he theraftire;   **Alexaunder seside** Alexandria seized
Affrike and Arraby and Egipt the noble,
15 Surry and Sessoyne sessede° he togedir,   **Surry . . .** Syria and Saxony seized
With alle the iles of the see appon iche a syde.
Thies thre were paynymes full priste and passed°   **paynymes . . .** greatly esteemed pagans
    alle othire.   and surpassed

Joshua

"Of thre Jewes full gentill juggen° we aftir,   **gentill juggen** noble consider
In the Olde Testament as the storye tellis
In a booke of the Bible that breves° of kynges,   tells
And renkes° that rede kane *Regum*° it callen.   men   Kings
5 The firste was gentill Josue that was a Jewe noble,
Was heryet° for his holynes into heven-riche.°   carried · the kingdom of heaven
When Pharaoo had flayede° the folkes of Israelle,   put to flight
Thay ranne into the Rede° See for radde° of   Red   fear
    hymselven,
And than Josue the Jewe Jhesu° he prayede   to Jesus
10 That the peple myghte passe unpereschede° that   unharmed
    tyme,
And than the see sett up appon sydes twayne
In the manere of a mode° walle that made were   mud
    with hondes.
And thay soughten° over the see, sownnde,° alle   went   sound
    togedir,
And Pharaoo full fersely followede thaym aftire.
15 And efte° Josue the Jewe Jhesus he prayede,   again
And the see sattillede° agayne and sanke thaym   flowed back
    thereinn—
A soppe for the Sathanas, unsele° have theire bones! **Sathanas, unsele** Satan, misfortune
And aftire Josue the Jewe full gentilly hym bere,°   **gentilly . . .** nobly bore himself
And conquerede kynges and kyngdomes twelve,
20 And was a conqueroure full kene° and most kyd°   bold   renowned
    in his tyme.

David

"Than David the doughty,° thurghe Drightynes   valiant one
    sonde,°   **Drightynes sonde** the Lord's comm
Was caughte° from kepyng of schepe and a kyng   taken
    made.

The grete grym Golyas° he to grounde broghte   Goliath
And sloughe° hym with his slynge and with no   slew
    sleghte° ells.   skill
5 The stone thurghe his stele helme stong° into his   pierced
    brayne,
And he was dede of that dynt°—the devyll hafe that   blow
    reche!°   **that reche** him who cares
And than was David full dere to Drightyn° hym-   the Lord
    selven
And was a prophete of pryse° and praysed full ofte.   excellence
Bot yit greved he° his God gretely theraftire,   **yit** . . . he still aggrieved
10 For Urye° his awnn° knyghte in aventure° he   Uriah own peril
    wysede°   sent
There° he was dede at° that dede° as dole° es to here;   Where **dede at** dead by deed grief it
For Bersabee his awnn birde° was alle that bale   lady
    rerede.°   **bale rerede** evil brought about

Judas Maccabeus

"The gentill° Judas Machabee was a Jewe kene°   noble bold
And thereto worthy in were° and wyse of his dedis.   war
Antiochus and Appolyne aythere° he drepide,°   both killed
And Nychanore, another kynge, full naytly°   dexterously
    thereaftir,
5 And was a conquerour kydde° and knawen with   renowned
    the beste.
Thies thre were Jewes full joly° and justers full noble   excellent
That full loughe° have bene layde sythen gane° full   low **sythen gane** since there has passed a
    longe tyme;
Of siche doughety° doers looke what es worthen.°   **siche doughety** such valiant become

King Arthur

"Of the thre Cristen to carpe couthely° thereaftir   **carpe couthely** speak knowledgeably
That were conquerours full kene and kyngdomes
    wonnen,
Areste° was Sir Arthure and eldeste of tyme,   First,
For alle Inglande he aughte° at his awnn° will   held own
5 And was kynge of this kythe° and the crowne hade.   country
His courte was at Carlele° comonly holden   Carlisle
With renkes° full ryalle of his rownnde table   knights
That Merlin with° his maystries° made in his tyme,   by powers

255

	And sett the sege° perilous so semely° one highte,	seat fairly
10	There° no segge° scholde sitt bot hym scholde schame tyde°	Where man **schame tyde** disgrace befall
	Owthir° dethe withinn the thirde daye demed° to hymselven,	Or adjudged
	Bot° Sir Galade° the gude that the gree wanne.°	Except for Galahad **gree wanne** Grace won
	There was Sir Launcelot de Lake full lusty in armes	
	And Sir Gawayne the gude that never gome° harmede,	man
15	Sir Askanore, Sir Ewayne, Sir Errake fytz Lake,	
	And Sir Kay the kene and kyd of° his dedis,	**kyd of** renowned for
	Sir Percevalle de Galeys that preved° had bene ofte,	tested
	Mordrede and Bedwere,° men of mekyll° myghte,	Bedivere great
	And othere fele° of that ferde,° folke of the beste.	many company
20	"Then Roystone the riche kyng, full rakill° of his werkes,	rash
	He made a blyot to° his bride of° the berdes of kynges	**blyot to** tunic for from
	And aughtilde° Sir Arthures berde one scholde be,	intended
	Bot Arthure, oure athell° kynge, another° he thynkes	noble otherwise
	And faughte with hym in the felde till he was fey worthen.°	**was . . .** became fated to die
25	And than Sir Arthure oure kyng ames hym° to ryde;	**ames hym** decides
	Uppon Sayn Michaells Mounte mervaylles he wroghte,	
	There° a dragone he dreped° that drede was full sore.	Where killed
	And than he sayled over the see into sere° londes	various
	Whils alle the beryns° of Bretayne bewede hym to fote.°	knights **Bretayne . . .** Brittany knelt at his feet
30	Gascoyne and Gyane° gatt he thereaftir	Guienne
	And conquered kyngdomes and contrees full fele.°	many
	"Then ames he into Inglonde into his awnn kythe;°	**awnn kythe** own country
	The gates° towardes Glassthenbery° full graythely° he rydes,	ways Glastonbury at once
	And ther Sir Mordrede hym mett by a more syde°	**by . . .** beside a moor
35	And faughte with hym in the felde to° alle were fey worthen°	until **were . . .** became fated to die
	Bot° Arthur oure athell° kyng and Wawayne° his knyghte.	Except noble Gawain

And when the felde was flowen and fey bot°   **flowen** ... fled and fated except for
    thaymselven,
Than Arthure Sir Wawayne athes° by his trouthe   makes swear
That he swiftely his swerde scholde swynge° in the   hurl
    mere,°   sea
40 And whatt selcouthes° he see° the sothe scholde   marvels   might see
    he telle.
And Sir Wawayne swith° to the swerde and   went quickly
    swange° it in the mere,   hurled
And ane hande by the hiltys hastely it grippes
And brawndeschet that brighte swerde and bere it
    awaye.
And Wawayne° wondres of this werke and wendes   Gawain
    bylyve°   **wendes bylyve** goes quickly
45 To his lorde there° he hym lefte and lokes abowte,   where
And he ne wiste° in alle this werlde where he was   knew
    bycomen.°   gone
And then he hyghes hym° in haste and hedis to the   **hyghes hym** hurries
    mere°   sea
And seghe° a bote from the banke and beryns   saw
    thereinn.
Thereinn was Sir Arthure and othire of his ferys°   companions
50 And also Morgn la Faye that myche couthe° of   **myche couthe** knew much
    sleghte,°   cunning
And there ayther segge seghe othir laste,° for sawe   **ayther** ... each man saw the other for
    he hym no more.   the last time

Godfrey of Bouillon

"Sir Godfraye de Bolenn siche° grace of God   such
    hade
That alle Romanye he rode and rawnnsunte it
    sone.°
The Amorelle of Antyoche aftire he drepit°   killed
That was called Corborant, kilwarde° of dedis.   treacherous
5 And aftir he was callede kynge and the crownn hade
Of Jerusalem and of the Jewes gentill° togedir,   noble
And with the wirchipe of this werlde he went to his
    ende.

2. That he rode over the whole Roman realm and put it to ransom at once.

Charlemagne

"Than was Sir Cherlemayne chosen chefe kynge
of Fraunce,
With his doghty doussypers,° to do als hym
lykede:°
Sir Rowlande the riche and Duke Raynere of
Jene,°
Olyver and Aubrye and Ogere Deauneys,°
5 And Sir Naymes at the nede that never wolde
fayle,
Turpyn and Terry, two full tryed° lordes,
And Sir Sampsone hymselfe of the Mounte Ryalle,
Sir Berarde de Moundres, a bold beryn in armes,
And gud Sir Gy de Burgoyne, full gracyous of
dedis.
10 The katur fitz Emowntez° were kydde° knyghtes
alle,
And other moo° than I may myne° or any man
elles.°
    "And then Sir Cherlles° the chefe ches° for to
ryde
And paste towardes Polborne° to proven his
strenghte.
Salamadyne the Sowdane° he sloghe° with his
handis,
15 And that cité he bysegede and saylede° it full ofte
While° hym his yernynge° was yett° and the yates°
opynede,
And Witthyne° thaire waryed° kynge wolde nott
abyde°
Bot soghte° into Sessoyne socoure° hym to gete,
And Cherlemayne, oure chefe kynge, cheses° into
the burgh,°
20 And dame Nioles anone he name° to hymselven
And maried hir to Maundevyle that scho hade
myche° lovede,
And spedd hym into hethyn Spayne spedely
thereaftire
And fittilled hym° by Flagott° faire for to loge.°
    "There Olyver the everous aunterede hymselven°
25 And faughte with Sir Ferambrace and fonge° hym
one were,°
And than they fologhed° hym in a fonte and
Florence hym callede.

doghty doussypers valiant twelve peers

als . . . as he pleased

Genoa

Ogere Deauneys Ogier the Dane

valiant

katur . . . four sons of Aymon   renowned

more   remember

else

Charlemagne   chose

Paderborn (Saxony)

Sultan   slew

attacked

Until   wish   granted   gates

Widukind   accursed

stay

went   **Sessoyne socoure** Saxony help

goes

town

took

greatly

fittilled hym prepared   the Flagot River

dwell

everous . . . eager for glory   ventured

took

one were in battle

baptized

And than moved he hym to Mawltryple Sir
    Balame to seche,°   seek
And that Emperour at Egremorte aftir he takes
And wolde hafe made Sir Balame a man of oure
    faythe,
30 And garte feche° forthe a founte byfore-with° his   had brought   before
    eghne,°   eyes
And he dispysede it and spitte and spournede it to
    the erthe,
And one° swyftely with a swerde swapped of° his   a man   **swapped of** chopped off
    hede.
And Dame Floripe the faire was cristened there-
    aftire
And kende° thaym to the corownne that Criste had   guided
    one hede
35 And the nayles, anone, nayttly° thereaftire,   properly
When He with passyoun and pyne° was naylede   torture
    one the rode.°   cross
And than those relikes so riche redely he takes,
And at Sayne Denys[1] he thaym dide° and dwellyd   put
    there for ever.
    "And than bod-worde° unto Merchill full boldly   message
    he sendys
40 And bade hym Cristyne bycome and one° Criste   in
    leve°   believe
Or he scholde bette° doun his borowes and brenn°   beat   **borowes ...** towns and burn
    hym thereinn,
And garte Genyone goo° that erande that grevede   **garte ...** made Ganelon go on
    thaym alle.
Than rode he to Rowncyvale, that rewed hym°   **rewed hym** he regretted
    aftire,
There° Sir Rowlande, the ryche Duke, refte° was   Where   bereft of
    his lyfe,
45 And Olyver, his awnn fere,° that ay° had bene   comrade   ever
    trewe,
And Sir Turpyn the trewe that full triste° was at   trusty
    nede,
And full fele othir folke, als ferly were elles.°   **als ...** who were otherwise as wonderful
Then suede° he the Sarazenes seven yere and more,   pursued
And the Sowdane° at Saragose full sothely° he   Sultan   **full sothely** indeed
    fyndis,
50 And there he bett° down the burghe,° and Sir   beat   town
    Merchill he tuke,

---

[1] St. Denis, north of Paris, where Charlemagne rebuilt the church of St. Denis, in which he was later buried.

And that daye he dide hym to the dethe als he had
    wele servede.°   *deserved*
"Bot by than his wyes° were wery and woundede *men*
    full many,
And he fared into France to fongen° thaire riste° *take rest*
And neghede° towarde Nerbone,° that noyede° *neared Narbonne grieved*
    thaym full sore,
55 And that cité he asseggede° appone sere halves° *besieged **sere halves** various sides*
While° hym the yates° were yette and yolden° *Until gates **yette**... surrendered and*
    the keyes,   *given up*
And Emorye° made Emperour even at that tyme, *Aymeri of Narbonne*
To kepe it and to holde it to hym and to his ayers.° *heirs*
And then thay ferden° into Fraunce to fongen° *went take*
    thaire ese,
60 And at Sayn Denys he dyede, at his dayes tyme.
"Now hafe I nevened° yow the names of nyne of *named*
    the beste
That ever were in this werlde wiste° appon erthe *known*
And the doghtyeste° of dedis in thaire dayes tyme, *most valiant*
Bot doghetynes,° when dede° comes, ne dare *valiance death*
    noghte habyde.°   ***ne***... dare not remain*

Wise Men

"Of wyghes° that were wyseste will ye now here, *men*
And I schall schortly yow schewe and schutt me° ***schutt me*** conclude*
    ful sone.
Arestotle he was arste° in Alexander° tyme, *first Alexander's*
And was a fyne philozophire and a fynour° noble, *refiner of metal*
5 The° grete Alexander to graythe° and gete golde *For the prepare*
    when hym liste,°   ***hym liste*** he pleased*
And multiplye metalles with mercurye watirs
And with his ewe ardaunt° and arsneke pouders, ***ewe ardaunt*** ardent spirit (alcohol)*
With salpetir and sal-jeme° and siche° many othire, *crystal salt such*
And menge° his metalles and make fyne silvere, *mix*
10 And was a blaunchere° of the best thurgh blaste of *alchemist who whitens metals*
    his fyre.
"Then Virgill, thurgh his vertus,° verrayle he *powers*
    maket°   *caused*
Bodyes of brighte brasse full boldely to speke,
To telle whate betydde° had and whate betyde° *happened happen*
    scholde,

When Dioclesyane was dighte° to be dere°   ordained noble
    emperour;
15 Of Rome and of Romanye the rygalté° he hade.   sovereignty
  "Than Sir Salomon hymselfe sett hym by hym
    one.°   **hymselfe ...** sat down by himself
  His Bookes in the Bible bothe bene togedirs;
  That one° of wisdome and of witte wondirfully   **That one** The one (Ecclesiastes)
    teches;
  His sampills° and his sawes bene sett in the tother.°   parables other (Proverbs)
20 And he was the wyseste in witt that ever wonnede° dwelled
    in erthe,
  And his techynges will bene trowede° whills the   believed
    werlde standes
  Bothe with° kynges and knyghtis and kaysers°   by emperors
    therinn.
  "Merlyn was a mervayllous man and made many
    thynges,
  And naymely nygromancye nayttede° he ofte   **naymely ...** especially necromancy
                            practiced
25 And graythed° Galyan[1] a boure° to gete hyr   prepared bower
    therin
  That no wy° scholde hir wielde° ne wynne from   man possess
    hymselven.
  Theis were the wyseste in the worlde of witt that
    ever yitt were,
  Bot dethe wondes° for no witt to wende were hym   hesitates
    lykes.°   **wende ...** go where he pleases

[1] *Galyan* is obscure; see *Nynyve* in Malory; *Niviene* in Old French *Merlin*; *Vivien* in Tennyson.

Famous Lovers

  "Now of the prowdeste in presse° that   **prowdeste ...** noblest in battle
    paramoures loveden
  I schalle titly° yow telle and tary° yow no lengere.   quickly delay
  Amadase and Edoyne,[1] in erthe are thay bothe,
  That in golde and in grene were gaye in thaire
    tyme.
5 And Sir Sampsone hymselfe, full savage of his dedys,
  And Dalyda° his derelynge,° now dethe has tham   Delilah darling
    bothe.

[1] Amadas and Idoine, famous hero and heroine of French romance, first mentioned in Middle English in the *Love Rune* of Thomas of Hailes (p. 158).

Sir Ypomadonn de Poele,[2] full priste° in his armes, quick
The faire Fere° de Calabre, now faren° are they Proud One gone
    bothe.
Generides[3] the gentill,° full joly° in his tyme, noble fair
10 And Clarionas, that was so clere,° are bothe now beautiful
    bot erthe.
Sir Eglamour of Artas, full everous° in armes, eager for glory
And Cristabelle the clere maye° es crept in hir grave. maid
And Sir Tristrem the trewe, full triste° of hym- trusty
    selven,
And Ysoute, his awnn lufe, in erthe are thay bothe.
15 Whare es now Dame Dido was° qwene of Cartage, who was
Dame Candace, the comly, was called quene of
    Babyloyne?
Penelopie, that was price° and pasten° alle othere excellent surpassed
And Dame Gaynore° the gaye, nowe graven° are Guinevere buried
    thay bothen,
And othere moo° than I may mene° or any man more tell
    elles.° else
20   "Sythen doughtynes° when dede° comes ne dare **Sythen doughtynes** Since valiance
    noghte habyde,° death
        ne ... dare not remain
Ne dethe wondes° for no witt to wende where hym **Ne ...** And death doesn't hesitate
    lykes,° **wende ...** go where he pleases
And thereto paramours and pride puttes he full
    lowe,
Ne there es reches° ne rent may° rawnsone your **Ne ...** Nor are there riches which can
    lyves,
Ne noghte es sekire° to youreselfe in certayne bot assured
    dethe,
25 And he es so uncertayne that sodaynly he comes.
Me thynke° the wele° of this werlde worthes° to **Me thynke** It seems to me wealth
    noghte. turns
Ecclesiastes the clerke declares in his booke
Vanitas vanitatum et omnia vanitas,°
That alle es vayne and vanytés, and vanyté es alle.
30 Forthi amendes° youre mysse° whills ye are men **Forthi amendes** Therefore reform si
    here,
Quia in inferno nulla est redempcio,°
For in helle es no helpe, I hete° yow for sothe.° promise **for sothe** indeed

---

[2] Ipomadon of Apulia after numerous adventures married the Duke of Calabria's daughter, known only as La Fière, The Proud One of Calabria. Three Middle English versions of the Anglo-Norman romance are extant.
[3] Generides and Clarionas, protagonists of a romance that survives in two late Middle English versions.
28. Vanity of vanities and all is vanity (Eccles. 1:2; 12:8)
31. Because in hell there is no redemption (free paraphrase, Job 7:9)

Als God in his gospelle graythely° yow teches,	fittingly
Ite ostendite vos sacerdotibus,°	
35 To schryve yow full schirle° and schewe yow to	completely
prestis.	
Et ecce omnia munda sunt vobis,°	
And ye that wronge wroghte° schall worthen° full	did become
clene.	
"Thou man in thi medill elde,° have mynde	middle age
whate I saye.	
I am thi sire and thou my sone, the sothe for to telle,	
40 And he the sone of thiselfe that sittis one the stede,°	steed
For Elde° es sire of Midill-Elde, and Midill-Elde of	Age
Youthe.	
"And haves gud daye, for now I go; to grave	
moste me wende;°	**moste . . .** I must go
Dethe dynges° one my dore; I dare no lengare	knocks
byde."°	remain

Epilogue

When I had lenged and layne a full longe while,	
I herde a bogle° one a bonke be blowen full lowde,	bugle
And I wakkened therwith and waytted° me umbe.°	looked around
Than the sone was sett and syled° full loughe,°	sunk low
5 And I founded° appon fote and ferkede° towarde	hastened hurried
townn.	
And in the monethe of Maye thies mirthes° me	delights
tydde°	befell
Als I schurtted° me in a schelfe° in the schawes°	amused bank thickets
faire,	
And belde me° in the birches with bewes° full smale,	**belde me** built myself a blind boughs
And lugede° me in the leves, that lighte were and	sheltered
grene.	
10 There, dere Drightyne,° this daye dele° us of thi	Lord give
blysse,	
And Marie that es mylde qwene amende° us of synn.	reform

Amen. Amen.

34. Go show yourselves to the priests (Luke 17:14)
36. And behold all the world is yours (free paraphrase, Luke 17:21)

Morte Arthure

(c. 1360, originally Northwest Midland?)

❦

The *Alliterative Morte Arthure* is a stirring epic dealing first with Arthur's attempt to win the mastery of the western world by conquering the Emperor of Rome and his tragic overthrow, brought about by the treachery of Mordred. It freely adapts the materials in Wace's Anglo-Norman version of Geoffrey of Monmouth's *History of the Kings of Britain*. A cohesive work written in the alliterative tradition of Lawman's earlier *Brut* (p. 49), the *Morte Arthure* is best known today for a number of brilliant passages—the banquet (ll. 167–230), Arthur's farewell to Guinevere (ll. 695–716), his dream (ll. 756–831), his slaying of the giant (ll. 941–1221), and his final battle with Mordred (ll. 4154–346, printed below). In each of these passages the unknown author displays his mastery not only of the plastic medium of his verse but also of his subject, in his rich profusion of specific details, in his heroic concept of Arthur's grandeur, and in his emphasis on the tragic workings of fate.

The first half of the poem, dealing with Arthur's defeat of the Roman Emperor Lucius, provided the basis for Malory's *The Tale of the Noble King Arthur That Was Emperor Himself* (*Works*, ed. Eugene Vinaver, Oxford, 1959), which appears as Book V in Caxton's version.

The poem is written in conventional alliterative verse; see Introduction, type 1, page 29.

The text of the *Morte Arthure* was edited by E. Brock, EETS 8 (London, 1871), by Mary M. Banks (London, 1900), and by Erich Björkman (London, 1915). A modernization appears in Andrew Boyle, *Morte Arthure*, ed. Lucy A. Paton (London, 1912). For bibliography see Sever, ch. 1.16.

[Lines 4154–346]

Than remys° the riche kynge with rewthe° at his herte,   *cries out* *pity*

Hevys° hys handys one heghte,° and to the hevene lokes: *Raises* *on high*

"Qwhythene hade Dryghttyne destaynede° at his dere wille   **Qwhythene** . . . O that the Lord ha[d] *destined*

That he hade demyd° me todaye to dy for yow alle.   *ordained*

5 That had I lever° than be lorde alle my lyfe tyme   *rather*

Off alle that Alexandere aughte qwhilles° he in erthe lengede."°   **aughte qwhilles** owned while *stayed*

Sir Ewayne and Sir Errake, thes excellente beryns,°   *men*

Enters in one° the oste,° and egerly strykes.   **Enters** . . . Enter together *host*

The ethenys° of Orkkenaye and Irische kynges,   *giants*

264

10 Thay gobone° of the gretteste with growndene°
        swerdes,

strike down sharpened

Hewes one° thas hulkes with theire harde wapyns,

on

Layed downe thas ledes° with lothely dynttys.°

men **lothely dynttys** horrible blows

Schuldirs and scheldys thay schrede° to the hawnches,°

slashed hips

And medilles° thourghe mayles° thay merkene in
        sondire.°

waists mail armor **merkene . . .** cut asunder

15 Siche° honoure never aughte° none erthely kyng

Such owned

At theire endyng daye, bot Arthure hyme selvene.

So the droughte° of the daye dryede° theire hertes,

dryness made to suffer

That bothe drynkles they dye. Dole° was the more.

Sorrow

    Now mellys° oure medillewarde,° and mengene°
        togedire.

joins center mixes

20 Sir Mordrede the Malebranche with his myche pöple°

myche pöple great people

He had hide hyme behynde within thas holte eynys,°

thas . . . that wood's narrow passages

With halle bataile one hethe, harme° es the more.

halle . . . whole army on the heath, suffering

He hade sene the conteke° al clene to the ende,

strife

How oure chevalrye chevyde be° chaunces of armes.

chevyde be prevailed by

25 He wiste° oure folke was forfoughttene° that thare
        was feye levede.°

knew weary of fighting **feye levede** fated to be left dead

To encowntere the kynge he castes hyme sone,°

castes . . . determines at once

Bot the churles chekyne° hade chaungyde his armes.

churles chekyne churlish chicken

He had sothely forsakene° the sawturoure engrelede,[1]

sothely forsakene truly abandoned

And laughte° upe thre lyons alle of whitte silvyre,

taken

30 Passande° in purpre° of perrie fulle° riche,

Surpassing purple **perrie fulle** precious stones very

Ffor° the kynge sulde° noghte knawe the cawtelous°
        wriche.

So that should cunning

Because of his cowardys he keste of° his atyre,

off

Bot the comliche° kyng knewe hym fulle swythe;°

comely quickly

Karpis° to Sir Cadors thes kyndly wordez:

Speaks

35   "I see the traytoure come yondyr trynande° fulle
        yerne;°

proceeding eagerly

Yone° ladde with the lyones es like to hyme selfene.

Yonder

Hym salle torfere betyde,° may I touche ones,°

Hym . . . Harm shall befall him once

Ffor alle his tresone and trayne, alls° I am trew lorde.

trayne, alls trickery, as

Today Clarente and Caliburne[2] salle kythe° theme
        togedirs

show

40 Whilke° es kenere of kerfe° or hardare of eghge.

Which sword cutting

Ffraiste° sall we fyne stele appone fyne wedis.°

Test garments

Itt° was my derlynge daynteuous and fulle° dere
        holdene,°

It (the steel sword) very held

[1] The 'engrailed saltire' is Mordred's usual coat of arms, consisting of the saltire, a device similar to the St. Andrew's cross, which is engrailed, or drawn with an edge ornamented with a series of concave indentations.

[2] King Arthur carried Caliburne; Mordred carried Clarente, which he had stolen with Guinevere's help from Arthur's effects.

Kepede fore encorownmentes° of kynges enoynttede.   coronations
One° dayes when I dubbyde dukkes and erlles,   On

45 It was burliche° borne be° the bryghte hiltes.   grandly by
I durste never dere° it in dedis of armes,   injure
Bot ever kepide clene because° of my selvene.   for the sake
Ffor I see Clarent unclede,° that crowne es of swerdes,   unsheathed
My wardrop° of Walyngfordhe I wate° es distroyede.   wardrobe know

50 Wist no wy° of wone° bot Waynor° hir selvene;   **Wist . . .** No man knew   dwelling Guinevere
Schö hade the kepynge hir selfe of that kydde° wapyne,   renowned
Off° cofres enclosede that to the crowne lengede,°   Of belonged
With rynges and relikkes and the regale° of Ffraunce,   crown jewels
That was ffowndene one° Sir Ffrolle, whene he was   on
   feye levyde."°   **feye levyde** left dead

55   Than Sir Marrike in malyncoly metys hym sone,°   at once
With a mellyd° mace myghtyly hym strykes.   hammerheaded
The bordoure of his bacenett° he bristes in sondire°   steel cap **bristes . . .** bursts asunder
That the schire° rede blode over his brene° rynnys.   bright cuirass (breast armor)
The beryne blenkes° for bale,° and alle his ble°   **beryne blenkes** man flinches pain
   chaunges,   color

60 Bot yitt he byddys° as a bore, and brymly° he strykes.   stands firm **bore . . .** boar, and fiercely
He braydes° owte a brande,° bryghte als° ever ony   draws sword as
   sylver,
That was Sir Arthure° awene, and Utere his fadirs,   Arthur's
In the wardrop° of Walyngfordhe was wonte to be   wardrobe
   kepede.
Tharewith the derfe° dogge syche° dynttes he rechede,°   stout such gave

65 The tother withdrewe one dreghe° and durste do none   **one dreghe** aside
   other;
Ffor Sir Marrake was mane merrede in elde,°   **mane . . .** man marred by age
And Sir Mordrede was myghty and in his moste
   strenghis.
Come none within the compas, knyghte ne none other,
Within the swyng of swerde, that ne he the swete
   levyd.°   **that . . .** who left not his life

70   That persayfes° oure prynce, and presses to° faste,   perceives **presses to** hurries there
Strykes into the stowre° by strenghe of hys handis,   battle
Metis with Sir Mordrede; he melis unfaire:°   **melis unfaire** speaks harshly
"Turne, traytoure untrewe, thee tydys no bettyre.°   **thee . . .** no better shall befall you
Be° gret Gode, thow salle° dy with dynt of my handys.   By shall

75 Thee schalle rescowe no renke ne reches° in erthe."   **renke . . .** man nor wealth
The kyng with Calaburne knyghtly hym strykes;
The cantelle° of the clere° schelde he kerfes in sondyre°   corner bright **in sondyre** asunder
Into the schuldyre of the schalke° a schaftmonde large,°   man **schaftmonde large** a half-foot deep
That the schire° rede blode schwede° on the maylys.°   bright showed mail

80 He° schodirde and schrenkys and schontes° bot lyttille,   He (Mordred) turns aside

Bott schokkes° in scharpely in his schene wedys.°   jumps   **schene wedys** bright garments (armor)

The ffelonne with the ffyne swerde freschely he strykes;

The ffelettes° of the fferere° syde he flassches in sondyre°   fillets   farther   **flassches . . .** rips asunder

Thorowe jopowne and jesserawnte[3] of gentille mailes.°   **gentille mailes** noble mail

85 The freke fichede° in the flesche an halfe fotte large.°   **freke fichede** man pierced   deep

That derfe° dynt was his dede,° and dole was the more   stout   **his dede** his (Arthur's) death

That ever that doughtty sulde° dy, bot at Dryghttyns° wylle.   **doughtty sulde** valiant one should   Lord's

Yitt° with Calyburne his swerde, fulle knyghtly he strykes,   Once more

Kastes ine° his clere° schelde, and coveres him fulle° faire,   **Kastes ine** Draws on   bright   very

90 Swappes of° the swerde hande, als° he by glentes;°   **Swappes of** Strikes off   as   **by glentes** glides by

Ane inche fro the elbowe he ochede° it in sondyre,°   hacked   **in sondyre** asunder

That he° swounnes one° the swarthe° and one swym° fallis—   he (Mordred)   on   sward   faint

Thorowe bracer° of browne stele and the bryghte mayles,°   brassart (arm piece)   mail

That the hilte and the hande appone the hethe ligges.°   lie

95 Thane frescheliche the freke the ffente upe rererys,°

Brochis hym° in with the bronde° to the bryghte hiltys,   **Brochis hym** Stabs him (Mordred)   sword

And he brawles one° the bronde, and bownes° to dye.   **brawles one** sprawls on   prepares

"In faye,"° says the feye° kynge, "sore me for-thynkkes   faith   dying

That ever siche° a false theefe so faire an ende haves."   such

100 Qwene° they had ffenyste° this feghte, thane was the felde wonnene,°   When   finished   won

And the false folke in the felde feye° are bylevede.°   dead   left

Tille° a fforeste they fledde and felle in the grevys,°   Into   groves

And fers feghtande folke folowes theme aftyre,

Howntes° and hewes downe the heythene tykes,°   Hunt   dogs

105 Mourtherys° in the mowntaygnes Sir Mordrede° knyghtes.   Murder   Mordred's

Thare chapyde° never no childe,° cheftayne, ne other,   escaped   man

Bot choppes theme downe in the chace—it chargys° bot littyle.   matters

Bot whene Sir Arthure anone° Sir Ewayne he fyndys,   next

And Errake the Avenaunt,° and other grett lordes,   Graceful

[3] 'Jupon,' a padded tunic, and 'jazeran,' velvet over iron on canvas, the whole ornamented with brass studs.

95. Then briskly the man (Arthur) raises up the flap (*ffente*, covering the slit in Mordred's coat of mail)

267

110 He kawghte up Sir Cador with care° at his herte,   sorrow
     Sir Clegis, Sir Cleremonde, thes clere° mene of armes,   illustrious
     Sir Lothe and Sir Lyonelle, Sir Lawncelott, and Lowes,
     Marrake and Meneduke, that myghty ware ever.
     With langoure° in the launde° thare he layes theme   sorrow   field
       togedire,
115 Lokede one° theyre lighames,° and with a lowde   on   bodies
       stevene,°   voice
     Alls lede° that liste° noghte lyfe and loste had his   **Alls lede** As a man   desired
       myrthis,
     Than he stotays for made,° and alle his strenghe faylez,   **stotays . . .** becomes dizzy from
                                                                                           madness
     Lokes upe to the lyfte,° and alle his lyre° chaunges.   sky   countenance
     Downne he sweys fulle swythe,° and in a swoune   **sweys . . .** sways very quickly
       fallys;
120 Upe he coveris° one kneys° and kryes fulle oftene: gets   his knees
       "Kyng comly with crowne, in care° am I levyde.°   grief   left
     Alle my lordschipe lawe° in lande es layde undyre   low
     That has me gyfene gwerdones be° grace of hym   **gwerdones be** rewards by
       selvene,°   **hym selvene** themselves
     Mayntenyde my manhede be myghte of theire handes,
125 Made me manly one molde° and mayster in erthe.   earth
     In a tenefulle° tyme this torfere was reraryde°   grievous   **torfere . . .** harm arose
     That for° a traytoure has tynte° alle my trewe lordys.   because of   lost
     Here rystys the riche blude of the Rownde Table,
     Rebukkede with a rebawde, and rewthe° es the more.   **rebawde . . .** rascal, and pity
130 I may helples one hethe house by myne one°   **house . . .** dwell by myself
     Alls° a wafulle wedowe that wanttes° hir beryne.°   As   lacks   lord
     I may werye° and wepe and wrynge myne handys,   curse
     Ffor my wytt and my wyrchipe° awaye es for ever.   honor
     Off alle lordchips I take leve to myne ende.
135 Here es the Bretones° blode broughte owt of lyfe,   Britons'
     And nowe in this journee alle my joy endys."
       Thane relyes° the renkes° of alle the Rownde Table;   rally   men
     To the ryalle roy° thay ride tham alle.   king
     Than assembles fulle sonne sevene score knyghtes
140 In sighte to thaire soverayne, that was unsownde
       levede.°   **unsownde levede** left unwell
     Than knelis the crownede kynge and kryes one
       lowde:°   **one lowde** aloud
       "I thanke thee, Gode, of thy grace, with a gud wylle,
     That gafe us vertue and witt to vencows° this beryns°   vanquish   men
     And us has grauntede the gree° of theis gret lordes.   ascendancy
145 He sent us never no schame ne schenchipe° in erthe   disgrace
     Bot ever yit the overhande of° alle other kynges.   **overhande of** mastery over
     We hafe no laysere° now these lordys to seke,   leisure

268

Ffor yone laythely° ladde me lamede so sore.   **yone laythely** yonder loathsome

Graythe° us to Glaschenbery;° us gaynes° none other;   Take   Glastonbury avails

150 Thare we may ryste° us with roo and raunsake° oure   rest **roo . . .** peace and search
      wondys.

Of this dere day° werke, the Dryghttene° be lovede°   day's Lord praised

That us has destaynede° and demyd to dye in oure   destined
      awene."°   own land

    Thane they holde at° his heste hally° at ones   **holde at** fulfill **heste hally** request wholly

And graythes to Glasschenberye the gate° at the   road
      gayneste;°   nearest

155 Entres the Ile of Aveloyne, and Arthure he lyghttes,°   alights

Merkes° to a manere° there, for myghte° he no   Goes manor could go
      forthire.

A surgyne of Salerne° enserches his wondes.   Salerno

The kyng sees by asaye° that sownde bese° he never,   examination will be

And sone to his sekire° mene he said theis wordes: trusty

160   "Do calle me a confessour, with Criste in his arms;

I wille be howselde° in haste, whate happe° so   **be howselde** receive the host **whate**
      betyddys.°   **happe** whatever fortune befalls

Constantyne my cosyne he salle° the corowne bere,   shall

Alls becommys him of kynde,° yife Criste wille hym   nature
      thole.°   permit

Beryne,° fore my benysone,° thowe berye yone° lordys   Man blessing **berye yone** bury yonder

165 That in baytaille with brondez° are broghte owte of   swords
      lyfe;

And sythene merke° manly to Mordrede childrene,°   **sythene merke** then go **Mordrede childrene** Mordred's men

That they bee sleghely° slayne and slongene° in watyrs.   cunningly slung

Latt no wykkyde wede° waxe ne wrythe° one this   **wykkyde wede** evil weed turn
      erthe.

I warne for thy wirchipe, wirke° alls I bydde.   do

170 I foregyffe° alle greffe° for Cristez lufe of hevene.   forgive injury

Yife Waynor° hafe wele wroghte, wele hir betydde."°   Guinevere befall

    He saide *In manus*° with mayne° one molde° whare   *In manus* Into thy hands strength
      he ligges,°   earth lies

And thus passes his speryt, and spekes he no more.

The baronage of Bretaygne° thane, bechopes, and   Britain
      othire

175 Graythes theme° to Glaschenbery, with   **Graythes theme** Go
      gloppynnande° hertes,   terror-struck

To bery thare the bolde kynge and brynge to the erthe

With alle wirchipe and welthe that any wy° scholde.   man

Throly° belles thay rynge and *Requiem* syngys,   Fervently

Dosse° messes and matyns with mournande notes.   Sing

180 Relygeous reveste° in theire riche copes,   dressed

Pontyficalles and prelates in precyouse wedys,°   garments

Dukes and dusszeperis° in theire dule-cotes,°   peers   mourning coats

Cowntasses knelande and claspande theire handes,

Ladys languessande and lowrande° to schewe°—   looking sad   appear

185 Alle was buskede° in blake, birdes° and othire,   **was buskede** were dressed   ladies

That schewede at the sepulture, with sylande° teris.   flowing

Whas never so sorowfulle a syghte seene in theire
     tyme.

Thus endis Kyng Arthure, as auctors alegges,

That was of Ectores blude, the kynge sone of Troye,

190 And of Sir Pryamous,° the prynce, praysede in erthe.   **Sir Pryamous** King Priam's

Ffro thethene° broghte the Bretons° alle his bolde   thence   Britons
     eldyrs

Into Bretaygne° the brode, as the *Bruytte*° tellys.   Britain   Lawman's *Brut*

The Bruce

(1375, Northern)

John Barbour was born about 1316, studied at Aberdeen and Oxford and probably also in France, and became an archdeacon of Aberdeen. He received various emoluments from King Robert II, presumably as a reward for his having undertaken the writing of *The Bruce*. He died in Aberdeen in 1395.

The Bruce, which Barbour completed in 1375, is a verse chronicle of more than 13,500 lines in length. It has two main heroes: King Robert the Bruce, who was born in 1274, crowned in 1306, and died in 1329, and his faithful supporter Sir James Douglas (1286–1330), who was called "The Good Douglas" by the Scots and "The Black Douglas" by the English. In a brief prologue Barbour outlines the attempts of King Edward I to control Scotland by his support of the claims of John de Balliol (1249–1315) against Bruce; in the following twenty books he recounts how Bruce decided to win the crown of Scotland, how he led his country to ultimate victory against the English at the battle of Bannockburn (1314), how he died, and how Douglas perished during a vain attempt to carry the heart of Bruce to the Holy Land. Perhaps out of consideration for his royal patron, Robert II (Bruce's grandson), Barbour concludes his work at the year 1332 and thus has no occasion to mention the Battle of Halidon Hill (see p. 231, above) and other subsequent disasters.

Barbour was well qualified for the task he undertook. He was familiar with all the appropriate Biblical, classical, and medieval models, and he had interviewed many informants of the older generation who had personally witnessed the events he described. *The Bruce* is well organized. Centered as it is on Bruce as the defender of liberty and Douglas as the exemplar of loyalty, it possesses a thematic unity seldom found in medieval chronicles. Yet, even if it transcends the chronicle, it is admittedly something less than an epic.

The selections printed below reveal both the strength and the weakness of *The Bruce*. The author's eloquent praise of freedom is related to the central problem of Scottish history. Presumably he remembered the argument of the Scottish Declaration of Independence (composed in Latin at Arbroath in 1320) and was inspired in particular by the noble passage within it, which the anonymous framer had drawn from Sallust:

> So long as a hundred of us are left alive, we will not yield in the slightest way to English domination. We do not fight for glory or wealth or honors; we fight solely for freedom, which no honest man will surrender excepting with his life.

But, not content with the validity of his own adaptation, Barbour spoils the effect by raising a scholarly quibble about the true definition of freedom. He boldly compares his hero, Douglas, to Hector but then gratuitously asserts the superiority of Hector. He recounts Bruce's speech at Bannockburn, presumably using his own imagination, since he was writing sixty-one years after the event, but he provides his hero with a very calm, low-keyed, common-sensical rhetoric. Seldom has a poet been so inhibited by his concern for plain fact. Yet, perhaps because of its very unpretentiousness, *The Bruce* is still cherished as Scotland's national epic. The meter is rhyming couplets; see Introduction, type 5, page 31.

The best edition is *Barbour's Bruce*, ed. W. W. Skeat, STS 31–33 (Edinburgh, 1894). As a dictionary use *DOST*. A good modernization is John Barbour, *The Bruce*, trans. A. A. H. Douglas (Glasgow, 1964). For bibliography see Wells, ch. 3.8; *CBEL*, 1.166–67, 5.118.

The Author's Prologue

[I, 1–36]

	Storyss to rede ar delitabill,°	delightful
	Supposs° that thai be nocht° bot fabill.°	Even supposing nothing fable
	Than suld° storyss that suthfast° wer,	should truthful
	And° thai war said° on gud maner,	If told
5	Have doubill plesance in heryng.	
	The fyrst plesance is the carpyng,°	recital
	And the tothir° the suthfastnes	second
	That schawys° the thing rycht as it wes;	portrays
	And suth° thyngis that ar likand°	true pleasing
10	Tyll° mannys heryng ar plesand.	To
	Tharfor I wald fayne set my will,	
	Giff° my wyt mycht suffice thartill,°	If thereto
	To put in wryt° a suthfast story	writing
	That it lest ay furth° in memory,	**lest . . .** may last evermore
15	Swa° that na lenth of tyme it let°	So impede
	Na ger° it haly° be foryet.°	**Na ger** Nor cause wholly to forgotten
	For aulde storys that men redys°	read
	Representis° to thaim the dedys	Portray
	Of stalwart folk that lyvyt ar°	**lyvyt ar** lived before
20	Rycht as° thai than in presence war.	**Rycht as** Just as if
	And, certis, thai suld weill have pryss°	esteem
	That in thar tyme war wycht° and wyss,	brave
	And led thar lyff in gret travaill,	
	And oft in hard stour off° bataill	**stour off** combat of
25	Wan richt gret price° off chevalry,	renown
	And war voydyt off cowardy,°	**voydyt . . .** free from cowardice
	As wes King Robert off Scotland,	
	That hardy wes off hart and hand,	
	And gud Schyr James off Douglas,	
30	That in his tyme sa° worthy was	so
	That off° hys price° and hys bounté°	for renown excellence
	In fer° landis renownyt wes he.	far
	Off° thaim I thynk this buk to ma.°	Of make
	Now God gyff grace that I may swa°	so
35	Tret° it and bryng it till° endyng	Manage to
	That I say nocht° bot suthfast° thing.	nothing truthful

The Scots Under Subjection to Edward I

[I, 219–80]

Alas, that folk that evir wes fre	
And in fredome wount° for to be,	accustomed
Throw° thar gret myschance and foly,	Through
War tretyt than sa° wykkytly	so
5 That thar fays° thar jugis° war.	foes judges
Quhat° wrechitnes may man have mar?°	What more
A! Fredome is a noble thing!	
Fredome mayss° man to haiff liking;°	causes pleasure in life
Fredome all solace to man giffis.	
10 He levys° at ess° that frely levys.	lives ease
A noble hart may° haiff nane° ess	can no
Na ellys nocht° that may him pless	**Na** . . . Or anything else
Gyff° fredome failyhe,° for fre liking°	If fails choice
Is yharnyt our° all othir thing;	**yharnyt our** yearned for over
15 Na° he that ay° hass levyt° fre	Nor always lived
May nocht knaw weill the propyrté,°	peculiar state
The angyr,° na the wrechyt dome°	anguish fate
That is cowplyt° to foule thyrldome°	coupled thralldom
Bot gyff° he had assayit it.	**Bot gyff** Unless
20 Than all *per quer*° he suld° it wyt°	***per quer*** by heart should know
And suld think fredome mar° to pryss°	more be prized
Than all the gold in warld that is.	
Thus contrar° thingis evirmar°	contrary always
Discoveryngis° off the tothir° ar;	Revelations opposite
25 And he that thryll° is has nocht his;°	thrall his own
All that he hass enbandownyt° is	subjected
Till° hys lord, quhatevir° he be.	To whatever
Yheyt° has he nocht sa mekill° fre	Yet **nocht** . . . not even so much
As fre liking° to leyve° or do	choice leave undone
30 That at° hys hart hym drawis to.	which
Than mayss clerkis° questioun	**mayss clerkis** scholars make
Quhen° thai fall in disputacioun	When
That, gyff° man bad° his thryll owcht° do,	if ordered **thryll owcht** thrall something to
And in the samyn° tym come° him to	same came
35 His wyff and askyt hym hyr det,°	debt
Quhethir° he his lordis neid suld let°	Whether **neid** . . . requirement should ignore
And pay fryst that° he awcht and syne°	**fryst that** first what **awcht** . . . owed and then
Do furth his lordis commandyne,	
Or leve onpayit his wyff and do	
40 It that commaundyt is him to.	
I leve all the solucioun	
Till° thaim that ar off mar° renoun,	To **off mar** of more

Bot, sen° thai mak sic comperyng° — since **sic comperyng** such comparison
Betwix the dettis off wedding

45 And lordis bidding till his threll,° — thrall
Ye may weile se, thoucht nane° yow tell, — **thoucht nane** though none
How hard a thing that threldome° is, — thralldom
For men may weile se that ar wyss
That wedding is the hardest band° — bond

50 That ony man may tak on hand.
And thryldome is weill wer° than deid,° — **weill wer** much worse death
For quhill° a thryll his lyff may leid, — as long as
It merrys° him, body and banys,° — mars bones
And dede anoyis° him bot anys.° — **dede anoyis** death troubles once

55 Schortly to say, is nane° can tell — **is nane** there is none who
The halle° condicioun off a threll. — whole
Thus-gat levyt thai and in sic thrillage,°
Bath pur° and thai off hey parage,° — **Bath pur** Both poor **off** ... of high rank
For off the lordis sum thai° slew, — they (the English)

60 And sum thai hangyt, and sum thai drew,
And sum thai put in hard presoune
Forowtyn° causs or enchesoun.° — Without reason

Sir James Douglas

[I, 360–406]

All men lufyt° him for his bounté,° — loved excellence
For he wes off full° fayr effer,° — **off full** of very behavior
Wyss, curtaiss, and deboner.
Larg° and luffand als° wes he — Generous **luffand als** kind also

5 And our° all thing luffyt lawté.° — above loyalty
Leawté to luff is gretumly.°
Throuch leawté liffis men rychtwisly.° — **liffis** ... men live righteously
With a vertu of leawté
A man may yeit sufficyand be

10 And, but° leawté, may nane haiff price° — without **nane** ... have no renown
Quhethir° he be wycht° or he be wyss, — Whether vigorous
For, quhar° it failyeys,° na vertu — where fails
May be off° price na° off valu — of nor
To mak a man sa gud° that he — **sa gud** so good

15 May symply gud man callyt be.
He wes in all his dedis lele,° — loyal

57. Thus lived they (the Scots) and in such thralldom
6. Loyalty is greatly to be loved.

For him dedeynyeit nocht° to dele — **him . . .** he deigned not
With trechery na with falset.° — falsehood
His hart on hey° honour wes set, — high
20 And hym contenyt° on sic° maner — **hym contenyt** he conducted himself   such
That all him luffyt° that war him ner. — loved
Bot he wes nocht sa° fayr that we — so
Suld° spek gretly off his beauté. — Should
In vysage wes he sumdeill° gray — somewhat
25 And had blak har,° as Ic hard° say; — hair   **Ic hard** I heard
Bot off lymmys he wes weill maid,
With banys° gret and schuldrys braid.° — bones   broad
His body wes weyll maid and lenye,° — lean
As thai that saw hym said to me.
30   Quhen he wes blyth, he wes lufly° — lovable
And meyk and sweyt in cumpany;
Bot quha° in battaill mycht him se, — whoever
All othir contenance had he.
And in spek wlispyt° he sumdeill,° — **spek wlispyt** speech lisped   somewhat
35 Bot that sat° him rycht wondre° weill. — suited   wondrously
   Till° gud Ector of Troy mycht he — To
In mony thingis liknyt° be. — likened
Ector had blak har° as he had, — hair
And stark° lymmys, and rycht weill maid, — strong
40 And wlispyt alswa as° did he, — **wlispyt . . .** lisped just as
And wes fullfillyt° of leawté,° — full   loyalty
And wes curtaiss and wyss and wycht.° — vigorous
Bot off manheid and mekill° mycht — **off . . .** for manhood and great
Till Ector dar° I nane° comper — dare   none
45 Off all that evir in warld wer.
The quhethyr,° in his tyme sa wrocht° he — **The quhethyr** Nevertheless   **sa wrocht** so wrought
That he suld° gretly lovyt be. — should

Bruce Addresses His Army at Bannockburn

[XII, 210–53]
   "Lordyngis, sen° ye will sa,° — since   so
Schapis° tharfor in the mornyng — Prepare
Swa that we be° the sonne-rysing — by
Haf herd mes,° and be buskit° weill, — mass   equipped
5 Ilk° man intill° his awne yscheill,° — Each   in   **awne yscheill** own squadron
Without° the palyownys arayit° — Outside   **palyownys arayit** tents arranged
In battale° with baneris displayit. — battle-order

And luk° yhe na° way brek aray.°	see to it in no order
And, as ye luf me, I yow pray	
10 That ilk man for his awne honour	
Purvay hym° a gud baneour,°	**Purvay hym** Provide himself banner-bea...
And, quhen° it cummys to the ficht,	when
Ilk° man set his hert and mycht	Each
To stynt° our fais mekill° pryd.	quench **fais mekill** foes' great
15 "On horss thai sall arayit° ryd	**sall arayit** shall in order
And cum on yow in weill° gret hy.°	very speed
Meit thame with speris hardely,°	bravely
And wreik° on thame the mekill° ill	avenge great
That thai and tharis has° done us till°	**tharis has** theirs have **us till** to us
20 And ar in will yeit for till° do	**in . . .** hoping still to
Gif° thai haf mycht till cum tharto.	If
"And, certis, me think° weill that we,	**certis . . .** certainly, it seems to me
Forout abasyng,° aucht till be	**Forout abasyng** Without flinching
Worthy and of gret vassalage,°	valor
25 For we have thre gret avantage.	
"The first is that we haf the richt,	
And for the richt ilk° man suld ficht.	each
"The tothir° is, thai ar cummyn heir,°	second **ar . . .** have come here
For lypnyng° in thair gret power,	**For lypnyng** Trusting
30 To seik° us in our awne° land	seek own
And has° broucht her° richt till our hand	have here
Richess into° so gret plentée	in
That the pouerest of yow sall° be	shall
Bath° rych and mychty tharwithall	Both
35 Gif that° we wyn, as weill may fall.°	**Gif that** If befall
"The thrid is that we for our lyvis	
And for our childer and our wifis	
And for the fredome of our land	
Ar strenyeit° in battale for to stand;	compelled
40 And thai, for° thair mycht anerly,°	because of alone
And for° thai leit° of us lichtly,°	because think lightly
And for thai wald° distroy us all,	would like to
Mais thame° to ficht. Bot yet ma fall°	**Mais thame** Force themselves **ma fall** it may befall
That thai sall rew° thar barganyng."°	**sall rew** shall regret undertaking

WILLIAM LANGLAND

Piers Plowman

(1372–79, Southwestern)

One of the greatest poems of the Middle Ages, *Piers Plowman* is at the same time one of the most complicated. Various clues suggest that the author, William Langland (ca. 1332–ca. 1400) was born at Cleobury Mortimer (Shropshire), was trained as a priest at the Benedictine monastery at Great Malvern (Worcestershire), took minor orders but acquired no benefice, was married, and lived with his wife and daughter at Cornhill, in London, where he secured a meager income by reciting prayers for benefactors.

Langland wrote about religion and human life with the fervor of an Old Testament prophet. In the process of writing he constantly discovered new material to incorporate into his message. Consequently, he revised *Piers Plowman* several times. His first version of *Piers Plowman* (Version A, ca. 1370) ran to 2,567 lines; this was soon followed by an extended second version (Version B, excerpted here, ca. 1377–79) containing 7,242 lines; and this in turn was revised in a slightly longer and considerably different final version (Version C, ca. 1387). It seems unlikely that the poet's restless mind ever considered any of these versions as truly completed works of art.

The poem is complicated by Langland's use of allegory. Like *The Romance of the Rose*, *Piers Plowman* is a dream vision, but though the poem is often personal and even autobiographical, the Poet is not simply to be thought of as Langland. Rather, the Poet is Everyman, baffled and perplexed, and his vision is an apocalyptic revelation of the destiny of mankind; allegorically, Will the Poet is a counterpart of the Human Will searching for his proper direction. The poem, furthermore, is lifted above the level of passive contemplation by the dramatic role of the Poet's mentor, Piers Plowman. Piers first enters into the vision as a simple man who faithfully performs his daily tasks—an exemplar of the laws of the Old Testament dispensation; then he appears as a counterpart of Christ and reveals the nature of charity—the Divine Love unfolded in the new dispensation of the Gospels; and finally he becomes the counterpart of St. Peter—the founder of Holy Church proclaimed in the Acts of the Apostles.

At the narrative level, all of the characters who appear in the Poet's dreams are allegorical. He dreams at first of an assembly of the people, who are visited by their king (Prologue). Lady Holy Church explains that the field where they have gathered is situated between Truth and Falsehood (Canto I); Lady Meed (Graft) is about to marry Falsehood (Canto II) but is tried before the king (Cantos III–IV). The Poet then dreams that Reason preaches to the people and causes the Seven Deadly Sins to repent; the people set out in search of Truth, and Piers Plowman describes the way (Canto V), but he requires that they first turn to work (Canto VI), and he rejects a pardon offered to him by a priest, whereupon the Poet learns that Do-well is better than any pardon (Canto VII).

Here the part usually referred to as "The Vision" concludes, and "The Life of Do-well, Do-better and Do-best" begins. The Poet seeks Do-well and is given counsel by Thought (Canto VIII), Wit (Intelligence) (Canto IX), Study (Canto X), Fortune, Loyalty, Scripture,

Nature, and Reason (Canto XI), Imagination (Canto XII), and Conscience and Patience (Canto XIII). Finally, the Poet learns how the Active Man can be saved from sin (Canto XIV).

Anima (Soul) teaches the Poet about Charity (Canto XV). Piers Plowman shows him the Tree of Charity; the Poet meets Abraham (Faith) (Canto XVI), Moses (Hope), and the Good Samaritan (Charity) (Canto XVII). The Poet dreams of Christ's death and the Harrowing of Hell, awakens on Easter morning, and takes his wife and daughter to mass (Canto XVIII).

In a dream he learns how Christ's life exemplifies Do-well, Do-better, and Do-best and how Piers Plowman as Holy Church serves as Christ's messenger (Canto XIX). Antichrist, however, overturns Truth and besieges Castle Unity, and Conscience must therefore set out on a pilgrimage to find Piers Plowman so that he may destroy the pride of the adversary (Canto XX).

There are many forerunners of Piers Plowman in medieval literature, such as *The Pilgrimage of Human Life, of the Soul, and of Jesus Christ* (ca. 1330–58), by the French Cistercian monk Guillaume de Deguilleville, but none can be said to rival Langland's poem. Despite its complete reliance on allegory, *Piers Plowman* is intensely vivid and realistically concerned with contemporary problems. Despite its heavy freight of dogma, its narrative is more lively than that of many a romance, and it thus escapes the aridity of systematic theological tracts. Its sermons are sympathetic, its satire humane, and its tone arrestingly witty.

Langland was a learned man, his mind saturated with Biblical, liturgical, and patristic lore. Yet the application of his message is inescapably clear. Neither Pope nor friar, king nor plowman, could have misunderstood the demands that Langland laid on their consciences. He rejoices in paradoxes, as when he perceives that Truth can be fallible (Canto XVIII, l. 142) and that Wisdom cannot of itself secure salvation (Canto X, l. 428), but his paradoxes are arresting rather than mystifying. For, learned though he was, Langland the theologian was never pedantic. If any one passage could provide a motto for his point of view, it would be the comment of Lady Study:

> Theology has tormented me ten score of times.
> The more I muse therein, the mistier it seems.
> And the deeper I divine, the darker it looks to me.
> It is, indeed, no science to subtilize in.
> A most idle thing would Theology be, if there were not Love,
> But since Theology esteems Love best, I love it the better,
> For where Love is leader, Grace never lacks.

> (X, 180–86, modernized)

There are, to be sure, serious obscurities in the poem, such as Piers's rejection of the pardon and the conceptual significance of Do-well, Do-better, and Do-best, but these are rich mysteries, and the Poet consistently presents these aspects of his dreams as revelations whose whole meaning he himself cannot immediately grasp. So too, the ending of the poem, which seems anticlimactically to leave Antichrist in power, effectively expresses the Poet's concern about the state of his corrupt and war-torn world and yet leaves hope in his reader's heart. Indeed, all of these difficult aspects—Piers, Do-well, Do-better, Do-best, and the reign of Antichrist—are distinguishing features of a highly original work of piety that is also a uniquely moving work of art.

The Prologue and Cantos I, V, VII, and parts of XVIII and XIX are printed below. The meter is alliterative verse; see Introduction, type 1, page 29.

Piers Plowman

The best complete edition is *The Vision of William concerning Piers the Plowman* (Text B), ed. W. W. Skeat, EETS (London, 1869), with Notes and Glossary, EETS 67, 81 (London, 1877, 1885), reprinted along with Versions A and C (Oxford, 1886), 2 vols. A new, definitive edition *Piers Plowman: The A Version*, ed. George Kane (London, 1960), will be followed by similar editions of the texts of B and C. For a modernization see William Langland, *Piers the Ploughman*, trans. J. F. Goodridge (Harmondsworth, 1959). For criticism see *Piers Plowman: Critical Approaches*, ed. S. S. Hussey (London, 1969), and *Style and Symbolism in Piers Plowman: A Modern Critical Anthology*, ed. Robert J. Blanch (Knoxville, 1969). For bibliography see Wells, ch. 4. 51; *CBEL*, 1.197–200, 5.126–28.

Prologue

In a somer seson whan soft was the sonne,
I shope° me in shroudes as° I a shepe° were,   dressed **shroudes as** rough clothes as if shepherd
In habite as an heremite unholy° of workes;   worldly
Went wyde in this world wondres to here.°   hear
5 Ac° on a May mornynge on Malverne hülles,°   But hills
Me byfel a ferly° of fairy, me thoughte.°   marvel **fairy ...** magic, it seemed to me
I was wery forwandred° and went me to reste   **wery forwandred** weary from wandering
Under a brode banke bi a bornes° side,   stream's
And as I lay and lened° and loked in the wateres,   leaned
10 I slombred in a slepyng; it sweyved° so merye.   flowed
Thanne gan° I to meten° a merveilouse swevene,°   began dream dream
That I was in a wildernesse, wist° I never where.   knew
As I bihelde° into the est an° hiegh to the sonne,   looked on
I seigh° a toure° on a toft trielich° y-maked;   saw tower **toft trielich** hill excellently
15 A depe dale° binethe, a dongeon° there-inne,   valley castle
With depe dyches and derke, and dredful of sight.
A faire felde ful of folke fonde I there bytwene,
Of alle maner of men, the mene and the riche,
Worchyng and wandryng as the worlde asketh.°   demands
20 Some putten hem° to the plow, pleyed ful selde,°   themselves **ful selde** very seldom
In settyng and in sowyng swonken° ful harde,   worked
And wonnen that° wastours with glotonye destruyeth.   **wonnen that** won what
And some putten hem to prüyde, apparailed° hem   **prüyde, apparailed** pride, dressed
     there-after,
In contenaunce° of clothyng comen° disgised.   display came
25 In prayers and in penance putten hem manye,
Al for love of owre Lorde lyveden ful streyte,°   **lyveden ...** lived very strictly
In hope for to have heveneriche° blisse,   heaven's
As ancres° and heremites that holden hem° in here   **As ancres** Such as anchorites **holden hem** stay
     selles°   **here selles** their cells
And coveiten° nought in contré to kairen° aboute   covet wander

279

30 For no likerous liflode her lykam° to plese. — **likerous ...** sensuous living their body
   And somme chosen chaffare;° they cheven° the bettere, — bargaining   succeed
As it semeth to owre syght that suche men thryveth;
And somme mürthes° to make as mynstralles conneth,° — mirth   can
And geten gold with here glee, synneles, I leve.° — believe
35 Ac japers and jangelers,° Judas chylderen, — **Ac ...** But jesters and clowns
Feynen° hem fantasies and foles hem maketh,° — Invent **foles ...** pose as fools
And han here witte° at wille to worche yif thei sholde.° — **han ...** have their wits must
That Poule° precheth of hem,° I nel° nought preve° it here! — **That Poule** What Paul them wi... say
   Qui turpiloquium loquitur[1] is Luciferes hyne.° — servant
40   Bidders° and beggeres fast about yede° — Beggars went
With her° belies and her bagges of bred ful y-crammed, — their
Fayteden° for here fode, foughten atte° ale; — Begged over
In glotonye, God it wote, gon hii° to bedde, — **wote ...** knows, they go
And risen with ribaudye, tho Roberdes° knaves. — **ribaudye ...** ribaldry, those vagabond
45 Slepe and sori sleuthe seweth hem° evre. — **sleuthe ...** sloth pursue them
   Pilgrymes and palmers plighted° hem togidere — pledged
To seke Seynt James° and seyntes in Rome. — **Seynt James** Santiago de Compostela, Spain
Thei went forth in here° wey with many wise tales — their
And hadden leve to lye al here lyf after.
50 I seigh° somme that seiden thei had y-sought seyntes; — saw
   To eche a tale that thei tolde, here tonge was tempred° to lye — tuned
More than to sey soth,° it semed bi here speche. — **sey soth** tell the truth
   Heremites on an heep° with hoked staves — heap
Wenten to Walsyngham,[2] and here° wenches after.° — their with them
55 Grete lobyes° and longe that loth were to swynke° — lubbers work
Clotheden hem in copis° to ben° knowen fram othere — capes be
And shopen hem° heremites, here ese to have. — **shopen hem** made themselves
   I fonde there Freris,° alle the foure ordres, — Friars
Preched the peple for profit of hemselven,
60 Glosed° the gospel as hem good lyked,° — Explained **hem ...** it well please... them
For coveitise of copis° construed it as thei wolde. — **coveitise ...** covetousness for cloth
Many of this maistres° Freris mowe° clothen hem at lykyng,° — master can their pleasure
For here money and marchandise marchen togideres.°
For sith° Charité hath be chapman and chief° to shryve° lordes, — since **be ...** been merchant and chiefly absolve
65 Many ferlis° han fallen in a fewe yeris. — marvels
But° Holy Chirche and hii holde° better togideres, — Unless **hii holde** they agree

[1] 'He who speaks filth.' Possibly reflects Eph. v.4 or Col. iii.8.
[2] Shrine of Our Lady, Walsingham, Norfolk.
63. For their money and their commodity (preaching) prosper mutually.

The moste myschief on molde° is mountyng wel° faste.   earth   very
   There preched a Pardonere as° he a prest were,   as if
   Broughte forth a bulle° with bishopes seles,   document
70 And seide that hymself myghte assoilen hem° alle   **myghte . . . could absolve them**
   Of falshed of fastyng,° of vowes y-broken.   **falshed . . . failure to fast**
   Lewed° men leved° hym wel and lyked his wordes,   Unlearned   believed
   Comen up knelyng to kisse his bulles.
   He bonched° hem with his brevet° and blered here eyes,   struck   document
75 And raughte° with his ragman° rynges and broches.   took in   document
   Thus they geven° here golde, glotones to kepe,°   give   support
   And leveth such loseles° that lecherye haunten.   scoundrels
   Were the bischop y-blissed° and worth bothe his eres,°   holy   ears
   His seel shulde nought be sent to deceyve the peple.
80 Ac° it is naught by° the bischop that the boy° precheth,   But   against   young pardoner
   For the parisch prest and the Pardonere parten° the   divide
      silver,
   That the poraille° of the parisch sholde° have yif thei   poor   ought to
      nere.°   were not there
   Persones° and parisch prestes pleyned hem° to the   Parsons   **pleyned hem** complained
      bischop,
   That here parisshes were pore sith° the pestilence tyme,   since
85 To have a lycence and a leve at London to dwelle,
   And syngen there for symonye, for silver is swete.
   Bischopes and bachelers, bothe maistres and doctours—
   That han cure° under Criste, and crounyng° in tokne°   **han cure** have charge   tonsure
      token
   And signe that thei sholden shryven° here paroschienes,°   absolve   parishioners
90 Prechen, and prey for hem,° and the pore fede—   them
   Liggen° in London, in Lenten and elles.°   Dwell   at other times
   Some serven the kyng and his silver tellen;°   count
   In cheker° and in chancerye chalengen° his dettes   exchequer   claim
   Of° wardes and wardmotes, weyves and streyues.°   From   **wardmotes . . . ward**
      meetings, waifs and estrays
95 And some serven, as servantz, lordes° and ladyes,   to lords
   And in stede of stuwardes sytten and demen.°   judge
   Here messe° and here matynes, and many of here oures°   **Here messe** Their mass
      canonical hours
   Arn don undevoutlych. Drede° is at the laste   Fear
   Lest Crist in consistorie acorse ful° manye.   very
100   I parceyved of the power that Peter had to kepe,
   To bynde and to unbynde, as the boke telleth,
   How he it left with Love, as owre Lorde hight,°   ordered
   Amonges foure vertues, the best of alle vertues,
   That cardinales ben° called, and closyng yatis,°   are   gates
105 There° Crist is in kyngdome, to close and to shutte,   Where
   And to opne it to hem° and hevene blisse shewe.   them
   Ac° of the cardinales atte Courte, that caught of° that   But   **caught of** took
      name,

And power presumed in hem a Pope to make,
To han° that power that Peter hadde, inpugnen° I nelle;°   *have   deny* / *will not*
110 For in love and letterure° the eleccioun bilongeth;   *learning*
    For-thi° I can, and can naughte, of courte speke more.   *Therefore*
        Thanne come there a kyng, knyghthod° hym ladde,°   *knights   led*
    Might of the comunes° made hym to regne,   *common-people*
    And thanne cam Kynde Wytte,° and clerkes he made,   **Kynde Wytte** Common Sense
115 For to conseille the kyng and the Comune° save.   *Commons*
        The kyng and knyghthode and clergye bothe°   *also*
    Casten° that the Comune shulde hemself fynde.°   *Decided* **hemself fynde** provide for themselves
    The Commune contreved of Kynde Witte craftes°   *skills*
    And, for profit of alle the poeple, plowmen ordeygned
120 To tilie and travaile as trewe lyf asketh.°   *demands*
    The kyng and the Comune and Kynde Witte the thridde°   **Comune . . .** Commons and Common Sense as the third
    Shope° Lawe and Lewté,° eche man to knowe his owne.   *Arranged   Loyalty*
        Thanne loked up a lunatik,[3] a lene thing withalle,
    And knelyng to the kyng, clergealy° he seyde: *seriously*
125 "Crist kepe thee, Sire Kyng, and thi kyngriche,°   *kingdom*
    And leve° thee lede° thi londe, so Leuté° thee lovye,°   *let   rule   Loyalty   love*
    And for thi rightful rewlyng be rewarded in hevene!"
        And sithen° in the eyre an° hiegh an angel of hevene   *then* **eyre an** air on
    Lowed° to speke in Latyn—for lewed° men ne coude   *Stooped   unlearned*
130 Jangle° ne jugge that° justifie hem shulde,   *Talk about   that which*
    But° suffren and serven—for-thi° seyde the angel: *But only   therefore*
        "*Sum Rex, sum Princeps; neutrum fortasse deinceps.*
    O qui jura regis Christi specialia regis,
    Hoc quod agas melius, justus es, esto pius!
135 *Nudum jus a te vestiri vult pietate;*
    Qualia vis metere talia grana sere.
    Si jus nudatur nudo de jure metatur.
    Si seritur pietas, de pietate metas!"°
        Thanne greved hym° a Goliardeys,° a glotoun of wordes,   **greved hym** was annoyed   *vagra*
140 And to the angel an° heigh answered after: *on*
    "*Dum rex a regere dicatur nomen habere,*
    Nomen habet sine re nisi studet jura tenere."°

---

[3] Presumably the Poet himself.

132–38. I am king, I am prince, you say; soon perhaps you may be neither. O you who administer the special laws of Christ the King, that you may better do this, as you are just, be merciful. Naked justice should be clothed by you with mercy; sow such grain as you wish to reap. If justice is stripped of mercy, you shall be dealt with by naked justice. If mercy is sown, you shall be dealt with by mercy.

141–42. Since the king is said to have the name of king from the act of ruling, he has the name without anything else unless he is careful to maintain the laws.

And thanne gan° alle the Comune crye in vers of Latin — did
To° the kynges conseille, construe ho-so° wolde: — For   howsoever he

145   *Precepta Regis sunt nobis vincula legis.°*

With that ran there a route° of ratones° at ones, — pack   rats
And smale mys with hem mo° then a thousande, — more
And comen to a conseille for here comune° profit; — common
For a cat of a courte cam whan hym lyked,° — it pleased
150 And overlepe° hem lyghtlich and laughte° hem at his — jumped over   seized
        wille,
And pleyde with hem perilouslych and possed° hem — pushed
        aboute.
    "For doute° of dyverse dredes we dar noughte wel — fear
        loke;° — look about
And yif we grucche° of his gamen,° he wil greve° us alle, — complain   games   harm
Cracche° us, or clowe us, and in his cloches holde, — Scratch
155 That us lotheth° the lyf or° he lete us passe. — **us lotheth** we loathe   before
Myghte we with any witte° his wille withstonde, — idea
We myghte be lordes aloft and lyven at owre ese." —
    A raton° of renon, most renable° of tonge, — rat   ready
Seide for a sovereygne help, to hymselve:° — **help** ... remedy, in his opinion
160 "I have y-sein segges,"° quod he, "in the cité of London — **y-sein segges** seen men
Beren bighes° ful brighte abouten here nekkes, — collars
And some colers of crafty° werk. Uncoupled° thei — skillful   Unleashed
        wenden
Bothe in wareine° and in waste° where hem leve — warren   open land
        lyketh;° — **leve lyketh** well it pleases
And otherwhile thei aren elles-where as I here telle. —
165 Were there a belle on here beigh, bi Jhesu, as me —
        thynketh,° — **me thynketh** it seems to me
Men myghte wite° where thei went and awei renne!° — know   run
And right so," quod that ratoun,° "reson me sheweth, — rat
To bügge° a belle of brasse or of brighte sylver, — buy
And knitten° on a colere for owre comune profit, — attach
170 And hangen it upon the cattes hals.° Thanne here we — neck
        mowen° — can
Where° he ritt° or rest or renneth° to playe. — Whether   rides   runs
And yif him list° for to laike,° thenne loke we mowen, — it pleases   play
And peren° in his presence ther while hym plaie liketh,° — appear   **plaie liketh** play pleases
And yif him wrattheth,° be y-war° and his weye — **him wrattheth** he becomes angry
        shonye."° —   aware   shun
175 Alle this route° of ratones° to this reson thei assented. — pack   rats
Ac° tho the belle was y-bought and on the beighe° — But   collar
        hanged,

145. The decrees of the king are to us as bonds of law.

There ne was ratoun in alle the route for alle the rewme° realm
    of Fraunce
That dorst have y-bounden the belle aboute the cattis
    nekke,
Ne hangen it aboute the cattes hals° al Engelonde to   neck
    wynne;
180 And helden hem unhardy° and here conseille feble,   **helden . . .** they considered themselves fearful
And leten° here laboure lost and alle here longe studye.   regarded
   A mous that moche° good couthe,° as me thoughte,°   much knew **me thoughte** it seemed to me
Stroke° forth sternly and stode biforn hem alle   Moved
And to the route° of ratons reherced° these wordes: pack **ratons reherced** rats pronounced
185 "Though° we cülled° the catte, yüt° sholde ther come   Even if killed yet
    another
To cracchy° us and al owre kynde though we croupe°   scratch crept
    under benches.
For-thi° I conseille alle the Comune° to lat the catte   Therefore Commons
    wörthe,°   be
And be we never so bolde the belle hym to shewe;
For I herde my sire seyn, is sevene yere y-passed,
190 There° the catte is a kitoun, the courte is ful elyng.°   Where **ful elyng** very miserable
That witnisseth Holi Write, who-so° wil it rede: whosoever

Vae terrae ubi puer rex est, etc.[4]

For may no renke° there rest have for° ratones bi nyghte.   man because of
The while he caccheth conynges,° he coveiteth nought   rabbits
    owre caroyne°   carrion
195 But fet° hym al with venesoun,° defame we hym nevere.   feeds game
For better is a litel losse than a longe sorwe.°   sorrow
The mase° amonge us alle, though° we mysse° a   **The mase** Confusion if lose
    schrewe!°   tyrant
For many mannüs° malt we mys wolde destrüye,   a man's
And also ye route° of ratones rende mennes° clothes,   pack men's
200 Nere° that cat of that courte that can yow overlepe;   Were it not for
For had ye rattes yowre wille, ye couthe° nought reule°   could rule
    yowreselve.
I sey° for me," quod the mous, "I se so mykel after,°   speak **mykel after** much in the future
Shal never the cat ne the kitoun bi my conseille be
    greved,°   offended
Ne carpyng° of this coler that costed me nevre.   **Ne carpyng** Nor shall there be tal[k]
205 And though it had coste me catel, biknowen° it I nolde,°   **catel, biknowen** goods, acknowled[ge] would not
But suffre as hymself wolde to do as hym liketh,°   it pleases
Coupled° and uncoupled, to cacche what thei mowe.°   Leashed can
For-thi° üche a wise wighte° I warne: wite° wel his   Therefore man guard
    owne."

[4] 'Woe to the land where the king is a child, etc.' Eccles. x.16.

What this meteles bemeneth,° ye men that be merye,
210 Devine ye, for I ne dar bi dere° God in hevene!
    Yit hoved° there an hondreth in houves° of selke,
Serjaunts° it semed that serveden atte barre,
Pleideden for penyes° and poundes the lawe,
And nought for love of owre Lorde unlese° here lippes onis.°
215 Thow myghtest better mete° the myste on Malverne hülles°
Than gete a momme of° here mouthe but° money were shewed.
    Barones and burgeis and bonde-men als°
I seigh° in this assemblé as ye shul here after.
Baxsteres and brewesteres and bocheres° manye,
220 Wollewebsteres° and weveres of lynnen,
Taillours and tynkeres and tolleres° in marketes,
Masons and mynours° and many other craftes.°
Of alkin libbyng° laboreres lopen° forth somme,
As dykers and delveres° that doth here dedes ille
225 And dryven forth the longe day with "*Dieu vous save, Dame Emma!*"[5]
Cokes° and here knaves crieden "Hote pies, hote!
Gode gris and gees, gowe dyne,° gowe!"
Taverners until° hem tolde the same;°
"White wyn of Oseye° and red wyn of Gascoigne,
230 Of the Ryne° and of the Rochel,° the roste to defye."°
Al this seigh° I slepyng and sevene sythes° more.

meteles bemeneth dream means
dear
hovered hoods
Law sergeants
pennies
unloosed
once
measure
hills
momme of sound from unless
bonde-men als peasants also
saw
Baxsteres . . . Bakers and brewers and butchers
Wool-weavers
toll-takers
miners skills
Of . . . Of all kinds of living strode
dykers . . . ditch-diggers and diggers
Cooks
gris . . . pigs and geese, come dine
to **tolde . . .** spoke similarly
Alsace
Rhine Rochelle digest
saw times

Canto I

    What this montaigne bymeneth° and the merke dale°
And the felde ful of folke, I shal yow faire schewe.
A loveli ladi of lere° in lynnen y-clothed
Come down fram a castel and called me faire
5 And seide, "Sone, slepestow? Sestow this° poeple,
How bisi thei ben° abouten the mase?°
The moste partie° of this poeple that passeth on this erthe,
Have thei worschip° in this worlde, thei wilne° no better;
Of other hevene than here holde thei no tale."°

means **merke dale** dark valley
face
slepestow . . . do you sleep? Do you see these
are confusion
moste partie greatest part
Have . . . If they have honor wish for
account

---

[5] 'God save you, Dame Emma.' Probably the refrain of some bawdy popular song.

10 I was aferd of her face, theigh° she faire were, — though
And seide, "Mercy, Madame, what is this to mene?"° — mean
　　"The toure up° the toft,"° quod she, "Treuthe is — **toure up** tower on hill
　　　there-inne,
And wolde that ye wroughte° as his worde techeth; — would do
For He is Fader of Feith, fourmed° yow alle, — created
15 Bothe with fel° and with face and yaf° yow fyve wittis° — skin gave senses
For to worschip hym ther-with the while that ye ben° — are
　　here.
And ther-fore he hyghte° the erthe to help yow üchone° — ordered each one
Of wollen, of lynnen, of lyflode° at nede, — food
In mesurable° manere to make yow at ese;° — moderate ease
20 And comaunded of his curteisye in comune° three — common
　　thinges;
Arne none nedful but tho, and nempne° hem I thinke,° — **tho** ... those, and name intend
And rekne° hem bi resoun, reherce° thow hem after. — count **bi** ... rightly, repeat
That one is vesture, from chele° thee to save, — chill
And mete° atte mele for myseise° of thiselve, — food **mele** ... meal against discomfort
25 And drynke whan thow dryest, ac° do nought out of — **dryest, ac** thirst, but
　　resoun,
That° thow wörth° the werse whan thow worche — Lest be
　　shuldest.
　　For Loth° in his lifdayes, for likyng of drynke, — Lot
Dede bi° his doughtres that° the devel lyked; — **Dede bi** Did with what
Delited hym in drynke, as the devel wolde,° — would wish
30 And lecherye hym laught,° and lay bi hem bothe; — seized
And al he witt it° wyn, that wikked dede. — **witt it** blamed it on

　　　Inebriamus eum vino, dormiamusque cum eo,
　　　Ut servare possimus de patre nostro semen.[1]

Thorw wyn and thorw women there was Loth
　　acombred,° — overcome
35 And there gat° in glotonye gerlis° that were cherlis.° — begot sons scoundrels
For-thi° drede delitable drynke and thow shalt do thee — Therefore
　　bettere;
Mesure° is medcyne though thow moche yerne. — Moderation
It is naught al gode to the goste° that the gutte axeth,° — spirit **gutte axeth** belly demand
Ne liflode° to thi likam° that leef° is to thi soule. — food body dear
40 Leve° not thi likam, for a lyer him techeth, — Believe
That is the wrecched worlde, wolde thee bitraye.
For the Fende° and thi flesch folweth thee togidere; — Fiend
This and that sueth° thi soule and seith it° in thin herte; — pursue **seith it** speak it (the lie)

[1] 'Let us make him drunk with wine, and let us sleep with him, that we may preserve the seed of our father.' Gen. xix.32.

And for° thow sholdest ben y-war,° I wisse° thee the
    beste."   *so that*   **ben y-war** *be aware*   *teach*

45 "Madame, mercy," quod I, "me liketh° wel yowre   *please*
    wordes,
Ac° the moneye of this molde° that men so faste holdeth,   *But earth*
Telle me to whom, Madame, that tresore appendeth"°   *belongs*
    "Go to the Gospel," quod she. "That God seide
    hymselven
Tho° the poeple Hym apposed° with a peny° in the   *When questioned penny*
    Temple,

50 Whether thei shulde ther-with worschip° the kyng   *honor*
    Sesar.
And God axed° of hem, of whome spake the lettre   *asked*
And the ymage i-lyke° that there-inne stondeth.   *alike*
'Cesaris,' thei seide. 'We sen° hym wel üchone.'°   *see each one*
'*Reddite Cesari*,'° quod God, 'that° *Cesari* bifalleth,   ***Reddite Cesari*** *Give to Caesar*
                                            what

55 *Et que sunt Dei, Deo*,° or elles ye done ille.'   ***Et* . . .** *And what is God's, to God*
For rightful reson shulde rewle yow alle,
And Kynde Witte° be wardeyne yowre welthe to kepe,   **Kynde Witte** *Common Sense*
And tutour° of youre tresore and take° it yow at nede;   *guardian bring*
For housbonderye° and hii° holden togideres."   *thrift they*

60 Thanne I frained° hir faire for° Hym that hir made: *asked for the sake of*
"That dongeoun in the dale° that dredful is of sighte,   *valley*
What may it be to mene, madame, I yow bische?"
    "That is the Castel of Care.° Who-so° cometh   *Sorrow Whosoever*
    ther-inne
May banne° that he borne was to body or to soule.   *curse*

65 Ther-inne wonieth° a wighte° that Wronge is y-hote,°   *dwells creature called*
Fader of Falshed, and founded it hymselve.
Adam and Eve he egged to ille,
Conseilled Cayn to küllen his brother;
Judas he japed° with Juwen° silver,   *tricked Jewish*

70 And sithen° on an eller° honged hym after.   *then elder tree*
He is letter° of love and lyeth° hem alle;   *hinderer lies to*
That° trusten on his tresor bitrayeth he sonnest."°   *Those who first*
    Thanne had I wonder in my witt what womman it
    were
That such wise wordes of Holy Writ shewed;

75 And asked hir on the hieghe Name, ar heo thennes
    yeode,°   **ar . . .** *before she went thence*
What she were, witterli,° that wissed° me so faire.   *truly taught*
    "Holi Cherche I am," quod she; "thow oughtest me
    to knowe.
I underfonge° thee firste and thee feyth taughte,   *received*
And broughtest me borwes,° my biddyng to fulfille,   *sponsors*

80 And to love me lelly° the while thi lyf dureth."°   loyally   endures
    Thanne I courbed° on my knees and cryed hir° of grace,   fell   to her
    And preyed hir pitousely prey for my synnes,
    And also kenne° me kyndeli° on Criste to bileve,   teach   properly
    That I mighte worchen° His wille that wroughte° me to man: do   made
85 "Teche° me to no tresore, but telle me this ilke,°   Direct   **this ilke** this very thing
    How I may save my soule, that° seynt art y-holden?"   you who
    "Whan alle tresores aren tried," quod she, "Trewthe is the best.
    I do it on° *Deus caritas*,[2] to deme° the sothe.°   **do** . . . appeal to   judge   truth
    It is as derworth° a drewery° as dere God hymselven.   dear   darling
90 Who-so° is trewe of his tonge and telleth none other,   Whosoever
    And döth the werkis ther-with and wilneth no man ille,
    He is a god bi the Gospel agrounde° and aloft,   on earth
    And y-like to owre Lorde, bi Seynte Lukes wordes.
    The clerkes that knoweth this shulde kenne° it aboute,   make known
95 For Cristene and uncristne clameth° it üchone.°   cry out for   each one
    "Kynges and knightes shulde kepe it bi resoun;°   **bi resoun** rightly
    Riden and rappe° down, in reumes° aboute,   strike   realms
    And taken *trangressores* and tyen hem faste,
    Til Treuthe had y-termyned° her trespas to the ende.°   determined   final result
100 And that is the professioun appertly° that appendeth for° knyghtes,   plainly   **appendeth for** pertains to
    And nought to fasten a° Fryday in fyve score wynter,   one
    But holden with him and with hir that wolden al Treuthe,°
    And never leve hem for love ne for lacchyng° of sylver.   getting
    "For David in his dayes dubbed knightes
105 And did° hem swere on here swerde° to serve trewthe evere;   made   sword
    And who-so passed° that poynte° was *apostata*° in the ordre.   **who-so passed** whosoever broke   vow   apostate
    But Criste, kingene° kynge, knighted ten,[3]   of kings
    Cherubyn and Seraphin, suche° sevene, and an othre,   of such
    And yaf° hem myghte in His majesté, the muryer hem thoughte,°   gave   **hem thoughte** it seemed to them
110 And over his mene meyné° made hem archangeles,   **mene meyné** common household
    Taughte hem bi the Trinitee Treuthe to knowe,

---

[2] 'God is love.' I John iv.8.
102. But support every man and woman who would wish for entire Truth
[3] Ten orders: Seraphim, Cherubim; Thrones, Dominions, Virtues, Powers, Principalities, Archangels, Angels; and Lucifer's Fallen Angels.

To be buxome° at his biddyng—he bad hem noughte elles.   obedient

"Lucifer with legiounes lerned it in hevene,
But, for° he brake buxumnesse,° his blisse gan he tyne,° because obedience **gan . . . he lost**
115 And fel fro that felawship in a fendes° liknes   fiend's
Into a depe derke helle to dwelle there for evre.
And mo° thowsandes with him than man couthe   more
 noumbre°   **couthe noumbre** could count
Lopen° out with Lucifer in lothelich° forme,   Leaped loathsome
For thei leveden upon° hym that lyed in this manere: **leveden upon** believed in

120   *Ponam pedem in aquilone, et similis ero altissimo.*[4]

And alle that hoped it mighte be so, none hevene
 mighte hem holde,
But fellen out in fendes° liknesse nyne dayes togideres, fiends'
Til God of his goodnesse gan stable and stynte,°   **gan . . .** steadied and stopped
And garte° the hevene to stekye° and stonden in quiete. made close
125 "Whan thise wikked went out, wonderwise thei
 fellen,
Somme in eyre, somme in erthe, and somme in helle
 depe.
Ac Lucifer lowest lith° of hem alle;   lies
For pryde that he pult out,° his peyne hath none ende. **pult out** put on
And alle that worche with wronge, wenden hii shulle° **wenden . . .** they must go
130 After her deth-day and dwelle with that shrewe.°   wretch
Ac tho° that worche wel, as Holi Writ telleth,   those
And enden, as I ere seide, in Treuthe, that is the best,
Mowe be siker° that her soule shal wende to hevene, **Mowe . . .** Can be sure
Ther° Treuthe is in Trinitee and troneth° hem alle. Where enthrones
135 For-thi I sey as I seide ere, bi sighte of thise textis,
Whan alle tresores arne y-tried, Treuthe is the beste.
Lereth° it this lewde° men, for lettred men it knowen, Teach **this lewde** to these unlearned
That Treuthe is tresore the triest° on erthe."   most proven
 "Yet have I no kynde° knowing," quod I. "Yet mote natural
 ye kenne° me better   teach
140 By what craft° in my corps° it comseth° and where." skill body originates
 "Thow doted daffe,"° quod she, "dulle arne thi **doted daffe** doting dolt
 wittes;
Too litel Latyn thow lernedest, lede,° in thi youthe: man

   Heu mihi, quod sterilem duxi vitam juvenilem!°

"It is a kynde knowyng," quod he,° "that kenneth° she teaches
 in thine herte

---

[4] 'I shall place my foot in the North, and I shall be like to the most high.' See Isaiah xiv.13, 14.
143. Woe is me that I have lived such a barren youth!

145 For to lovye° thi Lorde lever° than thiselve;   love   dearer
No dedly synne to do, dey though thow sholdest.
This I trowe° be Treuthe. Who° can teche thee better,   believe   Whoever
Loke thow suffre hym to sey,° and sithen lere° it after.   speak   **sithen lere** then teach
For thus witnesseth His worde, worche° thow   do
  there-after;°   accordingly
150 For Trewthe telleth that Love is triacle° of hevene;   remedy
May no synne be on him sene° that useth that spise,   seen
And alle his werkes he wroughte with Love as him
  liste;°   it pleased
And lered it Moises for the levest° thing and moste like   dearest
  to hevene,
And also the plenté of Pees,° moste precious of vertues.   Peace
155   "For hevene myghte noughte holden it, it was so
  hevy of hymself,°   itself (Love)
Tyl it hadde of the erthe yeten his° fylle.   **yeten his** eaten its
And whan it haved of this folde° flesshe and blode taken,   world
Was nevere leef upon lynde° lighter ther-after,   linden tree
And portatyf and persant° as the poynt of a nedle,   **portatyf . . .** easy to carry and
    piercing
160 That myghte non armure it lette,° ne none heigh   stop
  walles.
    "For-thi is Love leder of the Lordes folke of hevene,
And a mene,° as the maire° is, bitwene the kyng and the   mediator   mayor
  Comune,°   Commons
Right so is Love a ledere and the lawe shapeth;
Upon man for his mysdedes the merciment° he taxeth.°   fine   imposes
165 And, for to knowe it kyndely,° it comseth bi° myght,   naturally   **comseth bi** originates
    in
And in the herte, there is the hevede° and the heigh   head
  welle;°   fount
For in kynde knowynge in herte there a myghte
  bigynneth.
And that falleth° to the Fader that formed° us alle,   belongs   created
Loked on us with love and lete His Sone deye
170 Mekely for owre mysdedes to amende° us alle;   redeem
And yet wolde° He hem no woo° that wroughte Hym   wished   evil
  that peyne,
But mekelich with mouthe mercy He bisoughte
To have pité of that poeple that peyned° Hym to deth.   tortured
    "Here myghtow° see ensamples in Hymselve one,°   may you   alone
175 That He was mightful and meke, and mercy gan
  graunte°   **gan graunte** granted
To hem that hongen Him an° heigh and His herte   on
  thirled.°   pierced
    "For-thi I rede° yow riche, haveth reuthe° of the   advise   pity
  pouere;°   poor

290

Though ye be myghtful to mote,° beth meke in yowre
    werkes. **to mote** in court

For the same mesures that ye mete, amys other elles,° **mete** . . . measure, amiss or
    otherwise

180 Ye shullen ben° weyen ther-wyth whan ye wende be
    hennes:° **wende hennes** go hence

Eadem mensura qua mensi fueritis, remecietur vobis.[5]

For though ye be trewe of yowre tonge and trewliche
    wynne,° gain

And as chaste as a childe that in cherche wepeth,

But if° ye loven lelliche and lene° the poure, **But if** Unless **lelliche** . . . loyally
    and give to

185 Such good° as God yow sent, godelich parteth,° goods **godelich parteth**
    generously share

Ye ne have na more meryte in masse ne in houres

Than Malkyn of hire maydenhode that no man desireth.

    "For James the gentil° jugged in his bokes noble

That faith withoute the faite° is righte no thinge worthi deed

190 And as ded as a dore-tre, but yif° the dedes folwe. **dore-tre** . . . door bar, unless

Fides sine operibus mortua est, etc.[6]

For-thi chastité withoute charité wörth° cheyned in will be
    helle;

It is as lewed° as a laumpe that no lighte is inne. worthless

    "Many chapeleynes arne chaste, ac charité is awey;

195 Aren no men avarousere° than hii° whan thei ben more avaricious they
    avaunced;° **ben avaunced** are advanced

Unkynde to her kyn and to alle Cristene,

Chewen° here charité and chiden° after more. Swallow cry out

Such chastité withouten charité wörth° cheyned in will be
    helle!

    "Many curatoures° kepen hem clene of here bodies, curates

200 Thei° ben acombred° with coveitise—thei konne nought But they encumbered
    don° it fram hem, take

So harde hath avarice y-hasped° hem togideres. joined

And that is no treuthe of the Trinité but treccherye of
    helle,

And lernyng° to lewde° men the latter° for to dele.° teaching unlearned **the latter**
    later give

    "For-thi this wordes ben° wryten in the Gospel: are

205 '*Date et dabitur vobis*, for I dele yow alle.'[7]

And that is the lokke° of love and lateth oute° my grace lock **lateth oute** sets free

To conforte the careful,° acombred with synne. sorrowful

Love is leche° of lyf, and nexte owre Lorde selve, physician

And also the graith gate° that göth into hevene. **graith gate** straight way

---

[5] 'And with what measure you have measured out, it shall be measured to you.' Matt. vii.2.
[6] 'Faith without works is dead, etc.' James ii.26.
[7] 'Give and it shall be given to you for I gave you all you have.' Luke vi.38.

210 For-thi I sey as I seide ere by the textis,
    Whan alle tresores ben y-tryed, Treuthe is the beste.
    Now have I tolde thee what Treuthe is, that no tresore
        is bettere;
    I may no lenger lenge° thee with. Now loke° thee owre   stay   guard
        Lorde!"

Canto V

    The kyng and his knightes to the kirke° wente   church
    To here matynes of the day and the masse after.
    Thanne waked I of° my wynkynge° and wo was   from   sleeping
        withalle
    That I ne hadde sleped sadder° and y-seighen° more.   more soundly   seen
5 Ac er° I hadde faren° a fourlonge, feyntise° me hente,°   before gone faintness seized
    That I ne myghte° ferther a-foot for defaute° of   **ne myghte** couldn't go lack
        slepynge;
    And sat softly adown and seide my Bileve,°   Creed
    And so° I babeled on my bedes, thei broughte me   as
        aslepe.
    And thanne saw I moche more than I bifore tolde,
10 For I say° the felde ful of folke that I bifore of seyde,°   saw spoke
    And how Resoun gan arrayen hym° alle the reume°   **gan . . .** prepared himself realm
        to preche,
    And with a crosse afor the kynge comsed° thus to   commenced
        techen.
    He preved° that thise pestilences[1] were for° pure   showed because of
        synne,
    And the southwest wynde on Saterday at evene[2]
15 Was pertliche° for pure pryde and for no poynt elles.°   clearly other
    Piries° and plomtrees were puffed° to the erthe   Pears blown
    In ensample,° ye segges,° ye shulden do the bettere.   example men
    Beches and brode okes were blowen to the grounde,
    Torned upward her tailles in tokenynge of drede
20 That dedly synne at Domesday shal fordon° hem alle.   destroy
    Of this matere I myghte mamely ful° longe,   **mamely ful** mumble very
    Ac I shal seye as I saw, so me God helpe,
    How pertly° afor the poeple Resoun gan° to preche.   clearly began
    He bad Wastoure go worche what he best couthe,°   could
25 And wynnen° his wastyng° with somme manere crafte,°   earn back money wasted skill

[1] Pestilence of 1361–62.
[2] Storm of Saturday, January 15, 1362.

And preyed Peronelle° her purfyle° to lete,°   **preyed Peronelle** begged Lady
And kepe it in hir cofre° for catel° at hire nede.   Peacock furs let go
Thomme Stowue he taughte to take two staves   chest goods
And fecche Felice home fro the wyven-pyne.°   ducking stool
30 He warned Watt his wyf was to blame
    That hire hed° was worth halve a marke, his hode   headpiece
        noughte worth a grote,
    And bad Bette° kut a bow other tweyne°   Bart **bow** ... bough or two
    And bete Betoun° ther-with but if° she wolde worche.   Betty **but if** unless
     And thanne he charged chapmen° to chasten° her   merchants chastise
        childeren;
35 Late no wynnynge° hem forweny° whil thei be yonge,   profits spoil
    Ne, for no pouste° of pestilence, plese hem noughte out   **no pouste** any fear of attack
        of resoun.
    "My syre seyde so to me, and so did my dame,
    That the levere° childe, the more lore° bihoveth,   dearer the instruction
    And Salamon seide the same, that Sapience made,°   **Sapience made** wrote Proverbs

40   *Qui parcit virge, odit filium.*

    The Englich of this Latyn is, who-so° wil it knowe,   whosoever
    'Who-so spareth the sprynge spilleth° his children.'"   **sprynge spilleth** rod spoils
     And sithen° he preyed prelatz and prestes togideres,   then
    "That° ye prechen to the peple, preve° it on   What practice
        yowreselven,
45 And doth it in dede; it shal drawe yow to good.
    If ye lyven as ye leren° us, we shal leve° yow the   teach believe
        bettere."
     And sithen he radde Religioun° here reule to holde,   **radde Religioun** advised the
    "Leste the kynge and his conseille yowre comunes   religious orders
        appayre,°   **comunes appayre** provisions
    And ben° stuwardes of yowre stedes° til ye be ruled   reduce
        bettre."   be places
50   And sithen° he conseilled the kynge the Comune°   then Commons
        to lovye:°   love
    "It is thi tresore, if tresoun ne were, and triacle° at thi   remedy
        nede."
    And sithen he prayed the Pope have pité on Holi
        Cherche,
    And er° he gyve any grace governe firste hymselve.   before
     "And ye that han lawes to kepe, late° Treuthe be   let
        yowre covveytise°   desire
55 More than golde or other gyftes, if ye wil God plese.
    For who-so contrarieth Treuthe, He telleth in the
        Gospel,

That God knoweth hym noughte, ne no seynte of
  hevene,

Amen dico vobis, nescio vos.[3]

And ye that seke Seynte James[4] and seintes of Rome,
60 Seketh seynt Treuthe, for he may save yow alle,
Qui cum patre et filio. That feire hem bifalle°   follow   spoke
That suweth° my sermon." And thus seyde° Resoun.   declared   theme
    Thanne ran Repentance and reherced° his teme,°   made
And gert° Wille to wepe water with his eyen.

Superbia°   Pride
65   Peronelle° Proude-herte platte° hir to the erthe,   Lady Peacock   threw
And lay longe ar° she loked, and "Lorde, mercy!"   before
    cryed,
And byhighte° to Hym that us alle made,   promised
She shulde unsowen hir serke° and sette there an heyre°   **unsowen** . . . slit her shift   hair
                                                             shirt
To affaiten° hire flesshe that fierce was to synne: tame
70   "Shal nevere heighe herte me hente,° but holde me   seize
    lowe,
And suffre to be myssayde°—and so did I nevere.   abused
But now wil I meke me° and mercy biseche,   **meke me** humble myself
For al this I have hated in myne herte."

Luxuria°   Lechery
    Thanne Lecchoure seyde "Allas!" and on owre Lady
    he cryed
75 To make mercy for his misdedes bitwene God and his
    soule,
With that he shulde the Saterday sevene yere
    there-after°
Drynke but myd° the doke° and dyne but ones.   **but myd** only water with   duck

Invidia°   Envy
    Envye with hevy herte asked after scrifte,°   confession
And carefullich *mea culpa°* he comsed° to shewe.°   the Confiteor   commenced   say
80 He was as pale as a pelet,° in the palsye he semed,   stone pellet
    And clothed in a caurimaury,° I couthe° it noughte   coarse cloth   could
    discreve;
In kirtel and kourteby° and a knyf bi his syde;   **kirtel** . . . jacket and coat
Of a freres frokke° were the forsleves,   **freres frokke** friar's habit

---

[3] 'Amen I say to you, I know you not.' Matt. xxv.12.
[4] James of Compostella.
61. Who with the father and the son (lives and reigns). May good happen to them
76. With provision that he would every Saturday for seven years from that time

And as a leke° hadde y-leye longe in the sonne,   *leek which*

85 So loked he with lene chekes, lourynge foule.°   **lourynge foule** *scowling foully*

His body was to-bolle° for wratthe that he bote° his lippes,   *swollen bit*

And wryngynge he yede° with the fiste; to wreke° hymself he thoughte   *went avenge*

With werkes or with wordes whan he seighe° his tyme.   *saw*

Eche a worde that he warpe° was of an addres tonge;   *spoke*

90 Of chydynge and of chalangynge was his chief lyflode,°   *way of life*

With bakbitynge and bismer° and beryng of fals witnesse;   *slander*

This was al his curteisye° where that evere he shewed hym.°   *manners / himself*

"I wolde ben y-shryve,"° quod this schrewe,° "and° I for shame durst;   *confessed wretch if*

I wolde be gladder, bi God, that Gybbe had meschaunce

95 Than thoughe I had this wöke° y-wonne a weye° of Essex chese.   *week wey (two to three hundredweights)*

"I have a neighbore neyghe° me, I have ennuyed° hym ofte,   *near annoyed*

And lowen on° hym to lordes to don° hym lese° his silver,   **lowen on** *lied about make lose*

And made his frendes ben° his foon° thorw my false tonge;   *be foes*

His grace° and his good happes° greveth me ful° sore.   *favor luck very*

100 Bitwene many and many I make debate ofte,

That bothe lyf and lyme° is lost thorw my speche.   *limb*

And whan I mete him in market that I moste hate,

I hailse° hym hendeliche,° as I his frende were;   *greet courteously*

For he is doughtier° than I, I dar do non other.   *stronger*

105 Ac hadde I maystrye° and myghte, God wote° my wille!°   *mastery knows / intention*

"And whan I come to the kirke° and sholde knele to the Rode,°   *church / Cross*

And preye for the poeple as the prest techeth,

For pilgrimes and for palmers, for alle the poeple after,°   *besides*

Thanne I crye on my knees that Cryste yif° hem sorwe°   *may give sorrow*

110 That baren° awey my bolle° and my broke schete.°   *carried bowl **broke schete** torn sheet*

Awey fro the auter° thanne turne I my eyghen,°   *altar eyes*

And biholde how Eleyne hath a newe cote;

I wisshe thanne it were myne and al the webbe° after.   *cloth*

"And of mennes lesynge° I laughe; that liketh myn herte;   **mennes lesynge** *men's losses*

115 And for her wynnynge I wepe and waille the° tyme,   *all the*

And deme° that hii don° ille there° I do wel° worse; — judge | **hii don** they do | where | much

Who-so undernymeth° me here-of, I hate hym dedly after. — takes to task

I wolde that üche a wyght° were my knave,° — **a wyght** man | servant

For who-so hath more than I, that angreth me sore.

120 And thus I lyve lovelees lyke a lüther° dogge, — evil

That al my body bolneth° for bitter° of my galle. — swells | bitterness

   "I myghte noughte° eet, many yeres, as a man oughte, — **myghte noughte** could not

For envye and yvel wille is yvel to defye.° — digest

May no sugre ne swete thinge asswage my swellynge,

125 Ne no *diapenidion*° dryve it fro myne herte, — sweet medicine

Ne noyther schrifte° ne shame, but ho-so schrape° my mawe?"° — confession | **but . . .** unless someone | scrapes | stomach

   "Yüs, redili,"° quod Repentaunce, and radde° hym to the beste, — **Yüs, redili** Yes, indeed | advised

"Sorwe° of synnes is savacioun of soules." — Sorrow

   "I am sori," quod that segge." "I am but selde other,° — man | **selde other** seldom otherwise

130 And that maketh me thus megre,° for I ne may° me venge. — **thus megre** so thin | **ne may** cannot

Amonges burgeyses have I be dwellynge at Londoun,

And gert° Bakbitinge be a brocoure° to blame mennes ware.° — made | broker | **blame . . .** criticize men's wares

Whan he solde and I noughte, thanne was I redy

To lye and to loure° on my neighbore and to lakke° his chaffare.° — scowl | find fault with | merchandise

135 I wil amende this, yif I may, thorw myghte of God Almyghty."

Ira° — Anger

Now awaketh Wratthe with two whyte eyen,

And nyvelynge° with the nose, and his nekke hangynge. — snivelling

   "I am Wrath," quod he. "I was sum tyme a frere,° — friar

And the coventes° gardyner for to graffe ympes.° — convent's | **graffe ympes** graft shoots

140 On limitoures and listres lesynges I ymped° —

Tyl thei bere leves° of low° speche, lordes to plese, — **bere leves** bore leaves | humble

And sithen° thei blosmed obrode,° in boure° to here shriftes.° — then | out | bower | **here shriftes** hear confessions

And now is fallen therof a frute that folke han wel levere° — **han . . .** had much rather

Schewen° her schriftes to hem than shryve° hem to her persones.° — Tell | confess | parsons

145 And now persones han parceyved that freres parte° with hem; — **freres parte** friars share

   140. On mendicants and preachers I engrafted lies

Thise possessioneres° preche and deprave° freres,   beneficed priests   defame

And freres fyndeth hem in defaute,° as folke bereth witnes,   **in defaute** at fault

That whan thei preche the poeple in many place aboute,

I, Wrath, walke with hem and wisse° hem of° my bokes.   teach   from

150   "Thus thei speken of spiritualté, that eyther despiseth other,

Til thei be bothe beggers and by my spiritualté libben,°   live

Or elles alle riche and riden aboute.

I, Wrath, rest nevere, that I ne moste folwe°   **that . . .** because I must follow

This wykked folke, for suche is my grace.

155   "I have an aunte to nonne° and an abbesse bothe,°   **to nonne** as a nun   too

Hir were levere swowe or swelte° than suffre any peyne.   **Hir . . .** She would rather faint or die

I have be cook in hir kichyne and the covent° served   convent

Many monthes with hem, and with monkes bothe.

I was the Prioresses potagere° and other poure° ladyes,   pottage cook   poor

160 And made hem joutes° of jangelynge° that Dame° Johanne was a bastard,   broths   gossip   Mother

And Dame° Clarice a knightes doughter, ac a kokewolde° was hire syre,   Sister   cuckold

And Dame Peronelle° a prestes file.° Priouresse wörth° she nevere,   Peacock   wench   will be

For she had childe in chirityme,° al owre chapitere it wiste.°   cherry time   knew

     "Of wykked wordes I, Wrath, here wortes° i-made,   cooked vegetables

165 Til 'Thow lixte'° and 'Thow lixte' lopen° oute at ones,   **Thow lixte** You lie   leaped

And eyther hitte other under the cheke;

Hadde thei had knyves, bi Cryst, her° eyther had killed other.   of them

     "Seynt Gregorie was a gode Pope and had a gode forwit°   forethought

That no priouresse were° prest, for that he ordeigned.   would be

170 Thei had thanne ben *infamis*° the firste day; thei can so yvel hele conseille.°   disreputable   **yvel . . .** poorly keep a secret

Amonge monkes I might be, ac many tyme I shonye;°   shun them

For there ben many felle frekis° my feres° to aspye,°   **felle frekis** cruel fellows   sort   spy out

Bothe prioure and supprioure° and owre *Pater Abbas*.°   subprior   ***Pater Abbas*** Father Abbot

And if I telle any tales, thei taken hem° togyderes,   **taken hem** meet

175 And do° me faste Frydayes to bred and to water,   make

And am chalanged° in the chapitelhous as° I a childe were,   accused   **chapitelhous as** chapter house as if

And baleised° on the bare ers° and no breche° bitwene.   beaten   buttocks   breeches

For-thi have I no lykyng with tho leodes° to wonye.°   **tho leodes** those men   dwell

I ete there unthende° fisshe and fieble ale drynke;   half-grown
180 Ac other while,° whan wyn cometh, whan I drynke   **other while** sometimes
     wyn at eve,
   I have a fluxe of a foule mouthe wel fyve dayes after.
   Al the wikkednesse that I wote° bi any of owre   know
     bretheren,
   I couth° it in owre cloistre that al owre covent wote it."   make known
     "Now repent thee," quod Repentaunce, "and
     reherce° thow nevre   repeat
185 Conseille° that thow cnowest bi contenaunce° ne bi   Secrets   favor
     righte;
   And drynke noughte over delicatly° ne too depe   luxuriously
     noyther,
   That thi wille bicause therof to wrath myghte torne.
   Esto sobrius,"° he seyde, and assoilled° me after,   ***Esto sobrius*** Be sober   absolve
   And bad me wilne to wepe my wikkednesse to amende.

Avaricia

190   And thanne cam Coveytise, can I hym noughte
     descryve,°   describe
   So hungriliche and holwe,° Sire Hervy[5] hym loked.°   hollow   **hym loked** he seemed
   He was bitelbrowed and baberlipped° also,   thick-lipped
   With two blered eyghen° as a blynde hagge;   eyes
   And as a letheren purs lolled° his chekes;   sagged
195 Wel sydder° than his chyn thei chiveled for elde;°   **Wel sydder** Even lower   **chive** ... trembled because of old age
   And as a bondman of° his bacoun his berde was   with
     bidraveled.°   slobbered
   With an hode on his hed, a lousi hatte above,
   And in a tauny tabarde° of twelve wynter age,   short coat
   Al totorne and baudy° and ful of lys crepynge.   **totorne** ... torn apart and filthy
200 But if that a lous couthe° have lopen° the bettre,   could   leaped
   She sholde noughte have walked on that welche,° so   Welsh cloth
     was it thredebare.
     "I have ben coveytouse," quod this caityve,° "I   wretch
     biknowe° it here.   confess
   For some tyme I served Symme atte° Stile,   at the
   And was his prentis y-plighte,° his profit to wayte.°   **prentis y-plighte** apprentice pledged   look after
205 First I lerned to lye a leef other tweyne;°   **a** ... for a leaf of the lesson or tw
   Wikkedlich to weye° was my fürst lessoun.   weigh
   To Wy° and to Wynchestre I went to the faire,   Weyhill
   With many manere marchandise as my maistre me
     highte;°   ordered
   Ne had° the grace of gyle y-go° amonge my ware,   **Ne had** If   had not gone
210 It had be° unsolde this sevene yere, so me God helpe!   **had be** would have been

[5] A name apparently associated with avarice.

"Thanne drowe° I me amonges draperes, my donet°   went   grammar
    to lerne,
To drawe the lyser° alonge, the lenger it° semed.   selvage   it (the cloth)
Amonges the riche rayes° I rendred° a lessoun,   striped cloths   construed
To broche° hem with a pak-nedle, and plaited hem   pierce
    togyderes,
215 And put hem in a presse and pynned hem ther-inne,
Tyl ten yerdes or twelve hadde tolled° out threttene.   stretched
    "My wyf was a webbe° and wollen cloth made.   weaver
She spak to spynnesteres° to spynnen it oute.   **spak . . .** employed spinners
Ac the pounde that she payed by poised a quarteroun
    more°
220 Than myne owne auncere,⁶ who-so weyghed treuthe.
    "I boughte hir barly malte; she brewe it to selle.
Peny° ale and podyng° ale she poured togideres   Cheap   good
For laboreres and for low folke; that lay° by hymselve.°   was stored   itself
The best ale lay in my boure° or in my bedchambre,   bower
225 And who-so bummed° therof boughte it ther-after   tasted
A galoun for a grote, God wote,° no lesse;   knows
And yit it cam in cupmel,° this crafte° my wyf used.   cupfuls   trick
Rose the Regratere° was hir righte name;   Retailer
She hath holden hokkerye° al hire lyf-tyme.   huckstering
230   "Ac I swere now, so thee Ik,° that synne wil I lete,°   **so . . .** may I prosper   forgo
And nevere wikkedliche weye° ne wikke chaffare°   weight   bargaining
    use,
But wenden° to Walsyngham and my wyf als,°   go   also
And bidde° the Rode° of Bromeholme brynge me oute   pray to   Cross
    of dette."
    "Repentedestow thee° evere," quod Repentance,   **Repentedestow thee** Did you
    "ne restitucioun madest?"   repent
235   "Yüs, ones I was herberwed,"° quod he, "with an hep   lodged
    of chapmen,°   merchants
I roos whan thei were arest° and y-rifled here males."°   at rest   packs
    "That was no restitucioun," quod Repentance, "but
    a robberes thefte!
Thow haddest be better worthy be hanged ther-fore
Than for al that thow hast here shewed."
240   "I wende° ryflynge were restitucioun," quod he, "for   thought
    I lerned nevere rede on° boke,   in
And I can° no Frenche in feith but of° the ferthest ende   know   from
    of Norfolke."
    "Usedestow° evere usurie," quod Repentaunce, "in   Did you use
    alle thi lyf tyme?"

219. But the pound weight that she used to pay them by weighed a quarter more
⁶ 'Steelyard.' The Danish steelyard was a pound measure prohibited because of its indefiniteness.

"Nay, sothly,"° he seyde, "save in my youthe.　　　*truly*
I lerned amonge Lumbardes and Jewes a lessoun,
245　To wey pens° with a peys° and pare the hevyest,　　**wey pens** weigh pence　weight
And lene it for love of the crosse, to legge a wedde and
　　　lese it;°
Such dedes I did wryte yif he his day breke.°　　　**day breke** due day should miss
I have mo maneres° thorw rerages° than thorw *miseretur*　**mo maneres** more manors　arre[…]
　　　et comodat.°　　　　　　　　　　　　　　**miseretur . . .** have pity and lend[…]
"I have lent lordes and ladyes my chaffare°　　　*merchandise*
250　And ben her brocour° after and boughte it myself.　*broker*
Eschaunges and chevesances,° with suche chaffare I dele,　**Eschaunges . . .** Barter and loans
And lene° folke that lese wol a lyppe at° every noble.°　lend to　**lese . . .** will lose a part of
　　　　　　　　　　　　　　　　　　　　　　gold　noble
And with Lumbardes lettres I ladde° golde to Rome　*brought*
And toke it by taille° here and tolde° there lasse."°　tally　counted　less
255　"Lentestow° evre lordes for love° of her　　　Did you lend　desire
　　　mayntenaunce?"°　　　　　　　　　　　　*support*
"Ye, I have lent lordes loved° me nevere after,　　who loved
And have y-made many a knyghte bothe mercere and
　　　drapere
That payed nevere for his prentishode,° noughte a　*apprenticeship*
　　　peire gloves."
"Hastow° pité on pore men that mote° nedes　　Have you　must
　　　borwe?"
260　"I have as moche pité of pore men as pedlere hath of
　　　cattes,
That wolde kille hem, yf he cacche hem myghte for
　　　coveitise of here skynnes."
"Artow manlyche° amonge thi neighbores of thi　　**Artow manlyche** Are you charita[…]
　　　mete° and drynke?"　　　　　　　　　　*food*
"I am holden," quod he, "as hende° as hounde is in　kind
　　　kychyne;
Amonges my neighbores namelich° such a name Ich°　especially　I
　　　have."
265　"Now, God lene° nevre," quod Repentance, "but°　grant　unless
　　　thow repent thee rather,°　　　　　　　　*soon*
Thee grace on this grounde thi good wel to bisette,°　*employ*
Ne thine ysue after thee have joye of that thow wynnest,
Ne thi executours wel bisett the silver that thow hem
　　　levest;
And that° was wonne with wronge with wikked men　what
　　　be despended.°　　　　　　　　　　　　*spent*
270　"For were I frere° of that hous there° gode faith and　friar　where
　　　charité is,

---

246. And lend it for the love of the cross (on the reverse side of the coin), so that the borrower would deposit a pledge (security) and then lose it

I nolde cope° us with thi catel° ne owre kyrke amende,°   **nolde cope** would not clothe   goods

    kyrke amende church repair

Ne have a peny° to my pitaunce of thyne, bi my soule hele,°   penny

    soule hele soul's health

For the best boke in owre hous, theighe brent° golde were the leves,   **theighe brent** though burnished

And I wyst wytterly° thow were suche as thow tellest,   **And . . .** If I knew surely

275 Or elles that I kouthe° knowe it by any kynnes wise.°   could   **kynnes wise** kind of manner

> *Servus es alterius, cum fercula pinguia queris;*
> *Pane tuo pocius vescere, liber eris.°*

"Thow art an unkynde° creature. I can thee noughte assoille,°   unnatural

    absolve

Til thow make restitucioun and rekne° with hem alle;   settle

280 And sithen that° Resoun rolle° it in the regystre of hevene,   **sithen that** until   enrolls

That thow hast made üche man good, I may thee noughte assoille.

> *Non dimittitur peccatum, donec restituatur ablatum, etc.*[7]

For alle that have of thi good,° have God my trouthe,   wealth

Ben holden at the heighe dome° to helpe thee to restitue.   judgment

285 And who-so leveth° noughte this be soth,° loke in the Sauter Glose,°   believes   true

    Psalter Gloss

In *Miserere mei Deus*, where° I mene treuthe,   **In . . .** At *Have pity on me, oh God,* whether

> *Ecce enim veritatem dilexisti, etc.*[8]

Shal nevere werkman in this worlde thryve wyth that thow wynnest.

Cum sancto sanctus eris[9]—construe me that on Englische!"

290 Thanne wex° that shrewe° in wanhope and walde° have hanged himself,   fell   wretch   **wanhope . . .** despair and would

Ne hadde° Repentaunce the rather reconforted° hym in this manere: **Ne hadde** If had not   **the . . .** at once comforted

"Have mercye in thi mynde and with thi mouth biseche it,

For Goddes mercye is more than alle hise other werkes;

> *Misericordia eius super omnia opera eius, etc.*[10]

276–77. You are the slave of another when you seek dainty dishes; rather eat bread of your own and you shall be free.

[7] 'A sin is not forgiven until restitution is made, etc.' St. Augustine, *Epistles*, cliii.20.

[8] 'For behold you have desired truth, etc.' Ps. li.6.

[9] 'With the holy you shall be holy.' See Ps. xviii.25, 26.

[10] 'His mercy is above all His other works, etc.' Ps. cxlv.9.

295 And al the wikkednesse in this worlde that man myghte
worche or thynke
Ne is no more to the mercye of God than in the see a
glede:°   live coal

Omnis iniquitas quantum ad misericordiam Dei est quasi sintilla in
medio maris.[11]

"For-thi, have mercy in thi mynde; and
marchandise, leve it,
For thow hast no good grounde° to gete thee with a   justification
wastel°   fine bread
300 But if° it were with° thi tonge or ellis with thi two   **But if** Unless   by
hondes.
For the good° that thow hast geten bigan al with   wealth
falsehede,
And as longe as thow lyvest ther-with, thow yeldest°   give
noughte, but borwest.°   borrow
And if thow wite° nevere to whiche ne whom to   know
restitue,
Bere it to the bisschop and bidde° hym of his grace   ask
305 Bisette° it hymselve as best is for thi soule.   Employ
For he shal answere for thee at the heygh dome.°   judgment
For thee and for many mo,° that man shal yif° a   more   give
rekenynge,
What he lerned° yow in Lente—leve thow none   taught
other—
And what he lent yow of owre Lordes good to lette°   keep
yow fro synne."

Gula°   Gluttony

310   Now bigynneth Glotoun for to go to schrifte,°   confession
And kaires hym to-kirke-ward,° his coupe° to schewe.°   **kaires** . . . rambles to church   si
                                              tell
Ac Beton° the brewestere° bad hym good morwe,°   Betty   alewife   morning
And axed° of hym with that whiderward he wolde.°   asked   would go
"To Holi Cherche," quod he, "for to here° Masse,   hear
315 And sithen I wil be shryven° and synne namore."   confessed
"I have gode ale, gossib,"° quod she. "Glotown,   neighbor
wiltow assaye?"°   **wiltow assaye** will you try it
"Hastow° aughte in thi purs, any hote spices?"   Do you have
"I have peper and pionés,"° quod she, "and a pounde   peony seeds
of garlike,
A ferthyngworth of fenel-seed for fastyng dayes."
320   Thanne göth Glotoun in and Grete Othes after;

[11] 'All evil compared to the mercy of God is like a live coal in the middle of the sea.' Attributed to St.
Augustine.

Cesse the souteresse° sat on the benche, — *female shoemaker*
Watte the warner° and his wyf bothe,° — *gamekeeper   too*
Tymme the tynkere and tweyne° of his prentis,° — *two   apprentices*
Hikke the hakneyman° and Hughe the nedeler,° — *liveryman   needle-seller*
325 Clarice of Cokkes Lane and the clerke of the cherche,
Dawe the dykere,° and a dozeine other; — *ditch-digger*
Sire Piers of Pridie and Peronelle of Flaundres,°
A ribibour,° a ratonere,° a rakyer° of Chepe,° — *fiddler   rat-catcher   scavenger   Cheapside*
A ropere,° a redyngkyng,° and Rose the dissheres,° — *rope-maker   groom   dish-seller*
330 Godfrey of Garlekehithe and Gryfin the Walshe,° — *Welshman*
And upholderes° an hepe, erly bi the morwe, — *old-clothes-sellers*
Geven° Glotoun with glad chere° good ale to hansel.° — *Gave   appearance   **to hansel** as a gift*
    Clement the cobelere cast of his cloke,
And atte New Faire¹² he nempned° it to selle. — *offered*
335 Hikke the hakeneyman hitte° his hood after — ***hakeneyman hitte** liveryman threw down*
And badde Bette° the bochere° ben on his side. — *Bart   butcher*
There were chapmen° y-chose this chaffare° to preise;° — *merchants   merchandise   price*
Who-so haveth the hood shuld have amendes of° the cloke. — ***amendes of** compensation for*
    Two risen up in rape and rouned° togideres — ***rape** . . . haste and whispered*
340 And preised° these penyworthes apart bi hemselve. — *appraised*
Thei couth° noughte bi her conscience acorden in treuthe, — *could*
Tyl Robyn the ropere° arose bi the southe,° — *rope-maker   **bi** . . . for the truth*
And nempned hym for a noumpere that no debate nere,°
For to trye this chaffare° bitwixen hem thre. — ***trye** . . . decide this bargain*
345 Hikke the hostellere° hadde the cloke — *innkeeper*
In covenaunte that Clement shulde the cuppe fille
And have Hikkes hode hostellere° and holde hym y-served.° — ***Hikkes** . . . Hick the innkeeper's   hood   content*
And who-so repented rathest° shulde arise after — *soonest*
And grete Sire Glotoun with a galoun ale.
350   There was laughyng and louryng° and "Let go the cuppe." — *scowling*
And seten° so til evensonge° and songen umwhile° — *they sat   vespers   for a while*
Tyl Glotoun had y-globbed° a galoun and a jille.° — *gulped   gill (one-fourth pint)*
His guttis gunne° to gothely° as two gredy sowes; — *began   rumble*
His pissed a potel° in a *Pater-noster* while, — *pottle (two quarts)*
355 And blew his rounde ruwet° at his rigge-bon° ende — *horn   backbone's*
That alle that herde that horne held her nose after

327. Father Piers of Prie-Dieu and Lady Peacock of Flanders
¹² 'New Fair,' a game of barter. The deputies appointed by the principals Clement and Hick decide the terms of the barter, by which all must abide. Final arbitration rests with the umpire Robyn.
343. And named himself as an umpire so that there might be no quarrel

And wissheden° it had be wexed° with a wispe of
    firses.°   wished   plugged / furze

He myghte neither steppe ne stonde er° he his staffe
    hadde,   before

And thanne gan° he go, liche a glewmannes° bicche,   began minstrel's

360   Somme tyme aside, and somme tyme arrere,°   to the rear

As who-so leyth lynes° for to lacche foules.°   **leyth lynes** lays snares   **lacche foules** catch birds

And whan he drowgh° to the dore, thanne dymmed his
    eighen;°   drew near / eyes

He stumbled on the thresshewolde and threwe° to the
    erthe.   tumbled

Clement the cobelere caughte hym bi the myddel

365   For to lyfte hym alofte and leyde him on his knowes.°   knees

Ac Glotoun was a gret cherle° and a grym° in the
    liftynge,   fellow heavy one

And coughed up a caudel° in Clementis lappe.   mess

Is° non so hungri hounde in Hertford schire   There is

Durst lape of° the levynges, so unlovely thei smaughte.°   **lape of** lap up some of   tasted

370   With al the wo of this worlde his wyf and his wenche

Baren hym home to his bedde and broughte hym
    ther-inne.

And after al this excesse he had an accidie°   fit of sloth

That he slepe Saterday and Sonday til sonne yede° to
    reste.   went

Thenne waked he of his wynkyng and wiped his
    eyghen.°   eyes

375   The fyrste worde that he warpe° was "Where is the
    bolle?"°   uttered / bowl

His wif gan edwite° hym tho° how wikkedlich he lyved,   **gan edwite** rebuked   then

And Repentance righte so rebuked hym that tyme:

     "As thow with wordes and werkes hast wroughte
         yvel in thi lyve,

Shryve thee° and be shamed therof and shewe it with
    thi mouth."   **Shryve thee** Confess

380   "I, Glotoun," quod the gome,° "gylti me yelde,°   man confess

That I have trespassed with my tonge, I can noughte
    telle how ofte,

Sworen 'Goddes Soule' and 'So God me help and
    halidom'°   holy relics

There° no nede ne was nyne hundreth tymes,   Where

And overseye me° at my sopere° and some tyme at
    nones°   **overseye me** forgotten myself / supper noon meal

385   That I, Glotoun, girt° it up er° I hadde gone a myle,   threw before

And y-spilte that° myghte be spared and spended on
    somme hungrie;   what

Overdelicatly on fastyng dayes drunken and eten   **too**
    bothe,°

And sat some tyme so longe there that I slepe and ete at
    ones.

For love of tales in tavernes to drynke the more, I dyned,

190 And hyed° to the mete er none° whan fastyng-dayes   hurried   **mete ... food before**
    were.”   midday

    “This shewyng shrifte,”° quod Repentance, “shal be   **shewyng shrifte** frank confession
      meryte to thee.”

    And thanne gan° Glotoun grete° and gret doel to   began   to cry
      make

For his lither° lyf that he lyved hadde,   wicked

And avowed to fast: “For hunger or for thürst

195 Shal nevere fisshe on the Fryday defien° in my wombe,°   digest   belly

Tyl Abstinence myn Aunte have yive° me leve;   given

And yit have I hated hir al my lyf tyme.”

         Accidia°   Sloth

    Thanne come Sleuthe° al bislabered with two slymy   Sloth
      eighen,°   eyes

“I most° sitte,” seyde the segge,° “or elles shulde I   must   man
    nappe;

200 I may° noughte stonde, ne stoupe, ne withoute a stole°   can   stool
    knele.

Were I broughte abedde, but if° my taille-ende it   **but if** unless
    made,°   made me

Sholde no ryngynge do° me ryse ar° I were rype° to   make   before   ready
    dyne.”

He bygan *Benedicite*[13] with a bolke° and his brest   belch
    knocked,

And roxed and rored and rutte° atte laste.   **roxed ...** stretched and groaned and
      snored

205   “What! Awake, renke!”° quod Repentance, “and   man
    rape° thee to shrifte.”   hasten

    “If I shulde deye bi this day, me liste° noughte to   **me liste** it pleases me
      loke.°   watch

I can° noughte perfitly my *Pater-noster* as the prest it   know
    syngeth,

But I can rymes of Robyn Hood and Randolf Erle of
    Chestre,

Ac neither of owre Lorde ne of owre Lady the leste
    that evere was made.

210   I have made vowes fourty and foryete° hem on the   forgotten
    morne;

I parfourned° nevre penaunce as the prest me highte,°   performed   ordered

---

[13] ‘Bless me.’ Opening of confession formula.

Ne ryghte sori for my synnes yet was I nevere.
And yif I bidde° any bedes,° but if it be in wrath,   pray   rosary beads
That° I telle with my tonge is two myle fro myne herte.   What

415 I am occupied eche day, haliday and other,
With ydel tales atte ale and otherwhile in cherches;
Goddes peyne and his passioun ful selde thynke I
     there-on.
   "I visited nevere fieble men ne fettered folke in
     püttes,°   dungeons
I have levere° here an harlotrie° or a somer game[14] of   **have levere** would rather   baw-
     souteres,°   tale   shoemakers
420 Or lesynges° to laughe at and belye° my neighbore,   lies   slander
Than al that evere Marke made, Mathew, John, and
     Lucas.
And vigilies and fastyng dayes, alle thise late° I passe,   let
And ligge° abedde in Lenten and my lemman° in myn   lie   mistress
     armes,
Tyl matynes and masse be do,° and thanne go to the   done
     freres;
425 Come I to *Ite, missa est,°* I holde me y-served.°   **Ite . . .** Go, the mass is ended
I nam° noughte shryven some tyme but if sekenesse it   finished   am
     make,
Nought tweies in two yere, and thanne up gesse° I   **up gesse** at a guess
     schryve me.
   "I have be prest and parsoun passynge thretti wynter,
Yete can I neither solfé° ne synge ne seyntes lyves rede,   read notes
430 But I can fynde in a felde or in a fourlonge° an hare,   furrow
Better than in *Beatus vir*[15] or in *Beati omnes*[16]
Construe oon clause wel and kenne° it to my   teach
     parochienes.°   parishioners
I can holde lovedays and here° a reves rekenynge,°   **lovedays . . .** settlement days an-
Ac in canoun° ne in the decretales I can noughte rede a   audit   accounting
     lyne.   canon law
435 Yif I bigge° and borwe it, but yif it be y-tailled,°   buy   marked on a tally
I foryete° it as yerne,° and yif men me it axe   forget   eagerly
Sixe sithes° or sevene, I forsake° it with othes,   times   deny
And thus tene° I trewe° men ten hundreth tymes.   injure   honest
   "And my servauntz some tyme, her salarye is
     bihynde,
440 Reuthe° is to here° the rekenynge° whan we shal rede   Pity   hear   accounting
     acomptes;
So with wikked wille and wraththe my werkmen I paye.

[14] The 'summer game' was a midsummer athletic festival, often conducted indecorously.
[15] 'Blessed is the man.' Ps. i.1.
[16] 'Blessed are all.' Ps. ii.12.

"Yif any man döth me a benfait° or helpeth me at nede, — good deed

I am unkynde ayein° his curteisye and can noughte understonde it. — in return for

For I have and have hadde some dele haukes° maneres: — **dele haukes** part of the hunting hawk's

445 I nam noughte lured with love, but there ligge° aughte under the thombe. — **but . . .** except where lies

The kyndenesse that myne evene-Cristene kidde° me fernyere,° — **evene-Cristene kidde** fellow Christian showed   formerly

Sixty sythes° I, Sleuthe,° have foryete° it sith.° — times   Sloth   forgotten   since

In speche and in sparynge of speche, y-spilte° many a tyme — I have wasted

Bothe flesche° and fissche and many other vitailles; — meat

450 Bothe bred and ale, butter, melke, and chese

Forsleuthed° in my servyse til it myghte serve no man. — Wasted

"I ran aboute in youthe and yaf° me noughte to lerne, — gave

And evere sith° have be beggere for my foule sleuthe,° — since   sloth

Heu michi, quod sterilem vitam duxi juvenilem."°

455 "Repentestow thee° naughte?" quod Repentance, and righte with that he° swowned, — **Repentestow thee** Do you repent / he (Sloth)

Til *Vigilate*° the veille fette° water at his eyghen, — Watch   **veille fette** watcher brought

And flatte° it on his face, and faste on him criede — dashed

And seide, "Ware thee fram wanhope, wolde° thee bitraye. — **Ware . . .** Beware of despair, which would

'I am sori for my synnes,' sey so to thiselve,

460 And bete thiselve on the breste and bidde° Hym of grace; — pray

For is no gült here so grete that His goodnesse nys° more." — is not

Thanne sat Sleuthe° up and seyned° hym swithe,° — Sloth   blessed   quickly

And made avowe° to-fore God for his foule sleuthe; — vow

"Shal no Sondaye be this sevene yere, but sykenesse it lette,° — prevent

465 That I ne shal do° me er day to the dere cherche, — bring

And heren° matines and masse as° I a monke were. — hear   as if

Shal none ale after mete° holde me thennes,° — food   thence

Tyl I have evensonge herde, I behote° to the Rode.° — vow   Cross

And yete wil I yelde ayein,° if I so moche have, — **yelde ayein** give back

470 Al that I wikkedly wan sithen° I wytte° hadde. — since   reason

And though my liflode lakke, leten° I nelle,° — **liflode . . .** livelihood be lacking, stop   will not

That eche man ne shal have his ar° I hennes wende:° — before   **hennes wende** go hence

And with the residue and the remenaunt, bi the Rode of Chestre,

454. Woe is me that I have lived such a barren youth.

I shal seke Treuthe arst° ar I se Rome!"   first

475   Robert the robbere on *Reddite*[17] lokede,
And for° ther was noughte wher-of,° he wepe swithe°   because **noughte wher-of** no
sore.   wherewithal   very
Ac yet the synful shrewe° seyde to hymselve,   wretch
"Cryst that on Calvarye uppon the crosse deydest,
Tho° Dismas[18] my brother bisoughte yow of grace,   When

480   And haddest mercy on that man for *memento*° sake,   remember me
So rewe° on this robbere that *reddere*° ne have,   pity to repay
Ne nevere wene° to wynne with crafte that° I owe.   think **crafte that** skill what
But for thi mykel° mercy mitigacioun I biseche;   great
Ne dampne° me noughte at Domesday for that I did so   condemn
ille."

485   What bifel of this feloun I can noughte faire schewe.
Wel I wote° he wepte faste water with bothe his eyen,   know
And knowleched his gült to Cryst yete eftsones,°   soon after
That *penitencia* his pyke° he shulde polsche° newe,   pikestaff polish
And lepe with hym over londe al his lyf tyme,

490   For he had leyne° bi Latro,° Luciferes Aunte.   lain the Robber
And thanne had Repentaunce reuthe and redde° hem   **reuthe ...** pity and bade
alle to knele,
"For I shal biseche for al synful owre Saveoure of grace,
To amende us of owre mysdedes and do mercy to us
alle.
"Now God," quod he, "that of thi goodnesse gonne°   did
the worlde make,

495   And of naughte madest aughte and man moste liche to
thiselve,
And sithen suffredest° for to synne, a sikenesse to us alle,   suffered him
And al for the best, as I bileve, what evere the boke
telleth,

O felix culpa! O necessarium peccatum Ade! etc.[19]

For though that synne thi sone sent was to this erthe,

500   And bicam man of a mayde, mankynde to save,
And madest thiself with thi sone and us synful y-liche,°   **synful y-liche** sinful ones alike

Faciamus hominem ad ymaginem et similitudinem nostram;
Et alibi, qui manet in caritate, in Deo manet, et Deus in eo.[20]

"And sith° with thi self° sone in owre sute° deydest   then own suit of flesh

---

[17] 'Render to all men their dues.' Rom. xiii.7.
[18] Apocryphal name of the penitent thief crucified with Christ.
[19] 'O happy fault: O necessary sin of Adam! etc.' From Holy Saturday canticle *Exsultet*.
[20] 'Let us make man in our image and likeness; and elsewhere: he who dwells in love, dwells in God, and
God in him.' Gen. i.26, I John iv.16.

505 On Gode Fryday for mannes sake at ful tyme of the
      daye,
    There° thiself ne thi sone no sorwe in deth feledest;   Where
    But in owre secte° was the sorwe,° and thi sone it ladde,°   following sorrow led

      Captivam duxit captivitatem.[21]

    The sonne for sorwe therof les° syghte for a tyme   gave up
510 Aboute mydday whan most lighte is° and mele tyme of   there is
      seintes;
    Feddest with thi fresche blode owre forfadres in
      derknesse,

      Populus qui ambulabat in tenebris, vidit lucem magnam.[22]

    And thorw the lighte that lepe out of thee, Lucifer was
      blent,°   blinded
    And blewe° alle thi blissed into the blisse of Paradise.   you heralded
515   "The thrydde daye after thow yedest° in owre sute,°   went suit of flesh
    A synful Marie thee seighe ar° Seynte Marie thi dame,°   before mother
    And al to solace synful,° thow suffredest it so were:°   sinful ones to be

      Non veni vocare justos, sed peccatores ad penitenciam.[23]

    And al that Marke hath y-made, Mathew, Johan, and
      Lucas,
520 Of thyne doughtiest° dedes were don in owre armes.°   most valiant armor

      Verbum caro factum est, et habitavit in nobis.[24]

    And bi so moche, me semeth, the sikerere° we mowe°   more securely may
    Bydde° and biseche if it be thi wille,   Pray
    That art owre Fader and owre Brother, be merciable to
      us,
525 And have reuthe° on thise ribaudes° that repente hem   pity sinners
      here sore,
    That evere thei wratthed° thee in this worlde in worde,   angered
      thoughte, or dedes."
     Thanne hent° Hope an horne of *Deus, tu conversus*   seized
      vivificabis nos,[25]
    And blew it with *Beati quorum remisse sunt iniquitates,*[26]
    That alle seyntes in hevene songen at ones:

[21] 'He led captivity captive.' Eph. iv.8.
[22] 'The people who walked in darkness have seen a great light.' Isa. ix.2.
[23] 'I came to call not the just, but sinners to penitence.' Matt. ix.13.
[24] 'The word was made flesh and dwelt among us.' John i.14.
[25] 'God, You having turned shall refresh us.' Ps. lxxxi.20.
[26] 'Blessed are those whose sins are forgiven.' Ps. xxxii.1.

530   *Homines et jumenta salvabis, quemadmodum multiplicasti*
          misericordiam tuam, Deus, etc.[27]

A thousand of men tho° thrungen togyderes;   then
Criede upward to Cryst and to his clene° moder   pure
To have Grace to go with hem, Treuthe to seke.
    Ac there was wyghte° non so wys the wey thider   man
      couthe,°   knew
535 But blustreden forth as bestes over bankes and hilles,
Til late was and longe that thei a lede° mette,   man
Apparailled as a paynym° in pylgrymes wyse.°   Saracen guise
He bare a burdoun° y-bounde with a brode liste°   staff   strip of cloth
In a withewyndes wise° y-wounden aboute.   **withewyndes wise** bindweed's
                                                                       manner
540 A bolle° and a bagge he bare by his syde;   bowl
An hundreth° of ampulles° on his hatt seten,°   hundred   phials   were placed
Signes° of Synay,° and shelles of Galice.°   Emblems   Sinai   Galicia
And many a cruche° on his cloke and keyes of Rome,   cross
And the vernicle° bifore, for men shulde knowe   Veronica's veil
545 And se bi his signes whom he soughte hadde.
This folke frayned° hym firste fro whennes° he come.   asked   whence
    "Fram Synay," he seyde, "and fram owre Lordes
      sepulcre;
In Bethleem and in Babiloyne I have ben in bothe,
In Ermonye,° in Alisaundre, in many other places.   Armenia
550 Ye may se bi my signes° that sitten° on myn hatte   emblems   are placed
That I have walked ful wyde in wete and in drye
And soughte gode seyntes for my soules helth."
    "Knowestow° oughte a corseint° that men calle   Do you know   holy person
      Treuthe?
Coudestow° aughte wissen° us the weye where that wy°   Could you   teach   person
      dwelleth?"
555   "Nay, so me God helpe!" seide the gome° thanne,   man
"I seygh nevere palmere with pike ne with scrippe
Axen after hym er til° now in this place."   **er til** formerly until
"Peter!"° quod a plowman and put forth his hed,   By Peter
"I knowe hym as kyndely° as clerke döth his bokes;   intimately
560 Conscience and Kynde Witte kenned° me to his place,   **Kynde . . .** Common Sense direc
And deden° me suren° hym sikerly° to serve hym for   made   pledge   surely
      evere,
Bothe to sowe and to sette° the while I swynke° myghte. plant   work
I have ben his folwar al this fifty wyntre;
Bothe y-sowen his sede and sued° his bestes,   driven
565 Withinne and withouten wayted° his profyt.   looked after
I dyke° and I delve;° I do that Treuthe hoteth.°   dig ditches   dig   bids

[27] 'You shall save men and beasts, just as you have increased Your mercy, God, etc.' Ps. xxxvi.6, 7.

Some tyme I sowe and some tyme I thresche;
In tailoures crafte° and tynkares crafte what Treuthe can   skill
    devyse,
I weve and I wynde and do what Treuthe hoteth.
570   "For thoughe I seye it myself, I serve hym to paye.°   his satisfaction
Ich have my hüire° of hym wel and otherwhiles° more.   pay sometimes
He is the prestest° payer that pore men knoweth;   quickest
He ne withhalt° non hewe° his hyre that he ne hath it at   withholds laborer
    even.
He is as low° as a lombe and loveliche of speche,   meek
575 And yif ye wilneth to wite° where that he dwelleth,   know
I shal wisse° yow witterly° the weye to his place."   teach truly
    "Ye, leve° Pieres," quod this pilgrymes, and profered   dear
    hym hüire°   pay
For to wende with hem to Treuthes dwellyng place.
    "Nay, bi my soules helth," quod Pieres, and gan° for   began
    to swere,
580 "I nolde fange° a ferthynge, for Seynt Thomas shryne!   **nolde fange** would not take
Treuthe wolde love me the lasse a longe tyme
    there-after!
Ac if ye wilneth to wende° wel, this is the weye thider   go
That I shal say to yow and sette yow in the sothe.°   truth
    "Ye mote° go thourgh Mekenesse, bothe men and   must
    wyves,
585 Tyl ye come into Conscience, that Cryst wite° the   may know
    sothe,
That ye loven owre Lorde God levest° of alle thinges,   dearest
And thanne yowre neighbores nexte in non wise
    apeyre°   **wise apeyre** manner harm
Otherwyse than thow woldest he wroughte° to   did
    thiselve.
    "And so boweth° forth bi a broke,° *Beth-buxom°-*   go brook mild
    of-spech,
590 Tyl ye fynden a forth,° *Yowre-fadres-honoureth,*   ford

        Honora patrem et matrem,° etc.   ***Honora*** ... Honor father and mother

Wadeth in that water and wascheth yow wel there,
And ye shul lepe the lightloker° al yowre lyf tyme.   more lightly
And so shaltow° se *Swere-noughte-but-if it-be-for-nede-*   you will
595 *And-namelich-an-ydel°-the-name-of-God-Almyghti.*   **namelich** ... especially-in-vain
    "Thanne shaltow come by a crofte,° but come thow   enclosure
    noughte there-inne;
That crofte hat° *Coveyte-noughte-mennes-catel-ne-her-*   is called
    wyves-
Ne-none-of-her-servauntes-that-noyen°-hem-myghte.   **that-noyen** lest-you-injure

Loke ye breke no bowes° there but if it be yowre owne.　　boughs
600　Two stokkes° there stondeth, ac stynte° ye noughte　　stocks　stop
　　　　there;
　　They hatte *Stele-noughte, Ne-Slee°-noughte*; stryke°　　Slay　go
　　　　forth by bothe,
　　And leve hem on thi left halfe° and loke noughte　　side
　　　　there-after;
　　And holde wel thyne haliday heighe° til even.　　holy
　　Thenne shaltow blenche° at a berghe,° *Bere-no-false-*　　shaltow blenche you will turn　hill
　　　　witnesse.
605　He is frithed° in with floreines° and other fees many;　　enclosed　florins
　　Loke thow plukke no plante there for peril of thi soule.
　　Thanne shall ye se *Sey-soth°-so-it-be-to-done-*　　the truth
　　In-no-manere-ellis-naughte-for-no-mannes-biddynge.
　　　　"Thanne shaltow come to a courte° as clere as the　　mansion court
　　　　sonne;
610　The mote is of Mercy, the manere° aboute,　　manor
　　And alle the wallis ben of Witte° to holden Wille oute;　　Wisdom
　　And kerneled° with Crystendome, man-kynde to save,　　crenelated
　　Boterased° with *Bileve-so-or-thow-beest-noughte-y-saved.*　　Buttressed
　　　　"And alle the houses ben hiled,° halles and chambres,　　roofed
615　With no lede, but with Love and *Lowe°-speche-as-*　　Humble
　　　　bretheren.
　　The brügge° is of *Bidde°-wel-the-bette°-may-thow-spede*;°　　bridge　Pray　better　prosper
　　Eche piler° is of penaunce, of preyeres to seyntes;　　pillar
　　Of almes deeds ar the hokes that the gates hangen on.
　　　　"*Grace* hatte° the gateward,° a gode man for sothe,°　　is called　gatekeeper　for sothe indeed
620　Hys man hatte *Amende°-yow*, for many man him　　Reform
　　　　knoweth.
　　Telleth hym this tokene, that *Treuthe* wite° the sothe:　　may know
　　'I parfourned° the penaunce the prest me enjoyned　　performed
　　And am ful sori for my synnes, and so I shal evere
　　Whan I thinke there-on, theighe° I were a pope.'　　though
625　　　"*Biddeth*° *Amende-yow* meke him til° his maistre　　Ask　meke . . . to humble himsel[f]
　　　　ones,
　　To wayve° up the wiket that the womman shette　　raise
　　Tho° *Adam and Eve eten apples unrosted.*　　When

　　　　Per Evam cunctis clausa est, et per Mariam Virginem iterum
　　　　　　patefacta est;°

　　For he° hath the keye and the cliket° though the Kynge　　she　latch
　　　　slepe.
630　And if *Grace* graunte thee to go in this wise,°　　manner
　　Thow shalt see in thiselve *Treuthe* sitte in thine herte,

628. Through Eve the gate was closed to all, and through Mary the Virgin again it was opened

In a cheyne of charyté, as° thow a childe were,   as if

To suffre Hym and segge° noughte ayein° thi Sires   speak against
    wille.

   "Ac bewar thanne of Wraththe, that is a wikked
    shrewe;

635 He hath Envye to Hym that in thine herte sitteth

And pukketh° forth Pruyde to prayse thiselven.   pushes

The boldnesse° of thi bienfetes° maketh thee blynde   presumption good deeds
    thanne,

And thanne worstow° dryven oute as dew, and the dore   you will be
    closed,

Kayed and cliketed° to kepe thee withouten   **Kayed**... Locked and latched

640 Happily° an hundreth wyntre ar thow eft° entre.   Perhaps again

Thus myght thow lesen° His love, to late° wel by   lose think
    thiselve,

And nevere happiliche efte entre but grace thow have.

   "Ac there aren sevene sustren° that serven Treuthe   sisters
    evere

And aren porteres of the posternes that to the place
    longeth.°   belong

645 That one hat° Abstenence and Humilité an other,   is called

Charité and Chastité ben His chief maydenes,

Pacience and Pees,° moche poeple thei helpeth,   Peace

Largenesse° the lady, heo let° in ful manye,   Bounty **heo let** she lets

Heo hath hulpe a thousande oute of the develes
    ponfolde.°   pound

650 "And who° is sibbe° to this sevene, so me God helpe,   whoever akin

He is wonderliche° welcome and faire underfongen.°   wonderfully received

And but if ye be syb° to summe of thise sevene,   akin

It is ful harde bi myne heved,"° quod Peres, "for any of   head
    yow alle

To geten ingonge° at any gate there but grace be the   entrance
    more."

655 "Now, bi Cryst," quod a cutpurs, "I have no kynne
    there!"

   "Ne I," quod an apewarde,° "bi aughte that I   monkey-keeper
    knowe!"

   "Wite° God," quod a wafrestre,° "wist I° this for   Save us wafer-seller **wist I** if I
    sothe,°   knew **for sothe** indeed

Shulde° I nevere ferthere a fote for no freres   Should go
    prechynge."

   "Yüs," quod Pieres the Plowman, and pukked° hem   pushed
    alle to gode,°   **to gode** toward good behavior

660 "Mercy is a maydene there, hath myghte over hem
    alle.

And she is syb° to alle synful and her Sone also.　　akin
And thorughe the helpe of hem two—hope thow none
　　other—
Thow myghte gete grace there, bi so° thow go　　**bi so** provided
　　bityme."°　　in time
　　"By Seynt Poule," quod a Pardonere, "peraventure
　　I be noughte knowe° there.　　known
665　I wil go fecche my box with my brevettes° and a bulle°　　documents of indulgence
　　with bisshopes lettres!"　　document
　　"By Cryst," quod a comune womman,° "thi　　**comune womman** prostitute
　　companye wil I folwe,°　　follow
Thow shalt sey I am thi süstre." I ne wot° where thei　　know
　　bicome.°　　went

Canto VII

Treuthe herde telle her-of and to Peres he sent,
To taken his teme and tülyen° the erthe,　　till
And purchaced° hym a pardoun *a poena et a culpa*[1]　　provided
For hym and for his heires for evermore after.
5　And bad hym holde hym at home and eryen° his leyes;°　　plow　fields
And alle° that halpe hym to erie, to sette,° or to sowe,　　to all　plant
Or any other myster° that myghte Pieres availle,°　　trade　assist
Pardoun with° Pieres Plowman Treuthe hath　　along with
　　y-graunted.
Kynges and knyghtes that kepen° Holy Cherche　　guard
10　And ryghtfullych in reumes° reulen the peple　　realms
Han pardoun thourgh Purgatorie to passe ful lyghtly,
With patriarkes and prophetes in Paradise to be felawes.
Bisshopes y-blessed,° yif thei ben as thei shulden,　　consecrated
Legistres° of bothe the lawes,[2] the lewed° there-with to　　Advocates　unlearned
　　preche,
15　And in as moche as thei mowe, amende° alle synful,°　　**mowe, amende** can, correct
Aren peres° with the Apostles (this pardoun Piers　　sinful ones
　　sheweth),　　peers
And at the Day of Dome° atte heigh deyse° to sytte.　　Judgment　dais
Marchauntz in the margyne° hadden many yeres,°　　margin of the Bull　years of
Ac none *a poena et a culpa*[1] the Pope nolde° hem　　indulgence
　　graunte,　　would not

[1] 'From punishment and from guilt.' Indulgences usually removed only punishment.
[2] Both parts of the Ten Commandments: the laws concerning our duty to God and those concerning our duty to our fellow man.

20 For thei holde nought her halidayes as Holi Cherche
    techeth,
And for° thei swere "By her° soule" and "So God   *because   their*
    moste hem helpe"
Ayein° clene conscience her catel° to selle.   *Against   goods*
    Ac under his secret seel Treuthe sent hem a lettre,
That they shulde bügge° boldely that° hem best liked,°   *buy   what   pleased*
25 And sithenes selle it ayein° and save the wynnynge,   *again*
And amende *mesondieux* there-myde and myseyse°   **amende . . .** repair hospitals
    folke helpe,   therewith and unfortunate
And wikked wayes wightlich° hem amende;°   **wikked . . .** bad roads quickly
And do bote° to brügges° that to-broke were,   improve
Marien° maydenes or maken hem nonnes;   **do bote** make repairs   bridges
30 Pore peple and prisounes° fynden hem here fode,°   *Dower*
And sette scoleres to scole or to somme other craftes;   *prisoners   food*
Releve Religioun and renten° hem bettere—   **Releve . . .** Assist religious orders
"And I shal sende yow, myselve, Seynt Michel myn   and endow
    archangel,
That no devel shal yow dere ne fere° yow in yowre   **dere . . .** harm nor frighten
    deyinge,°   *dying*
35 And witen° yow fro wanhope° if ye wil thus worche,°   *guard   despair   do*
And sende yowre sowles in safté° to my seyntes in joye."   *safety*
    Thanne were Marchauntz mery; many wepten for
    joye,
And preyseden Pieres the Plowman that purchaced°   *provided*
    this bulle.°   *document*
    Men of lawe lest° pardoun hadde that pleteden° for   *least   pleaded*
    mede,°   *bribe*
40 For the Sauter° saveth hem noughte such as taketh   *Psalter*
    yiftes,°   *gifts*
And namelich of° innocentz that none yvel ne   **namelich of** especially from
    kunneth:°   *know*

    Super innocentem munera non accipies.[3]

Pledoures° shulde peynen hem° to plede for such, and   *Pleaders*   **peynen hem** trouble
    helpe;   themselves
Prynces and prelates shulde paye for her° travaille: *their (the pleaders')*

45   *A regibus et pryncipibus erit merces eorum.*°

Ac many a justice and juroure wolde for Johan° do   *friend John*
    more
Than *pro Dei pietate,*° leve thow none other!   ***pro . . .*** for devotion to God

[3] 'Against the innocent you shall accept no bribes.' See Ps. xv.5.
45. From kings and princes shall be their wages.

Ac he that spendeth his speche and speketh for the
    pore

That is innocent and nedy and no man appeireth,°   harms
50 Conforteth hym in that cas withoute coveytise of
    yiftes,°   gifts
And scheweth° lawe for owre Lordes love as he it hath   explains
    lerned,
Shal no devel at his ded-day deren° hym a myghte°   harm   bit
That he ne wörth sauf° and his sowle. The Sauter°   ne . . . will not be saved   Psalter
    bereth witnesse:

    Domine, quis habitabit in tabernaculo tuo, etc.[4]

55   Ac to bügge° water, ne wynde, ne witte,° ne fyre the   buy   intelligence
    fierthe!°—   fourth
Thise foure the Fader of hevene made to this folde° in   earth
    comune.
Thise ben Treuthes tresores, trewe folke to helpe,
That nevere shal wax ne wanye withoute God
    hymselve.
Whan thei drawen on to deye, and indulgences wolde
    have,
60 Her pardoun is ful petit° at her partyng hennes,°   little   hence
That° any mede° of mene° men for her motyng° taketh.   If   bribe   poor   pleading
Ye legistres° and lawyers holdeth this for treuthe,   advocates
That, yif that I lye, Mathew is to blame,
For he bad me make° yow this, and this proverbe me   compose
    tolde,

65   *Quodcumque vultis ut faciant vobis homines, facite eis.*[5]

    Alle lybbyng° laboreres that lyven with° her hondes,   living   by
That trewlich taken and trewlich wynnen,
And lyven in love and in lawe for her lowe° hertis,   humble
Haveth the same absolucioun that sent was to Peres.°   Piers
70   Beggeres ne bidderes° ne beth noughte in the bulle,°   spongers   document
But if the suggestioun° be soth° that shapeth hem to   reason   honest
    begge.
For he that beggeth or bit,° but if he have nede,   asks
He is fals with° the Fende° and defraudeth the nedy,   along with   Fiend
And also he bigileth the gyvere ageines his wil.
75 For if he wist° that he were noughte nedy, he wolde   knew
    yive° that another   give
That were more nedy than he so the nediest shuld be
    hulpe.

[4] 'Lord, who shall dwell in Thy tabernacle, etc.' Ps. xv.1.
[5] 'Whatever you wish that men should do to you, do to them.' Matt. vii.12.

Catoun kenneth° men thus and the clerke of the stories,[6]   **Catoun kenneth** Cato teaches
Cui des, videto[7] is Catounes techynge,
And in the stories he techeth to bistowe thyn almes:

80   *Sit elemosina tua in manu tua, donec studes cui des.*°

    Ac Gregori was a gode man, and bad us gyven alle
    That asketh, for His love that us alle leneth:°   gave

    Non eligas cui miserearis, ne forte pretereas illum qui meretur
    accipere; quia incertum est pro quo Deo magis placeas.[8]

    For wite ye nevere who is worthi, ac God wote who
        hath nede.
85 In hym that taketh is the treccherye if any tresoun
        wawe;°   goes about
    For he that yiveth, yeldeth, and yarketh° hym to reste,   **yiveth** ... gives, repays God, and
    And he that biddeth,° borweth, and bryngeth hymself   prepares
        in dette.   begs
    For beggeres borwen evermo,° and her borghe° is God   evermore   security
        Almyghti
    To yelden hem that yiveth hem and yet usure° more: pay interest

90   *Quare non dedisti peccuniam meam ad mensam, ut ego veniens*
        cum usuris exegissem illam?[9]

    For-thi biddeth nought, ye beggeres, but if ye have
        gret nede;
    For who-so hath to büggen° hym bred, the boke bereth   buy
        witnesse,
    He hath ynough that hath bred ynough though he have
        nought elles:

    Satis dives est qui non indiget pane.[10]

95 Late° usage be yowre solace of seyntes lyves redynge.   Let
    The boke banneth beggarie and blameth hem in this
        manere:

    Junior fui, etenim senui; et non vidi justum derelictum, nec semen
        eius querens panem.[11]

---

[6] A reference to Peter Comestor (d. 1198), author of *Historia Scholastica*, a miscellaneous collection of narratives from the Bible and other sources.
[7] 'Watch to whom you give.' Breves Sententiae 23, *Distichs*.
80. Let your alms be in your hand until you study to whom you give.
[8] 'Choose not whom you shall pity, nor by chance pass over that one who deserves to receive; because it is uncertain in virtue of whom you are more pleasing to God.' St. Jerome, *Commentary on Eccl.*, xi.6.
[9] 'Why have you not given my money to the bank, so that I, coming, might have required it with interest?' Luke xix.23.
[10] 'He is rich enough who does not lack bread.' St. Jerome, *Epistles*, cxxv.
[11] 'I have been young; now I am old; and I have not seen the just abandoned, nor his seed begging bread.' Ps. xxxvii.25.

For ye live in no love ne no lawe holde;
Many of yow ne wedde nought the wommen that ye
   with delen,
100 But as wilde bestis with wehe wörthen uppe° and   **wehe** . . . a neigh mount
   worchen,
And bryngeth forth barnes° that bastardes men calleth.   children
Or° the bakke or some bone he breketh in his youthe,°   Either offspring
And sitthe gon faiten° with youre fauntes° for evermore   **sitthe** . . . then go begging
   after.   children
There is moo° mysshape peple amonge thise beggeres   more
105 Than of alle maner men that on this molde° walketh,   earth
And thei that lyve thus here lyf mowe° lothe the tyme   may
That evere he was man wrought whan he shal hennes°   hence
   fare.
Ac olde men and hore,° that helplees ben of   hoary
   strengthe,
And women with childe, that worche ne mowe,°   **ne mowe** cannot
110 Blynde and bede-red° and broken here membres,   bedridden
That taketh this myschief mekelych, as meseles° and   **as meseles** such as lepers
   othere,
Han° as pleyne° pardoun as the plowman hymself.   Have full
For love of her lowe° hertis owre Lorde hath hem   humble
   graunted
Here penaunce and her purgatorie here on this erthe.
115 "Pieres," quod a prest tho,° "thi pardoun most° I rede,   then must
For I wil construe eche clause and kenne° it thee on   teach
   Engliche."
And Pieres at his preyere° the pardoun unfoldeth,   request
And I bihynde hem bothe bihelde al the bulle.°   document
Al in two lynes it lay and nought a leef more,
120 And was writen right thus, in witnesse of Treuthe:

    Et qui bona egerunt, ibunt in vitam eternam;
    Qui vero mala, in ignem eternum.[12]

"Peter!"° quod the prest tho.° "I can no pardoun   By Peter then
   fynde,
But 'Dowel,'° and have wel, and God shal have thi   Do-well
   sowle,
125 And do yvel, and have yvel, hope thow non other,
But after thi ded-day the devel shal have thi sowle!' "
And Pieres for pure tene° pulled it atweyne,   vexation

---

[12] 'And those who have done good shall go into eternal life, those who have done evil, into eternal fire.'
Athanasian Creed, from Matt. xxv.46.

And seyde: "*Si ambulavero in medio umbrae mortis,*
Non timebo mala; quoniam tu mecum es.[13]

130 I shal cessen of my sowyng," quod Pieres, "and swynk°   work
     nought so harde,
Ne about my bely joye so bisi be namore!
Of preyers and of penaunce my plow shal ben herafter,
And wepen whan I shulde slepe, though whete° bred   wheat
     me faille.
    "The prophete his payn° ete in penaunce and in   bread
     sorwe;°   sorrow

135 By that° the Sauter° seith, so dede° other manye.   **By that** What   Psalter   did
That° loveth God lelly,° his lyflode° is ful esy: He who   loyally   livelihood

    Fuerunt mihi lacrimae meae panes die ac nocte.[14]

And but if Luke lye, he lereth° us bi foules,°   teaches   birds
We shulde nought be too bisy aboute the worldes
     blisse.

140 *Ne solliciti sitis*[15] he seyth in the gospel,
And sheweth us bi ensamples us selve to wisse.°   direct
The foules on the felde, who fynt° hem mete° at   finds   food
     wynter?
Have thei no gernere° to go to but God fynt hem alle."   barn
    "What!" quod the prest to Perkyn, "Peter, as me
     thinketh,°   **me thinketh** it seems to me

145 Thow art lettred a litel. Who lerned thee on° boke?"   in
    "Abstinence the Abbesse," quod Pieres, "myne
     A B C me taughte,
And Conscience come afterward and kenned me moche
     more."
    "Were thow a prest, Pieres," quod he, "thow
     mighte preche where thow sholdest,
As devynour° in devynyté with *dixit insipiens*[16] to thi   teacher
     teme."°   **to . . . as** your theme

150   "Lewed lorel!"° quod Pieres. "Litel lokestow° on the   **Lewed lorel** Unlearned fellow   do
     Bible,   you look
On Salomones sawes seldon thow biholdest,

    Eice derisores et jurgia cum eis, ne crescant, etc."[17]

The prest and Perkyn apposeden eyther° other,   each
And I thorw here wordes awoke and waited° aboute   looked

[13] 'If I shall walk in the middle of the shadow of death, I shall not fear evil, because You are with me.' Ps. xxiii.4.
[14] 'My tears have been food for me day and night.' Ps. xlii.3.
[15] 'Be not solicitous.' Matt. vi.25, 31.
[16] 'The fool has spoken.' Ps. xiv.1, liii.1.
[17] 'Cast out the scorners and contention with them, so that they may not increase, etc.' Prov. xxii.10.

155 And seigh the sonne in the south sitte° that tyme,   *set*
    Metelees and monelees° on Malverne hülles,°   **Metelees . . .** Foodless and
                                            moneyless   hills
    Musyng on this meteles;° and my waye Ich yede.°   *vision   went*
      Many tyme this meteles hath maked me to studye
      Of that° I seigh slepyng if it so be myghte,   *what*
160 And also for Peres the Plowman, ful pensyf in herte,
    And which a pardoun Peres hadde, alle the peple to
         conforte,
    And how the prest impugned it with two propre°   *distinct*
         wordes.
    Ac I have no savoure in songwarie,° for I se it ofte faille.   **savoure . . .** delight in dream-
                                             interpretation
    Catoun and Canonistres° conseilleth us to leve°   **Catoun . . .** Cato and the Canonists
                                             stop
165 To sette sadnesse° in songewarie, for *sompnia ne cures*.[18]   **To . . .** Putting faith
      Ac for° the boke Bible bereth witnesse   *as*
    How Danyel devyned the dremes of a kynge
    That was Nabugodonosor nempned of° clerkis,   **nempned of** named by
    Daniel seyde, "Sire Kynge, thi dremeles° bitokneth   *dream*
170 That unkouth° knyghtes shul come thi kyngdom to   *strange*
         cleve;
    Amonges lowere lordes thi londe shal be departed."°   *divided*
    And as Danyel devyned, in dede it felle° after;   *befell*
    The kynge lese° his lordship and lower men it hadde.   *lost*
      And Joseph mette° merveillously how the mone and   *dreamed*
         the sonne
175 And the ellevene sterres hailsed° hym alle.   *greeted*
    Thanne Jacob jugged Josephes swevene:°   *dream*
      "Beau filtz,"° quod his fader, "for defaute° we   **Beau filtz** Fair son   want
         shullen,°   *must*
    I myself and my sones, seche° thee for nede."   *seek*
      It bifel as his fader seyde in Pharaoes tyme,
180 That Joseph was justice Egipte to loken;°   *look after*
    It bifel as his fader tolde; his frendes there hym soughte.
      And al this maketh me on this meteles° to thynke,   *vision*
    And how the prest preved° no pardoun to Dowel°   *proved*   **to Dowel** like Do-well
    And demed that Dowel indulgences passed,°   *surpassed*
185 Biennales, and triennales,° and bisschopes lettres,   **Biennales . . .** Biennial and trienni[al]
                                             masses for the dead
    And how Dowel at the day of dome° is dignelich   *judgment*
         underfongen,°   **dignelich underfongen** worthily
                                             received
    And passeth al the pardoun of Seynt Petres Cherche.
      Now hath the Pope powere pardoun to graunte the
         peple
    Withouten eny penaunce to passen into hevene.
190 This is owre bileve as lettered men us techeth:

---

[18] 'Pay no heed to dreams.' Cato, *Distichs*, ii.31.

Quodcumque ligaveris super terram, erit ligatum et in celis, etc.[19]

And so I leve lelly° (Lordes forbode ellis!)   loyally
That pardoun and penaunce and preyeres don save
Soules that have synned sevene sithes° dedly.   times
195 Ac to trust to thise triennales° trewly me thinketh°   triennial masses for the dead   **me thinketh** it seems to me
Is nought so syker° for the soule, certis,° as is Dowel.°   sure   certainly   Do-well
For-thi I rede° yow renkes° that riche ben on this erthe,   advise   men
Uppon trust of yowre tresoure triennales to have,
Be ye never the balder° to breke the ten hestes.°   bolder   commandments
200 And namelich,° ye maistres,° mayres, and jugges,   especially   lords
That han the welthe of this worlde and for wyse men ben holden,°   considered
To purchace yow pardoun and the popis bulles,
At the dredeful dome° whan dede shullen° rise,   judgment   shall
And comen alle bifor Cryst acountis to yelde,°   render
205 How thow laddest thi lyf here and His lawes keptest,
And how thow dedest day bi day, the dome wil reherce.°   declare
A poke° ful of pardoun there ne Provinciales lettres,   sack
Theigh° ye be founde in the fraterneté of alle the foure ordres,   Though
And have indulgences double-folde, but if Dowel° yow helpe,   Do-well
210 I sette yowre patentes and yowre pardounz at one pies-hele!°   pea pod
For-thi I conseille alle Cristene to crye God mercy,
And Marie His moder be owre mene° bitwene,   intermediary
That God gyve us grace here, ar we gone hennes,°   hence
Suche werkes to werche while we ben here
215 That after owre deth-day, Dowel reherce,°   **Dowel reherce** Do-well may declare
At the day of dome, we dede° as he highte.°   did   ordered

Canto XVIII

[Lines 228–431]
Thanne was there a wighte° with two brode eyen,   person
Boke highte° that beupere,° a bolde man of speche.   **Boke highte** Bible was called   reverend father
"By Godes body," quod this Boke, "I wil bere witnesse,
That tho° this barne° was y-bore° there blased a sterre,   when   child   born

[19] 'Whatever you have bound upon earth it shall be bound also in heaven, etc.' Matt. xvi.19.

5 That alle the wyse of this worlde in o witte° acordeden   **o witte** one mind
That such a barne was borne in Bethleem Citee
That mannes° soule sholde save and synne destroye.   man's
   "And alle the elementz,"° quod the Boke, "her-of   four elements
    bereth witnesse.
That He was God that al wroughte, the walkene° firste   welkin
    shewed;
10 Tho° that weren in hevene token *stella comata*°   Those   **token . . .** took a comet
And tendeden° hir as a torche to reverence his birthe.   kindled
The lyghte folwed° the Lorde into the lowe erthe.   followed
The water witnessed that He was God, for He went on it.
Peter the Apostel parceyved his gate,°   going
15 And as He went on the water, wel Hym knewe and
    seyde,

       'Jube me venire ad te super aquas.'[1]

   "And lo! how the sonne gan louke° her lighte in   **gan louke** locked up
    herself
Whan she seye° Hym suffre that sonne and se made.   saw
The erthe, for hevynesse that He wolde suffre,
20 Quaked as quykke° thinge and al biquashte° the roche.°   a living   crushed   rock
Lo! Helle mighte noughte holde,° but opened tho° God   hold together   when
    tholed,°   suffered
And lete oute Symondes° sons to seen Hym hange on   Simeon's
    Rode.°   Cross
And now shal Lucifer leve it, thowgh hym loth thinke.°   **hym . . .** it disgusts him
For Gygas the geaunt° with a gynne engyned°   giant   **gynne engyned** engine contrived
25 To breke and to bete doune that° ben ayeines° Jhesus.   those who   against
   "And I, Boke, wil be brent° but Jhesus rise to lyve   burned
In alle myghtes° of man, and His moder gladye,°   the powers   gladden
And conforte al His kynne° and out of care° brynge,   kin   sorrow
And al the Juwen° joye unjoignen and unlouken,°   Jews'   **unjoignen . . .** disjoin and undo
30 And, but thei reverencen His Rode° and His resurexioun   Cross
And bileve on a newe lawe, be lost lyf and soule."
   "Suffre we," seide Treuth. "I here and se bothe
How a spirit speketh to helle and bit unspere° the yatis,°   **bit unspere** orders them to unbar gates

     Attollite portas, etc."[2]

35   A voice loude in that lighte to Lucifer cryeth,
"Prynces of this place, unpynneth and unlouketh!
For here cometh with croune That° kynge is of glorie."   He Who
    Thanne syked° Sathan and seyde to hem alle: sighed
"Suche a lyghte, ayeines° owre leve, Lazar° it fette;°   against   Lazarus   fetched

[1] 'Order me to come to you upon the waters.' Matt. xiv.28.
[2] 'Lift up the gates etc.' Ps. xxiv.9.

40 Care and combraunce° is comen to us alle.   **Care . . .** Sorrow and trouble
    If this Kynge come in, mankynde wil he fecche,
    And lede it ther Hym lyketh, and lyghtlych° me bynde.   easily
    Patriarkes and prophetes han parled° her-of longe   spoken
    That such a lorde and a lyghte shulde lede hem alle
        hennes."°   hence
45   "Lysteneth," quod Lucifer, "for I this Lorde knowe—
    Bothe this Lorde and this Lighte; is longe ago I knewe
        Hym.
    May no deth hym dere,° ne no develes queyntise,°   harm   cunning
    And where He wil, is His waye. Ac war Hym° of the   **war Hym** let Him beware
        periles;
    If He reve° me my righte, He robbeth me by maistrye,°   rob   force
50 For by right and bi resoun, tho renkes° that ben here,   **tho renkes** those men
    Bodye and soule ben myne, bothe gode and ille.
    For Hymself seyde, that Sire is of hevene,
    Yif Adam ete the apple, alle shulde deye,
    And dwelle with us develes. This thretynge° He made,   threat
55 And He that sothenesse° is seyde thise wordes.   truth
    And sitthen° I seised° sevene hundreth wyntre,   since   have been in possession
    I leve° that Lawe nil° naughte lete° Hym the leest."   believe   will   allow
        "That is sothe,"° seyde Sathan, "but I me sore drede,   true
    For thow gete° hem with gyle and His gardyne breke,°   got   broke into
60 And in semblaunce of a serpent sat on the appel-tre,
    And eggedest hem to ete, Eve by hirselve,
    And toldest hir a tale, of tresoun were the wordes;
    And so thow haddest hem oute and hider atte laste.
    It is noughte graythely° geten there° gyle is the rote."°   properly   where   source
65   "For God wil nought be bigiled," quod Gobelyn,
        "ne bijaped.°   tricked
    We have no trewe title to hem, for thorwgh tresoun
        were thei dampned."°   condemned
        "Certes,° I drede me," quod the devel, "leste Treuth   Certainly
        wil hem fecche.
    This thretty° wynter, as I wene,° hath he gone and   thirty   think
        preched;
    I have assailled hym with synne, and some tyme
        y-asked
70 Where° he were God or Goddes sone. He gaf me shorte   Whether
        answere.
    And thus hath he trolled° forth this two and thretty   wandered
        wynter,
    And whan I seighe it was so, slepyng, I went
    To warne Pilates wyf what dones° man was Jhesus.   sort of
    For Juwes hateden Hym, and han done Hym to deth.

323

75 I wolde have lengthed His lyf, for I leved, yif He
　　　　deyede,
　　That His soule wolde suffre no synne in His syghte.
　　For the body, whil it on bones yede aboute, was evere
　　To save men fram synne yif hemself wolde.
　　　　"And now I se where a soule cometh hiderward
　　　　seyllynge°　　　　　　　　　　　　　　　　　sailing
80 With glorie and gret lighte; God it is, I wote wel.
　　I rede° we flee," quod he, "faste alle hennes.　　advise
　　For us were better noughte be than biden° His syghte.　endure
　　For thi lesynges,° Lucifer, loste is al owre praye.°　lies　prey
　　Firste thorw thee we fellen fro hevene so highe.
85 For° we leved thi lesynges, we loupen° oute alle with　Because　leaped
　　　　thee;
　　And now for thi last lesynge y-lore° we have Adam,　lost
　　And al owre lordeship, I leve, a° londe and a water.　on

　　　　　　Nunc princeps hujus mundi ejicietur foras."[3]

　　　　Efte° the Lighte bad unlouke and Lucifer answered.　Again
90　　"What lorde artow?"° quod Lucifer. "*Quis est iste?*"[4]　are you
　　"*Rex glorie*"[5] the Lighte sone° seide,　　　　　　at once
　　"And Lorde of myghte and of mayne and al manere
　　　　vertues, *Dominus virtutum.*[6]
　　Dukes of this dym place, anon° undo this yates,°　at once　gates
　　That Cryst may come in, the Kynges Sone of hevene."
95　　And with that breth,° helle brake,° with Beliales　speech　burst
　　　　barres;
　　For° any wye or warde° wide opene the yatis.　Before　**wye** . . . man or guard
　　Patriarkes and prophetes, *populus in tenebris,*[7]
　　Songen° Seynt Johanes songe, *Ecce Agnus Dei.*[8]　Sang
　　Lucyfer loke ne myghte° so Lyghte hym ableynte.°　**ne myghte** could not　blinded
100 And tho° that owre Lorde loved, into His lighte He　those
　　　　laughte,°　　　　　　　　　　　　　　　　　took
　　And seyde to Sathan, "Lo, here my soule to amendes°　ransom
　　For alle synneful soules, to save tho that ben worthy.
　　Myne thei be and of me; I may the bette° hem clayme.　better
　　Although resoun recorde° and right of Myself　declare
105 That if thei ete the apple alle shulde deye,
　　I bihyghte° hem nought here helle for evere.　promised
　　For the dede that thei dede,° thi deceyte it made;　did

---

[3] 'Now the prince of this world shall be cast out.' John xii.31.
[4] 'Who is that one?' Ps. xxiv.8.
[5] 'King of Glory.' Ibid.
[6] 'Lord of virtues.' Ibid.
[7] 'People in the darkness.' Isa. ix.2; Matt. iv.16.
[8] 'Behold the Lamb of God.' John i.36.

With gyle thow hem gete° agayne al resoun.   *gained*
For in my paleys,° Paradys, in persone of an addre,   *palace*
10 Falseliche thow fettest° there thynge that I loved.   *took*
"Thus y-lyke a lüsarde° with a lady° visage,   *serpent lady's*
Thevelich° thow me robbedest. The Olde Law graunteth   *Thievishly*
That gylours be begiled, and that is gode resoun:

Dentem pro dente, et oculum pro oculo.[9]

15 *Ergo,°* soule shal soule quyte,° and synne to synne wende,°   *Therefore requite correspond*
And al that man hath mysdo, I, man, wyl amende.°   *make amends for*
Membre for membre bi the Olde Lawe was amendes,°   *reparation*
And lyf for lyf also; and by that lawe I clayme it:
Adam and al his issue at my wille her-after.
20 And that Deth in hem fordid° my deth shal releve,°   *destroyed redeem*
And bothe quykke and quyte that queynte was° thorw synne.   **quykke** ... *revive and requite what was destroyed*
And, that grace gyle destruye, Good Feith it asketh.°
"So leve° it noughte, Lucifer, ayeine° the lawe I fecche hem,   *think against*
But bi right and by resoun raunceoun° here my lyges:°   *ransom subjects*

25 *Non veni solvere legem, sed adimplere.*[10]

Thow fettest° myne in my place, ayeines al resoun,   *took*
Falseliche and felounelich.° Gode Faith me it taughte,   *wickedly*
To recovre hem thorw raunceoun and bi no resoun elles,°   *other*
So, that with gyle thow gete,° thorw grace it is y-wone.   *gained*
30 Thow, Lucyfer, in lyknesse of a lüther° addere,   *evil*
Getest by gyle tho° that God loved;   *those*
And I, in lyknesse of a leode,° that Lorde am of hevene,   *man*
Graciousliche thi gyle have quytte. Go gyle ayeine gyle!
And as Adam and alle thorw a tre deyden,
35 Adam and alle thorwe a tree shal torne ayeine° to lyve;   *again*
And gyle is bigyled and in his gyle fallen:

Et cecidit in foveam quam fecit.[11]

Now bygynneth thi gyle ageyne thee to tourne,
And my grace to growe ay gretter and wyder.

[9] 'A tooth for a tooth, and an eye for an eye.' Matt. v.38.
122. And Good Faith (Justice) demands that grace destroy guile.
[10] 'I have not come to destroy the law, but to fulfill it.' Matt. v.17.
[11] 'And he has fallen into the pit that he made.' Ps. vii.15.

140	The bitternesse that thow hast browe, brouke° it thiselven;	**browe, brouke** brewed, enjoy
	That° art doctour of deth, drynke that thow madest!	You who
	"For I, that am Lorde of lyf, love is my drynke,	
	And for that drynke today, I deyde upon erthe.	
	I faughte so, me threstes° yet, for mannes° soule sake.	**me threstes** I thirst man's
145	May no drynke me moiste, ne my thrüste slake,	
	Tyl the vendage° falle in the vale of Josephath,¹²	vintage
	That I drynke righte ripe must *resureccio mortuorum*,¹³	
	And thanne shal I come as a kynge crouned with angeles	
	And han out of helle alle mennes soules.	
150	Fendes and fendekynes° bifor me shulle° stande,	**Fendes . . .** Fiends and little fiends will
	And be at my biddynge wheresoevre me lyketh.	
	And to be merciable to man, thanne my kynde° it asketh,	nature
	For we beth bretheren of blode but noughte in Baptesme alle.	
	Ac alle that beth myne hole° bretheren in blode and in Baptesme	whole
155	Shal noughte be dampned° to the deth that is withouten ende:	condemned

*Tibi soli peccavi, etc.*¹⁴

	"It is nought used in erthe to hangen a feloun	
	Ofter than ones, though he were a tretour.	
	And yif the Kynge of that kyngedome come in that tyme,	
160	There the feloun thole° sholde, deth or otherwyse,	suffer
	Lawe wolde,° he yeve° hym lyf if he loked on hym.	would have it may give
	And I that am Kynge of kynges, shal come such a tyme,	
	There dome° to the deth dampneth° al wikked.	sentence condemns
	And yif lawe wil° I loke on hem, it lithe° in my grace,	decides that lies
165	Whether thei deye or deye noughte for that thei deden° ille.	did
	Be it any thinge aboughte° the boldnesse of her synnes,	**any . . .** in any way atoned
	I may do mercy thorw rightwisnesse° and alle my wordes trewe.	righteousness
	And though Holi Writ wil that I be wroke° of hem that deden ille—	avenged

¹² Scene of the Last Judgment. See Joel iii.2, 12, 13.
¹³ 'That I may drink truly ripe new wine of resurrection of the dead.' See Joel iii.18.
¹⁴ 'Against you alone I have sinned, etc.' Ps. li.4.

326

Nullum malum impunitum, etc.[15]

170 Thei shul be clensed clereliche and wasshen of her
    synnes
    In my prisoun purgatorie til *parce* it hote,°   ***parce* . . .** spare them is commanded
    And my mercy shal be shewed to manye of my
    bretheren.
    For blode° may suffre blode, bothe hungry and a-kale,°   kin   cold
    Ac blode may nought se blode blede,° but hym rewe."°   bleed   **hym rewe** he grieve for him

175   *Audivi archana verba, quae non licet homini loqui.*[16]

    "Ac my rightwisnesse° and right shal reulen al helle,   righteousness
    And mercy al mankynde bifor me in hevene.
    For I were° an unkynde° Kynge but I my kynde holpe,°   would be   unnatural   **kynde
                                                                 holpe** kin helped
    And namelich° at such a nede ther nedes helpe bihoveth: especially

180   *Non intres in judicium cum servo tuo, domine.*[17]

    Thus bi lawe," quod owre Lorde, "lede I will fro hennes
    Tho° that me loved and leved in my comynge.   Those
    And for thi lesynge° that thow lowe° til Eve,   lie   told
    Thow shalt abye° it bittre"—and bonde hym with   atone for
    cheynes.
185   Astaroth and al the route° hidden hem in hernes.°   pack   corners
    They dorste noughte loke on owre Lorde, the boldest
    of hem alle,
    But leten Hym lede forth what Hym lyked and lete°   allowed
    what Hym liste.°   **Hym liste** He wished
    Many hundreth of angeles harpeden and songen,

        Culpat caro, purgat caro;
190   *Regnat Deus Dei caro.*[18]

    Thanne piped Pees° of poysye° a note: Peace   poetry

        "Clarior est solito post maxima nebula Phebus,
        Post inimicitias clarior est et amor.°

    After sharpe shoures,"° quod Pees, "moste shene° is the **sharpe shoures** heavy showers
    sonne;   bright
195 Is no weder warmer than after watery cloudes.
    Ne no love levere ne lever frendes,

[15] 'No evil unpunished, etc.' An allusion to Pope Innocent III, *De Contempto Mundi*, Book 3, ch. 15: "He
only is a just judge . . . who leaves no evil unpunished, no good unrewarded."
[16] 'I have heard secret words, which it is not permitted to man to speak.' II. Cor. xii.4.
[17] 'Enter not into judgment with thy servant, O Lord.' Ps. cxliii.2.
[18] 'The flesh sins, the flesh atones; the Flesh of God reigns as God.' From *Aeterne Rex Altissime*, an Ascension Matins hymn.
192-93. Brighter is the sun after the greatest cloud of Phoebus, after enmities even brighter is love.

Than after werre° and wo, whan Love and Pees° be   war Peace
    maistres.
Was nevere werre in this worlde ne wykkednesse so
    kene,°   cruel
That ne Love, an hym lüste,° to laughynge ne   **an** . . . if it pleased him
    broughte,°   turned
200 And Pees thorw pacience alle periles stopped."
    "Trewes,"° quod Treuth. "Thow tellest us soth, bi   Truce
    Jhesus!
Clippe° we in covenaunt and üch of us cüsse° other."   Embrace kiss
    "And lete no peple," quod Pees,° "perceyve that we   Peace
    chydde,
For inpossible is no thyng to Hym that is almyghty."
205   "Thow seist soth," seyde Ryghtwisnesse,° and   Righteousness
    reverentlich hir kyste,
Pees, and Pees here, *per saecula saeculorum.*°   **here** . . . kissed her, world withou
     end

Misericordia et veritas obviaverunt sibi, justicia et pax osculatae sunt.[19]

Treuth tromped tho and songe *Te Deum Laudamus,*°
And thanne luted° Love in a loude note,   played a lute

210   *Ecce quam bonum, et quam jocundum, etc.*[20]

Tyl the daye dawed,° this damaiseles° daunced,   dawned maidens
That men rongen° to the Resurexioun; and right with   rang bells
    that I waked,
And called Kitte my wyf and Kalote my doughter:
"Ariseth and reverenceth Goddes Resurrexioun,
215 And crepeth to the Crosse on knees, and kisseth it for a
    juwel!
For Goddes blissed body it bar° for owre bote.°   bore benefit
And it afereth° the Fende, for suche is the myghte,   frightens
May no grysly gost° glyde there it shadweth!"   spirit

Canto XIX

Thus I awaked and wrote what I had dremed,
And dighte° me derely and dede me° to cherche,   dressed **derely** . . . neatly and w
To here holy° the masse and to be houseled° after.   wholly **be houseled** receive
In myddes of the masse tho men yede to offrynge,   Communion

[19] 'Mercy and Truth have met each other; Justice and Peace have kissed.' Ps. lxxxv.10.
208. Truth blew a trumpet then and sang *We Praise Thee, God*
[20] 'Behold how good and how pleasant, etc.' Ps. cxxxiii.1.

5 I fel eftsones° aslepe, and sodeynly me mette°   *again*   **me mette** *I dreamed*
    That Pieres the Plowman was paynted° al blody   *stained*
    And come in with a crosse bifor the comune peple
    And righte lyke in alle lymes to owre Lorde Jhesu.
    And thanne called I Conscience to kenne me the sothe.
10   "Is this Jhesus the Juster?"° quod I, "that Juwes did to   *Jouster (Knight)*
        deth?
    Or is it Pieres the Plowman? Who paynted hym so
        rede?"°   *red*
        Quod Conscience, and kneled tho, "Thise aren
          Pieres armes,
    His coloures and his cote-armure, ac He that cometh so
        blody
    Is Cryst with His crosse, Conqueroure of Crystene."
15   "Why calle ye Hym Cryst?" quod I, "sithenes°   *since*
        Juwes calle Hym Jhesus?
    Patriarkes and prophetes prophecyed bifore
    That alkyn° creatures shulden knelen and bowen   *all kinds of*
    Anon° as men nempned° the name of God, Jhesu.   *At once   named*
    Ergo° is no name to° the name of Jhesus,   *Therefore   like*
20 Ne none so nedeful to nempne by nyghte ne by daye.
    For alle derke develles aren adradde° to heren it,   *afraid*
    And synful aren solaced and saved bi that name.
    And ye callen Hym Cryst, for what cause, telleth me?
    Is Cryst more of myghte, and more worthy name
25 Than Jhesu or Jhesus that al owre joye come of?"
        "Thow knowest wel," quod Conscience, "and° thow   *if*
        konne° resoun,   *understand*
    That knyghte, kynge, conqueroure may be o° persone.   *one*
    To be called a knighte is faire, for men shal knele to
        hym.
    To be called a kynge is fairer, for he may knyghtes
        make;
30 Ac to be conquerour called, that cometh of special
        grace,
    And of hardynesse° of herte, and of hendenesse°   *firmness   courtesy*
        bothe,
    To make lordes of laddes of° londe that he wynneth,   **of . . .** *out of lads over*
    And fre men foule thralles that folweth nought his
        lawes.
        "The Juwes, that were gentil° men, Jhesu thei   *noble*
        dispised,
35 Bothe His lore and His lawe; now ar thei lowe cherlis.°   *serfs*
    As wyde as the worlde is, wonyeth° there none   *dwells*
    But under tribut and taillage° as tykes° and cherles.   *taxation   low people*

And tho that bicome Crysten by conseille of the
    Baptiste,
Aren frankeleynes,° fre men thorw fullyng° that thei   *freemen baptism*
    toke,
40 And gentel° men with Jhesu, for Jhesus was y-fulled,°   *noble baptized*
And uppon Calvarye on crosse y-crouned Kynge of
    Jewes.
    "It bicometh° to a Kynge to kepe and to defende,   *is becoming*
And conquerour of conquest, his lawes and his large.°   *liberality*
And so dide Jhesus the Jewes. He justified and taughte
    hem
45 The lawe of lyf that last shal evere;
And fended fram foule yveles, feveres, and fluxes,
And fro fendes that in hem were, and fals bileve.°   *belief*
Tho° was He Jhesus of Jewes called, gentel° prophete,   *Then noble*
And Kynge of her kyngdome, and croune bar° of   *bore*
    thornes.
50   "And tho° conquered He on crosse as conquerour   *when*
    noble,
Myght no deth Hym fordo° ne adown brynge,   *destroy*
That He ne aros and regned and ravysshed helle.
And tho° was He conquerour called of quikke° and of   *then living*
    ded,
For he yaf° Adam and Eve and other mo° blisse   *gave **other mo** others more*
55 That longe hadde leyne bifore as Lucyferes cherles.°   *serfs*
And sith he yaf largely alle his lele lyges°   **lele lyges** *loyal liegemen*
Places in paradys at her partynge hennes,
He may wel be called Conquerour, and that is Cryst to
    mene.°   *mean*
    "Ac the cause that He cometh thus, with crosse of
    His passioun,
60 Is to wissen us there-wyth that whan that we ben
    tempted,
Ther-with to fyghte and fenden us fro fallyng into
    synne,
And se bi His sorwe° that who-so loveth joye,   *sorrow*
To penaunce and to poverté he moste putten
    hymselven,
And moche wo in this worlde willen° and suffren.   *desire*
65   "Ac to carpe° more of Cryst, and how He come to   *speak*
    that name,
Faithly forto speke, His firste name was Jhesus.
Tho He was borne in Bethleem as the boke telleth,
And cam to take mankynde,° kynges and aungeles   **take mankynde** *take on human*
Reverenced Hym faire with richesse of erthe.   *nature*

330

70 Angeles out of hevene come knelyng and songe

> *Gloria in excelsis Deo, etc.*[1]

Kynges come after, kneled, and offred
Mirre° and moche golde withouten mercy° askynge,   Myrrh   thanks
Or any kynnes catel,° but knowlechyng Hym   **kynnes catel** kinds of goods
    soevereigne
75 Bothe of sonde,° sonne, and see; and sithenes° thei went   sand (earth)   then
Into her kyngene kyth° by conseille of angeles.   **kyngene kyth** country of kings
And there was that worde fulfilled the which thow of
    speke,

> *Omnia celestia, terrestria, flectantur in hoc nomine Jhesu.*[2]

For alle the angeles of hevene at His bürth kneled,
80 And al the witte° of the worlde was in tho thre kynges.   wisdom
Resoun and Rightwisnesse and Reuth° thei offred;   **Rightwisnesse . . .** Righteousness and Pity
Wherfore and whi,° wyse men that tyme,   **Wherfore . . .** Thus and so
Maistres and lettred men, *Magy*° hem called.   Magi
    "That o° kynge cam with Resoun kevered° under   **That o** The first   symbolized
    sense.°   incense
85 The secounde kynge sitthe sothliche° offred   **sitthe sothliche** then truly
Rightwisnesse under red golde, Resouns felawe.
Golde is likned to Leuté° that last shal evere,   Loyalty
And Resoun to riche golde, to Righte and to Treuthe.
The thridde kynge tho cam, knelyng to Jhesu,
90 And presented Hym with Pitee, apierynge by° myrre;   as
For mirre is mercy to mene° and mylde speche of tonge.   signify
Thre y-liche honest° thinges were offred thus at ones,   **y-liche honest** equally valuable
Thorw thre kynne kynges,° knelynge to Jhesu.   **thre . . .** kings of three races
    "Ac for° alle thise preciouse presentz, owre Lorde   despite
    Prynce Jhesus
95 Was neyther kynge ne conquerour til He gan to wexe°   grow
In the manere of a man, and that by moche sleight,°   skill
As it bicometh a conquerour to konne° many sleightes,   know
And many wyles and witte, that wil ben a leder;
And so did Jhesu in His dayes, who-so had tyme to telle
    it.
00 Sum tyme He suffred and sum tyme He hydde Hym;
And sum tyme He faughte faste, and fleigh otherwhile.°   **faste . . .** hard, and fled sometimes
And some tyme He gaf good° and graunted hele bothe,°   wealth   **hele bothe** healing too
Lyf and lyme, as Hym lyste,° He wrought.   it pleased
As kynde° is of a conquerour, so comsed° Jhesu   nature   commenced
05 Tyle He had alle hem that He fore bledde.°   **fore bledde** bled for

---

[1] 'Glory to God in the highest, etc.' Luke ii.14.
[2] 'All in heaven and on earth must genuflect at this name, Jesus.' Phil. ii.10.

"In His juvente° this Jhesus, atte Juwen feste, youth
Water into wyn tourned, as Holy Writ telleth,
And there bigan God of His grace to do-wel.
For wyn is lykned to lawe and lyf of holynesse,
110 And lawe lakked tho,° for men loved nought her **lakked tho** was lacking then
  enemys.
And Cryst conseilleth thus and commaundeth bothe,° too
Bothe to lered° and to lewed to lovye owre enemys. learned
So atte feste firste, as I bifore tolde,
Bygan God, of His grace and goodnesse, to do-wel.
115 And tho was He cleped° and called nought Holy Cryst, named
  but Jhesu,
A faunt° fyn, ful of witte, *filius Mariae.*° child ***filius Mariae*** son of Mar
  "For bifor His moder Marie made He that wonder,
That she fürste and formest° ferme shulde bileve, foremost
That He thorw grace was gete° and of no gome elles.° begotten **gome elles** other mar
120 He wrought that bi no witte,° but thorw worde one, trick
After the kynde° that He come of, there comsed He nature
  do-wel.
And whan He was woxen° more in His moder° absence, grown mother's
He made lame to lepe and yave° lighte to blynde, gave
And fedde with two fisshes and with fyve loves
125 Sore afyngred° folke mo than fyve thousande. famished
Thus He conforted carful° and caughte a gretter name, sorrowful
The whiche was Do-bet° where that He went. Do-better
For defe thorw His doynges to here, and dombe speke
  He made,
And alle He heled and halpe that Hym of grace asked.
130 And tho was He called in contré of° the comune peple by
For the dedes that He did, *fili David, Jhesus!*° ***fili ...*** Jesus, the son of David
For David was doughtiest° of dedes in his tyme, mightiest
The berdes° tho songe:° *Saul interfecit mille, et David bards sang
  decem milia.*[3]
For-thi the contré there Jhesu cam called Hym *fili
  David*
135 And nempned° Hym of Nazereth, and no man so called
  worthi
To be kaisere or kynge of the kyngedome of Juda,
Ne over Juwes justice, as Jhesus was, hem thoughte.° **hem thoughte** it seemed to them
  "Where-of Caiphas hadde envye and other of the
  Jewes,
And for to done Hym to deth day and nyght thei
  casten.° plotted
140 Külleden° Hym on crosse-wys at Calvarie on Fryday They killed

[3] 'Saul killed thousands and David, tens of thousands.' I Sam. xviii.7.

And sithen buryden His body and beden° that men
    sholde   bade

Kepen it fro night-comers with knyghtes y-armed,

For no frendes shulde Hym fecche. For prophetes hem
    tolde

That that blessed body of burieles° shulde rise   **of burieles** from the tomb

145 And gone into Galilé and gladen His Apostles

And His moder Marie—thus men bifore demed.°   declared

The knyghtes that kepten° it biknewe° it hemselven   guarded   confessed

That angeles and archangeles, at° the day spronge,   before

Come knelynge to the corps and songen *Christus
    resurgens.*[4]

150 Verrey° man bifor hem alle and forth with hem He   True
    yede.

    "The Jewes preyed hem pees° and bisoughte the   **hem pees** them (the guards) silence
    knyghtes

Telle the comune° that there cam a compaignye of His   common people
    Aposteles

And bywicched hem as thei woke and awey stolen it.

Ac Marie Magdeleyne mette Hym bi the wey,

155 Goynge toward Galilé, in Godhed° and manhed,   Godhood

And lyves° and lokynge, and she aloude cryde   alive

In eche a compaignye there she cam, *Christus resurgens!*°   **Christus resurgens** Christ being
                                                                                    raised

Thus cam it out that Cryst overcam, rekevered, and
    lyved:

                Sic oportet Christum pati, et intrare, etc.[5]

160 For that that° wommen witeth° may noughte wel be   **For . . .** For what   know
    conseille!°   secret

    "Peter perceyved al this and pursued after,

Bothe James and Johan, Jhesu for to seke,

Tadde° and ten mo, with Thomas of Ynde.   Thaddeus

And as alle thise wise wyes° weren togideres   men

165 In an hous al bishette° and her dore y-barred,   shut

Cryst cam in—and al closed bothe dore and yates°—   gates

To Peter and to His Aposteles and seyde *Pax vobis!*°   **Pax vobis** Peace to you

And toke Thomas by the hande and taughte hym to
    grope

And fele with his fyngres His flesshelich herte.

170 Thomas touched it and with his tonge seyde,

           '*Deus meus et Dominus meus.*[6]

---

[4] 'Christ being raised.' See Rom. vi.9.
[5] 'Thus it behooved Christ to suffer and rise, etc.' Luke xxiv.46.
[6] 'My God and My Lord.' John xx.28.

Thow art my Lorde, I bileve, God, Lorde Jhesu!
Thow deydest and deth tholedest and deme° shalt us
    alle,
And now art lyvynge and lokynge and laste shalt evere!'

175 "Crist carped° thanne and curteislich seyde,
'Thomas, for thow trowest° this, and trewliche bilevest
    it,
Blessed mote° thow be, and be shalt for evere,
And blessed mote thei alle be in body and in soule
That nevere shal se me in sighte, as thow doste nouthe,°
180 And lellich° bileven al this; I love hem and blesse hem:

        Beati qui non viderunt, et crediderunt, etc.'[7]

"And whan this dede was done, Do-best He taughte,
And yaf° Pieres power—and pardoun He graunted
To alle manere man, mercy and foryyfnes°—
185 Hym° myghte men to assoille° of alle manere synnes,
In covenant that thei come and knowleche° to paye
To Pieres pardon the Plowman,° *redde quod debes*.[8]
Thus hath Pieres powere, be° his pardoun payed,
To bynde and to unbynde both here and elleswhere,
190 And assoille men of alle synnes save of dette one.°
    "Anone° after, an° heigh up into hevene
He went and wonyeth° there and wil come atte laste
And rewarde hym righte wel that *reddit quod debet*°—
Payeth parfitly° as pure Trewthe wolde.
195 And what persone payeth it nought, punysshen He
    thinketh
And demen° hem at Domes daye, bothe quikke° and
    ded;
The gode to the Godhede° and to grete joye,
And wikke° to wonye° in wo withouten ende."
Thus Conscience of Crist and of the crosse carped°
200 And conseilled me to knele ther-to. And thanne come,
    me thoughte,
One *spiritus paraclitus*° to Pieres and to his felawes;
In lyknesse of a lightnynge he lyghte on hem alle
And made hem konne° and knowe alkyn° langages.
I wondred what that was and wagged° Conscience
205 And was afered of the lyghte, for in fyres lyknesse
Spiritus paraclitus overspradde hem alle.
    Quod Conscience, and kneled, "This is Crystes
    messager,

	tholedest . . . suffered and judge
	spoke
	believe
	may
	now
	yet truly
	gave
	forgiveness
	That he **to assoille** absolve
	acknowledge
	Pieres . . . Piers the Plowman's pardon
	if be
	dette one debt alone
	At once on
	went . . . wends and dwells
	reddit . . . pays back what he owes
	completely
	judge living
	Godhood
	wicked dwell
	spoke
	the Paraclete
	understand all kinds of
	nudged

[7] 'Blessed are they who have not seen and have believed, etc.' John xx.29.
[8] 'Pay back what you owe.' Matt. xviii.28.

And cometh fro the grete God and Grace is his name.
Knele now," quod Conscience, "and if thow canst
   synge,
210 Welcome hym and worshipe hym with *Veni*,° *Creator*   Come
   Spiritus."
Thanne songe° I that songe, and so did many hundreth,   sang
And cryden with Conscience, "Help us, God of Grace!"
   And thanne bigan Grace to go with Piers Plowman
And conseilled hym and Conscience the comune° to   common people
   sompne,°   summon
215 "For I wil dele todaye and dyvyde grace
To alkynnes° creatures that han her fyve wittes,°   all kinds of senses
Tresore to lyve by to her lyves ende,
And wepne° to fyghte with that wil nevre faille.   weapon
For Antecryst and his al the worlde shal greve
220 And acombre° thee, Conscience, but if Cryst thee   overwhelm
   helpe.
And fals prophetes fele,° flatereres and glosers°   many deceivers
Shullen come and be curatoures over kynges and erlis,
And Pryde shal be Pope, prynce of Holy Cherche,
Coveytyse and Unkyndenesse Cardinales hym to lede.
225 For-thi," quod Grace, "er I go, I wil gyve yow tresore,
And wepne to fighte with whan Antecryst yow
   asailleth."
And gaf eche man a grace to gye° with hymselven,   govern
That Ydelnesse encombre hym nought, Envye ne
   Pryde,

Divisiones graciarum sunt, etc.[9]

230   Some he yaf Wytte,° with wordes to shewe,   **yaf Wytte** gave Intelligence
Witte to wynne her lyflode° with, as the worlde asketh,   livelihood
As prechoures and prestes and prentyces of lawe,
Thei lelly° to lyve by laboure of tonge,   faithfully
And bi witte to wissen other° as Grace hem wolde   others
   teche.
235 And some he kenned Crafte° and kunnynge of syghte,   **kenned Crafte** taught Trade
With sellyng and büggynge° her bylyf° to wynne,   buying livelihood
And some he lered to laboure, a lele° lyf and a trewe,   honest
And somme he taughte to tilie,° to dyche° and to   till dig ditches
   thecche,°   thatch
To wynne with her lyflode° by lore of his techynge.   livelihood
240 And somme to dyvyne and divide, noumbres to kenne;°   know
And some to compas craftily° and coloures to make;   **compas craftily** plan skillfully
And some to se and to saye what shulde bifalle,

[9] 'Diversities of gifts there are, etc.' I Cor. xii.4.

335

Bothe of wel° and of wo, telle it or° it felle,°   weal   before   happens

As astronomyenes thorw astronomye and philosophres
   wyse.

245 And some to ryde and to recoevre° that unrightfully   recover
   was wonne;

He wissed° hem wynne it ayeyne° thorw wightnesse°   taught   again   quickness
   of handes,

And fecchen it fro fals men, with Folvyles lawes.[10]

   And some he lered to lyve in longynge to ben hennes,

In poverté and in penaunce to preye for alle Crystene.

250 And alle he lered to be lele° and eche a crafte° love   loyal   handicraft
   other,

And forbad hem alle debate° that none were amonge   struggle
   hem.

   "Thowgh some be clenner than somme, ye se wel,"
   quod Grace,

   "That he that useth the fairest crafte, to the foulest I
   couth° have put hym.   could

Thinketh° alle," quod Grace, "that grace cometh of my   Remember
   yifte;°   gift

255 Loke that none lakke° other, but loveth alle as   find fault with
   bretheren.

And who that moste maistries can° be myldest of   **who . . .** whoever has the greatest
   berynge,   achievements

And crouneth Conscience kynge and maketh Crafte°   Skill
   yowre stuward,

And after° Craftes conseille, clotheth yow and fede.   according to

For I make Pieres the Plowman my procuratour° and   proctor
   my reve,°   steward

260 And regystrere° to receyve *redde quod debes.*°   registrar   **redde . . .** pay back wh[at]
    you owe

My prowor° and my plowman Piers shal ben on erthe,   purveyor

And for to tülye° Treuthe a teme° shal he have."   till   team

   Grace gave Piers a teme, foure gret oxen.

That on° was Luke, a large beste and a lowe-chered,°   **That on** The one   meek-manner[ed]

265 And Marke, and Mathew the thrydde, myghty bestes
   bothe,

And joigned to hem one Johan, most gentil° of alle,   noble

The prys nete° of Piers' plow, passyng° alle other.   **prys nete** chief ox   surpassing

   And Grace gave Pieres of his goodnesse foure stottis,°   bullocks

Al that his oxen eryed,° they to harwe° after.   plowed   harrow

270 On hyghte Austyne,° and Ambrose another,   **On . . .** One was called Augustine

Gregori the grete clerke, and Jerome the gode.

Thise foure, the feithe to teche, folweth° Pieres teme,   follow

And harwed in an handwhile° al Holy Scripture   short time

[10] An uncertain reference, probably signifying something like the modern lynch laws.

Wyth two harwes that thei hadde, an olde and a newe,

275   *Id est, vetus testamentum et novum.*°

And Grace gave greynes,° the cardynales vertues,   seeds
And sewe° hem in mannes soule, and sithen he tolde her   sowed
names.
Spiritus Prudenciae° the firste seed hyghte,°   **Spiritus Prudenciae** Prudence
And who-so eet that, ymagyne he shulde,   is called
280 Ar he did any dede, devyse° wel the ende.   consider
And lerned men a ladel bügge° with a longe stele°   buy   handle
That cast° for to kepe a crokke° to save the fatte aboven.°   plan   **kepe**...watch a pot   on top
The secounde seed highte *Spiritus Temperanciae.*°   **Spiritus Temperanciae** Temperance
He that ete of that seed hadde suche a kynde,
285 Shulde nevere mete ne mochel° drynke make hym to   much
swelle,
Ne sholde no scorner ne scolde° oute of skyl hym   scold
brynge,
Ne wynnynge ne welthe of worldeliche ricchesse,
Waste worde of ydelnesse, ne wykked speche meve;°   speak
Shulde no curyous clothe comen on hys rügge,°   back
290 Ne no mete in his mouth that Maister Johan spiced.
The thridde seed that Pieres sewe was *Spiritus
Fortitudinis.*°   **Spiritus Fortitudinis** Fortitude
And who so eet of that seed hardy was evre
To suffre al that God sent, sykenesse and angres.°   troubles
Myghte no lesynge° ne lyere ne losse of worldely catel°   lie   goods
295 Maken hym for any mournynge that he nas° merye in   was not
soule,
And bolde, and abydynge bismeres° to suffre,   insults
And playeth al with pacyence *et parce mihi, Domine,*[11]
And covered hym under conseille of Catoun° the wyse: Cato

Esto forti animo, cum sis dampnatus inique.[12]

300   The fierthe seed that Pieres sewe was *Spiritus
Justiciae,*°   **Spiritus Justiciae** Justice
And he that eet of that seed shulde be evere trewe
With God, and nought agast but of gyle one.°   only
For gyle göth so pryvely° that Good Faith otherwhile°   secretly   sometimes
May noughte ben aspyed for *Spiritus Justiciae.*
305 *Spiritus Justiciae* spareth noughte to spille°   destroy
Hem that ben gulty and for to correcte
The Kynge, yif he falle in gylte or in trespasse.

275. That is, the Old and New Testaments.
[11] 'Spare me, O Lord.' Possibly Ps. xvi.1.
[12] 'Be strong in spirit when you are unjustly blamed.' Cato, *Distichs*, ii.14.

For counteth he no kynges wratthe whan he in courte
    sitteth
To demen° as a Domes Man.° Adradde° was he nevre,   *judge* **Domes Man** *Judge* / *Afraid*
310 Noither of duke ne of deth that he ne dede° the lawe,   **ne dede** *administered*
For present or for preyere° or any prynces lettres;   *petition*
He dede equité° to alle, evene forth° his powere.   *justice*   **evene forth** *to the exten[t]*
  Thise foure sedes Pieres sewe, and sitthe he did hem
    harwe°   *harrow*
Wyth olde lawe and newe lawe that Love myghte wexe°   *grow*
315 Amonge the foure vertues and vices destroye.
For communelich° in contrees kammokes[13] and wedes   *commonly*
Fouleth the fruite in the felde there thei growe
    togyderes;
And so don vices vertues worthy.
  Quod Piers, "Harweth alle that kunneth Kynde
    Witte bi° conseille of this° doctours,   **kunneth . . .** *know Common Sens[e]* / *with* *these*
320 And tülyeth° after her techynge the cardinale vertues."   *till*
    "Ayeines° thi greynes,"° quod Grace, "bigynneth for   *Before* *seeds*
    to ripe,
Ordeigne thee an hous, Piers, to herberwe° in thi   *stow*
    cornes."
    "By God! Grace," quod Piers, "ye moten° gyve   *must*
    tymbre
And ordeyne that hous ar ye hennes wende."
325   And Grace gave hym the crosse with the croune of
    thornes
That Cryst upon Calvarye for mankynde on pyned,°   *suffered*
And of His baptesme and blode that He bledde on
    Rode°   *Cross*
He made a maner° morter and Mercy it highte.°   *kind of* *called*
And there-with Grace bigan to make a good
    foundement,°   *foundation*
330 And watteled it and walled it with His peynes° and His   *suffering*
    passioun,
And of al Holy Writ he made a rofe after,
And called that hous Unité, Holi Cherche on
    Englisshe.
And whan this dede was done, Grace devised
A carte, hyghte Cristendome, to carye Pieres' sheves;
335 And gaf hym caples° to his carte, Contricioun and   *horses*
    Confessioun,
And made presthode haywarde, the while hymself went
As wyde as the worlde is with Pieres to tülye° Treuthe.   *till*

---

[13] 'Cammock,' or 'rest harrow,' a low shrub with pink flowers and tough crooked roots that hinder a plow or harrow.

The Pearl

(ca. 1380, West Midland)

The Pearl was written in the northern part of the West Midlands. Other works attributed to the same author because of similarities in dialect and style are *Cleanness, Patience,* and *Sir Gawain and the Green Knight* (p. 376, below). Like *The Romance of the Rose*, with which the author shows acquaintance, the poem is a dream vision. Its seriousness of tone, however, recalls Dante's *Divine Comedy*, and its imagery is largely drawn from the Book of Revelation. Literally, the pearl in the poem is the poet's infant daughter, who died before reaching her second year. Like Dante's Beatrice, she not only reveals to the poet her blissful state in heaven but also corrects his human misunderstanding of the divine plan. Whether the poet, like Dante, intends other allegorical levels of meaning has been widely but inconclusively debated, but the pearl, or *margery*, is also the pearl (*margarita*) of great price that in Matthew xiii.45–46 is an analogue of the Kingdom of Heaven.

Stylistically, *The Pearl* is a remarkable *tour de force*. At least three-fourths of the total number of lines are decorated with the traditional, native-English device of alliteration. At the same time, the poem is composed of carefully wrought stanzas, rhyming ababababbcbc. The stanzas are bound together by an intricate concatenation in groups of five, except for the fifteenth group, which contains six stanzas. Concatenation is maintained by the repetition of a freely varied refrain in the last stanza of each group, by the use of the same c-rhyme (in the tenth and twelfth lines) in all the stanzas comprising a group, and by the repetition, within the first line of each stanza, of some thematic word from the refrain in the preceding stanza. For example, in group II, the last line of each stanza in the group (stanzas vi–x) carries a refrain based on the word *adubbement* ('adornment'); lines 10 and 12 of all five stanzas rhyme together on the syllable *ent*; and the first line of stanza vi echoes the refrain of the last line of stanza v, in group I, by the word *jewel*; the first lines of stanzas vii–x and xi, in group III, echo the refrain of group II with some form of the word *dub*. As a crowning touch, the refrain of the final group in the poem concatenates with the first line of the first stanza, thus fulfilling the self-imposed requirements of the perfect design. The meter type is twelve-line stanzas; see Introduction, type 22, page 33.

The poet also seems to have attempted to reinforce the symmetry of his vision by a numerological connection between his metrical form and his Biblical imagery. The proportions of the Heavenly Jerusalem (as in Revelation xxi) are based on the number twelve; its foundations consist of the twelve precious stones; its gates are twelve *margeries* ('pearls'); and the innocents among whom the pearl has found a place (as in Revelation xiv) number twelve times twelve thousand. Correspondingly, the number of lines in a stanza is twelve; the only break in concatenation (l. 721 lacks the word *right*) occurs immediately after the twelfth group; the total number of lines (because of the supernumerary stanza in group XV) is 1,212. That *The Pearl*, like *Sir Gawain*, contains 101 stanzas may also be part of a symbolic plan, though its purpose is no longer apparent.

Mere style alone, however, will not account for the charm of the poem. Numerology is likely to remain for most readers a hidden ingredient akin to the esoteric patterns of

Gothic architecture—a feature that satisfies the artist but is appreciated only dimly by the observer. More accessible is the poet's personal feeling of grief, his puzzled piety, and the universality of his vision. Like Milton in *Lycidas* or Tennyson in *In Memoriam*, he passionately expresses mankind's eternal questions concerning the deepest mysteries of providence.

The best edition is *Pearl*, ed. E. V. Gordon (Oxford, 1953). Among many modernizations, that in *Medieval English Verse*, trans. Brian Stone (Harmondsworth, 1964), pp. 136–74, is particularly satisfactory. The poem survives, along with *Cleanness, Patience*, and *Sir Gawain*, in a single manuscript, of which a facsimile is available in *Facsimile of MS. Cotton Nero A.x*, EETS 162 (London, 1923), folios 39–55. For bibliography see Severs, ch. 2.2. For criticism see John Conley, ed., *The Middle English Pearl: Critical Essays* (Notre Dame, 1970).

I

i

Perle, plesaunte° to prynces paye°   pleasing   pleasure
Too clanly clos° in golde so clere;°   **clanly clos** fairly set   bright
Oute of Oryent, I hardyly saye,
Ne proved I never° her precios pere.°   **Ne** . . . I never proved   peer
5 So rounde, so reken° in üche araye,°   fresh   **üche araye** each setting
So smal, so smothe her sydes were,
Where-so-ever I jugged° gemmes gaye,°   judged   fair
I sette hyr sengeley in synglere.°   **sengeley** . . . apart as unique
Allas! I leste° hyr in on erbere;°   lost   **on erbere** a garden
10 Thurgh gresse° to grounde hit fro me yot.°   grass   went
I dewyne, fordolked of luf-daungere°
Of that pryvy° perle wythouten spot.   my own

ii

Sythen° in that spote hit fro me sprange,   Since
Ofte haf I wayted, wyschande° that wele,°   wishing for   precious thing
15 That wont was whyle devoyde° my wrange°   **whyle devoyde** formerly to drive away   grief
And heven° my happe° and al my hele.°   raise up   happiness   well-being
That dos bot thrych° my hert thrange,°   **bot thrych** only weigh down   heavily
My breste in bale° bot bolne and bele.°   sorrow   **bolne** . . . swells and burns
Yet thoght me° never so swete a sange°   **thoght me** there seemed to me   song
20 As stylle stounde° let to me stele;   **stylle stounde** that quiet time
For sothe° ther fleten° to me fele,°   **For sothe** Indeed   flowed   many song
To thenke hir color° so clad in clot.°   complexion   clay
O moul,° thou marres a myry° juele,   earth   pleasant
My privy perle wythouten spotte.

11. I pine away, grievously wounded by love power

iii

25　That spot of spyses mot° nedes sprede,°
　　Ther° such ryches to rot is runne;
　　Blomes blayke° and blwe and rede
　　Ther schynes ful schyr° agayn the sunne.
　　Flor° and fryte may° not be fede°
30　Ther hit doun drof° in moldes dunne;°
　　For üch gresse mot grow of graynes dede°—
　　No whete° were elles to wones wonne.°
　　Of goud üche goude is ay° bygonne;
　　So semly a sede moght fayly° not,
35　That spryngande spyces up ne sponne°
　　Of that precios perle wythouten spotte.

mot must　*nedes sprede* be covered
Ther Where
blayke yellow
schyr brightly
Flor Flower　*fryte may* fruit can　*fede* faded
drof sank　*moldes dunne* brown earth
graynes dede
whete wheat　*wones wonne* dwellings brought
ay ever
moght fayly could fail
up . . . would not spring up

iv

　　To that spot that I in speche expoun
　　I entred in that erber° grene,
　　In Auguste in a hygh seysoun,°
40　When corne is corven° wyth crokes° kene.
　　On hüyle ther° perle hit trendeled° doun,
　　Schadowed this wortes ful schyre and schene,°
　　Gilofre,° gyngure, and gromylyoun,°
　　And pyonys powdered ay° bytwene.
45　Yif hit was semly on to sene,°
　　A fayr reflayr° yet fro hit flot.°
　　Ther wonys° that worthyly,° I wot and wene,°
　　My precious perle wythouten spot.

erber garden
hygh seysoun festival time
corven cut　*crokes* sickles
hüyle ther the hill where　*trendeled* rolled
this . . . these plants very bright and fair
Gilofre Gillyflower　*gromylyoun* gromwell
pyonys . . . peonies scattered ever
sene look
reflayr fragrance　*flot* flowed
wonys dwells　*worthyly* precious one　*wot . . .* know and suppose

v

　　Bifore that spot my honde I spenned°
50　For care ful° colde that to me caght.°
　　A devely dele° in my hert denned,°
　　Thagh° resoun sette myselven saght.°
　　I playned° my perle, that ther was spenned,°
　　Wyth fyrce skylles° that faste faght.°
55　Thagh kynde° of Kryst me comfort kenned,°
　　My wreched wylle in wo ay wraghte.°
　　I felle upon that floury flaght,°
　　Suche odour to my hernes° schot.
　　I slode upon° a slepyng-slaghte°
60　On that precios perle wythouten spot.

spenned clasped
For . . . Because of sorrow very　*caght* seized
devely dele desolate grief　*denned* lay deep
Thagh Though　*saght* at peace
playned lamented　*spenned* confined
skylles arguments　*faste faght* stubbornly fought
kynde nature　*kenned* taught
ay wraghte ever suffered
flaght turf
hernes brains
slode upon slid into　*slepyng-slaghte* sudden sleep

31. For each blade of grass must grow from dead grains

II

vi

Fro spot my spyryt ther sprang in space.°
My body on balke° ther bod° in sweven.°
My goste° is gon in Godes grace
In aventure ther° mervayles meven.°
65 I ne wyste° in this worlde where that hit wace,°
Bot I knew me keste° ther klyfes cleven.°
Towarde a foreste I bere° the face,
Where rych° rokkes wer to dyscreven.°
The lyght of hem° myght no mon leven,°
70 The glemande° glory that of hem glent;°
For wern never webbes° that wyghes weven°
Of half so dere adubbemente.°

> in space after a while
> a mound   stayed   dreams
> spirit
> where   take place
> ne wyste didn't know   was
> cast   klyfes cleven cliffs soared
> turned
> splendid   be discerned
> them   believe
> gleaming   glinted
> fabrics   wyghes weven men wove
> dere adubbemente glorious adornmen[t]

vii

Dubbed° wern alle tho downes sydes°
Wyth crystal klyffes° so cler of kynde.°
75 Holtewodes° bryght aboute hem bydes°
Of bolles° as blwe as ble of Ynde.°
As bornyst° sylver the lef onslydes,°
That thike con trylle° on üch a tynde.°
When glem of glodes° agayns hem glydes,
80 Wyth schymeryng schene ful schrylle° thay
      schynde.°
The gravayl that on grounde con grynde°
Wern precious perles of Oryente;
The sunnebemes, bot blo and blynde°
In respecte of that adubbement.°

> Adorned   tho . . . those hillsides
> cliffs   nature
> Woods   hem bydes them stand
> trunks   blwe . . . indigo
> burnished   unfolds
> con trylle quivers   üch . . . each branch
> bright patches of sky
> schymeryng . . . bright gleam very
>   dazzingly   shone
> con grynde ground
>
> bot . . . only dark and dim
> adornment

viii

85 The adubbemente of tho downes dere°
Garten° my goste° al greffe foryete.°
So frech flavores° of frytes° were
As fode° hit con° me fayre refete.°
Fowles ther flowen° in fryth in fere,°
90 Of flaumbande hwes,° bothe smale and grete.
Bot sytole-stryng and gyternere°
Her reken° myrthe moght° not retrete;°
For when those bryddes° her wynges bete,
Thay songen° wyth a swete asent.°
95 So gracios gle couthe° no mon gete
As here° and se her adubbement.°

> tho . . . those glorious hills
> Made   spirit   greffe foryete grief forg[ot]
> fragrances   fruits
> food   did   revive
> flew   fryth . . . woods together
> flaumbande hwes flaming hues
> sytole-stryng . . . citole string and
>   cithern-player
> Her reken Their ready   could   imita[te]
> birds
> sang   harmony
> could
> hear   adornment

ix

So al was dubbet on dere asyse°
That fryth ther° Fortwne forth me feres.°
The derthe° therof for to devyse°
100 Nis no wygh° worthy that tonge beres.°
I welke ay° forth in wely wyse;°
No bonk° so byg that did me deres.°
The fyrre° in the fryth, the feirer con ryse°
The playn, the plonttes, the spyse, the peres,°
105 And rawes and randes and rych reveres°—
As fyldor° fyn her bonkes brent.°
I wan° to a water by schore° that scheres.°
Lorde, dere° was hit adubbement!°

dubbet . . . adorned in a glorious manner
fryth ther wood where   leads
glory   picture
Nis . . . There is no man   has
welke ay walked ever   **wely wyse** a blissful manner
slope   harm
farther   **con ryse** rose
pears

gold thread   steep
came   bank   courses
glorious   **hit adubbement** its adornment

x

The dubbemente of tho derworth depe°
110 Wern bonkes bene° of beryl bryght.
Swangeande° swete the water con swepe,°
Wyth a rownande rourde raykande aryght.°
In the founce° ther stonden stones stepe,
As glente° thurgh glas that glowed and glyght,°
115 As stremande sternes,° when strothe-men° slepe,
Staren° in welkyn° in wynter nyght.
For üche a pobbel° in pole° ther pyght°
Was emerad, saffer, other° gemme gente,°
That alle the loghe lemed° of lyght,
120 So dere° was hit adubbement.°

tho . . . those splendid depths
fair
Swirling   **con swepe** swept
rownande . . . whispering voice rolling straight on
bottom
light   shone
stremande sternes streaming stars   valley men (mortals)
Shine   sky
üche . . . each pebble   stream   set
emerad . . . emerald, sapphire, or   noble
loghe lemed pool gleamed
glorious   **hit adubbement** its adornment

III

xi

The dubbement dere of doun and dales,°
Of wod and water and wlonk° playnes,
Bylde° in me blys, abated my bales,°
Fordidden° my stresse, dystryed° my paynes.
125 Doun after a strem that dryghly hales°
I bowed° in blys, bredful° my braynes.
The fyrre° I folghed° those floty° vales,
The more strenghthe of joye myn herte straynes.°

doun . . . hill and valleys
splendid
Aroused   sorrows
Did away with   **stresse, dystryed** grief, destroyed
dryghly hales steadily flows
went   brimful
farther   followed   watery
stirs

105. And hedgerows and borders and splendid river banks

As Fortune fares ther as hö fraynes,°   **hö fraynes** she makes trial
130 Whether solace hö sende other° elles sore,°   or   pain
     The wygh° to wham° her wylle hö waynes°   man   whom   grants
     Hyttes° to have ay° more and more.   Chances   ever

xii

     More of wele° was in that wyse°   delight   manner
     Then I cowthe° telle thagh° I tom° hade,   could   though   leisure
135 For ürthely° herte myght not suffyse   earthly
     To the tenthe döle° of tho gladnes glade.°   part   **tho ...** those joyful joys
     For-thy° I thoght that Paradyse   Therefore
     Was ther over gayn° tho bonkes brade.°   against   **bonkes brade** broad slopes
     I hoped° the water were a devyse°   supposed   division
140 Bytwene myrthes° by meres° made.   delights   pools
     Byyonde the broke, by slente other slade,°   **slente ...** slope or valley
     I hoped that mote merked wöre.°   **mote ...** castle would be situated
     Bot the water was depe, I dorst not wade,
     And ever me longed° ay more and more.   **me longed** I longed

xiii

145 More and more and yet wel mare,°   **wel mare** much more
     Me lyste° to se the broke byyonde;   **Me lyste** I wished
     For if hit was fayr ther I con fare,°   **con fare** went
     Wel loveloker° was the fyrre° londe.   lovelier   farther
     Abowte me con I stote° and stare;   **con ...** I did halt
150 To fynde a forthe° faste con I fonde;°   ford   **con ...** I tried
     Bot wothes mo, i-wysse,° ther ware,   **wothes ...** dangers more, indeed
     The fyrre I stalked by the stronde.°   bank
     And ever me thoght° I schulde not wonde°   **me thoght** it seemed to me   flinch
     For wo° ther weles° so wynne wöre.°   **For wo** From danger   delights   **wynne**
         wöre joyful were
155 Thenne new note° me com on honde   matter
     That meved my mynde ay more and more.

xiv

     More mervayle con my dom adaunt.°   **con ...** subdued my reason
     I segh° byyonde that myry mere°   saw   **myry mere** pleasant pool
     A crystal clyffe ful relusaunt;°   **ful relusaunt** very shiny
160 Mony ryal ray con fro hit rere.°   **con ...** rose from it
     At the fote therof ther sete° a faunt,°   sat   child
     A mayden of menske,° ful debonere.°   grace   gracious
     Blysnande° whyt was hyr bleaunt.°   Gleaming   mantle
     I knew hyr wel, I hade sen hyr ere.

165 As glysnande° golde that man con schere,°
So schon that schene an-under shore.°
On lenghe° I loked to° hyr there;
The lenger, I knew hyr more and more.

glistening   **man** ... one cut
schene ... fair one under the hill
On lenghe For a long time   at

xv

The more I frayste° hyr fayre face,
170 Her fygure fyn when I had fonte,°
Suche gladande° glory con to me glace°
As lyttel° byfore therto was wonte.°
To calle hyr lyste con me enchace,°
Bot baysment gef° myn hert a brunt.°
175 I segh° hyr in so strange a place,
Such a bürre myght° make myn herte blunt.°
Thenne veres hö° up her fayre frount,°
Hyr vysayge whyt as playn yvore.°
That stonge myn hert, ful stray atount,°
180 And ever the lenger, the more and more.

scanned
noticed
gladdening   **con** ... glided to me
seldom   accustomed
lyste ... longing urged me
baysment gef ... bewilderment gave blow
saw
bürre myght shock could   stunned
veres hö she lifts   forehead
ivory
ful ... very much astounded to distraction

IV

xvi

More then me lyste,° my drede aros.
I stod ful° stylle and dorste not calle.
Wyth yghen° open and mouth ful clos
I stod as hende° as hawk in halle.
185 I hoped° that gostly° was that porpose;°
I dred onende° what schulde byfalle,
Lest hö° me eschaped° that I ther chos,°
Er° I at steven° hir moght stalle.°
That gracios gay° wythouten galle,°
190 So smothe, so smal, so seme slyght,°
Ryses up in hir araye ryalle,
A precios pyece in perles pyght.°

me lyste I wished
very
eyes
quiet
supposed   spiritual   significance
concerning
she   eluded   saw
Before   **at steven** for a meeting   **moght stalle** could stop
fair one   flaw
seme slyght becomingly slender

adorned

xvii

Perles pyghte of ryal prys°
There moght mon° by grace haf sene
195 When that° frech as flor-de-lys
Doun the bonke con boghe bydene.°

excellence
moght mon could one
that one
bonke ... slope came straightway

Al blysnande° whyt was hir beau biys,°   gleaming **beau biys** beautiful mantle
Upon° at sydes, and bounden bene°   Open **bounden bene** bordered beautifully
Wyth the myryeste margarys,° at my devyse,°   **myryeste margarys** fairest pearls opinion
200 That ever I segh° yet with myn ene;°   saw eyes
Wyth lappes° large, I wot° and I wene,°   folds know suppose
Dubbed° with double perle and dyghte;°   Set adorned
Her cortel of self sute schene,°
Wyth precios perles al umbepyghte.°   adorned around

xviii

205 A pyght coroune° yet wer° that gyrle   **pyght coroune** adorned crown wore
Of marjorys° and non other ston,   pearls
Highe pynakled of cler whyt perle,
Wyth flurted° flowres perfet° upon.   figured perfect
To hed° hade hö° non other werle.°   **To hed** On her head she attire
210 Her here leke, al hyr umbegon,
Her semblaunt sade for doc other erle,°
Her ble° more blaght° then whalles bon.   complexion white
As schorne° golde schyr° her fax° thenne schon,   cut bright hair
On schylderes° that leghe unlapped lyghte.°   shoulders **leghe . . .** lay unbound lightly
215 Her depe colour yet wonted° non   lacked
Of° precios perle in porfyl pyghte.°   In comparison to **in . . .** on an embroidered border set

xix

Pyght° was poyned° and üche a° hemme   Adorned wristband **üche a** each
At honde, at sydes, at overture,°   opening
Wyth whyte perle and non other gemme,
220 And bornyste° whyte was hyr vesture.   burnished
Bot a wonder° perle wythouten wemme°   wonderful flaw
Inmyddes hyr breste was sette so sure.
A mannes dom moght dryghly demme,°   **dom . . .** reason could completely be baffled
Er° mynde moght malte° in hit mesure.°   Before comprehend value
225 I hope° no tong moght endure°   suppose suffice
No saverly saghe say° of that syght,   **No . . .** Any fitting word to say
So was hit clene and cler and pure,
That precios perle ther hit was pyght.°   set

xx

Pyght° in perle, that precios pyece   Adorned
230 On wyther half° water com doun the schore.°   **wyther half** the opposite side bank
No gladder gome hethen° into Grece   **gome hethen** man from here
Then I, when hö° on brymme wöre.°   she **brymme wöre** bank was

203. Her kirtle of the same fair style
210–11. Her hair, encircled all around her, enclosed her face, grave as a duke's or an earl's

Hö was me nerre° then aunte or nece;   nearer
My joy for-thy° was much the more.   therefore
235 Hö profered me speche, that special spece,° **special spece** excellent person
Enclynande° lowe in wommon lore,° Bowing **wommon lore** womanly manner
Caghte of° her coroun of grete tresore **Caghte of** Took off
And haylsed° me wyth a lote lyghte.° greeted **lote lyghte** joyous word
Wel was me° that ever I was bore° **Wel . . . I** was happy born
240 To sware° that swete° in perles pyghte!° answer sweet one adorned

V

xxi

"O perle," quod I, "in perles pyght,
Art thou my perle that I haf playned,°   mourned
Regretted by myn one on° nyghte? **myn . . .** myself alone at
Much longeyng haf I for thee layned,° concealed
245 Sythen° into gresse° thou me aglyghte.° Since grass slipped from
Pensyf, payred,° I am forpayned,° broken tormented
And thou in a lyf of lykyng lyghte,° **lykyng lyghte** joy came
In Paradys erde,° of stryf unstrayned.° land untroubled
What wyrde° has hyder my juel vayned,° fate sent
250 And don° me in thys del° and gret daunger?° put sorrow subjection
Fro we in twynne wern towen and twayned,°
I haf ben a joyles juelere."

xxii

That juel thenne in gemmes gente°   noble
Vered° up her vyse° wyth yghen° graye, Raised face eyes
255 Set on hyr coroun° of perle orient, crown
And soberly after thenne con hö say:
"Sir, ye haf your tale mysetente,° misstated
To say your perle is al awaye,° gone away
That is in cofer so comly clente° **comly clente** beautifully enclosed
260 As in this gardyn gracios gaye,° fair
Here-inne to lenge° for ever and play, stay
Ther mys nee mornyng° com never nere. **mys . . .** loss nor mourning
Her were a forser for thee, in faye,°
If thou were a gentyl° jueler. noble

251. Since we were drawn asunder and parted
263. Here would be a treasure casket for you, in faith

xxiii

265   "Bot, jueler gente,° if thou schal lose   noble
      Thy joy for a gemme that thee was lef,°   dear
      Me thynk° thee put in a mad porpose,°   **Me thynk** It seems to me   intention
      And büsyes thee aboute a raysoun bref;°   **raysoun bref** reason soon gone
      For that° thou lestes° was bot° a rose   what   lost   only
270   That flowred and fayled as kynde° hyt gef.°   nature gave
      Now thurgh kynde of the kyste° that hyt con   casket
            close°   **con close** encloses
      To a perle of prys hit is put in pref.°
      And thou has called thy wyrde° a thef,   fate
      That oght of noght° has mad thee cler.°   **oght ...** something from nothing   clearl
275   Thou blames the bote of° thy meschef;°   **bote of ...** cure for   misfortune
      Thou art no kynde° jueler."   gentle

xxiv

      A juel to me then was thys geste,°   guest
      And jueles wern hyr gentyl sawes.°   **gentyl sawes** noble words
      "I-wyse,"° quod I, "my blysfol beste,°   Indeed   noblest one
280   My grete dystresse thou al todrawes.°   draw away
      To be excused I make requeste;
      I trawed° my perle don out of dawes.°   believed   days
      Now haf I fonde hyt, I schal ma feste,°   **ma feste** make rejoicing
      And wony° wyth hyt in schyr wod-schawes,°   dwell   **schyr wod-schawes** bright gro
285   And love° my Lorde and al his lawes   praise
      That has me broght thys blys ner.
      Now were I at° yow byyonde thise wawes,°   with   waves
      I were a joyful jueler."

xxv

      "Jueler," sayde that gemme clene,°   pure
290   "Why borde° ye men? So madde ye be!   jest
      Thre wordes has thou spoken at ene;°   one time
      Unavysed, for sothe,° wern alle thre.   **Unavysed ...** Ill-advised, indeed
      Thou ne woste° in worlde what on dos mene;° **ne woste** do not know **on ...** one mea
      Thy worde byfore thy wytte con fle.°   **con fle** did fly
295   Thou says thou trawes° me in this dene°   believe   valley
      Bycawse thou may wyth yghen° me se;   eyes
      Another° thou says, in thys countré   Another thing
      Thyself schal won° wyth me ryght here;   dwell
      The thrydde, to passe thys water fre,°   noble
300   That may no joyfol jueler.

272. It has proved to be an excellent pearl.

xxvi

"I halde that jueler lyttel to prayse
That leves° wel that° he ses wyth yghe,
And much to blame and uncortayse°
That leves oure Lorde wolde make a lyghe,°
305 That lelly hyghte° your lyf to rayse,
Thagh° fortune dyd your flesch to dyghe.°
Ye setten Hys wordes ful westernays°
That leves nothynk bot° ye hit syghe.°
And that is a poynt o sorquydryghe°
310 That üche° god mon° may evel byseme,°
To leve no tale be true to tryghe°
Bot that° hys one skyl° may dem.°

believes what
discourteous
lie
lelly hyghte faithfully promised
Though die
ful westernays very contrariwise
unless see
o sorquydryghe of pride
to each man **evel byseme** ill befit
test
that which **one skyl** reason alone judge

xxvii

"Deme now thyself if thou con dayly°
As man to God wordes schulde heve.°
315 Thou says thou schal won° in this bayly.°
Me thynk thee bürde° fyrst aske leve,
And yet of graunt° thou myghtes fayle.
Thou wylnes° over thys water to weve.°
Er moste° thou cever° to other counsayle:°
320 Thy corse° in clot mot calder keve.°
For hit was forgarte° at Paradys greve;°
Oure yorefader° hit con mysseyeme.°
Thurgh drüry° deth bös° üch man dreve,°
Er° over thys dam° hym Dryghtyn deme."°

con dayly spoke
lift
dwell domain
Me ... It seems to me you ought to
permission
wish go
Er moste Before that must attain
course
body **clot ...** clay must colder sink
ruined grove
forefather **con mysseyeme** neglected
cruel it behooves to pass
Before stream **Dryghtyn deme** the
Lord may allow

xxviii

325 "Demes thou° me," quod I, "my swete,
To döl° agayn, thenne I dowyne.°
Now haf I fonte that° I forlete;°
Schal I efte° forgo hit er ever I fyne?°
Why schal I hit bothe mysse and mete?°
330 My precios perle dos me gret pyne.°
What serves tresor, bot gares° men grete°
When he hit schal efte° wyth tenes tyne?°
Now rech° I never for to declyne,°
Ne how fer of folde° that man° me fleme.°
335 When I am partles° of perle myne,
Bot durande doel° what may men deme?"°

Demes thou If you condemn
sorrow pine away
fonte that found what lost
again die
mysse ... lose and find
sorrow
makes cry
later **tenes tyne** pains lose
care fall
fer ... far from earth one may drive
deprived
durande doel lasting sorrow call it

xxix

"Thow demes noght bot° doel-dystresse,"   demes . . . talk of only
Thenne sayde that wyght.° "Why dos thou so?   person
For dyne of doel of lüres lesse°
340 Ofte mony° mon forgos the mo.°   many a   greater
Thee oghte better thyselven blesse,
And love ay God, in wele and wo,°   wele . . . prosperity and adversity
For anger gaynes thee not a cresse.°   watercress
Who nedes schal thole,° be not so thro.°   nedes . . . must suffer   bold
345 For thogh thou daunce as any do,°   doe
Braundysch° and bray thy brathes breme,°   Toss about   **brathes breme** agonies
                                                                                     fierce
When thou no fyrre may,° to ne° fro,   **fyrre may** farther can   or
Thou moste abyde that° He schal deme.°   **moste** . . . must suffer what   judge

xxx

"Deme Dryghtyn,° ever hym adyte,°   **Deme Dryghtyn** Judge the Lord   indic
350 Of° the way a fote ne wyl He wrythe.°   From   ne . . . He will not swerve
Thy mendes mountes° not a myte,   **mendes mountes** rewards will increase
Thagh° thou for sorwe° be never blythe.°   Though   sorrow   happy
Stynt of thy strot and fyne to flyte,°
And sech Hys blythe° ful swefte and swythe.°   sech . . . seek His mercy   quickly
355 Thy prayer may Hys pyté byte,°   move
That mercy schal hyr craftes kythe.°   **craftes kythe** powers show
Hys comforte may thy langour lythe°   **langour lythe** grief assuage
And thy lüres of lyghtly leme;°   **lüres** . . . sorrows gently dispose of
For, marre other madde,° morne and mythe,°   **marre** . . . lament or rage   hide feelings
360 Al lys in Hym to dyght and deme."°   **dyght** . . . ordain and appoint

VII

xxxi

Thenne demed° I to that damyselle:°   said   maiden
"Ne worthe° no wraththe unto my Lorde,   **Ne worthe** Let there be
If rapely° I rave, spornande in spelle.°   rashly   **spornande** . . . stumbling in
                                                                               speech
My herte was al wyth mysse remorde,°   **mysse remorde** loss tormented
365 As wallande° water gos out of welle.   welling
I do me° ay in hys myserecorde.°   **do me** put myself   mercy
Rebuke me never wyth wordes felle,°   cruel
Thagh° I forloyne,° my dere endorde,°   Though   go astray   adored one

339. For sound of lamentation of lesser sorrows
353. Stop your arguing and cease chiding

Bot kythes° me kyndely your coumforde,°   show   comfort
370 Pytosly thenkande° upon thysse: thinking
Of care° and me ye made acorde°   sorrow   agreement
That er° was grounde of alle my blysse.   **That er** Who before

xxxii

"My blysse, my bale,° ye han ben bothe,   sorrow
Bot much the bygger yet was my mon;°   grief
375 Fro° thou was wroken° fro üch a wothe,°   Since   banished   danger
I wyste° never where my perle was gon.   knew
Now I hit se, now lethes° my lothe.°   abates   woe
And, when we departed,° we wern at on;°   parted   one
God forbede we be now wrothe,
380 We meten so selden° by stok other° ston.   seldom   **stok other** trunk or
Thagh° cortaysly ye carp con,°   Though   **carp con** can speak
I am bot mol° and maneres mysse.°   **bot mol** only dust   lack
Bot Crystes mersy and Mary and Jon,
Thise arn the grounde of alle my blisse.

xxxiii

385 "In blysse I se thee blythely blent,°   set
And I a man al mornyf mate.°   **mornyf mate** mournful and dejected
Ye take theron ful° lyttel tente,°   very   attention
Thagh I hente° ofte harmes hate.°   get   **harmes hate** sorrows burning
Bot now I am here in your presente,°   presence
390 I wolde bysech, wythouten debate,
Ye wolde me say in sobre asente
What lyf ye lede erly and late.
For I am ful fayn° that your astate°   glad   estate
Is worthen to worschyp and wele, i-wysse.°
395 Of alle my joy the hyghe gate°   road
Hit is, and grounde of alle my blysse."

xxxiv

"Now blysse, bürne, mot° thee bytyde,"°   **bürne, mot** man, may   befall
Then sayde that lufsom° of lyth and lere,°   lovely   **lyth . . .** limb and face
"And welcum here to walk and byde,°   stay
400 For now thy speche is to me dere.
Maysterful mod° and hyghe pryde,   **Maysterful mod** Lordly spirit
I hete° thee, arn heterly° hated here.   assure   bitterly
My Lorde ne loves not° for to chyde,   **ne . . .** does not love
For meke arn alle that wones° Hym nere;   dwell

394. Has become one of honor and prosperity, indeed.

351

405 And when in Hys place thou schal apere,
    Be dep devote in hol° mekenesse.   all
    My Lorde the Lamb loves ay such chere,°   mien
    That is the grounde of alle my blysse.

XXXV

    "A blysful lyf thou says I lede;
410 Thou woldes knaw therof the stage.°   state
    Thow wost° wel when thy perle con schede°   know **con schede** fell
    I was ful yong and tender of age.
    Bot my Lorde the Lombe thurgh Hys godhede,
    He toke myself to Hys maryage,
415 Corounde° me quene in blysse to brede°   Crowned flourish
    In lenghe° of dayes that ever schal wage;°   length endure
    And sesed in° alle Hys herytage°   **sesed in** put in possession of inheritance
    Hys lef° is. I am holy° Hysse: beloved wholly
    Hys prese,° Hys prys,° and Hys parage°   worth excellence high rank
420 Is rote and grounde of alle my blysse."

VIII

XXXVI

    "Blysful," quod I, "may thys be trewe?
    Dyspleses not if I speke errour.
    Art thou the quene of hevenes blwe,
    That al thys worlde schal do honour?
425 We leven on° Marye that grace of grewe,°   **leven on** believe in **that** ... from whom grace came
    That ber a barne of° vyrgyn flour;   **barne of** child in
    The croune fro hyr who moght remewe°   **moght remewe** could remove
    Bot hö hir passed° in sum favour?   **Bot** ... Unless she surpassed her
    Now, for synglerty o° hyr dousour,°   **synglerty o** uniqueness of sweetness
430 We calle hyr Fenyx of Arraby,
    That, freles, fleghe of° hyr Fasor,°   **freles** ... flawless, flew from Creator
    Lyk to the Quen of cortaysye."

XXXVII

    "Cortayse Quen," thenne sayde that gaye,°   fair one
    Knelande° to grounde, folde° up hyr face,   Kneeling turned
435 "Makeles° Moder and myryest May,°   Matchless **myryest May** fairest Maiden
    Blessed bygynner of üch a grace!"

Thenne ros hö up and con restay,°   **con restay** paused

And speke me towarde° in that space:°   **me towarde** to me   time

"Sir, fele° here porchases and fonges pray,°   many   **porchases . . .** seek and get a prize

440 Bot supplantores° none wythinne thys place.   usurpers

That emperise° al hevens has,   empress

And ürthe, and helle, in her bayly;°   rule

Of erytage° yet non wyl hö chace,   **Of erytage** From heritage

For hö is Quen of cortaysye.

xxxviii

445 "The court of the kyndom of God alyve°   living

Has a property in hytself° beyng: its own

Alle that may ther-inne aryve

Of alle the reme° is quen other kyng,   realm

And never other° yet schal depryve,   another

450 Bot üchon fayn° of otheres hafyng,°   **üchon fayn** each one glad   possession

And wolde her corounes wern° worthe tho fyve,°   **her . . .** their crowns might be   **tho fyve** five of them

If possyble were her mendyng.°   improvement

Bot my Lady of whom Jesu con spryng,

Hö haldes the empyre over uus ful hyghe;

455 And that dyspleses non of oure gyng,°   company

For hö is Quene of cortaysye.

xxxix

"Of courtaysye, as says Saynt Poule,

Al arn we membres of Jesu Kryst;

As heved° and arme and legg and naule°   head   navel

460 Temen° to hys body ful trew and tryste,°   Are joined   faithfully

Ryght° so is üch a Krysten sawle   Just

A longande lym° to the Mayster of myste.°   **longande lym** limb belonging   mysteries

Thenne loke what hate other any gawle°   bitterness

Is tached other tyghed° thy lymmes bytwyste.°   **tached . . .** attached or tied   between

465 Thy heved° has nauther greme ne gryste,°   head   **greme . . .** anger nor spite

On arme other fynger thagh thou ber byghe.°   **ber byghe** wear a ring

So fare we alle wyth luf and lyste°   joy

To kyng and quene by cortaysye."

xl

"Cortaysé," quod I, "I leve,°   believe

470 And charyté grete, be yow among,

Bot my speche that yow ne greve,°   **yow . . .** may not grieve you

. . . . .¹

---

¹ Line omitted by scribe.

Thyself in heven over hygh thou heve,°   raise
To make thee quen that was so yonge.
475 What more honour moghte he acheve
That hade endured in worlde stronge,°   firmly
And lyved in penaunce hys lyves longe
Wyth bodyly bale° hym blysse to byye?°   harm buy
What more worschyp° moght he fonge°   honor get
480 Then corounde° be kyng by cortaysé?   crowned

IX

xli

"That cortaysé is too fre° of dede,°   lavish deed
Yyf hyt be soth° that thou cones saye.°   true **cones saye** say
Thou lyfed not two yer in oure thede;°   land
Thou cowthes° never God nauther plese ne pray,   could
485 Ne never nawther° Pater ne Crede;   **Ne ...** Nor ever knew either
And quen mad on the fyrst day!
I may not traw,° so God me spede,   **may ...** cannot believe
That God wolde wrythe° so wrange° away.   turn wrong
Of countes, damysel, par ma fay,°
490 Wer° fayr in heven to halde asstate,°   It would be rank
Other elles a lady of lasse aray;°   **lasse aray** lesser position
Bot a quene! Hit is too dere a date."°   end

xlii

"Ther is no date of Hys godnesse,"
Then sayde to me that worthy wyghte,°   person
495 "For al is trawthe that He con dresse,°   **con dresse** established
And He may do nothynk bot ryght.
As Mathew meles° in your messe°   speaks mass
In sothfol° gospel of God almyght,   truthful
In sample° He can ful graythely gesse,°   parable **graythely gesse** fittingly devise
500 And lyknes hit to heven lyghte.°   bright
'My regne,'° He says, 'is lyk on hyght°   realm high
To a lorde that hade a vyne,° I wate.°   vineyard know
Of tyme of yere the terme was tyght,°   **terme ...** time was come
To labor° vyne was dere° the date.°   cultivate good time

489. Of countess, maiden, by my faith

xliii

505 " 'That date of yere wel knawe thys hyne.°   **thys hyne** these workers
    The lorde ful erly up he ros
    To hyre werkmen to hys vyne,°   vineyard
    And fyndes ther summe to hys porpos.
    Into acorde thay con declyne°   **con declyne** consented
510 For a pené° on a day, and forth thay gos,   penny
    Wrythen° and worchen and don gret pyne,°   Twist   toil
    Kerven and caggen° and man° hit clos.°   **Kerven** . . . Cut and bind   make   secure
    Aboute under° the lorde to marked tos,°   the third hour (9 A.M.)   **marked tos** market goes
    And ydel men stande° he fyndes ther-ate.   standing
515 " ' "Why stande ye ydel?" he sayde to thos.
    "Ne knawe ye of this day no date?" '°   end

xliv

    " ' "Er° date of daye hider arn we wonne," '°   Before   come
    So was al samen her° answar soght.°   **samen her** together their   given
    "We haf standen her syn° ros the sunne,   **standen** . . . stood here since
520 And no mon byddes uus do ryght noght."
    " ' "Gos° into my vyne,° dos that° ye conne," '°   Go   vineyard   what   can
    So sayde the lorde, and made hit toght:°   an agreement
    "What resonabele hyre be naght be runne°   **hyre** . . . wage by night has accumulated
    I yow pay in dede and thoghte." '°   **dede** . . . deed and intention (in full)
525 Thay wente into the vyne and wroghte,°   worked
    And al day the lorde thus yede° his gate,°   went   way
    And new men to hys vyne° he broghte   vineyard
    Welnegh whyl° day was passed date.°   **Welnegh whyl** Almost until   its end

xlv

    " 'At the date° of day of evensonge   time
530 On oure° byfore the sonne go doun,   **On oure** One hour
    He segh° ther ydel men ful stronge   saw
    And sade° to hem° wyth sobre soun,°   said   them   **sobre soun** earnest voice
    " ' "Why stonde ye ydel thise dayes longe?"
    Thay sayden her hyre° was nawhere boun.°   **her hyre** their wage   made ready
535 "Gos to my vyne, yemen° yonge,   **vyne, yemen** vineyard, yeomen
    And wyrkes and dos that at° ye moun." '°   **dos** . . . do what   can
    Sone the worlde bycom wel broun;°   dark
    The sunne was doun and hit wex° late   grew
    To take her hyre he mad sumoun;°   **mad sumoun** gave summons
540 The day was al apassed date.°   its end

X

xlvi

" "The date° of the daye the lorde con knaw,°   time   **con knaw** knew
Called to the reve:° "Lede,° pay the meyny.°   steward   Man   company
Gyf hem° the hyre° that I hem owe,   them   wage
And fyrre,° that non me may repreny,°   further   reprove
545 Set hem alle upon a rawe°   row
And gyf üchon inlyche° a peny.   **gyf** . . . give each one alike
Begyn at the laste that standes lowe,
Tyl to the fyrste that thou atteny."°   reach
And thenne the fyrst bygonne to pleny°   complain
550 And sayden that thay hade travayled° sore: worked
" ' "These bot on oure hem con streny;°   **bot** . . . only one hour exerted themselves
Uus thynk uus oghe° to take more.   **Uus** . . . It seems to us we ought

xlvii

" ' "More haf we served, uus thynk so,
That suffred han° the dayes hete,   have
555 Thenn thyse that wroght° not houres two,   worked
And thou dos hem° uus to counterfete."°   **dos hem** make them   resemble
Thenne sayde the lorde to on° of tho:°   one   those
" ' "Frende, no waning° I wyl thee yete;°   lessening   grant
Take that° is thyn owne, and go.   what
560 And I hyred thee for a peny agrete,°   all together
Why bygynnes thou now to threte?°   quarrel
Was not a pené° thy covenaunt thore?°   penny   **covenaunt thore** agreement there
Fyrre° then covenaunde° is noght to plete.°   Further   agreement   plead
Why schalte thou thenne ask more?

xlviii

565 " ' "More, whether lawely is me my gyfte,
To do wyth myn what-so me lykes?°
Other elles thyn yghe° to lyther° is lyfte,°   eye   evil   turned
For I am goude and non byswykes?"°   **non byswykes** cheat no one
" 'Thus schal I,' quod Kryste, 'hit skyfte:°   ordain
570 The laste schal be the fyrst that strykes,°   goes
And the fyrst the laste, be he never so swyft;
For mony ben° called, thagh fewe be mykes.'°   are   friends of Christ
Thus pore men her part° ay pykes,°   **her part** their share   get
Thagh thay com late and lyttel wöre;°   **lyttel wöre** humble were
575 And thagh her sweng° wyth lyttel atslykes,°   toil   is spent
The merci of God is much the more.

565–66. Moreover, is my act of giving lawful for me, my act of doing with my own whatever I please?

xlix

"More haf I of joye and blysse here-inne,
Of ladyschip gret and lyves blom,°   **lyves blom** bloom of life
Then alle the wyghes° in the worlde myght   men
    wynne
580 By the way of ryght to aske dome.°
Whether welnygh° now I con bygynne,   **Whether welnygh** Though almost
In eventyde into the vyne I come,°   came
Fyrst of my hyre° my Lorde con mynne;°   wage   **con mynne** remembered
I was payed anon of al and sum.°   **anon . . .** at once in full
585 Yet other ther werne that toke more tom,°   time
That swange and swat° for long yore,°   **swange . . .** toiled and sweated   past
That yet of hyre nothynk thay nom,°   got
Paraunter° noght schal to-yere° more."   And perhaps   this year

l

Then more I meled° and sayde apert:°   spoke   openly
590 "Me thynk° thy tale° unresounable.   **Me thynk** Seems to me   account
Goddes ryght° is redy and evermore rert,°   justice   exalted
Other Holy Wryt is bot a fable.
In Sauter° is sayd a verce overte°   the Psalter   plain
That spekes a poynt determynable:
595 'Thou quytes üchon° as hys desserte,   **quytes üchon** reward each one
Thou hyghe kyng ay pretermynable.'°   foreordaining
Now he that stod the long day stable,°   firm
And thou to payment com hym byfore,
Thenne the lasse in werke, to take more able,
600 And ever the lenger the lasse, the more."°

XI

li

"Of more and lasse in Godes ryche,"°   kingdom
That gentyl° sayde, "lys no jöparde,°   noble one   **lys . . .** lies no doubt
For ther is üch mon payed inlyche,°   alike
Whether lyttel other much be hys rewarde.
605 For the gentyl Cheventayn° is no chyche,°   Chieftain   niggard
Whether-so-ever he dele nesch° other harde;   soft
He laves° hys gyftes as water of dyche,°   pours   **of dyche** from a ditch
Other gotes° of golf° that never charde.°   streams   a gulf   would cease

580. If they were to ask judgment according to strict justice.
599–600. Then the less work done, the greater the ability to earn; and thus continually, the less work, the more earning.

Hys fraunchyse° is large that ever dard°   freedom   has shown fear
610 To° Hym that mas° in synne rescoghe;°   Toward   makes   rescue
No blysse bes° fro hem reparde,°   is   withheld
For the grace of God is gret inoghe.°   enough

lii

"Bot now thou motes,° me for to mate,°   argue   confuse
That I my peny haf wrang tan° here;   **wrang tan** wrongly taken
615 Thou says that I that come too late
Am not worthy so gret fere.°   rank
Where wystes° thou ever any bourne abate,°   knew   **bourne abate** man lived
Ever so holy in hys prayere,
That he ne forfeted by sumkyn gate°   **sumkyn gate** some kind of way
620 The mede° sumtyme of hevenes clere?°   reward   bright
And ay the ofter,° the alder thay were   oftener
Thay laften° ryght and wroghten woghe.°   left   **wroghten woghe** did evil
Mercy and grace moste hem° then stere,°   **moste hem** must them   guide
For the grace of God is gret innoghe.°   enough

liii

625 "Bot innoghe of grace has innocent.°   the innocent
As sone as thay arn borne, by lyne°   **by lyne** in order
In the water of babtem° thay dyssente;°   baptism   descend
Then arne thay broght into the vyne.
Anon° the day, wyth derk endente,°   At once   **derk endente** darkness inlaid
630 The myght of deth dos° to enclyne.°   causes   sink
That wroght never wrang er thenne thay wente,°
The gentyle° Lorde thenne payes hys hyne.°   noble   **hys hyne** as his workers
Thay dyden° hys heste,° thay wern there-ine;   followed   commandment
Why schulde he not her labour alow,°   credit
635 Yys,° and pay hem at the fyrst fyne?°   Indeed   **at ...** at once completely
For the grace of God is gret innoghe.°   enough

liv

"Inoghe is knawen° that mankyn° grete   known   mankind
Fyrste was wroght to blysse parfyt;°   perfect
Oure forme fader° hit con forfete°   **forme fader** first father   **con forfete** forfeited
640 Thurgh an apple that he upon con byte.
Al wer we dampned° for that mete°   damned   food
To dyghe in doel out of delyt,°
And sythen wende° to helle hete,°   **sythen wende** then go   **helle hete** hell's heat
Ther-inne to won° wythoute respyt.   dwell

631. Those who never did wrong before they went thence
642. To die in sorrow away from joy

645 Bot theron com a bote as-tyt.° **bote as-tyt** remedy at once
Ryche blod ran on rode° so roghe,° the cross cruel
And wynne° water then at that plyt;° precious perilous time
The grace of God wex° gret innoghe.° grew enough

lv

"Innoghe ther wax° out of that welle, flowed
650 Blod and water of brode wounde.
The blod uus boght° fro bale° of helle redeemed suffering
And delyvered uus of the deth secounde;
The water is baptem,° the sothe° to telle, baptism truth
That folghed° the glayve° so grymly° grounde, followed spear cruelly
655 That wasches away the gyltes felle° **gyltes felle** sins deadly
That Adam wyth° inne deth uus drounde. **That...** With which Adam
Now is ther noght° in the worlde rounde nothing
Bytwene uus and blysse bot that° he wythdrogh,° **bot that** except what removed
And that° is restored in sely stounde,° that bliss **sely stounde** a blessed hour
660 And the grace of God is gret innogh.° enough

XII

lvi

"Grace innogh the mon may have
That synnes thenne new, yif him repente,
Bot wyth sorw and syt° he mot° hit crave, **sorw...** sorrow and grief must
And byde° the payne therto is bent.° suffer **therto...** which is with it bound
665 Bot resoun, of ryght that con noght rave° **con...** cannot stray
Saves evermore the innossent.
Hit is a dom° that never God gave, judgment
That ever the gyltles° schulde be schente.° innocent discomfited
The gyltyf may° contryssyoun hente° **gyltyf may** guilty can find
670 And be thurgh mercy to grace thryght;° led
Bot he to gyle that never glente,° turned
That inoscente is saf and ryghte.

lvii

"Ryght° thus I knaw wel in this cas Just
Two men° to save is god by skylle:° kinds of men reason
675 The ryghtwys° man schal se hys face, righteous
The harmles hathel° schal com hym tylle.° man to

359

The Sauter° hyt sas° thus in a pace:°   *Psalter says passage*
"'Lorde, who schal klymbe Thy hygh hylle,
Other rest wythinne Thy holy place?'
680 Hymself to onsware He is not dylle:°   *slow*
"'Hondelynges harme that dyt not ille,°
That is of hert bothe clene and lyght,°   *pure*
Ther schal hys step stable stylle.'°   **stable stylle** stand firm
The innosent is ay saf by ryght.

lviii

685 "The ryghtwys° man also sertayn°   *righteous certainly*
Aproche he schal that proper pyle,°   **proper pyle** fair castle
That takes not her lyf in vayne,
Ne glaveres° her nieghbor wyth no gyle.   *cheats*
Of thys ryghtwys sas° Salamon playn   *says*
690 How Koyntise° onoure con aquyle.°   *Wisdom* **con aquyle** obtained
By wayes ful streght hö con hym strayn,°   *guide*
And schewed° hym the rengne° of God awhyle,   *showed kingdom*
As who° says, 'Lo, yon lovely yle!   *one who*
Thou may hit wynne if thou be wyghte.'°   *brave*
695 Bot, hardyly,° wythoute peryle,   *surely*
The innosent is ay save° by ryghte.   *redeemed*

lix

"Anende ryghtwys° men yet says a gome,°   **Anende ryghtwys** About righteous *man*
David in Sauter, if ever ye segh° hit: *saw*
"'Lorde, thy servaunt dragh° never to dome,°   *bring judgment*
700 For non lyvyande° to thee is justyfyet.'   **non lyvyande** no one living
For-thy° to corte when thou schal com,   *Therefore*
Ther alle oure causes schal be tryed,
Alegge thee ryght,° thou may be innome°   **Alegge . . .** If you plead privilege for yourself refuted
By thys ilke° spech I have asspyed.°   *same observed*
705 Bot He on rode° that blody dyed,   *the cross*
Delfully° thurgh hondes thryght,°   *Grievously pierced*
Gyve° thee to passe, when thou arte tryed,   *May He grant*
By innocens and not by ryghte.

lx

"Ryghtwysly° who con rede,°   *Rightly* **con rede** can read
710 He loke° on bok and be awayed°   **He loke** May he look *instructed*
How Jesus Hym welke in are-thede,°   **Hym . . .** walked among ancient people
And bürnes° her barnes° unto hym brayde.°   *persons children brought*

681. He who with hands harmfully did not perform evil

360

For happe and hele° that fro Hym yede,°   happe . . . good fortune and healing
To touch her chylder° thay fayr Hym prayed.   issued
715 His dessypeles wyth blame let be hem bede°   children
And wyth her resounes ful fele restayed.°   blame . . . rebuke bade them cease
Jesus thenne hem swetely sayde: fele restayed many restrained
    "'Do way,° let chylder unto me tyght.°   Do way Cease come
To suche is hevenryche arayed.'°   hevenryche arayed heaven's kingdom
720 The innocent is ay saf by ryght.   prepared

XIII

lxi

"Jesus con calle to Hym Hys mylde,°   gentle ones
And sayde Hys ryche° no wygh° myght wynne   kingdom man
Bot° he com thyder ryght° as a chylde,   Unless even
Other elles nevermore com ther-inne.
725 Harmles, trewe, and undefylde,
Wythouten mote other mascle° of sulpande°   mote . . . stain or spot polluting
    synne,
When such ther cnoken° on the bylde,°   knock dwelling
Tyt° schal hem men the yate unpynne.°   Quickly yate unpynne gate unbolt
Ther is the blys that con° not blynne°   can end
730 That the jueler soghte thurgh perré pres,°   perré pres gems of value
And solde alle hys goud,° bothe wolen and lynne,°   goods linen
To bye hym a perle was mascelles.°   was mascelles that was spotless

lxii

"This makelles° perle, that boght is dere,   matchless
The joueler gef° fore alle hys god,   gave
735 Is lyke the reme° of hevenesse clere°—   kingdom bright
So sayde the Fader of folde and flode.°   folde . . . earth and water
For hit is wemles,° clene, and clere,   spotless
And endeles rounde, and blythe of mode,°   spirit
And commune° to alle that ryghtwys° were.   common righteous
740 Lo, even inmyddes° my breste hit stode.   in the middle of
My Lorde the Lombe, that schede Hys blode,
He pyght° hit there in token of pes.°   put peace
I rede° thee, forsake the worlde wode°   advise crazy
And porchace thy perle maskelles."°   spotless

lxiii

745 "O maskeles perle in perles pure,
   That beres," quod I, "the perle of prys,°   excellence
   Who formed thee thy fayre fygure?
   That° wroght thy wede,° he was ful wys.   He who   garment
   Thy beauté com never of nature;
750 Pymalyon° paynted never thy vys,°   Pygmalion   face
   Ne Arystotel nawther by hys lettrure°   learning
   Of carped° the kynde° these propertés.   **Of carped** Spoke of   nature of
   Thy colour passes° the flour-de-lys,   surpasses
   Thyn angel-having° so clene cortes.°   angelic manner   **clene cortes** purely gracious
755 Breve° me, bryght, what kyn offys°   Tell   **kyn offys** kind of rank
   Beres the perle so maskelles?"°   spotless

lxiv

   "My makeles° Lambe that al may bete,"°   matchless   amend
   Quod schö,° "my dere destyné,   she
   Me ches to° Hys make,° althagh unmete°   **ches to** chose as   spouse   unfitting
760 Sumtyme semed that assemblé.°   union
   When I wente fro yor worlde wete,°   damp
   He calde me to Hys bonerté:°   beatitude
      "'Cum hyder to me, my lemman° swete,   beloved one
   For mote° ne spot is non in thee.'   stain
765 He gef° me myght and als° bewté;   gave   **myght . . .** power and also
   In Hys blod He wesch° my wede° on dese,°   washed   garment   a dais
   And coronde clene° in vergynté,   **coronde clene** crowned me pure
   And pyght me in perles maskelles."°   spotless

lxv

   "Why, maskelles bryd° that bryght con flambe,°   bride   **con flambe** shines
770 That reiates° has so ryche and ryf,°   royal attributes   **ryche . . .** splendid an- plentiful
   What kyn° thyng may be that Lambe   kind of
   That thee wolde wedde unto Hys wyf?
   Over alle other so hygh thou clambe
   To lede wyth Hym so ladyly° lyf.   ladylike a
775 So mony a comly on-uunder cambe°   **comly . . .** beautiful one under comb
   For Kryst han lyved in much stryf;
   And thou con alle tho dere° out dryf   **tho dere** those dear ones
   And fro that maryage al other depres,°   drive away
   Al-only° thyself so stout and styf,°   Exclusively   **stout . . .** brave and strong
780 A makeles may and maskelles."°   **makeles . . .** matchless and spotless ma-

lxvi

"Maskelles," quod that myry° quene,   fair
"Unblemyst I am, wythouten blot,
And that may I wyth mensk menteene.°   **mensk menteene** grace maintain
Bot 'makeles quene' thenne sade° I not.   said
785 The Lambes wyves in blysse we bene,°   are
A hondred and forty-fowre thowsande flot,°   company
As in the Apocalyppes hit is sene.
Sant John hem sygh° al in a knot   saw
On the hyl of Syon,° that semly clot;°   Zion   hill
790 The apostel hem segh in gostly drem°   **gostly drem** spiritual vision
Arayed to the weddyng in that hyl-coppe,° hilltop
The newe cyté o Jerusalem.

lxvii

"Of Jerusalem I in speche spelle.°   tell
If thou wyl knaw what kyn° he be,   kind
795 My Lombe, my Lorde, my dere juelle,
My joy, my blys, my lemman fre,°   **lemman fre** beloved noble
The profete Ysaye of Hym con melle°   **con melle** spoke
Pitously° of Hys debonerté:°   Compassionately   meekness
   "'That gloryous gyltles° that mon con quelle°   innocent   **mon...** was killed
800 Wythouten any sake° of felonye,   charge
As a schep to the slaght ther lad was He;
And, as lombe that clypper° in hande nem;'°   shearer   took
So closed He Hys mouth fro üch query,
When Jues Hym jugged in Jerusalem.

lxviii

805 "In Jerusalem was my lemman° slayn,   beloved one
And rent on rode wyth boyes° bolde.   **rode...** a cross by wretches
Al oure bales° to bere ful bayn,°   sorrows   willing
He toke on Hymself oure cares° colde.   sorrows
Wyth boffetes was Hys face flayn°   flayed
810 That was so fayr on to byholde.
For synne, He set° Hymself in vayn°   valued   **in vayn** at nothing
That never hade non° Hymself to wolde.°   any sin   own
For uus He lette hym flyghe and folde°   **hym...** himself be torn and bent
And brede° upon a bostwys bem.°   stretched   **bostwys bem** rough beam
815 As meke as lomb that no playnt° tolde,   complaint
For uus He swalt° in Jerusalem.   died

lxix

"In Jerusalem, Jordan, and Galalye,
Ther as° baptysed the goude Saynt Jon, — Ther as Where
His wordes acorded to° Ysaye. — with
820 When Jesus con to hym warde° gon, — to ... toward him
He sayde of Hym thys professye:
" 'Lo, Godes Lombe as trewe as ston,
That dos° away the synnes dryghe° — takes   heavy
That alle thys worlde has wroght upon.° — wroght upon practiced
825 Hymself ne wroght never yet non,
Whether° on Hymself He con al clem.'° — Yet   con ... claimed them all
Hys generacyoun° who recen con,° — ancestry   recen con can tell
That dyghed for uus in Jerusalem?

lxx

"In Jerusalem thus my lemman° swete — beloved
830 Twyes for° lombe was taken thare, — Twyes for Twice as
By trew recorde of ayther° prophete, — each (Isaiah, John)
For mode° so meke and al Hys fare.° — spirit   demeanor
The thryde tyme is therto ful mete,° — fitting
In Apokalypes¹ wryten ful yare:° — clearly
835 Inmydes° the trone, there sayntes sete,° — In the middle of   sat
The apostel John Hym sagh° as bare,° — saw   clearly
Lesande° the boke with leves sware° — Opening   square
There seven syngnettes° wern sette in seme;° — seals   the border
And at that syght üche douth con dare° — douth ... man feared
840 In helle, in erthe, and Jerusalem.

XV

lxxi

"Thys Jerusalem Lombe hade never pechche° — a speck
Of other huee bot whyt jolyf,° — fair
That mot ne masklle° moght on streche,° — mot ... stain nor spot   on streche res
For wolle° whyte so ronk and ryf.° — For wolle Because of wool   ronk ... and plentiful
845 For-thy° üche saule that hade never teche° — Therefore   a stain
Is to that Lombe a worthyly° wyf; — worthy
And thagh üch day a store° He feche,° — multitude   brings
Among uus commes nouther strot° ne stryf; — wrangling
Bot üchon enlé° we wolde° were fyf— — üchon enlé each one singly   wish
850 The mo° the myryer, so God me blesse. — more
In compayny gret our luf con thryf
In honour more and never the lesse.

¹ See Rev. v.6.

The Pearl

lxxii

"Lasse of blysse may non uus bryng
That beren thys perle upon oure bereste,°   breast
855 For thay of mote° couthe never mynge°   dispute   think
Of spotles perles that beren the creste.
Althagh oure corses° in clottes clynge,°   bodies   **clottes clynge** the earth waste away
And ye remen for rauthe° wythouten reste,   **remen** . . . cry out in grief
We thurghoutly° haven cnawyng.°   thoroughly   knowledge
860 Of on° dethe, ful oure hope is drest.°   one   drawn up
The Lombe uus glades,° oure care is kest;°   gladdens   driven away
He myrthes uus alle° at üch a mes.°   **myrthes** . . . makes us all rejoice   mass
Üchones° blysse is breme° and beste,   **Üchones** Each one's   glorious
And never ones honour yet never the les.

lxxiii

865 "Lest les thou leve° my tale farande,°   believe   **tale farande** enumeration fitting
In Appocalyppece is wryten in wro:°   a passage
" 'I seghe,'° says John, 'the Loumbe Hym stande°   saw   **Hym stande** standing
On the mount of Syon° ful thryven and thro,°   Zion   **thryven** . . . mighty and strong
And wyth Hym maydennes an hundrethe thowsande,
870 And fowre and forty thowsande mo.°   more
On alle her forhedes wryten I fande°   found
The Lombes nome,° Hys Faderes also.   name
A hue° from heven I herde thoo,°   cry   then
Lyk flodes fele laden runnen on resse,°
875 And as thunder throwes° in torres blo,°   rolls   **torres blo** dark hills
That lote,° I leve,° was never the les.   sound   believe

lxxiv

" 'Nautheles,° thagh hit schowted scharpe,°   Nevertheless   **schowted scharpe** sounded strongly
And ledden° loude althagh hit were,   a voice
A note ful newe I herde hem warpe,°   utter
880 To lysten that was ful lufly dere.°   **lufly dere** delightfully pleasant
As harpores harpen in her harpe,
That newe songe thay songen ful cler,
In sounande° notes a gentyl carpe.°   resounding   **gentyl carpe** noble discourse
Ful fayre the modes° thay fonge in fere.°   melodies   **fonge** . . . got all together
885 Ryght byfore Godes chayere°   throne
And the fowre bestes that hym obes°   reverence
And the aldermen° so sadde° of chere,°   elders   serious   countenance
Her songe thay songen never the les.

874. Like the sound of many rivers run together in a rush

lxxv

" 'Nowthelese° non was never so quoynt,°   Nevertheless   skillful
890 For alle the craftes° that ever thay knewe,   skills
That of that songe myght synge a poynt°   note
Bot° that meyny° the Lombe that sewe;°   Except   company   follow
For thay arn boght° fro the ürthe aloynte°   redeemed   far removed
As newe fryt° to God ful due,   **newe fryt** first fruit
895 And to the gentyl° Lombe hit° arn anjoynt,°   noble   they   united
As lyk to Hymself of lote and hwe;°   **lote** . . . appearance and color
For never lesyng° ne tale untrewe   lie
Ne towched her tonge for no dysstresse.
That moteles meyny° may never remewe°   **moteles meyny** spotless company   pa
900 Fro that maskeles mayster, never the les.' "

lxxvi

"Never the les let be my thonc,"°   **be** . . . my thanks be
Quod I, "my perle, thagh I appose.°   question
I schulde not tempte thy wyt so wlonc,°   noble
To Krystes chambre that art i-chose.
905 I am bot mokke and mul among,°   **mokke** . . . muck and dust mixed
And thou so ryche° a reken° rose,   splendid   fresh
And bydes° here by thys blysful bonc°   stay   slope
Ther lyves lyste° may never lose.°   **lyves lyste** life's joy   fade
Now, hynde,° that sympelnesse cones enclose,°   gracious one   **cones enclose** enclose
910 I wolde thee aske a thynge expresse,°   plainly
And thagh I be bustwys° as a blose,°   rough   churl
Let my bone vayl,° neverthelese.   **bone vayl** prayer avail

XVI

lxxvii

"Neverthelese, cler° I yow bycalle,°   clearly   call on
If ye con se hyt be to done;°
915 As thou art gloryous wythouten galle,°   spot
Wythnay° thou never my ruful° bone.   Deny   piteous
Haf ye no wones° in castel-walle,   dwellings
Ne maner° ther ye may mete and won?°   manor   dwell
Thou telles me of Jerusalem the ryche ryalle,°   **ryche ryalle** royal kingdom
920 Ther David dere was dyght° on trone,   set

914. If you can see that it be done

Bot by thyse holtes° hit con not hone,°   woods   **con . . .** can't be situated
Bot in Judee hit is, that noble note.°   structure
As ye ar maskeles under mone,°   **under mone** under the moon (on earth)
Your wones schulde be wythouten mote.°   stain

lxxviii

925   "Thys moteles meyny° thou cones of mele,°   **moteles meyny** spotless company
     Of thousandes thryght° so gret a route°—   **cones . . .** spoke of
     crowded   company
     A gret ceté,° for ye arn fele,°   city   many
     Yow byhod° have, wythouten doute.°   **Yow byhod** It behooved you   doubt
     So cumly° a pakke of joly° juele   beautiful   fair
930   Wer evel° don, schulde lygh ther-oute;°   ill   **schulde . . .** should they lie outside
     And by thyse bonkes° ther I con gele°   slopes   **con gele** linger
     I se no bygyng° nawhere aboute.   dwelling
     I trowe° alone ye lenge and loute°   suppose   **lenge . . .** linger and walk
     To loke on the glory of thys gracious gote.°   stream
935   If thou has other bygynges stoute,
     Now tech me to that myry mote."°   **myry mote** fair city

lxxix

     "That mote thou menes° in Judy° londe,"   mean   Judea
     That specyal spyce° then to me spakk,   **specyal spyce** excellent person
     "That is the cyté that the Lombe con fonde
940   To soffer inne sor° for manes° sake,   sorrow   man's
     The olde Jerusalem, to understonde;°   **to understonde** that is to say
     For there the olde gülte was don° to slake.°   brought   an end
     Bot the newe, that lyght° of Godes sonde,°   came down   sending
     The apostel in Apocalyppce in theme con take.°   **in theme . . .** adopted as a theme
945   The Lombe ther wythouten spottes blake
     Has feryed° thyder Hys fayre flote;°   led   company
     And as Hys flok is wythouten flake,°   spot
     So is Hys mote° wythouten moote.°   city   stain

lxxx

     "Of motes° two to carpe clene°—   cities   **carpe clene** speak exactly
950   And Jerusalem hyght° bothe nawtheles°—   are called   nevertheless
     That nys° to yow no more to mene°   is   mean
     Bot 'ceté of God' other 'syght° of pes.'°   vision   peace
     In that on oure pes was mad° at ene;°   made   once
     Wyth payne to suffer the Lombe hit chese.°   chose
955   In that other is noght bot pes to glene°   glean
     That ay schal laste wythouten reles.°   cessation

That is the borgh° that we to pres°   city   hurry
Fro that° oure flesch be layd to rote;°   **Fro that** After   rot
Ther glory and blysse schal ever encres
960 To the meyny° that is wythouten mote."°   company   stain

lxxxi

"Moteles may° so meke and mylde,"   **Moteles may** Spotless maiden
Then sayde I to that lufly flor,°   flower
"Bring me to that bygly bylde,°   **bygly bylde** pleasant dwelling
And let me se thy blysful bor."°   bower
965   That schene° sayde: "That God wyl schylde.°   fair one   prevent
Thou may not enter wythinne hys tor,°   tower
Bot of the Lombe I have thee aquylde°   obtained permission
For a syght therof thurgh gret favor.
Utwyth° to se that clene cloystor°   From without   **clene cloystor** pure enclosure
970 Thou may, bot inwyth° not a fote;   from within
To strech° in the strete thou has no vygour,°   walk   power
Bot° thou wer clene° wythouten mote.   Unless   pure

XVII

lxxxii

"If I this mote° thee schal unhyde,°   city   reveal
Bow° up towarde thys bornes heved,°   Go   **bornes heved** stream's head
975 And I anendes° thee on this syde   opposite
Schal sue,° tyl thou to a hil be weved."°   follow   brought
Then wolde I no lenger byde,°   tarry
Bot lurked° by launces° so lufly leved,°   stole   branches   **lufly leved** delightfu leaved
Tyl on a hyl that I asspyed
980 And blusched° on the burghe,° as I forth dreved,°   gazed   city   rushed
Byyonde the brok fro me warde keved,°   **fro . . .** which away from me sank
That schyrrer° then sunne wyth schaftes° schon.   brighter   rays
In the Apokalypce is the fasoun preved,°   **fasoun preved** fashion shown
As devyses° hit the apostel Jhon.   pictures

lxxxiii

985 As John the apostel hit sygh° wyth syght,   saw
I syghe that cyty of gret renoun,
Jerusalem so newe and ryally dyght,°   **ryally dyght** royally adorned
As° hit was lyght° fro the heven adoun.   As if   **was lyght** had come

The borgh° was al of brende° golde bryght   city   refined
990 As glemande° glas burnist broun,°   gleaming   bright
Wyth gentyl gemmes an-under° pyght   underneath
Wyth banteles° twelve on basyng boun,°   coursings   **basyng boun** foundation fixed
The foundementes° twelve of riche tenoun;°   foundations   joining
Üch tabelment° was a serlypes° ston;   tier   single
995 As derely devyses° this ilk° toun   pictures   same
In Apocalyppes the apostel John.

lxxxiv

As John thise stones in writ con nemme,°   **con nemme** named
I knew the name after his tale:
Jasper hyght° the fyrst gemme   is called
1000 That I on the fyrst basse con wale,°   **basse ...** base perceived
He glente° grene in the lowest hemme;°   **He glente** It glinted   course
Saffer° helde the secounde stale;°   Sapphire   place
The calsydoyne° thenne wythouten wemme°   chalcedony   flaw
In the thryd table con purly pale;°   **table ...** tier shone pure and pale
1005 The emerade the furthe so grene of scale;°   surface
The sardonyse° the fyfthe ston;   sardonyx
The sexte,° the rybé,° he con hit wale°   sixth   ruby   **con ...** noted it
In the Apocalyppce, the apostel John.

lxxxv

Yet joyned° John the crysolyt,°   added   chrysolite
1010 The seventhe gemme in fundament;°   the foundation
The aghtthe° the beryl cler and whyt;   eighth
The topasye twynne-hew,° the nente endent;°   **topasye twynne-hew** topaz twin-hued   **nente endent** ninth set
The crysopase° the tenthe is tyght;°   chrysoprase   fixed
The jacynght,° the enleventhe gent;°   jacinth   noble
1015 The twelfthe, the gentyleste in üch a plyt,°   state
The amatyst purpre° wyth ynde blente;°   **amatyst purpre** amethyst purple   **ynde blente** indigo mixed
The wal abof the bantels bent°   **bantels bent** coursings set
O jasporye,° as glas that glysnande° schon;   **O jasporye** Of jasper   glistening
I knew hit by his devysement°   description
1020 In the Apocalyppes, the apostel John.

lxxxvi

As John devysed yet sagh° I thare   saw
Thise twelve degres wern° brode and stayre;°   which were   steep
The cyté stod abof ful sware,°   square
As longe as brode as hyghe ful fayre;°   **ful fayre** exactly

1025 The stretes of golde as glasse al bare,
　　　 The wal of jasper that glent° as glayre;°   glinted　egg-white glaze
　　　 The wones wythinne enurned° ware   adorned
　　　 Wyth alle kynnes perré° that moght repayre.°   **kynnes perré** kinds of gems　come together
　　　 Thenne helde üch sware° of this manayre°   square　manor
1030 Twelve forlonge space, er ever hit fon,°   ceased
　　　 Of heght,° of brede,° of lenthe to cayre,°   height　breadth　extend
　　　 For meten° hit sygh° the apostel John.   measured　saw

XVIII

lxxxvii

　　　 As John hym wrytes yet more I syghe:°   saw
　　　 Üch pane° of that place had thre yates;°   side　gates
1035 So twelve in poursent° I con asspye,   the encompassing wall
　　　 The portales pyked° of rych° plates,   adorned　splendid
　　　 And üch yate of a margyrye,°   pearl
　　　 A parfyt perle that never fates.°   fades
　　　 Üchon in scrypture a name con plye°   **con plye** showed forth
1040 Of Israel barnes,° folewande her dates,   **Israel barnes** Israel's children
　　　 That is to say, as her byrth-whates;°   fortunes of birth
　　　 The aldest ay fyrst theron was done.
　　　 Such lyght ther lemed° in alle the strates°   gleamed　streets
　　　 Hem nedde° nawther sunne ne mone.°   **Hem nedde** They needed　moon

lxxxviii

1045 Of sunne ne mone had thay no nede;
　　　 The self God° was her lombe-lyght,°   **The . . .** God Himself　lamplight
　　　 The Lombe her lantyrne, wythouten drede;°   doubt
　　　 Thurgh hym blysned° the borgh° al bryght.   shone　city
　　　 Thurgh woghe° and won my lokyng yede,°   wall　**lokyng yede** gaze pierced
1050 For sotyle, cler, noght lette no lyght.°
　　　 The hyghe trone ther moght ye hede°   behold
　　　 Wyth alle the apparaylmente umbepyghte,°   **apparaylmente umbepyghte** adornm[?] set around
　　　 As John the appostel in termes tyghte;°   **termes tyghte** exact words set forth
　　　 The hyghe Godes self° hit set upone.   Himself
1055 A rever° of the trone ther ran outryghte,   river
　　　 Was bryghter then bothe the sunne and mone.°   moon

1050. For being transparent, clear, nothing hindered any light.

lxxxix

Sunne ne mone schon never so swete
As that foysoun flode° out of that flet;°
Swythe° hit swange° thurgh üch a strete°
060 Wythouten fylthe other galle other glet.°
Kyrk° ther-inne was non yete,°
Chapel, ne temple that ever was set;
The Almyghty was her mynyster mete,°
The Lombe the sakerfyse ther to reget.°
065 The yates stoken° was never yet,
Bot evermore upen° at üche a lone;°
Ther entres non to take reset°
That beres any spot an-under mone.°

foysoun flode abundant river   floor
Swiftly   rushed   street
galle . . . scum or slime
Church   yet

fitting
redeem
yates stoken gates shut
open   lane
refuge
an-under mone under the moon (on earth)

xc

The mone may therof acroche° no myghte;
070 Too spotty hö is, of body too grym,°
And also ther ne is never nyght.
What° schulde the mone ther compas° clym
And to even° wyth that worthly° lyght
That schynes upon the brokes brym?°
075 The planates arn in too pouer a plyght,°
And the self° sunne ful fer° too dym.
Aboute that water arn tres ful schym,°
That twelve frytes° of lyf con bere ful sone;°
Twelve sythes on° yer thay beren ful frym,°
080 And renowles° newe in üche a mone.

acquire
ugly

Why   circuit
vie   glorious
brokes brym river's bank
state
very   far
bright
fruits   quickly
sythes on times in a   richly
renew

xci

An-under mone° so great mervayle°
No fleschly hert ne myght° endeure,
As when I blusched° upon that bayle,°
So ferly° therof was the fasure.°
085 I stod as stylle as dased quayle
For ferly° of that freuch fygure,°
That felde° I nawther reste ne travayle,°
So was I ravyste° wyth glymme° pure.
For I dar say wyth conciens sure,
090 Hade bodyly bürne abiden° that bone,°
Thagh alle clerkes hym hade in cure,°
His lyf were loste an-under mone.°

An-under mone under the moon (on earth)
marvel
ne myght could
looked   wall (city)
wondrous   fashion

wonder   freuch fygure delicate form
felt   labor
ravished   radiance

bürne abiden man endured   favor
care
an-under mone under the moon (on earth)

xcii

Ryght° as the maynful° mone con rys — Just   mighty
Er thenne° the day-glem dryve° al doun, — **Er thenne** Before   goes
1095 So sodanly on a wonder wyse° — **wonder wyse** wonderful manner
I was war° of a prosessyoun. — aware
This noble cité of ryche enpryse° — **ryche enpryse** splendid renown
Was sodanly ful, wythouten sommoun,° — summons
Of such vergynes in the same gyse° — guise
1100 That was my blysful an-under° croun. — under
And coronde wern alle of the same fasoun,° — fashion
Depaynt° in perles and wedes° whyte; — Arrayed   garments
In üchones breste was bounden boun° — **bounden boun** fixed firmly
The blysful perle wyth gret delyt.

xciii

1105 Wyth gret delyt thay glod in fere° — **glod . . .** glided in company
On golden gates° that glent° as glasse. — streets   glinted
Hundreth thowsandes I wot° ther were, — know
And alle in sute° her livres wasse;° — **in sute** to match   **livres wasse** garmen were
Tor° to knaw the gladdest chere.° — Hard   expression
1110 The Lombe byfore con proudly passe
Wyth hornes seven of red golde cler;° — bright
As praysed° perles His wedes° wasse. — precious   garments
Towarde the throne thay trone a tras.° — **trone . . .** made their way
Thagh thay wern fele, no pres in plyt.° — **pres . . .** crowding in their order
1115 But mylde as maydenes seme at mas
So drogh° thay forth wyth gret delyt. — went

xciv

Delyt that His come encroched° — **come encroched** coming brought
Too much hit were of for to melle° — **of . . .** to tell of
Thise aldermen,° when He aproched, — elders
1120 Grovelyng to His fete thay felle.
Legyounes of aungeles togeder voched° — summoned
Ther kesten° ensens of swete smelle. — cast
Then glory and gle was newe abroched;° — uttered
Al songe° to love° that gay° juelle. — sang   praise   fair
1125 The steven° moght stryke thurgh the ürthe to — sound
helle
That the Vertues of heven of° joye endyte.° — for   sing out
To love the Lombe His meyny in melle° — midst
I-wysse,° I laght° a gret delyt. — Indeed   took

xcv

Delit the Lombe for to devise°   look on
130 Wyth much mervayle° in mynde went.   wonder
Best was He, blythest, and moste to pryse°   esteem
That ever I herde of speche spent;°   **of** . . . speech spent on
So worthly° whyt wern wedes° Hys,   gloriously   garments
His lokes symple,° Hymself so gent.°   humble   noble
135 Bot a wounde fyl wyde and weete con wyse°   **weete** . . . wet showed
Anende° Hys hert, thurgh hyde torente.°   Over   **hyde torente** skin all torn
Of His whyte syde his blod outsprent.°   gushed forth
Alas, thoght I, who did that spyt?°   evil
Ani breste for bale aght haf forbrent°   **bale** . . . sorrow ought to have burned up
140 Er he therto hade had delyt.

xcvi

The Lombe° delyt non lyste° to wene.°   Lamb's   **non lyste** no one wished   doubt
Thagh He were hurt and wounde hade,
In His sembelaunt° was never sene,   demeanor
So wern His glentes° gloryous glade.   looks
145 I loked among His meyny schene°   bright
How thay wyth lyf wern laste and lade;°   **laste** . . . filled and laden
Than sagh I ther my lyttel quene
That I wende° had standen° by me in sclade.°   thought   stood   a valley
Lorde, much of mirthe was that hö made
150 Among her feres° that was so whyt!   companions
That syght me gart° to thenk to wade   made
For luf-longyng in gret delyt.

XX

xcvii

Delyt me drof in yghe and ere,°   **yghe** . . . eye and ear
My manes° mynde to maddyng malte.°   man's   melted
55 When I segh my frely,° I wolde be there,   fair one
Byyonde the water thagh hö were walte.°   set
I thoght that nothyng myght me dere°   harm
To fetch me bür and take° me halte,   **bür** . . . blow and make
And to start° in the strem schulde non me stere,°   plunge   hinder
60 To swymme the remnaunt,° thagh I ther swalte.°   remainder   might die
Bot of that münt° I was bitalt;°   intention   shaken
When I schulde° start in the strem astraye,   was about to
Out of that caste° I was bycalt:°   purpose   called
Hit was not at my Prynces paye.°   pleasure

xcviii

1165 Hit payed° Hym not that I so flonc°
 Over mervelous meres,° so mad arayde.°
 Of raas° thagh I were rasch and ronk,°
 Yet rapely° ther-inne I was restayed.°
 For, ryght° as I sparred° unto the bonc,
1170 That braththe° out of my drem me brayde.°
 Then wakned I in that erber wlonk;°
 My hede upon that hylle was layde
 Ther as° my perle to grounde strayd.
 I raxled,° and fel in gret affray,°
1175 And, sykyng,° to myself I sayd,
  "Now al be to that Prynces paye."°

pleased flung myself

*waters **mad arayde** madly conditioned*
rush overbearing
quickly restrained
just rushed
violence roused
***erber wlonk** garden splendid*

***Ther as** Where*
stretched myself dismay
sighing

pleasure

xcix

 Me payed° ful ille to be outfleme°
 So sodenly of that fayre regioun,
 Fro alle tho syghtes so quyke and queme.°
1180 A longeyng hevy me strok in swone,°
 And rewfully thenne I con to reme:°
  "O perle," quod I, "of rych° renoun,
 So was hit me dere that° thou con deme°
 In this veray avysyoun.°
1185 If hit be veray and soth sermoun°
 That thou so stykes° in garlande gay,°
 So wel° is me in thys doel°-doungoun
 That thou art to that Prynces paye."°

pleased outcast

quyke . . . lifelike and pleasant
a swoon
con . . . cried out
splendid
*me . . . dear to me what **con deme** sp*
 of
veray avysyoun true vision
veray . . . real and true account
are set fair
happy sorrow
pleasure

c

 To that Prynces paye hade I ay bente,°
1190 And yerned no more then was me gyven,
 And halden me° ther in trewe entent,°
 As the perle me prayed that was so thryven,°
 As helde,° drawen to Goddes present,°
 To mo° of His mysterys I hade ben dryven.°
1195 Bot ay wolde man of happe° more hente°
 Then moghte by ryght upon° hem clyven.°
 Therfore my joye was sone toriven,°
 And I kaste of kythes° that lastes aye.
 Lorde, mad hit° arn that agayn thee stryven,
1200 Other proferen thee oght agayn thy paye.°

hade . . . if I had ever bowed

halden me stayed intention
fair
likely as possible presence
more brought
good fortune seize
to belong
torn apart
kaste . . . cast from regions
they
pleasure

ci

To pay the Prince other sete saghte°   **sete saghte** set at peace
Hit is ful ethe° to the god Krystyin;   easy
For I haf founden Hym, bothe day and naghte,°   night
A God, a Lorde, a frende ful fyin.°   noble
205 Over this hyül° this lote° I laghte,°   hill   fortune   took
For pyty of my perle enclyin,°   lying prostrate
And sythen° to God I hit bytaghte°   then   committed
In Krystes dere blessyng and myn,
That in the forme of bred and wyn
210 The preste uus schewes üch a daye.
He gef° uus to be His homly hyne°   granted   **homly hyne** household servants
Ande precious perles unto His pay.
    Amen. Amen.

Sir Gawain and the Green Knight

(ca. 1390, West Midland)

☙

Sir Gawain is generally attributed to the author of *The Pearl* (see p. 339). Like *The Pearl*, it is a work of considerable finesse. The plot of the romance is derived ultimately from *The Feast of Bricriu*, an Irish heroic legend glorifying Cuchulainn and the magical Curoi; but the wild magic of Celtic legend has been transformed into a courtly Arthurian romance, set within the dramatic framework of the British legendary history that Geoffrey of Monmouth had created in his *History of the Kings of Britain*, which Lawman had already popularized for English audiences (see p. 49). As in many romances, the hero is a paragon of bravery and a master of the art of courtly love. But the author of *Sir Gawain* is a moralist as well as a romancer, and, as in the other writings attributed to him, he is essentially concerned with human behavior and sets greater store on his hero's acquirement of self-knowledge than on knightly self-aggrandizement.

The romance shows the same sense of symmetry that appears in *The Pearl*. The conclusion echoes the opening lines (compare l. 1, Part I, and l. 2255, Part IV). The progress of the hero's adventures is marked by the passing of the four seasons. Gawain's heraldic device, the pentangle, or five-pointed star, has a fivefold signification: the five wits, the five fingers, the five wounds of Christ, the five joys of Mary, and the five virtues. The sequence of the three quarries hunted by the host—the noble deer, the savage bear, and the foul fox—match the decline of Gawain's resolve in his three encounters with the host's wife.

The stanzas are composed in the traditional English alliterative measure, and each is decorated with a final set of five rhyming lines, known as a bob-and-wheel. The bob contains one stress; the following lines of the wheel contain generally three stresses and at least two alliterations; and the rhyme is ababa. (See also Introduction, type 2, p. 30.)

To satisfy alliteration, the poet uses a number of etymologically distinct words for *man*, sometimes without any clear distinction of meaning: *bürn* ('warrior'), *freke* ('knight'), *gome* ('man'), *grome* ('servant'), *hathel* ('leader'), *knight, lede, l(e)ude* ('man'), *lord, mon, prince, renk* ('warrior'), *schalk* ('servant'), *segge* ('man'), *syr(e)* ('sire'), *tulk* ('speaker'), *wyghe* ('person').

Two useful editions of *Sir Gawain and the Green Knight* are ed. J. R. R. Tolkien and E. V. Gordon, rev. Norman Davis (Oxford, 1967) and ed. I. Gollancz, M. Day, and M. S. Serjeantson, EETS 210 (London, 1938). A facsimile of the manuscript will be found in *Facsimile of MS. Cotton Nero A x*, EETS 162 (London, 1923), fols. 91–124. For bibliography see Severs, ch. 1.25. For criticism see *Critical Studies of Sir Gawain and the Green Knight*, ed. Donald R. Howard and Christian Zacher (Notre Dame, 1968).

Part I

i

Sithen° the sege and the assaut was sesed° at Troye,　　After　ceased

The burgh brittened and brent° to brondes and askes,°　　**burgh** ... city destroyed and burned　ashes

The tulk° that the trammes° of tresoun ther wroght　　man　plots

Was tried for his tricherie, the trewest on erthe.

5　Hit was Ennias° the athel° and his highe kynde°　　Aeneas　splendid　**highe kynde** noble kin

That sithen depreced° provinces, and patrounes° bicome　　**sithen depreced** later conquered　lords

Welneghe° of al the wele° in the west iles.　　Almost　wealth

Fro riche° Romulus to Rome ricchis hym swythe,°　　**Fro riche** When noble　**ricchis** ... proceeds quickly

With gret bobbaunce° that burghe° he biges upon fyrst°　　pride　city　**biges** ... builds at first

10　And nevenes° hit his awne nome,° as hit now hat;°　　names　**awne nome** own name　is called

Ticius° to Tuskan, and teldes bigynnes;°　　Ticius goes　**teldes bigynnes** begins to build houses

Langaberde in Lumbardie lyftes up homes;

And fer° over the French flod° Felix Brutus　　far　sea (English Channel)

On many bonkkes ful° brode Bretayn he settes,　　**bonkkes ful** slopes very

15　　　wyth wynne;°　　joy

Where werre and wrake° and wonder　　**werre** ... war and vengeance

Bi sythes has wont° ther-inne,　　**Bi** ... At times have dwelled

And oft bothe blysse and blunder°　　confusion

Ful skete° has skyfted synne.°　　quickly　**skyfted synne** shifted since

ii

20　Ande when this Bretayn was bigged° bi this bürn rych,°　　built　**bürn rych** noble man

Bolde bredden° ther-inne, baret that lofden,°　　**Bolde bredden** Brave men bred　**baret** ... who loved strife

In mony turned tyme tene° that wroghten.　　**turned** ... a time come to pass grief

Mo ferlyes° on this folde han° fallen here oft　　**Mo ferlyes** More marvels　**folde han** land have

Then in any other that I wot,° syn that ilk° tyme.　　know of　same

25　Bot, of alle that here bult,° of Bretaygne kynges　　dwelt

Ay° was Arthur the hendest,° as I haf herde telle.　　Ever　most courteous

For-thi° an aunter in erde° I attle° to schawe,　　Therefore　**aunter** ... adventure actually intend

That a selly° in sight summe men hit holden,　　marvel

And an outtrage° aventure of Arthures wonderes.　　extraordinary

30　If ye wyl lysten this laye bot on° littel while,　　**bot on** only a

I schal telle hit as-tit,° as I in toun herde,　　at once

　　　with tonge;

As hit is stad and stoken°   **stad** ... placed and written
In stori stif° and stronge,   brave
35   With lel° lettres loken,°   true   linked
In londe so° has ben longe.   as it

iii

This kyng lay at Camylot upon Krystmasse
With mony luflych° lorde, ledes° of the best,   comely   men
Rekenly° of the Rounde Table alle tho rich°   Nobly   **tho rich** those noble
    brether,
40   With rych revel oryght and rechles° merthes.   **oryght** ... fitting and carefree
Ther tournayed tulkes° by tymes ful° mony,   knights   very
Justed ful jolilé thise gentyle° knightes,   noble
Sythen kayred° to the court, caroles to make.   **Sythen kayred** Then rode
For ther the fest° was i-lyche° ful fiften dayes,   festival   the same
45   With alle the mete° and the mirthe that men   food
    couthe avyse,°   **couthe avyse** knew how to devise
Such glaum° ande gle glorious to here,°   merry sounds   hear
Dere dyn° upon day, daunsyng on nyghtes.   **Dere dyn** Pleasant noise
Al was hap° upon heghe in halles and chambres,   happiness
With lordes and ladies, as levest him thoght.°   **levest** ... it seemed most delightful to
        them
50   With alle the wele° of the worlde thay woned°   joy   dwelled
    ther samen,°   together
The most kyd° knyghtes under Krystes selven,°   famous   **Krystes selven** Christ himself
And the lovelokkest° ladies that ever lif haden,   fairest
And he the comlokest° kyng that the court   comeliest
    haldes;°   rules
For al was this fayre folk in her first age,°   **her** ... their prime
55   on sille,°   the floor
    The hapnest° under heven,   most fortunate
    Kyng hyghest° mon of wylle;°   noblest   mind
    Hit were now gret nye° to neven°   difficulty   name
    So hardy a here° on hille.   **hardy** ... bold a company

iv

60   Wyle New Yer was so yep° that hit was newe   fresh
    cummen
That day doubble on the dece° was the douth°   dais   company
    served.
Fro° the kyng was cummen with knyghtes into   When
    the halle,
The chauntré of° the chapel cheved° to an ende.   **chauntré of** singing from   came
Loude crye was ther kest° of clerkes and other,   cast
65   Nowel nayted° onewe, nevened ful° ofte;   **Nowel nayted** Noel celebrated
    nevened ful named very

And sythen riche° forth runnen to reche   **sythen riche** then nobles
    hondeselle,°   **reche hondeselle** give New Year's gifts
Yeghed yeres° giftes on high, yelde hem° bi   **Yeghed yeres** Cried the year's   **yelde**
    hond,   **hem** gave them
Debated busyly aboute tho° giftes.   those
Ladies laghed ful loude, thogh thay lost haden,
70 And he that wan° was not wrothe, that may ye   won
    wel trawe.°   believe
Alle this mirthe thay maden to the mete° tyme.   meal
When thay had waschen worthyly,° thay wenten   fittingly
    to sete,
The best bürne ay° abof, as hit best semed,   **bürne ay** man ever
Quene Guenore ful gay, graythed° in the myddes,   **Guenore . . .** Guinevere very fair, set
75 Dressed° on the dere des, dubbed° al aboute,   Placed   **dere . . .** glorious dais, adorned
Smal sendal° bisides, a selure° hir over,   **Smal sendal** Fine silk   canopy
Of tryed Tolouse, of Tars tapites innoghe,°
That were enbrawded and beten° wyth the best   **enbrawded . . .** embroidered and set
    gemmes
That myght be preved° of prys° wyth penyes° to   proved   value   money
    bye,
80   in daye.°   **in daye** ever
    The comlokest° to discrye°   comeliest   look on
    Ther glent° with yghen° gray;   glanced   eyes
    A semloker° that ever he syghe,°   comelier one   might see
    Soth moght° no mon say.°   **Soth moght** Truly could   speak of

              v

85   Bot Arthure wolde not ete til al were served,
He was so joly of his joyfnes,° and sumwhat   youth
    child-gered;°   boyish
His lif liked° hym lyght,° he lovied the lasse°   pleased   when active   less
Auther° too longe lye or too longe sitte,   Either
So bisied° him his yonge blod and his brayn   stirred
    wylde.°   restless
90 And also another maner meved° him eke°   **maner meved** habit moved   as well
That he thurgh nobelay° had nomen:° he wolde   magnificence   undertaken
    never ete
Upon such a dere° day er° hym devised° were   pleasant   before   related
Of sum aventurus thyng an uncouthe° tale   strange
Of sum mayn° mervayle that he myght trawe°   great   **myght trawe** could believe
95 Of alderes,° of armes, of other aventurus;   princes
Other° sum segg° hym bisoght of sum siker°   Or   man   trusty
    knyght
To joyne wyth hym in justyng, in jöpardé to lay,

77. Of fine fabric from Toulouse, of many tapestries from Tharsia (Turkestan)

Lede lif for° lyf, leve üchon° other,
As fortune wolde fulsun höm,° the fayrer° to have.
100 This was the kynges countenance° where he in
court were,
At üch farand fest° among his fre meny°
in halle.
Therfore of face so fere°
He stightles stif in stalle;°
105 Ful yep° in that New Yere,
Much mirthe he mas° with alle.

vi

Thus ther stondes in stale° the stif kyng hisselven,
Talkkande° bifore the hyghe table of trifles ful
hende,°
There gode Gawan was graythed Gwenore°
bisyde,
110 And Agravayn à la dure mayn° on that other syde
sittes,
Bothe the kynges sister° sunes, and ful siker°
knightes.
Bischop Bawdewyn abof bigines the table,
And Ywan, Uryn° son, ette with hymselven.
Thise were dight° on the des, and derworthly°
served,
115 And sithen° mony siker segge° at the sidbordes.
Then the first cors come° with crakkyng° of
trumpes,°
Wyth mony baner ful bryght that ther-bi henged,
Newe nakryn noyse° with the noble pipes,
Wylde werbles° and wyght-wakned lote,°
120 That mony hert° ful highe hef° at her
towches.°
Dayntes dryven° ther-wyth of ful dere metes,°
Foysoun° of the fresche,° and on so fele° disches
That pine° to fynde the place the peple biforne
For to sette the sylveren that sere sewes° halden,
125 on clothe.
Iche lede° as he loved° hymselve
Ther laght° withouten lothe;°
Ay° two had disches twelve,
Good ber and bryght wyn bothe.°

Glosses:

Lede . . . Risk life against leve üchon let each
fulsun höm help them advantage behavior
farand fest splendid festival fre meny noble company
proud
stightles . . . stands up fearlessly
bold
makes

in stale up
Talking
ful hende very courteous
graythed Gwenore set Guinevere
à . . . of the hard hand

sister's trusty

Urien's
set des . . . dais, and honorably
then men
came blaring
trumpets

nakryn noyse clamor of kettledrums warblings wyght-wakned lote loud-stirred sound
mony hert many a heart lifted
her towches their tunes
come dere metes precious foods
Abundance fresh foods many
it was difficult
sere sewes different stews

Iche lede Each man pleased
took displeasure
Each
too

vii

130 Now wyl I of hör° servise say yow no more,   their
For üch wyghe° may wel wit° no wont that ther   man   know
    were.
Another noyse° ful newe neghed bilive,°   clamor   **neghed bilive** neared quickly
That the lüde° myght haf leve liflode° to cach.°   man   food   get
For unethe° was the noyce not a whyle sesed,°   hardly   ceased
135 And the fyrst cource in the court kyndely° served,   properly
Ther hales° in at the halle dor an aghlich mayster,°   comes   **aghlich mayster** dreadful knight
On° the most on the molde on mesure° hyghe;   One   **molde** ... earth in stature
Fro the swyre° to the swange° so sware° and so   neck   waist   square
    thik,
And his lyndes° and his lymes so longe and so   loins
    grete,
140 Half etayn in erde° I hope° that he were;   **etayn** ... giant actually   suppose
Bot mon most° I algate mynn° hym to bene,°   must   **algate mynn** at any rate think   be
And that the myriest° in his muckel° that myght   fairest   size
    ride;
For of bak and of brest al were° his bodi sturne,°   was   strong
Both his wombe° and his wast were worthily°   belly   fittingly
    smale,
145 And all his fetures folghande° in forme° that he   following   manner
    hade,
        ful clene.°   fair
    For wonder of his hewe° men hade,   hue
    Set in his semblaunt sene;°   **semblaunt sene** appearance clearly
    He ferde° as freke were fade,°   acted   **freke** ... a man who would be hostile
150   And overal enker° grene.   very

viii

Ande al graythed° in grene this gome° and his   clothed   man
    wedes,°   garments were
A strayt° cote ful streght that stek on his sides,   tight
A meré° mantile abof, mensked° withinne   fair   adorned
With pelure pured apert,° the pane° ful clene,°   **pelure** ... fur trimmed clearly   fur lining   fair
155 With blythe blaunner° ful bryght, and his hod   **blythe blaunner** gay white fur
    bothe,°   too
That was laght° fro his lokkes and layde on his   caught back
    schulderes;
Heme, wel-haled° hose of that same grene,   **Heme, wel-haled** Neat, well-drawn
That spenet° on his sparlyr,° and clene spures   were fastened   calf
    under

Of bryght golde, upon silk bordes barred° ful ryche,   striped

160 And scholes° under schankes, there° the schalk° rides.   pointed shoes   **schankes, there** legs, whe[re] man

And alle his vesture verayly was clene verdure,°   **clene verdure** pure green

Bothe the barres of his belt and other blythe° stones   gay

That were richely rayled° in his aray clene°   arranged   fair

Aboutte hymself and his sadel, upon silk werkes,°   embroidery

165 That were too tor° for to telle of tryfles° the halve   hard   details

That were enbrauded° abof, wyth bryddes and flyghes,°   embroidered   **bryddes** ... birds and flies

With gay gaudi° of grene, the golde ay inmyddes.°   **gay gaudi** fair color   **ay inmyddes** ever in the middle

The pendauntes of his payttrure,° the proude cropure,°   horse trappings   cropper

His molaynes° and alle the metail anamayld° was thenne,   bit studs   enameled

170 The steropes that he stod on, stayned of the same,

And his arsouns° al after, and his athel skurtes,°   saddlebows   **athel skurtes** splendid saddle skirts

That ever glemered and glent° al of grene stones.   glinted

The fole° that he ferkkes° on, fyn° of that ilke,° sertayn;°   horse   rides   completely   same   certainly

175   A grene hors gret and thikke,

A stede ful stif to strayne,°   **stif** ... hard to restrain

In brawden° brydel quik;°   embroidered   lively

To the gome° he was ful gayn.°   man   ready

ix

Wel gay° was this gome gered° in grene,   **Wel gay** Very fairly   clothed

180 And the here° of his hed, of his hors suete.°   hair   **of** ... matched that of his horse

Fayre fannand fax umbefoldes° his schulderes;   **fannand** ... waving hair hangs about

A much° berd as a busk° over his brest henges,   great   bush

That wyth his highlich° here that of° his hed reches,   splendid   from

Was evesed° al umbetorne,° abof his elbowes,   clipped   around

185 That half his armes ther-under were halched° in the wyse°   enclosed   manner

Of a kinges capados° that closes his swyre.°   hood   neck

The mane of that mayn° hors, much to hit lyke,   great

Wel cresped and cemmed° wyth knottes ful mony,   **cresped** ... curled and combed

Folden in° wyth fildore° aboute the fayre grene,   Entwined   gold thread

190 Ay a herle° of the here,° an other of golde;   **Ay** ... Ever one strand   hair

The tayl and his toppyng twynnen of° a sute,°   **toppyng** ... forelock joined in   match

And bounden bothe wyth a bande of a bryght grene,

382

Dubbed° wyth ful dere° stones, as the dok lasted;°   Adorned   glorious   **dok lasted** tail

Sythen thrawen° wyth a thwong,° a thwarle° knot   extended
    alofte,   twisted   thong   intricate

195   Ther° mony belles ful bryght of brende° golde   Where   burnished
    rungen.

Such a fole° upon folde, ne freke° that hym rydes,   horse   **folde** . . . earth, or man

Was never sene in that sale° wyth syght er° that   hall   before
    tyme,

      with yghe.°   eye

He loked as layt° so lyght,°   lightning   bright

200   So sayd al that hym syghe;°   might see

Hit semed as no mon myght°   could

Under his dynttes dryghe.°   **dynttes dryghe** blows survive

         x

Whether° hade he no helme, ne hawbergh   Yet
    nauther,°   **helme** . . . helmet, nor coat of mail either

Ne no pysan,° ne no plate that pented° to armes,   breastplate   pertained

205   Ne no schafte,° ne no schelde, to schuve° ne to   spear   thrust
    smyte,

Bot in his on° honde he hade a holyn bobbe,°   one   **holyn bobbe** holly branch

That is grattest in grene when greves° ar bare,   groves

And an ax in his other, a hoge and unmete,°   **hoge** . . . huge and monstrous

A spetos sparthe,° to expoun° in spelle who-so   **spetos sparthe** cruel ax   describe
    myght.°   **spelle** . . . speech whosoever could

210   The hede of an elnyerde° the large lenkthe° hade,   ell (45″ measure)   length

The grayn° al of grene stele and of golde hewen,°   spike   hammered

The bit burnyst° bryght, with a brod egge,°   **bit burnyst** blade polished   edge

As wel schapen to schere° as scharp rasores.   cut

The stele° of a stif staf—the sturne° hit bigrypte°   handle   grim one   gripped

215   That was wounden wyth yrn° to the wandes°   iron   handle's
    ende,

And al bigraven° with grene, in gracios° werkes;   engraved   beautiful

A lace° lapped aboute, that louked° at the hede,   thong   fastened

And so after the halme halched° ful ofte,   **halme halched** shaft looped

Wyth tryed° tasseles therto tacched innoghe°   fine   **tacched innoghe** fastened many

220   On botouns° of the bryght grene brayden° ful   **On botouns** To bosses   embroidered
    ryche.

This hathel heldes hym° in and the halle entres,   **hathel** . . . knight goes

Drivande° to the heghe dece; dut° he no wothe,°   Coming   **dece; dut** dais; feared   danger

Haylsed° he never one, bot heghe he over loked.   Greeted

    The fyrst word that he warp,° "Wher is," he   uttered
      sayd,

225   "The governour of this gyng?° Gladly I wolde   assembly

Se that segg° in syght, and with hymself speke raysoun."	man
To knyghtes he kest his yghe,°	eye
And reled hym° up and doun,	**reled hym** swaggered
230 He stemmed and con studie°	**stemmed** . . . stopped and looked closely
Who walt° ther most renoun.	had

xi

Ther was lokyng on lenthe,° the lüde° to beholde,	**lokyng** . . . gazing at length man
For üch man had mervayle what hit mene myght,°	**mene myght** could mean
That a hathel° and a horse myght such a hewe lach,°	knight **hewe lach** hue take
235 As growe° grene as the gres,° and grener hit semed	to grow grass
Then grene aumayl° on golde glowande° bryghter;	enamel glowing
Al studied° that ther stod, and stalked° hym nerre,°	watched moved carefully nearer
Wyth al the wonder of the worlde what he worch° schulde.	do
For fele sellyes° had thay sen, bot such never are,°	**fele sellyes** many marvels before
240 For-thi° for fantoum and fayryghe° the folk there hit demed;	Therefore **fantoum** . . . illusion and magic
Therfore to answare was arghe mony athel freke,°	**arghe** . . . afraid many a noble man
And al stouned° at his steven, and ston-stil seten°	amazed **steven** . . . voice, and sat still as stone
In a swoghe°-sylence thurgh the sale riche.°	dead **sale riche** splendid hall
As al were slypped upon slepe, so slaked hör lotes°	
245 in hyghe;°	haste
I deme° hit not al for doute,°	judge fear
Bot sum for cortaysye,	
Bot let hym° that al schulde loute,°	him (Arthur) bow to
Cast° unto that wyghe.°	Speak man

xii

250 Thenn Arthour, bifore the high dece,° that aventure byholdes	dais
And rekenly° hym reverenced, for rad° was he never,	nobly afraid
And sayde, "Wyghe, welcum i-wys° to this place.	indeed
The hede of this ostel Arthour I hat;°	am called
Light luflych° adoun and lenge,° I thee praye,	**Light luflych** Alight graciously stay
255 And what-so° thy wylle is, we schal wyt° after."	whatsoever know
"Nay, as help me," quoth the hathel,° "he that on hyghe syttes,	knight
To wone° any whyle in this won,° hit was not myn ernde;°	stay dwelling mission

244. As if all fell asleep, so ceased their cries

Bot for the los° of thee, lede,° is lyft up so hyghe,   °renown °sir

And thy burgh° and thy bürnes° best ar holden,   °city °men

260 Stifest under stel-gere° on stedes to ryde,   **Stifest . . .** Most fearless in armor

The wyghtest° and the worthyest of the worldes kynde,   °strongest

Preve° for to play wyth in other pure laykes,°   °Valiant   **pure laykes** noble sports

And here is kydde° cortaysye, as I haf herd carp,°   °shown   **herd carp** heard said

And that has wayned° me hider, i-wyis,° at this tyme.   °brought °indeed

265 Ye may be seker° bi this braunch that I bere here,   °sure

That I passe as in pes,° and no plyght seche;°   °peace   **plyght seche** danger seek

For had I founded in fere,° in feghtyng wyse,°   **founded . . .** come in company   °manner

I have a hauberghe° at home and a helme bothe,°   °coat of mail   **helme bothe** helmet too

A schelde, and a scharp spere, schinande bryght,

270 Ande other weppenes to welde, I wene wel, als;°   **wene . . .** know well, also

Bot for I wolde no were,° my wedes° ar softer;   °fighting °clothes

Bot if thou be so bold as alle bürnes° tellen,   °men

Thou wyl grant me godly the gomen° that I ask, bi ryght."   °sport

275   Arthour con onsware,°   **con onsware** answered

And sayd, "Sir cortays knyght,

If thou crave batayl bare,°   °unarmed

Here fayles° thou not to fyght."°   °lack   **to fyght** fighting

xiii

"Nay, frayst° I no fyght, in fayth I thee telle.   °seek

280 Hit arn° aboute on this bench bot° berdles chylder;   **Hit arn** There are °only

If I were hasped° in armes on a heghe° stede,   °buckled °noble

Here is no mon me to mach,° for myghtes° so wayke.°   °match   **for myghtes** because of your °powers °weak

For-thy° I crave in this court a Crystemas gomen,°   °Therefore °sport

For hit is Yol° and Newe Yer, and here ar yep° mony;   °Yule °brave men

285 If any so hardy in this hous holdes hymselven,

Be so bolde in his blod, brayn° in hys hede,   °mad

That dar stifly° strike a strok for an other,   °fearlessly

I schal gif hym of my gyft thys giserne ryche,°   **giserne ryche** noble ax

This ax, that is hevé innogh,° to hondele as hym lykes,°   **hevé innogh** heavy enough   °it pleases

290 And I schal bide the fyrst bür,° as bare° as I sitte.   °blow °unarmed

If any freke° be so felle to fonde° that I telle,   °man   **felle . . .** fierce as to try

Lepe lyghtly me to, and lach° this weppen—   °take

I quit-clayme hit for ever; kepe° hit as his awen°—   °let him keep °own

And I schal stonde° hym a strok, stif° on this flet;°   °endure °fearless °floor

295 Elles° thou wyl dight° me the dom° to dele hym   Then   appoint   judgment
     another,
         barlay,°   none hindering
     And yet gif hym respite
     A twelmonyth and a day.
     Now hyghe,° and let se tite,°   hurry   **se tite** me see quickly
300   Dar any her-inne oght° say."   anything

               xiv
     If he hem stowned° upon fyrst, stiller were   amazed
       thanne
     Alle the hered-men° in halle, the hygh° and the   retainers   noble
       loghe;°   low
     The renk° on his rouncé hym rüched° in his sadel,   man   **rouncé . . .** steed turned himself
     And rünischly° his rede yghen° he reled aboute,   fiercely   eyes
305 Bende his bresed° browes, blycande° grene,   bristling   shining
     Wayved his berde for to wayte who-so° wolde   **wayte who-so** see whosoever
       ryse.
     When non wolde kepe° hym with carp,° he   engage   talk
       coghed ful hyghe,°   loud
     Ande rimed hym° ful richly, and ryght hym° to   **rimed hym** cleared his throat   **ryght
       speke: hym** prepared
     "What, is this Arthures hous," quoth the hathel°   knight
       thenne,
310 "That al the rous rennes of thurgh ryalmes so
       mony?°
     Where is now your sourquydrye° and your   pride
       conquestes,
     Your gryndel-layk° and your greme° and your   fierceness   anger
       grete wordes?
     Now is the revel and the renoun of the Rounde
       Table
     Overwalt° wyth a worde of on wyghes° speche;   Overturned   **on wyghes** one man's
315 For al dares° for drede, withoute dynt° schewed!"   shrink   blow
     Wyth this he laghes so loude that the lorde
       greved;
     The blod schot for scham into his schyre° face   bright
       and lere;°   flesh
     He wex as wroth as wynde,
320 So° did alle that ther were.   As
     The kyng, as kene bi kynde,°   **kene . . .** one bold in nature
     Then stod that stif° mon nere,°   fearless   nearer

---

310. Of whom all the fame runs throughout so many realms?

xv

Ande sayde, "Hathel,° by heven thyn askyng is
    nys,°
And as thou foly° has frayst,° fynde thee bihoves;°
325 I know no gome° that is gast° of thy grete wordes.
Gif me now thy geserne, upon Godes halve,°
And I schal baythen° thy bone° that thou boden
    habbes."°
Lyghtly lepes he hym to, and laght at° his honde;
Then feersly that other freke° upon fote lyghtis.
330 Now has Arthure his axe, and the halme° grypes,
And sturnely stüres° hit aboute, that stryke wyth
    hit thoght.
The stif mon hym bifore stod upon hyght,°
Herre° then ani in the hous by the hede and more.
Wyth sturne schere° ther he stod; he stroked his
    berde,
335 And wyth a countenaunce dryghe° he drogh°
    doun his cote,
No more mate° ne dismayd for hys mayn dintes°
Then any bürne° upon bench hade broght hym to
    drynk
       of wyne.
    Gawan, that sate bi the quene,
340   To the kyng he can enclyne,°
    "I beseche now with saghes sene°
    This melly mot° be myne.

xvi

"Wolde ye,° worthilych lorde," quoth Wawan
    to the kyng,
"Bid me boghe° fro this benche and stonde by
    yow there,
345 That I wythoute vylanye moght voyde° this table,
And that° my legge° lady lyked not ille,
I wolde com to your counseyl, bifore your cort
    ryche.
For me think hit not semly—as hit is soth°
    knawen,
Ther° such an askyng is hevened° so hyghe in your
    sale,°
350 Thagh° ye yourself be talenttyf°—to take hit to
    yourselven

Glosses:
- Hathel,° Knight
- nys,° foolish
- foly° folly; frayst,° sought; **fynde . . .** it behooves you to find out
- gome° man; gast° afraid
- upon Godes halve,° **geserne . . .** ax, for God's sake
- baythen° grant; bone° boon
- **boden habbes** have asked
- laght at° took
- freke° man
- halme° shaft
- stüres° brandishes
- upon hyght,° **upon hyght** on high
- Herre° Taller
- schere° expression
- dryghe° unchanging; drogh° drew
- mate° daunted; mayn dintes° **mayn dintes** strong blows
- bürne° man
- can enclyne,° **can enclyne** bowed
- saghes sene° **saghes sene** words clear
- melly mot° **melly mot** contest may
- Wolde ye,° **Wolde ye** If you would
- boghe° go
- voyde° quit
- that° if; legge° liege
- soth° the truth
- Ther° Where; hevened° raised
- sale,° hall
- Thagh° Though; talenttyf° desirous

Whil mony so bolde yow aboute upon bench
     sytten
That under heven, I hope, non hagherer of wylle,°
Ne better bodyes on bent° ther baret° is rered;°   field   strife   raised
I am the wakkest,° I wot,° and of wyt feblest,   weakest   know

355 And lest lür° of my lyf, who laytes° the sothe,°   **lest lür** least loss   seeks   truth
Bot, for as much as ye ar myn em,° I am only to   uncle
     prayse;
No bounté bot your blod I in my bodé° knowe;   body
And sythen° this note° is so nys° that noght hit   since   business   foolish
     yow falles,°   is fitting
And I have frayned° hit at° yow fyrst, foldes° hit   sought   from   grant
     to me;
360 And if I carp° not comlyly, let alle this cort rych,°   speak   decide
     bout° blame."   without
     Ryche° togeder con roun,°   Nobles   **con roun** whispered
     And sythen° thay redden° alle same,   then   advised
     To ryd° the kyng wyth croun,   relieve
365   And gif Gawan the game.

          xvii
    Then comaunded the kyng the knyght for to
     ryse;
And he ful radly° up ros, and rüchched° hym   promptly   prepared
     fayre,
Kneled doun bifore the kyng, and caches that
     weppen;
And he luflyly° hit hym laft,° and lyfte up his   graciously   gave
     honde,
370 And gef hym Goddes blessyng, and gladly hym
     biddes
That his hert and his honde schulde hardi be
     bothe.
    "Kepe thee,° cosyn," quoth the kyng, "that   **Kepe thee** Take care
     thou on kyrf sette,°   **kyrf sette** cutting apply yourself
And if thou redes° hym right, redly I trowe   deal with
That thou schal byden° the bür° that he schal   survive   blow
     bede° after."   offer
375   Gawan gos to the gome,° with giserne° in   man   ax
     honde,
And he baldly hym bydes, he bayst° never the   was abashed
     helder.°   more
Then carppes° to Sir Gawan the knyght in the   speaks
     grene,

352. Than whom there are under heaven, I suppose, none more sound of mind

"Refourme° we oure forwardes, er° we fyrre°   Restate   **forwardes, er** agreements,
     passe.   before   farther
Fyrst I ethe° thee, hathel, how that thou hattes,°   entreat   are called
380 That thou me telle trewly, as I tryst° may."   trust
     "In god fayth," quoth the goode knyght,
       "Gawan I hatte,
That bede° thee this buffet, what so bifalles after,   offer
And at this tyme twelmonyth take at° thee   from
     another,
Wyth what weppen so thou wylt, and wyth no
     wygh° elles   man
385   on lyve."°   **on lyve** alive
     That other onswares agayn,
     "Sir Gawan, so mot° I thryve,   may
     As I am ferly fayn°   **ferly fayn** marvelously glad
     This dint° that thou schal dryve.   blow

xviii

390 "Bigog!" quoth the grene knyght, "Sir Gawan,
     me lykes,°   it pleases
That I schal fange at° thy füst° that I haf frayst°   **fange at** receive from   fist   sought
     here;
And thou has redily rehersed, bi resoun ful trewe,
Clanly° al the covenaunt that I the kynge asked,   Wholly
Saf that thou schal siker° me, segge,° bi thi   assure   man
     trawthe,
395 That thou schal seche° me thiself, where-so° thou   seek   **where-so** wherever
     hopes°   suppose
I may be funde upon folde, and foch° thee such   **folde . . .** earth, and fetch
     wages
As thou deles me today bifore this douthe° ryche."   company
     "Where schulde I wale° thee?" quoth Gawan.   seek
       "Where is thy place?
I wot° never where thou wonyes,° bi hym that me   know   dwell
     wroght,
400 Ne I know not thee, knyght, thy cort ne° thi   nor
     name.
Bot teche° me trewly therto, and telle me howe°   direct   what
     thou hattes,°   are called
And I schal ware° alle my wyt to wynne me   spend
     thider,
And that I swere thee for sothe,° and by my seker   truth
     traweth."°   **seker traweth** sure truth
     "That is innogh° in Newe Yer, hit nedes no   enough
     more,"

389

405 Quoth the gome° in the grene to Gawan the   man
       hende,°   courteous
     "Yif I thee telle trewly when I the tape° have,   blow
     And thou me smothely° has smyten, smartly° I   duly   promptly
       thee teche°   shall direct
     Of my hous and my home and myn owen nome.
     Then may thou frayst° my fare, and forwardes°   ask   **fare** . . . condition, and covenants
       holde,
410 And if I spende° no speche, thenne spedes° thou   utter   succeed
       the better,
     For thou may leng° in thy londe, and layt° no   stay   seek
       fyrre,°   farther
         bot slokes;°   **bot slokes** without cease
       Ta° now thy grymme tole° to thee,   Take   weapon
     And let se how thou cnokes."°   strike
415   "Gladly, sir, for sothe,"°   truth
     Quoth Gawan; his ax he strokes.°   whets

              xix

     The grene knyght upon grounde graythely°   speedily
       hym dresses,°   arranges
     A littel lut° with the hede, the lere° he discoveres;   bowed   flesh
     His longe lovelych lokkes he layd over his croun,
420 Let the naked nec to the note° schewe.   blow
     Gawan gripped to his ax, and gederes° hit on   lifts
       hyght,°   high
     The kay° fot on the folde° he before sette,   left   earth
     Let hit doun lyghtly lyght° on the naked,°   **lyghtly lyght** swiftly alight   bare flesh
     That the scharp° of the schalk schyndered° the   sharp blade   **schalk schyndered** man
       bones,   shattered
425 And schrank° thurgh the schyire grece, and scade°   sank   **schyire** . . . white flesh, and severe
       hit in twynne,
     That the bit° of the broun stel bot on° the   edge   **bot on** bit into
       grounde.
     The fayre hede fro the halce° hit to the erthe   neck
     That fele° hit foyned° wyth her° fete there hit   **That fele** So that many   spurned   their
       forth roled;
     The blod brayd° fro the body, that blykked° on   spurted   shone
       the grene;
430 And nawther faltered ne° fel the freke never the   nor
       helder,°   more
     Bot stythly° he start forth upon styf schonkes,°   firmly   **styf schonkes** strong legs
     And rünyschly° he raght° out, there as renkkes°   fiercely   reached   knights
       stoden,
     Laght° to his lufly hed, and lyft hit up sone,   Took

And sythen boghes° to his blonk;° the brydel he cachches,   **sythen boghes** then goes   horse

435 Steppes into stel-bawe° and strydes alofte,   stirrup

And his hede by the here in his honde haldes;

And as sadly° the segge° hym in his sadel sette   steadily man

As non unhap had hym ayled, thagh° hedles he were,   though

    in stedde;°   place

440   He brayde° his bluk° aboute,   twisted body

    That ugly bodi that bledde;

    Moni on° of hym had doute,°   **Moni on** Many a one fear

    Bi° that his resouns° were redde.°   By the time words declared

        xx

For the hede in his honde he haldes up even,°   straight

445 Toward the derrest° on the dece° he dresses the face,   noblest dais

And hit lyfte° up the yghe-lyddes,° and loked ful brode,   lifted eyelids

And meled° thus much with his muthe, as ye may now here.   spoke

"Loke, Gawan, thou be graythe° to go as thou hettes,°   set / promised

And layte° as lelly° til thou me, lüde,° fynde,   seek faithfully man

450 As thou has hette in this halle, herande° thise knyghtes.   hearing

To the grene chapel thou chose,° I charge thee, to fotte°   go / get

Such a dünt° as thou has dalt°—disserved thou habbes°—   blow dealt / **disserved...** as you have deserved

To be yederly yolden° on New Yeres morn;   **yederly yolden** quickly given

The Knyght of the Grene Chapel men knowen me mony;

455 For-thi° me for to fynde if thou fraystes,° fayles thou never.   Therefore seek

Therfore com, other° recreaunt be calde thee behoves."°   or / **be...** you must be called

With a rünisch rout° the raynes he tornes,   **rünisch rout** fierce rush

Halled° out at the hal dor, his hed in his hande,   Rushed

That the fyr° of the flynt flaghe° fro fole° hoves.   fire flew the horse's

460 To what kyth° he becom,° knewe non there,   region went

Nevermore then thay wyste° fram whethen° he was wonnen.°   knew whence / come

    What thenne?

    The kyng and Gawen thare,

	At that grene° thay laghe and grenne,°	green man grin
465	Yet breved° was hit ful bare°	made known plainly
	A mervayl among tho° menne.	those

xxi

	Thagh° Arther the hende° kyng at hert hade wonder,	Though courteous
	He let no semblaunt be sene, bot sayde ful hyghe°	nobly
	To the comlych quene, wyth cortays speche,	
470	"Dere dame, today demay° yow never;	be dismayed
	Wel bycommes such craft° upon Cristmasse,	skill
	Laykyng° of enterludes, to laghe and to syng,	Playing
	Among thise kynde° caroles of knyghtes and ladyes.	noble
	Never-the-lece to my mete° I may me wel dres,°	food turn
475	For I haf sen a selly,° I may not forsake."°	marvel deny
	He glent° upon Sir Gawen, and gaynly° he sayde,	glanced graciously
	"Now sir, heng up thyn ax, that has innogh° hewen."	enough
	And hit was don° abof the dece, on doser° to henge,	put a tapestry
	Ther alle men for mervayl myght° on hit loke,	could
480	And bi trewe tytel° therof to telle the wonder.	description
	Thenne thay boghed° to a borde,° thise bürnes° togeder,	went table men
	The kyng and the gode knyght, and kene° men hem served	bold
	Of alle dayntyes double, as derrest° myght falle,°	noblest befall
	Wyth alle maner of mete° and mynstralcie bothe;°	food too
485	Wyth wele walt° thay that day, til worthed° an ende in londe.	**wele walt** joy enjoyed came
	Now thenk wel, Sir Gawan,	
	For wothe° that thou ne wonde°	peril hesitate
	This aventure for to frayn,°	seek
490	That thou has tan on° honde.	**tan on** taken in

Part II

xxii

This hanselle° has Arthur of aventurus on° fyrst | gift   at
In yonge yer, for he yerned yelpyng° to here; | vaunting
Thagh hym° wordes were wane° when thay to | **Thagh hym** Though to him   wanting
    sete wenten,
Now ar thay stoken of° stürne work, staf-ful° her | **stoken of** fully provided with   very full
    hond.
495 Gawan was glad to begynne those gomnes° in | sports
    halle,
Bot thagh the ende be hevy, haf ye no wonder;
For thagh men ben mery in mynde, when thay
    han mayn° drynk, | **han mayn** have strong
A yere yernes° ful yerne,° and yeldes never lyke;° | passes   quickly   the same
The forme° to the fynisment foldes° ful selden.° | beginning   **fynisment foldes** end
    | accords   seldom
500 For-thi° this Yol overyede,° and the yere after, | Therefore   **Yol overyede** Yule passed over
And üche sesoun serlepes sued° after other; | **serlepes sued** in turn followed
After Crysten-masse com the crabbed Lentoun,
That fraystes flesch° wyth the fysche and fode | **fraystes flesch** tries meat
    more symple;
Bot thenne the weder of the worlde wyth wynter
    hit threpes,° | struggles
505 Colde clenges° adoun, cloudes up lyften, | shrinks
Schyre schedes° the rayn in schowres ful warme, | **Schyre schedes** Brightly falls
Falles upon fayre flat,° flowres there schewen, | field
Bothe groundes° and the greves,° grene ar her | fields   woods
    wedes,° | **her wedes** their garments
Bryddes busken° to bylde and bremlych° syngen | **Bryddes busken** Birds prepare   loudly
510 For solace of the softe somer that sues° ther-after, | follows
    bi bonk;° | slope
    And blossumes bolne° to blowe,° | swell   bloom
    Bi rawes° rych and ronk,° | hedge rows   luxuriant
    Then notes noble innoghe,° | many
515   Ar herde in wod so wlonk.° | lovely

xxiii

After the sesoun of somer wyth the soft wyndes,
When Zeferus syfles° hymself on sedes and erbes | blows
Welawynne° is the wort° that waxes° ther-oute, | Very joyful   plant   grows
When the donkande° dewe dropes of the leves, | dripping
520 To bide a blysful blusch° of the bryght sunne. | gleam
Bot then hyghes hervest, and hardenes hym° sone, | **hyghes . . .** hastens autumn, and becomes
    | severe
Warnes hym° for the wynter to wax ful rype; | it (plant)
He dryves wyth droght the dust for to ryse

Fro the face of the folde° to flyghe° ful hyghe.   earth fly

525 Wrothe° wynde of the welkyn wrasteles with the sunne,   Fierce

The leves lancen° fro the lynde and lyghten° on the grounde,   fall **lynde** . . . lime tree and alight

And al grayes° the gres, that grene was ere;   becomes gray

Thenne al rypes and rotes° that ros upon fyrst,   **rypes** . . . ripens and rots

And thus yirnes° the yere in yisterdayes mony,   passes

530 And wynter wyndes° ayayn, as the worlde askes,° no fage.°   returns demands / **no fage** in truth

Til Meghelmas mone°   **Meghelmas mone** Michaelmas (harvest) moon

Was cumen wyth wynter wage;°   challenge

Then thenkkes Gawan ful sone

535 Of his anious vyage.°   **anious vyage** wearisome journey

xxiv

Yet whyl Al-hal-day° with Arther he lenges,°   **whyl Al-hal-day** until All Saints' Day / stays

And he made a fare° on that fest, for the frekes sake,   observance

With much revel° and ryche° of the Rounde Table;   revelry splendid

Knyghtes ful cortays and comlych ladies,

540 Al for luf of that lede in longynge° thay were;   grief

Bot never-the-lece ne the later° thay nevened bot° merthe;   **ne** . . . nor the less readily / **nevened bot** spoke only of

Mony joyles° for that jentyle japes° ther maden.   joyless ones **jentyle japes** noble one jests

For aftter mete,° with mournyng he meles° to his eme,°   meal speaks / uncle

And spekes of his passage, and pertly° he sayde,   plainly

545 "Now, lege lorde of my lyf, leve° I yow ask;   leave

Ye knowe the cost° of this cace; kepe° I no more   terms care

To telle yow tenes° therof never bot° trifel;   troubles **never bot** but only

Bot I am boun to° the bür barely to-morne,°   **boun to** ready for **bür** . . . blow without fail tomorrow morning

To sech the gome of the grene, as God wyl me wysse."°   guide

550 Thenne the best of the burgh boghed° togeder,   **burgh boghed** city went

Aywan and Errik and other ful mony,

Sir Doddinaval de Savage, the duk of Clarence,

Launcelot and Lyonel and Lucan the gode,

Sir Boos and Sir Bydver, big men bothe,

555 And mony other menskful,° with Mador de la Port.   dignified ones

Alle this compayny of court com the kyng nerre,

For to counseyl the knyght, with care at her° hert;   **care** . . . sorrow in their

There was much derve doel driven° in the sale°   **derve** . . . severe sorrow suffered hall

That so worthy as Wawan schulde wende° on that   go
    ernde,°   mission
560 To dryghe° a delful dynt,° and dele no more   suffer   **delful dynt** doleful blow
    wyth bronde.°   sword
    The knyght mad ay° god chere,   ever
    And sayde, "What schuld I wonde°   fear
    Of destinés derf and dere?°   **derf**...severe and harsh
565   What may mon do bot fonde?"°   try

             xxv
    He dowelles° ther al that day, and dresses on the   stays
    morn,
    Askes erly hys armes, and alle were thay broght;
    Fyrst a tulé tapit, tyght° over the flet,°   **tulé**...rich red carpet, spread   floor
    And miche was the gyld gere° that glent° ther   **gyld gere** gilded armor   glinted
    alofte;
570 The stif° mon steppes theron, and the stel   strong
    hondeles,
    Dubbed° in a dublet of a dere tars,°   Adorned   **dere tars** glorious silk from
        Tharsia (Turkestan)
    And sythen° a crafty capados,° closed aloft, then   **crafty capados** skillfully-made hood
    That wyth a bryght blaunner° was bounden white fur
    withinne;
    Thenne set thay the sabatouns° upon the segge°   steel shoes   man's
    fotes,
575 His leges lapped° in stel with luflych greves,°   wrapped   greaves
    With polaynes piched° therto, policed ful clene,°   **polaynes piched** kneepieces fixed
        policed...polished very bright
    Aboute his knes knaged° wyth knotes of golde; riveted
    Queme quyssewes° then, that coyntlych° closed   **Queme quyssewes** Good thighpieces
        cunningly
    His thik, thrawen° thyghes, with thwonges   brawny
    to-tachched;°   **thwonges to-tachched** thongs attached
580 And sythen the brawden bryny° of bryght stel   **brawden bryny** woven coat of mail
    rynges
    Umbeweved° that wygh,° upon wlonk° stuffe;   Enclosed   man   lovely
    And wel bornyst brace° upon his bothe armes,   **bornyst brace** burnished armpieces
    With gode cowters and gay,° and gloves of plate,   **cowters**...elbowpieces and fair
    And alle the godlych gere° that hym gayn° schulde   armor   benefit
585   that tyde;°   time
    Wyth ryche cote-armure,°   surcoat
    His gold spores spend with pryde,°   **spend**...fastened splendidly
    Gürde° wyth a bront° ful sure   Girt   sword
    With silk sayn umbe° his syde.   **sayn umbe** girdle around

             xxvi
590 When he was hasped° in armes, his harnays was   buckled
    ryche,
    The lest lachet° over loupe lemed° of golde;   **lest lachet** smallest clasp   shone

	So harnayst as he was, he herknes° his masse,	hears
	Offred and honoured at the heghe auter.°	altar
	Sythen he comes to the kyng and to his cort-feres,°	court companions
595	Laches lufly° his leve at° lordes and ladyes;	**Laches lufly** Takes graciously from
	And thay hym kyst and conveyed, bikende° hym to Kryst.	**conveyed, bikende** conducted on his wa commending
	Bi that was Gryngolet grayth,° and gürde wyth a sadel	set
	That glemed ful gayly° with mony golde frenges,	brightly
	Aywhere naylet° ful newe, for that note ryched;°	**Aywhere naylet** Everywhere nailed **note ryched** occasion enriched
600	The brydel barred° aboute, with bryght golde bounden;	striped
	The apparayl of the payttrure° and of the proude skyrtes,	neck armor
	The cropore° and the covertor° acorded wyth the arsounes;°	crupper cloth cover saddlebows
	And al was rayled° on red ryche golde nayles,	arrayed
	That al glytered and glent° as glem of the sunne.	glinted
605	Thenne hentes° he the helme,° and hastily hit kysses,	takes helmet
	That was stapled stifly, and stoffed withinne;	
	Hit was hyghe on his hede, hasped° bihynde,	buckled
	Wyth a lightly urysoun° over the aventayle,°	**lightly urysoun** light cover visor
	Enbrawden° and bounden wyth the best gemmes	Embroidered
610	On brode sylkyn borde,° and bryddes° on semes°	hem birds seams
	As papjayes° paynted pernyng bitwene,°	parrots **pernyng bitwene** preening at intervals
	Tortors and trulofes, entayled° so thyk	**Tortors . . .** Turtledoves and true-lovers' knots, embroidered
	As mony bürde ther-aboute° had ben seven wynter	**mony . . .** many a lady engaged on it
	in toune;	
615	The cercle was more o prys°	**o prys** of excellence
	That umbeclypped° hys croun	encircled
	Of diamauntes *à devys*,°	**à devys** perfect
	That bothe were bryght and broun.°	shining

xxvii

	Then thay schewed hym the schelde, that was of schyr goules,°	**schyr goules** bright gules
620	Wyth the pentangel depaynt° of pure golde hewes;°	**pentangel depaynt** five-pointed star depicted hues
	He braydes° hit by the bauderyk,° aboute the hals kestes,°	swings shield strap **hals kestes** neck casts
	That bisemed° the segge semlyly° fayre.	befitted becomingly
	And why the pentangel apendes° to that prynce noble,	belongs

I am intent yow to telle, thof tary° hyt me schulde.   **thof tary** though delay
625 Hit is a syngne that Salamon set sumwhyle,°   once upon a time
In bytoknyng of trawthe, bi tytle° that hit habbes;   right
For hit is a figure that haldes fyve poyntes,
And üche lyne umbelappes and loukes° in other,   **umbelappes . . .** overlaps and locks
And aywhere° hit is endeles, and Englych hit   everywhere
    callen
630 Overal, as I here,° the endeles knot.   hear
For-thy hit acordes to this knyght and to his cler°   bright
    armes,
For ay faythful in fyve and sere° fyve sythes,°   separately   times
Gawan was for gode knawen and as golde pured,°   refined
Voyded of üche vylany, wyth vertues ennourned°   adorned
635   in mote;°   chivalry
    For-thy the pentangel° newe   five-pointed star
    He ber in schelde and cote,
    As tulk° of tale° most trewe   man   word
    And gentylest° knyght of lote.°   noblest   aspect

            xxviii
640   Fyrst he was funden fautles in his fyve wyttes,°   senses
And efte° fayled never the freke in his fyve   then
    fyngres,
And alle his afyaunce° upon folde° was in the fyve   trust   earth
    woundes
That Cryst kaght° on the croys, as the crede telles;   received
And where-so-ever thys mon in melly° was stad,°   battle   placed
645 His thro° thoght was in that, thurgh alle other   earnest
    thynges,
That alle his fersnes° he fong at° the fyve joyes   power   **fong at** took from
That the hende° heven quene had of hir chylde;   noble
At this cause the knyght comlyche° hade   fittingly
In the more° half of his schelde hir ymage   larger (upper)
    depaynted,
650 That when he blusched° therto, his belde° never   looked   courage
    payred.°   failed
The fyft fyve that I finde that the frek used
Was fraunchyse° and felawschyp forbe° al thyng;   liberality   surpassing
His clannes° and his cortaysye croked° were never,   chastity   astray
And pité, that passes alle poyntes—thyse pure fyve
655 Were harder happed° on that hathel then on any   fastened
    other.
Now alle these fyve sythes,° forsothe, were fetled   times
    on° this knyght,   **fetled on** joined in
And üchone halched° in other, that non ende hade,   **üchone halched** each one fastened

And fyched° upon fyve poyntes, that fayled never,	fixed
Ne samned° never in no syde, ne sundred° nouther;	joined **ne sundred** nor separated
660 Withouten ende at any noke aiwhere° I fynde,	**noke aiwhere** corner anywhere
Where-ever the gomen° bygan or glod° to an ende.	device glided
Therfore on his schene° schelde schapen was the knot	bright
Ryally wyth red golde upon rede gowles,°	gules
That is the pure pentangel wyth° the peple called,	**pentangel wyth** five-pointed star by
665 with lore.°	learning
Now graythed° is Gawan gay,	set
And laght° his launce ryght thore,°	took there
And gef hem alle goud day,	
He wende° for ever more.	thought

xxix

670 He sperred the sted with the spures, and sprong on his way	
So stif° that the ston-fyr stroke° out therafter;	hard **ston-fyr stroke** sparks flew
Al that segh° that semly syked° in hert,	saw **semly syked** seemly one sighed
And sayde sothly al same° segges til° other,	together to
Carande° for that comly, "Bi Kryst, hit is scathe°	Anxious a grievous thing
675 That thou, leüde,° schal be lost, that art of lyf noble!	man
To fynde hys fere° upon folde, in fayth, is not ethe;°	equal easy
Warloker° to haf wroght° had more wyt° bene,	More warily acted **more wyt** wiser
And haf dyght° yonder dere a duk to have worthed;°	made become
A lowande° leder of ledes° in londe hym wel semes,	shining men
680 And so had better haf ben then britned° to noght,	broken
Hadet° wyth an alvisch° mon, for angardes° pryde.	Beheaded elfish arrogance's
Who knew ever any kyng such counsel to take,	
As knyghtes in cavelaciouns° on Crystmasse gomnes?"°	disputes sport
Wel° much was the warme water that waltered of° yghen	Very **waltered of** flowed from
685 When that semly syre soght° fro tho wones° thad° daye;	went **tho wones** the dwelling that
He made non abode,°	delay
Bot wyghtly° went hys way;	quickly
Mony wylsum° way he rode,	**Mony wylsum** Many a wild
690 The bok as I herde say.	

398

xxx

Now rides this renk° thurgh the ryalme of   knight
   Logres,°   Britain
Sir Gawan, on Godes halve, thagh hym no
   gomen thoght;°
Oft leüdles,° alone he lenges° on nyghtes,   companionless   dwells
Ther° he fonde noght hym byfore the fare° that   Where   food
   he lyked.
695 Hade he no fere° bot his fole° bi frythes° and   companion   horse   woods
   dounes,
Ne no gome bot God bi gate° wyth to karp,°   road   speak
Til that he neghed° ful neghe in to the Northe   neared
   Wales;
Alle the iles of Anglesay on lyft half° he haldes,   side
And fares over the fordes by the forlondes,°   lowlands
700 Over at the Holy Hede,[1] til he hade eft bonk°   **hade . . .** reached the shore again
In the wyldrenesse of Wyrale;[2] wonde° ther bot   there dwelled
   lyte
That auther God other° gome wyth goud hert   or
   lovied.
And ay he frayned,° as he ferde,° at frekes that he   asked   went
   met,
If thay hade herde any karp° of a knyght grene   talk
705 In any grounde ther-aboute, of the grene chapel;
And al nykked° hym wyth nay, that never in   denied
   her lyve
Thay seghe° never no segge that was of suche   saw
   hewes°   hues
     of grene.
   The knyght tok gates° straunge   roads
710   In mony a bonk unbene;°   **bonk unbene** unpleasant slope
   His cher° ful oft con chaunge,°   mood   **con chaunge** changed
   That chapel er° he myght sene.°   before   see

xxxi

Mony° klyf he overclambe in contrayes   Many a
   straunge;
Fer floten° fro his frendes fremedly° he rydes;   **Fer floten** Far removed   as a stranger
715 At üche warthe other° water ther° the wyghe   **warthe other** shore or   where
   passed,
He fonde a foo° hym byfore, bot ferly° hit were,   foe   marvel

---

692. Sir Gawain, for God's sake, though it seemed no game to him
[1] A promontory in the vicinity of Flint, not Holyhead in Anglesey.
[2] A district in the west midlands of England, between the Dee and Mersey rivers.

And that so foule and so felle° that feght hym   fierce
    byhode.°   behooved
So mony mervayl bi mount° ther the mon   **bi mount** in the mountains
    fyndes,
Hit were too tore° for to telle of the tenthe döle.°   difficult   part
720 Sumwhyle° wyth wormes° he werres,° and wyth   Sometimes   dragons   fights
    wolves als,°   also
Sumwhyle wyth wodwos° that woned° in the   wild men   dwelled
    knarres,°   rocks
Bothe wyth bulles and beres and bores
    otherwhyle,
And etaynes° that hym anelede, of° the heghe   giants   **anelede, of** attacked, from
    felle;°   rocks
Nade he° ben dughty and dryghe,° and Dryghten°   **Nade he** Had he not   **dughty** ... brave
    had served,   and enduring   the Lord
725 Douteles he hade ben ded and dreped° ful ofte.   killed
For werre wrathed° hym not so much, that   troubled
    wynter was wors,
When the colde, cler water fro the cloudes
    schadde,
And fres er° hit falle myght to the fale° erthe;   **fres er** froze before   pale
Ner° slayn wyth the slete he sleped in his yrnes°   Nearly   irons
730 Mo° nyghtes then innoghe° in naked rokkes,   More   enough
Ther-as claterande° fro the crest the colde borne°   clattering   stream
    rennes,
And henged° heghe over his hede in hard   hung
    iisseikkles.
Thus in peryl and payne and plytes° ful harde,   straits
Bi contray cayres° this knyght tyl Krystmasse   **Bi** ... Over the land rides
    even,
735   alone.
    The knyght wel that tyde°   time
    To Mary made his mone,°   complaint
    That hö° hym red° to ryde,   she   might advise where
    And wysse° hym to sum wone.°   guide   dwelling

xxxii

740   Bi a mounte on the morne meryly he rydes
Into a forest ful dep, that ferly° was wylde,   marvelously
Highe hilles on üche a halve, and holtwodes°   woods
    under
Of hore° okes ful hoge° a hundreth togeder.   hoary   huge
The hasel and the hawthorne were harled al
    samen,°   **harled** ... twisted together
745 With roghe, raged mosse rayled° aywhere,   arrayed

With mony bryddes° unblythe upon bare twyges,	birds
That pitosly ther piped for pyne of the colde.	
The gome upon Gryngolet glydes hem° under	them (birds)
Thurgh mony misy° and myre, mon al hym one,°	**mony misy** many a quagmire **al** . . . all alone
750 Carande° for his costes,° lest he ne kever° schulde	Worrying devotions arrive
To se the servyse of that Syre, that on that self° nyght	same
Of a bürde° was borne, oure baret° to quelle.	maiden grief
And therfore sykyng° he sayde, "I beseche thee, Lorde,	sighing
And Mary, that is myldest° moder so dere,	gentlest
755 Of sum herber ther heghly° I myght here masse	**herber** . . . lodging where devoutly
Ande thy matynes tomorne;° mekely I ask,	tomorrow morning
And ther-to prestly° I pray my *pater* and *ave* and *crede*."	promptly
He rode in his prayere	
760 And cryed for his mysdede,	
He sayned hym in sythes sere°	**sayned** . . . crossed himself several times
And sayde, "Cros-Kryst me spede!"°	help

xxxiii

Nade° he sayned hymself, segge, bot thrye,°	Had not thrice
Er° he was war° in the wod of a won° in a mote,°	Before aware dwelling moat
765 Abof a launde,° on a lawe, loken° under boghes	plain **lawe, loken** hill, enclosed
Of mony borelych bole,° aboute bi the diches,	**borelych bole** burly tree
A castel the comlokest° that ever knyght aghte,°	comeliest owned
Pyched° on a prayere,° a park al aboute,	Set meadow
With a pyked palays, pyned° ful thik,	**pyked** . . . spiked palisade, fastened
770 That umbeteghe° mony tre mo° then two myle.	enclosed more
That holde° on that on° syde the hathel avysed,°	castle one observed
As hit schemered and schon thurgh the schyre° okes.	white
Thenne has he hendly of° his helme, and heghly he thonkes	**has** . . . he courteously takes off
Jesus and sayn Gilyan,° that gentyle ar bothe,	St. Julian
775 That cortaysly° hade hym kydde° and his cry herkened.	courtesy shown
"Now bone hostel,"° quoth the bürne, "I beseche yow yette!"°	**bone hostel** good lodging to grant
Thenne gederes° he to Gryngolet with the gilt heles,	spurs
And he ful chauncely° has chosen° to the chef gate°	by chance gone **chef gate** main road

That broght bremly° the bürne to the brygge°　　　clearly　bridge's
　　　ende
780　　　　　in haste.
　　　The brygge was breme upbrayde,°　　　**breme upbrayde** stoutly pulled up
　　　The yates° wer stoken° faste,　　　gates　shut
　　　The walles were wel arayed,°　　　constructed
　　　Hit dut° no wyndes blaste.　　　feared

xxxiv

785　The bürne bode° on bonk,° that on blonk hoved,°　waited　the slope　**blonk hoved** horse
　　　　　　　　　　　　　　　　　　　　　　　halted
　　　Of the depe double dich that drof to° the place;　**drof to** enclosed
　　　The walle wod° in the water wonderly depe,　stood
　　　Ande eft° a ful huge heght° hit haled upon lofte°　again　height　**haled** ... rose aloft
　　　Of harde hewen ston up to the tables,°　cornices
790　Enbaned° under the abataylment, in the best lawe,°　Buttressed　style
　　　And sythen garytes° ful gaye gered bitwene,°　towers　**gered bitwene** built at interval
　　　Wyth mony luflych loupe° that louked° ful clene°—　loophole　shut　neatly
　　　A better barbican that bürne blusched° upon　looked
　　　　　never.
　　　And innermore he behelde that halle ful hyghe,
795　Towres telded° bytwene, trochet° ful thick,　erected　battlemented
　　　Fayre fylyoles° that fyghed,° and ferlyly° long,　pinnacles　fitted　marvelously
　　　With corvon coprounes, craftyly sleghe.°　**corvon** ... carved tops, skillfully ingeni
　　　Chalk-whyt chymnees ther ches° he innoghe,°　saw　many
　　　Upon bastel roves° that blenked° ful whyte;　**bastel roves** tower roofs　shone
800　So mony pynakle payntet was poudred aywhere°　**poudred aywhere** scattered everywher
　　　Among the castel carneles, clambred° so thik,　**carneles, clambred** embrasures,
　　　　　　　　　　　　　　　　　　　　　　　clustered
　　　That pared° out of papure purely hit semed.　cut
　　　The fre° freke on the fole° hit fayr innoghe thoght,　noble　horse
　　　If he myght kever° to com the cloyster wythinne,　succeed
805　To herber° in that hostel,° whyl halyday lested,　lodge　dwelling
　　　　　avinant.°　pleasant
　　　　　He calde, and sone ther com
　　　　　A porter pure plesaunt;
　　　　　On the wal his ernd° he nome°　message　took
810　　　　And haylsed° the knyght erraunt.　greeted

xxxv

　　　"Gode sir," quoth Gawan, "woldes thou go°　go with
　　　　　myn ernde
　　　To the hegh lorde of this hous, herber° to crave?"　lodging
　　　"Ye, Peter," quoth the porter, "and purely I
　　　　　trowee°　believe
　　　That ye be, wyghe, welcum to won° whyle yow　dwell here
　　　　　lykes."

815   Then yede° that wyghe ayayn swythe,°   went   quickly
       And folke frely° hym wyth, to fonge° the knyght.   readily   receive
       Thay let doun the grete draght and derely° out   **draght** ... drawbridge and courteously
         yeden
       And kneled doun on her knes upon the colde erthe
       To welcum this ilk° wygh, as worthy höm   same
         thoght.°   **höm thoght** ... seemed to them
820 Thay yolden° hym the brode yate, yarked° up   yielded   **yate, yarked** gate, opened
         wyde,
       And he hem raysed rekenly° and rod over the   **raysed rekenly** bade rise courteously
         brygge;
       Sere° segges hym sesed° by sadel, whel he lyght,°   Several   took   alighted
       And sythen stabeled his stede stif° men innoghe.°   strong   many
       Knyghtes and swyeres° comen doun thenne   squires
825 For to bryng this bürne wyth blys into halle.
       When he hef° up his helme,° ther highed° innoghe   raised   helmet   hastened
       For to hent° hit at his honde, the hende° to serven;   take   noble one
       His bronde° and his blasoun bothe° thay token.   sword   **blasoun bothe** shield too
       Then haylsed° he ful hendly tho hatheles üch one,   greeted
830 And mony proud mon ther presed, that prynce to
         honour.
       Alle hasped° in his hegh wede,° to halle thay hym   buckled   **hegh wede** noble armor
         wonnen,°   brought
       Ther fayre fyre upon flet° fersly brenned.°   the hearth   burned
        Thenne the lorde of the lede loutes° fro his   **lede loutes** people turns
         chambre
       For to mete wyth menske° the mon on the flor.   courtesy
835 He sayde, "Ye are welcum to welde° as yow lykes;   take
       That° here is, al is yowre awen,° to have at   That (which)   own
         yowre wylle
         and welde."°   control
         "Graunt mercy,"° quoth Gawayn,   **Graunt mercy** Many thanks
         "Ther Kryst hit yow foryelde."°   reward
840 As frekes that semed fayn°   glad
       Ayther other in armes con felde.°   **con felde** embraced

xxxvi

       Gawayn glyght° on the gome that godly hym   looked
         gret,°   greeted
       And thught hit a bolde bürne that the burgh
         aghte,°   **burgh aghte** city owned
       A hoge hathel for the nones, and of hyghe eldee;°   **for** ... indeed, and in prime of life
845 Brode, bryght was his berde, and al bever-hewed,
       Sturne, stif on the stryththe° on stalworth   **stif** ... firm standing
         schonkes,°   legs

Felle° face as the fyre, and fre° of hys speche.　　　Fierce　noble
And wel hym semed forsothe, as the segge thught,
To lede a lortschyp in lee° of leüdes° ful gode.　　　lede ... hold a lordship as protector　m
850　The lorde hym charred° to a chambre and chefly°　　turned　particularly
　　　cumaundes
To delyver hym a leüde, hym loghly° to serve.　　　**hym loghly** him (Gawain) humbly
And there were boun° at his bode° bürnes　　　ready　command
　　　innoghe°　　　many
That broght hym to a bryght boure,° ther　　　bedroom
　　　beddyng was noble
Of cortaynes of clene° sylk wyth cler golde　　　pure
　　　hemmes,
855　And covertores° ful curious with comlych panes,°　coverlets　panels
Of bryght blaunmer° above, enbrawded bisydes,°　white fur　**enbrawded bisydes**
　　　　　　　　　　　　　　　　　　　　　　　embroidered at the sides
Rüdeles rennande° on ropes, red golde rynges,　　**Rüdeles rennande** Curtains running
Tapytes tyght to the woghe, of Tuly and Tars,°
And under fete, on the flet,° of folghande sute.°　　floor　**folghande sute** matching sort
860　Ther he was dispoyled,° wyth speches of myerthe,　disrobed
The bürn of his brüny° and of his bryght wedes.°　coat of mail　armor
Ryche robes ful rad renkkes° hym broghten,　　　**rad renkkes** quickly men
For to charge° and to chaunge and chose of the　　put on
　　　best.
Sone as he on hent, and happed° ther-inne,　　　**on** ... took one, and enclosed himself
865　That sete on hym semly, wyth saylande° skyrtes;　flowing
The ver° by his visage° verayly hit semed　　　springtime　appearance
Wel negh° to üche hathel, alle on hewes,　　　**Wel negh** Very near
Lowande° and lufly, alle his lymmes under.　　　Brilliant
That a comloker° knyght never Kryst made,　　　comelier
870　　　hem thoght.°　　　　　　　　　　　　　　**hem thoght** it seemed to them
　　　Whethen° in worlde he were,　　　　　　　From wherever
　　　Hit semed as° he moght°　　　　　　　　　as if　could
　　　Be prynce withouten pere
　　　In felde ther felle° men foght.　　　　　　fierce

xxxvii

875　A cheyer° byfore the chemné,° ther charcole　　chair　fireplace
　　　brenned,
Was graythed° for Sir Gawan graythely° with　　ready　speedily
　　　clothes,°　　　　　　　　　　　　　　　coverings
Quyssynes° upon queldepoyntes,° that koynt°　　Cushions　quilted covers　cunningly
　　　wer bothe.　　　　　　　　　　　　　　made
And thenne a meré° mantyle was on that mon　　fair
　　　cast,
Of a broun bleeaunt, enbrauded° ful ryche,　　　**bleeaunt, enbrauded** silk, embroidere

858.Tapestries hung on the wall, from Toulouse and Tharsia (Turkestan)

880 And fayre furred wythinne with felles° of the   skins
     best,
   Alle of ermyn, in erde,° his hode of the same.   **in erde** actually
   And he sete in that settel semlych° ryche,   excellently
   And achaufed hym chefly,° and thenne his cher°   **achaufed ...** warmed himself quickly
     mended.   mood
   Sone was telded° up a tabil on trestes° ful fayre,   set   trestles
885 Clad wyth a clene clothe that cler whyt schewed,
   Sanap and salure° and sylverin spones.   **Sanap ...** Napkin and saltcellar
   The wyghe wesche° at his wylle, and went to his   washed
     mete.°   food
   Segges hym served semly° innoghe   properly
   Wyth sere sewes and sete,° sesounde of the best,   **sere ...** various stews and fitting
890 Double-felde, as hit falles, and fele kyn fisches,°   **falles ...** is fitting, and many kinds of fish
   Summe baken in bred, summe brad° on the   grilled
     gledes,°   coals
   Summe sothen,° summe in sewe, savered wyth   boiled
     spyces,
   And ay sawses so sleghe,° that the segge lyked.   cunningly made
   The freke calde hit a feste° ful frely° and ofte   feast   readily
895 Ful hendely,° when alle the hatheles rehayted°   courteously   exhorted
     hym at ones
       as hende:°   courteously
     "This penaunce³ now ye take,
     And eft° hit schal amende."°   later   improve
     That mon much merthe con make,°   **con make** made
900   For wyn in° his hed that wende.°   to   went

xxxviii

   Thenne was spyed and spüred, upon spare
     wyse°   **spyed ...** inquired and asked, in a tactful
   Bi prevé° poyntes, of that prynce, put to   manner
     hymselven,   discreet
   That° he beknew° cortaysly, of the court that he   So that   acknowledged
     were
   That athel° Arthure the hende haldes hym one,°   noble   **haldes ...** rules alone
905 That is the ryche, ryal kyng of the Rounde Table;
   And hit was Wawen hymself that in that won°   dwelling
     syttes,
   Comen to° that Krystmas, as case° hym then   **Comen to** Having arrived   chance
     lymped.°   befell
   When the lorde hade lerned that he the leüde hade,
   Loude laghed he ther-at, so lef° hit hym thoght;°   pleasant   **hym thoght** seemed to him

---

³ Gawain's feast of fish is only penitential fare (*penaunce*) required by the fact that the Vigil of Christmas is a fast day; the real feast will be served on Christmas day.

910 And alle the men in that mote° maden much joye   castle
To apere in his presence prestly that tyme,
That alle prys and prowes and pured thewes
Apendes to hys persoun, and praysed is ever;°
Byfore alle men upon molde° his mensk° is the   earth   courtesy
      most.
915   Üch segge ful softly sayde to his fere,°   companion
"Now schal we semlych° se sleghtes° of thewes°   pleasantly   skillful acts   manners
And the teccheles° termes of talkyng noble.   spotless
Which spede° is in speche, unspürd° may we lerne,   **Which spede** What success   unasked
Syn we haf fonged° that fyne fader of nurture.°   received   good breeding
920 God has geven uus his grace godly, forsothe,
That such a gest as Gawan grauntes uus to have,
When bürnes blythe of His bürthe schall sitte
      and synge.
      In menyng° of maneres meré°   understanding   fair
925   This bürne now schal uus bryng,
      I hope that° may hym here°   **hope that** suppose that one who   hear
      Schal lerne of luf-talkyng."

xxxix

      Bi-that° the diner was done, and the dere° up,   When   noble ones
Hit was negh° at the niyght neghed° the tyme.   almost   drawn near
930 Chaplaynes to the chapeles chosen the gate,°   **chosen . . .** took the way
Rungen° ful rychely, ryght as thay schulden,   Rang the bells
To the hersum° evensong of the hyghe tyde.°   devout   festival
The lorde loutes° therto, and the lady als;°   goes   also
Into a comly closet coyntly hö° entres.   **closet . . .** pew graciously she
935 Gawan glydes° ful gay and gos theder sone;   hastens
The lorde laches° hym by the lappe° and ledes   takes   fold of his garment
      hym to sytte,
And couthly° hym knowes° and calles hym his   familiarly   recognizes
      nome,°   name
And sayde he was the welcomest wyghe of the
      world.
And he hym thonkked throly,° and ayther   earnestly
      halched° other,   embraced
940 And seten soberly samen° the servise-whyle.   together
Thenne lyst° the lady to loke on the knyght;   it pleased
Thenne com hö° of hir closet° with mony cler   **com hö** she came   pew
      bürdes.°   **cler bürdes** fair maidens
Hö was the fayrest in felle,° of flesche and of lyre,°   skin   face

911–13. To appear appropriately at that time in the presence of him to whose person belongs all excellence
and prowess and refined manners, and who is ever praised

And of compas° and colour and costes,° of alle   proportion manners
    other,
945 And wener° then Wenore,° as the wyghe thoght.   fairer Guinevere
He ches° thurgh the chaunsel to cheryche° that   went greet
    hende.°   courteous one
Another lady[4] hir lad bi the lyft honde,
That was alder then hö,° an auncian° hit semed,   she aged one
And heghly honowred with° hatheles aboute.   by the
950 Bot unlyke° on to loke tho° ladyes were,   dissimilar those
For if the yonge was yep, yölwe° was that other;   **yep, yölwe** fresh, yellow
Riche red on that on rayled aywhere,°   **on rayled . . .** one arrayed everywhere
Rugh ronkled chekes that other on rolled.°   hung
Kerchöfes of that on wyth mony cler perles,
955 Hir brest and hir bryght throte, bare displayed,
Schon schyrer° then snawe that schedes° on   whiter falls
    hilles;
That other wyth a gorger° was gered° over the   neckerchief clothed
    swyre,°   neck
Chymbled° over hir blake chyn with mylk-whyte   Wrapped
    vayles,
Hir frount° folden in sylk, enfoubled aywhere,°   forehead **enfoubled aywhere** muffled everywhere
960 Toret and trejeted° with tryfles aboute,°   **Toret . . .** Turreted and adorned
That° noght was bare of that bürde° bot the blake   So that lady
    browes,
The tweyne° yghen and the nase,° the naked   two nose
    lyppes,
And those were soure to se and sellyly° blered;   marvelously
A mensk° lady on molde° mon may hir calle,   dignified earth
965   for° Gode!   before
    Hir body was schort and thik,
    Hir buttokes balgh° and brode;   round
    More lykkerwys on to lyk
    Was that schö hade on lode.°

        xl
970 When Gawayn glyght° on that gay° that   looked fair one
    graciously loked,
Wyth leve laght° of the lorde he went hem   **leve laght** permission granted
    ayaynes.°   **hem ayaynes** toward them
The alder he haylses, heldande° ful lowe;   **haylses, heldande** greets, bowing
The loveloker° he lappes° a lyttel in armes,   lovelier one embraces
He kysses her comlyly, and knyghtly he meles.°   speaks

[4] The first lady is the wife of the lord of the castle; this second is Morgne (Morgan le Fay), as we learn later (Part IV, l. 2446).
968–69. One more sweet to the taste was the one whom she had in her company.

975 Thay kallen° hym of aquoyntaunce, and he hit   beg
       quyk askes
   To be her° servaunt sothly, if hemself lyked.°   their   **hemself lyked** it pleased them
   Thay tan° hym bytwene hem,° wyth talkyng   take   them
       hym leden
   To chambre, to chemné,° and chefly° thay asken   fireplace   particularly
   Spyces, that unsparely° men speded höm° to   eagerly   **speded höm** hastened
       bryng,
980 And the wynnelych° wyne therwith üche tyme.   joyous
   The lorde luflych° aloft lepes ful ofte,   graciously
   Mynned° merthe to be made upon mony sythes,°   Devised   times
   Hent heghly of° his hode, and on a spere henged,   **Hent . . .** Took gaily off
   And wayned höm° to wynne the worschip°   **wayned höm** directed them   honor
       therof
985 That most myrthe myght meve° that Crystenmas   make
       whyle.
    "And I schal fonde,° bi my fayth, to fylter° wyth   try   contend
       the best,
   Er me wont° the wede,° with help of my frendes."   **Er . . .** Before I lack   garment
   Thus wyth laghande lotes° the lorde hit tayt°   **laghande lotes** laughing words   merry
       makes,
   For to glade° Sir Gawayn with gomnes° in halle   gladden   sports
990   that nyght,
     Til that hit was tyme
     The lord comaundet lyght.°   lights
     Sir Gawen his leve con nyme°   **con nyme** took
     And to his bed hym dight.°   went

         xli
995   On the morne, as üch mon mynes° that tyme   recalls
   That Dryghten° for oure destyné to deghe° was   the Lord   die
       borne,
   Wele waxes° in üche a won° in worlde for his sake.   **Wele waxes** Joy grows   dwelling
   So did hit there on that day, thurgh dayntés°   courtesies
       mony;
   Both at mes° and at mele, messes° ful quaynt°   lunch   **mele, messes** dinner, food
       cunningly made
1000 Derf° men upon dece drest° of the best.   Strong   arranged
   The olde, auncian wyf° heghest hö° syttes;   **auncian wyf** aged woman   she
   The lorde lufly her by lent,° as I trowe.°   stayed   believe
   Gawan and the gay bürde° togeder thay seten   maiden
   Even in-myddes, as the messe metely come;°
1005 And sythen thurgh al the sale,° as hem° best   hall   to them
       semed,
   Bi üche grome° at his degré graythely° was served.   person   speedily

1004. Equally in the middle, as the food properly came

Ther was mete, ther was myrthe, ther was much
    joye,
That for to telle therof hit me tene° were,   *trouble*
And° to poynte° hit yet I pyned° me paraventure.°   *If describe troubled perhaps*
010   Bot yet I wot° that Wawen° and the wale bürde°   *know Gawain **wale bürde** fair maiden*
Such comfort of her compaynye caghten° togeder   *got*
Thurgh her dere dalyaunce° of her derne° wordes,   *conversation private*
Wyth clene,° cortays carp closed° fro fylthe,   *pure **carp closed** talk free*
That hör° play was passande° üche prynce gomen,°   *their surpassing **prynce gomen***
015   in vayres.°   *princely sport truth*
     Trumpes and nakerys,°   **Trumpes ...** Trumpets and kettledrums
     Much pypyng ther repayres;°   *is present*
     Üche mon tented hys,°   **tented hys** attended to his business
     And thay two tented thayres.

xlii

020   Much dut° was ther dryven° that day, and that   *mirth made*
     other°   *the next*
And the thryd° as thro thronge° in therafter.   *third day **thro thronge** equally delightful*
The joye of Sayn Jones° day was gentyle to here,   **Sayn Jones** St. John's (December 27)
And was the last of the layk, leüdes° ther thoghten.   **layk, leüdes** entertainment, people
Ther wer gestes° to go, upon the gray morne,   *guests*
025   For-thy° wonderly thay woke,° and the wyn   *So stayed awake*
     dronken,
Daunsed ful dreghly° wyth dere caroles.   *unceasingly*
At the last, when hit was late, thay lachen° her   *took*
     leve,
Üchon° to wende° on his way that was wyghe   *Each one go*
     strange.°   **wyghe strange** a stranger
Gawan gef° hym god day, the god mon° hym   *bade **god mon** host*
     lachches,°   *takes*
030   Ledes hym to his awen° chambre, the chymné°   *own fireplace*
     bysyde,
And there he draghes° hym on dryghe,° and   *draws **on dryghe** aside*
     derely hym thonkkes
Of the wynne worschip° that he hym wayned°   **wynne worschip** pleasant honor *brought*
     hade,
As to honour his hous on that hyghe tyde,°   **hyghe tyde** festival
And enbelyse his burgh° with his bele chere.°   *castle **bele chere** good company*
035   "I-wysse,° Sir, whyl I leve, me worthes° the   *Indeed **leve ...** live, I will be*
     better
That Gawayn has ben my gest° at Goddes awen   *guest*
     fest."°   **awen fest** festival
     "Grant merci, Sir," quoth Gawayn, "in god
     fayth hit is yowres,

Al the honour is your awen, the Heghe Kyng
  yow yelde.°   reward
And I am, wyghe,° at your wylle, to worch°   sir do
  youre hest,°   behest
1040 As I am halden° therto in hyghe and in loghe,°   bound low
  bi right."
  The lorde fast can hym payne°   **fast . . .** earnestly troubled himself
  To holde lenger the knyght.
  To hym answares Gawayn
1045   Bi non way that he myght.°   could hold him longer

xliii

  Then frayned° the freke ful fayre at himselven°   asked him (Gawain)
What derve° dede had hym dryven, at that dere   brave
  tyme,
So kenly° fro the kynges kourt to kayre° al his   boldly ride
  one,°   **his one** alone
Er the halidayes holly° were halet° out of toun.   wholly gone
1050 "For sothe, Sir," quoth the segge, "ye sayn bot°   only
  the trawthe,
A heghe ernde° and a hasty° me hade fro tho   errand urgent one
  wones,°   **tho wones** the dwelling
For I am sumned myselfe to sech° to a place,   seek
I ne wot° in worlde whederwarde to wende° hit   **ne wot** don't know go
  to fynde.
I nolde bot if° I hit negh° myght on New Yeres   **nolde . . .** would not unless reach
  morne
1055 For alle the londe inwyth Logres,° so me oure   **inwyth Logres** in England
  Lorde help!
For-thy, Sir, this enquest I require yow here,
That ye me telle with trawthe, if ever ye tale
  herde
Of the grene chapel, where hit on grounde stondes,
And of the knyght that hit kepes, of colour of
  grene.
1060 Ther was stabled bi statut° a steven° uus bytwene,   **stabled . . .** established by agreement
       tryst
To mete that mon at that mere,° yif I myght last;   appointed place
And of that ilk° New Yere bot neked° now   same **bot neked** only a little
  wontes,°   it wants
And I wolde loke on that lede,° if God me let   man
  wolde,
Gladloker,° bi Goddes Son, then any god welde!°   More gladly **god welde** good thing
       possess
1065 For-thi, i-wysse,° bi yowre wylle, wende me   indeed
  bihoves.°   **wende . . .** it behooves me to go
Naf° I now to busy° bot bare° thre dayes,   Have not be active **bot bare** except
       barely

And me als fayn to falle feye° as fayly° of myyn   als . . . as fain doomed to death   fail
   ernde."

    Thenne laghande° quoth the lorde, "Now leng°   laughing   stay
   thee byhoves,

For I schal teche° yow to that terme° bi the tymes   direct   appointed place
   ende.

1070 The grene chapayle upon grounde greve° yow no   let it grieve
   more.

Bot ye schal be in yowre bed, bürne, at thyn ese,

Whyle forth dayes, and ferk° on the fyrst of the   Whyle . . . Till late in the day, and go
   yere,

And cum to that merk° at mydmorn, to make   appointed place
   what yow likes

      in spenne.°   **in spenne** there (on that turf)

1075   Dowelles° whyle New Yeres daye,   Remain

    And rys and raykes° thenne.   leave

    Mon schal yow sette in waye;

    Hit is not two myle henne."°   hence

         xliv

    Thenne was Gawan ful glad, and gomenly° he   happily
   laghed:

1080 "Now I thonk yow thryvandely thurgh° alle   **thryvandely thurgh** heartily beyond
   other thynge;

Now acheved is my chaunce;° I schal at your   adventure
   wylle

Dowelle,° and elles do what ye demen."°   Remain   think fit

    Thenne sesed° hym the syre and set hym bysyde,   grasped

Let the ladies be fette,° to lyke hem° the better.   brought   **lyke hem** please them

1085 Ther was seme solace° by hemself stille;°   **seme solace** seemly pleasure   **hemself**
       stille themselves privately

The lorde let° for luf lotes° so myry,°   uttered   words   fair

As wygh that wolde of his wyte, ne wyst what he
   myght.°

    Thenne he carped° to the knyght, criande° loude: spoke   crying

"Ye han demed° to do the dede that I bidde.   **han demed** have determined

1090 Wyl ye halde° this hes° here at thys ones?"°   keep   promise   time

    "Ye, Sir, forsothe," sayd the segge trewe,

"Whyl I byde in yowre borghe, be bayn° to   **borghe** . . . castle, I'll be obedient
   yowre hest."°   behest

    "For° ye haf travayled," quoth the tulk,°   Since   man
    "towen° fro ferre,°   come   far

And sythen waked° me wyth, ye arn not wel   kept vigil
   waryst°   recovered

1095 Nauther of sostnaunce ne of slepe, sothly I knowe.

1087. As someone who was going to go out of his wits and didn't know what he was doing.

411

Ye schal lenge° in your lofte and lyghe° in your ese   stay   **lofte** ... room and lie

To-morn whyle the messe-whyle,° and to mete wende,°   **To-morn** ... This morning till mass time / go

When ye wyl, wyth my wyf, that wyth yow schal sitte

And comfort yow with compayny, til I to cort torne.°   return

1100   Ye lende,°   stay

And I schal erly ryse;

On huntyng wyl I wende."

Gawayn grantes alle thyse,

Hym heldande,° as the hende.°   **Hym heldande** Bowing to him / courteous one does

xlv

1105   "Yet firre,"° quoth the freke,° "a forwarde° we make: further   man   agreement

What-so-ever I wynne in the wod, hit worthes to° youres;   **worthes to** becomes

And what chek° so ye acheve, chaunge me° ther-forne.   fortune   **chaunge me** exchange with me

Swete, swap° we so—sware° with trawthe—   **Swete, swap** Good sir, bargain   answer

Whether, leüde,° so lymp lere other° better."   sir   **lymp** ... befall loss or

1110   "Bi God," quoth Gawayn the gode, "I grant ther-tylle,

And that yow lyst for to layke, lef hit me thynkes."°

"Who brynges uus this beverage,° this bargayn is maked."   drink (to seal the bargain)

So sayde the lorde of that lede.° Thay laghed üchone.°   people / every one

Thay dronken and daylyeden and dalten untyghtel,°   **daylyeden** ... dallied and dealt pleasantries

1115   Thise lordes and ladyes, whyle that hem lyked.°   **hem lyked** pleased them

And sythen with Frenkysch fare and fele° fayre lotes°   **Frenkysch** ... French behavior and many / words

Thay stoden and stemed and stylly° speken,   **stoden** ... arose and stopped and softly

Kysten ful comlyly, and kaghten° her leve.   took

With mony leüde ful lyght and lemande° torches,   **lyght** ... active and gleaming

1120   Üche bürne to his bed was broght at the laste ful softe.

To bed yet er thay yede,°   went

Recorded° covenauntes ofte.   They repeated

The olde lorde of that leüde°   people

1125   Cowthe° wel halde layk alofte.°   Could   **halde** ... carry on a game

1111. And that which it pleases you to play, it seems pleasant to me.

412

Part III

xlvi

Ful erly bifore the day the folk up rysen;
Gestes that go wolde, hör gromes° thay calden,   **hör gromes** their servants
And thay busken up bilyve, blonkkes° to sadel,   **busken** ... hurry up quickly, horses
Tyffen° her takles, trussen° her males.°   Prepare   **takles, trussen** gear, pack   bags
1130 Richen hem° the rychest, to ryde alle arayde,   **Richen hem** Dress
Lepen up lightly, lachen° her brydeles,   **lightly, lachen** swiftly, grasp
Üche wyghe on his way ther hym wel lyked.°   pleased
The leve° lorde of the londe was not the last   dear
Arayed for the rydyng, with renkkes° ful mony;   knights
1135 Ete a sop° hastyly, when he hade herde masse;   light meal
With bugle to bent-felde° he buskes bylyve;°   open field   **buskes bylyve** hurries quickly
By° that any daylyght lemed° upon erthe,   By the time   shone
He with his hatheles on hyghe horsses weren.
Thenne thise cacheres° that couthe, cowpled° hör   hunters   **couthe, cowpled** knew how, leashed
      houndes,
1140 Unclosed the kenel dore and calde hem ther-oute,
Blewe bygly in bugles thre bare mote.°   **bare mote** single notes
Braches° bayed therfore, and breme° noyse maked,   Hounds   fierce
And thay chastysed and charred, on chasyng that°   **charred** ... turned back, astray those hounds that
      went,
A hundreth of hunteres, as I haf herde telle,
1145   of the best.
      To trystors vewters yod;°   **trystors** ... stations deerhound-keepers went
      Couples huntes of kest.°   **Couples** ... Leashes huntsmen cast off
      Ther ros for blastes gode
      Gret rürd° in that forest.   noise

xlvii

1150 At the fyrst quethe° of the quest° quaked the   sound   baying
      wylde;°   wild animals
Der drof° in the dale, doted° for drede,   rushed   grew mad
Highed° to the hyghe,° bot heterly° thay were   Sped   high ground   quickly
Restayed with° the stablye,° that stoutly ascryed.°   **Restayed with** Turned by   beaters shouted
Thay let the herttes haf the gate,° with the hyghe   **haf** ... go free
      hedes,
1155 The breme° bukkes also with hör° brode paumes;°   brave   their   antlers
For the fre° lorde hade defende° in fermysoun   noble   forbidden
      tyme°   **fermysoun tyme** closed season
That ther schulde no mon meve to° the male dere.   **ther** ... anyone should hunt
The hindes were halden in, with "hay!" and
      "war!"
The does dryven with gret dyn to the depe slades.°   valleys

413

1160 Ther myght mon se, as thay slypte, slentyng° of
    arwes;°   **slypte, slentyng** were loosed, a rush
                                               arrows
    At üche wende° under wande wapped° a
    flone,°   turn   **wande wapped** branches flew
                                            arrow
    That bigly bote° on the broun,° with ful brode
    hedes.°   bit   brown hides
                                             arrowheads
    What! thay brayen and bleden, bi bonkkes° thay
    deghen,°   slopes
                                             die
    And ay rachches° in a res radly hem folghes,°   hounds   **res** ... rush swiftly follow the►
1165 Hunteres wyth hyghe horne hasted hem after,
    Wyth such a crakkande° kry as° klyffes haden   blaring   as if
    brusten.°   burst
    What wylde so atwaped wyghes° that schotten   **What** ... Whatever animal escaped the r►
    Was al toraced° and rent at the resayt,°   seized   receiving station
    Bi° thay were tened° at the hyghe, and taysed° to   After   worried   driven
    the wattres.
1170 The ledes° were so lerned° at the loghe trysteres,°   men   skilled   **loghe trysteres** low
                                               stations
    And the grehoundes so grete that geten hem
    bylyve°   **geten** ... seized them quickly
    And hem tofylched° as fast as frekes myght loke,   pulled down
    ther ryght.
      The lorde, for blys abloy,°   carried away
1175   Ful oft con launce and lyght,°   **con** ... did gallop and alight
      And drof° that day wyth joy   spent
      Thus to the derk nyght.

xlviii

      Thus laykes° this lorde by lynde-wodes eves,°   plays   **lynde-wodes eves** lime wood's
                                               edge
    And Gawayn the god mon in gay bed lyges,°   lies
1180 Lurkkes whyl° the daylyght lemed° on the   **Lurkkes whyl** Lies concealed until   sh►
    wowes,°   walls
    Under covertour ful clere,° cortyned aboute;   fair
    And as in slomeryng° he slode, sleghly° he herde   slumbering   **slode, sleghly** glided, wa►
    A littel dyn° at his dor, and derfly upon;°   sound   **derfly upon** (heard) it quickly
                                               open
    And he heves up his hed out of the clothes,
1185 A corner of the cortyn he caght up a lyttel,
    And waytes° warly thiderwarde, what hit be   looks
    myght.
    Hit was the ladi, loflyest to beholde,
    That drogh° the dor after hir ful dernly° and   drew   secretly
    stylle,
    And boghed° towarde the bed; and the bürne   turned
    schamed°   was embarrassed
1190 And layde hym doun lystyly and let as° he slepte.   **lystyly** ... craftily and behaved as if
    And hö stepped stilly and stel° to his bedde,   stole

Kest up the cortayn and creped withinne
And set hir ful softly on the bed-syde
And lenged° there selly° longe to loke when he   stayed   very
     wakened.
1195   The lede° lay lurked° a ful longe whyle,   man   hidden
Compast° in his concience° to what that cace°   Pondered   mind   happening
     myght
Meve other amount, to mervayle hym thoght;°
Bot yet he sayde in hymself, "More semly hit were
To aspye° wyth my spelle in space° what hö   discover   **spelle** . . . words soon
     wolde."°   might want
1200   Then he wakenede and wroth° and to-hir-warde   stretched
     torned
And unlouked his yghe-lyddes and let as hym
     wondered,°   **let** . . . pretended to be surprised
And sayned hym,° as bi his saghe° the saver° to   **sayned hym** crossed himself   prayer
     worthe,°   safer   become
       with hande.
       Wyth chynne and cheke ful swete,
1205   Bothe whit and red in blande,°   **in blande** together
       Ful lufly con hö lete,°   **lufly** . . . graciously she behaved
       Wyth lyppes smal laghande.°   laughing

         xlix
    "God moroun, Sir Gawayn," sayde that fayr
     lady,
"Ye are a sleper unslyghe,° that mon° may slyde°   unwary   one   steal
     hider.
1210   Now ar ye tan as-tyt; bot true° uus may schape,°   **tan** . . . taken in a moment, unless truce
I schal bynde yow in your bedde, that be ye   be arranged
     trayst."°   sure
Al laghande the lady lanced tho bourdes.°   **lanced** . . . uttered those jests
    "God moroun, gay," quoth Gawayn the blythe.°   happy
"Me schal worthe° at your wille, and that me wel   **Me** . . . It shall be with me
     lykes;°   pleases
1215   For I yelde me yederly and yeghe° after grace,°   **yederly** . . . promptly and cry   mercy
And that is the best, be my dome,° for me   judgment
     byhoves nede."°   **byhoves nede** necessity compells
    And thus he bourded° ayayn with mony a blythe   jested
     laghter.
"Bot wolde ye,° lady lovely, then leve me grante   **Bot** . . . If you would
And deprece° your prysoun° and pray hym to   release   prisoner
     ryse,
1220   I wolde boghe° of this bed and busk° me better,   go   dress

1197. Result in or mean, as a marvel it seemed to him

I schulde kever° the more comfort to karp° yow   get   speak
    wyth."
    "Nay, for sothe, beau° sir," sayd that swete,   fair
"Ye schal not rise of your bedde; I rych° yow   intend
    better;
I schal happe° yow here that other half als,°   wrap   **that . . .** on the other side also
1225 And sythen karp wyth my knyght that I kaght
    have;
For I wene° wel, i-wysse,° Sir Wowen° ye are,   know   indeed   Gawain
That alle the worlde worschipes, where-so° ye   **worschipes, where-so** honors, wherever
    ride.
Your honour, your hendelayk° is hendely praysed   courtesy
With lordes, wyth ladyes, with alle that lyf bere.
1230 And now ye ar here, i-wysse, and we bot oure
    one.°   **oure one** alone
My lorde and his ledes ar on lenthe faren,°   **ar . . .** have gone afar
Other bürnes in her bedde, and my bürdes als,°   **bürdes als** maidens also
The dor drawen, and dit° with a derf haspe.°   locked   **derf haspe** strong buckle
And sythen° I have in this hous hym that al lykes,   since
1235 I schal ware° my whyle wel whyl hit lastes,   spend
    with tale.°   speech
    Ye ar welcum to my cors,°   body
    Yowre awen won° to wale;°   will   take
    Me behoves of fyne force°   **fyne force** absolute necessity
1240   Your servaunt be, and schale."°   I shall

                        1

    "In god fayth," quoth Gawayn, "gayn° hit me   good
        thynkkes,
Thagh° I be not now he that ye of speken;   Though
To reche to such reverence as ye reherce° here   relate
I am wyghe° unworthy, I wot wel myselven.   a person
1245 Bi God, I were glad, and yow god thoght°   **and . . .** if it seemed good to you
At saghe° other at servyce° that I sette° myght   **At saghe** By word   deed   set myself
To the pleasaunce° of your prys°—hit were a   pleasure   excellence
    pure joye."
    "In god fayth, Sir Gawayn," quoth the gay lady,
    "The prys and the prowes that pleses al other,
1250 If I hit lakked° other set at lyght, hit were littel   belittled
    daynté.°   courtesy
Bot hit ar ladyes innoghe that lever wer° nowthe   **that . . .** to whom it might be more
Haf thee, hende, in hör holde, as I thee habbe   delightful
    here,
To daly with derely° your daynté wordes,   pleasantly
Kever° hem comfort and colen° her cares,°   Get   relieve   sorrows

1255 Then much of the garysoun° other golde that thay   treasure
       haven.
    Bot I lowe° that ilk° Lorde that the lyfte° haldes,   praise   same   sky
    I haf hit holly° in my honde that al desyres,   wholly
       thurghe grace."
      Schö° made hym so gret chere,°   She   entertainment
1260   That was so fayr of face.
      The knyght with speches skere°   pure
      Answared to üche a cace.°   speech

li

    "Madame," quoth the myry° mon, "Mary yow   fair
      yelde,°   reward
    For I haf founden, in god fayth, yowre fraunchis°   liberality
      nobele.
1265 And other° ful much of other folk fongen hör   others
      dedes,°   **fongen** . . . pattern their own actions
    Bot the daynté° that thay delen for my disert   courtesy
      nysen.°   they exaggerate
    Hit is the worschyp° of yourself that noght bot   honor
      wel connes."°   knows how to say
     "Bi Mary," quoth the menskful,° "me thynk hit   honorable lady
      another;°   otherwise
    For were I worth al the wone° of wymmen alyve,   multitude
1270 And al the wele° of the worlde were in my honde,   joy
    And° I schulde chepen° and chose, to cheve° me a   If   bargain   obtain
      lorde,
    For the costes° that I haf knowen upon thee,   manners
      knyght, here,
    Of bewté and debonerté° and blythe semblaunt,°   courtesy   appearance
    And that I haf er herkkened° and halde hit here°   heard of   now
      trewe,
1275 Ther schulde no freke upon folde bifore yow be
      chosen."
     "I-wysse, worthy," quoth the wyghe, "ye haf
      waled° wel better;   taken
    Bot I am proude of the prys° that ye put on me,   esteem
    And soberly, your servaunt, my soverayn I holde
      yow,
    And yowre knyght I becom, and Kryst yow
      foryelde!"°   reward
1280 Thus thay meled° of muchwhat° til mydmorn   spoke   many things
      paste,
    And ay the lady let lyk as° hym loved mych.   **let** . . . behaved as if
    The freke ferde° with defence and feted° ful fayre.   acted   **defence** . . . caution and behaved

417

"Thagh I were bürde° bryghtest," the bürde in
 mynde hade,°   maiden **in** ... thought
"The lasse° luf in his lode"°—for lür° that he soght   less **in** ... with him **for lur** because of
1285 boute hone,°   the disaster **boute hone** without dela[y]
The dünte° that schulde hym deve,°   blow stun
And nedes hit most be done.
The lady thenn spek of leve,°   leaving
He graunted hir ful sone.°   at once

       lii

1290 Thenne hö gef hym god day, and wyth a glent°   glance
  laghed,
And as hö stod, hö stonyed° hym wyth ful stor°   astonished stern
  wordes:
"Now He that spedes° üche spech, this disport   blesses
  yelde° yow!   **disport yelde** entertainment reward
Bot that ye be Gawan, hit gos in mynde."°   **gos** ... is debated
  "Wherfore?" quoth the freke, and freschly° he   eagerly
  askes,
1295 Ferde° lest he hade fayled in fourme of his costes.°   Afraid manners
  Bot the bürde° hym blessed, and bi this skyl°   maiden manner
  sayde:
"So god° as Gawayn gaynly° is halden—   good a man fittingly
And cortaysye is closed so clene° in hymselven—   fully
Couth° not lyghtly haf lenged° so long wyth a   Could stayed
  lady
1300 Bot he had craved a cosse° bi his courtaysye,   kiss
Bi sum towch° of summe tryfle at sum tales°   hint speech's
  ende."
  Then quoth Wowen,° "I-wysse, worthe° as   Gawain let it be
  yow lykes;
I schal kysse at your comaundement, as a knyght
  falles,°   is fitting for
And fire,° lest he displese yow, so plede hit no   further
  more."
1305 Hö comes nerre with that, and caches hym in
  armes,
Loutes° luflych adoun and the leüde kysses.   Bends
Thay comly bykennen° to Kryst ayther° other.   commend each
Hö dos hir° forth at the dore withouten dyn°   **dos hir** goes sound
  more,
And he ryches° hym to ryse and rapes° hym sone,   readies hastens
1310 Clepes° to his chamberlayn, choses his wede,°   Calls garments
Boghes forth, when he was boun,° blythely to   ready
  masse.

And thenne he meved° to his mete° that menskly° — went   meal   duly
    hym keped,° — occupied
And made myry al day til the mone rysed,
    with game.
1315   Was never freke fayrer fonge° — received
    Bitwene two so dyngne° dame, — worthy
    The alder and the yonge;
    Much solace° set thay same.° — delight   together

liii

And ay the lorde of the londe is lent° on his — gone
    gamnes,° — sports
1320 To hunt in holtes° and hethe at hyndes barayne.° — woods   barren
Such a sowme° he ther slowe° bi that the sunne — number   slew
    heldet,° — set
Of dos and of other dere, to deme° were wonder. — tell
Thenne fersly° thay flokked in, folk at the laste, — quickly
And quykly of the quelled° dere a querré° thay — slain   pile
    maked.
1325 The best° boghed therto with bürnes innoghe;° — noblest   many
Gedered the grattest of gres° that ther were, — **grattest . . .** fattest
And didden hem derely° undo as the dede askes.° — neatly   **dede askes** task demands
Serched hem at the asay° summe that ther were, — trial
Two fyngeres° thay fonde of the fowlest° of alle. — fingers thickness   poorest
1330 Sythen thay slyt the slot,° sesed the erber,° — hollow in the breast   first stomach
Schaved° wyth a scharp knyf, and the schyre — Cut it away
    knitten.° — **schyre knitten** tied up the white flesh
Sythen rytte° thay the foure lymmes and rent off — cut
    the hyde;
Then brek thay the balé,° the bales° out token, — belly   bowels
Lystily forlancyng, and lere of the knot.°
1335 Thay gryped to° the gargulun,° and graythely — **gryped to** seized   throat
    departed° — **graythely departed** promptly separated
The wesaunt° fro the wynt-hole, and walt° out — gullet   **wynt-hole . . .** windpipe and flung
    the guttes.
Then scher° thay out the schulderes with her — cut
    scharp knyves,
Haled° hem by a lyttel hole, to have hole° sydes. — Drew   whole
Sithen britned° thay the brest and brayden° hit in — cut   pulled
    twynne.
1340 And eft° at the gargulun bigynes on thenne, — again
Ryves° hit up radly° ryght to the byght,° — Rips   quickly   fork of the legs
Voydes out the avanters,° and verayly therafter — intestines
Alle the rymes° by the rybbes radly thay lance.° — membranes   cut

1334. Skillfully emptying them, and the flesh of the knot of the neck.

	So ryde thay off by resoun° bi the rygge° bones,	**ryde . . .** they cleared off rightly back
1345	Evenden° to the haunche, that henged alle samen,°	Down together
	And heven hit up al hole° and hewen° hit of there;	whole hewed
	And that thay neme for° the noumbles° bi nome,° as I trowe,° bi kynde.°	**neme for** name as entrails name believe nature
	Bi the byght° al of the thyghes	fork
1350	The lappes° thay lance bihynde;	folds
	To hewe hit in two thay hyghes,°	hasten
	Bi° the bakbon to unbynde.°	Along cut open

liv

	Bothe the hede and the hals° thay hewen° off thenne,	neck hewed
	And sythen sunder thay the sydes swyft fro the chyne,°	backbone
1355	And the corbeles fee° thay kest in a greve.°	**corbeles fee** raven's fee (gristle) thicket
	Thenn thurled° thay ayther° thik side thurgh bi the rybbe,	pierced each
	And henged thenne ayther bi hoghes° of the fourches,°	hocks haunches
	Üche freke° for his fee as falles° for to have.	man working is fitting
	Upon a felle° of the fayre best,° fede thay thayr houndes	skin beast
1360	Wyth the lyver and the lyghtes,° the lether° of the paunches,	lungs lining
	And bred bathed in blod blende° ther-amonges.	mixed
	Baldely thay blew prys,° bayed thayr rachches;°	**blew prys** sounded the kill hounds
	Sythen fonge° thay her flesche folden° to home,	took packed
	Strakande° ful stoutly mony stif motes.°	Sounding **stif motes** loud notes
1365	Bi that the daylyght was done, the douthe° was al wonen°	company come
	Into the comly castel, ther the knyght bides ful stille,	
	Wyth blys and bryght fyr bette.°	**fyr bette** fire kindled
	The lorde is comen ther-tylle;	
1370	When Gawayn wyth hym mette,	
	Ther was bot wele° at wylle.	joy

lv

	Thenne comaunded the lorde in that sale to samen° alle the meny,°	gather company

Bothe the ladyes on loghe to lyght° with her bürdes.°   on ... come downstairs / maidens

Bifore alle the folk on the flette,° frekes he beddes°   floor / bids

375 Verayly his venysoun to fech hym byforne;

And al godly in gomen° Gawayn he called,   sport

Teches hym to° the tayles° of ful tayt° bestes,   **Teches** ... Shows to him / tally / lively

Schewes hym the schyree grece° schorne upon rybbes.   **schyree grece** white flesh

"How payes° yow this play? Haf I prys° wonnen?   pleases / praise

380 Have I thryvandely° thonk thurgh my craft served?"°   heartily / **craft served** skill deserved

"Ye, i-wysse," quoth that other wyghe. "Here is wayth° fayrest   hunting spoils

That I segh° this seven yere in sesoun of wynter."   saw

"And al I gif yow, Gawayn," quoth the gome thenne,

"For by acorde of covenaunt ye crave° hit as your awen."   may ask for

385 "This is soth,"° quoth the segge. "I say yow that ilke;°   true / same

That° I haf worthyly wonnen this wones° wythinne,   That which / dwelling

I-wysse with as god wylle hit worthes to° youres."   **worthes to** becomes

He hasppes° his fayre hals° his armes wythinne,   grasps / neck

And kysses hym as comlyly as he couthe avyse:°   devise

390 "Tas yow° there my chevicaunce,° I cheved° no more.   **Tas yow** Take / winnings / won

I vowche hit saf fynly,° thagh feler° hit were."   **vowche** ... would grant it completely / more

"Hit is god," quoth the god mon.° "Grant mercy° therfore;   **god mon** host / **Grant mercy** Much thanks

Hit may be such, hit is the better, and° ye me breve° wolde   **better, and** better of the two, if / tell

Where ye wan this ilk wele,° bi wytte° of yorselven."   joy / cleverness

395 "That was not forward,"° quoth he. "Frayst° me no more;   an agreement / Ask

For ye haf tan° that yow tydes; trawe ye° non other ye mowe."°   taken / **tydes** ... is due; be sure / can get

Thay laghed and made hem blythe

Wyth lotes° that were to lowe;°   words / praise

400 To soper thay yede as swythe,°   **as swythe** straightaway

Wyth dayntés° newe innowe.°   courtesies / many

lvi

And sythen by the chymné° in chamber thay
seten.　　　　　　　　　　　　　　　　　fireplace
Wyghes the walle° wyn weghed° to hem oft,　choice　carried
And efte° in her bourdyng° thay baythen° in the　again　jesting　agree
morn.
1405 To fylle the same forwardes that thay byfore
maden;
What chaunce so bytydes,° hör chevysaunce° to　befalls　winnings
chaunge,°　　　　　　　　　　　　　　　　　exchange
What newes° so thay nome,° at naght° when thay　new things　took　night
metten.
Thay acorded of the covenauntes byfore the
court alle;
The beverage° was broght forth in bourde° at　drink to seal the bargain　jest
that tyme.
1410 Thenne thay lovelych leghten° leve at the last,　took
Üche bürne to his bedde busked bylyve.°　　**busked bylyve** hurried quickly
Bi that the coke hade crowen and cakled bot
thryse,
The lorde was lopen° of his bedde, the leüdes üch　**was lopen** leaped
one,
So that the mete and the masse was metely°　duly
delyvered;
1415 The douthe dressed° to the wod, er any day　**douthe dressed** company repaired
sprenged,°　　　　　　　　　　　　　　　　broke
to chace.
　Hegh° with hunte° and hornes　　　　Loudly　huntsman
　Thurgh playnes thay passe in space;°　a short while
　Uncoupled,° among tho thornes,　　　Unleashed
1420　Raches° that ran on race.°　　　　　Hounds　**on race** in haste

lvii

Sone thay calle of° a quest in a ker° syde,　for　marsh
The hunt rehayted° the houndes that hit fyrst　**hunt rehayted** huntsman urged
mynged,°　　　　　　　　　　　　　　　　noted
Wylde wordes° hym warp° wyth a wrast° noyce.　cries　uttered　loud
The howndes that hit herde hastid thider swythe,°　quickly
1425 And fellen as fast to the fuyt,° fourty at ones.　trail
Thenne such a glaver ande glam° of gedered　**glaver ande glam** clamor and noise
rachches°　　　　　　　　　　　　　　　　hounds
Ros that the rocheres° rungen aboute.　　　rocks
Hunteres hem hardened° with horne and wyth　urged
muthe.
Then al in a semblé sweyed° togeder　　　**semblé sweyed** pack rushed

1430 Bitwene a flosche° in that fryth° and a foo° cragge.   *pool   wood   forbidding*
    In a knot,° bi a clyffe, at the kerre° syde,   *rocky hill   marsh*
    Ther-as° the rogh rocher unrydely° was fallen,   *Where   ruggedly*
    Thay ferden° to the fyndyng, and frekes hem after.   **Thay ferden** They (the hounds) went
    Thay umbekesten° the knarre° and the knot bothe,   *cast about   crag*
1435 Wyghes, whyl° thay wysten° wel wythinne hem   *until   knew*
      hit were,
    The best° that ther breved° was wyth° the   *beast   announced   by*
      blodhoundes.
    Thenne thay beten on the buskes and bede° hym   **buskes ...** bushes and bade
      up ryse,
    And he unsoundyly out soght segges overthwert.°
    On° the sellokest° swyn swenged° out there.   *One of   most wonderful   rushed*
1440 Long sythen fro the sounder° that wight forolde,°   *herd   **wight forolde** creature grew old*
    For he was breme° bor alther grattest,°   *a fierce   **alther grattest** greatest of all*
    Ful grymme when he gronyed. Thenne greved
      mony,
    For thre at the fyrst thrast° he thryght° to the erthe,   *thrust   threw*
    And sped hym° forth good sped, boute spyt°   **sped hym** rushed   **good ...** quickly,
      more.   *without injury*
1445 Thise other halowed "Hyghe!" ful hyghe,° and   *loudly*
      "Hay! Hay!" cryed,
    Haden hornes to mouthe, heterly rechated.°   **heterly rechated** quickly sounded the recall
    Mony was the myry mouthe° of men and of   *voice*
      houndes
    That buskkes° after this bor with bost° and wyth   *hurry   outcry*
      noyse,
        To quelle.°   *kill*
1450 Ful ofte he bydes° the baye   *stands at*
    And maymes the mute inn melle;°   **mute ...** pack on all sides
    He hurtes of the houndes, and thay
    Ful yomerly° yaule and yelle.   *piteously*

lviii

    Schalkes° to schote at hym schoven to° thenne,   *Men   **schoven to** pushed forward*
1455 Haled° to hym of her arewes,° hitten hym oft.   *Loosed   arrows*
    Bot the poyntes payred° at the pyth° that pyght°   *failed   toughness   struck*
      in his scheldes,°   *flanks*
    And the barbes of his browen° bite non wolde;   *flesh*
    Thagh the schaven schaft schyndered° in peces,°   *splintered   pieces*
    The hede hypped° ayayn, were-so-ever hit hitte.   *bounded*
1460 Bot when the dyntes° hym dered° of her dryghe°   *blows   hurt   heavy*
      strokes,
    Then, braynwod° for bate,° on bürnes he rases,°   *frenzied   strife   rushes*

1438. And he dangerously sought out the men athwart his way.

Hurtes hem ful heterly° ther he forth hyghes,°   *fiercely hastens*
And mony arghed° ther-at and on lyte droghen.°   *grew afraid on... somewhat drew back*
Bot the lorde on a lyght° horce launces° hym after,   *swift gallops*
1465 As bürne bolde upon bent° his bugle he blowes,   *battlefield*
He rechated,° and rode thurgh rones° ful thyk,   *sounded the recall bushes*
Suande° this wylde swyn til the sunne schafted.°   *Pursuing shone forth*
This day wyth this ilk dede° thay dryven on° this wyse,°   *task **dryven on** spend in manner*
Whyle oure luflych lede lys in his bedde,
1470 Gawayn graythely° at home, in geres° ful ryche of hewe.   *properly clothes*
   The lady noght foryate,°   *forgot*
   Com to hym to salue;°   *greet*
   Ful erly hö was hym ate
1475   His mode° for to remewe.°   *mood alter*

     lix

  Hö commes to the cortyn and at the knyght totes.°   *peeps*
Sir Wawen° her welcumed worthy on fyrst,   *Gawain*
And hö hym yeldes ayayn° ful yerne° of hir wordes,   ***yeldes ayayn** replies eagerly*
Settes hir sofly° by his syde, and swythely° hö laghes,   *gently much*
1480 And wyth a luflych loke hö layde° hym thyse wordes: *set forth to*
"Sir, yif ye be Wawen, wonder me thynkkes,
Wyghe that is so wel wrast° alway to god,   *disposed*
And connes° not of companye° the costes undertake,°   *can society **costes undertake** manners understand*
And if mon kennes° yow höm to knowe, ye kest° höm of your mynde.   *teaches put*
1485 Thou has foryeten yederly that° yisterday I taghtte   ***foryeten...** forgotten quickly what*
Bi alder truest° token of talk that I cowthe."°   ***alder truest** truest of all know*
  "What is that?" quoth the wyghe. "I-wysse, I wot never;
If hit be sothe that ye breve,° the blame is myn awen."   *declare*
  "Yet I kende° yow of kyssyng," quoth the clere° thenne,   *taught fair one*
1490 "Where-so countenaunce° is couthe,° quikly to clayme;   ***Where-so countenaunce** Wherever fa evident*
That bicumes üche a knyght that cortaysy uses."
  "Do way,"° quoth that derf mon, "my dere, that speche,   ***Do way** Cease from*

For that I durst not do, lest I denayed were.
If I were werned,° I were wrang, i-wysse, yif I   refused
    profered."
495 "Ma fay!"° quoth the meré wyf.° "Ye may not   **Ma fay** My faith   **meré wyf** fair woman
    be werned!
Ye ar stif° innoghe to constrayne wyth strenkthe,   strong
    yif yow lykes,
Yif any were so vilanous that yow devaye°   deny
    wolde."
    "Ye, be God," quoth Gawayn, "good is your
    speche,
Bot threte° is unthryvande,° in thede° ther I lende,°   force   unlucky   the country   live
500 And üche gift that is geven not with goud wylle.
I am at your comaundement, to kysse when yow
    lykes;
Ye may lach° when yow lyst, and leve° when yow   take   leave
    thynkkes,
        in space."°   a short time
    The lady loutes adoun
505   And comlyly kysses his face.
    Much speche thay ther expoun
    Of druryes greme and grace.°   **druryes** ... love's grief and joy

lx

"I woled wyt at° yow, wyghe," that worthy   **woled** ... would learn from
    ther sayde,
"And° yow wrathed° not ther–wyth, what were   If   be angry
    the skylle°   reason
510 That so yong and so yepe° as ye at this tyme,   brisk
So cortayse, so knyghtly, as ye ar knowen oute.°   widely
(And of alle chevalry to chose, the chef thyng
    alosed°   praised
Is the lel layk° of luf, the lettrure° of armes;   **lel layk** faithful game   science
For to telle of this tevelyng° of this trewe   deeds
    knyghtes,
515 Hit is the tytelet token° and tyxt of her werkkes,   **tytelet token** inscribed title
How ledes for her lele° luf hör lyves han auntered,°   **her lele** their true   have ventured
Endured for her drury dulful stoundes,°   **drury** ... love doleful times
And after venged° with her valour and voyded   avenged themselves
    her care°   sorrow
And broght blysse into boure° with bountees°   bower   virtues
    hör awen)
520 And ye ar knyght comlokest kyd° of your elde,°   **comlokest kyd** comeliest known   age
Your worde and your worschip° walkes aywhere,   honor
And I haf seten by yourself here sere twyes,°   **sere twyes** two separate times

Yet herde I never of your hed° helde no wordes   **of** . . . from you

That ever longed to luf, lasse° no more.   less

1525 And ye, that ar so cortays and coynt° of your   polite

hetes,°   vows

Oghe to a yonke thynk yern° to schewe   **yonke** . . . young girl eagerly

And teche sum tokenes of treweluf craftes.°   skills

Why! Ar ye lewed,° that alle the los weldes,°   unlearned   **los weldes** renown have

Other elles ye demen° me too dille° your   judge   silly

dalyaunce° to herken?   conversation

1530   For schame!

I com hider sengel and sitte

To lerne at° yow sum game;   from

Dos teches° me of your wytte,   **Dos teches** Do teach

Whil my lorde is fro hame."

         lxi

1535   "In goud faythe," quoth Gawayn, "God yow

foryelde!°   reward

Gret is the gode gle, and gomen° to me huge,   sport

That so worthy as ye wolde wynne° hidere   come

And pyne° yow with so pouer° a mon, as play   trouble   poor

wyth your knyght

With anyskynnes countenaunce°—hit keveres°   **anyskynnes countenaunce** any kind o[f]

me ese.   favor   brings

1540 Bot to take the torvayle° to myself to trewluf   travail

expoun

And towche the temes° of tyxt° and tales of armes   themes   that text

To yow that, I wot wel, weldes° more slyght°   has   skill

Of that art, bi the half, or a hundreth of seche°   such

As I am, other ever schal, in erde ther I leve°—   **in** . . . on earth while I live

1545 Hit were a folé fele-folde,° my fre,° by my   **folé fele-folde** foolishness manifold

trawthe.°   noble one   word

I wolde yowre wylnyng worche° at my myght,°   **wylnyng worche** will do   power

As I am hyghly bihalden, and evermore wylle

Be servaunt to yourselven, so save me

Dryghtyn!"°   the Lord

Thus hym frayned° that fre and fondet° hym   asked   tempted

ofte,

1550 For to haf wonnen hym to woghe, what-so

schö° thoght elles.   **woghe** . . . sin, whatsoever she

Bot he defended hym so fayr° that no faut semed,°   graciously   **faut semed** fault appeared

Ne non evel on nawther halve;° nawther thay   side

wysten°   knew

bot blysse.

Thay laghed and layked° longe;   played

426

1555 At the last schö con hym kysse.°   **con** ... kissed him
     Hir leve fayre con schö fonge,°   **con** ... she took
     And went hir waye, i-wysse.

lxii

     Then rüthes° hym the renk and ryses to the   bestirs
       masse,
     And sithen° hör diner was dyght and derely°   later **dyght** ... prepared and nobly
       served.
1560 The lede with the ladyes layked° alle day,   played
     Bot the lorde over the londes launced° ful ofte, spurred
     Sues° his uncely° swyn, that swynges° bi the   Follows   ill-fated   rushes
       bonkkes
     And bote° the best of his braches° the bakkes in bit   hounds
       sunder
     Ther he bode in his bay,° tel bawemen hit   **bode** ... stood at bay
       breken,°   overcame
1565 And madee hym, mawgref his hed,° for to meve   **mawgref** ... despite himself
       utter,°   **meve utter** move out
     So felle flones° ther flete° when the folk gedered. **felle flones** many arrows   sped
     Bot yet the styffest° to start bi stoundes° he made, bravest   **start** ... flinch at times
     Til at the last he was so mat,° he myght no more exhausted
       renne,
     Bot in the hast that he myght, he to a hole wynnes° goes
1570 Of a rasse,° bi a rokk, ther rennes the boerne.° bank   stream
     He gete the bonk at his bak, bigynes to scrape,° scrape the ground
     The frothe femed° at his mouth unfayre° bi the   foamed   horribly
       wykes,°   corners
     Whettes his whyte tusches.° With hym then irked° tusks   were weary
     Alle the bürnes so bolde that hym by stoden
1575 To nye° hym on-ferum,° bot neghe° hym non   **To nye** Of annoying   from afar   to
       durst   approach
         for wothe.°   danger
     He hade hurt so mony byforne
     That al thught thenne ful lothe°   dangerous
     Be more° wyth his tusches torne   **Be more** To be any more
1580 That breme° was and brayn-wod° bothe.   fierce   frenzied

lxiii

     Til the knyght com° hymself, kachande° his   came   spurring
       blonk,°   horse
     Sygh° hym byde at the bay, his bürnes bysyde.   Saw
     He lyghtes luflych adoun, leves his corsour,
     Braydes° out a bryght bront° and bigly forth   Draws   sword
       strydes,

1585 Foundes° fast thurgh the forth° ther the felle°   Comes   stream   fierce one
      bydes.
      The wylde was war° of the wyghe with weppen   aware
        in honde,
      Hef° hyghly the here,° so hetterly° he fnast,°   Rose   bristles   fiercely   snorted
      That fele ferde° for the freke, lest felle° hym the   **fele ferde** many feared   befall
        worre.°   worse
      The swyn settes hym out on° the segge even,°   **settes ...** rushes out at   straight
1590 That the bürne and the bor were bothe upon
        hepes°   **upon hepes** in heaps
      In the wyghtest° of the water. The worre° hade   strongest   worst of it
        that other;
      For the mon merkkes° hym wel, as thay mette   aims at
        fyrst,
      Set sadly° the scharp° in the slot° even,   firmly   sharp blade   hollow of the breast
      Hit hym up to the hült, that the hert schyndered,
1595 And he yarrande° hym yelde,° and yed doun° the   snarling   yielded   **yed doun** went down
        water   in
           ful tyt.°   quickly
        A hundreth houndes hym hent,°   caught
        That bremly° con hym bite;   fiercely
        Bürnes him broght to bent°   the bank
1600   And dogges to dethe endite.°   **to ...** put to death

                lxiv
      Ther was blawyng of prys° in mony breme°   the kill   loud
        horne,
      Heghe halowing on highe with hatheles that
        myght.
      Brachetes° bayed that best,° as bidden the   Hounds   beast
        maysteres,
      Of that chargeaunt° chace that were chef huntes.°   difficult   huntsmen
1605 Thenne a wyghe that was wys upon° wodcraftes   in
      To unlace° this bor lufly bigynnes.   cut up
      Fyrst he hewes of his hed and on highe settes,
      And sythen° rendes him al roghe° bi the rygge°   then   roughly   backbone
        after,
      Braydes° out the boweles, brennes° höm on glede,°   Pulls   broils   coals
1610 With bred blent° therwith his braches° rewardes.   **bred blent** bread mixed   hounds
      Sythen he britnes° out the brawen° in bryght   cuts   flesh
        brode scheldes,°   slabs
      And has out the hastlettes,° as hightly° bisemes.   entrails   fitly
      And yet hem halches° al hole the halves togeder,   fastens
      And sythen on a stif stange° stoutly hem henges.   pole
1615 Now with this ilk swyn thay swengen° to home.   hurry

The bores hed was borne bifore the bürnes
  selven°   **bürnes selven** very man
That him forferde° in the forthe° thurgh forse of   slew   stream
  his honde
      so stronge.
  Til he segh° Sir Gawayne   saw
620 In halle hym thoght ful longe,
  He calde, and he com gayn°   **com gayn** came promptly
  His fees ther for to fonge.°   take

                    lxv

  The lorde ful lowde with lote° laghed myry   word
When he seghe Sir Gawayn; with solace° he   delight
  spekes.
625 The goude ladyes were geten,° and gedered the   brought
  meyny,°   company
He schewes hem the scheldes and schapes° hem   **scheldes** . . . slabs of flesh and gives
  the tale°   tally
Of the largesse° and the lenthe, the lithernes alse,°   size   **lithernes alse** ferocity also
Of the were° of the wylde swyn, in wod° ther he   fight   wood
  fled.
That other knyght ful comly comended his dedes,
630 And praysed hit as gret prys° that he proved   excellence
  hade;
For suche a brawne° of a best,° the bolde bürne   flesh   beast
  sayde,
Ne such sydes of a swyn segh he never are.°   before
Thenne hondeled thay the hoge hed; the hende
  mon hit praysed,
And let lodly° ther-at, the lorde for to here.°   **let lodly** showed horror   praise
635 "Now, Gawayn," quoth the god mon, "this
  gomen is your awen
Bi fyn forwarde and faste, faythely° ye knowe,"   **fyn** . . . final agreement and firm, truly
  "Hit is sothe," quoth the segge, "and as siker°   surely
  trewe
Alle my get° I schal yow gif agayn,° bi my   booty   in return
  trawthe."°   word
He hent° the hathel aboute the halse° and   took   neck
  hendely hym kysses,
640 And eftersones° of the same he served hym there.   again
  "Now ar we even," quoth the hathel, "in this
  eventide,
Of alle the covenauntes that we knyt, sythen° I   since
  com hider,
      bi lawe."

The lorde sayde, "Bi Saynt Gile,
1645 Ye ar the best that I knowe.
Ye ben° ryche in a whyle,   *will be*
Such chaffer and° ye drowe!"°   **chaffer and** *trade if*   *carry on*

lxvi

Thenne thay teldet° tables trestes alofte,°   *erected*   **trestes alofte** *on trestles*
Kesten° clothes upon. Clere° lyght thenne   *Put*   *Bright*
1650 Wakned° bi woghes;° waxen torches   *Shone*   *walls*
Segges sette, and served in sale° al aboute.   *the hall*
Much glam° and gle glent° up ther-inne   *merry noise*   *sprang*
Aboute the fyre upon flet° and on fele wyse,°   **upon flet** *in the hall*   *ways*
At the soper and after, mony athel° songes,   *splendid*
1655 As coundutes° of Krystmasse and caroles newe,   *songs*
With alle the manerly merthe that mon may of
    telle,
And ever oure luflych knyght the lady bisyde.
Such semblaunt° to that segge semly hö made,   *manner*
Wyth stille, stollen° countenaunce, that stalworth   **stille, stollen** *secret, stealthy*
    to plese,
1660 That al forwondered° was the wyghe, and wroth   *astonished*
    with hymselven;
Bot he nolde° not for his nurture nurne hir   *would*
    ayaynes,°   **nurne ... refuse her**
Bot dalt with hir al in daynté,° how-se-ever the   *courtesy*
    dede turned
      to-wrast.°   *amiss*
When thay hade played in halle
1665 As longe as hör wylle höm last,
To chambre he° con hym calle,   *he (the lord of the castle)*
And to the chemné° thay past.°   *fireplace*   *passed*

lxvii

Ande ther thay dronken and dalten, and demed°   **dalten ... spoke, and decided**
    eft newe°   **eft newe** *once again*
To norne on° the same note° on Newe Yeres   **norne on** *propose*   *fashion*
    even;
1670 Bot the knyght craved leve to kayre° on the morn,   *go*
For hit was negh at° the terme that he to schulde.°   **negh at** *near*   **to schulde** *must go*
The lorde hym letted° of that, to lenge° hym   *deterred*   *stay*
    resteyed,°   *bade*
And sayde: "As I am trewe segge, I siker° my   *assure*
    trawthe°   *word*
Thou schal cheve° to the grene chapel, thy   *come*
    charres° to make,   *affairs*

675	Leude, on New Yeres lyght,° longe bifore pryme.°	dawn prime (6:00–9:00 A.M.)
	For-thy, thow lye in thy loft,° and lach thyn ese,	room
	And I schal hunt in this holt and halde° the	**holt . . .** wood and keep
	towches,°	terms
	Chaunge° wyth thee chevicaunce,° bi that I	Exchange winnings
	charre° hider;	return
	For I haf fraysted° thee twys,° and faythful I	tried twice
	fynde thee.	
680	Now 'Thrid° tyme, throwe° best,' thenk on the	Third prove
	morne;	
	Make we mery whyl we may, and mynne° upon	think
	joye,	
	For the lür° may mon lach when-so° mon lykes."	**the lür** sorrow **lach when-so** get whenever
	This was graythely° graunted, and Gawayn is	speedily
	lenged.°	**is lenged** stayed
	Blithe° broght was hym drynk, and thay to bedde	Happily
	yeden°	went
685	with light.	
	Sir Gawayn lis and slepes	
	Ful stille and softe al night,	
	The lorde that his craftes° kepes,	affairs
	Ful erly he was dight.°	ready

lxviii

690	After messe° a morsel he and his men token;	mass
	Miry° was the mornyng, his mounture° he askes.	Fair mount
	Alle the hatheles that on horse schulde helden°	go
	hym after	
	Were boun busked° on hör blonkkes,° bifore the	**boun busked** already dressed horses
	halle yates.°	gates
	Ferly° fayre was the folde,° for the forst clenged,°	Wondrously ground **forst clenged** frost clung to it
695	In rede rudede° upon rak° rises the sunne	**rede rudede** redness fiery cloud drift
	And ful clere costes° the clowdes of the welkyn.	**clere costes** brightly passes above
	Hunteres unhardeled° bi a holt° syde;	unleashed hounds wood
	Rocheres roungen bi rys,° for rürde° of her	**Rocheres . . .** Rocks rang in woods noise
	hornes.	
	Summe fel in° the fute° ther the fox bade°—	**fel in** hit on track waited
700	Trayles ofte a traveres°—bi traunt° of her wyles.	**a traveres** crisscross the skill
	A kenet° kryes therof, the hunt° on hym calles;	small hound huntsman
	His felawes fallen hym to, that fnasted° ful thike,	panted
	Runnen forth in a rabel in his ryght fare.°	track
	And he fyskes° hem byfore; thay founden hym	rushes
	sone,	
705	And when thay seghe° hym wyth syght, thay	saw
	sued° hym fast,	followed

Wreghande° hym ful weterly° wyth a wroth° noyse. — Reviling   clearly   angry

And he trantes and tornayees° thurgh mony tene greve,° — trantes . . . dodges and doubles / tene greve rough thickets

Havilounes and herkenes° bi hegges ful ofte. — Havilounes . . . Doubles back and listen

At the last bi a littel dich he lepes over a spenné,° — thorn hedge

1710 Steles out ful stilly° bi a strothe rande,° — quietly   strothe rande wood side

Went haf wylt° of the wode with wyles fro the houndes. — Went . . . Thought to have escaped

Thenne was he went,° er he wyst, to a wale tryster,° — gone / wale tryster choice hunting station

Ther thre thro° at a thrich thrat° hym at ones, al graye. — fierce ones   thrich thrat rush attacked

1715 He blenched° ayayn bilyve° — drew back   quickly

And stifly start onstray.° — aside

With alle the wo on lyve° — earth

To the wod he went away.

lxix

Thenne was hit list° upon lif to lythen° the houndes, — joy   hear

1720 When alle the mute° hade hym met, menged° togeder. — pack   mingled

Suche a sorwe° at that syght thay sette on his hede — imprecation

As° alle the clamberande° clyffes hade clatered° on hepes. — As if   clustering   clattered down

Here he was halawed when hatheles hym metten,

Loude he was yayned° with yarande° speche. — met   snarling

1725 Ther he was threted° and ofte thef called, — threatened

And ay the titleres° at his tayl, that tary he ne myght. — hounds

Ofte he was runnen at when he out rayked,° — out rayked went for the open

And ofte reled° in ayayn, so Reniarde was wylé.° — turned   wily

And ye,° he lad hem bi lag-mon,° the lorde and his meyny,° — indeed   bi lag-mon astray (?) / company

1730 On this maner bi the mountes, whyle mid-over-under° — mountes . . . hills, until midmorning

Whyle the hende knyght at home holsumly slepes

Withinne the comly cortynes, on the colde morne.

Bot the lady for luf let° not to slepe, — allowed herself

Ne the purpose to payre,° that pyght° in hir hert, — fail   was set

735 Bot ros hir up radly, rayked hir° theder,　　*radly . . .* quickly, went
In a mery mantyle, mete° to the erthe,　　extending
That was furred ful fyne with felles° wel pured.°　　pelts　trimmed
No hewes goud° on hir hede, bot the hagher°　　**hewes goud** precious decorations
　　stones　　well-wrought
Trased° aboute hir tressour° be twenty in　　Entwined　hairnet
　　clusteres;
740 Hir thryven° face and hir throte throwen° al　　fair　exposed
　　naked,
Hir brest bare bifore, and bihinde eke.°　　also
Hö comes withinne the chambre dore and closes
　　hit hir after,
Wayves° up a wyndow and on the wyghe calles,　　Throws
And radly° thus rehayted° hym with hir riche　　quickly　rallied
　　wordes,
745　　with chere:°　　good cheer
　　"A! mon, how may thou slepe?
　　This morning is so clere."
　　He was in drowping° depe,　　drowsing
　　Bot thenne he con hir here.°　　**con . . .** heard her

　　　　　　lxx
750　　In dregh° droupyng of dreme draveled° that　　heavy　muttered
　　noble,
As mon that was in mournyng of mony thro°　　heavy
　　thoghtes,
How that destiné schulde that day dele hym his
　　wyrde°　　fate
At the grene chapel, when he the gome metes
And bihoves° his buffet abide° withoute debate°　　must　suffer　defense
　　more;
755 Bot when-that comly° he kevered° his wyttes,　　fittingly　recovered
Swenges° out of the swevenes and swares° with　　He hastens　**swevenes . . .** dreams and
　　hast.　　answers
The lady luflych com, laghande swete,
Felle° over his fayre face, and fetly° hym kyssed.　　Bent　gracefully
He welcumes hir worthily with a wale chere.°　　**wale chere** fair cheer
760 He segh hir so glorious and gayly atyred,
So fautles of hir fetures and of so fyne hewes,
Wight wallande° joye warmed his hert.　　**Wight wallande** Ardently welling up
With smothe smylyng and smolt° thay smeten°　　gentle　fell
　　into merthe,
That al was blis and bonchef° that breke hem　　happiness
　　bitwene,
765　　and wynne.°　　joy

Thay lanced° wordes gode,   uttered
Much wele then was ther-inne;
Gret perile bitwene hem stod,
Nif Maré° of hir knyght mynne.°   **Nif Maré** If not Mary   may be mindful

lxxi

1770   For that prynces of pris depresed° hym so   **prynces . . .** noble princess importuned
       thikke,°   hard
     Nurned° hym so neghe° the thred,° that nede   Urged   near   limit
       hym bihoved
     Other° lach ther hir luf other lodly° refuse.   Either   **other lodly** or offensively
     He cared° for his cortaysye, lest crathayn° he were,   feared   villain
     And more for his meschef,° yif he schulde make   evil plight
       synne
1775 And be traytor to that tolke° that that telde aght.°   lord   **telde aght** house owned
      "God schylde,"° quoth the schalk.° "That schal   forbid   man
       not befalle!"
     With luf-laghyng° a lyt° he layd hym bysyde°   loving laugh   little   **layd . . .** parried
     Alle the speches of specialté° that sprange of her   partiality
       mouthe.
     Quoth that bürde to the bürne: "Blame ye
       disserve,
1780 Yif ye luf not that lyf° that ye lye nexte,   person
     Bifore alle the wyghes in the worlde wounded in
       hert;
     Bot if° ye haf a lemman,° a lever,° that yow lykes   Unless   sweetheart   dearer one
       better,
     And folden° fayth to that fre, festned so harde   plighted
     That yow lausen ne lyst,° and that I leve° nouthe.   wish   believe
1785 And that ye telle me that, now trewly I pray yow.
     For alle the lufes upon lyve, layne° not the sothe   **upon . . .** alive, hide
       for gile."°   guile
     The knyght sayde, "Be Sayn Jon,"
     And smethely° con he smyle,   gently
1790   "In fayth I welde right non,°   **welde . . .** have none at all
     Ne non wil welde the while."°   **the while** at present

lxxii

     "That is a worde," quoth that wyght,° "that   person
       worst is of alle;
     Bot I am swared forsothe,° that sore° me   **swared forsothe** answered truly   pain
       thinkkes.
     Kysse me now comly, and I schal cach hethen;°   **cach hethen** go hence
1795 I may but mourne upon molde,° as may° that   earth   maiden
       much lovyes."

Sykande° hö sweghe° doun and semly hym kyssed,	Sighing stooped
And sithen hö severes° hym fro, and says as hö stondes:	parts
"Now, dere, at this departyng, do me this ese,°	comfort
Gif me sumwhat of thy gifte, thi glove if hit were,	
800 That I may mynne° on thee, mon, my mournyng to lassen."°	think / lessen
"Now i-wysse,"° quoth that wyghe, "I wolde I hade here	indeed
The levest° thing for thy luf that I in londe welde;°	dearest / have
For ye haf deserved, forsothe, sellyly° ofte	very
More rewarde bi resoun° then I reche° myght;	rights offer
805 Bot to dele° yow for drurye,° that dawed° bot neked.°	give **for drurye** a token for love would avail little
Hit is not your honour to haf at this tyme	
A glove for a garysoun° of Gawaynes giftes;	warrant
And I am here on an erande in erdes uncouthe,°	**erdes uncouthe** lands unknown
And have no men wyth no males° with menskful° thinges.	bags valuable
810 That mislykes° me, ladé,° for your luf at this tyme;	displeases lady
Iche tolke mon° do as he is tan, tas to° non ille ne pine."°	**Iche** ... Each man must **tan** ... placed, take it as **ne pine** nor grief
"Nay, hende of hyghe honours,"	
Quoth that lufsum under lyne,°	**lufsum** ... lovely linen-clad lady
815 "Thagh I hade noght of youres,	
Yet schulde ye have of myne."	

lxxiii

Hö raght° hym a riche rynk° of red golde werkes,	offered ring
Wyth a starande° ston stondande alofte,	shining
That bere° blusschande bemes as the bryght sunne.	cast
820 Wyt° ye wel, hit was worth wele° ful hoge,°	Know wealth huge
Bot the renk hit renayed,° and redyly he sayde,	refused
"I wil no giftes for gode,° my gay,° at this tyme;	my own fair lady
I haf none yow to norne,° ne noght wyl I take."	offer
Hö bede° hit hym ful bysily,° and he hir bode wernes,°	offered eagerly **bode wernes** offer refuses
825 And swere swyfte by his sothe° that he hit sese nolde;°	word **sese nolde** would not take
And hö sore° that he forsoke,° and sayde ther-after,	grieved refused
"If ye renay my rynk, too ryche° for hit semes,	costly
Ye wolde not so hyghly halden° be to me,	**hyghly halden** greatly beholden

435

I schal gif yow my girdel, that gaynes° yow lasse." — profits

1830 Hö laght° a lace lyghtly that leke umbe° hir sydes, — grasped   **leke umbe** was fastened arour

Knit° upon hir kyrtel,° under the clere° mantyle; — Knotted   gown   bright

Gered° hit was with grene sylke, and with golde schaped, — Made

Noght bot arounde brayden, beten° with fyngres; — **arounde ...** embroidered all around, decorated

And that hö bede° to the bürne,° and blythely bisoght, — offered   man

1835 Thagh hit unworthi were, that he hit take wolde.

And he nay that he nolde neghe in no wyse°

Nauther golde ne garysoun,° er God hym grace sende — **Nauther ...** Either gold or treasure

To acheve to the chaunce° that he hade chosen° there. — adventure   undertaken

"And ther-fore, I pray yow, displese yow noght,

1840 And lettes be° your bisinesse,° for I baythe° hit yow never — **lettes be** cease from   beseeching   will consent

   to graunte.

I am derely° to yow biholde — deeply

Bicause of your sembleaunt,° — manner

And ever in hot and colde

1845   To be your trewe servaunt."

lxxiv

"Now forsake° ye this silke," sayde the bürde thenne, — refuse

"For hit is symple in hitself, and so hit wel semes?

Lo! So hit is littel, and lasse hit is worthy;° — valuable

Bot who-so° knew the costes° that knit ar ther-inne, — whosoever   qualities

1850 He wolde hit prayse at more prys, paraventure;° — **prys, paraventure** excellence, perhaps

For what gome so is gorde° with this grene lace, — girt

While he hit hade hemely halched° aboute, — **hemely halched** neatly looped

Ther is no hathel° under heven to-hewe° hym that myght; — man   cut down

For he myght not be slayn for slyght° upon erthe." — **for slyght** by any means

1855   Then kest° the knyght, and hit come to his hert, — considered

Hit were a juel for the jöpardé that hym jugged° were, — adjudged

When he acheved to the chapel, his chek° for to fech;° — fortune / get

Myght he haf slypped° to be unslayn, the sleght were noble. — escaped

---

1836. And he said that he would not (literally, 'denied that he would') in any way touch

Thenne he thulged° with hir threpe, and tholed°   was patient   **threpe ...** argument, and
   hir to speke,   suffered

860 And hö bere on hym the belt and bede° hit hym   offered
   swythe°—   earnestly

And he granted°—and hym gafe with a goud   agreed
   wylle,

And bisoght hym, for hir sake, discever° hit never,   reveal

Bot to lelly layne° fro hir lorde; the leüde hym   **lelly layne** loyally hide (it)
   acordes°   **hym acordes** agrees

That never wyghe° schulde hit wyt, i-wysse, bot   anyone
   thay twayne,°   two

865   for noghte.

He thonkked hir oft ful swythe,

Ful thro° with hert and thoght.   heartily

Bi-that, on thrynne sythe°   **thrynne sythe** three times

Hö has kyst the knyght so toght.°   strong

lxxv

870 Thenne lachches hö hir leve and leves hym
   there,

For more myrthe of that mon moght hö not gete;

When hö was gon, Sir Gawayn geres° hym sone,   dresses

Rises and riches° hym in araye noble,   dresses

Lays up° the luf-lace the lady hym raght,°   **Lays up** Puts away   gave

875 Hid hit ful holdely,° ther he hit eft fonde.°   carefully   might find

Sythen chevely° to the chapel choses° he the   quickly   takes
   waye,

Prevely° aproched to a prest, and prayed hym   Privately
   there

That he wolde lyfte° his lyf and lern hym better   lift up

How his sawle schulde be saved when he schuld
   seye hethen.°   **seye hethen** go hence

880 There he schrof hym schyrly° and schewed his   fully
   misdedes

Of the more° and the mynne,° and merci beseches,   greater   less

And of absolucioun he on the segge° calles;   priest

And he asoyled° hym surely and sette hym so   absolved
   clene°   pure

As° Domesday schulde haf ben dight° on the   As if   appointed
   morn.

885 And sythen he mace° hym as mery among the   makes
   fre ladyes,

With comlych° caroles and alle kynnes° joye,   sweet   kinds of

As never he did bot that daye, to the derk nyght,
   with blys.

Úche mon hade daynté° thare — courtesy
1890 Of° hym, and sayde, "I-wysse, — From
Thus myry he was never are,° — before
Syn he com hider, er this."

lxxvi

Now hym lenge° in that lee,° ther luf hym bityde!° — **hym lenge** may he stay shelter / may befall
Yet is the lorde on the launde,° ledande his gomnes.° — field / sports
1895 He has forfaren° this fox that he folghed° longe. — slain followed
As he sprent over a spenné,° to spye the schrewe,° — thorn hedge villain
Ther as° he herd the howndes that hasted° hym swythe,° — **Ther as** Where pressed / quickly
Renaud com richchande° thurgh a roghe greve,° — running **roghe greve** rough thicket
And alle the rabel in a res,° ryght at his heles. — rush
1900 The wyghe was war° of the wylde° and warly abides° — aware creature / waits
And braydes° out the bryght bronde° and at the best castes.° — pulls sword / thrusts
And he schunt for° the scharp and sculde° haf arered;° — **schunt for** swerved from would / retreated
A rach rapes° hym to, ryght er he myght,° — **rach rapes** hound rushes could retreat
And ryght bifore the hors fete thay fel on hym alle
1905 And woried me⁵ this wyly° wyth a wroth° noyse. — wily one angry
The lorde lyghtes bilyve and laches° hym sone, — **lyghtes . . .** alights quickly and seizes
Rased° hym ful radly° out of the rach mouthes, — Snatched quickly
Haldes heghe over his hede, halowes° faste, — halloes
And ther bayen hym mony brath° houndes; — fierce
1910 Huntes° hyghed hem theder, with hornes ful mony, — Huntsmen
Ay rechatande aryght° til thay the renk seghen; — **rechatande aryght** sounding the recall properly
Bi-that° was comen his compeyny noble, — When
Alle that ever ber bugle blowed at ones,
And alle thise other halowed, that hade no hornes;
1915 Hit was the myriest mute° that ever men herde, — baying
The rich rürd° that ther was raysed for Renaude° saule — noise Reynard's
with lote;° — cries
Hör houndes thay ther rewarde,
Her hedes thay fawne and frote,° — **fawne . . .** fondle and stroke
1920 And sythen thay tan° Reynarde — take
And tyrven° off his cote. — strip

⁵ Here *me* is the ethic dative of *I* and must be omitted in translation; see also lines 1932, 2014, 2144, and 2459.

lxxvii

And thenne thay helden to° home, for hit was   **helden to** went
    niegh nyght,
Strakande° ful stoutly in hör store° hornes.   Sounding   mighty
The lorde is lyght° at the laste at hys lef° home,   **is lyght** alighted   dear
1925 Fyndes fire upon flet,° the freke ther byside,   **upon flet** in the hall
Sir Gawayn the gode that glad was withalle;
Among the ladies for luf he ladde° much joye.   had
He were° a bleaunt° of blewe that bradde° to the   wore   mantle   reached
    erthe;
His surkot semed° hym wel, that softe was   suited
    forred,°   furred
1930 And his hode of that ilke° henged on his schulder;   same material
Blande° al of blaunner° were bothe al aboute.   Decorated   white fur
  He metes me this god mon inmyddes the
    flore,
And al with gomen° he hym gret,° and goudly he   sport   greeted
    sayde,
"I schal fylle upon fyrst° oure forwardes nouthe,°   **fylle . . .** fulfill first of all   **forwardes nouthe** agreements now
1935 That we spedly han spoken° ther spared was no   spoken of
    drynk."
Then acoles° he the knyght, and kysses hym   embraces
    thryes
As saverly and sadly as he hem sette couthe.°
  "Bi Kryst," quoth that other knyght, "ye cach
    much sele°   luck
In chevisaunce of° this chaffer,° yif ye hade goud   **chevisaunce of** winning from   trade
    chepes."°   bargains
1940 "Ye, of the chepe no charg,"° quoth chefly° that   importance   quickly
    other,
"As is pertly° payed the chepes that I aghte."°   plainly   owed
  "Mary," quoth that other mon, "myn is
    bihynde,°   lesser
For I haf hunted al this day, and noght haf I geten
Bot this foule fox felle°—the fende° haf the   skin   fiend
    godes!°—   goods
1945 And that is ful pore for to pay for suche prys°   excellent
    thinges
As ye haf thryght° me here thro, suche thre cosses°   thrust   kisses
    so gode."
  "Inogh," quoth Sir Gawayn,
  "I thonk yow, bi the rode,"°   cross
1950 And how the fox was slayn
He tolde hym as thay stode.

1937. As pleasantly and firmly as he could place them.

lxxviii

With merthe and mynstralsye, wyth metes at hör
    wylle,
Thay maden as mery as any men moghten—
With laghyng of ladies, with lotes° of bordes,°   words jests
1955 Gawayn and the gode mon so glad were thay
    bothe—
Bot if° the douthe° had doted other° dronken ben   Unless company or
    other.°   else
Bothe the mon and the meyny° maden mony   company
    japes,°   jests
Til the sesoun° was seghen° that thay sever   time come
    moste;°   **sever moste** must part
Bürnes to hör bedde behoved° at the laste.   must go
1960   Thenne loghly° his leve at the lorde fyrst   humbly
Fochches° this fre mon, and fayre he hym   Takes
    thonkkes:
"Of such a selly° sojorne as I haf hade here,   marvelous
Your honour at this hyghe fest, the hyghe kyng
    yow yelde!°   reward
I yef yow me° for on of youres, if yowreself   **yef** . . . surrender myself to you
    lykes—
1965 For I mot° nedes, as ye wot, meve to-morne—   must
And° ye me take° sum tolke,° to teche, as ye   If give man
    hyght,°   promised
The gate° to the grene chapel, as God wyl me   way
    suffer
To dele° on New Yeres day the dome° of my   perform doom
    wyrdes."°   fate
    "In god faythe," quoth the god mon, "wyth a
    goud wylle,
1970 Al that ever I yow hyght, halde schal I redé."°   ready
Ther asyngnes he a servaunt to sett hym in the
    waye
And coundue° hym by the downes, that he no   conduct
    drechch° had,   trouble
For to ferk° thurgh the fryth° and fare at the   go wood
    gaynest°   **at** . . . most directly
    bi greve.°   thicket
1975   The lorde, Gawayn con thonk,°   **con thonk** thanked
Such worchip° he wolde hym weve;°   honor offer
Then at tho ladyes wlonk°   lovely
The knyght has tan° his leve.   taken

lxxix

With care° and wyth kyssyng he carppes° hem   sorrow speaks
    tille,
1980 And fele thryvande° thonkkes he thrat° höm to   hearty urged
    have,
And thay yelden° hym ayayn yeply° that ilk;   return promptly
Thay bikende° hym to Kryst, with ful colde   commended
    sykynges.°   **colde sykynges** grievous sighs
Sythen fro the meyny° he menskly° departes;   company courteously
Üche mon that he mette, he made hem a thonke
1985 For his servyse and his solace° and his sere pyne°   kindness **sere pyne** individual trouble
That thay wyth busynes had ben aboute hym to
    serve;
And üche segge as sore to sever with hym there
As° thay hade wonde° worthyly with that wlonk°   As if lived lovely one
    ever.
Then with ledes° and lyght he was ladde to his   servants
    chambre
1990 And blythely broght to his bedde to be at his
    rest.
Yif he ne slepe soundyly, say ne dar I,
For he hade muche on the morn to mynne,° yif   think of
    he wolde,
      in thoght.
    Let hym lyghe° there stille,   lie
1995   He has nere that° he soght.   **nere that** nearby what
    And° ye wyl a whyle be stylle,   If
    I schal telle yow how thay wroght.°   did

Part IV

lxxx

Now neghes° the New Yere, and the nyght   draws near
    passes,
The day dryves° to the derk, as Dryghtyn° biddes.   follows the Lord
2000 Bot wylde wederes° of the worlde wakned   weather
    ther-oute,°   outside
Clowdes kesten kenly° the colde to the erthe,   **kesten kenly** cast bitterly
Wyth nyghe innoghe of the northe, the naked to
    tene.°   punish

The snawe snitered° ful snart,° that snayped° the   shivered down bitterly nipped
wylde;°   wild animals
The werbelande° wynde wapped° fro the hyghe   whistling rushed
2005 And drof üche dale ful of dryftes ful grete.
The leüde lystened ful wel, that legh in his bedde,
Thagh he lowkes° his liddes, ful lyttel he slepes;   closes
Bi üch kok that crewe he knewe wel the steven.°   appointed time
Deliverly° he dressed up er the day sprenged,   Quickly
2010 For there was lyght of a laumpe that lemed° in   shone
his chambre.
He called to his chamberlayn, that cofly° hym   promptly
swared,°   answered
And bede hym bryng hym his brüny° and his   mail shirt
blonk sadel.°   **blonk sadel** horse saddle
That other ferkes° hym up and feches hym his   gets
wedes°   clothes
And graythes° me Sir Gawayn upon° a grett wyse.°   clothes in **grett wyse** magnificent manner
2015 Fyrst he clad hym in his clothes, the colde for to
were;°   ward off
And sythen his other harnays, that holdely° was   faithfully
keped,
Bothe his paunce° and his plates, piked° ful clene,°   stomach armor polished bright
The rynges rokked° of the roust° of his riche   cleaned rust
brüny;°   mail shirt
And al was fresch as upon° fyrst, and he was fayn°   at glad
thenne
2020   to thonk.°   give thanks
He hade upon° üche pece,   on him
Wypped° ful wel and wlonk,°   Wiped beautifully
The gayest into° Grece.   from here to
The bürne bede bryng his blonk.

lxxxi

2025 Whyle the wlonkest° wedes he warp° on   loveliest put
hymselven—
His cote wyth the conysaunce° of the clere   badge (pentangle)
werkes°   **clere werkes** fair embroidery
Ennurned° upon velvet, vertuus° stones,   Set potent
Aboute beten° and bounden, enbrauded° semes,   set embroidered
And fayre furred withinne wyth fayre pelures°—   furs
2030 Yet laft° he not the lace,° the ladies gifte;   left belt
That forgat not Gawayn, for gode of hymselven.
Bi° he hade belted the bronde° upon his balghe   When sword
haunches,°   **balghe haunches** smooth hips
Thenn dressed he his drurye° double hym aboute.   love token

Swythe swethled umbe° his swange° swetely that   **Swythe . . .** Quickly wrapped around
    knyght   waist
2035 The gordel of the grene silke that gay wel bisemed
Upon that ryol,° red clothe that ryche° was to   regal   splendid
    schewe.°   look at
Bot wered not this ilk wyghe° for wele° this   man   wealth
    gordel,
For pryde of the pendauntes, thagh polyst thay
    were,
And thagh the glyterande golde glent° upon   glinted
    endes,
2040 Bot for to saven hymself, when suffer hym
    byhoved,
To byde bale° withoute dabate° of bronde° hym   **byde bale** suffer death   defense   sword
  to were°   defend
      other knyffe.
    Bi-that° the bolde mon boun°   Then   ready
    Wynnes ther-oute° bilyve;   **Wynnes ther-oute** Goes outside
2045   Alle the meyny of renoun
    He thonkkes ofte ful ryve.°   much

lxxxii

    Thenne was Gryngolet graythe,° that gret was   made ready
    and huge,
And hade ben sojourned saverly° and in a siker   pleasantly
  wyse;°   **siker wyse** sure manner
Hym lyst prik° for poynt,° that proude hors   **lyst prik** it pleases to gallop   good
    thenne.   condition
2050 The wyghe wynnes° hym to, and wytes° on his   goes   looks
  lyre,°   coat
And sayde soberly hymself, and by his soth
  sweres,°   **by . . .** on his word swears
"Here is a meyny in this mote° that on menske°   castle   courtesy
    thenkkes.
The mon hem maynteines, joy mot° he have!   may
The leve° lady, on lyve° luf hir bityde!°   dear   **on lyve** during life   befall
2055 Yif thay for charyté cherysen° a gest,°   cherish   guest
And halden honour in her honde, the Hathel°   Lord
  hem yelde°   reward
That haldes the heven upon hyghe, and also yow
    alle!
And yif I myght lyf° upon londe° lede any whyle,   life   earth
I schuld rech yow sum rewarde redyly, if I
    myght."
2060 Thenn steppes he into stirop and strydes alofte.

His schalk schewed° hym his schelde; on schulder he hit laght,	**schalk schewed** servant brought
Gordes to° Gryngolet with his gilt heles,	**Gordes to** Spurs
And he startes° on the ston, stod he no lenger to praunce;	leaps forward
2065 His hathel° on hors was thenne,	master
That bere his spere and launce.	
"This kastel to Kryst I kenne,°	commend
He gef hit ay god chaunce!"°	luck

lxxxiii

The brygge was brayde° doun, and the brode yates°	pulled / gates
2070 Unbarred and born open upon bothe halve.	
The bürne blessed hym bilyve, and the bredes° passed;	planks
Prayses the porter, bifore° the prynce kneled,	who before
Gef° hym God and goud day, that Gawayn he save;	And who gave
And went on his way with his wyghe° one	servant
2075 That schulde teche hym to tourne to that tene° place	dangerous
Ther the ruful race° he schulde resayve.°	attack receive
Thay boghen° bi bonkkes ther boghes° ar bare;	went boughs
Thay clomben bi clyffes ther clenges the colde.	
The heven was up halt,° bot ugly ther-under	**heven . . .** clouds were high
2080 Mist muged° on the mor, malt° on the mountes;	drizzled melted
Üch hille hade a hatte, a myst-hakel° huge.	cloak of mist
Brokes byled and breke bi bonkkes aboute,	
Schyre schaterande° on schores,° ther thay doun schouved.°	**Schyre schaterande** Brightly breaking banks rushed
Wela wylle° was the way ther thay bi wod schulden,°	**Wela wylle** Very wild must go
2085 Til hit was sone sesoun° that the sunne ryses that tyde.°	time time
Thay were on a hille ful hyghe,	
The whyte snaw lay bisyde;	
The bürne° that rod hym by	man
2090 Bede° his mayster abide.°	Bade wait

lxxxiv

"For I haf wonnen° yow hider, wyghe, at this tyme,	brought
And now nar° ye not fer° fro that note° place	are far noted
That ye han spied and spüryed° so specially after.	**han . . .** have looked for and asked

Bot I schal say yow forsothe, sythen I yow knowe,		
2095 And ye ar a lede upon lyve° that I wel lovy,°	**upon lyve** alive love	
Wolde ye worch° bi my wytte,° ye worthed° the better.	do advice would be	
The place that ye prece° to ful perelous is halden;°	hurry held	
Ther wones a wyghe in that waste, the worst upon erthe,		
For he is stiffe° and sturne, and to strike lovies.	strong	
2100 And more he is then any mon upon myddel-erde,°	earth	
And his body bigger then the best fowre		
That ar in Arthures hous, Hestor, other other.°	**Hestor . . .** Hector, or any other	
He cheves° that chaunce° at the chapel grene,	brings about fortune	
Ther passes non bi that place so proude in his armes		
2105 That he ne dynges° hym to dethe with dynt° of his honde;	**ne dynges** doesn't smite blow	
For he is a mon methles,° and mercy non uses,	immoderate	
For be hit chorle other chaplayn that bi the chapel rydes,		
Monk other masseprest other any mon elles,		
Hym thynk as queme° hym to quelle as quyk go° hymselven.	pleasant **quyk go** alive to go	
2110 For-thy I say thee, as sothe° as ye in sadel sitte,	sure	
Com ye there,° ye be kylled, may the knyght rede,°	**Com . . .** If you come manage it	
Trawe° ye me that trewely, thagh ye had twenty lyves	Believe	
to spende;		
He has wonyd here ful yore,°	long	
2115 On bent° much baret bende.°	field **baret bende** strife has led	
Ayayn his dyntes sore		
Ye may not yow defende."		

lxxxv

"For-thy, goude Sir Gawayn, let the gome one,°	alone	
And gos away sum other gate,° upon Goddes halve.°	way sake	
2120 Cayres° bi sum other kyth,° ther Kryst mot° yow spede;°	Ride land may help	
And I schal hygh me hom ayayn and hete° yow fyrre°	promise further	
That I schal swere bi God and alle his gode halghes,°	saints	
As help me God and the halydam° and othes innoghe,	holy relic (on which oaths were sworn)	
That I schal lelly° yow layne and lance° never tale	faithfully **layne . . .** conceal and utter	
2125 That ever ye fondet° to fle for freke that I wyst."°	hastened knew of	

445

"Grant merci," quoth Gawayn, and gruchyng°   reluctantly
    he sayde,
"Wel worth° thee, wyghe, that woldes° my gode;   be wished
And, that lelly me layne, I leve° wel thou woldes.°   believe would
Bot helde thou hit never so holde, and° I here   **holde, and** faithfully, if
    passed,
2130 Founded° for ferde° for to fle, in fourme° that thou   Came fear manner
    telles,
I were a knyght kowarde; I myght not be
    excused.
Bot I wyl to the chapel, for chaunce that may
    falle,
And talk wyth that ilk tulk the tale° that me lyste,°   account pleases
Worthe° hit wele other wo, as the wyrde° lykes   Be fate
2135   hit hafe.
    Thaghe he be a sturn knape°   man
    To stightel, and stad with stave,°
    Ful wel con Dryghtyn schape°   **con . . .** the Lord arranged
    His servauntes for to save."

          lxxxvi
2140 "Mary!" quoth that other mon, "now thou so
    much spelles°   say
That thou wylt thyn awen nye nyme° to   **nye nyme** harm take
    thyselven,
And thee lyst lese thy lyf, thee lette I ne kepe.°
Haf here thi helme° on thy hede, thi spere in thi   helmet
    honde,
And ryde me doun this ilk rake,° bi yon rokke   path
    syde,
2145 Til you be broght to the bothem° of the brem   bottom
    valay.°   **brem valay** wild valley
Thenne loke a littel on the launde,° on thi lyfte   field
    honde,
And thou schal se in that slade° the self° chapel   valley very
And the borelych° bürne on bent° that hit kepes.   burly field
Now fares wel on Godes half,° Gawayn the noble.   sake
2150 For alle the golde upon grounde I nolde° go wyth   wouldn't
    thee
Ne bere thee felawschyp thurgh this fryth° on fote   wood
    fyrre."°   farther
Bi-that° the wyghe in the wod wendes° his brydel,   Then turns
Hit the hors with the heles as harde as he myght,

2137. To master, and armed with a club
2142. If it pleases you to lose your life, I don't care to hinder you.

446

Lepes hym over the launde and leves the knyght
    there
2155   al one.°   *alone*
      "Bi Goddes self," quoth Gawayn,
      "I wyl nauther grete° ne grone;   *weep*
      To Goddes wylle I am ful bayn,°   *obedient*
      And to hym I haf me tone."°   *committed*

lxxxvii

2160   Thenne gyrdes° he to Gryngolet and gederes°   **puts spurs follows**
      the rake,°   *path*
    Schouves° in bi a schore° at a schawe° syde,   **Pushes bank wood**
    Rides thurgh the roghe bonk ryght to the dale.
    And thenne he wayted° hym aboute, and wylde   *looked*
      hit hym thoght,
    And seghe no syngne of resette bisydes° nowhere,   **resette bisydes** shelter around
2165   Bot hyghe bonkkes and brent° upon bothe halve,°   **steep sides**
    And rughe knokled knarres° with knorned°   **knokled knarres** rugged crags **gnarled**
      stones;
    The skewes of° the scowtes skayned,° hym thoght.   **skewes of** skies by **scowtes skayned** rocks touched
    Thenne he hoved° and wythhylde his hors at that   *halted*
      tyde,°   *time*
    And ofte chaunged his cher° the chapel to seche.°   **chaunged...** looked in different directions **seek**
2170   He segh non suche in no syde, and selly° hym   **syde...** direction, and marvelous
      thoght,
    Save a lyttel on a launde,° a lawe° as hit were,   **field mound**
    A balgh bergh° bi a bonke, the brymme° bysyde,   **balgh bergh** smooth mound **water's edge**
    Bi a fors° of a flode that ferked° thare;   **waterfall ran**
    The borne blubred° ther-inne as hit boyled hade.   **borne blubred** stream bubbled
2175   The knyght kaches his caple° and com to the lawe,   **kaches...** spurs his horse
    Lightes doun lufyly, and at a lynde taches°   **lynde taches** tree ties
    The rayne, and his riche, with° a roghe braunche.   **riche, with** noble steed, to
    Thenne he boghes to the berghe, aboute hit he
      walkes,
    Debatande with hymself what hit be myght.
2180   Hit hade a hole on the ende and on ayther syde,
    And overgrowen with gresse in glodes° aywhere,   *patches*
    And al was holgh° inwith—nobot° an olde cave   **hollow nothing but**
    Or a crevisse of an olde cragge; he couthe° hit   *could*
      noght deme°   *tell*
      with spelle.°   *word*
2185   "We!° Lorde," quoth the gentyle knyght.   *Alas*
      "Whether° this be the grene chapelle?   *Can*
      Here myght aboute mydnyght
      The Dele° his matynnes telle."°   **Devil recite**

lxxxviii

"Now i-wysse," quoth Wowayn,° "wysty° is   Gawain desolate
    here;
2190 This oritore is ugly, with erbes overgrowen.
    Wel bisemes the wyghe wruxled° in grene   wrapped
    Dele° here his devocioun on the Develes wyse;   Perform
    Now I fele hit is the Fende,° in my fyve wyttes,°   Fiend senses
    That has stoken° me this steven,° to strye° me   fixed tryst destroy
    here.
2195 This is a chapel of meschaunce—that chekke° hit misfortune
    bytyde!
    Hit is the corsedest kyrk° that ever I com° inne." **corsedest kyrk** most accursed church
      With heghe helme on his hede, his launce in his   came
      honde,
    He romes° up to the roffe of tho rogh wones.   makes his way
    Thene herde he of that hyghe hil, in a harde
      roche
2200 Biyonde the broke in a bonk, a wonder breme°   fierce
    noyse.
    What! hit clatered in the clyff as hit cleve°   break
    schulde,
    As one upon a gryndelston° hade grounden a   grindstone
    sythe.
    What! hit wharred and whette° as water at a   **wharred** ... whirred and ground
    mulne.°   mill
    What! hit rusched and ronge, rawthe° to here.   **ronge, rawthe** rang, terrible
2205   Thenne "Bi Godde," quoth Gawayn, "that
      gere,° as I trowe,°   apparatus believe
    Is ryched at the reverence me, renk, to mete
      bi rote!°
      Let God worche; 'We loo,'°   **worche** ... do His will; to say 'Alas'
      Hit helppes me not a mote.°   bit
2210   My lif thagh I forgoo,
      Drede dos me no lote."°

lxxxix

    Thenne the knyght con calle° ful hyghe,°   **con calle** called loudly
    "Who stightles° in this sted, me steven° to holde? rules **sted** ... place, with me tryst
    For now is gode Gawayn goande ryght here.
2215 If any wyghe oght wyl, wynne° hider fast,   **oght** ... wishes anything, come
    Other now other never, his nedes° to spede."° business help
      "Abyde," quoth on on the bonke aboven
      over his hede,

2206. Is being readied out of respect to greet me, a knight, in due manner!
2211. No noise will make me fear.

"And thou schal haf al in hast that I thee hyght
    ones."°   **hyght ones** promised once
Yet he rusched on that rürde rapely a throwe,°
2220 And wyth° whettyng awharf,° er he wolde lyght;   for   turned aside
And sythen he keveres° bi a cragge and comes of a   goes
    hole,
Whyrlande out of a wro° wyth a felle° weppen,   nook   fierce
A Denes° ax newe dyght,° the dynt with to yelde,°   Danish   sharpened   repay
With a borelych bytte bende° by the halme,°   **borelych ...** huge blade curved   handle
2225 Fyled° in a fylor,° fowre fote large°—   Sharpened   filing bench   wide
Hit was no lasse, bi that lace° that lemed° ful   thong   gleamed
    bryght—
And the gome in the grene gered as fyrst,°   **gered ...** dressed as at first
Bothe the lyre° and the legges, lokkes and berde,   face
Save that fayre° on his fote he foundes° on the   well   goes
    erthe,
2230 Sette the stele° to the stone° and stalked bysyde.   handle   stony ground
When he wan° to the watter, ther he wade nolde!°   came   wouldn't
He hypped° over on hys ax, and orpedly° strydes,   hopped   boldly
Bremly brothe,° on a bent° that brode was aboute,   **Bremly brothe** Fiercely savage   field
    on snawe.
2235   Sir Gawayn the knyght con mete;°   **con mete** greeted
    He ne lutte hym no thyng lowe.°   **ne ...** didn't bow at all low
    That other sayde, "Now, sir swete,
    Of steven° mon may thee trowe."°   agreement   trust

            xc
    "Gawayn," quoth that grene gome, "God thee
    mot loke!°   **mot loke** may look after
2240 I-wysse, thou art welcom, wyghe, to my place,
And thou has tymed thi travayl° as trewe mon   journey
    schulde;
And thou knowes the covenauntes kest° uus   made
    bytwene:
At this tyme twelmonyth thou toke that° thee   **toke that** took what
    falled,°   befell
And I schulde at this Newe Yere yeply° thee   quickly
    quyte.°   repay
2245 And we ar in this valay° verayly oure one.°   valley   **oure one** alone
Here are no renkes us to rydde, rele° as us likes.   **rydde, rele** part, reel
Haf° thy helme off thy hede, and haf here thy   Take
    pay;
Busk° no more debate° then I thee bede° thenne   Make   defense   offered
When thou wypped° off my hede at a wap° one."   slashed   blow
2219. Yet he kept on making that noise quickly for a while

2250   "Nay, bi God," quoth Gawayn, "that me gost
        lante,°   **gost lante** a spirit gave
    I schal gruch° thee no grue° for grem° that falles;   begrudge   **no grue** not a bit   harm
    Bot styghtel thee upon° on strok, and I schal   **styghtel . . .** limit yourself to
        stonde stylle
    And warp° thee no wernyng° to worch° as thee   give   resistance   do
        lykes,
            nowhare."
2255   He lened with the nek and lutte°   bowed
    And schewed that schyre° al bare   white flesh
    And lette° as he noght dutte;°   acted   feared
    For drede° he wolde not dare.°   fear   shrink

xci

    Then the gome in the grene graythed° hym   readied
        swythe,°   quickly
2260 Gederes up hys grymme tole, Gawayn to smyte.
    With alle the bür° in his body he ber hit on lofte,   strength
    Münt° as maghtyly° as marre° hym he wolde;   Aimed   mightily   destroy
    Hade hit° dryven adoun as dregh° as he atled,°   **Hade hit** If it had   fiercely   intended
    Ther hade ben ded of his dynt that° doghty was   he who
        ever.
2265 Bot Gawayn on that giserne glyfte° hym bysyde,   **giserne glyfte** axe glanced
    As hit com glydande adoun on glode° hym to   ground
        schende,°   destroy
    And schranke a lytel with the schulderes for the
        scharp yrne.
    That other schalk° wyth a schunt° the schene°   man   swerve   blade
        wythhaldes,
    And thenne repreved° he the prynce with mony   reproved
        prowde wordes:
2270 "Thou art not Gawayn," quoth the gome,
        "that is so goud halden,
    That never arghed° for no here° by hylle ne be   quailed   army
        vale,
    And now thou fles° for ferde° er thou fele harmes.   flinch   fear
    Such cowardise of that knyght cowthe I never
        here.
    Nawther fyked° I ne flaghe,° freke, when thou   flinched   fled
        myntest,°   aimed
2275 Ne kest° no kavelacion° in kynges hous Arthor.   made   cavilling
    My hede flagh° to my fote, and yet flagh I never;   flew
    And thou, er any harme hent, arghes° in hert;   **hent, arghes** taken, quail
    Wherefore the better bürne me bürde° be called   **me bürde** I ought to
        therfore."

2280	Quoth Gawayn, "I schunt ones,°	**schunt ones** flinched once
	And so wyl I no more.	
	Bot, thagh° *my* hede falle on the stones,	if
	I con not hit restore!	

xcii

	"Bot busk,° bürne, bi thi fayth, and bryng me to the poynt,	hurry
2285	Dele to me my destiné, and do hit out of honde,	
	For I schal stonde thee a strok, and start no more	
	Til thyn ax have me hitte; haf here my trawthe."°	word
	"Haf at thee thenne," quoth that other, and heves hit alofte,	
	And waytes° as wrothely as he wode° were.	looks mad
2290	He myntes° at hym maghtyly,° bot not the mon ryves,°	aims mightily cuts
	Withhelde heterly° his honde er hit hurt myght.	quickly
	Gawayn graythely° hit bydes and glent° with no membre,	properly flinched
	Bot stode stylle as the ston other a stubbe auther°	**other** . . . or else a stump
	That ratheled° is in roché° grounde with rotes a hundreth.	entwined rocky
2295	Then müryly efte con he mele,° the mon in the grene,	**efte** . . . again he spoke
	"So now thou has thi hert holle,° hitte me bihoves.	**hert holle** courage whole
	Halde thee now the hyghe hode° that Arthur thee raght,°	dignity gave
	And kepe° thy kanel° at this kest,° yif hit kever° may."	save neck blow survive
	Gawayn ful gryndelly° with greme° thenne sayde,	fiercely wrath
2300	"Wy, thresch° on, thou thro° mon; thou thretes too longe.	smite fierce
	I hope° that thi hert arghe wyth° thyn awen selven!"	believe **arghe wyth** quails at
	"Forsothe," quoth that other freke, "so felly° thou spekes,	fiercely
	I wyl no lenger on lyte lette° thin ernde° right nowe."	**on** . . . in delay hinder errand
2305	Thenne tas° he hym strythe° to stryke	takes a stance
	And frounses° bothe lyppe and browe.	wrinkles
	No mervayle thagh hym myslyke°	it displeases
	That hoped of no rescowe.	

451

xciii

He lyftes lyghtly his lome and let° hit doun fayre	**lome ...** weapon and lets
2310 With the barbe° of the bitte° bi the bare nek;	edge blade
Thagh he homered heterly,° hurt hym no more	**homered heterly** struck fiercely
Bot snyrt° hym on that on syde, that severed the hyde.	nicked
The scharp schrank° to the flesche thurgh the schyre° grece,	**scharp schrank** sharp blade sank white
That the schene° blod over his schulderes schot to the erthe.	bright
2315 And when the bürne° segh the blode blenk° on the snawe,	man (Gawain) gleam
He sprit° forth spenne-fote° more then a spere lenthe,	sprang feet together
Hent heterly° his helme and on his hed cast,°	**Hent heterly** Seized quickly put it
Schot° with his schulderes his fayre schelde under,	Slung
Braydes° out a bryght sworde, and bremely he spekes—	Pulls
2320 Never syn that he was bürne borne of his moder,	
Was he never in this worlde wyghe half so blythe—	
"Blynne,° bürne, of thy bür; bede° me no mo;	Cease **bür; bede** violence; offer
I haf a stroke in this sted° withoute stryf hent,	place
And if thow reches° me any mo,° I redyly schal quyte°	give more repay
2325 And yelde yederly° ayayn, and therto ye tryst,°	quickly be sure
And foo.°	fiercely
Bot on° stroke here me falles,	**Bot on** Only one
The covenaunt schop° ryght so,	appointed
Fetled° in Arthures halles,	Arranged
2330 And therfore, hende, now hoo!"°	stop

xciv

The hathel heldet hym fro° and on his ax rested,	**heldet ...** turned
Sette the schaft upon schore° and to the scharp° lened,	ground sharp blade
And loked to the leüde that on the launde yede,°	**launde yede** field went
How that doghty dredles dervely° ther stondes,	**dredles dervely** fearless one boldly
2335 Armed, ful aghles;° in hert hit hym lykes.	fearless
Thenn he meles° müryly wyth a much steven,°	speaks **much steven** big voice
And wyth a rynkande rürde° he to the renk sayde,	**rynkande rürde** ringing noise
"Bolde bürne, on this bent° be not so gryndel;°	field fierce
No mon here unmanerly thee mysboden habbes,°	**mysboden habbes** has mistreated

2340 Ne kyd° bot as covenaunde°at kynges kort schaped.°   *acted   the covenant / directed*

I hyght° thee a strok, and thou hit has; halde° thee wel payed.   *promised   consider*

I relece thee of the remnaunt of ryghtes° alle other.   *duties*

Yif I deliver° had bene, a boffet, paraunter,°   *nimble   **boffet, paraunter** blow, perhaps*

I couthe wrotheloker° haf waret,° to thee haf wroght anger.°   ***couthe wrotheloker** could more harshly dealt   **wroght anger** done harm*

2345 Fyrst I mansed° thee müryly with a mynt one,°   *threatened   **mynt one** feint only*

And rove° thee wyth no rof° sore—with ryght I thee profered   *ripped   gash*

For the forwarde° that we fest° in the fyrst nyght;   *agreement   agreed on*

And thou trystyly° the trawthe° and trewly me haldes:°   *faithfully   promise / keep*

Al the gayne thow me gef,° as god mon schulde.   *gave*

2350 That other münt° for the morne, mon, I thee profered;   ***other münt** second feint*

Thou kyssedes my clere° wyf, the cosses me raghtes.°   *fair / you returned*

For bothe two here I thee bede° bot two bare myntes° boute scathe.°   *offered / feints / **boute scathe** without harm*

Trewe mon trewe° restore,   ***Trewe** . . . A true person must honestly*

2355 Thenne thar° mon drede no wathe.°   *need   danger*

At the thrid,° thou fayled thore,°   *third exchange   there*

And therfor that tappe ta° thee.   ***tappe ta** blow take*

xcv

"For hit is my wede that thou weres, that ilke woven girdel;

My owen wyf hit thee weved,° I wot wel forsothe.   *gave*

2360 Now know I wel thy cosses° and thy costes° als   *kisses   manners*

And the wowyng° of my wyf; I wroght° hit myselven.   *wooing   arranged*

I sende hir to asay° thee, and sothly me thynkkes,   *test*

On the fautlest freke° that ever on fote yede.°   ***On** . . . One of the most faultless men went*

As perle bi° the white pese° is of prys° more,   *compared to   pea   excellence*

2365 So is Gawayn, in god fayth, bi other gay knyghtes.

Bot here yow lakked a lyttel, sir, and lewté° yow wonted,   *loyalty*

Bot that was for no wylyde° werke, ne wowyng° nauther,   *guileful   wooing*

453

Bot for° ye lufed your lyf. The lasse° I yow
    blame!"
                                                          because   less

That other stif mon in study stod a gret whyle,
2370 So agreved for greme,° he gryed° withinne.   *grief   trembled*
Alle the blode of his brest blende° in his face,   *rushed*
That° al he schrank for schome that° the schalk   *So that   while*
    talked.
The forme° worde upon folde that the freke   *first*
    meled:°   *spoke*
"Corsed worth° cowarddyse and covetyse   **Corsed worth** *Cursed be*
    bothe!
2375 In yow is vylany and vyse that vertue disstryes."°   *destroy*
Thenne he kaght° to the knot, and the kest lawses,°   *caught   * **kest lawses** *fastening loosens*
Brayde brothely° the belt to the bürne selven:°   **Brayde brothely** *Flung fiercely   hims*
"Lo! ther the falssyng, foule mot° hit falle!°   **falssyng . . .** *betrayer, evil may   befall*
For care° of thy knokke, cowardyse me taght   *fear*
2380 To accorde° me with covetyse,° my kynde° to   *associate   covetousness   nature*
    forsake,
That is larges and lewté° that longes° to knyghtes.   **larges . . .** *liberality and loyalty   belong*
Now am I fawty° and falce, and ferde° haf ben   *faulty   yet afraid*
    ever
Of trecherye and untrawthe°—bothe bityde   *faithlessness*
    sorwe°   **bothe . . .** *may both have sorrow*
        and care!
2385   I biknowe° yow, knyght, here stylle,°   *confess to   privately*
    Al fawty is my fare.°   *behavior*
    Letes me overtake° your wylle,°   *gain   good will*
    And efte° I schal be ware."°   *afterward   careful*

               xcvi
    Thenn loghe° that other leüde, and luflyly   *laughed*
        sayde:
2390 "I halde hit hardily hole,° the harme that I hade;   **hardily hole** *certainly healed*
Thou art confessed so clene, beknowen° of thy   *absolved*
    mysses,°   *faults*
And has the penaunce apert° of the poynt of myn   *evident*
    egge.°   *sword*
I halde thee polysed° of that plyght and pured° as   *cleaned   * **plyght . . .** *offense and purified*
    clene°   *pure*
As thou hades never forfeted sythen° thou was   **forfeted sythen** *transgressed since*
    fyrst borne.
2395 And I gif thee, sir, the gurdel that is golde-
    hemmed.
For° hit is grene as my goune, Sir Gawayn, ye   *Since*
    maye

Thenk upon this ilke threpe° ther thou forth thrynges°	contest hasten
Among prynces of prys,° and this a pure token	esteem
Of the chaunce° of the grene chapel, at° chevalrous knyghtes.	adventure among
400 And ye schal in this Newe Yer ayayn to my wones,	
And we schyn° revel the remnaunt of this ryche fest°	shall festival
ful bene."°	pleasantly
Ther lathed° hym fast° the lorde,	invited earnestly
And sayde: "With my wyf, I wene,°	suppose
405 We schal yow wel acorde,°	reconcile
That was your enmy kene."°	bold

xcvii

"Nay, forsothe," quoth the segge, and sesed hys helme	
And has° hit off hendely and the hathel thonkkes:	takes
"I haf sojorned sadly.° Sele° yow bytyde,	enough Good luck
410 And He yelde° hit yow yare° that yarkkes° al menskes.°	**He yelde** May he repay fully dispenses dignities
And comaundes° me to that cortays,° your comlych fere,°	commend courteous one wife
Bothe that on and that other, myn honoured ladyes,	
That thus hör knyght wyth hör kest° han koyntly° bigyled.	trick cunningly
Bot hit is no ferly thagh° a fole madde°	**ferly thagh** marvel if **fole madde** fool act madly
415 And thurgh wyles of wymmen be wonen° to sorwe;°	brought sorrow
For so was Adam in erde° with one bigyled,	**in erde** actually
And Salamon with fele sere,° and Samson eftsones°—	**fele sere** many different ones besides
Dalyda dalt hym hys wyrde!°—and Davyth ther-after	fate
Was blended° with Barsabe, that much bale tholed.°	deluded **bale tholed** woe suffered
420 Now° these were wrathed wyth° her wyles, hit were a wynne° huge	Since **wrathed wyth** undone by gain
To luf höm wel and leve° hem not, a° leüde that couthe.°	believe for a could
For° thes wer forne° the freest, that folghed° alle the sele,°	Because of old **that folghed** whom followed good luck

Exellently° of alle thyse other under heven-ryche°   Preeminently heaven's kingdom
    that mused,°   were bemused
2425 And alle thay were biwyled°   beguiled
    With wymmen that thay used.
    Thagh I be now bigyled,
    Me think me bürde° be excused!   **me bürde** I ought to

xcviii

    "Bot your gordel," quoth Gawayn, "God yow
    foryelde!°   reward
2430 That wyl I welde° wyth good wylle, not for the   wear
    wynne° golde   pleasant
    Ne the saynt° ne the sylk ne the syde   girdle
    pendaundes,°   **syde pendaundes** long pendants
    For wele° ne for worschyp° ne for the wlonk   costliness worth
    werkkes,°   **wlonk werkkes** lovely workmanship
    Bot in syngne of my surfet.° I schal se hit ofte   fault
    When I ride in renoun, remorde° to myselven   remorsefully recall
2435 The faut and the fayntyse° of the flesche crabbed,°   frailty perverse
    How tender° hit is to entyse teches° of fylthe;°   liable **entyse teches** attract stains ev
    And thus when pryde schal me pryk° for prowes   spur
    of armes,
    The loke to this luf-lace schal lethe° my hert.   humble
    Bot on° I wolde yow pray, displeses° yow never: one thing **pray, displeses** ask, offend
2440 Syn ye be lorde of the yonde° londe ther I haf   yonder
    lent° inne   stayed
    Wyth yow, wyth worschyp—the Wyghe° hit   Lord
    yow yelde
    That uphaldes the heven and on hygh sittes—
    How norne° ye yowre ryght nome? And thenne   call
    no more?"
    "That schal I telle thee trewly," quoth that other
    thenne.
2445 "Bercilak de Hautdesert I hat° in this londe.   am called
    Thurgh myght of Morgne la Faye, that in my
    hous lenges,
    And koyntyse° of clergye,° bi craftes° wel   cunning magic skills
    lerned . . .[6]
    The maystrés° of Merlyn, mony hö has taken;°   arts acquired
    For hö has dalt drury° ful dere° sum tyme   **dalt drury** made love pleasant
2450 With that conable° klerk, that knowes alle your   excellent
    knyghtes
    at hame.

---

[6] A line seems to have been lost by the copyist. In substance, it would be, 'It is possible for me to transform my
into the invulnerable Green Knight.'

Morgne the Goddes,
Therfore hit is hir name;
Weldes non° so hyghe hawtesse°   **Weldes non** No one has   pride
2455 That hö ne con make ful tame.

xcix

"Hö wayned° me upon this wyse° to your   sent   manner
  wynne° halle,   pleasant
For to assay the surquidré,° yif hit soth were **assay . . .** test your pride
That rennes° of the grete renoun of the Rounde **That rennes** What is current
  Table.
Hö wayned me this wonder, your wyttes to
  reve,°   take away
2460 For to haf greved Gaynour and gart° hir to **Gaynour . . .** Guinevere and made
  dyghe°   die
With glopnyng° of that ilke gome that gostlych horror
  speked
With his hede in his honde bifore the hyghe
  table.
That is hö that is at home, the auncian° lady. aged
Hö is even thyn aunt, Arthures half-suster,
2465 The duches° doghter of Tyntagelle, that dere° duchess's   noble
  Uter after
Hade Arthur upon, that athel° is nowthe.[7]   glorious
Therfore I ethe° thee, hathel, to com to thy   ask
  naunt,°   aunt
Make myry in my hous; my meny thee lovies,
And I wol° thee as wel, wyghe, bi my faythe,   wish
2470 As any gome under God, for thy grete trauthe."° faithfulness
  And he nikked° hym naye, he nolde° bi no   said   would not
  wayes.
Thay acolen° and kyssen and kennen ayther other° embrace   **kennen . . .** commend each other
To the Prynce of Paradise, and parten ryght there
  on coolde.°   cold ground
2475 Gawayn on blonk ful bene°   fair
  To the kynges burgh buskes bolde,
  And the knyght in the enker° grene   bright
  Whiderwarde-so-ever he wolde.

---

[7] Morgan had transformed Bercilak into the Green Knight so that he might thus test the pride of the members of the Round Table, take away their senses (*your* in l. 2459 is plural), and terrify Guinevere. The audience would have known from other romances the reason for the sorceress' spite, namely, that Guinevere had expelled her from court because of a love affair. Morgan is Arthur's half-sister (l. 2464) because their mother was the duchess of Tintagel (l. 2465; Morgan's father was the duke of Tintagel; Arthur's father was Uther Pendragon). Morgan is also Gawain's aunt because his mother was another daughter of the duke and duchess of Tintagel.

C

Wylde wayes in the worlde Wowen° now rydes   Gawain
2480 On Gryngolet, that the grace° hade geten of his   gift
          lyve.
     Ofte he herbered in house and ofte al ther-oute,°   outside
     And mony aventure in vale, and venquyst° ofte   **in . . .** he had en route, and conquered
     That I ne tyght° at this tyme in tale to remene.°   intend   recount
     The hurt was hole that he hade hent° in his nek,   received
2485 And the blykkande° belt he bere theraboute,   shining
     A-belef° as a bauderyk,° bounden bi his syde,   Crosswise   baldric
     Loken° under his lyfte arme, the lace,° with a   Tied   belt
          knot,
     In tokenyng he was tane° in tech° of a faute;   taken   stain
     And thus he commes to the court, knyght al in
          sounde.°   safety
2490 Ther wakned° wele in that wone when wyst°   arose   learned
          the grete°   great one
     That gode Gawayn was commen; gayn° hit hym   good
          thoght.
     The kyng kysses the knyght, and the quene alce,°   also
     And sythen mony syker° knyght that soght hym   trusty
          to haylce,°   greet
     Of his fare that hym frayned;° and ferlyly° he   asked   marvelously
          telles,
2495 Biknowes° alle the costes° of care° that he hade—   Confesses   conditions   sorrow
     The chaunce° of the chapel, the chere° of the   adventure   behavior
          knyght,
     The luf of the ladi, the lace° at the last.   belt
     The nirt° in the nek he naked hem schewed,   nick
     That he laght° for his unleuté° at the leüdes   got   disloyalty
          hondes
2500   for blame.
     He tened° when he schulde telle,   grieved
     He groned for gref and grame.°   shame
     The blod in his face con melle°   **con melle** rushed
     When he hit schulde schewe, for schame.

ci

2505 "Lo! lorde," quoth the leüde, and the lace
          hondeled,
     "This is the bende° of this blame I bere in my nek,   band
     This is the lathe° and the losse that I laght° have   harm   received
     Of cowardise and covetyse° that I haf caght thare.   covetousness
     This is the token of untrawthe that I am tan° inne,   taken
2510 And I mot° nedes hit were° wyle I may last;   must   wear

458

For non may hyden his harme bot unhap ne may
   hit,°   **unhap . . .** that misfortune may befall

For ther hit ones° is tachched, twynne° wil hit   once   **tachched, twynne** attached,
   never."   separate

  The kyng comfortes the knyght, and alle the
    court als

  Laghen° loude ther-at, and luflyly acorden°   Laugh   agree

2515 That lordes and ladis that longed° to the Table,   belonged

  Üche burne of the brotherhede, a bauderyk°   baldric
    schulde have,

  A bende a-belef° hym aboute, of a bryght grene,   **bende a-belef** band crosswise

  And that, for sake of that segge, in suete° to were.°   following suit   wear

  For that was acorded the renoun of the Rounde
    Table,

2520 And he honoured that hit hade, evermore after,

  As hit is breved° in the best boke of romaunce.   written

  Thus in Arthurus day this aunter bitidde;°   **aunter bitidde** adventure befell

  The Brutus bokes therof beres wyttenesse.

  Sythen° Brutus, the bolde bürne, boghed° hider   Since   came
    fyrst,

2525 After the segge° and the asaute was sesed° at Troye,   siege   ceased
      i-wysse,

    Mony aunteres here biforne

    Haf fallen suche er this.

    Now that bere° the croun of thorne,   **that bere** He that bore

2530   He bryng uus to his blysse!   AMEN.

JOHN GOWER

The Lover's Confession

(ca. 1393, East Midland)

༕

Little is known definitely about the life of John Gower (ca. 1330–1408). He was reared in Kent, came of a well-connected family, became active in real estate, probably served in the Court of Chancery, and lived in St. Mary Overeys Priory, at Southwark. He was married, apparently for the first time, in 1398. A friend of Chaucer, he was supported in turn by Richard II and Henry IV.

His major work is a loosely articulated trilogy of poems in three languages. In the period between 1374 and 1378 he wrote first an Anglo-Norman poem, *The Mirror of Man* (*Mirour de l'Omme*, or *Speculum Hominis*), which moves from a general exposition of the virtues and vices to a specific condemnation of his sinful contemporaries. By 1381 he had completed the first version of a Latin poem, *The Voice of the Complainant* (*Vox Clamantis*), which deals with the evils that beset the state. By 1390 he had completed the first version of his English poem *The Lover's Confession* (*Confessio Amantis*), which deals with what he calls "the fatuous passions of lovers." All three works are bound together by Gower's search for the "common good" of mankind, which, he felt, men destroy by a selfish regard for their own "singular profit."

Despite the dominance of this basic theme, *The Lover's Confession* progresses discursively. In the Prologue the Poet laments the failure of rulers, the corruption of churchmen, and the lawlessness of the commons. In Book I, like Chaucer in *The Legend of Good Women*, Gower dreams that he meets the God of Love and the Queen of Love. He is smitten by their dart, learns that he is to fail in love, and submits to the queen's priest, Genius, to whom he confesses.

Genius first warns the Lover against the dangers of the assaults of love through the two senses of sight and hearing; then he embarks on a long series of illustrative stories relating to the Seven Deadly Sins. The story dealing with Pride concludes Book I. Envy is the subject of Book II; Wrath, Book III; Sloth, Book IV; Avarice, Book V; and Gluttony, Book VI. Gower digresses in Book VII to summarize the wisdom that Aristotle imparted to Alexander, emphasizing the five points of governing policy—Truth, Largess, Justice, Pity, and Chastity. In Book VIII he deals with some aspects of the seventh Deadly Sin, Lechery.

The Poet ultimately finds himself relieved of the pains of love and resolutely turns to the pursuit of moral virtue and of that divine love confirmed by charity. Returning then to the theme of the Prologue, he concludes the poem with a prayer for the attainment of peace and unity within his troubled land.

The logic of the work will necessarily seem tenuous to a modern reader. The confessor Genius, who is drawn from Jean de Meun's thirteenth-century *Roman de la Rose*, is the priest of nature's propagative principle. Frequently Gower's Genius shows the Poet how the commission of a sin has impeded love and how the exercise of a corresponding virtue may secure love, but he does not share with his Old French predecessor any great concern about the necessity of fecundity, and he evinces no real interest in the Poet's amatory success. Yet, the difference between the two Geniuses is merely a matter of emphasis and poetic

460

enthusiasm. Jean de Meun's Genius admits that the joys of fleshly love, though essential, are

> . . . fables—vain imaginings—
> No stable facts, but fictions that will fade.
> Dances will reach their end, and dancers fail.

The joys of heavenly love, in contrast, are "everlasting joys, sincere and great"; and "all things" in Heaven are "delightful, permanent, and true." And that is Gower's point, too.

Many of the illustrative tales narrated as examples by Genius may seem to be somewhat irrelevant to the substance of the Lover's confession, but ultimately at least, they are for the most part concerned with the role of heavenly love in human affairs, and Gower clearly considered that only heavenly love could secure human salvation.

Chaucer called his friend the "moral Gower," and both poets certainly must have thought of the term *moral* as a compliment. Gower was, admittedly, a lesser poet than his great contemporary, but his works were held in high esteem for two centuries. Sixty-nine manuscripts of *The Lover's Confession*, in whole or part, are still extant; Caxton printed the work in 1483, and Berthelette printed it twice in the sixteenth century; and it was translated into both Spanish and Portuguese during Gower's lifetime. Shakespeare or perhaps a collaborator borrowed the plot of *Pericles* from it and chose Gower as the speaker of his Prologue.

The combination of a clear, simple narrative style and fluent versification joined to enduringly popular stories may in part explain the longevity of *The Lover's Confession*, but Gower also won the instinctive respect of his medieval audience for his moral earnestness. Chaucer, in comparison, characteristically allows comedy or irony to complicate the tone of his narratives. In this respect it is instructive to compare Gower's treatment of Ovid's tale of Ceyx and Halcyon (*Metamorphoses*, xi.266–748) with Chaucer's adaptation of the same source in his *Book of the Duchess*.

The meter is rhyming couplets; see Introduction, type 5, page 31.

The best edition is *The English Works of John Gower*, ed. G. C. Macaulay, EETS 81, 82 (London, 1900, 1901), appearing also in *The Complete Works of John Gower*, ed. Macaulay (Oxford, 1899–1902), vols. 2 and 3. For modernizations see John Gower, *Confessio Amantis: The Lover's Shrift*, trans. Terence Miller (Harmondsworth, 1963); Eric W. Stockton, *The Major Latin Works of John Gower* (Seattle, 1962); and William Burton Wilson, *A Translation of John Gower's Mirour de l'Omme* (University Microfilms 70–18, 159, Ann Arbor, 1970). For criticism see John H. Fisher, *John Gower: Moral Philosopher and Friend of Chaucer* (New York, 1964). For bibliography see Wells, ch. 15.13; *CBEL*, 1.205–08, 5.129–30.

Prologue

[Lines 1–92]

THE POET

Of hem that writen ous tofore,°	before
The bokes dwelle, and we ther-fore	
Ben tawht° of that was written tho.°	taught then
For-thi,° good is that we also	Therefore

461

5	In oure tyme among ous hiere
	Do wryte of newe som matiere
	Ensampled° of the olde wise,°
	So that it myhte in such a wyse,
	Whan we ben° dede and elleswhere,
10	Beleve° to the worldes ere°
	In tyme comende° after this.
	Bot for men sein, and soth° it is,
	That who that al of wisdom writ°
	It dulleth ofte a mannes wit
15	To him that schal it aldai rede,
	For thilke° cause, if that ye rede,°
	I wolde go the middel weie
	And wryte a bok betwen the tweie,°
	Somwhat of lust,° somwhat of lore,
20	That of the lasse or of the more
	Som man mai lyke of that° I wryte.
	And for that fewe men endite°
	In oure Englissh, I thenke° make
	A bok for King Richardes sake,
25	To whom belongeth my ligeance
	With al myn hertes obeissance
	In al that evere a liege man
	Unto his king may doon° or can.
	So ferforth° I me recomande
30	To him which al me may comande,
	Preyende unto the Hihe Regne°
	Which causeth every king to regne
	That his corone° longe stonde.
	I thenke and have it understonde,
35	As it bifel upon a tyde°
	As thing which scholde tho° betyde,
	Under the town of Newe Troye,°
	Which tok of° Brut[1] his ferste joye,
	In Temse° whan it was flowende,
40	As I by bote cam rowende,
	So as Fortune hir tyme sette,
	My liege lord parchaunce I mette.
	And so befel as I cam nyh°
	Out of my bot, whan he me syh,°
45	He bad me come into his barge.
	And whan I was with him at large,
	Amonges other thinges seid

Glosses (right margin):

- Ensampled° ... wise° — Illustrative manner
- ben° — are
- Beleve° ... ere° — Remain ... hearing ear
- comende° — coming
- soth° — sein ... say, and true
- writ° — writes
- thilke° ... rede° — this ... approve
- tweie° — two
- lust° — pleasure
- that° — of that some of what
- endite° — compose
- thenke° — intend to
- doon° — do
- ferforth° — far
- Regne° — King
- corone° — crown
- tyde° — time
- tho° — then
- Newe Troye° — Newe Troye London
- of° — from
- Temse° — Thames
- nyh° — near
- syh° — saw

[1] Brutus, according to Geoffrey of Monmouth, was a descendant of Aeneas of Troy and founded New T
(London), in Britain.

He hath this charge upon me leid
And bad me do my besynesse,
50 That to his hihe worthinesse
Som newe thing I scholde boke,°   record
That he himself it mihte loke°   examine
After the forme of my writynge.
And thus upon his comandynge
55 Myn herte is wel° the more glad   very much
To write so as he me bad.
And eek° my fere° is wel the lasse   also   fear
That non envye schal compasse
Withoute a resonable wite°   blame
60 To feyne and blame that I write.
A gentil herte his tunge stilleth
That it malice non distilleth
But preyseth that° is to be preised.   what
But he that hath his word unpeysed°   unweighed
65 And handleth onwrong° everything,   wrongly
I pray unto the Hevene King
Fro suche tunges He me schilde,°   shield
And, natheles,° this world is wilde   nevertheless
Of such jangling;° and what° befalle,   evil talk   whatever
70 My kinges heste° schal nought falle°   command   happen
That° I, in hope to deserve   So that
His thonk, ne schal° his wil observe;   **thonk . . .** thanks, may not
And elles were I nought° excused,   **elles . . .** otherwise I would not be
For that thing may nought be refused
75 What that° a king himselve bit.°   **What that** That   asks
   For-thi,° the symplesse of my wit   Therefore
I thenke if that it myhte avayle
In his service to travaile,
Though I seknesse have upon honde
80 And longe have had, yit wol° I fonde,°   will   try
So as I made my beheste,°   promise
To make a bok after his heste°   command
And write in such a maner wise°   **maner wise** kind of manner
Which may be wisdom to the wise
85 And pley° to hem that lust° to pleye.   amusement   wish
But in proverbe I have herd seye
That who that wel his werk begynneth,
The rather° a good ende he wynneth.   sooner
   And thus the prologe of my bok
90 After the world that whilom tok,°   **whilom tok** formerly took place
And eek somdel° after the newe,   **eek somdel** also somewhat
I wol begynne for to newe.°   produce

Book I

[Lines 1-228]

THE POET MEETS VENUS AND GENIUS

I may noght strecche up to the hevene
Min hand, ne setten al in evene
This world, which ever is in balance;
It stant° noght in my sufficance°   rests   ability
5   So grete thinges to compasse.
But I mot° lete it overpasse   must
And treten upon other thinges.
For-thi,° the stile of my writinges   Therefore
Fro this day forth I thenke change,
10   And speke of thing° is noght so strange,   something that
Which every kinde° hath upon honde,   race
And wherupon the world mot° stonde   must
And hath done sithen° it began   since
And schal whil ther is any man,
15   And that is Love, of which I mene
To trete, as after schal be sene.
In which ther can no man him reule,
For Loves lawe is out of reule,
That of too moche or of too lite.°   little
20   Wellnyh° is every man to wyte,°   Nearly   blame
And natheles° ther is no man   nevertheless
In al this world so wys that can
Of Love temper the mesure,
Bot as it falleth in aventure.°   **falleth** . . . happens by chance
25   For wit ne° strengthe may noght helpe,   nor
And he which elles° wolde him yelpe°   otherwise   **him yelpe** boast
Is rathest° throwen under fote;   soonest
Ther can no wiht° therof do bote.°   man   **do bote** remedy
For yet was nevere such covine°   device
30   That couthe° ordeine a medicine   could
To thing which God in lawe of kinde°   nature
Hath set, for ther may no man finde
The rihte salve of such a sor.
It hath and schal ben° evermor   be
35   That Love is maister wher he wile—
Ther can no lif make other skile°—   reasoning
For wher-as evere him list° to sette,°   it pleases   settle
Ther is no myht° which him may lette.°   power   stop
Bot what schal fallen° ate laste,   happen
40   The sothe° can no wisdom caste,°   truth   forecast

Bot as it falleth upon chance;
For if ther evere was balance
Which of Fortune stant° governed,   remains
I may wel lieve° as I am lerned°   believe   taught
45 That Love hath that balance on honde
Which wol no reson understonde.
For Love is blind and may noght se,
For-thi may no certeineté
Be set upon his jugement;
50 Bot as the whiel aboute went,°   turns
He yifth° his graces° undeserved,   gives   favors
And fro that man which hath him served
Ful ofte he takth aweye his fees
As he that pleieth ate dees;°   **ate dees** at dice
55 And ther-upon what schal befalle
He not,° til that the chance falle,°   knows not   happens
Wher° he schal lese° or he schal winne. Whether   lose
And thus ful° ofte men beginne,   very
That if thei wisten° what it mente   knew
60 Thei wolde change al here entente.°   **here entente** their purpose
    And for to proven it is so
I am miselven on° of tho°   one   those
Which to this scole am underfonge.°   received
For it is siththe go noght longe,°   **siththe . . .** not long ago
65 As for to speke of this matiere
I may you telle, if ye woll hiere,
A wonder hap° which me befell,   **wonder hap** wondrous chance
That was to me bothe hard and fell,°   cruel
Touchende of° Love and his fortune,   **Touchende of** Touching upon
70 The which me liketh° to commune°   it pleases   share
And pleinly for to telle it oute.
To hem° that ben lovers aboute,°   them   **ben . . .** are busily engaged as lovers
Fro point to point I wol declare
And wryten of my woful care,°   sorrow
75 Mi wofull day, my wofull chance,
Than men mowe° take remembrance   may
Of that° thei schall hierafter rede.   what
For in good feith this wolde I rede,°   advise
That every man ensample° take   example
80 Of wisdom which him is betake,°   entrusted
And that he wot of good aprise°   **wot . . .** knows to be worth teaching
To teche it forth, for such emprise°   courage
Is for to preise. And ther-fore I
Woll wryte and schewe al openly
85 How Love and I togeder mette,

465

Wherof the world ensample fette°   **ensample fette** get example
Mai after this, whan I am go,°   gone
Of thilke unsely, jolif° wo,   **thilke** ... this unhappy, merry
Whos reule stant° out of the weie,   stands
90   Now glad, and now gladnesse aweie,
And yet it may° noght be withstonde   can
For oght that men may understonde.
     Upon the point that is befalle
Of love, in which that I am falle,°   fallen
95   I thenke° telle my matiere.   intend to
Now herken, who that wol it hiere,
Of my fortune how that it ferde°   fared
This enderday,° as I forth ferde   past day
To walke, as I you telle may.
100   And that was in the monthe of Maii,
Whan every brid° hath chose his make°   bird   mate
And thenkth° his merthes for to make   intends
Of love that he hath achieved.
Bot so was I no thing relieved,
105   For I was further fro my love
Than erthe is fro the hevene above.
And for to speke of eny sped,°   success
So wiste° I me non other red,°   knew   counsel
Bot as it were a man forfare°   worn out
110   Unto the wode I gan° to fare,   began
Noght for to singe with the briddes,°   birds
For whanne I was the wode amiddes
I fond a swote,° grene pleine,   fair
And ther I gan° my wo compleigne,   did
115   Wisshinge and wepinge al myn one,°   **myn one** by myself
For other merthes made I none.
     So hard me was that ilke throwe,°   **ilke throwe** same time
That ofte sithes° overthrowe   **ofte sithes** many times
To grounde I was, withoute breth;
120   And evere I wisshide after deth,
Whanne I out of my peine awok,
And caste up many a pitous lok
Unto the hevene, and seide thus:

            THE POET
     "O thou Cupide, O thou Venus,
125   Thou god of love, and thou goddesse,
Wher is pité? Wher is meknesse?
Now doth° me pleinly live or dye,   make
For certes° such a maladie   certainly

As I now have and longe have had,
130   It myhte make a wis man mad,
If that it scholde longe endure.
O Venus, Queene of loves cure,°   care
Thou lif, thou lust,° thou mannes hele,°   pleasure   health
Behold my cause and my querele
135   And yif° me som part of thi grace,°   give   favor
So that I may finde in this place
If thou be gracious or non!"
    And with that word I sawh anon
The Kyng of Love and Queene bothe.
140   Bot he, that kyng, with yhen° wrothe   eyes
His chiere° aweiward fro me caste,   face
And forth he passede ate laste.
Bot natheles, er he forth wente,
A firy dart me thoghte° he hente°   **me thoghte** it seemed to me   took
145   And threw it thurgh min herte rote.°   root
In him fond I non other bote,°   remedy
For lenger list° him noght to dwelle.   it pleased
Bot sche, that is the source and welle
Of wel° or wo that schal betide   joy
150   To hem° that loven, at that tide°   them   time
Abod; but, for to tellen hiere,
Sche cast on me no goodly chiere.°   countenance
Thus, natheles,° to me sche seide: nevertheless

VENUS

"What art thou, sone?" And I abreide°   started
155   Riht as a man doth out of slep,
And therof tok sche riht good kep°   heed
And bad me nothing ben adrad;°   **ben adrad** be afraid
Bot for al that I was noght glad,
For I ne sawh° no cause why.   **ne sawh** did not see
160   And eft° sche asketh, what was I?   again

THE POET

I seide: "A caitif that lith hiere.
What wolde° ye, my ladi diere?   wish
Schal I ben hol° or elles dye?"   **ben hol** be safe

VENUS

    Sche seide: "Tell thi maladie.
165   What is thy sor of which thou pleignest,°   complain
Ne° hyd it noght, for if thou feignest,   Do not
I can do thee no medicine."

467

THE POET

   "Madame, I am a man of thyne
   That in thi court have longe served
170 And aske that° I have deserved—   for what
   Som wele° after my longe wo."   joy
   And sche began to loure tho°   **loure tho** scowl then

VENUS

   And seide: "There is manye of you
   Faitours,° and so may be that thou   Dissemblers
175 Art riht such on,° and by feintise°   a one feigning
   Seist that thou hast me do° service."   done
   And natheles° sche wiste° wel   nevertheless knew
   My world° stod on an other whiel   fortune
   Withouten any faiterie.°   false pretense
180 Bot algate° of my maladie   in any case
   Sche bad me telle and seie hir trowthe.

THE POET

   "Madame, if ye wolde have rowthe,"°   pity
   Quod I, "than wolde I telle you."

VENUS

   "Sey forth," quod sche, "and tell me how,
185 Schew me thi seknesse every del."°   part

THE POET

   "Madame, that can I do wel,
   Be so° my lif ther-to wol laste."   **Be so** Provided
   With that, hir lok on me sche caste

VENUS

   And seide, "In aunter if° thou live,   **In . . .** If it happen that
190 Mi will is ferst that thou be schrive;°   confessed
   And, natheles,° how that it is   nevertheless
   I wot° miself, bot for al this   know
   Unto my prest, which comth anon,
   I woll thou telle it on and on,°   **on . . .** one by one
195 Bothe all thi thoght and al thi werk.
   O Genius, myn oghne° clerk,   own
   Come forth and hier this mannes schrifte,"° confession
   Quod Venus tho.° And I uplifte   then
   Min hefd° with that, and gan beholde° head **gan beholde** beheld
200 The selve° prest, which as sche wolde, same
   Was redy there and sette him doun

To hiere my confessioun.
   This worthi prest, this holy man,
To me spekende thus began

GENIUS

205 And seide, "Benedicité.°   Bless you
My sone, of the felicité
Of Love and ek° of all the wo   also
Thou schalt be schrive of bothe two.
What thou er° this for Loves sake   before
210 Hast felt, let nothing be forsake;°   concealed
Tell pleinliche as it is befalle."
   And with that word I gan° doun falle did
On knees, and with devocioun
And with full gret contricioun

THE POET

215 I seide thanne: "Dominus,
Min holi fader Genius,
So as thou hast experience
Of Love, for whos reverence
Thou schalt me schriven° at this time, absolve
220 I prai thee let me noght mistime
Mi schrifte,° for I am destourbed   confession
In al myn herte and so contourbed,° confused
That I ne may° my wittes gete;° **ne may** cannot   recover
So schal I moche thing foryete.°   forget
225 Bot if thou wolt my schrifte oppose° question
Fro point to point, thanne I suppose
Ther schal no thing be left behinde.
Bot now my wittes ben so blinde,
That I ne can° miselven teche."   **ne can** cannot
230   Tho° he began anon to preche,   Then
And with his wordes debonaire
He seide to me softe and faire:

GENIUS

"Thi schrifte° to oppose° and hiere, confession   question
My sone, I am assigned hiere
235 By Venus the goddesse above,
Whos prest I am, touchende of° love. **touchende of** touching upon
Bot natheles for certein skile°   reason
I mot algate°—and nedes° wile— **mot algate** must always   necessarily
Noght only make my spekynges
240 Of Love, bot of other thinges,

469

That touchen to the cause of Vice.
For that belongeth to th'office
Of prest, whos ordre that I bere,
So that I wol nothing forbere

245 That I the vices on and on°   **on** . . . one by one
Ne schal thee schewen everychon;°   everyone
Wherof thou myht take evidence
To reule with thi conscience.
Bot of conclusion final

250 Conclude I wol in special
For Love, whos servant I am,
And why the cause is that I cam.
So thenke° I to don bothe two: intend
Ferst that° min ordre longeth° to,   what   pertains

255 The vices for to telle a rewe;°   **a rewe** in a row
Bot next, above alle other, schewe
Of Love I wol the propretés,°   characteristics
How that thei stonde by degrés
After the disposicioun

260 Of Venus, whos condicioun
I moste folwe,° as I am holde.°   follow   bound
For I with Love am al witholde,°   retained
So that the lasse° I am to wyte,°   less   blame
Thogh I ne conne° bot a lyte°   know   little

265 Of other thinges that ben° wise;   are
I am noght tawht° in such a wise.   taught
For it is noght my comun us°   use (custom)
To speke of vices and vertus,
Bot al of Love and of his lore,

270 For Venus bokes° of no more   books
Me techen, nowther° text ne glose.°   neither   **ne glose** nor gloss
Bot for als° moche as I suppose   as
It sit° a prest to be wel thewed,°   suits   mannered
And schame it is if he be lewed.°   unlearned

275 Of my presthode after the forme
I wol thi schrifte° so enforme,°   confession   instruct
That ate leste thou schalt hiere
The vices, and to thi matiere
Of Love I schal hem° so remene°   them   apply

280 That thou schalt knowe what thei mene.°   mean
For what a man schal axe or sein°   **axe** . . . ask or say
Touchende of schrifte,° it mot° be plein.   **Touchende** . . . Touching on confession
                                                      must
It nedeth noght to make it queinte,°   cunning
For Trowthe hise wordes wol noght peinte.

285 That° I wole axe of thee for-thi,°   What   therefore

470

My sone, it schal be so pleinly,
That thou schalt knowe and understonde
The pointz of schrifte° how that thei stonde."   confession

Book IV

[Lines 2701–3180]

GENIUS DESCRIBES SOMNOLENCE[1]

   "Toward° the slowe progenie   With regard to
Ther is yit on° of compaignie,   one
And he is cleped° Sompnolence,   called
Which doth to Slouthe° his reverence   Sloth
5   As he which is his Chamberlein,
That many an hundrid time hath lein
To slepe whan he scholde wake.
He hath with Love trewes° take,   truce
That wake who-so° wake wile,   **who-so** whosoever
10 If he mai couche° adown his bile,°   lay   bill
He hath al wowed what° him list,°   **al** ... wooed everything that   pleased
That° ofte he goth to bedde unkist   So that
And seith that for no druerie°   lovemaking
He wol noght leve his sluggardie.
15 For thogh no man it wole allowe,
To slepe lever° than to wowe   rather
Is his manere, and thus on nyhtes
Whan that he seth the lusti knyhtes
Revelen wher these wommen are,
20 Awey he skulketh as an hare,
And goth to bedde and leith him softe,
And of his Slouthe° he dremeth ofte,   Sloth
How that he stiketh in the myr,
And how he sitteth by the fyr
25 And claweth on his bare schanckes,
And how he clymbeth up the banckes
And falleth in the slades° depe.   valleys
Bot thanne who-so° toke kepe°   **who-so** whosoever   care
Whanne he is falle in such a drem,
30 Riht as a schip ayein° the strem   against
He routeth° with a slepi noise   snores
And brustleth° as a monkes froise°   rustles   pancake
Whanne it is throwe into the panne.

[1] Somnolence here represents one aspect of the deadly sin of Slothfulness in love.

	And otherwhile sieldewhanne°	seldom
35	That he mai dreme a lusti swevene,°	dream
	Him thenkth° as thogh he were in hevene	**Him thenkth** It seems to him
	And as the world were holi° his.	wholly
	And thanne he spekth of that and this	
	And makth his exposicioun	
40	After the disposicioun	
	Of that° he wolde,° and in such wise°	what might wish manner
	He doth to Love all his service;	
	I not° what thonk he schal deserve!	know not
	Bot, sone, if thou wolt Love serve,	
45	I rede° that thou do noght so."	advise

THE POET

	"Ha, goode fader, certes° no.	certainly
	I hadde levere,° by mi trowthe,°	rather word
	Er° I were set on such a slouthe	Before
	And bere such a slepi snoute,	
50	Bothe yhen° of myn hed were oute.	eyes
	For me were betre° fulli die	**me ... I would sooner**
	Thanne I of such a slugardie	
	Hadde eny name, God me schilde.²	

.   .   .

71	"For certes,° fader Genius,	certainly
	Yit unto now it hath be thus,	
	At alle time if it befelle ·	
	So that I mihte come and dwelle	
75	In place ther° my ladi were,	where
	I was noght slow ne slepi there.	
	For thanne I dar wel undertake°	pledge
	That whanne hir list° on nyhtes wake°	**hir list** it pleased her vigil
	In chambre as to carole and daunce,	
80	Me thenkth° I mai me more avaunce	**Me thenkth** it seems to me
	If I mai gon upon hir hond,°	**gon ... submit to her**
	Thanne if I wonne a kinges lond.	
	For whanne I mai hire° hand beclippe,°	her embrace
	With such gladnesse I daunce and skippe,	
85	Me thenkth I touche noght the flor,	
	The ro,° which renneth on the mor,°	roe moor
	Is thanne noght so lyht as I.	
	So mow° ye witen° wel for-thi,°	may know therefore
	That, for the time, slep I hate.	
90	And whanne it falleth othergate,°	otherwise
	So that hire like° noght to daunce	**hire like** it pleases her

² Lines 2754–70 have been omitted.

472

Bot on the dees° to caste chaunce,   dice
Or axe° of love som demaunde,   ask
Or elles that hir list° comaunde   **hir list** it pleases her
95   To rede and here of Troilus
Riht as sche wole, or so or thus,
I am al redi to consente.
And if so is, that I mai hente°   take
Somtime among° a good leisir,°   at   opportunity
100 So as I dar of mi desir
I telle a part, but whanne I preie,
Anon sche bidt me go my weie
And seith: 'It is ferr in° the nyht.'   **ferr in** far into
And I swere, 'It is even° liht.'   still
105 Bot as it falleth ate° laste   **falleth ate** happens at
Ther mai no worldes joie laste,
So mot° I nedes° fro hire wende°   must   necessarily   go
And of my wachche make an ende.
And if sche thanne hiede° toke   heed
110 How pitousliche on hire I loke,
Whan that I schal my leve take,
Hire oghte° of mercy for to slake°   **Hire oghte** She ought   lessen
Hire daunger,° which seith ever nay.   **Hire daunger** Her resistance
    "Bot he seith often, 'Have good day,'
115 That loth is for to take his leve.
Ther-fore, while I mai beleve,°   remain
I tarie° forth the nyht along.   delay
For it is noght on me along°   **on . . .** owing to me
To slep that I so sone go
120 Til that I mot algate° so,   **mot algate** must in any case
And thanne I bidde° 'God hire se,'   pray
And so down knelende on mi kne
I take leve, and if I schal,
I kisse hire and go forth withal.
125 "And otherwhile, if that I dore,°   dare
Er I come fulli to the dore,
I torne ayein° and feigne a thing   again
As thogh I hadde lost a ring
Or somwhat elles, for I wolde
130 Kisse her eftsones,° if I scholde,   again
Bot selden is that I so spede.°   succeed
And whanne I se that I mot nede
Departen, I departe, and thanne
With al my herte I curse and banne°   denounce
135 That ever slep was mad for yhe.°   eye
For, as me thenkth,° I mihte dryhe°   **me thenkth** it seems to me   endure

473

Withoute slep to waken evere
So that I scholde noght dissevere
Fro hire in whom is al my liht.
140   "And thanne I curse also the nyht
With al the will of mi corage°   heart
And seie: 'Awey thou blake ymage,
Which of thi derke, cloudy face
Makst al the worldes lyht deface
145 And causest unto slep a weie,
By which I mot now gone aweie
Out of mi ladi° compaignie.   lady's
O slepi nyht, I thee defie,
And wolde° that thou leye in presse°   wish **leye**...lie down below
150 With Proserpine the goddesse
And with Pluto the helle king.
For til I se the daies spring,
I sette slep noght at a risshe.'°
And with that word I sike° and wisshe   sigh
155 And seie: 'Ha, whi ne were it° day?   **whi**...would it were
For yit my ladi thanne I may
Beholde, thogh I do no more.'³

        .   .   .

    "Bot slep—I not° wherof it serveth,   know not
Of which no man his thonk° deserveth   thanks
165 To gete him love in eny place,
Bot is an hindrere of his grace°   favor
And makth him ded as for a throwe,°   short time
Riht as a stok° were overthrowe.   log
And so, mi fader, in this wise°   manner
170 The slepi nyhtes I despise
And evere amiddes of mi tale
I thenke upon the nyhtingale,
Which slepeth noght by weie of kinde°   nature
For love, in bokes as I finde.
175 Thus ate° last I go to bedde   at
And yit min herte lith° to wedde   is disposed
With hire wher as I cam fro;
Thogh I depart, he wol noght so.°   do so
Ther is no lock mai schette° him oute,   **mai schette** that can shut
180 Him nedeth noght to gon° aboute,   go
That perce mai the harde wall;
Thus is he with hire overall,

153. I consider sleep not worth a rush.
³ Lines 2858–62 have been omitted.

That be hire lief or be hire loth,°
Into hire bedd myn herte goth,
185 And softly takth hire in his arm
And fieleth how that sche is warm,
And wissheth that his body were
To fiele that° he fieleth there.   what
And thus miselven I tormente
190 Til that the dede slep me hente.°   seizes
　　"Bot thanne by a thousand score
Wel more than I was tofore°   before
I am tormented in mi slep,
Bot that° I dreme is noght of schep,   what
195 For I ne thenke noght on wulle,
Bot I am drecched° to the fulle   tormented
Of° love that I have to kepe,°   By　wait for
That now I lawhe° and now I wepe,   laugh
And now I lese° and now I winne,   lose
200 And now I ende and now beginne.
And otherwhile I dreme and mete°   dream
That I alone with hire mete
And that Danger° is left behinde.   Resistance
And thanne in slep such joie I finde
205 That I ne bede° never awake.   **ne bede** might ask for
　　"Bot after, whanne I hiede° take   heed
And schal arise upon the morwe,°   morning
Thanne is al torned into sorwe,°   sorrow
Noght for the cause I schal° arise,   **Noght**... Not because I must
210 Bot for I mette° in such a wise,   dreamed
And ate° laste I am bethoght,°   at　remembered
That al is vein and helpeth noght,
Bot yit me thenketh° by my wille   **me thenketh** it seems to me
I wold have leie and slepe stille,
215 To meten evere of such a swevene,°   dream
For thanne I hadde a slepi hevene."

GENIUS
　　"Mi sone, and for thou tellest so,
A man mai finde of time ago°   past
That many a swevene° hath be certein,   dream
220 Al be it so that som men sein°   say
That swevenes ben° of no credence.   are
Bot for to schewe in evidence
That thei ful° ofte sothe° thinges   very　true
Betoken, I thenke° in my wrytinges   intend

183. That be it (my heart) pleasing to her, or be it hateful to her

225 To telle a tale ther-upon,
Which fell by olde daies gone.
   "This finde I writen in poesie:
Ceix the king of Trocinie
Hadde Alceone to his wif,
230 Which as hire oghne° hertes lif   own
Him loveth. And he hadde also
A brother which was cleped tho°   **cleped tho** called then
Dedalion, and he per cas°   **per cas** by chance
Fro kinde° of man forschape° was   nature   transformed
235 Into a goshauk for liknesse.
Wherof the king gret hevynesse°   sorrow
Hath take, and thoghte in his corage°   heart
To gon° upon a pelrinage°   go   pilgrimage
Into a strange regioun,
240 Wher he hath his devocioun
To don° his sacrifice and preie   make
If that he mihte in eny weie
Toward° the goddes° finde grace   From   gods
His brother hele° to pourchace,°   **brother hele** brother's cure   procure
245 So that he mihte be reformed
Of that° he hadde be transformed.   what
   "To this pourpos and to this ende
This king is redy for to wende°   go
As he which wolde go by schipe.
250 And for to don him felaschipe,°   **don . . .** give him company
His wif unto the see him broghte
With al hire herte, and him besoghte
That he the time hire wolde sein°   say
Whan that he thoghte come ayein.°   **thoghte . . .** expected to return
255 'Withinne,' he seith, 'two monthe day.'
And thus in al the haste he may
He tok his leve and forth he seileth,
Wepende, and sche hirself beweileth,
And torneth hom ther° sche cam fro.   where
260   "Bot whan the monthes were ago°   past
The whiche he set of his comynge,
And that sche herde no tydinge,
Ther was no care° for to seche.°   sorrow   seek
Wherof the goddes to beseche
265 Tho° sche began in many wise   Then   **many wise** many a manner
And to Juno hire sacrifise
Above alle other most° sche dede,°   particularly   made
And for hir lord sche hath so bede°   prayed
To wite° and knowe how that he ferde°   discover   fared

270	That Juno the goddesse hire herde	
	Anon, and upon this matiere	
	Sche bad Yris hir Messagere	
	To Slepes hous that sche schal wende°	go
	And bidde him that he make an ende	
275	By swevene,° and schewe al the cas°	vision affair
	Unto this ladi, how it was.	
	"This Yris, fro the hihe stage,°	place
	Which undertake hath the message,	
	Hire reyny cope dede upon,°	**reyny** ... rain cloak put on
280	The which was wonderli begon,°	worked
	With colours of diverse hewe,	
	An hundred mo° than men it knewe.	more
	The hevene° lich unto a bowe	skies
	Sche bende, and so sche cam down lowe,	
285	The God of Slepe wher that sche fond.°	found
	And that was in a strange lond	
	Which marcheth° upon Chymerie.	borders
	For ther, as seith the poesie,	
	The God of Slep hath mad his hous,	
290	Which of entaille° is merveilous.	sculpture
	"Under an hell° ther is a cave	hill
	Which of the sonne mai noght have,	
	So that no man mai knowe ariht	
	The point betwen the dai and nyht.	
295	Ther is no fyr,° ther is no sparke,	fire
	Ther is no dore which mai charke,°	creak
	Wherof an yhe° scholde unschette,°	eye open
	So that inward ther is no lette.°	hindrance (to sleep)
	And for to speke of that withoute,	
300	Ther stant° no gret tree nyh° aboute,	stands near
	Wheron ther myhte crowe or pie°	magpie
	Alihte for to clepe° or crie.	call
	Ther is no cok to crowe day,	
	Ne beste non° which noise° may	**Ne** ... Nor any beast disturb
305	The hell,° bot al aboute round	hill
	Ther is growende° upon the ground	growing
	Popi, which berth the sed of slep,	
	With other herbes suche an hep.°	large quantity
	"A stille water for the nones°	time
310	Rennende° upon the smale stones,	Running
	Which hihte of Lethes the rivere,°	
	Under that hell in such manere	
	Ther is, which yifth° gret appetit	gives

311. Which is called the river of Lethe

477

To slepe. And thus ful of delit
315   Slep hath his hous, and of his couche
  Withinne his chambre, if I schal touche,°   treat
  Of hebenus° that slepi tree   ebony
  The bordes° al aboute be;   boards
  And for he scholde slepe softe,
320   Upon a fether bed alofte
  He lith° with many a pilwe° of down.   lies   pillow
  The chambre is strowed up and down
  With swevenes° many thousend fold.   dreams
  Thus cam Yris unto this hold,°   stronghold
325   And to the bedd, which is al blak,
  Sche goth, and ther with Slep sche spak,
  And in the wise° as sche was bede°   manner   ordered
  The message of Juno sche dede.°   brought
    "Ful ofte hir wordes sche reherceth,°   repeats
330   Er° sche his slepi eres perceth.   Before
  With mochel wo,° bot ate laste   **mochel wo** much suffering
  His slombrende yhen° he upcaste   eyes
  And seide hir, that it schal be do,°   done
  Wherof, among a thousand tho
335   Withinne his hous that slepi were,
  In special he ches° out there   chose
  Thre, whiche scholden do this dede.
  The ferst of hem,° so as I rede,   them
  Was Morpheus, the whos nature
340   Is for to take the figure
  Of what persone that him liketh,°   pleases
  Wherof that he ful° ofte entriketh°   very   ensnares
  The lif which slepe schal by nyhte.
  And Ithecus that other hihte,°   **that . . .** the other is called
345   Which hath the vois of every soun,
  The chiere° and the condicioun   looks
  Of every lif, what-so° it is.   **what-so** whatsoever
  The thridde, suiende° after this,   **thridde, suiende** third, following
  Is Panthasas, which may transforme
350   Of every thing the rihte forme
  And change it in an other kinde.
  Upon hem thre, so as I finde,
  Of swevenes stant al th'apparence,
  Which other while is evidence
355   And other while bot a jape.°
    "Bot natheles it is so schape

352–55. From these three, as I find, stems all the form (**apparence**) of dreams, which form at one time is a s
(**evidence**), at another time but a jest.

478

That Morpheus by nyht alone
Appiereth until Alceone
In liknesse of hir housebonde
360   Al naked, ded upon the stronde,°   shore
     And how he dreynte° in special   was drowned
     These other two° it schewen al.   two (Ithecus and Panthasas)
     The tempeste of the blake cloude,
     The wode° see, the wyndes loude,   raging
365   Al this sche mette, and sih° him dyen;   **mette . . . dreamed, and saw**
     Wherof that sche began to crien
     Slepende° abedde ther° sche lay.   Sleeping   where
     And with that noise of hire affray°   fright
     Hir wommen sterten° up aboute,   leaped
370   Whiche of here° ladi were in doute,°   their   fear
     And axen° hire how that sche ferde.   ask
     And sche riht as sche syh° and herde   saw
     Hir swevene hath told hem every del.°   part
     And thei it halsen° alle wel   explain
375   And sein° it is a token of goode.   say
       "Bot til sche wiste° how that it stoode,   knew
     Sche hath no confort in hire herte.
     Upon the morwe,° and up sche sterte°   morning   leaped
     And to the see wher that sche mette°   dreamed
380   The bodi lay, withoute lette°   delay
     Sche drowh,° and whan that sche cam nyh,° approached   near
     Stark ded, hise armes sprad, sche syh°   saw
     Hire lord flietende° upon the wawe.°   floating   wave
     Wherof hire wittes ben° withdrawe,   are
385   And sche, which tok of deth no kepe,°   heed
     Anon forth lepte into the depe
     And wolde have cawht him in hire arm.
       "This infortune° of double harm   misfortune
     The goddes° fro the hevene above   gods
390   Behield, and for the trowthe° of love   loyalty
     Which in this worthi ladi stod,
     Thei have upon the salté flod
     Hire dreinte° lord and hire also   drowned
     Fro deth to lyve torned so
395   That thei ben schapen into briddes°   birds
     Swimmende° upon the wawe° amiddes.   Swimming   wave
     And whan sche sih° hire lord livende   saw
     In liknesse of a bridd swimmende,
     And sche was of the same sort,
400   So as sche mihte do desport°   **do desport** make merry
     Upon the joie which sche hadde,

Hire wynges bothe abrod sche spradde,
And him, so as sche mai suffise°   be able
Beclipte and keste° in such a wise°   **Beclipte** ... Embraced and kissed   man:
405   As sche was whilom° wont to do.   formerly
Hire wynges for hire armes two
Sche tok, and for hire lippes softe
Hire harde bile, and so ful° ofte   very
Sche fondeth° in hire briddes° forme   tries   bird's
410   If that sche mihte hirself conforme
To do the plesance° of a wif°   pleasant behavior   woman
As sche did in that other lif.
For thogh sche hadde hir power lore,°   lost
Hir will stod as it was tofore°   before
415   And serveth him so as sche mai.
      "Wherof into° this ilke° day   unto   same
Togeder upon the see thei wone,°   dwell
Wher many a dowhter and a sone
Thei bringen forth of briddes kinde.°   **briddes kinde** birds' nature
420   And for men scholden take in mynde
This Alceoun° the trewe queene,   Halcyon (kingfisher)
Hire briddes yit, as it is seene,
Of Alceoun the name bere.
      "Lo thus, mi sone, it mai thee stere°   move
425   Of swevenes for to take kepe;°   heed
For ofte time a man aslepe
Mai se what after schal betide.
For-thi it helpeth at som tyde°   time
A man to slepe as it belongeth,°   is fitting
430   Bot Slouthe° no lif underfongeth°   Sloth   receives
Which is to Love appourtenant."°   appertaining

THE POET
      "My fader, upon covenant°   agreement
I dar wel make this avow,
Of all mi lif into now
435   Als fer° as I can understonde   **Als fer** As far
Yit tok I nevere slep on honde
Whan it was time for to wake;
For thogh min yhe it wolde take,
Min herte is evere ther ayein.°   again
440   Bot natheles, to speke it plein,
Al this that I have seid you hiere
Of my wakinge, as ye mai hiere,
It toucheth to° mi lady swete,   upon
For otherwise, I you behiete,°   promise

480

445 In straunge place whanne I go
Me list° no thing to wake so.   pleases
For whan the wommen listen° pleie   desire to
And I hir se noght in the weie
Of whom I scholde merthe take,
450 Me list noght longe for to wake,
Bot if° it be for pure schame   **Bot if** Unless
Of that I wolde eschuie° a name   avoid
That thei ne scholde have cause non
To seie: 'Ha, lo, wher goth such on°   a one
455 That hath forlore° his contenaunce?'   lost
And thus among I singe and daunce
And feigne lust ther as non is.
For ofte sithe° I fiele this   **ofte sithe** many times
Of thoght which in mi herte falleth
460 Whanne it is nyht, myn hede appalleth,°   grows weak
And that is for I se hire noght
Which is the wakere° of mi thoght.   awakener
And thus as tymliche as I may
Ful° ofte, whanne it is brod day,   Very
465 I take of all these other leve
And go my weie, and thei beleve°   remain
That sen per cas here° loves there.   **That...** Who see perhaps their
    "And I go forth as noght ne were°   **noght...** though it were nothing
Unto mi bedd, so that alone
470 I mai ther ligge,° sighe, and grone,   lie
And wisshen al the longe nyht,
Til that I se the daies lyht.
I not° if that be Sompnolence,   know not
Bot upon youre conscience,
475 Min holi fader, demeth° ye."   judge

                    GENIUS
    "My sone, I am wel paid° with thee,   pleased
Of slep that thou the sluggardie
By nyhte in Loves compaignie
Eschuied° hast, and do thi peine°   Avoided   endeavor
480 So that thi love thar° noght pleine."°   should   complain

Book VIII

[Lines 2870–939, 2940–70]

VENUS DISMISSES THE POET

	Venus behield me than and lowh,°	laughed
	And axeth,° as it were in game,°	asks sport
	What love was. And I for schame	
	Ne wiste° what I scholde answere,	knew
5	And natheles I gan° to swere	began
	That by my trouthe° I knew him noght,	word
	So ferr° it was out of mi thoght,	far
	Riht as it hadde never be.	

VENUS

	"Mi goode sone," tho quod sche,	
10	"Now at this time I lieve° it wel,	believe
	So goth the fortune of my whiel.	
	For-thi mi conseil is, thou leve."°	leave

THE POET

	"Madame," I seide, "by your leve,	
	Ye witen° wel, and so wot° I,	know know
15	That I am unbehovely°	unfitting
	Your court fro this day forth to serve.	
	And for° I may no thonk° deserve,	because thanks
	And also for I am refused,	
	I preie you to ben° excused.	be
20	And natheles as for the laste,	
	Whil that my wittes with me laste,	
	Touchende° my confessioun,	Touching
	I axe° an absolucioun	ask
	Of Genius, er that° I go."	**er that** before
25	The prest anon was redy tho,	

GENIUS

	And seide, "Sone, as of thi schrifte,°	confession
	Thou hast ful pardoun and foryifte.°	forgiveness
	Foryet° it thou, and so wol I."	Forget

THE POET

	"Min holi fader, grant mercy,"	
30	Quod I to him, and to the queene	
	I fell on knes upon the greene,	
	And tok my leve for to wende.°	go

Bot sche, that wolde make an ende
As ther-to which I was most able,
35   A peire of bedes blak as sable
Sche tok and heng my necke aboute.
Upon the gaudes° al withoute   large beads
Was write of gold, *Por reposer*.°   ***Por reposer*** For resting

VENUS

"Lo," thus sche seide, "John Gower
40   Now thou art ate° laste cast.°   at   defeated
This have I for thin ese cast,°   planned
That thou no more of love sieche.°   seek
Bot my will is that thou besieche
And preie hierafter for the pes,°   peace
45   And that thou make a plein° reles   full
To Love, which takth litel hiede°   heed
Of olde men upon the niede,
Whan that the lustes ben° aweie.   **lustes ben** pleasures are
For-thi to thee nys bot o° weie,   **nys . . .** is only one
50   In which let Reson be thi guide;
For he may sone himself misguide,
That seth noght the peril tofore.°   before
"Mi sone, be wel war ther-fore
And kep the sentence of my lore°   teaching
55   And tarie° thou mi court no more,   tarry in
Bot go ther° vertu moral dwelleth,   where
Wher ben thi bokes, as men telleth,
Whiche of long time thou hast write.
For this I do° thee wel to wite,°   make   know
60   If thou thin hele° wolt pourchace,   salvation
Thou miht noght make suite° and chace,   pursuit
Wher that the game is nought pernable.°   worth catching
It were a thing unresonable,
A man to be so overseie.°   careless
65   For-thi, tak hede of that I seie.°   say
For in the lawe of my commune°   community
We be noght schape° to commune,°   intended   communicate
Thiself and I, nevere after this.
Now have Y seid al that ther is
70   Of love, as for thi final ende.
Adieu, for Y mot° fro thee wende.°   must   go
And gret° wel Chaucer whan ye mete,   greet
As mi disciple and mi poete.
For in the floures of his youthe,
75   In sondri wise, as he wel couthe,°   could

483

Of ditees and of songes glade,
The whiche he for mi sake made,
The lond fulfild is over al.
Wherof to him in special
80 Above alle other I am most holde.°   indebted
For-thi, now in hise daies olde
Thou schalt him telle this message,
That he upon his latere age—
To sette an end of alle his werk,
85 As he which is myn owne clerk—
Do° make his testament of love,   Should
As thou hast do° thi schrifte above,   made
So that mi court it mai recorde."

THE POET

"Madame, I can me wel acorde,"°   agree
90 Quod I, "to telle as ye me bidde."
And with that word it so betidde,
Out of my sihte al sodeynly,
Enclosed in a sterred sky,
Up to the hevene Venus straghte.°   went
95 And I my rihte weie cawhte°   took
Hom fro the wode, and forth I wente;
Wher as with al myn hole° entente,   whole
Thus with mi bedes upon honde,
For hem that trewe love fonde°   experience
100 I thenke bidde° whil I lyve,   pray
Upon the poynt which I am schryve.°   absolved

The Wyclyfite Bible

(ca. 1395, East Midland)

John Wyclyf (ca. 1320–84) collaborated with his Lollard followers in preparing an English translation of the Bible (completed ca. 1390) for the benefit of laymen unfamiliar with Latin. John Purvey (ca. 1354–ca. 1428), along with others, produced a later, improved version (ca. 1395) of this pioneering work shortly after Wyclyf's death.

The *Prologue for All the Books of the Old Testament*, briefly excerpted here from the later version, contains an extensive discussion not only of the techniques of exegesis but also of the problems of translation.

For the sake of illustrating the prose style of the translation, the Lord's Prayer is also excerpted from the later version.

The best edition is *The Wycliffite Versions of the Holy Bible*, ed. Josiah Forshall and Frederic Madden (Oxford, 1850), 4 vols. For bibliography see *CBEL*, 1.202–05, 5.129; Severs, ch. 3, ch. 4.52.

Prolog for Alle the Bokis of the Oolde Testament

CHAPTER XII

But it is to wite° that Holy Scripture hath foure understondingis: literal, allegorik, moral, and anagogik. [be known]

The literal understonding techith the thing
5 don in dede,° and literal undirstonding is ground [actual fact] and foundament of thre goostly° undirstond- [spiritual] ingis, in so myche as Austyn in his *Pistle to Vincent*[1] and othere doctouris seyn° oonly bi the [say that] literal undirstonding a man may argue ayens° an [against]
10 adversarie.

Allegorik is a goostly undirstonding that techith what thing men owen for to° bileeve of [**owen ...** ought to] Crist either° of Hooly Chirche. Moral is a [or] goostly° understonding that techith men what [spiritual]
15 vertues thei owen to sue° and what vices thei [strive for] owen to flee. Anagogik is a goostly undir-stonding that techith men what blisse thei schal have in Hevene.

[1] St. Augustine, *Letters*, XCIII (A.D. 408).

And these foure undirstondingis moun° be — can
20 taken in this word 'Jerusalem,' for-whi,° to the — because
literal undirstonding, it signefieth an erthly citée,
as Loundoun either° such another. To allegorie, — or
it signefieth Hooly Chirche in erthe, that fightith
ayens° synnes and fendis.° To moral undir- — against fiends
25 stondinge, it signefieth a Cristen soule. To
anagogik it signefieth Hooly Chirche regnynge° — reigning
in blisse either in Hevene and tho° that be — those
therinne.

And these thre goostly° understondingis ben° — spiritual are
30 not autentik:° either of beleeve,° no-but tho — authoritative **of beleeve** for belief
ben° groundid opynly° in the text of Holy — **no-but . . .** unless they are clearly
Scripture in oo° place other° other; either° in — one or or
opin resoun that may not be distroied;° either — overturned
whanne the gospelris° either other apostlis taken — evangelists
35 allegorie of° the Eelde Testament and con- — from
feermyn it, as Poul in the *Pistle to Galatians* (in
the fourth *capitulo°*) preveth° that Sara, the free — chapter proves
wiif and principal of Abraham, with Isaac hir
sone signefieth bi allegorie the Newe Testament
40 and the sones of biheeste,° and Agar, the hand- — the new dispensation
mayde, with hir sone Ismael signefieth bi
allegorie the Elde Testament and fleschly men
that schulen° not be resseyved° into the eritage — shall received
of God with the sones of biheeste that holden the
45 treuthe and freedom of Cristis gospel with
endeles charité.

Also, Holy Scripture hath many figuratif
spechis, and as Austyn seith in the thridde book
of *Cristen Teching*[2] that autouris° of Hooly — authors
50 Scripture usiden moo° figuris (that is, moo — **usiden moo** used more
figuratif spechis) than gramariens moun° gesse — can
that reden° not tho° figuris in Holy Scripture. — interpret those

[2] St. Augustine, *Christian Doctrine*, III, xxix, 40.

The Lord's Prayer

[MATT. vi.9–13]
Oure fadir that art in hevenes, halewid be thi
name. Thi kyngdoom come to. Be thi wille don
in erthe as in hevene. Yyve to us this day oure

breed over othir substaunce, and foryyve to us
5 oure dettis as we foryyven to oure dettouris, and
lede us not into temptacioun, but delyvere us fro
yvel.
        Amen.

JOHN PURVEY (?)

A Defense of Translation

(ca. 1382–95, East Midland)

❧

The following passage is excerpted from a Middle English translation, probably by John Purvey, of Wyclyf's Latin tract *De Officio Pastorali*. This passage (Chapter 15), which is inserted by the translator in the middle of Wyclyf's complaint against friars, has no counterpart in the original Latin.

The best edition is *The English Works of Wyclif*, ed. F. D. Matthew, EETS 74 (London, 1880). For bibliography see Severs, ch. 3.50.

Heere the freris° with ther fautours seyn° that   friars   **fautours seyn** abettors say
it is heresye to write thus Goddis lawe in English
and make it knowun to lewid° men. And fourty   unlearned
signes that they bringen for to shewe an heretik
5   ben° not worthy to reherse,° for nought ground-   are   repeat
ith° hem but nygromansye.°   supports   necromancy
     It semyth first that the wit° of Goddis lawe   knowledge
shulde be taught in that tunge that is more
knowun, for this wit is Goddis word. Whanne
10   Crist seith in the Gospel[1] that bothe hevene and
erthe shulen° passe, but his wordis shulen not   shall
passe, he undirstondith° bi his woordis his wit.°   means   **his wit** a knowledge of him
And thus Goddis wit is hooly writ, that may on
no maner be fals.
15   Also, the Hooly Gost yaf° to apostlis wit at   gave
Wit-Sunday[2] for to knowe al maner langagis to
teche the puple Goddis lawe therby, and so God
wolde° that the puple were taught Goddis lawe in   wished
dyverse tungis. But what man on Goddis half°   behalf
20   shulde reverse Goddis ordenaunse and his wille?
     And for this cause Seynt Jerom travelide° and   labored
translatide the Bible fro dyverse tungis into
Lateyn that it myghte be aftir translatid to othere
tungis. And thus Crist and his apostlis taughten

[1] Matt. v.18.
[2] Whitsunday (Pentecost), actually 'White Sunday,' not 'Wit Sunday.'

488

25 the puple in that tunge that was moost knowun
to the puple. Why shulden not men do now so?

And herfore° autours of the New Law,° that *therefore Testament*
weren apostlis of Jesu Crist, writen° ther gospels *wrote*
in dyverse tungis that weren more knowun to the
30 puple.

Also, the worthy reume° of Fraunse, notwith- *realm*
stondinge alle lettingis,° hath translatid the Bible *hindrances*
and the Gospels with othere trewe sentensis° of *commentaries*
doctours° out of Lateyn into Freynsch. Why *scholars*
35 shulden not Engliysche men do so? As lordis of
Englond han° the Bible in Freynsch, so it were not *have*
ayenus° resoun that they hadden the same *against*
sentense° in Engliysch, for thus Goddis lawe *meaning*
wolde be betere knowun and more trowid° for *believed*
40 onehed° of wit,° and more acord be° bitwixe *unity knowledge would be*
reumes. *realms*

And herfore freris han° taught in Englond the **herfore . . .** *therefore friars have*
Paternoster° in Engliysch tunge, as men seyen,° in *Lord's Prayer say*
the pley° of York and in many othere cuntreys.° *miracle play districts*
45 Sithen° the Paternoster is part of Matheus Gospel, *Since*
as clerkis knowen, why may not al be turnyd to
Engliysch trewely, as is this part? Specialy sithen
alle Cristen men, lerid and lewid,° that shulen° be **lerid . . .** *learned and unlearned shall*
savyd moten algatis sue° Crist and knowe his lore **moten . . .** *must anyway follow*
50 and his lif. But the comyns of Engliyschmen
knowen it best in ther modir tunge, and thus it
were al oon° to lette° siche knowing of the **were . . .** *would be the same thing*
Gospel and to lette Engliysch men to sue Crist and *prevent*
come to hevene.

55 Wel Y woot, defaute° may be in untrewe **woot, defaute** *know, fault*
translating, as myghten have be° many defautis in *been*
turnyng fro Ebrew into Grew,° and fro Grew *Greek*
into Lateyn, and from o° langage into another. *one*
But lyve men° good lif, and studie many persones **lyve men** *let men live*
60 Goddis lawe, and whanne chaungyng of wit° is *knowledge*
foundun, amende they° it as resoun wole.° **foundun . . .** *found, let them amend will*

489

JOHN DE TREVISA

The Properties of Things

(1398, East Midland)

ॐ

John de Trevisa (1326–1402) was born in Cornwall, presumably of Cornish-speaking parents. He was a fellow of Exeter College and later of Queen's College, Oxford, and was appointed vicar of Berkeley in Gloucestershire. Under the patronage of Thomas, Lord Berkeley, he completed his two major works, a translation in 1387 of Higden's Latin *Polychronicon* (1327), and a translation in 1398 of the widely used encyclopedia *De Proprietatibus Rerum* (ca. 1250), excerpted here.

The author of the encyclopedia was Bartholomew de Glanville, better known as Bartholomew the Englishman or Bartholomaeus Anglicus, who had joined the Franciscan order in France and had gained renown on the Continent as a scholar. The fundamental purpose of his work was to enumerate the properties of things within the universe, for as the author points out, it is only by an allegorical understanding of the material universe that we can comprehend God's invisible universe. *De Proprietatibus Rerum* became extremely popular and was translated into numerous European languages.

Much of the material is derived from purveyors of "unnatural natural history," such as Isidore of Seville (seventh century) and the authors of bestiaries (see p. 150), lapidaries, and the like. Bartholomew's account of the owl (below) contains none of the rich symbolism implicit in *The Owl and the Nightingale* (p. 54, above), and his enumeration of the properties of the pearl gives no inkling of the allegorical possibilities of the subject as developed by the master poet in *The Pearl* (p. 339, above). Yet Shakespeare, when he wanted a one-volume encyclopedia, is known to have used Batman's version (1582) of Bartholomew, and the work is still curiously interesting because of its characteristically medieval mingling of classical and contemporary beliefs and of learned and popular traditions.

The abridged and somewhat inaccurate printed version of Trevisa published by Wynkyn de Worde (Westminster, 1491) has been used here with some emendations. Another abridgment printed by Berthelet in 1535 has been excerpted in modernized form in *Medieval Lore from Bartholomew Anglicus*, ed. Robert Steele (London, 1893). Trevisa's translation is extant in several manuscripts, but it has never been published in its entirety; two manuscripts are available as microprints: MLA Rotograph 261 (Addit. 27944) and Rotograph 317 (Tollemache), Library of Congress, Washington, D.C. For bibliography see Wells, ch. 10.35 (cf. ch. 3.9); H. S. Bennett, "Science and Information in English Writings of the Fifteenth Century," *Modern Language Review*, 39 (1944), 1–8; Bennett, *OHEL*, p. 299; *CBEL*, 1.167, 880, 5.118.

Translator's Prologue

Merveyle not, ye witty° and eloquent reders,   wise
that I, thynne of wytte and voyde of cunnynge,°   ingenuity
have translatid this boke from Latin into our
vulgare langage as a thynge profitable to me and,
5 peraventure, to many other whyche understonde
not Latyne nor have not the knowlege of the
proprytées of thynges, whiche thynges ben
approved° by the bookes of grete and cunnynge   **ben approved** are attested to
clerkes° and by the experience of moost wytty° and   **cunnynge clerkes** ingenious scholars
10 noble phylosophres.   wise

Alle thyse propritées of thynges ben full°   very
necessary and of grete value to them that wyll, or
be desyrous to, understonde the obscuretées or
derknesse of Holy Scriptures, whiche be yeven° to   given
15 us under fygures, under parables and semblaunces
or liklihodes° of thynges naturelles and arty-   similitudes
fycyelles.

Saynt Denys, that grete philosopher and
solempne clerke,° in his boke namyd *Of the Hevenly*   **solempne clerke** distinguished
20 *Ierarchies of Aungelles*,[1] testyfieth and wytnesseth the   scholar
same, sayenge in this manere:

"Whatsoever ony man wyll conjecte, feyne,°   **conjecte, feyne** conjecture, pretend
ymagyne, suppose, or saye, it is a thynge impos-
syble that the lyghte of the hevenly dyvyne clareté,
25 coverte and closid° in the deyté or in the godhede,   enclosed   deity
sholde shyne upon us yf it were not bi the
dyversitées of holy covertures.° Alls° it is not   coverings   As
possyble that our wytte or entendement° myghte   **wytte ...** knowledge or understanding
ascende unto the contemplacyon of the hevenly
30 ierarchyes immaterielles yf our wytte be not ledde
by some materyell thynge as a man is ledde by the
honde, soo by thyse fourmes visibles our wytte may
be led to the consyderacyon of the gretnesse or
magnytude of the moost excellent, bewteuous
35 clareté dyvyne and invysyble."

Reciteth this also the blessyd appostle Poul in his
Epistles,[2] sayeng that, by thise thynges visybles
whyche ben° made and ben visyble, man may se   are
and knowe by his inwarde syghte intellectuall the
40 divyne, celestyall, and godly thynges whiche ben
invisibles to this our naturall sighte.

[1] Pseudo-Dionysius Areopagiticus, *De Celesti Hierarchia* (ca. A.D. 500), I, 2.
[2] Rom. i.20.

Devowte doctours of theologye or dyvinyté for
this consyderatyon prudently and wysely rede and
use natural philosophye and moral—and poetes in
45 ther ficcions and feyned informacyons—unto this
fyne° or ende so that, by the lyklyhode or simyli-   purpose
tude of thynges visible, our wit° or our under-   knowledge
stondynge spirytuelly by clere and crafty° utter-   compelling
aunce of wordes may be so well ordred and uttred
50 that thyse thynges corporelles maye be cowplid
wyth thynges spyrytuelles, and thyse thynges
visybles may be conjoyned wyth thynges in-
vysybles.

The Owl

BOOK XII, vi

The owle hyghte° *bubo* and hath the name of°   is called   **name of** name (*bubo*) from
the sowne of her voyce, as Ysydre° sayth, and is a   Isidore
wylde byrde, chargyd° wyth fethers. But he° is   covered   she
alway holde° wyth slouthe,° and is feble to fle,° and held back   sloth   fly
5 dwellyth by graves by daye and by nyghte and in
chymnés.

And divynours° tell that they betoken evyl, for   soothsayers
they tell that, yf the owle be sette° in a cytée, it   settled
sygnyfyeth dystruccion and waste,° as Ysydre°   devastation   Isidore
10 sayth.

Arystotle sayth of the owle that the chough°   red-beaked crow
fyghtyth with the owle, for he° is feble of syghte at   she (the owl)
myddaye and seeth more clerely by nyghte than by
daye. And the owle etyth the choughes egges by
15 nyghte, for the owle is stronger by nyghte than by
daye, and the chough is stronger by daye thanne by
nyghte.

And other foules fle° abowte the owle by daye   **foules fle** birds fly
and pulle hym;° and therfore wyth° the owle   **pulle hym** pluck at her   by means of
20 foulars take° other byrdes and foules. The fyght-   **foulars take** fowlers catch
ynge of thise byrdes, as the fightinge of other
beestes, is not but° for meete other° for dwellynge   **not but** only   or
places.

Cryenge of the owle by nyght tokenyth dethe,
25 as divynours conject and deme.° The owle is fedde   **divynours . . .** soothsayers conjecture
wyth dyrte and wyth other unclene thynges, and is   and judge

hatyd of other byrdes, and hauntyth temples by
nyghte to have her fylle of oyle of lampes.

And namely° in fetheres and in becke° she semyth   especially beak
30 lyke to foules° of pray, but she is all unlyke to   birds
theym in boldnesse and in vertue;° and, whan   power
byrdes and foules assaylleth the owle, she lyeth
upright° and deffendyth herself wyth her becke and   facing up
wyth her fete. And they hounte° and ete myes and   hunt
35 rere-myes° and fle° abowte by nyghte and hyde   bats fly
theim in chymnés and walles by daye.

The Pearl

BOOK XVI, lxi

Margarita° is chyef of alle whyte precyous stones,   The pearl
as Ysydre° sayth, and hath that name Margarita for°   Isidore because
it is founde in shelles and in shellefyssh of the see.[1]
It bredyth in flesshe of shellefyssh and is somtyme
5 founde in the brayne of the fysshe and is gendred
of the dewe of heven, the whyche dewe shelfysh
receyve in certayn tymes of the yere.

Of the whyche margarites,° some ben° callyd   pearls are
uniones[2] and have a covenable° name, for oonly one   appropriate
10 is founde, and never two or moo° togyder.   more

And whyte margarites ben better than yelowe.
And those that ben conceyved of the morowe°   morning
dewe ben made dymme wyth the ayre of the
evyntyde. And some ben° founde kyndly percyd,°   are **kyndly percyd** pierced by nature
15 and those ben better than other; and some ben
percyd by crafte,° as Plato sayth. And they ben best   craftsmanship
that ben whyte and clere, bryght and rounde.

And they have vertue of comforte, other by°   **vertue…** comforting power, either with
alle the kyndes° therof, as some men meaneth,° or   kinds of pearls believe
20 for they ben byspr…onge° wyth certayne kynde; and   associated
it comfortith lymmes and membres, for it clensyth
them of superfluyté of humour,[3] and fastnyth° the   strengthens
lymmes, and helpeth ayenst° the cardiacle passion°   against **cardiacle passion** heart pain
and ayenst swounynge of hert and ayenst febly-
25 nesse that comyth of flyxe° of medycyn, and   flux

[1] This is a fanciful etymology that derives *margarita* from the Latin *mare* 'sea.'
[2] From Latin *unus* 'one.'
[3] Excess of any one of the four humors.

helpeth also ayenst rennynge of bloode and ayenst
flyxe of the wombe,° as Plato sayth.   stomach

And, in Plato it is sayd, the margarites ben°   **margarites ben** pearls are
gendryd of dewe. The more dewynge is founde,
30 the more and the gretter they ben. The margarite
is gendryd of the dewe, but it is trowed° that no   believed
margarite growyth passyng of° half a fote.   **passyng of** exceeding

Also, it is sayd there, yf the lyghtnyng or
thondrynge falle whan the margarite sholde° brede   is about to
35 of the dewe that is take,° the shell closyth by   received
sodayn strengthe, and so the gendrynge faylyth and
is caste out.

The beste margarites° come oute of Ynde° and   pearls   India
oute of the Olde Brytayn,° as it is sayd.   **Olde Brytayn** Great Britain

Thomas of Erceldoun

(ca. 1388–1401, Northern)

Thomas of Erceldoun is a peculiarly medieval work. It contains a romance that has fascinated readers from the time of Sir Walter Scott down to the present. For its fourteenth-century audience, however fascinating the narrative, the romance served primarily to fortify the authenticity of the political prophecies embedded in the work. The hero is an actual historical person, Thomas Rymor of Earlston, in Berwickshire, who within his own lifetime (ca. 1210–ca. 1286) had gained a remarkable reputation for his prophetic powers. He became known as Thomas the Rimer, though Rymor may have originally been a mere surname, and prophecies attributed to him circulated orally in Scotland until the nineteenth century.

The poem, inconsistently shifting between first person and third person narration, explains in the first part, or fytte, how Thomas received the gifts of minstrelsy and prophecy by winning the love of an otherworld queen. The second part records the queen's predictions concerning identifiable events in the fourteenth-century struggles between Scotland and England, including Bannockburn (1314; see *The Bruce*, p. 271, above), Halidon Hill (1333; see *Halidon Hill*, p. 231, above), and Otterburn (1388). The third part recounts the queen's ambiguous and vague prophecies of events that do not seem to have occurred in the fourteenth century or, for that matter, at any later period.

Most of the narrative elements in the romance are strikingly similar to counterparts in Celtic legends: the otherworld queen visits this world on a hunt; the hero wins supernatural knowledge from her because of his sexual potency; the queen is capable of changing from beautiful to loathly form; the hero visits the otherworld with the queen despite the power of her husband. The minstrels who transmitted the romance and the scribes who recorded it did not fully understand its primitive background, so the road that leads Thomas to the otherworld is confused with the Christian concept of three alternate roads that lead to heaven (l. 149), purgatory (l. 157), and hell (l. 162). Yet the romance preserves much of the glamor associated with ancient belief. Chaucer may have intended to parody this very poem when he composed *Sir Thopas*, but if so, his parody betrays his affection for his source.

The prophetic elements of the poem are part of a deliberate political technique universally employed in western Europe throughout the Middle Ages. Propagandists would attribute to some ancient and honored seer prophecies concerning events in the immediate past already consummated and then would add appropriate predictions concerning whatever they particularly wished to happen in the immediate future. The scribes clearly understood this utilitarian aspect of *Thomas of Erceldoun*, even though they did not always record the names of people and places correctly. In any case, the literary appeal of the poem has readily outlived its obscure folkloristic origins and its devious political purposes.

The meter is four-line stanzas; see Introduction, type 9, page 31.

James A. H. Murray has edited *The Romance and Prophecies of Thomas of Erceldoun*, EETS 62 (London, 1875) with full introduction and notes. The present selection is based whenever possible on the Thornton Manuscript; it omits a late prologue and includes all of the first fytte, the beginning of the second, and the end of the third (Murray's composite line numbers

25–338, 673–700). See also Child, No. 37; H. M. Flasdieck, *Tom der Reimer: Von keltischen Feen und politischen Propheten* (Breslau, 1934); and Rupert Taylor, *The Political Prophecy in England* (New York, 1911), pp. 62–71. For bibliography see Wells, ch. 4.25; *CBEL*, 1.168, 5.118.

I

Als° I me° wente this endres° daye — As   by myself   former
Full° faste in mynd makand° my mone° — Very   making   complaint
In a mery mornynge of Maye
By Huntlé[1] bankkes myselfe allone,
5   I herde the jaye and the throstyll° cokke; — song thrush
The mavys menyde hir of° hir songe; — **mavys . . .** song thrush bemoaned with
The wodewale beryde als° a belle, — **wodewale . . .** wood lark rang like
That alle the wode abowte me ronge.
Allonne in longynge thus als I laye
10 Undyrenethe a semely tree,
Saw I whare a lady gaye° — fair
Cam rydyng over a lovely lee.° — meadow
If I solde° sytt to domesdaye, — should
With my tonge, to wrobbe and wrye,° — **wrobbe . . .** wriggle and twist
15 Certanely that lady gaye,
Never bese scho askryede for° mee. — **bese . . .** would she be described by
Hir palfraye was a dappill graye;
Swylke° one ne saghe° I never none. — Such   **ne saghe** saw
Als dose° the sonne on someres daye, — **Als dose** As does
20 That faire lady hirselfe scho schone.
Hir selle° it was of roelle° bone— — saddle   rewel
Full semely was that syghte to see—
Stefly° sett with precyous stones — Firmly
And compaste° all with crapotée,° — encircled   toadstone
25 Stones of oryente, grete plenté.
  Hir hare abowte hir hede it hange.° — hung
Scho° rade over that lovely lee; — She
A° whylle scho blewe, another scho sange. — One
Hir garthes° of nobyll sylke thay were, — girths
30 The bukylls were of berelle stone;
Hir steraps were of crystalle clere
And all with perelle over-by-gone.° — **perelle over-by-gone** pearl covered
Hir payetrelle° was of yral° fyne, — horse's breastplate   precious stone
Hir cropoure was of orpharé;° — gold embroidery

[1] Huntley Brae is located near Melrose, below the Eildon Hills, not far from Abbotsford, which overlooks Tweed.

35 And als clere° golde hir brydill it schone.   **als clere** as bright
One aythir° syde hange bellys three.   **One aythir** On each
Scho° led three grehoundis in a lesshe,°   She   leash
And sevene raches° by hir thay rone.°   hounds   ran
Scho bare an horne abowte hir halse°   neck
40 And undir hir belte full° many a flone.°   very   arrow
　Thomas laye and sawe that syghte
Undirnethe ane semly tree.
He sayd, "Yone es° Marye, moste of myghte,   **Yone es** Yonder is
That bare that Childe that dyede for mee.
45 Bot if° I speke with yone lady bryghte,   **Bot if** Unless
I hope° myne herte will bryste in three!   expect
Now sall° I go with all my myghte,   shall
Hir for to mete at Eldoune Tree."²
　Thomas rathely° upe he rase,   quickly
50 And he rane over that mountayne hye.
Gyff° it be als° the storye sayes,   If   as
He hir mette at Eldone Tree.
He knelyde downe appone his knee
Undirnethe that grenwode spraye°   branch
55 And sayd, "Lufly ladye! rewe one° me,   **rewe one** pity on
Qwene of Hevene, als thou wele maye!"
　Than spake that lady milde of thoghte:
"Thomas, late swylke° wordes be.   such
Qwene of Hevene ne am° I noghte,   **ne am** am
60 For I tuke° never so heghe degré,   took
Bote I ame of ane other countrée.
If I be payrelde° most of prysse,°   appareled   excellence
I ryde aftyre this wylde fee;°   game
My raches rynnys° at my devyse."°   **raches rynnys** hounds run   command
65　"If thou be parelde moste of prysse,
And here rydis thus in thy folye,
Of lufe, lady, als° thou erte wysse,°   as   wise
Thou gyffe me leve to lye thee bye."
　Scho° sayde, "Thou mane, that ware folye.   She
70 I praye thee, Thomas, thou late me bee;
For I saye thee full sekirlye,°   surely
That synne will fordoo° all my beauté."   destroy
　"Now, lufly ladye, rewe one° mee,   **rewe one** pity on
And I will ever more with thee dwelle—
75 Here my trouthe I will thee plyghte°—   pledge
Whethir thou will in hevene or helle."
　"Mane of Molde,° thou will me marre,°   Earth   mar
Bot yitt° thou sall hafe all thy will;   yet

² The Eildon Tree was on the slope of the easternmost of the three Eildon Hills.

And trowe° it wele, thou chevys the werre,°   believe   **chevys . . . come off the wor**
80 For alle my beauté will thou spylle."°   destroy
     Downe thane lyghte° that lady bryghte   alighted
Undirnethe that grenewode spraye;°   branch
And als° the storye tellis full° ryghte,   as   very
Sevene sythis° by hir he laye.   times
85   Scho sayd, "Mane, thee lykes° thy playe.°   pleases   play
Whate byrde° in boure° maye delle° with thee?   maiden   bower   deal
Thou merrys° me all this longe daye;   mar
I praye thee, Thomas, late me bee!"
     Thomas stode upe in that stede,°   place
90 And he byhelde that lady gaye.°   fair
Hir hare it hange° all over hir hede;   hung
Hir eghne° semede owte that are° were graye;   eyes   formerly
And alle the riche clothynge was awaye
That he byfore sawe in that stede;
95 Hir a schanke° blake, hir other graye,   **a schanke** one leg
And all hir body lyke the lede.°   lead
     Thomas laye and sawe that syghte
Undirnethe that grenewod tree.
Than said Thomas, "Allas! Allas!
100 In faythe this es° a dullfull° syghte.   is   doleful
How arte thou fadyde thus in the face,
That schane° byfore als the sonne so bryghte!"   shone
     Scho sayd, "Thomas, take leve at° sonne and   of
       mone°   moon
And als° at lefe that grewes on tree.   also
105 This twelmoneth sall° thou with me gone,°   shall   go
And medill-erthe° sall thou none see."   earth
     He knelyd downe appone his knee
Undirnethe that grenewod spraye
And sayd, "Lufly lady, rewe° on mee,   pity
110 Mylde qwene of Hevene, als thou beste maye.°   may be
Allas," he sayd, "and wa° es mee!   woe
I trowe° my dedis wyll wirke me care;°   believe   sorrow
My saulle, Jhesu, byteche° I thee,°   commit   to you
Whedir-some that ever° my banes° sall fare."   **Whedir-some . . .** Wherever   bones
115   Scho° ledde hym in at Eldone Hill   She
Undirnethe a derne° lee   secret
Whare it was dirke als mydnyght myrke,°   murk
And ever the water till° his knee.   up to
The montenans° of dayes three   period
120 He herd bot swoghynge° of the flode.   **bot swoghynge** only roaring
At the laste, he sayde, "Full wa° es mee!   **Full wa** Much woe
Almaste I dye, for fawte° of fode."   lack

Scho lede hym intill a faire herbere,°   garden
Whare frwte was growand gret plentée:
125 Pere and appill, bothe ryppe thay were,
The date, and als° the damasée;°   also damson plum
The fygge, and alsso the wyneberye;°   grape
The nyghtgales byggande° on thair neste.   building
The papejoyes° faste abowte gane flye,°   parrots **gane flye** flew
130 And throstylls sange° wolde hafe no reste.   **throstylls sange** thrushes' song
        He pressede° to pulle frowyte° with his hande,   hurried **pulle frowyte** pick fruit
Als mane° for fude that was nere faynt.   a man
        Scho sayd, "Thomas, thou late thame stande,
Or ells the fende° thee will atteynt.°   fiend seize
135 If thou it plokk, sothely° to saye,   truly
Thi saule gose to the fyre of helle.
It commes never owte or° domesdaye,   before
Bot ther in payne ay° for to dwelle.   ever
Thomas, sothely, I thee hyghte,°   bid
140 Come lygge° thyne hede downe on my knee,   lay
And thou sall se the fayreste syghte
That ever sawe mane of thi contrée."
        He did in hye° als scho hym badde.   haste
Appone hir knee his hede he layde,
145 For hir to paye° he was full° glade.   please very
        And thane that lady to hym sayde:
"Seese° thou nowe yone° faire waye   Seest yonder
That lygges° over yone heghe mountayne?   lies
Yone es° the waye to hevene for aye,°   is ever
150 Whene synfull sawles are passede ther payne.
        "Seese thou nowe yone other° waye,   second
That lygges lawe° bynethe yone rysse?°   low underbrush
Yone° es the waye, the sothe° to saye,   Yonder truth
Unto the joye of paradyse.
155 "Seese thou yitt yone thirde waye
That ligges° undir yone grene playne?   lies
Yone es° the waye, with tene and traye,°   is **tene . . .** pain and trouble
Whare synfull saulis suffiris thaire payne.
        "Bot seese thou nowe yone° ferthe waye   yonder
160 That lygges over yone depe delle?
Yone es the waye, so waylaraye,°   alas
Unto the birnande fyre of helle.
        "Seese thou yitt yone faire castelle
That standis over yone heghe hill?
165 Of towne and towre, it beris the belle;³
In erthe es none lyke it untill.

³ 'Stands in first place.' The lead animal in a herd usually carried a bell.

499

Forsothe, Thomas, yone es° myne awenne,°   **yone es** yonder is   own
And the kynges of this countrée.
Bot me ware lever° be hanged and drawene   **me** . . . I would rather
170 Or that° he wyste° thou laye me by.   **Or that** Before   knew
When thou commes to yone castelle gaye,°   fair
I pray thee curtase° mane to bee.   a courteous
And whate-so° any mane to thee saye,   whatsoever
Luke° thou answere none bott mee.   Look
175 My lorde es servede at ylk a mese°   **ylk** . . . each course
With thritty° knyghttis faire and free.   **With thritty** By thirty
I sall saye, syttande at the desse,°   dais
I tuke° thi speche byyonde the see."   captured
    Thomas still als stane he stude,
180 And he byhelde that lady gaye.°   fair
Scho come° agayne als faire and gude   became
And also ryche one° hir palfraye,   **ryche one** splendid on
Hir grewehoundis fillide° with dere° blode,   filled   deer's
Hir raches couplede,° by my faye.°   **raches couplede** hounds leashed   fai
185 Scho blewe hir horne with mayne and mode;°   **mayne** . . . might and spirit
Unto the castelle scho tuke the waye.
Into the haulle sothely° scho went.   **haulle sothely** hall truly
Thomas folowed at hir hande.
Than ladyes come, bothe faire and gent,°   noble
190 With curtassye to hir knelande.
Harpe and fethill° bothe thay fande,°   fiddle   found
Getterne,° and alsso the sawtrye,°   Gittern   psaltery
Lutte and rybybe° bothe gangande,°   rebeck   going
And all manere of mynstralsye.
195   The moste mervelle° that Thomas thoghte   **moste mervelle** greatest marvel
Whene that he stode appone the flore,
For feftty hertis° in were broghte   stags
That were bothe grete and store.°   mighty
Raches° laye lapande in the blode.   Hounds
200 Cokes° come with dryssynge knyfe;   Cooks
Thay brittened° thame als° thay were wode.°   cut up   as if   crazy
Revelle amanges thame was full° ryfe.   very
Knyghtis dawnsede by three and three.
There was revelle, gamene,° and playe,   sport
205 Lufly ladyes faire and fre°   noble
That satte and sange one° riche araye.   in
Thomas dwellide in that solace
More thane I yowe saye, pardé,°   indeed
Till one a daye, so hafe I grace,
210 My lufly lady sayde to mee:
    "Do buske° thee, Thomas. Thee buse° agayne,   ready   it behooves to go

For thou may here no lengare be.
Hye° thee faste with myghte and mayne.   Hasten
I sall thee brynge till Eldone Tree."
215   Thomas sayde thane with hevy chere,°   **hevy chere** sad countenance
"Lufly lady, nowe late me bee,
For certis,° lady, I hafe bene here   certainly
Noghte bot° the space of dayes three!"   **Noghte bot** Only
     "Forsothe, Thomas, als I thee telle,
220 Thou hase bene here thre yere and more,
Bot langere here thou may noghte dwelle.
The skylle° I sall° thee telle wharefore.   reason   shall
Tomorne° of helle the foulle fende[4]   Tomorrow
Amange this folke will feche his fee;
225 And thou arte mekill° mane and hende;°   a large   courteous
I trowe° full wele he wolde chese° thee.   expect   choose
For alle the golde that ever may bee
Fro hethyne° unto the worldis ende,   hence
Thou bese° never betrayede for° mee.   will be   by
230 Therefore with me I rede° thou wende."°   advise   to go
     Scho broghte hym agayne to Eldone Tree
Undirnethe that grenewode spraye.
In Huntlee bannkes es mery to bee,
Whare fowles synges bothe nyght and daye.
235   "Ferre° owtt in yone° mountane graye,   Far   yonder
Thomas, my fawkone bygges° a neste.   builds
A fawconne es an erlis praye;°   **erlis praye** earl's prey
For-thi° in na place may he reste.   Therefore
Fare wele, Thomas, I wend° my waye,   go
240 For me byhoves° over yon benttis° browne."   it behooves to go   slopes
     Loo here a fytt. More es to saye,
All of Thomas of Erselldowne.

[4] The fiend of Hell exacts an annual tribute from the otherworld creatures.

II

"Fare wele, Thomas, I wend my waye.
I may no lengare stande with thee."
     "Gyff me a tokynynge, lady gaye,°   fair
That I may saye I spake with thee."
5   "To harpe or carpe, whareso° thou gose,   **carpe, whareso** speak, wherever
Thomas, thou sall hafe the chose sothely."°   **chose sothely** choice truly
     And he saide, "Harpynge kepe° I none,   regard

For tonge es chefe of mynstralsye."
  "If thou will spelle,° or tales telle,   narrate
10 Thomas, thou sall never lesynge lye.°   **lesynge lye** tell a lie
   Whare-ever thou fare, by frythe or felle,° **frythe . . .** field or hill
   I praye thee, speke none evyll of me.
   Fare wele, Thomas, withowttyne gyle,
   I may no lengare dwelle with thee."
15   "Lufly lady, habyde° a while,   wait
   And telle thou me of some ferly!"°   marvel
     "Thomas, herkyne what I thee saye:
   Whene a tree rote es dede,
   The leves fadis thane and wytis° awaye,   die
20 And froyte° it beris nane thane, whyte ne° rede. fruit   nor
   Of the Baylliolse blod[1] so sall° it falle: shall
   It sall be lyke a rotyne tree.
   The Comyns and the Barlays alle,
   The Russells and the Fresells free,[2]
25 All sall thay fade and wyte awaye.
   Na ferly° if that froyte than° dye.   **Na ferly** No wonder **froyte than** fru
                                            then
   And mekill bale sall° after spraye,°   **mekill . . .** much woe shall   spread
   Whare joye and blysse was wonte to bee.
   Fare wele, Thomas, I wende° my waye;   go
30 I may no langer stand with thee."

           .   .   .

---

[1] 'Baliols' blood,' descendants of John Baliol, rivals of the Bruce family.
[2] Comyns (Cumyns), Barclays, Russells, and Frasers, four families involved in the Baliol-Bruce controversy
the fourteenth century.

III

   Thomas drere° mann was he;   a dreary
   Teares fell over his eyen so graye.
     "Nowe, lovly lady, tell thou me
   If we shall parte for ever and aye."°   ever
5   "Naye," she saide, "Thomas, *par dé*.°   *par dé* indeed
   When thow sitteste° in Erseldown,   are settled
   To Huntlee Bankkis thou take the waye.
   There sall I sekirly° be bowne°   surely   ready to go
   And mete thee, Thomas, whene I maye.
10 I sall thee kenne,° whare-ever thou gaa,°   teach go
   To bere the pryce of° curtaysye;   **pryce of** esteem for
   For tunge es wele,° and tunge es waa,°   joy woe

And tunge es chefe of mynstrallsye."
Sche blewe hir horne on hir palfraye
15 And lefte Thomas undirnethe a tre.
To Helmesdale° sche tuke the waye,   Helmsdale (Sutherland)
And thus departede sche and hee.
Of swilke° an hirdmane° wolde I here°   such   retainer   hear
That couth° me telle of swilke ferly.°   could a marvel
20 Jhesu, corounde° with a crowne of brere,°   crowned briar
Brynge us to his hevene so hyee.
         Amene, Amene.

THE
FIFTEENTH
CENTURY

The Tale of Beryn

(ca. 1405, East Midland)

❧

The anonymous author of *The Tale of Beryn* calls himself "a son of Thomas's church" (Canterbury Cathedral). His is the first known work after Chaucer's death to attempt a continuation of *The Canterbury Tales*, for which Chaucer had intended to provide further tales told by the pilgrims on the road back from Canterbury. As a resident familiar with Canterbury, he realistically and wittily describes in his prologue (ll. 1–732) the activities of the simpler pilgrims within the town; and then he provides a second tale (ll. 733–4024) for Chaucer's Merchant.

The tale appropriately concerns Beryn, the son of a Roman senator, who himself becomes a merchant and, after trials in Falsetown, marries a duke's daughter. The romance, derived from a French source, is refreshingly bourgeois but, in the halting septenary lines of the English adaptation, is an inadequate competitor for a place among Chaucer's skillfully wrought narratives.

The meter is seven-beat couplets; see Introduction, type 7, page 31.

The best edition is *The Tale of Beryn*, ed. F. J. Furnivall and W. G. Stone, Chaucer Society, 2nd Series, 17, 24 (London, 1876, 1887), reprinted EETS 105 (London, 1909). For the manuscript see Manly-Rickert, I, 387–95 (Northumberland MS. 55 of *The Canterbury Tales*). For bibliography see Hammond, p. 412; *CBEL* 1.254; Bennett, *OHEL*, 17, 70, 317.

[Prologue, lines 130–90]

The knyght and al the feleshipp—and no thing
    for to ly°—   *misrepresent*
When they wer all i-loggit,° as skill wold and reson,   *lodged*
Everich° aftir his degré, to chirch then was seson°   *Each time*
To passen and to wend,° to maken hir° offringis,   *go their*
5 Righte° as hir devocioune was, of sylvir broch and   *According*
    ryngis.
Then atte chirche dorr the curtesy gan° to ryse,   *began*
Tyl the knyght, of gentilnes,° that knewe righte   *nobility*
    wele the guyse,°   *manner*
Put forth the prelatis, the person, and his fere,°   *companions*
A monk, that toke the spryngill° with a manly   *sprinkler*
    chere,°   *countenance*
10 And did, right as the manner is, moillid° al hir   *wet*
    patis,°   *pates*

506

Everich° aftir othir, righte as they wer of states.°   Each   ranks

The ffrere feynyd fetously° the spryngil for to hold   ffrere ... friar   tried neatly

To spryng oppon the remnaunt, that for his cope he nold°   wouldn't

Have lafft that occupacioune in that holy plase,

15 So longid his holy conscience to se the nonnys° fase.   nun's

The knyghte went with his compers° toward the holy shryne,   comrades

To do that° they were com fore and aftir for to dyne.   what

The pardoner and the miller and othir lewde sotes°   lewde sotes unlearned dolts

Sought hem° selffen in the chirch right as lewde gotes;°   them   goats

20 Pyrid° fast and pourid highe oppon the glase,°   Peered   stained glass

Countirfeting gentilmen,° the armys for to blase,°   Countirfeting gentilmen Imitating nobles   proclaim

Diskyveryng fast the peyntour, and for the story mourned.°   meditated

And a° red it also right° as wolde rammys° horned.   one   also right as correctly   rams

"He berith a balstaff,"[1] quod the toon,° "and els° a rakis ende."   one   besides

25 "Thow faillist," quod the miller; "thowe hast nat wel thy mynde.

It is a spere, yf thowe canst se, right with a prik tofore,°   in front

To bussh° adown his enmy and thurh the sholdir bore."   thrust

"Pese!"° quod the hoost of Southwork, "let stond the wyndow glasid.   Peace

Goith up and doith yeur offerynge. Yee semeth half amasid.

30 Sith° yee be in company of honest men and good,   Since

Worchith somwhat aftir, and let the kynd of brode°

Pas for a tyme. I hold it for the best,

Ffor who doith after company, may lyve the bet° in rest."   better

Then passid they forth boystly, goglyng° with hir° hedis,   boystly, goglyng crudely, staring   their

35 Knelid adown tofore the shryne, and hertilich hir bedis°   beads

They preyd to Seynt Thomas in such wise° as they couth;°   manner   knew how

And sith° the holy relikis ech man with his mowith   then

---

[1] 'Quarterstaff,' here possibly in an illustration of a saint with a staff.

31. Let this go until later (literally 'do somewhat later'), and let the natural disposition

Kissid, as a goodly monke the names told and
    taught;

And sith to othir placis of holynes they raughte°   reached

40 And were in hir devocioun tyl service wer al doon;

And sith they drowgh° to dynerward as it drew to   drew
    noon.

    Then, as manere and custom is, signes° there they   souvenir tokens
        boughte,

Ffor men of contré shulde know whom they hadde
    oughte.°

Ech man set his sylvir in such thing as they likid;

45 And in the meenewhile the miller had i-pikid°   picked

His bosom ful of signys of Cauntirbury brochis,

Huch° the pardoner and he pryvely in hir° pouchis   Which   their

They put hem° aftirward, that noon of hem it wist,°   them   knew

Save the sompnour seid° somwhat and seyde to   **sompnour seid** summoner saw
    ham,° "List,   them

50 Halff part," quod he, pryvely rownyng on° hir ere.   **rownyng on** whispering in

    "Hussht! Pees!"° quod the miller. "Seist thowe   Peace
        nat the frere,

Howe he lowrith undir his hood with a doggish ey?

Hit shuld be° a pryvy thing that he coude nat aspy;   **shuld be** would have to be

Of every crafft he can° somwhat, Our Lady gyve   knows
    him sorowe!"

55   "Amen," quod the sompnour,° "on eve and eke°   summoner   also
      on morowe.°   morning

So cursid a tale he told of me, the devil of hell hym
    spede!²

And me, but yf I pay hym wele and quyte° wele his   repay
    mede,°   reward

Yf it happene homward that ech man tell his tale

As wee did hiderward, thoughe wee shuld set at
    sale°   **set . . .** make use of

60 Al the shrewdnes that I can, I wol hym no thing
    spare,

That I nol° touch his taberd,° somwhat of his   won't   cloak
    care."°   sorrow

---

43. So that their countrymen might know from whom they had anything.

² A reference to Chaucer's "Friar's Tale," in *The Canterbury Tales*, directed against the Summoner, who ha[s]
countered the attack in Chaucer's "Summoner's Tale."

THOMAS HOCCLEVE

The Regiment of Princes

(ca. 1412, East Midland)

In the autobiographical introduction to this poem Hoccleve (ca. 1368–ca. 1437) expresses his weariness with the French-English wars and laments the financial insecurity of his annuity, which he finds inadequate as a reward for all his years of service as clerk at the Office of the Privy Seal. He decides to prepare a treatise on the duties of princes, which he will submit to Prince Hal, crowned Henry V in 1413, but he regrets that Chaucer and Gower are no longer alive to inspire him. Freely adapting Jacobus de Cessolis's *Moralized Chess* to this purpose, he advocates dignity, truth, justice, lawfulness, pity, mercy, patience, chastity, magnanimity, generosity (which should guarantee the payment of Hoccleve's annuity), prudence (on which Chaucer has given good advice), and peacefulness (which should lead Henry to marry Catherine of Valois—as he did, in 1420—and to bring peace between England and France).

The literary interest of the poem lies much more in its historical background than in its style. Throughout the work (cf. ll. 1867, 1962, 2078, 4983), Hoccleve praises Chaucer (who had died in 1400), hailing him as a "flower of eloquence" and as his "master dear." He provided at least one manuscript copy of his poem with a miniature of Chaucer, which, it is assumed, was painted from memory by some artist who had known Chaucer.

The meter is seven-line stanzas; see Introduction, type 17, page 32.

The best edition is ed. F. J. Furnivall, EETS 72, (London, 1897). The Harley 4866 folio containing the miniature of Chaucer and the surrounding stanzas is reproduced here in Plate 5, page 24. For bibliography see Bennett, *OHEL*, 123, 148, 150, 285–86; Hartung, ch. 8.2.

[Lines 4978–5019]

The firste fyndere° of oure faire langage   founder
Hath seyde in caas semblable° and othir moo°   similar more
So hyly° wel, that it is my dotage°   very foolishness
Ffor to expresse or touche any of thoo.°   those
5   Alasse! my fadir fro the worlde is goo°—   gone
    My worthi maister Chaucer, hym I mene.
    Be thou advoket for hym, Hevenes Quene.

As thou wel knowest, O Blissid Virgyne,
    With lovyng hert and hye devocioun
10 In thyne honour he wroot ful° many a lyne.   very
    O now thine helpe and thi promocioun,
    To God thi Sone make a mocioun°   proposal

How he thi servaunt was, Mayden Marie,
And lat his love floure and fructifie.

15   Althogh his lyfe be queynt,° the resemblaunce   quenched
Of him hath in me so fressh lyflynesse
That, to putte othir men in remembraunce
Of his persone, I have heere his lyknesse
Do make,° to this ende in sothfastnesse,°   **Do make** Caused to be made   trut‍
20   That thei that have of him lest° thought and mynde lost
By this peynture may ageyn him fynde.

The ymages that in the chirche been
Maken folk thenke on God and on his seyntes,
Whan the ymages thei beholden and seen;
25   Wereas unsyte° of hem° causith restreyntes   not seeing   them
Of thoughtes gode. When a thing depeynt° is   painted
Or entailed,° if men take of it heede,   figured
Thoght of the lyknesse it wil in hem brede.°   increase

Yit somme holden oppynyoun and sey
30   That none ymages schuld i-maked° be.   made
Thei erren foule and goon out of the wey;°   **erren**...blunder and err
Of trouth have thei scant sensibilité.
Passe over that. Now, Blessid Trinité,
Uppon my maistres soule, mercy have;
35   Ffor him, Lady, eke° thi mercy I crave.   also

More othir thing wolde I fayne speke and touche
Heere in this booke, but such is my dulnesse—
Ffor that al voyde and empty is my pouche—
That al my lust° is queynt° with hevynesse,°   desire   quenched   grief
40   And hevy spirit commaundith stilnesse.
And have I° spoke of pees,° I schal be stille.   **have I** when I have   peace
God sende us pees, if that it be his wille.

JOHN LYDGATE

The Siege of Thebes

(ca. 1421, East Midland)

ໝ

John Lydgate (ca. 1370–ca. 1450) spent most of his life as a Benedictine monk in the wealthy monastery of Bury St. Edmunds, in West Suffolk. With the assistance of the great monastic library there, he wrote numerous lengthy and highly derivative works for a variety of distinguished patrons.

The Siege of Thebes deals with the rivalry between Eteocles and Polyneices, the two sons of Oedipus, over the kingship of Thebes—a classical theme still popular in the Middle Ages. His source was a now lost French prose romance adapted from the Old French poem *Le Roman de Thebes*.

His amusing prologue depicts Daun John Lydgate joining Chaucer's pilgrims at Canterbury just as they set out on the return journey to Southwark. Within this context, his tale provides an appropriate counterpart to Chaucer's "Knight's Tale," and it has been argued in its justification that Lydgate intended his narrative to provide the company with a fitting moral exemplification. As with Chaucer's "Monk's Tale," however, the moral intentions of his pedestrian recital do not suffice to guarantee the enthusiasm of a worldly audience.

The meter is five-beat couplets; see Introduction, type 6, page 31.

The best edition is *The Siege of Thebes*, ed. A. Erdmann and E. Ekwall, Chaucer Society, 2nd Series, 46, and EETS 108, 125 (London, 1911, 1930). The most recent study is Derek A. Pearsall, *John Lydgate* (London, 1970). For the manuscript see Plate 6 and accompanying notes, pages 26–28. For bibliography see *CBEL*, 1.250–52, 5.146; Bennett, *OHEL*, pages 298–93.

[Lines 66–193]
And this while that the pilgrymes leye
At Canterbury well logged on° and all, **logged on** lodged one
I not° in soth° what I may it call, know not truth
Hap or fortune in conclusioun,° judgment
5 That me byfil to entren° into toun, **byfil** ... it befell that I entered
The holy seynt[1] pleynly to visite
Aftere siknesse, my vowes to aquyte,° fulfill
In a cope° of blak and not of grene, cape
On a palfrey slender, long, and lene,
10 With rusty brydel mad nat for the sale,
My man toforn° with a voide male° in front **voide male** empty pack
Which° of fortune took myn inne° anon Who inn

[1] St. Thomas Becket, of Canterbury.

511

Wher the pylgrymes were logged everichon.°　　　　**logged everichon** lodged everyone
　　The same tyme her° governour, the host,　　　　their
15　Stonding in halle, ful of wynde and bost,
　　Lich° to a man wonder° sterne and fers,　　　　Like　wondrously
　　Which spak° to me and seide anon, "Daun Pers,°　spoke　**Daun Pers** Sir Piers
　　Daun Domynyk, Dan Godfrey or Clement,
　　Ye be welcom newly into Kent,
20　Thogh youre bridel have neither boos° ne belle.　boss
　　Besechinge you that ye wil me telle
　　First youre name and of what contré,
　　Withoute more, shortely that° ye be　　　　　that which
　　That loke so pale, al devoyde of blood,
25　Upon youre hede a wonder° thred-bar hood,　　wondrously
　　Wel araied for to ride late."
　　　　I answerde, "My name was Lydgate,
　　Monk of Bery, nygh° fyfty yere of age,　　　　nearly
　　Come to this toune to do my pilgrimage
30　As I have hight;° I have therof no shame."　　vowed
　　　　"Daun° John," quod he, "wel broke° ye youre name.　Sir　uttered
　　Thogh ye be soul, beth° right glad and light,　　**soul, beth** alone, be
　　Preiyng you soupe with us tonyght,
　　And ye shal have mad at youre devis°　　　　wish
35　A gret puddyng° or a rounde hagys,°　　　　sausage　haggis
　　A Franchemole, a tansey, or a froyse.²
　　To ben° a monk, sclender° is youre koyse;°　　be　slim　rump
　　Ye han be° seke, I dar myn hede assure,　　　been
　　Or late fed in a feynt pasture.
40　Lift up youre hed; be glad, tak no sorowe,
　　And ye shal hom ride with us tomorowe.
　　　　"I seye, whan ye rested han° your fille,　　have
　　Aftere soper slepe wil do non ille.
　　Wrappe wel youre hede with clothes rounde aboute.
45　Strong notty° ale wol make you to route.°　　　nutty　snore
　　Tak a pylow, that ye lye not lowe.
　　Yif nede be, spare not to blowe.°　　　　　pass wind
　　To holde wynde, by myn opynyoun,
　　Wil engendre collikes passioun°　　　　　suffering
50　And make men to greven° on her roppys°　　suffer　**her roppys** their guts
　　Whan thei han° filled her mawes and her croppys.°　have　bellies
　　But toward nyght ete some fenel rede,°　　　**fenel rede** red fennel
　　Annys, comyn,° or coriandre sede.　　　　**Annys, comyn** Anise, cumin
　　And lik as I power have and myght,

---

² 'Fraunchemole,' a mixture boiled (like haggis) or roasted in a sheep's stomach; 'tansy,' a bitter, aromatic plant much used for stomach ailments and as a vegetable in cooking; 'froise,' a pancake containing chopped meat or fish.

55 I charge yow rise not at mydnyght,
Thogh it so be the moone shyne cler.
I wol mysilf be youre orloger°   horologist
Tomorrow erly whan I se my tyme,
For we wol forth parcel afore pryme,°
60 A company, pardé,° shal do you good.   indeed
   "What! Look up, Monk, for, by kokkis° blood,   God's
Thow shalt be mery, who-so that sey nay.°   **who-so . . .** no matter who says not
For tomorowe, anoon as° it is day,   **anoon as** as soon as
And that it gynne° in the est to dawe,°   begins   dawn
65 Thow shalt be bounde to a newe lawe
Att goyng oute of Canterbury toune
And leyn° aside thy professioun.   lay
Thow shalt not chese° nor thisilf withdrawe   choose
Yif eny myrth be founden in thy mawe,
70 Lyk° the custom of this compenye.   As is
For non so proude that dar me denye,
Knyght nor knave, canon, prest, ne° nonne,   nor
To telle a tale pleynly as thei konne,
Whan I assigne and se tyme opportune.
75 And for that we our purpoos wil contune,°   continue
We wil homward the same custome use,
And thow shalt not platly° thee excuse.   flatly
Be now wel war.° Stody wel tonyght.   aware
But, for al this, be of herte light;
80 Thy wit shal be the sharper and the bet."°   better
   And we anon were to soper sett
And served wel unto oure plesaunce;°   pleasure
And sone after, be° good governaunce,   by
Unto bed goth every maner wight.°   **maner wight** kind of person
85 And towarde morowe, anon as° it was light,   **morowe . . .** morning, as soon as
Every pilgryme bothe bet° and wors,   better
As bad° oure hoste, toke anon his hors,   ordered
Whan the sonne roos in the est ful clyere,°   bright
Fully in purpoos to come to dynere
90 Unto Osspryng° and breke ther our faste.   Ospringe (Kent)
   And whan we weren from Canterbury paste
Noght the space of a bowe-draught,°   bowshot
Our hoost in hast hath my bridel rauht°   seized
And to me seide, as° it were in game,°   as if   jest
95 "Come forth, Daun° John, be° your Cristene name,   Sir   by
And lat us make some manere° myrth or play.   kind of
Shet° youre portoos° a twenty develway.   Shut   breviary
It is no disport° so to patere and seie;   entertainment

59. For we will go forth in a group (literally, 'in part') before prime (6:00 to 9:00 A.M.)

It wol make youre lippes wonder° dreye. — wondrously

100 Tel some tale and make therof a jape,° — jest
For, be° my rouncy,° thow shalt not eskape. — by / horse
But preche not of non holynesse.
Gynne° some tale of myrth or of gladnesse, — Begin
And nodde not with thyn hevy bekke.° — **hevy bekke** sad beak

105 Telle us some thing that draweth to effecte
Only of joye. Make no lenger lette."° — delay
  And whan I saugh it wolde be no bette,° — better
I obeyed unto his biddynge,
So as the lawe me bonde in al thinge,

110 And as I coude,° with a pale cheere,° — **as** ... as best I could / countenanc[e]
My tale I gan° anon as ye shal here.° — began / hear
  "Sirs," quod I, "sith° of your curtesye — since
I entred am into your companye
And admitted a tale for to telle

115 By him that hath power to compelle—
I mene our hoste, governour, and guyde
Of yow echon,° ridyng her° beside— — each one / here
Thogh that my wit barayn be and dul,
I wol reherce a story wonderful

120 Touchinge the siege and destruccioun
Of worthy Thebees, the myghty royal toun,
Bylt and begonne of olde antiquité,
Upon the tyme of worthy Josué,
Be dyligence of Kyng Amphioun,

125 Chief cause first of his° fundacioun, — its
For which his fame, which nevere shal away,
In honure floureth yit unto this day,
And in story remembred is and preised."

Christ and His Mother

(ca. 1450, East Midland)

∽

This simple yet subtle lyric is a striking example of the religious use of the genre known as the reverdie, the song inspired by the return of spring (see *Spring*, p. 210, above). Its first and last stanzas are derived ultimately from an earlier religious lyric, "Nu this fules singet hand maket hüre blis" (ca. 1250); but in their total poetic effect its five restrained stanzas outshine the twelve stanzas of its prototype.

The meter is four-line stanzas; see Introduction, type 8, page 31.

The best edition is Carleton Brown, *Religious Lyrics of the Fifteenth Century* (Oxford, 1939), page 119. See also Stephen Manning, "I Syng of a Myden," *PMLA*, 75 (1960), 8–12. The only manuscript is British Museum Sloane 2593, which also contains *St. Stephen and Herod* (p. 516, below) and *Robyn and Gandeleyn* (p. 518, below); it has been published complete in *Songs and Carols from a Manuscript in the British Museum of the Fifteenth Century*, ed. Thomas Wright, Warton Club, 4 (London, 1856). For bibliography see Wells, ch. 13.205.

I syng of a myden	
that is makeles.°	matchless/mateless
Kyng of alle kynges	
to here° sone sche ches.°	**to here** as her chose
5 He cam also° stylle	as
ther° his moder was	where
As dew in Aprylle	
that fallyt° on the gras;	falls
He cam also stylle	
10 to his moderes bowr	
As dew in Aprille	
that fallyt on the flour;	
He cam also stylle	
there his moder lay	
15 As dew in Aprille	
that fallyt on the spray.	
Moder and maydyn	
was never non but sche.	
Wel may swych° a lady	such
20 Godes moder be.	

515

St. Stephen and Herod

(ca. 1450, East Midland)

❧

The origin of this ballad, like that of *Judas* (p. 153, above), lies in the ancient apocryphal material that accumulated around the narratives of the New Testament. In another ballad, *The Carnal and the Crane* (Child, No. 55), the same motif of the crowing cock is associated with the Wise Men and Christmas rather than with St. Stephen and the evening before St. Stephen's Day (December 26).

The meter is seven-beat couplets; see Introduction, type 7, page 31.

The best edition is Child, No. 22. Child also provides bibliographical references. The only manuscript is British Museum Sloane 2593, published in *Songs and Carols from a Manuscript in the British Museum of the Fifteenth Century*, ed. Thomas Wright, Warton Club, 4 (London, 1856).

	Seynt Stevene was a clerk	
	In kyng Herowdes halle	
	And servyd him of bred and cloth	
	As every kyng befalle.°	it befalls
5	Stevyn out of kechone cam	
	Wyth boris° hed on honde;	a boar's
	He saw a sterre was° fayr and bryght	that was
	Over Bedlem° stonde.	Bethlehem
	He kyst° adoun the boris hed	cast
10	And went into the halle.	
	"I forsak thee, kyng Herowdes,	
	And thi werkes alle.	
	"I forsak thee, kyng Herowdes,	
	And thi werkes alle.	
15	Ther is a chyld in Bedlem° born	Bethlehem
	Is° beter than we alle."	Who is
	"Quat eylyt° thee, Stevene?	**Quat eylyt** What ails
	Quat is thee befalle?°	**is . . .** has befallen you
	Lakkyt thee° eyther mete° or drynk	**Lakkyt thee** Do you lack food
20	In kyng Herowdes halle?"	

516

"Lakkyt me neyther mete ne° drynk   nor
   In kyng Herowdes halle.
Ther is a chyld in Bedlem° born   Bethlehem
   Is beter than we alle."

25 "Quat eylyt° thee, Stevyn?   **Quat eylyt** What ails
   Art thu wod,° or thu gynnyst° to brede?°   crazy begin rave
Lakkyt thee° eyther gold or fe°   **Lakkyt thee** Do you lack
   Or ony ryche wede?"°   property
                                                             garment

"Lakyt me neyther gold ne fe
30   Ne non ryche wede.
Ther is a chyld in Bedlem° born   Bethlehem
   Xal° helpyn us at our nede."   Who shall

"That is also soth,° Stevyn,   **also soth** as true
   Also soth, i-wys,°   indeed
35 As this capoun° crowe xal   capon
   That lyth here in myn dysh."

That word was not so sone seyd,
   That word in that halle,
The capoun crew "*Cristus natus est*"°   **Cristus** . . . Christ is born
40   Among the lordes alle.

"Rysyt° up, myn turmentowres,°   Rise   torturers
   Be to and als be on,°
And ledyt° Stevyn out of this town,   lead
   And stonyt° hym wyth ston."   stone

45 Tokyn he° Stevene   **Tokyn he** They took
   And stonyd hym in the way;
And therfore is his evyn
   On Crystes owyn day.

42. By two and also by one

Robyn and Gandeleyn

(ca. 1450, East Midland)

This is one of the two earliest recorded nonreligious English ballads, the other being *Robin Hood and the Monk* (Child, No. 119). It obviously belongs to a period in which a wide audience was interested in tales of such heroic outlaws as Robin Hood, about whom a whole cycle of ballads developed, and Gamelyn, who is the subject of a romance, *The Tale of Gamelyn* (ca. 1350–70). The resemblance of the name *Robyn* to *Robin Hood* and of *Gandeleyn* to *Gamelyn* is perhaps coincidental, but in its concern for popular justice, the ballad is unmistakably similar to the Robin Hood ballads and the Gamelyn romance. Its terse, impersonal, self-contained, and restrained yet dramatic style is typical of the best ballads that have been recorded in more recent times and presumably also of the innumerable ballads of an earlier age that were never recorded. (According to Piers Plowman in the late fourteenth century, Sloth knew rhymes of Robin Hood better than he knew his paternoster; unfortunately no one at that time bothered to write them down.)

The meter of *Robyn and Gandeleyn* is seven-beat couplets with a repeated refrain; see Introduction, type 7, page 31.

The best edition is Child, No. 115 (cf. No. 117 and No. 119). Child also provides bibliographical material. See also Chambers, *OHEL*, pp. 131–32, 136, 153. The only manuscript is British Museum Sloane 2593, published in *Songs and Carols from a Manuscript in the British Museum of the Fifteenth Century*, ed. Thomas Wright, Warton Club, 4 (London, 1856).

I herde a carpyng° of a clerk   story
    Al at yone° wodes ende   that
Of gode Robyn and Gandeleyn;
    Was ther non other thynge.

5   *Robynn lyth° in grene wode bowndyn.°*   lies   bound

Stronge° thevys wern tho chylderin non°   Confirmed   **tho . . .** those youths not
    But bowmen gode and hende.°   courteous
He° wentyn to wode to getyn hem fleych°   They   **hem fleych** themselves meat
    If God wold it hem° sende.   to them

10   Al day wentyn tho chylderin too°   two
    And fleych fowndyn he non°   none
Til it were ageyn° evyn;   toward
    The chylderin wold gon° hom.   **chylderin . . .** youths were about to go

Half an honderid of fat falyf° der   fallow
15   He comyn ayon,°   **comyn ayon** came upon
And alle he° wern fayr and fat inow,°   they (the deer)   enough
     But markyd° was ther non.°   marked   none (of them)
"By dere God," seyde gode Robyn,
     "Hereof we xul° have on."°   shall   one

20   Robyn bent his joly bowe;
     Therin he set a flo.°   arrow
The fattest der of alle
     The herte he clef a to.°   **clef . . .** split in two

He hadde not the der i-flawe°   flayed
25   Ne° half out of the hyde,   Nor
There cam a schrewde arwe° out of the west   **schrewde arwe** evil arrow
     That felde Robertes pryde.

Gandeleyn lokyd hym est and west
     Be° every syde.   On
30   "Hoo hat° myn mayster slayin?   **Hoo hat** Who has
     Ho hat don this dede?
Xal I° never out of grene wode go   **Xal I** I shall
     Til I se sydis blede."

Gandeleyn lokyd hym est and lokyd west
35   And sowt° under the sunne.   south
He saw a lytil boy°   churl
     He clepyn° Wrennok of Donne,   **He clepyn** They call

A good bowe in his hond,
     A brod arwe° therine,   arrow
40   And fowre-and-twenti goode arwys
     Trusyd° in a thrumme.°   Placed   holder
"Be war thee,° war thee, Gandeleyn,   **Be . . .** Beware
     Herof thu xalt han° summe.   **xalt han** shall have

"Be war thee, war thee, Gandeleyn,
45   Herof thu gyst plenté."°   **gyst plenté** will get plenty
"Ever on° for another," seyde Gandeleyn;   one
     "Mysaunter have he° xal fle!"   **Mysaunter . . .** Disaster may he have who

"Qwerat° xal our marke be?"   At what
     Seyde Gandeleyn.
50   "Everyche° at otheris herte,"   Each
     Seyde Wrennok ageyn.°   in reply

"Ho xal yeve° the ferste schote?"   **xal yeve** shall give
 Seyde Gandeleyn.
"And I xul yeve° thee on beforn,"°   give **on beforn** one at first
55 Seyde Wrennok ageyn.

Wrennok schette a ful° good schote— very
 And he schet not too hye°—   high
Throw the sanchothis° of his bryk;° fork (?) breeches
 It towchyd neyther thye.°   thigh

60 "Now hast thu yovyn° me on beforn,"° given **on beforn** one at first
 Al thus to Wrennok seyde he,
"And throw the myght of Our Lady
 A bettere I xal yeve° thee."   **xal yeve** shall give

Gandeleyn bent his goode bowe
65 And set therin a flo.°   arrow
He schet throw his grene certyl;° short tunic
 His herte he clef on too.°   **clef** . . . split in two

"Now xalt thu never yelpe,° Wrennok, boast
 At ale ne° at wyn   nor
70 That thu hast slawe° goode Robyn slain
 And his knave° Gandeleyn.   retainer

"Now xalt thu never yelpe, Wrennok,
 At wyn ne at ale
That thu hast slawe goode Robyn
75 And Gandeleyn his knave."

Robyn lyghth° in grene wode bowndyn.° lies bound

The Blacksmiths

(ca. 1450, Northeast Midland)

❦

This indignant satire is directed against the blacksmiths who kept the poet awake at night. Their assaults on his senses inspired a rich vocabulary of invective, the force of which the modern reader may occasionally miss. The poet calls his tormentors "water-burners" (l. 22) because of their practice of plunging the glowing iron in cold water in order to temper it. He calls them "horse-clothiers" (l. 21) perhaps because they prepared stylish armor for horses or perhaps simply because they prepared shoes and harnesses for farmhorses.

The poem is written in conventional alliterative verse; see Introduction, type 1, page 29.

The best edition is Kenneth Sisam, *Fourteenth Century Verse and Prose* (Oxford, 1921), pp. 169–70, 257–58. For bibliography see Wells, ch. 4.41.

Swarte, smekyd° smethes, smateryd wyth smoke,	**Swarte, smekyd** Black, smoky	
Dryve me to deth wyth den° of here dyntes.°	din **here dyntes** their blows	
Swech° noys on nyghtes ne herd° men never.	Such **ne herd** heard	
What knavene cry° and clateryng of knockes!	**knavene cry** shouting of workmen	
5 The cammede kongons° cryen after col,° col,	**cammede kongons** twisted monsters **after col** for coal	
And blowen here bellewys that° al here brayn brestes.°	so that bursts	
"Huf, puf," seith that on.° "Haf, paf," that other.	**that on** the one	
Thei spyttyn and spraulyn and spellyn° many spelles.	**spraulyn** . . . shamble and recite	
Thei gnauen and gnacchen;° thei gronys° togydere	**gnauen** . . . grind and gnash their teeth groan	
10 And holdyn hem hote° wyth here° hard hamers.	**holdyn** . . . keep hot their	
Of a bole° hyde ben° here barm-fellys;°	bull are leather aprons	
Here schankes ben schakeled° for the fere-flunderys.°	protectively covered flaming sparks	
Hevy hamerys thei han° that hard ben handled;	have	
Stark° strokes thei stryken on a stelyd stokke.°	Strong **stelyd stokke** steel anvil	
15 "Lus, bus, las, das," rowtyn be rowe.°	**rowtyn** . . . they strike in turn	
Swech dolful a dreme°—the devyl it todryve!°	**dolful** . . . a dreary noise confound	
The mayster longith° a lityl and lascheth° a lesse,°	lengthens hammers smaller piece	
Twyneth hem tweyn and towchith a treble.°		
"Tik, tak, hic, hac, tiket, taket, tyk, tak,		
20 Lus, bus, lus, das." Swych° lyf thei ledyn,°	Such lead	
Alle clothe-merys.° Cryst hem gyve sorwe!°	these horse-clothiers sorrow	
May no man for bren-waterys° on nyght han° hys rest?	water-burners have	

18. Twists them in two and reaches a treble note.

THE
SCOTTISH
RENAISSANCE

ROBERT HENRYSON

The Testament of Cresseid

(ca. 1470, Northern)

≈

All that is known with certainty of Robert Henryson (ca. 1425–ca. 1505) is that his literary career flourished in the last three decades of the fifteenth century and that he lived in Dunfermline. He was probably a master at the Benedictine Abbey grammar school there, but was not necessarily a cleric. Nothing is known for certain of his literary career apart from the surviving works identified with him: *Moral Fables, Orpheus and Eurydice, Robene and Makyne, The Testament of Cresseid,* and a number of other shorter pieces. Like many of his contemporaries, including King James I of Scotland, who wrote *The Kingis Quair,* Henryson was an ardent admirer of Chaucer. *The Testament of Cresseid* particularly expresses this admiration, and the poem soon found its way into the early printed editions of Chaucer as a fitting supplement to *Troilus and Criseyde.*

With stern realism but considerable sympathy Henryson relates the pathetic end of Cresseid, a fate that the more tolerant Chaucer would have hesitated to assign her. Written in rhyme royal, the meter of Chaucer's *Troilus* and of *The Kingis Quair, The Testament of Cresseid* adds Henryson's own Renaissance scholarship, as seen in the descriptions of the gods (stanzas xxi ff.), to Chaucer's style. The meter is seven-line stanzas; see Introduction, type 17, page 32.

The best recent edition is Robert Henryson, *Testament of Cressid,* ed. Denton Fox (London, 1968). For bibliography see *CBEL,* 1.257–58, 5.147; Bennett, *OHEL,* pages 122, 173–76, 285; Geddie, *BMSP,* pages 166–86.

i

Ane doolie sessoun to ane cairfull dyte°
Suld° correspond and be equivalent.
Richt sa° it wes quhen° I began to wryte
This tragedie, the wedder richt fervent,°
5 Quhen Aries in middis° of the Lent
Schouris° of haill can fra° the north discend,°
That scantlie° fra the cauld I micht defend.°

	Should
	so when
	wedder . . . weather being very severe
	the middle
	Showers **can fra** did from send down
	That scantlie So that hardly protect myself

ii

Yit nevertheles within myne oratur°
I stude, quhen° Titan had his bemis° bricht
10 Withdrawin doun and sylit° under cure,°

	chapel
	stude, quhen stood, when beams
	concealed cover

1. A doleful season to a sorrowful poem

And fair Venus, the bewtie of the nicht,
Uprais° and set unto the west full° richt   Rose up   very
Hir goldin face in oppositioun
Of God Phebus direct discending doun.

iii

15 Throw° out the glas hir bemis brast sa° fair   Through   **bemis . . .** beams burst so
That I micht se, on everie syde me by,
The northin wind had purifyit the air
And sched° the mistie cloudis fra° the sky.   scattered   from
The froist freisit,° the blastis bitterly   **froist freisit** frost froze
20 Fra Pole Artick come quhisling° loud and schill,°   whistling   shrill
And causit me remuse aganis° my will.   **remuse aganis** leave against

iv

For I traistit° that Venus, luifis° Quene,   trusted   love's
To quhome sum tyme° I hecht° obedience,   **quhome . . .** whom formerly   promised
My faidit° hart of lufe scho wald° mak grene.   faded   **scho wald** she would
25 And ther-upon with humbill reverence
I thocht° to pray hir hie° Magnificence,   intended   great
Bot for greit cald as than I lattit was°
And in my chalmer° to the fyre can pas.°   chamber   **can pas** passed

v

Thocht° lufe be hait,° yit in ane° man of age   Though   hot   a
30 It kendillis nocht sa° sone as in youtheid°   so   youth
Of quhome° the blude is flowing in ane rage;   whom
And in the auld the curage doif° and deid,   **curage doif** heart dull
Of quhilk the fyre outward is best remeid.
To help be phisike quhair that nature faillit
35 I am expert, for baith I have assaillit.°

vi

I mend the fyre and beikit° me about,   warmed
Than tuik ane° drink my spreitis° to comfort,   a   spirits
And armit me weill fra° the cauld thair-out.   from
To cut the winter nicht and mak it schort,
40 I tuik ane quair°—and left all uther sport—   book
Writtin be° worthie Chaucer glorious   by
Of fair Creisseid and worthie Troylus.

---

27. Except that I was prevented for the time being by the great cold
33–35. For which external heat is the best remedy. In helping through physic when nature's power fails I am expert, for I have known both.

vii

    And thair I fand,° efter that Diomeid   found
    Ressavit° had that lady bricht of hew,°   Received   hue
45 How Troilus neir out of wit abraid°   jumped
    And weipit soir° with visage° paill of hew;   sorrowfully   face
    For quhilk wanhope° his teiris can renew°   **quhilk wanhope** which despair **can renew** flowed
    Quhill° Esperus rejoisit° him agane.   Until   gladdened
    Thus quhyle° in joy he levit,° quhyle in pane.°   for a while   lived   torment

viii

50 Of hir behest° he had greit comforting,   promise
    Traisting° to Troy that scho suld° mak retour,°   Trusting   **scho suld** she should   return
    Quhilk he desyrit maist of eirdly° thing,   earthly
    For-quhy° scho was his only paramour.   Because
    But quhen° he saw passit baith day and hour   when
55 Of hir ganecome,° than sorrow can oppres°   return   **can oppres** oppressed
    His wofull hart in cair and hevines.°   **cair . . .** sorrow and grief

ix

    Of his distres me neidis nocht reheirs,°   **me . . .** I need not relate
    For worthie Chauceir in the samin° buik,   same
    In gudelie termis and in joly veirs,°   **joly veirs** pleasant verse
60 Compylit hes° his cairis, quha° will luik.   has   whoever
    To brek my sleip ane uther quair° I tuik   book
    In quhilk° I fand the fatall destenie   which
    Of fair Cresseid, that endit wretchitlie.

x

    Quha wait gif° all that Chauceir wrait was trew?   **Quha . . .** Who knows if
65 Nor I wait nocht gif this narratioun
    Be authoreist or fenyeit° of the new   **authoreist . . .** authorized or feigned
    Be° sum Poeit, throw° his inventioun,   By   through
    Maid to report the lamentatioun
    And wofull end of this lustie Creisseid,
70 And quhat° distres scho thoillit,° and quhat deid.°   what   **scho thoillit** she suffered   did

xi

    Quhen° Diomeid had all his appetyte   When
    And mair° fulfillit of this fair ladie,   more
    Upon ane uther he set his haill° delyte   whole
    And send to hir ane lybell° of repudie°   bill   divorce
75 And hir excludit fra° his companie.   from
    Than desolait scho° walkit up and doun,   she
    And sum men sayis into the court commoun.°   **court commoun** streets

xii

O fair Cresseid, the flour and A per se° A ... matchless one
Of Troy and Grece, how was thow fortunait° destined
80 To change in filth all thy feminitie,
And be with fleschelie lust sa maculait,° **sa maculait** so stained
And go amang the Greikis air and lait,° **air** ... early and late
Sa giglotlike takand thy foull plesance?°
I have pietie° thow suld fall sic° mischance. pity such

xiii

85 Yit nevertheles quhat° ever men deme° or say, what judge
In scornefull langage, of thy brukkilnes,° frailty
I sall° excuse als far furth° as I may° shall **als** ... as far can
Thy womanheid, thy wisdome and fairnes,
The quhilk° Fortoun hes° put to sic° distres **The quhilk** Which has such
90 As hir pleisit°—and nathing throw° the gilt pleased **nathing throw** not through
Of thee—throw wickit langage to be spilt.° destroyed

xiv

This fair lady, in this wyse° destitute manner
Of all comfort and consolatioun,
Richt privelie, but° fellowschip, on fute° **Richt** ... Very secretly, without foot
95 Disgysit,° passit far out of the toun Disguised
Ane myle or twa,° unto ane° mansioun two a
Beildit° full gay, quhair° hir father Calchas Adorned **gay, quhair** fair, where was
Quhilk° than amang the Greikis dwelland was. Who

xv

Quhen° he hir saw, the caus he can inquyre° When **can inquyre** inquired
100 Of hir cumming. Scho° said, siching full soir:° She **siching** ... sighing very sorrowfully
"Fra° Diomeid had gottin his desyre, When
He wox werie and wald° of me no moir." **wox** ... grew weary and wished
  Quod Calchas: "Douchter, weip° thow not **Douchter, weip** Daughter, weep
   thair-foir.
Peraventure° all cummis° for the best. Perhaps happens
105 Welcum to me; thow art full deir ane gest."° **deir** ... dear a guest

xvi

This auld Calchas, efter° the law was tho,° according to **was tho** which was then
Was keiper of the tempill as ane priest
In quhilk° Venus and hir sone Cupido which
War honourit, and his chalmer° was thame neist,° chamber **thame neist** next to them
110 To quhilk Cresseid with baill aneuch° in breist **baill aneuch** sorrow enough
Usit° to pas,° hir prayeris for to say, Used go
Quhill° at the last, upon ane solempne° day, Until feast

83. Like a harlot taking your foul pleasure?

xvii

As custome was, the pepil far and neir,
Befoir the none,° unto the tempill went   noon
115 With sacrifice devoit° in thair maneir.   devout
Bot still Cresseid, hevie° in hir intent,°   sad   mind
Into the kirk wald° not hir self present   **kirk wald** church would
For giving of the pepill ony deming°   suspicion
Of hir expuls fra° Diomeid the King,   from

xviii

120 Bot past° into ane secreit orature°   she went   chapel
Quhair° scho micht weip° hir wofull desteny.   Where   **micht weip** could weep for
Behind hir bak scho cloisit fast the dure
And on hir kneis bair° fell doun in hy.°   **kneis bair** bare knees   haste
Upon Venus and Cupide angerly
125 Scho cryit out, and said on this same wyse,°   manner
"Allace° that ever I maid you sacrifice.   Alas

xix

"Ye gave me anis° ane devine responsaill°   once   response
That I suld° be the flour of luif° in Troy.   should   love
Now I am maid ane unworthie outwaill,°   outcast
130 And all in cair° translatit is my joy.   **in cair** into sorrow
Quha sall° me gyde?° Quha sall me now convoy   **Quha sall** Who shall   guide
Sen° I fra Diomeid and nobill Troylus   Since
Am clene° excludit, as abject° odious.   completely   outcast

xx

"O fals Cupide, is nane to wyte° bot thow   blame
135 And thy mother, of lufe° the blind Goddes.°   love   Goddess
Ye causit me alwayis understand and trow°   believe
The seid of lufe was sawin° in my face,   sown
And ay° grew grene throw° your supplie and   ever   through
    grace.
Bot now allace° that scid with froist° is slane,   alas   frost
140 And I fra luifferis° left and all forlane."°   lovers   forgotten

xxi

Quhen° this was said, doun in ane extasie,   When
Ravischit in spreit, intill° ane dreame scho fell;   **spreit, intill** spirit, into
And be° apperance hard, quhair° scho did ly,   by   **hard, quhair** heard, where
Cupide the King ringand° ane silver bell,   ringing
145 Quhilk° men micht heir fra hevin unto hell,   Which
At quhais° sound befoir Cupide appeiris°   whose   appear
The sevin planetis[1] discending fra thair spheiris,

[1] Seven planets, namely Saturn, Jupiter, Mars, Sun (Phoebus), Venus, Mercury, Moon (Cynthia).

xxii

Quhilk hes power of all thing generabill°   created
To reull and steir° be thair greit influence   **reull** ... rule and steer
150 Wedder° and wind and coursis variabill.   Weather
And first of all Saturne gave his sentence,
Quhilk gave to Cupide litill reverence,
Bot as ane busteous° churl on° his maneir   rough   in
Come crabitlie° with auster° luik and cheir.°   sourly   severe   countenance

xxiii

155 His face fronsit,° his lyre° was lyke the leid.°   wrinkled   complexion   lead
His teith chatterit, and cheverit° with the chin;   shook
His ene° drowpit, how° sonkin in his heid;   eyes   hollow
Out of his nois° the meldrop° fast can rin,°   nose   mucous   **can rin** ran
With lippis bla° and cheikis leine and thin.   livid
160 The iceschoklis° that fra his hair doun hang   icicles
Was wonder° greit, and as ane speir als° lang.   wonderfully   as

xxiv

Atouir° his belt his lyart lokkis° lay   Over   **lyart lokkis** gray locks
Felterit° unfair, ouirfret° with froistis hoir,°   Tangled   decorated   **froistis hoir** white frost
His garmound° and his gyis full gay° of gray;   garment   **gyis** ... very fair attire
165 His widderit weid° fra him the wind out woir.°   **widdereit weid** withered garment   blew
Ane busteous° bow within his hand he boir,°   stout   carried
Under his girdill ane flasche° of felloun flanis°   sheaf   **felloun flanis** deadly arrows
Fedderit° with ice, and heidit° with hailstanis.°   Feathered   headed   hailstones

xxv

Than° Juppiter, richt fair and amiabill,   Then (came)
170 God of the starnis° in the firmament,   stars
And nureis° to all thing generabill,°   nourisher   created
Fra his father Saturne far different,
With burelie° face, and browis bricht and brent,°   strong   **browis** ... brows fair and smooth
Upon his heid ane garland wonder gay°   **wonder gay** wonderfully fair
175 Of flouris fair as it had bene in May.

xxvi

His voice was cleir, as cristall were his ene,°   eyes
As goldin wyre sa glitterand was his hair,
His garmound° and his gyis° full gay of grene,   garment   attire
With goldin listis° gilt on everie gair.°   borders   gore
180 Ane burelie brand° about his middil bair,°   **burelie brand** stout sword   bore
In his richt hand he had ane groundin° speir,   sharpened
Of his Father the wraith° fra us to weir.°   anger   defend

xxvii

Nixt efter him come Mars the God of ire,
Of strife, debait, and all dissensioun,
185 To chide and fecht, als feirs° as ony fyre,   **fecht** . . . fight, as fierce
In hard harnes, hewmound, and habirgeoun,°
And on his hanche° ane roustie fell fachioun;°   hip **fell fachioun** cruel falchion
And in his hand he had ane roustie sword.
Wrything° his face with mony° angrie word,   Twisting many an

xxviii

190 Schaikand° his sword, befoir Cupide he come   Shaking
With reid visage,° and grislie glowrand ene,°   face **glowrand ene** glowering eyes
And at his mouth ane bullar stude° of fome   **bullar stude** bubble stood
Lyke to ane bair quhetting° his tuskis kene,   **bair quhetting** boar whetting
Richt tuilyeour-lyke, but° temperance in tene;°   **tuilyeour-lyke, but** like a bully, without anger
195 Ane horne he blew, with mony bosteous brag,°   **mony** . . . many a rough blast
Quhilk all this warld with weir° hes maid to wag.°   fear shiver

xxix

Than° fair Phebus, lanterne and lamp of licht,   Then came
Of man and beist, baith frute and flourisching,°   **frute** . . . harvest and growth
Tender nureis,° and banischer of nicht,   nourisher
200 And of the warld causing, be° his moving   by
And influence, lyfe in all eirdlie° thing,   earthly
Without comfort of quhome, of force to nocht°
Must all ga° die that in this warld is wrocht.°   go made

xxx

As king royall he raid° upon his chair   rode
205 The quhilk Phaeton gydit sum tyme, upricht.°   **gydit** . . . drove formerly, indeed
The brichtnes of his face quhen it was bair
Nane micht behald for peirsing° of his sicht.   blinding
This goldin cart with fyrie bemis° bricht   beams
Four yokkit steidis full° different of hew°   very hue
210 But bait° or tyring throw° the spheiris drew.   **But bait** Without stopping through

xxxi

The first was soyr,° with mane als° reid as rois,   reddish brown as
Callit Eoye into the Orient.
The secund steid to name hecht° Ethios,   is called
Quhitlie° and paill, and sum deill ascendent;°   Whitish **sum** . . . somewhat dominant
215 The thrid Peros, richt hait and richt fervent;°   **richt hait** . . . very hot and very fiery

186. In strong armor, helmet, and coat of mail
202. Without whose comfort, of necessity to nothing

The feird° was blak, callit Phlegoney,[2]   fourth
Quhilk rollis Phebus doun into the sey.°   sea

xxxii

Venus was thair present, that goddes gay,°   fair
Hir sonnis querrell° for to defend, and mak   case
220 Hir awin° complaint, cled in ane nyce° array,   own   odd
The ane half grene, the uther half sabill blak;
Quhyte° hair as gold kemmit and sched° abak,   Fair **kemmit** ... combed and parted
Bot in hir face semit° greit variance,   appeared
Quhyles° perfyte treuth, and quhyles inconstance.°   For a while   inconstancy

xxxiii

225 Under° smyling scho was dissimulait,°   When   dissembling
Provocative, with blenkis° amorous,   glances
And suddanely changit and alterait,
Angrie as ony serpent vennemous,
Richt pungitive,° with wordis odious.   stinging
230 Thus variant° scho was, quha list tak keip;°   inconstant **quha** ... whoever pleases take heed
With ane eye lauch,° and with the uther weip,   laughs

xxxiv

In taikning° that all fleschelie paramour   tokening
Quhilk Venus hes in reull° and governance,   rule
Is sum tyme sweit, sum tyme bitter and sour,
235 Richt° unstabill, and full of variance,   Very
Mingit° with cairfull° joy and fals plesance,°   Mixed   sorrowful   delight
Now hait,° now cauld, now blyith,° now full of   hot   happy
    wo,
Now grene as leif, now widderit and ago.°   **widderit** ... withered and gone

xxxv

With buik in hand than come Mercurius,
240 Richt eloquent, and full of rethorie,°   rhetoric
With polite termis and delicious,°   charming
With pen and ink to report all reddie,
Setting sangis and singand° merilie.   **sangis** ... songs and singing
His hude° was reid heklit atouir° his croun,   hood   **reid** ... red fringed around
245 Lyke to ane poeit of the auld fassoun.

xxxvi

Boxis he bair with fyne electuairis,°   electuaries
And sugerit syropis for digestioun,
Spycis belangand° to the pothecairis,   belonging

[2] The names of the four horses of the sun are here derived from Ovid, *Metamorphoses*, ii. 153–54: Eous, Aethon, Pyroeis, and Phlegon.

With mony hailsum° sweit confectioun; **mony hailsum** many a wholesome
250 Doctour in Phisick° cled in ane skarlot goun, Medicine
And furrit° weill, as sic ane aucht° to be, furred ought
Honest and gude, and not ane word culd lie.

xxxvii

Nixt efter him come Lady Cynthia,
The last of all, and swiftest in hir spheir,
255 Of colour blak, buskit° with hornis twa,° dressed two
And in the nicht scho listis° best appeir, is pleased to
Haw° as the leid,° of colour nathing cleir,° Dull in color lead bright
For all hir licht scho borrowis at° hir brother from
Titan, for of hirself scho hes nane uther.

xxxviii

260 Hir gyse° was gray, and full of spottis blak, gown
And on hir brest ane churle³ paintit full evin,° **full evin** very precisely
Beirand° ane bunche of thornis on his bak, Bearing
Quhilk° for his thift° micht clim na nar° the hevin. Who theft **na nar** no nearer
Thus quhen thay gadderit war, thir° goddes sevin, **war, thir** were, these
265 Mercurius thay cheisit with ane assent° **cheisit . . .** chose unanimously
To be foirspeikar° in the Parliament. spokesman

xxxix

Quha° had been thair, and liken° for to heir Whoever minded
His facound° toung, and termis exquisite, eloquent
Of rethorick the prettick° he micht leir° practice learn
270 In breif sermone° ane pregnant sentence wryte.° discourse to write
Befoir Cupide veiling° his cap alyte,° doffing a little
Speiris° the caus of that vocatioun;° He asks summons
And he anone schew° his intentioun. showed

xl

"Lo!" quod Cupide, "quha° will blaspheme the whoever
name
275 Of his awin god, outher° in word or deid, either
To all goddis he dois baith lak° and schame, **baith lak** both fault
And suld° have bitter panis° to his meid.° should torments reward
I say this by yone° wretchit Cresseid, **by yone** of yonder
The quhilk throw° me was sum tyme flour° of through **sum . . .** formerly flower
lufe,° love
280 Me and my mother starklie can reprufe,° **starklie . . .** severely she reproved

³ The Man in the Moon.

xli

"Saying of hir greit infelicitie
I was the caus, and my mother Venus,
Ane blind goddes° hir cald that micht° not se,   goddess   could
With sclander and defame° injurious.   **sclander** ... slander and defamation
285 Thus hir leving° unclene and lecherous   **hir leving** her own living
Scho wald returne on me and my mother,
To quhome° I schew my grace abone° all uther.   whom   above

xlii

"And sen° ye ar all sevin deificait°   since   deified
Participant of devyne sapience,
290 This greit injurie done to our hie estait°   rank
Me think with pane we suld mak recompence.°
Was never to goddes done sic° violence.   such
As weill for yow, as for my self I say,
Thair-foir ga° help to revenge I yow pray."   go

xliii

295 Mercurius to Cupide gave answeir
And said: "Schir° King, my counsall is that ye   Sir
Refer yow to the hiest planeit heir,
And tak to him the lawest° of degre,   lowest
The pane° of Cresseid for to modifie;°   torment   judge
300 As God Saturne, with him tak Cynthia."
"I am content," quod he, "to tak thay twa."°   two

xliv

Than thus proceidit, Saturne and the Mone,
Quhen thay the mater rypelie° had degest,°   fully   considered
For the dispyte° to Cupide scho had done,   contempt
305 And to Venus oppin° and manifest,   clear
In all hir lyfe with pane° to be opprest,   torment
And torment sair° with seiknes incurabill,   sorrowful
And to all lovers be abhominabill.

xlv

This duleful sentence Saturne tuik on hand,
310 And passit doun quhair cairfull° Cresseid lay,   **quhair cairfull** where sorrowful
And on hir heid he laid ane frostie wand.
Than lawfullie on° this wyse can° he say: **lawfullie on** by law in **wyse can** manner did
"Thy greit fairnes and all thy bewtie gay,°   fair
Thy wantoun blude, and eik° thy goldin hair,   also
315 Heir° I exclude fra thee for evermair.   Here

291. It seems to me that with torment we should exact atonement.

xlvi

"I change thy mirth into melancholy,
Quhilk is the mother of all pensivenes;
Thy moisture and thy heit in cald° and dry;   **in cald** into cold
Thyne insolence, thy play and wantones
320 To greit diseis; thy pomp and thy riches
In mortall neid; and greit penuritie
Thow suffer sall,° and as ane beggar die."   shall

xlvii

O cruel Saturne, fraward and angrie!
Hard is thy dome,° and too malitious.   judgment
325 On fair Cresseid quhy° hes thow na mercie,   why
Quhilk° was sa° sweit, gentill, and amorous?   Who so
Withdraw thy sentence and be gracious
As thow was never; sa schawis thow thy deid,°   **schawis . . .** your deed reveals you
Ane wraikfull° sentence gevin on fair Cresseid.   vengeful

xlviii

330 Than Cynthia, quhen Saturne past away,
Out of hir sait discendit doun belyve,°   quickly
And red ane bill° on Cresseid quhair scho lay,   decree
Contening this sentence diffinityve:
"Fra heit of bodie I thee now depryve,
335 And to thy seiknes sall° be na recure,°   shall recovery
Bot in dolour thy dayis to indure.

xlix

"Thy cristal ene° minglit with blude I mak;   eyes
Thy voice sa cleir unplesand, hoir, and hace;°   **unplesand . . .** unpleasing, rough, and
                                                       hoarse
Thy lustie lyre° ouirspred with spottis blak;   **lustie lyre** beautiful face
340 And lumpis haw° appeirand in thy face.   livid
Quhair thow cummis, ilk° man sall° fle the place.   each shall
This° sall thow go begging fra hous to hous,   Thus
With cop° and clapper lyke ane lazarous."°   cup leprous one

l

This doolie° dreame, this uglye visioun   doleful
345 Brocht to an end, Cresseid fra it awoik.
And all that court and convocatioun
Vanischit away; than rais scho up and tuik
Ane poleist° glas, and hir schaddow culd luik.°   polished **culd luik** looked at
And quhen scho saw hir face sa deformait,
350 Gif° scho in hart was wa aneuch,° God wait!°   Whether **wa aneuch** woe enough know

534

li

Weiping full sair,° "Lo quhat° it is," quod sche,   sorrowfully   what
With fraward° langage for to mufe° and steir   perverse   move
Our craibit goddis,° and sa is sene on me!   **craibit goddis** irritable gods
My blaspheming now have I bocht full° deir.   **bocht full** paid for very
355 All eirdlie° joy and mirth I set areir.°   earthly   **set areir** leave behind
Allace° this day, allace this wofull tyde,°   Alas   time
Quhen I began with my goddis for to chyde."

lii

Be° this was said, ane chyld come fra the hall   When
To warne Cresseid the supper was reddy,
360 First knokkit at the dure, and syne culd call:°   **syne . . .** then called
"Madame, your father biddis yow cum in hy.°   haste
He hes mervell° sa lang on grouf° ye ly,   wonder   **on grouf** in groveling
And sayis your prayers bene too lang sum deill.°   **too . . .** somewhat too long
The goddis wait° all your intent full weill."   know

liii

365 Quod scho: "Fair chyld, ga° to my father deir,   go
And pray him cum to speik with me anone."°   at once
And sa he did, and said, "Douchter, quhat cheir?"°   **quhat cheir** how are you
"Allace,"° quod scho, "Father, my mirth is gone."   Alas
"How sa?" quod he; and scho can all expone°   **can . . .** set forth everything
370 As I have tauld, the vengeance and the wraik°   punishment
For hir trespas Cupide on hir culd tak.°   **culd tak** took

liv

He luikit on hir uglye lipper° face,   leper
The quhylk befor was quhite° as lillie flour,   white
Wringand his handis, oftymes he said allace°   alas
375 That he had levit° to se that wofull hour,   lived
For he knew weill that thair was na succour
To hir seiknes, and that dowblit° his pane.°   doubled   torment
Thus was thair cair aneuch° betwix thame twane.   **cair aneuch** sorrow enough

lv

Quhen thay togidder murnit° had full lang,°   mourned   long
380 Quod Cresseid: "Father, I wald° not be kend.°   would   known
Thair-foir in secret wyse° ye let me gang°   manner   go
Unto yone hospitall at the tounis end.
And thidder sum meit° for cheritie me send   food
To leif° upon, for all mirth in this eird°   live   earth
385 Is fra me gane; sic° is my wickit weird."°   such   fate

lvi

Than in ane mantill and ane baver° hat,   beaver
With cop° and clapper wonder prively,°   cup **wonder prively** very secretly
He opnit° ane secreit yet,° and out thair at   opened gate
Convoyit hir, that na man suld° espy,   should
390 Unto ane village half ane myle thair-by,
Delyverit hir in at the spittaill° hous,   leper
And daylie sent hir part of his almous.°   sustenance

lvii

Sum knew hir weill, and sum had na knawledge
Of hir becaus scho was sa deformait,
395 With bylis° blak ouirspred in her visage,°   boils face
And hir fair colour faidit and alterait.
Yit thay presumit,° for hir hie regrait°   suspected **hie regrait** great sorrow
And still murning,° scho was of nobill kin; **still murning** quiet mourning
With better will thair-foir they tuik hir in.

lviii

400 The day passit, and Phebus went to rest;
The cloudis blak ouirquhelmit° all the sky.   overwhelmed
God wait gif° Cresseid was ane sorrowfull gest,° **wait gif** knows if guest
Seeing that uncouth fair and harbery.°   **uncouth...** unaccustomed fare and lodgin̩
But meit° or drink scho dressit° hir to ly   **But meit** Without food prepared
405 In ane dark corner of the house allone.
And on° this wyse° weiping, scho maid hir mone.° in manner lamentation

THE COMPLAINT OF CRESSEID

lix

"O sop of° sorrow, sonkin into cair:°   **sop of** one immersed in sorrow
O cative° Creisseid, for now and ever mair,   wretched
Gane is thy joy and all thy mirth in eird;°   earth
410 Of all blyithnes° now art thou blaiknit bair.° happiness **blaiknit bair** pale bereft
Thair is na salve may saif° thee of thy sair;° **may saif** that can cure sorrow
Fell° is thy fortoun, wickit is thy weird.°   Evil fate
Thy blys is baneist,° and thy baill on breird.° banished **baill...** sorrow overflowing
Under the eirth, God gif° I gravin° wer,   grant buried
415 Quhair° nane of Grece nor yit of Troy micht Where
    heird.°   **micht heird** could hear

lx

"Quhair is thy chalmer° wantounlie besene,° chamber adorned
With burely° bed and bankouris browderit bene,° well-made **bankouris...** covers embroidered beautifully
Spycis and wyne to thy collatioun,

The cowpis° all of gold and silver schene,°	cups bright
420 The sweit meitis,° servit in plaittis clene,	foods
With saipheron sals° of ane gude sessoun,°	**saipheron sals** saffron sauce seasoning
Thy gay garmentis with mony° gudely goun,	many a
Thy plesand lawn° pinnit with goldin prene?°	**plesand lawn** pleasing fine cloths pin
All is areir,° thy greit royall renoun.	past

lxi

425 "Quhair is thy garding° with thir greissis° gay,	garden grasses
And fresche flowris, quhilk the Quene Floray	
Had paintit plesandly in everie pane,°	flowerbed
Quhair thou was wont full merilye in May,	
To walk and tak the dew be° it was day	when
430 And heir° the merle° and mavis mony ane,°	hear blackbird **mony ane** many a one
With ladyis fair in carrolling to gane,°	go
And se the royal rinkis° in thair array,	men
In garmentis gay garnischit on everie grane?°	color

lxii

"Thy greit triumphand° fame and hie honour,	triumphant
435 Quhair thou was callit of eirdlye wichtis flour,°	**of** ... flower of earthly creatures
All is decayit; thy weird° is welterit° so.	fate reversed
Thy hie estait° is turnit in darknes dour.°	rank severe
This lipper ludge° tak for thy burelie bour,°	**lipper ludge** leper lodging **burelie bour** goodly bower
And for thy bed tak now ane bunche of stro;°	straw
440 For waillit° wyne and meitis° thou had tho,°	choice food which then
Tak mowlit° breid, peirrie,° and ceder sour.	mouldy pear cider
Bot cop° and clapper, now is all ago.°	**Bot cop** Except for cup gone

lxiii

"My cleir voice and courtlie carrolling,	
Quhair I was wont with ladyis for to sing,	
445 Is rawk° as ruik,° full hiddeous hoir and hace.°	harsh rook **hoir** ... rough and hoarse
My plesand port° all utheris precelling,°	bearing excelling
Of lustines° I was hald maist conding.°	beauty excellent
Now is deformit the figour of my face;	
To luik on it, na leid° now lyking hes.	person
450 Sowpit° in syte,° I say with sair siching,°	Drowned sorrow **sair siching** sorrowful sighing
Ludgeit° amang the lipper leid, 'Allace!'°	Lodged **lipper** ... leper people, Alas

lxiv

"O ladyis fair of Troy and Grece, attend	
My miserie, quhilk nane may comprehend:	
My frivoll° fortoun, my infelicitie;	miserable
455 My greit mischeif quhilk na man can amend.	

Be war° in tyme, approchis neir the end;   careful
And in your mynd ane mirrour mak of me,
As I am now, peradventure that ye
For all your micht may cum to that same end,
460 Or ellis war, gif ony° war may be.   **ellis** . . . else worse, if any

lxv

"Nocht is your fairnes bot ane faiding flour,
Nocht is your famous laud° and hie honour   praise
Bot wind inflat° in uther mennis eiris.°   blown   ears
Your roising reid° to rotting sall retour.°   **roising reid** rosy red   return
465 Exempill mak of me in your memour,
Quhilk of sic° thingis wofull witnes beiris;   such
All welth in eird,° away as wind it weiris.°   **in eird** on earth   wastes away
Be war° thair-foir; approchis neir the hour.   careful
Fortoun is fikkill, quhen scho beginnis and steiris."°   rules

lxvi

470 Thus chydand° with hir drerie° destenye,   finding fault   sad
Weiping, scho woik° the nicht fra end to end.   lay awake
Bot all in vane; hir dule,° hir cairfull cry   lament
Micht not remeid,° nor yit hir murning mend.°   cure her   **murning mend** mourning
                                                                      relieve
Ane lipper° lady rais and till° hir wend,°   leper   **rais** . . . rose and to   went
475 And said: "Quhy spurnis thow° aganis the wall,   **Quhy** . . . Why do you hurl yourself
To sla° thy self, and mend nathing at all?   slay

lxvii

"Sen° thy weiping dowbillis bot° thy wo,   Since   **dowbillis bot** only doubles
I counsall thee mak vertew of ane neid,
To leir° to clap thy clapper to and fro,   learn
480 And leir efter° the law of lipper leid."°   according to   **lipper leid** leper people
Thair was na buit,° bot furth with thame scho   remedy
      yeid°   went
Fra place to place, quhill° cauld and hounger sair°   while   sore
Compellit hir to be ane rank beggair.

lxviii

That samin° tyme, of Troy the garnisoun,°   same   warriors
485 Quhilk had to° chiftane worthie Troylus,   as
Throw jeopardie of weir° had strikken doun   war
Knichtis of Grece in number mervellous.
With greit tryumphe and laude° victorious   praise
Agane° to Troy richt° royallie thay raid°   Back   very   rode
490 The way quhair Cresseid with the lipper baid.°   stayed

lxix

Seeing that companie, thai come; all with ane
     stevin.°   **ane stevin** one voice
Thay gaif° ane cry, and schuik coppis gude speid;°   gave   **schuik . . .** shook their cups rapidly
Said: "Worthie Lordis, for Goddis lufe° of hevin,   love
To us lipper, part of° your almous-deid."°   **part of** distribute   charity
495 Than to thair cry nobill Troylus tuik heid,
Having pietie, neir by the place can pas°   **can pas** passed
Quhair Cresseid sat, not witting° quhat scho was.   knowing

lxx

Than upon him scho kest up baith° hir ene,°   **kest . . .** raised both   eyes
And with ane blenk° it come into his thocht   glance
500 That he sumtime hir face befoir had sene.
Bot scho was in sic plye° he knew hir nocht.   state
Yit than hir luik° into his mynd it brocht   appearance
The sweit visage and amorous blenking°   expression
Of fair Cresseid, sumtyme° his awin° darling.   formerly   own

lxxi

505 Na wonder was, suppois in mynd that he°
Tuik° her figure° sa sone, and lo now quhy?°   Recognized   appearance   why
The idole° of ane thing in cace° may be   image   **in cace** by chance
Sa deip imprentit in the fantasy
That it deludis the wittis° outwardly,   senses
510 And sa appeiris in forme and lyke estait,°   condition
Within the mynd as it was figurait.°   pictured

lxxii

Ane spark of lufe° than till° his hart culd spring,°   love   to   **culd spring** sprang
And kendlit all his bodie in ane fyre.
With hait° fevir ane sweit° and trimbling   hot   sweat
515 Him tuik, quhill° he was reddie to expyre.   until
To beir his scheild his breist began to tyre.
Within ane quhyle° he changit mony hew,°   while   **mony hew** many a hue
And nevertheles not ane ane uther knew.°   **not . . .** one knew not the other

lxxiii

For knichtlie pietie and memoriall
520 Of fair Cresseid, ane gyrdill can° he tak,   did
Ane purs of gold, and mony gay jowall,
And in the skirt of Cresseid doun can swak;°   **can swak** threw
Than raid° away, and not ane word he spak,   rode
Pensive in hart, quhill° he come to the toun,   until
525 And for greit cair° oft syis° almaist fell doun.   sorrow   times

505. It was no wonder if he in his own mind

lxxiv

The lipper folk to Cresseid than can draw°   **can draw** drew
To se the equall distributioun
Of the almous,° bot quhen the gold thay saw, alms
Ilk° ane to uther prevelie can roun,°   Each **prevelie** . . . secretly whispered
530 And said: "Yone lord hes mair affectioun,
How ever it be, unto yone lazarous,°   leprous one
Than to us all. We knaw be° his almous." by

lxxv

"Quhat lord is yone," quod scho; "have ye na
   feill,°   knowledge
Hes done to us so greit humanitie?"
535 "Yes," quod a lipper man, "I knaw him weill.
Schir Troylus it is, gentill and fre."°   **gentill** . . . noble and generous
Quhen Cresseid understude that it was he,
Stiffer° than steill° thair stert° ane bitter stound° Stronger steel leapt pang
Throwout hir hart, and fell doun to the ground.

lxxvi

540 Quhen scho ouircome,° with siching° sair and sad, came to sighing
With mony° cairfull cry and cald° "Ochane": many a cold
"Now is my breist with stormie stoundis stad,° beset
Wrappit in° wo, ane wretch full will of wane."° **Wrappit in** Enveloped by **will** . . . devoi
            of purpose
Than swounit scho oft or° scho culd refrane,° before restrain herself
545 And ever in hir swouning cryit scho thus:
"O fals Cresseid and trew knicht Troylus.

lxxvii

"Thy lufe,° thy lawtie,° and thy gentilnes, love faithfulness
I countit small in my prosperitie,
Sa elevait I was in wantones,
550 And clam° upon the fickill quheill° sa hie. climbed wheel of fortune
All faith and lufe I promissit to thee
Was in the self° fickill and frivolous: same promise
O fals Cresseid, and trew knicht Troilus.

lxxviii

"For lufe of me thow keipt gude continence,
555 Honest and chaist in conversatioun.
Of all wemen protectour and defence
Thou was, and helpit thair opinioun.°   reputation
My mind in fleschelie foull affectioun
Was inclynit to lustis lecherous:
560 Fy fals Cresseid, O trew knicht Troylus.

lxxix

"Lovers, be war,° and tak gude heid° about   careful   heed
Quhome° that ye lufe,° for quhome ye suffer   Whom   love
    paine.°   torment
I lat° yow wit,° thair is richt few thair-out   let   know
Quhome ye may traist to have trew lufe agane.°   back from
565 Preif° quhen ye will, your labour is in vaine.   Try
Thair-foir, I reid,° ye tak thame as ye find,   advise
For thay ar sad° as widdercok° in wind!   steady   weathervane

lxxx

"Becaus I knaw the greit unstabilnes
Brukkill° as glas, into° my self I say,   Frail   unto
570 Traisting in uther als° greit unfaithfulnes,   as
Als unconstant, and als untrew of fay:°   faith
Thocht° sum be trew, I wait° richt few ar thay.   Though   know
Quha findis treuth,° lat him his lady ruse.°   faithfulness   praise
Nane but my self as now I will accuse."

lxxxi

575 Quhen this was said, with paper scho sat doun,
And on this maneir maid hir testament:
"Heir I beteiche° my corps and carioun   bequeath
With° wormis and with taidis° to be rent.   By   toads
My cop° and clapper and myne ornament,°   cup   jewels
580 And all my gold the lipper folk sall have,
Quhen I am deid, to burie me in grave.

lxxxii

"This royall ring, set with this rubie reid,°   red
Quhilk Troylus in drowrie° to me send,°   **in drowrie** as a love token   sent
To him agane I leif it quhen I am deid,
585 To mak my cairfull deid° unto him kend.°   death   known
Thus I conclude schortlie and mak ane end;
My spreit° I leif to Diane quhair scho dwellis,   spirit
To walk with hir in waist woddis° and wellis.°   **waist** ... desolate woods   springs

lxxxiii

"O Diomeid, thou hes baith° broche and belt,   both
590 Quhilk Troylus gave me in takning°   tokening
Of his trew lufe," and with that word scho swelt.°   died
And sone ane lipper man tuik off the ring,
Syne° buryit hir withouttin tarying;   Then
To Troylus furthwith the ring he bair,
595 And of Cresseid the deith he can declair.°   **can declair** declared

lxxxiv

Quhen he had hard° hir greit infirmitie,   heard of
Hir legacie and lamentatioun,
And how scho endit in sic povertie,
He swelt° for wo, and fell doun in ane swoun;   fainted
600 For greit sorrow his hart to brist° was boun;°   break   ready
Siching° full sadlie, said: "I can no moir,   Sighing
Scho was untrew, and wo is me thair-foir."

lxxxv

Sum said he maid ane tomb of merbell gray,
And wrait° hir name and superscriptioun,   wrote
605 And laid it on hir grave quhair that scho lay,
In goldin letteris, conteining this ressoun:°   statement
"Lo, fair ladyis, Cresseid, of Troyis toun,
Sumtyme° countit the flour of womanheid,   Formerly
Under this stane, lait° lipper, lyis deid."   **stane, lait** stone, formerly a

lxxxvi

610 Now worthie wemen, in this ballet° schort   ballad
Maid for your worschip° and instructioun,   honor
Of cheritie, I monische° and exhort,   admonish
Ming° not your lufe° with fals deceptioun.   Mix   love
Beir in your mynd this schort conclusioun°   **schort conclusioun** rapid end
615 Of fair Cresseid, as I have said befoir.
Sen° scho is deid, I speik of hir no moir.   Since

542

WILLIAM DUNBAR

The Dance of the Seven Deadly Sins

(1496 or 1507, Northern)

William Dunbar (ca. 1460–ca. 1521) was born in Scotland, apparently attended St. Andrews University (in Fife), served in the brilliant Scottish court of King James IV, and, evidently late in life, entered the priesthood. In his use of traditional poetic genres, particularly the religious lyric and the satire, he may be said to be one of the last great medieval poets. In his eclectic imitations both of the old alliterative measure and of the intricately rhymed new stanzas of Chaucer, in his experiments with aureate diction, and in his aggressive individualism he is a pioneer of the Renaissance.

Literary personifications of the Seven Deadly Sins were commonplace even before Langland animated them in *Piers Plowman* (p. 277, above), but in *The Dance* Dunbar recreates his own personal vision of them as if he himself had discovered each sin individually, and as a Lowlander, he concludes the poem by directing a characteristically personal satire against his Gaelic-speaking neighbors in the Highlands.

The meter is twelve-line, tail-rhyme stanzas, with two six-line stanzas interspersed; see Introduction, type 21, page 33.

The Poems of William Dunbar, ed. W. M. MacKenzie (Edinburgh, 1932), contains all of the attributed works; *William Dunbar: Poems*, ed. James Kinsley (Oxford, 1958), though only a selection, is very useful. For a dictionary use *DOST*. For the topic of this selection see Morton W. Bloomfield, *The Seven Deadly Sins* (East Lansing, Mich., 1952), pages 236–38. For bibliography see Lewis, *OHEL*; *CBEL*, 1.255–59, 5.147.

Off° Februar the fyiftene° nycht,   Of   fifteenth
Full lang° befoir the dayis lycht,   long
I lay intill° a trance;   in
And then I saw baith° hevin and hell.   both
5 Me thocht,° amangis the feyndis fell°   **Me thocht** It seemed to me   **feyndis fell** fell fiends
Mahoun gart cry ane° dance   **Mahoun** ... Mohammed called out a
Off schrewis° that wer nevir schrevin°   **Off schrewis** Of wretches   absolved
Aganis° the feist of Fasternis Evin°   For   **Fasternis Evin** Shrove Tuesday
To mak thair observance.
10 He bad gallandis ga graith° a gyis°   **gallandis** ... gallants go prepare masquerade
And kast up gamountis° in the skyis   gambols
That last° came out of France.   just

"Lat se," quod he, "now quha° begynnis."   who
With that, the fowll Sevin Deidly Synnis
15 Begowth° to leip at anis.°   Began once
And first of all in dance wes Pryd
With hair wyld° bak and bonet on syd,   dressed
Lyk° to mak waistie wanis.°   Likely **waistie wanis** homes impoverished
And round abowt him as a quheill°   wheel
20 Hang° all in rumpillis to the heill   Hung
His kethat° for the nanis.°   clothing occasion
Mony prowd trumpour° with him trippit;°   cheater danced
Throw skaldand° fyre ay° as thay skippit,°   scalding ever skipped
Thay gyrnd° with hiddous granis.°   grimaced groans

25 Heilie° harlottis on hawtane wyis°   Scornful **on . . .** in disdainful manner
Come in with mony sindrie gyis,°   **sindrie gyis** varied style
Bot yit luche° nevir Mahoun.°   laughed Mohammed
Quhill° preistis come in with bair-schevin nekkis,   When
Than all the feyndis lewche° and maid gekkis,°   laughed faces
30 Blak Belly and Bawsy Brown.

Than Yre come in with sturt° and stryfe.   disturbance
His hand wes ay° upoun his knyfe;   ever
He brandeist° lyk a beir.°   menaced boar
Bostaris, braggaris, and barganeris°   wranglers
35 Eftir him passit into° pairis,   in
All bodin° in feir° of weir,°   ready equipment war
In jakkis and stryppis° and bonettis of steill;   **jakkis . . .** padded jackets and bands
Thair leggis wer chenyeit° to the heill.   chainmailed
Frawart° wes thair affeir.°   Aggressive behavior
40 Sum upoun udir° with brandis beft;°   others **brandis beft** swords beat
Sum jaggit° uthiris to the heft°   stabbed hilt
With knyvis that scherp cowd scheir.°   **cowd scheir** could cut

Nixt in the dance followit Invy,
Fild full of feid° and fellony,   feud
45 Hid° malyce and dispyte.°   Hidden spite
For pryvie hatrent° that tratour trymlit.°   **pryvie hatrent** secret hatred trembled
Him followit mony freik dissymlit°   **mony . . .** many a dissembling man
With fenyeit wirdis quhyte,°   **fenyeit . . .** feigned fair words
And flattereris into° menis facis,   to
50 And bakbyttaris in secreit places
To ley° that had delyte,   lie
And rownaris° of fals lesingis.°   whisperers lies
Allace that courtis of noble kingis
Of thame can nevir be quyte!°   quit

Nixt him in dans come Cuvatyce,
Rute of all evill and grund° of vyce,
That nevir cowd be content.
Catyvis,° wrechis, and ockeraris,°
Hud-pykis, hurdaris, and gadderaris°
60 All with that warlo° went.
Out of thair throttis thay schot on udder°
Hett° moltin gold, me thocht° a fudder,°
As fyreflawcht° maist fervent.
Ay° as thay tomit thame° of schot,
65 Feyndis° fild thame new up to the thrott
With gold of allkin prent.°

    Syne Sweirnes,° at the secound bidding,
Come lyk a sow out of a midding;°
Full slepy wes his grunyie.°
70 Mony sweir, bumbard belly-huddroun,°
Mony slute daw° and slepy duddroun°
Him servit ay° with sounyie.°
He drew thame furth intill° a chenyie,°
And Belliall with a brydill renyie°
75 Evir lascht thame on the lunyie.°
In dance thay war so slaw of° feit,
Thay° gaif thame in the fyre a heit°
And maid tham quicker of counyie.°

    Than Lichery, that lathly cors,°
80 Come berand° lyk a bagit° hors,
And Ydilnes did him leid.
Thair wes with him ane ugly sort°
And mony stynkand,° fowll tramort°
That had in syn bene deid.
85 Quhen° thay wer entrit° in the dance,
Thay wer full strenge° of countenance
Lyk turkas birnand reid.°
All° led thay uthir° by the tersis,°
Suppois° thay fyllt with thair ersis,°
90 It mycht° be na remeid.°

    Than the fowll monstir Glutteny
Off wame unsasiable° and gredy
To dance he did him dres.°
Him followit mony fowll drunckart°
95 With can and collep, cop °and quart,
In surffet and exces.

70. Many a slothful, oafish fat hulk

Glosses:

grund° source
Catyvis° Scoundrels ockeraris° userers
Hud-pykis ... Misers, hoarders, and gatherers
warlo° deceiver
udder° others
Hett° Hot **me thocht** it seemed to me fudder° mass
As fyreflawcht Like lightning
Ay° Ever **tomit thame** emptied themselves
Feyndis° Fiends
allkin prent every kind of impression

Syne Sweirnes Then Sloth
midding° dung heap
grunyie° snout
belly-huddroun°
slute daw a sluttish slattern duddroun° sloven
ay° ever sounyie° attention
intill° in chenyie° chain
renyie° rein
lunyie° hindquarters
of° on their
Thay° They (the fiends) heit° heating
counyie° response (?)

lathly cors loathsome body
berand° neighing bagit° gelded
sort° group
mony stynkand many a stinking tramort° corpse
Quhen° When entrit° entered
full strenge very strange
turkas ... tongs glowing red
All° Though uthir° others tersis° penises
Suppois° Which though **with** ... ersis° their bottoms with
It mycht There could **na remeid** no remedy

Off ... Of unsasiable° belly insatiable
him dres prepare himself
drunckart° drunkard
collep, cop flagon, cup

545

Full° mony a waistles wallydrag°   Very   wastrel
With wamis unweildable° did furth wag   **wamis unweildable** bellies unwieldy
In creische° that did incres.   blubber
100 "Drynk!" ay° thay cryit with mony a gaip.°   ever   gasp
The feyndis° gaif thame hait leid° to laip;°   fiends   **hait leid** hot lead   lap up
Thair lovery° wes na° les!   allowance   no

     Na menstrallis playit to thame, but° dowt,   without
For glemen thair wer haldin owt°   **haldin owt** kept out
105 Be° day and eik° by nycht,   By   also
Except a menstral that slew a man;
Swa till° his heretage he wan°   **Swa till** So to   won
And entirt° be breif° of richt.°   entered   writ   right

     Than cryd Mahoun° for a Heleand padyane;°   Mohammed   **Heleand padyane**
                                             Highland pageant
110 Syne° ran a feynd° to feche MakFadyane¹   Then   fiend
Far northwart in a nuke.
Be° he the correnoch° had done schout,   When   lament
Erschemen° so gadderit him abowt   Ersemen (Highlanders)
In Hell grit rowme° thay tuke.   **grit rowme** great space
115 Thae tarmegantis° with tag and tatter   **Thae tarmegantis** Those savages
Full° lowd in Ersche begowth° to clatter   Very   **Ersche begowth** Erse (Gaelic) began
And rowp° lyk revin and ruke.°   croaked   **revin . .** raven and rook
The devill sa devit° wes with thair yell   **sa devit** so dazed
That in the depest pot of hell
120 He smorit° thame with smuke.   smothered

---

¹ 'MacFadyan,' that is, some typical Highland Scot, or perhaps the traitor MacFadyan, who, according to Henry the Minstrel's *Wallace*, was slain by Wallace.

WILLIAM DUNBAR

On the Resurrection of Christ

(ca. 1500–12, Northern)

As in the previous selection from Dunbar (see p. 543), the topic here is commonplace, but the pealing organ notes of this Ascension Day lyric represent the particular hymnodic genius of Dunbar.

The meter is eight-line stanzas; see Introduction, type 19, page 33.

The Poems of William Dunbar, ed. W. M. MacKenzie (Edinburgh, 1932), contains all the attributed works; *William Dunbar: Poems*, ed. James Kinsley (Oxford, 1958), though only a selection, is very useful. For a dictionary use *DOST*. For bibliography see Lewis, *OHEL*; *CBEL*, 1.258–59, 5.147.

Done° is a battell on the dragon blak;	Completed	
Our campioun° Christ confountet hes° his force.	champion	has
The yettis° of Hell ar brokin with a crak;	gates	
The signe triumphall ras't° is of the Croce;°	raised	Cross
5 The divillis trymmillis° with hiddous voce;°	tremble	voice
The saulis ar borrowit° and to the blis can go;	redeemed	
Christ with his blud our ransonis does indoce.°	ensure	
Surrexit Dominus de sepulchro.°		
Dungin° is the deidly dragon Lucifer,	Stricken	
10 The crewall serpent with the mortall stang,°	sting	
The auld, kene tegir° with his teith on-char,°	**kene tegir** bold tiger ajar	
Quhilk° in await hes lyne° for us so lang,	Who lain	
Thinking to grip us in his clowis strang.°	**clowis strang** strong claws	
The mercifull Lord wald nocht° that it wer so;	**wald nocht** did not wish	
15 He maid him for to felye of that fang.°	**felye . . .** miss that grasp	
Surrexit Dominus de sepulchro.		
He for our saik that sufferit to be slane		
And lyk a lamb in sacrifice wes dicht°	prepared	
Is lyk a lyone rissin up agane		
20 And as gyane raxit Him on hicht.°		

8. The Lord has risen from the sepulchre.
20. And like a giant has raised Himself on high.

547

Sprungin is Aurora radius° and bright,   radiant
On-loft° is gone the glorius Appollo,   Aloft
The blisfull day depairtit fro the nycht.
Surrexit Dominus de sepulchro.

25   The grit° victour agane is rissin on hicht°   great   high
That, for our querrell,° to the deth was woundit.   cause
The sun that wox° all paill now schynis bricht,   grew
And, dirknes clerit, our faith is now refoundit.°   restored
The knell of mercy fro the hevin is soundit,
30   The Cristin° ar deliverit of thair wo,   Christians
The Jowis and thair errour ar confoundit.
Surrexit Dominus de sepulchro.

The fo is chasit, the battell is done ceis,°   **done ceis** ceased
The presone brokin, the jewellouris fleit and flemit,°   **jewellouris** . . . jailors expelled and routed
35   The weir° is gon, confermit is the peis,   war
The fetteris lowsit,° and the dungeoun temit,°   loosed   emptied
The ransoun maid, the presoneris redemit.
The feild is win, ourcumin° is the fo,   overcome
Dispulit° of the tresur that he yemit.°   Despoiled   guarded
40   *Surrexit Dominus de sepulchro.*

WILLIAM DUNBAR

The Golden Targe

(ca. 1500–12, Northern)

❧

The Golden Targe is an allegorical dream vision heavily indebted to Chaucer. The poet falls asleep on a May morning, is attacked by the forces of Venus, is overcome by Beauty despite the protection of Reason's Golden Shield, is delivered over to Heaviness, and then awakens. Graceful though this highly conventional vision may be, the main point of interest is the modest conclusion excerpted below. Here Dunbar (see p. 543) acknowledges his indebtedness to Chaucer, Gower, and Lydgate as the masters who have inspired him.

The meter is nine-line stanzas; see Introduction, type 20, page 33.

The Poems of William Dunbar, ed. W. M. MacKenzie (Edinburgh, 1932), contains all the attributed works; *William Dunbar: Poems*, ed. James Kinsley (Oxford, 1958), though only a selection, is very useful. For a dictionary use *DOST*. For bibliography see Lewis, *OHEL*; *CBEL*, 1.258–59, 5.147.

[Lines 253–79]

O reverend Chaucere, rose of rethoris° all—   rhetoricians
As in° oure tong ane flour imperiall—   **As in** In
    That raise° in Britane evir, quho redis° richt,   arose   **quho redis** whoever interprets
Thou beris of makaris° the tryumph riall.°   **beris . . .** carry off from poets   royal
5   Thy fresch, anamalit° termes celicall°   enameled   celestial
    This mater coud illumynit° have full° brycht.   illuminated   very
    Was thou noucht of oure Inglisch all the lycht,
Surmounting eviry tong terrestriall,
    Alls fer° as Mayis morow° dois mydnycht?   **Alls fer** As far   morning

10   O morall Gower and Ludgate laureate,
Your sugurit lippis and tongis aureate
    Bene° to oure eris cause of grete delyte.   Are
Your angel mouthis most mellifluate
Oure rude langage has clere illumynate°   **clere illumynate** brightly illuminated
15   And faire ourgilt° oure speche that imperfyte   overgilded
    Stude or° your goldyn pennis schupe° to wryte.   **Stude or** Stood before   **pennis schupe** pens began
This ile before° was bare and desolate   **ile before** isle previously
    Off° rethorike or lusty, fresch endyte.°   Of   composition

Thou lytill quair,[1] be evir obedient,
20   Humble, subject, and symple of entent
      Before the face of eviry connyng wicht.°   **connyng wicht** competent critic
    I knaw quhat° thou of rethorike hes spent.°   what   **hes spent** have expended
    Off all hir lusty rosis redolent
      Is none into thy gerland sett on hicht.°   high
25   Eschame tharof,° and draw thee° out of sicht.   **Eschame tharof** Be modest therefore
    Rude is thy wede, disteynit,° bare, and rent.   **draw thee** withdraw
      Wele aucht° thou be aferit° of the licht.   **wede, disteynit** garment, stained
                                                           ought   afraid

[1] Either the manuscript booklet containing this poem or a volume of the poet's collected works.

LINGUISTIC APPENDICES

LINGUISTIC SYMBOLS

The following symbols are used throughout the discussion in Appendices 1, 2, and 3. To clarify the ambiguities of Middle English spelling, diacritical marks have been added to the Middle English examples listed in the center column of Appendix 1 and elsewhere in the linguistic commentary and to the letters *ö* and *ü* printed in the text though these were not used by medieval scribes.

[ ] [:]	Brackets enclose the standard International Phonetic Association Alphabet symbols. Modern approximations of the sounds represented have been provided in Appendix 1. Brackets with no symbol enclosed represent the absence of any sound. A colon after a symbol represents a long sound.
ā ē ī ō ū	represent long vowels contrasting in length of duration with ă ĕ ĭ ŏ ŭ.
ă ĕ ĭ ŏ ŭ	represent short vowels.
ė	represents the final, unstressed *schwa* sound, described under Phoneme 16.
ę̄	represents the close *e* sound [e:], described under Phoneme 3.
ę̄ ę̆	represent the open *e* sounds [ɛ:] and [ɛ], described under Phonemes 4 and 15.
ọ	represents the *u* sound of Modern English *pull*, for which Middle English scribes used an *o* in native words such as *son* and *lŏvė* (Phoneme 19).
ọ̄	represents the close *o* sound [o:], described under Phoneme 8.
ǭ ǫ̆	represent the open *o* sounds [ɔ:] and [ɔ], described under Phonemes 9 and 18.
ȫ ȫ̆	represent the Western Middle English sounds of the mid-position *o* vowels described under the alternate Phonemes 3A and 15A.
ü ü̆	represent the Western Middle English sounds of the mid-position *u* vowels described under the alternate Phonemes 7A and 17A.

Appendix 1: The Pronunciation of Middle English

The term *pronunciation* inevitably tends to convey by association the classical fallacy that letters have "values" that we award to them when we pronounce them. Actually, however, letters serve only to indicate what sound groups the writer intends us to utter when we reproduce his words in speech. Speakers of the influential dialect of Middle English in the Southeast Midland area (including London) around 1400, such as Chaucer and Gower, used over forty contrasting sounds, which are listed below as individual phonemes (including, for the sake of clarifying the arbitrary spelling system, some items such as [ks] that are clusters of phonemes).

To represent these sounds, Middle English scribes used the modern alphabet, except that *j* was not usually differentiated from *i*, and *v* was not usually differentiated from *u*, and they employed in addition the Old English letters þ (thorn, for *th*) and ȝ (yogh, used for *gh* and *y* and for some other purposes). Early scribes also used Old English Ƿ (wen, for *w*). In the printing of the texts in this anthology, the thorn, yogh, and wen symbols have been replaced by *th*, *gh* or *y* (or other appropriate phonetic representation), and *w* respectively. (See Plates 1–6, pp. 16–28.)

Early Middle English scribes did not always distinguish between *c* and *ch* and between *g* and *y*. In ambiguous cases occurring in the first two selections *c* meaning *ch* has been printed *ċ* (Phoneme 22, below), and *g* meaning *y* has been printed as *ġ* (Phoneme 48). The following list of phonemes, however, does not attempt to list all the phonemes and graphemes of Early Middle English.

Speakers of Western Middle English dialects, such as the author of *The Pearl* (West Midland) and Langland (Southwestern), used four vowels (Phonemes 3A, 7A, 15A, and 17A) as phonetically distinct variants that did not occur in the Southeast Midland area. In our texts, to help the reader recognize and pronounce these vowels, we have specially marked them with umlauts as *ö* and *ü* (without indication of length). There are many other phonetic differences between the various Middle English dialects, but a discussion of them lies beyond the scope of this work.

Middle English scribes did not use a distinct symbol for each distinct sound (the letter *a*, for instance, was used for long Phoneme 1 [ɑ:] *nāmė* and for short Phoneme 14 [a] *măn*). Neither did they represent one phoneme consistently by one spelling (Phoneme 3 was spelled indifferently *e* or *ee*, *bę̄* or *bę̄e* '[to] be'), and usage varied from area to area, even when scribes were representing the same phonetic values (as with *shę̄* and *schę̄*). Middle English sounds not only varied from dialect to dialect and from social level to social level but also altered during the development of the language. The word 'boat,' for instance, which was spelled *bāt* in Old English and Early Middle English, was pronounced with Phoneme 1 [ɑ:]; in Later Middle English it was spelled *bǭot* and pronounced with Phoneme 9 [ɔ:]; the vowel in Modern English *boat* has shifted to Phoneme 8 [o:].

Middle English phoneme in phonetic spelling (with modern approximation)	Middle English spelling(s) with Middle English example	(Modern English derivative [with modern phoneme])
LONG VOWELS AND DIPHTHONGS		
1. [ɑ:] (father)	a (aa) nāmė	(name [e:])
2. [au] (house)	au (aw) cáusė	(cause [ɔ:])
3. [e:] (bay)	e (ee) bẹ̄	(be [i:])
3A. [ö:] (Germ. schön)	o (eo) bọ̄	(be [i:])
4. [ɛ:] (ebb, prolonged)	e (ee) hẹ̄eth	(heath [i:])
5. [ɛi] (e of ebb gliding to i of it)	ai (ay), ei (ey) dāi	(day [e:])
6. [ɛu] (e of ebb gliding to u of pull)	eu (ew) knẹ̄w	(knew [ju:]
7. [i:] (fear)	i (y) fȳr	(fire [ai])
7A. [ü:] (Germ. Führer)	u (ui) fǖr	(fire [ai])
8. [o:] (note)	o (oo) fọ̄dė	(food [u:])
9. [ɔ:] (naught)	o (oo) bọ̄ot	(boat [o:])
10. [ɔi] (boy)	oi (oy) bōy	(boy [ɔi])
11. [ɔu] (o of oft gliding to u of pull)	ou (ow) sọ̄wlė	(soul [o:])
12. [u:] (rule)	ou (ow) hōus	(house [au])
13. [ju:] (cure)	eu (ew), u reūlė, cūrė	(rule [u:], cure [ju])
SHORT VOWELS		
14. [a] (Germ. Mann)	a măn	(man [æ])
15. [ɛ] (heaven)	e hĕvenė	(heaven [ɛ])
15A. [ö] (Germ. öffnen)	o (eo) hĕvenė	(heaven [ɛ])
16. [ə] (Stella, with un-stressed final)	e nāmĕ	(name [ ])
17. [i] (sin)	i sĭnnė	(sin [ɪ])

Middle English phoneme in phonetic spelling (with modern approximation)	*Middle English spelling(s) with Middle English example*	*(Modern English derivative [with modern phoneme])*
17A. [ü] (Germ. Gl*ü*ck)	u s*ŭ*nnė	(s*i*n [ɪ])
18. [ɔ] (*o*ften)	o *ǫ*ften	(*o*ften [ɔ])
19. [u] (p*u*ll)	o, u s*ŏ*nė, p*ŭ*llė	(s*o*n [ʌ], p*u*ll [u])
CONSONANTS		
20. [b] (*b*oy)	b *b*oy	(*b*oy [b])
21. [k] (*c*alm, *k*eep)	c, k *c*almė, *k*epė, *k*nowė	(*c*alm, *k*eep [k], *k*now [ ])
22. [tʃ] (*ch*ild)	ch (cch), *ċ* *ċ*ild, *ch*ild, fe*cch*ė	(*ch*ild, fet*ch* [tʃ])
23. [d] (*d*eem)	d *d*emė	(*d*eem [d])
24. [f] (*f*eel)	f *f*elė, o*f*	(*f*eel [f], o*f* [v])
25. [g] (*g*ame)	g (gg) *g*amė, do*gg*ė, *g*nawė	(*g*ame, do*g* [g], *g*naw [ ])
26. [dʒ] (*g*entle, *j*udge)	g (gg), j *g*entil, *j*ugge	(*g*entle, *j*udge [dʒ])
27. [x] (Scot. lo*ch*, Germ. Ba*ch*)	gh ni*gh*t	(ni*gh*t [ ])
28. [h] (*h*ome)	h *h*oom	(*h*ome [h])
29. [ ] (*h*onest)	h *h*onest	(*h*onest [ ])
30. [l] (*l*arge)	l *l*argė	(*l*arge) [l])
31. [m] (*m*ore)	m *m*orė	(*m*ore [m])
32. [n] (*n*ame, si*g*n)	n, gn, *n*amė, si*gn*ė	(*n*ame, si*g*n [n])
33. [ŋg] (fi*n*ger)	ng fi*ng*er, thi*ng*	(fi*ng*er [ŋg], thi*ng* [ŋ])
34. [ŋk] (thi*n*k)	nk thi*nk*ė	(thi*nk* [ŋk])
35. [p] (*p*age)	p *p*agė	(*p*age [p])
36. [kw] (*qu*een)	qu *qu*enė	(*qu*een [kw])
37. [r] (*r*age)	r *r*agė	(*r*age [r])
38. [s] (*s*ervice)	s, c *s*ervicė, wa*s*	(*s*ervice [s], wa*s* [z])
39. [z] (*z*odiac, cau*s*e)	s, z cau*s*e, *z*odiac	(cau*s*e, *z*odiac [z])

Middle English phoneme in phonetic spelling (with modern approximation)	Middle English spelling(s) with Middle English example	(Modern English derative [with modern phoneme])
40. [ʃ] (*ship*)	sh (sch) *ship*	(*ship* [ʃ])
41. [t] (*teach*)	t *teche*	(*teach* [t])
42. [θ] (*thin*)	th *thynnė, thennė*	(*thin* [θ], *then* [ð])
43. [ð] (*other*)	th *other*	(*other* [ð])
44. [v] (*vice*)	v *vicė*	(*vice* [v])
45. [w] (*was*)	w *was, wrecchė*	(*was* [w], *wretch* [ ])
46. [hw] (*what*, not *watt*)	wh *what, who*	(*what* [hw], *who* [h])
47. [ks] (*six*)	x *six*	(*six* [ks])
48. [j] (*your*)	y, ġ *your, ġaet*	(*your, yet* [j])

Appendix 2: The Middle English Verb

Like their Modern English counterparts, Middle English verbs relied on two different contrast systems to signal differences in tense. Weak verbs added a *d* or *t* to mark the past tense (modern *love: loved*), and strong verbs altered the root vowel to mark the past (*ride: rode*). The Southeast Midland dialect of Middle English (that of Chaucer and Gower) showed the following typical forms around 1400:

WEAK   STRONG

PRESENT INDICATIVE

Ī   lóvė   wē lóvė(n)   Ī   rīdė   wē rīdė(n)
thōu lóvest   yē lóvė(n)   thōu rīdest/rītt yē rīdė(n)
hē lóveth   they lóvė(n)   hē   rīdeth/rītt   they rīdė(n)

PRESENT SUBJUNCTIVE

(if) Ī   lóvė   wē lóvė(n)   Ī   rīdė   wē rīdė(n)
thōu lóvė   yē lóvė(n)   thōu ride   yē rīdė(n)
hē   lóvė   they lóvė(n)   hē   ride   they rīdė(n)

PAST INDICATIVE

Ī   lóvedė   wē lóvedė(n)   Ī   rōd   wē rĭdė(n)
thōu lóvedest yē lóvedė(n)   thōu rĭde   yē rĭdė(n)
hē lóvedė   they lóvedė(n)   hē   rōd   they rĭdė(n)

555

PAST SUBJUNCTIVE

(if)	Ī lóvedė	wē lóvedė(n)	Ī rĭdė	wē rĭdė(n)
	thou lóvedė	yē lóvedė(n)	thou rĭdė	yē rĭdė(n)
	hē lóvedė	thēy lóvedė(n)	hē rĭdė	thēy rĭdė(n)

COMPOUND PAST

Ī havė (y-) lóved   Ī am (y-) rĭden

Although most of the differences between the verb system of Southeast Midland Middle English and that of the Received Standard of Modern English are self-evident, the following important differences should be noted.

(1) The *thou* forms, now archaic, were regularly used in intimate conversation.
(2) The third person singular *hē* present forms, regularly ended in the now archaic *eth*, not *s*, as in Modern English.
(3) All verbs, weak and strong, with roots ending in *d* or *t* could form contracted *thou* and *hē* forms in the present indicative: *hē sendeth* or *hē sent* (the past would be *hē sentė*).
(4) All plural forms, present and past, of weak and strong verbs ended in *en*, now archaic, and this ending could be contracted to a final unstressed but pronounced *ė*.
(5) Contrasting subjunctive forms, now largely archaic, were regularly used with *if* clauses and similar hypothetical expressions (*if hē cómė*, Modern English, *if he comes*).
(6) In the past indicative of many strong verbs there was a vowel contrast (now eliminated) between the root vowel of the *Ī-hē* forms and the root vowel of the *thou-wē-yē-thēy* forms: *Ī rǫd: wē rĭdė(n)* (Modern English, *I rode, we rode*); *Ī flē: wē flŭė(n)* (modern *flew*); *Ī drănk: wē dronkė(n)* (modern *drank*); *Ī stăl: wē stę̄lė(n)* (modern *stole*); *Ī ăt: wē ētė(n)* (modern *ate*).
(7) In the compound past tense of intransitive verbs, forms of the verb *bē* were used with the past participle instead of, as in Modern English, forms of the verb *have*: thus, *hē is vanished, hē is (y-) rĭden*, instead of *he has vanished, he has ridden*.

IRREGULAR VERBS

The only other frequently occurring irregularities that are likely to seem unfamiliar to the modern reader are the verb *tō bę̄*, which has the forms *wē, yē, thēy bę̄* or *bę̄en* in addition to the familiar *arė(n)*; and the following group of verbs that are peculiar both in form and meaning: *Ī căn, thou cănst, hē căn; wē, yē, thēy cónnė(n); Ī cŏudė; wē cŏudė(n)* (conjugated like *lóvedė*) (modern *I can, know how*); *Ī māy, thou māyst, hē māy; wē mǫu̯ė(n); Ī mĭghtė* (modern *I can, am able*); *Ī mǫot, thou mǫost, hē mǫot; wē mǫote(n); Ī mǫstė* (modern *I may, must*); *Ī wǫot, thou wǫost, hē wǫot; wē wĭtė(n); Ī wĭstė* (modern *I know*).

Appendix 3: Dialect Variations

There was no one Received Literary Dialect of Middle English, and, as a result, manuscripts vary remarkably in recording literary texts. Some authors probably did not even attempt to write their works in a consistent manner that truly represented their own speech, and scribes in recopying texts tended to introduce dialect variations of their own. It is possible, nevertheless, to generalize about broad dialect areas in the fourteenth century, and it is especially useful for the student of literature to recognize the peculiarities of four highly productive areas:

(1) *Southeast Midland* (including London), represented by Gower (*The Lover's Confession*);
(2) *Northern*, represented by Minot (*Halidon Hill*) in Northern England and Barbour (*The Bruce*) in Scotland;
(3) *West Midland*, represented by the author of *The Pearl* and *Sir Gawain and the Green Knight*; and
(4) *Southwestern*, represented by Langland (*Piers Plowman*).

These four dialects, as well as the less productive Southeastern, though individually neither permanent nor homogeneous, differed consistently from one another in numerous ways. In particular they differed in the endings of the third person singular, present indicative, and of the third person plural, present indicative, and in the forms of certain pronouns. Two sentences, *She loves them*, and *They love her*, can be used to display these verbal endings and at the same time to show the variations in the pronouns *she*, *they*, and *them* (*her* was stable). Ignoring a multitude of possible spelling variations and schematizing the geography, the following chart thus presents a reliable guide to characteristic contrasts that occur with high relative frequency:

WEST MIDLAND (*Pearl*)	NORTHERN (Barbour)
hō lóves hĕm	schō lŭfis thāim
thāy lŭv hĭr	thāi lŭv hĭr

SOUTHWESTERN (Langland)	SOUTHEAST MIDLAND (Gower)
hēo lóveth hĕm	shē lóveth hĕm
hĭ lóveth hĭr	thēy lóvė(n) hĭr

Appendix 4: Glossary of Common Words and Phrases

The following words and phrases appear frequently in Middle English in senses unfamiliar to modern readers and are therefore worthy of particular attention.

ac   1. but; 2. and.
again, ayain   1. again; 2. in return, often equivalent to Modern English *re-*, *i.e.*, "yelde . . . again" (*Gawain*, 1. 2325), repay; 3. against.

als, also, alswa 1. also; 2. as.
and 1. and; 2. if.
anon (*lit., in one*) at once.
as 1. as; 2. in combinations: *so as*, so; *ther as*, where; *wher as*, where.
ay aye, always.

bi–that 1. *adv.* by that time; 2. *conj.* by the time that.
but 1. but; 2. without.
but if unless.

can, con 1. can; 2. sometimes used like *gan* to form past tense, *i.e., he con ride*, he rode.

eek also.
eft 1. again; 2. then.
er, er that before.

for the nones (*lit., for the once*) indeed.
for–thi therefore.
fro from.

gan (I *ginne*, I *gan*, we *gonnen*) 1. began to; 2. often used to form past tense, *e.g., he gan ride*, he did ride, he rode.

her(e), hir(e) 1. her (see Appendix 3, p. 553); 2. their.

ilk, ilke same.
i–wiss(e) indeed.

lesteth, listeth, lüsteth (it) pleases. The real subject is usually expressed in the dative, *him lesteth*, or in the contracted form, *him lest* (see Introduction, p. 13). The past tense is *him leste*, it pleased him.
liketh 1. *he liketh*, he likes; 2. *him liketh*, it pleases him.

men 1. men; 2. one (*sing.*), which also occurs in the form *man* or *mon*.
mid with.
mo more.

namelich particularly.
natheles nevertheless.
ne 1. not; 2. *ne . . . ne*, neither . . . nor.

o(o), oon one (*o(o)* occurs before consonants, *oon* before vowels).
of "The Kynges son of Rome" is equivalent to modern English "The King of Rome's son."
other 1. other; 2. or; 3. *other . . . other*, either . . . or.

sith, sith that since.
sithen 1. *adv.* then; 2. *conj.* since.
sone soon.
swich such.

swithe   very.
syn, syn that   since.

ther   1. there; 2. where (also *ther as*).
thinketh   1. thinks; 2. *me thinketh*, it seems to me.
tho   1. those; 2. then; 3. when.

wel   1. well; 2. very.
wher   1. where (also *wher as*); 2. whether.

yede   went.

SELECTIVE CRITICAL BIBLIOGRAPHY

BASIC REFERENCES

(referred to in the headnotes by abbreviated titles)

Bennett, *OHEL*
   Bennett, H. S. *Chaucer and the Fifteenth Century.* Oxford History of English Literature, vol. 2, pt. 1. Oxford, Eng., 1947. Extensive bibliography.

Brown and Robbins, *Index*
   Brown, Carleton, and Rossell Hope Robbins. *The Index of Middle English Verse.* New York, 1943. *Supplement.* Lexington, Ky., 1965. Index by first line of all Middle English poems, listing manuscript and printed sources.

CBEL
   Cambridge Bibliography of English Literature, The. Ed. F. W. Bateson. 4 vols. Cambridge, Eng., 1941. *Supplement.* Ed. George Watson. Cambridge, Eng., 1957. References to this work have been given here in those headnotes dealing with those items that have not been treated in Wells or in Severs and Hartung. Indispensable.

Chambers, *OHEL*
   Chambers, Sir Edmund K. *English Literature at the Close of the Middle Ages.* Oxford History of English Literature, vol. 2, pt. 2. Oxford, Eng., 1945.

Child
   Child, Frances James. *The English and Scottish Popular Ballads.* 10 vols. Boston, 1882–98. Available in various reprints. The ballads included in *Middle English Literature* are referred to by Child's numbers. The one-volume abridgment, edited by Helen C. Sargent and G. L. Kittredge (Cambridge, Boston, 1904), contains at least one version of each of the ballads.

DOST
   Dictionary of the Older Scottish Tongue, A. Ed. Sir William A. Craigie. Chicago, 1931– . In progress; necessary for Scottish texts, which are not covered in *Middle English Dictionary.*

EETS
   Early English Text Society. Original series. London, 1864– .

EETSES
   Early English Text Society. Extra Series. London, 1867– .

Geddie, *BMSP*
   Geddie, William. *A Bibliography of Middle Scots Poets.* Scottish Text Society Publications, 61. Edinburgh, 1912.

Hammond
   Hammond, Elizabeth P. *Chaucer: A Bibliographical Manual.* New York, 1908. Contains detailed information about many aspects of fourteenth-century literature.

Hartung
   Manual of the Writings in Middle English, 1050–1500, A. Ed. Albert E. Hartung. New Haven, 1972. Continuation in progress of Severs' revision of Wells; referred to by chapter and item numbers. (Volume III consists of Chapters 7–9.)

Legge
   Legge, M. Dominica. *Anglo-Norman Literature and Its Background.* Oxford, Eng., 1963.

Lewis, *OHEL*
> Lewis, C. S. *English Literature in the Sixteenth Century.* Oxford History of English Literature, Vol. III. Oxford, Eng., 1954.

Manly-Rickert
> Manly, John M., and Edith Rickert. *The Text of the Canterbury Tales.* 8 vols. Chicago, 1940. Volume I contains unusually complete descriptions of manuscripts containing the *Canterbury Tales* and often additional works; Volume II, pages 1–45, contains a useful discussion of the establishment of a text.

MED
> *Middle English Dictionary.* Ed. Hans Kurath and Sherman M. Kuhn. Ann Arbor, 1952– . In progress. *Plan and Bibliography.* A summary of dates, dialects, and sources of materials abstracted for the *MED.* Ann Arbor, 1954.

Severs
> *Manual of the Writings in Middle English, 1050–1500, A.* Ed. J. Burke Severs. 2 vols. New Haven, 1967, 1970. A revision of Wells' *Manual.* Works included in *Middle English Literature* are referred to by chapter and item numbers. (Volume I consists of Chapter 1, Volume II of Chapters 2–8.) Contains historical and critical commentaries and bibliography on each item.

STS
> Scottish Text Society. Publications. Edinburgh, 1884– .

Wells
> *Manual of the Writings in Middle English, 1050–1400, A.* Ed. John Edwin Wells. New Haven, 1916. *Supplements, I–IX.* New Haven, 1916–52. Works included in *Middle English Literature* are referred to by chapter and item numbers. Contains historical and critical summaries and an exhaustive bibliography on each item.

BIBLIOGRAPHIES

Ackerman, Robert W. "Middle English Literature to 1400." *The Medieval Literature of Western Europe: A Review of Research.* Ed. John H. Fisher. New York, 1966, pp. 73-123. A useful summary of scholarship from 1930 to 1960; the volume deals with related topics such as Latin, French, and Celtic.

PMLA: Annual International Bibliography. New York, 1957– . Each volume covers the preceding year's scholarship; Middle English literature is treated separately from the Middle English language. Indispensable for keeping abreast of the latest research.

Recent Middle English Scholarship and Criticism. Ed. J. Burke Severs. Pittsburgh, 1971. Suggestive interpretations of new critical trends by D. C. Fowler, D. R. Howard, Lillian H. Hornstein, and Helaine Newstead.

Tucker, Lena L., and R. Benham. *A Bibliography of Fifteenth-Century Literature.* Seattle, 1928. Covers a field not dealt with by Wells, but already largely replaced by *CBEL;* will be completely outdated by Severs and Hartung.

Zesmer, David M., and Stanley B. Greenfield. *Guide to English Literature from Beowulf through Chaucer.* New York, 1961. Greenfield's critical bibliography of Middle English is particularly useful.

LANGUAGE

Baugh, Albert C. *A History of the English Language.* 2nd ed. New York, 1957. Treats not only the linguistic development but also the cultural aspects of English.

Denholm-Young, N. *Handwriting in England and Wales.* Cardiff, Wales, 1954.

Hector, L. C. *The Handwriting of English Documents.* 2nd ed. London, 1966.

Johnson, Charles, and Hilary Jenkinson. *English Court Hand, A.D. 1066 to 1500*. 2 vols. Oxford, Eng. 1915.

Jones, Charles. *An Introduction to Middle English*. New York, 1972. Attempt at a modern structural and generative analysis of sounds, forms, and syntax in Middle English dialects.

Moore, Samuel. *Historical Outlines of English Sounds and Inflections*. Rev. Albert H. Marckwardt. Ann Arbor, 1951; rpt. 1966. Useful systematization of forms.

Mossé, Fernand. *A Handbook of Middle English*. Trans. James A. Walker. Baltimore, 1952. An anthology of brief excerpts with a useful and extensive grammar, particularly helpful on dialects.

Oxford English Dictionary, The. Ed. James A. H. Murray. *Supplement*. 13 vols. Oxford, Eng., 1933. This corrected reissue of *A New English Dictionary* (*NED*) will remain useful because of its scope even with the completion of the *MED* and the *DOST*.

Parkes, Malcolm B. *English Cursive Book Hands, 1250–1500*. Oxford, Eng., 1969.

Saintsbury, George A. *Historical Manual of English Prosody*. London, 1910; rpt. New York, 1926.
———. *History of English Prosody*. 3 vols. London, 1906–10; rpt. New York, 1961.

Serjeantson, Mary S. *A History of Foreign Words in English*. London, 1935; rpt. New York, 1961.

Stratmann, Francis H. *A Middle English Dictionary*. Rev. Henry Bradley. Oxford, Eng., 1891. Will be necessary until the completion of the *MED*.

Wright, C. E. *English Vernacular Hands from the Twelfth to the Fifteenth Centuries*. Oxford, Eng., 1960.

Wright, Joseph. *An Elementary Middle English Grammar*. 2nd ed. Oxford, Eng., 1928. Still useful.

LITERARY HISTORY

Ackerman, Robert W. *Backgrounds to Medieval English Literature*. New York, 1966. Excellent summary of the relationships between literature and society.

Age of Chaucer, The. Ed. Boris Ford. A Guide to English Literature. Vol. I. Rev. ed. Harmondsworth, Eng., 1963. Contains a number of interpretative essays by various specialists.

Arthurian Literature in the Middle Ages. Ed. R. S. Loomis. Oxford, Eng., 1959. Important collection of essays by experts on Celtic, English, French, and other sources of Middle English literature.

Atkins, J. W. H. *English Literary Criticism: The Medieval Phase*. New York, 1952.

Bronson, Bertrand Harris. *The Traditional Tunes of the Child Ballads with Their Texts*. 4 vols. Princeton, N. J., 1959–72. Should be used in conjunction with Child.

Critical Approaches to Medieval Literature. Ed. Dorothy Bethurum. New York, 1960. Critical methods represented include patristic exegesis and folkloristic methods.

Everett, Dorothy. *Essays on Middle English Literature*. Oxford, Eng., 1955. Important essays by a distinguished critic.

Hibbard, Laura H. *Mediaeval Romance in England*. New York, 1924; rpt. with bibliography added, New York, 1960.

Jackson, W. T. H. *Literature of the Middle Ages*. New York, 1960. A good brief survey of continental medieval literature, touching occasionally on Middle English literature.

Kane, George. *Middle English Literature: A Critical Study of the Romances, the Religious Lyrics, Piers Plowman*. London, 1951

Ker, W. P. *Medieval English Literature*. New York, 1942. Reissue of *English Literature, Medieval*, 1912.

Literary History of England, A. Ed. Albert C. Baugh. New York, 1948. Baugh's section, also published separately along with Kemp Malone's section on Old English, provides an excellent survey of Middle English and Anglo-Norman literature.

Middle English Survey: Critical Essays. Ed. Edward Vasta. Notre Dame, Ind., 1965. Important essays by experts on imagery, *Owl and Nightingale, Gawain, Pearl, Piers Plowman,* Gower, the ballad, and other topics.

Moore, Arthur K. *The Secular Lyric in Middle English.* Lexington, Ky., 1951.

Schlauch, Margaret. *English Medieval Literature and Its Social Foundations.* Warsaw, 1956. Literary criticism with Marxist commentary.

Speirs, John. *Medieval English Poetry: The Non-Chaucerian Tradition.* London, 1957. Opposed to the philological approach.

Valency, Maurice J. *In Praise of Love: An Introduction to the Love Poetry of the Renaissance.* New York, 1958. Wide survey from the Provençal poets to Dante.

Ward, A.W., and A. R. Waller. *The Cambridge History of English Literature.* 15 vols. Cambridge, Eng., 1907–08. Thorough study of Old English and Middle English literature in Volumes I and II.

Wilson, R. M. *Early Middle English Literature.* 3rd ed. London, 1968.

————. *The Lost Literature of Medieval England.* 2nd ed. London, 1970. Examines important though fragmentary evidence of the cultural vitality of the period.

Wimsatt, James I. *Allegory and Mirror: Tradition and Structure in Middle English Literature.* New York, 1970. A compact survey of the allegorical aspects of Middle English literature.

CULTURAL HISTORY

Auerbach, Erich. *Mimesis: The Representation of Reality in Western Literature.* Princeton, N. J., 1953. A profound study of the changes of style, attitude, and philosophy from classical times through later Christian eras.

Bloomfield, Morton W. *The Seven Deadly Sins.* Lansing, Mich., 1952.

Chaucer's World. Ed. Edith Rickert. Chicago, 1948. A fascinating collection of documents illustrating everyday phases of medieval life.

Curry, Walter Clyde. *Chaucer and the Medieval Sciences.* 2nd ed. New York, 1960.

Curtius, Ernst Robert. *European Literature and the Latin Middle Ages.* Trans. W. R. Trask. New York, 1953. Traces survival of the Classical tradition in the rhetorical motifs (*topoi*) of later literature.

Dawson, Christopher H. *Medieval Essays.* London, 1953. Concentrates on religious aspects of medieval culture.

Gilson, Étienne. *History of Christian Philosophy in the Middle Ages.* New York, 1955. The best single book on the medieval scholastic philosophers.

Huizinga, Johann. *The Waning of the Middle Ages.* London and New York, 1924; rpt. Harmondsworth, Eng., 1955. Cultural changes in the late fourteenth and fifteenth centuries.

Katzenellenbogen, Adolf. *Allegories of the Virtues and Vices in Medieval Art.* New York, 1964.

Knowles, David. *The English Mystical Tradition.* London, 1961.

————. *The Monastic Order in England, 943–1216.* 2nd ed. Cambridge, Eng., 1963.

————. *The Religious Orders in England.* 3 vols. Cambridge, Eng., 1948–59. A sequel to *The Monastic Order.*

Lewis, C. S. *The Allegory of Love.* Oxford, Eng., 1936. Highly readable, though in some respects no longer accepted.

————. *The Discarded Image: An Introduction to Medieval and Renaissance Literature.* Cambridge, Eng., 1964. The postclassical origins of the medieval *Weltanschauung.*

Lord, Albert B. *The Singer of Tales.* New York, 1965. An influential study of the role of themes and formulas in oral narrative.

Lubac, Henri de. *Exégèse Médiévale: Les Quatre Sens de l'Écriture.* 2 vols. in 4 parts. Paris, 1959–64. A massive study of the four-part medieval interpretation of the Scriptures.

Meaning of Courtly Love, The. Ed. F. X. Newman. Albany, 1968. Important theoretical papers; brief concluding discussion between participants in conference; useful bibliography.

Mosher, Joseph A. *The Exemplum in the Early Religious and Didactic Literature of England.* New York, 1911.

Owst, Gerald R. *Literature and Pulpit in Medieval England.* 2nd ed. Cambridge, Eng., 1961. A standard work on the relation of popular pulpit styles to literature.

Oxford History of English Art, The. Ed. T. S. R. Boase. Oxford, Eng., 1949– . In progress; relevant volumes are III, T. S. R. Boase, *English Art, 1100–1216;* IV, Peter Brieger, *English Art, 1216–1307;* V, Joan Evans, *English Art, 1307–1461.*

Patch, Howard R. *The Tradition of Boethius.* New York, 1935. On the question of God's providence, Boethius's *Consolation of Philosophy* was probably the most widely read work in the Middle Ages and the Renaissance.

Patterns of Love and Courtesy: Essays in Memory of C. S. Lewis. Ed. John Lawlor. Evanston, Ill., 1966. By various authorities on *Gawain,* Gower Chaucer, Malory, and other topics.

Thompson, Stith. *Motif-Index of Folk-Literature.* Rev. ed. 6 vols. Bloomington, Ind., 1955–58. Provides international parallels for many medieval motifs.

Utley, Francis L. *The Crooked Rib: An Analytical Index to the Argument about Women in English and Scots Literature.* Columbus, Ohio, 1944. An essential key to antifeminist satire.

Works of Geoffrey Chaucer, The. Ed. F. N. Robinson. 2nd ed. Cambridge, Mass., 1957. Though the references are now somewhat outdated, this is still an encyclopedia of Middle English culture.

SOCIAL AND POLITICAL HISTORY

Myers, Alec R. *England in the Late Middle Ages.* Rev. ed. Harmondsworth, Eng., 1956.

Oxford History of England, The. 15 vols. Oxford, Eng., 1934– . Relevant volumes are III, Austin L. Poole, *From Domesday Book to Magna Carta, 1087–1216;* IV, Maurice Powicke, *The Thirteenth Century, 1216–1307;* V, May McKisack, *The Fourteenth Century, 1307–99;* and VI, E. F. Jacob, *The Fifteenth Century.*

Poole, Austin L. *Medieval England.* Rev. ed. 2 vols. Oxford, Eng., 1958. Nineteen encyclopedic essays by various experts on different aspects of medieval English life.

Powicke, Frederick M. *Medieval England, 1066–1485.* London, 1948. An authoritative historical survey.

Stenton, Doris M. *English Society in the Early Middle Ages, 1066–1307.* Harmondsworth, Eng., 1951. A compact and readable history.

RECORDINGS OF MIDDLE ENGLISH

Dunn, Charles W. *The Changing English Language: Changing Literary Style.* Folkways FL 9852. New York, 1959. Includes Lawman, *Alliterative Morte Arthure,* Wyclyf, Chaucer, Caxton, Malory.

———. *Early English Poetry.* Folkways FL 9851. New York, 1958. Includes *Sir Gawain* and Chaucer.

A	3
B	4
C	5
D	6
E	7
F	8
G	9
H	0
I	1
J	2